Keywords for Latina/o Studies

Keywords for Latina/o Studies

Edited by
Deborah R. Vargas, Nancy Raquel Mirabal, and
Lawrence La Fountain-Stokes

NEW YORK UNIVERSITY PRESS New York

NEW YORK UNIVERSITY PRESS
New York
www.nyupress.org

References to Internet websites (URLs) were accurate at the time of writing.
Neither the author nor New York University Press is responsible for URLs that may have expired or changed since the manuscript was prepared.

Library of Congress Cataloging-in-Publication Data
Names: Vargas, Deborah R., editor. | Mirabal, Nancy Raquel, 1966– editor. | La Fountain-Stokes, Lawrence M. (Lawrence Martin), 1968– editor.
Title: Keywords for Latina/o studies / edited by Deborah R. Vargas, Nancy Raquel Mirabal, and Lawrence La Fountain-Stokes.
Description: New York: New York University Press, 2017. | Includes bibliographical references and index.
Identifiers: LCCN 2017012907| ISBN 9781479866045 (cl: alk. paper) | ISBN 9781479883301 (pb: alk. paper)
Subjects: LCSH: Hispanic Americans—Study and teaching.
Classification: LCC E184.S75 K48 2017 | DDC 973/.0468—dc23
LC record available at https://lccn.loc.gov/2017012907

New York University Press books are printed on acid-free paper, and their binding materials are chosen for strength and durability. We strive to use environmentally responsible suppliers and materials to the greatest extent possible in publishing our books.

Manufactured in the United States of America

10 9 8 7 6 5 4 3 2 1

Also available as an ebook

Contents

Acknowledgments   vii

Introduction: Deborah R. Vargas, Nancy Raquel
    Mirabal, and Lawrence La Fountain-Stokes   1
1. Afro-Latinas/os: Tanya Katerí Hernández   7
2. Americas: Alexandra T. Vazquez   10
3. Art: Rita Gonzalez   12
4. Assimilation: Catherine S. Ramírez   14
5. Barrio: Gina M. Pérez   18
6. Borderlands: Nicole M. Guidotti-Hernández   21
7. Brown: Joshua Javier Guzmán   25
8. Capitalism: Ramona Hernández   28
9. Chicana, Chicano, Chican@, Chicanx
    Sheila Marie Contreras   32
10. Citizenship: Nicholas De Genova   36
11. Culture: Arlene Dávila   40
12. Decolonial: María Lugones   43
13. Diaspora: Ricardo L. Ortíz   47
14. Education: Angela Valenzuela   51
15. Empire: Lázaro Lima   55
16. Exile: José Quiroga   58
17. Family: Richard T. Rodríguez   61
18. Feminisms: María Eugenia Cotera   64
19. Film: Sergio de la Mora   68
20. Food: Zilkia Janer   71
21. Gender: Sandra K. Soto   75
22. Health: John Mckiernan-González   79
23. History: Gerald E. Poyo   83
24. Housing: Zaire Z. Dinzey-Flores   86
25. Hyphen: Frederick Luis Aldama   89

26. Illegality: Cecilia Menjívar   93
27. Incarceration: Michael Hames-García   96
28. Indigeneity: Maylei Blackwell   100
29. Labor: Shannon Gleeson   105
30. Language: John Nieto-Phillips   109
31. Latinidad/es: Frances R. Aparicio   113
32. Law: Enid Trucios-Haynes   118
33. Literature: Ana Patricia Rodríguez   122
34. Maquiladoras: Norma Iglesias-Prieto   125
35. Media: Mari Castañeda   129
36. Mestizaje: Alicia Arrizón   133
37. Militarism: Manuel G. Avilés-Santiago   136
38. Modernity: José F. Aranda Jr.   140
39. Music: María Elena Cepeda   144
40. Nationalism: Raúl Coronado   147
41. Performance: Ramón H. Rivera-Servera   152
42. Philosophy: Linda Martín Alcoff and
    Rolando Pérez   156
43. Poetry: Urayoán Noel   159
44. Politics: John A. García   163
45. Popular Culture: Curtis Marez   167
46. Poverty: Patricia Zavella   171
47. Race: Silvio Torres-Saillant and Nancy Kang   175
48. Radio: Dolores Inés Casillas   181
49. Rasquachismo: Laura G. Gutiérrez   184
50. Raza: B. V. Olguín   188
51. Religion: Anne M. Martínez   192
52. Sexuality: Juana María Rodríguez   196
53. Social Movements: Randy J. Ontiveros   200
54. Sovereignty: Nelson Maldonado-Torres   204

55. Spanglish: Ana Celia Zentella   209

56. Spirituality: Theresa Delgadillo   212

57. Sterilization: Alexandra Minna Stern   217

58. Television: Mary Beltrán   221

59. Territoriality: Mary Pat Brady   224

60. Testimonio: Arnaldo Cruz-Malavé   228

61. Theater: Lillian Manzor   232

62. Transnationalism: Ginetta E. B. Candelario   236

63. White: Julie A. Dowling   239

Bibliography   243

About the Contributors   287

Acknowledgments

We wish to thank, first and foremost, the sixty-five contributors to this volume on *Keywords for Latina/o Studies*, without whom we would never have been able to create this book. We are also enormously thankful to Eric Zinner, Alicia Nadkarni, and Alexia Traganas at New York University Press for their enormous encouragement and support at all stages of production. We also want to thank Ricardo Bracho for his editorial assistance compiling the list of works cited.

Deborah R. Vargas would like to thank Eric Zinner for giving the three of us this opportunity to engage the field, to struggle over meanings and ideas, and to learn to apply a politics of *cariño y respeto* in our debates. Thanks so much to Alicia Nadkarni for all of her expertise and assistance. I consider it a privilege to have had the opportunity to collaborate with and learn so much from Nancy Raquel Mirabal and Lawrence La Fountain-Stokes. I addition to our work meetings I will always cherish sweet memories of ordering too many dumplings in San Francisco, inventing cheaterquiles in L.A., and being introduced to "Cuba H.P."

Nancy Raquel Mirabal, *mil gracias* to Deborah Vargas for inviting me to be part of this project and to both Deb and Lawrence M. La Fountain-Stokes for being exceptional co-editors. I learned so much from working with both of you and felt honored to witness your hard work, cooperative spirit, generosity, and humor. I also want to thank all of the contributors who participated in this project and provided us with brilliant entries; to the external readers for their thoughtful suggestions and critiques; and to the New York University Press editors, especially Eric Zinner, for giving us the room to expand, complicate, and rethink. In the process of putting together this project, it was clear that this field we call Latina/o/x studies is dynamic, powerful, and more important than ever.

Lawrence M. La Fountain-Stokes echoes Deb's and Nancy's sentiments. It has been an adventure completing this book, from figuring out what keywords to include and reaching out to our authors, to offering words of encouragement and keeping track of the multiple revisions! Latina/o (or Latinx) studies is a field near and dear to my heart and becomes more crucial every day. Thanks to my colleagues in American Culture, Latina/o studies, Romance Languages and Literatures, and Women's studies at the University of Michigan for their support, and to my great co-editors Deb and Nancy. I also wish to thank all of the authors—those whose work appears here, as well as those who were a part of this process at some moment and perhaps might join in the future. We all greatly hope that this book will make a difference.

Introduction

Deborah R. Vargas, Nancy Raquel Mirabal, and
Lawrence La Fountain-Stokes

Over the last five decades, Latina/o studies has rapidly evolved and expanded. An amalgamation of multiple disciplines, theories, and methods, Latina/o studies has generated an expansive, innovative, and ever-evolving framework to understand the experiences of persons of Latin American and Caribbean descent in the United States as well as broader sociohistorical, political, and cultural processes. By using the knowledges and methodologies of such diverse fields as American studies, anthropology, art, cultural studies, economics, education, ethnic studies, geography, history, labor, language and literary studies (particularly English and Spanish), Latin American and Caribbean studies, linguistics, media studies, medicine, music, political science, public health, religion, social work, sociology, and women's and gender studies, among others, Latina/o studies reveals facts and truths that had previously not been visible or accessible.

In naming this book, we have chosen the term "Latina/o" with the full understanding that during the past decade a number of theoretical, epistemological, and identity projects have used "Latin@" and "Latinx" in seeking to challenge and overcome the gender binary implicit in the Spanish-language feminine and masculine endings of Latina/o (Scharrón-del Río and Aja 2015; Padilla 2016; Ramirez and Blay 2016; de Onís 2017). It is also important to point out that there have been varying forms of resistance to these terms (Taylor et al. 2012;

Guerra and Orbea 2015). Some of the contributors to this book pick up and expand these discussions. Our use of "Latina/o" does not dismiss these new terms or the productive critiques they represent. Instead, we welcome and support the future evolution and transformation of multiple meanings and iterations. Our choice to use "Latina/o" is intended to honor interventions by feminist scholars to disrupt the Spanish-language masculine use of "o" as a default in "Latino" (Chabram-Dernersesian 2013). We also read the forward slash (/) as a productive tension rather than reaffirming a gendered binary.

Born out of struggles, protests, and demands for community-engaged politics and interdisciplinary methodologies, Latina/o studies emerged from conversations with knowledge models created by third-world liberation, civil rights, feminist, decolonial, social justice, LGBTQ, and immigration rights movements, to name a few, as well as in relation to critiques of U.S. foreign policy in Latin America and the Caribbean. It is also a field that, in interrogating definitions of citizenship, borders, territories, migrations, labor, self, language, performance, sexuality constructions, social identities, gender performance, and legitimacy, has given rise to powerful and influential theories and methods, many of which have redefined traditional disciplines.

Latina/o studies has also been defined as much by what it is not: it is neither an extension nor a corollary of Latin American and Caribbean area studies nor a simple fusion of Chicano, Boricua, Central American and other similar ethnic studies fields. The major contention informing this distinction is that area and international studies funded and organized under Title VI of the National Defense Education Act (NDEA) of 1958 were part of a larger Cold War politics to stem communism in the region, especially during and after the Cuban Revolution of 1959 (Delpar 2008). This is not to say that Latina/o studies is not influenced or shaped by Latin American and Caribbean theories and methods or by the problematics of establishing the field of Latin American and Caribbean studies in the U.S. academy. Early generations of scholars working in Latina/o studies were trained in Latin American, Caribbean, and Chicano/Boricua studies (as well as in American studies and other ethnic studies fields) and identified with progressive Latin Americanists and Caribbeanists who denounced United States policies and military interventions in the region (Cabán 2003a, 2003b). Instead, this is to acknowledge that Latina/o studies is a field of its own making. With close ties to ethnic, gender, and regional studies, it draws from but is distinct from other fields. It is inventive, multidisciplinary, and grounded in transnational and trans-American connections that speak to the uses of territorialities, borderlands, and the realities of shared histories, geographies, and sites that both encompass and eschew artificial borders (Brady 2002; Gruesz 2002).

The emergence of what would be referred to as "Latina/o studies" can be arguably traced to two particular social movements, the Chicana/o *movimiento* and the Puerto Rican movement of the 1960s and 1970s, which correspond to the two historically largest and oldest Latina/o demographic groups in the United States. Both demanded that universities establish Chicana/o and Puerto Rican studies departments and programs and hire more Chicana/o and Puerto Rican professors. In April of 1969, *El Plan de Santa Barbara: A Chicano Plan for Higher Education* was adopted at the University of California, Santa Barbara. It was drafted by the Chicano Coordinating Council on Higher Education as a manifesto for the implementation of Chicano studies throughout the state of California (C. Muñoz 1999; Chavez 2002; Blackwell 2011). That same year, African American and Latina/o students, influenced by the Black Panthers and Young Lords, demanded that the City University of New York system create departments and hire African American and Puerto Rican faculty (Cabán 2003a, 2003b; Beltrán 2010; Kynard 2014).

The nationwide demand for Chicano and Boricua studies departments was directly related to the shared belief that not only did Latinas/os deserve to have their history taught, but that this history, along with the histories of other marginalized and silenced communities of color, *is* the history of the United States, specifically of U.S. imperialism and territorial expansion (Ruiz 2006b). Moreover, by establishing a field and pushing for recognition, early Chicana/o and Puerto Rican scholars cultivated a critical space for knowledge and cultural productions. This was not the first time that Latina/o organizations called for the creation of courses that examined and reflected the history of the different populations and communities that constitute what we currently refer to as Latinas/os. Formed in 1939 and led in part by the Guatemalan-born labor activist Luisa Moreno, the delegates of El Congreso de Pueblos de Habla Española, as the historian Vicki L. Ruiz writes, "emphasized the importance of preserving Latina-Latino cultures and called upon universities to create departments of Latino Studies" (Ruiz 2006a, 226).

The movements of the 1960s and 1970s made impressive gains, and within a relatively short time, Chicano and Puerto Rican studies departments and programs were established at a number of colleges and universities (particularly public institutions), including those created at San Francisco State University (as part of the only College of Ethnic Studies), the University of California, Berkeley, the University of Minnesota, Lehman and Hunter Colleges (CUNY), Rutgers University, and the University of Connecticut. There were also locations in the Midwest, in particular Chicago and Detroit (for example, at Wayne State University), which called for the rise of Chicano-Boricua studies to address the needs of Mexican American and Puerto Rican communities (Padilla 1985; C. Muñoz 1999, 2007). By the 1990s, a significant number of universities had established centers, programs, and departments focused on Latina/o studies. This, however, was not without controversy or difficulties. The institutional inclusion of Latina/o with ethnic studies at certain universities has been seen as a strategy to dilute the field by subsuming it under centers and programs that do not offer undergraduate majors or train doctoral students in Latina/o studies (Cabán 2003b).

The evolution and growth of the field also gave rise to Cuban American (Pedraza-Bailey 1985; Poyo 1989; Pérez Firmat 1994; Torres 2001; Ortíz 2007), Central American-American (Arias 2003; A. P. Rodríguez 2009; Stoltz Chinchilla and Hamilton 2013), and Dominican American studies (Torres-Saillant and Hernández 1998; Candelario 2007; Méndez 2012; García-Peña 2016). Albeit developed through different trajectories, historical narratives, and methodologies, their inclusion within the larger discourse on Latinidad complicated the field and allowed scholars to move past singular and binary definitions of Latinidad to one that echoed the rise in population of migrants who were not from Mexico or Puerto Rico (Oboler 1995; C. Rodríguez 2000; Cabán 2003a, 2003b; Aparicio 2007; Mora 2014). The Communist Revolution in Cuba, the civil wars in Central America, the end of the Trujillo dictatorship in the Dominican Republic, and the passage of the Hart Cellar Act (1965) in the United States, to name a few events, prompted a rapid and dramatic increase in the number of migrants, exiles, and refugees arriving to the United States during the late twentieth century.

Salvadoran and Dominican migrants are fast becoming one of the largest Latina/o populations in the United States, with Dominican migrants possibly surpassing Puerto Ricans as the largest Latina/o population in New York City (G. López 2013; Bergad 2014). Los Angeles is the second largest Mexican-descent city in the world, second only to Mexico City. Simultaneously—and signaling the dynamic changes in who we come to define within the term "Latina/o"—in the past five years one of the largest groups of Mexicans immigrating to Los Angeles are Indigenous peoples who do not speak Spanish and contest their Mexican nation-state status. All of these demographic changes among Latinas/os are notable and have already shifted the field. Latina/o studies courses, programs, and departments are making room not only for Central American and Dominican studies, but also for the study of Afro-Latinas/os, Latinas/os of Asian descent, Arab and Muslim Latinas/os (for example the ones portrayed in the 2009 documentary *New Muslim Cool*), and South American migrations. We understand these dynamics as productive tensions contributing to the growth and expansion of the field itself; some of these receive more attention that others in this keywords volume.

The recent demographic changes have spurred a debate on whether numbers translate into political and electoral power, what many refer to as the "Latino vote." According to 2015 Census Bureau statistics, Latinas/os make up 17 percent of the overall United States population (U.S. Census Bureau 2015). States such as California, New Mexico, Texas, Arizona, Colorado, Illinois, New

York, New Jersey, and Florida boast the largest Latina/o populations in the United States (Pew Research Center 2013; U.S. Census Bureau 2015). These demographic shifts have compelled many to see this trend as a sign of impending Latina/o political empowerment and potential dominance (Santa Ana 2002; Beltrán 2010; Gutiérrez 2013; García Bedolla 2014; J. García 2016). At the same time, however, Latinas/os are often depicted as passive and forever foreign; they are described as a "perpetually emergent" population, one that is continually characterized as having "untapped potential" (Beltrán 2010, 4). Implicit in such a discourse is the complexity of what indeed determines a shared Latina/o identity and community, and if so, whether such a diverse community translates into a sense of common political empowerment (Beltrán 2010).

The essays included in *Keywords for Latina/o Studies* are part of a larger project of envisioning and defining an ever-evolving and changing field. Echoing these changes, the essays vary in theory, methodology, and scope. Some reflect the disciplinary training and interests of their contributors, while others exhibit a willingness to experiment and push traditional boundaries of what constitutes Latina/o or Latinx studies. There is no right way, just recognition that a field in transition cannot be categorized, fixed, or forced to compromise. Thus, we hope that readers will be attentive to tensions and divergences as well as commonalities and shared viewpoints and that they will also be incited to envision their own additional keywords (or rewritings or expansions of the ones in this volume) as part of the evolving conversation that we seek to foster and generate.

It was not easy choosing keywords that best captured this elusive and dynamic field. With Latina/o studies being grounded in multiplicity, dislocation, and transnationalism, one of the major challenges of the field is the need for it to be elastic and expansive enough to speak to the histories and experiences of multi-generational migrants from Latin America and the Caribbean, citizens from Puerto Rico, Indigenous citizens of tribal nations who persist in their struggle for sovereignty from nation-states, and longstanding residents and communities born in territories expropriated by the Treaty of Guadalupe Hidalgo, while at the same time, remaining narrow enough to denote a shared identity, movement, and politics (Oboler 1995; Aparicio 2007; Beltrán 2010).

Like Bruce Burgett and Glenn Hendler, who cite Raymond Williams's reading of keywords as a "record of an inquiry into a *vocabulary*" in their *Keywords for American Cultural Studies* (2007, 2), we too imagine this volume as part of a larger vocabulary, and more accurately a dialogue where contributors can and do extrapolate, reinvent, and in some cases, use specific keywords to reinterpret, challenge, contest, and complicate the field named "Latina/o studies." We also envision this volume in critical dialogue with other Latina/o keyword projects such as Paul Allatson's *Key Terms in Latino/a Cultural and Literary Studies* (2007) and Yolanda Martínez-San Miguel, Ben. Sifuentes-Jáuregui, and Marisa Belausteguigoitia's *Critical Terms in Caribbean and Latin American Thought: Historical and Institutional Trajectories* (2016); with Latina/o keyword essays such as Juana María Rodríguez's (2014a) "Latino, Latina, Latin@" in the second edition of *Keywords for American Cultural Studies*; and with the multiple Latina/o studies encyclopedias, anthologies, and readers coedited over the last decades by Frederick Luis Aldama, Frances R. Aparicio, Juan Flores, Deena González, Suzanne Oboler, Renato Rosaldo, Vicki L. Ruiz, Virginia Sánchez Korrol, and Ilan Stavans, among others.

Readers of *Keywords for Latina/o Studies* will be struck by the juxtaposition of general critical terms along with highly specific ones (such as Barrio, Chicana/Chicano/Chican@/Chicanx, Latinidad/es, Maquiladoras,

Mestizaje, Rasquache, Raza, and Spanglish), by the dialogue between many of the pieces, and by the shared bibliography, as well as by striking differences. Particularly interesting are the relational links or thematic groupings that appear among clusters of essays, for example around Culture (including Art, Culture, Food, Language, Literature, Music, Performance, Poetry, Popular Culture, and Theater, among others), Decolonial (including Citizenship, Decolonial, Modernity, Nationalism, and Sovereignty), Gender (including Decolonial, Gender, and Feminisms), Health (also including Sterilization), Housing (also including Barrio), Language (also including Spanglish), Media (including Film, Media, Radio, and Television), Labor (including Capitalism, Labor, Maquiladoras, and Poverty), Politics (including Illegality, Incarceration, Law, Politics, Social Movements, and Sovereignty), Race (including Afro-Latinas/os, Brown, Indigeneity, Mestizaje, Race, Raza, and White), Religion (also including Spirituality), Sexuality (also including Gender, Feminisms, and Sterilization), and Territoriality (also including Americas, Barrio, Borderlands, Diaspora, Exile, and Transnationalism). There are many additional possible, overlapping clusters, and it is our hope that readers will make these connections.

Readers might also be struck by missing terms: some of these correspond to limits of space, others to invited authors' inability to complete their requested essays. It is absolutely incorrect to assume that the absence of a term in this volume indicates the editors' lack of interest in specific discussions, and it is our hope that a future edition will include additional terms such as AIDS, ageing, archive, Boricua, Central American-American, DominicanYork, DREAMer (which is extensively discussed by Randy J. Ontiveros in his entry on "Social Movements"), hemispheric, Latinx, migration, Nuyorican (and/or Diasporican), queer, revolution, sanctuary, UndocuQueer, and youth. Because this book is meant

for a general readership as well as for college students, scholars, and professors, the list of works cited includes multiple sources and is designed to expand and complement the discussions in our book. As co-editors who approach our work from an interdisciplinary perspective, we also acknowledge that our approach to this book project is situated in and credits feminist, women of color, third world women's, and queer studies.

It is never a good idea to define a dynamic field, to decide what it is and what it is not, given its very engagement with a rapidly changing world and the various modes of accountability scholars in the field have to changing questions and shifts in power. Thus, we acknowledge and embrace our role as co-editors who may have fallen short or been short-sighted in compiling this text. Yet, we embrace the places where there are gaps and the need to reexamine, seeing them as a reminder that Latina/o studies should never be understood as a closed, finite, or cohesively established field. Its dynamism, pliability, and promiscuity are, after all, where its political potential lies.

The authors assembled here, we believe, provide us with an extremely powerful start to new conversations about the project and future of Latina/o studies, especially given changes to the U.S. academy in an era of neoliberalization, increased xenophobia, anxieties about immigration, massive deportation campaigns such as those experienced under the Obama and Trump presidencies, which have included those of youth and young adults protected under the Obama administration's Deferred Action for Childhood Arrivals (DACA), unspeakable numbers of tragedies at the border (de León 2015), and rising levels of social violence and intolerance, including President Trump's efforts to build a wall on the Mexican and United States border.

Under these conditions, it was critical for us, the editors, to compile a volume that speaks to multiple politics of resistance and resilience and includes the dreams of DREAMers, UndocuQueers, antiracists, and immigration activists. It follows the models of past civil rights struggles in an effort to present empowering critical concepts that can bring about social justice, something that is extraordinarily challenged currently in the United States. This book is then our invitation to reach across fluid constellations of possibilities, desires, and potential and allow the critical thinkers among us to speak and reveal their thoughts of where the field of Latina/o studies, as archive and political project, is intellectually imagined, knowing full well that that too will change.

I

Afro-Latinas/os

Tanya Katerí Hernández

The terms "Afro-Latina" and "Afro-Latino" refer to those Latinas/os in the United States who are of African ancestry and choose blackness as a racial identity in addition to identifying along ethnic lines with their Latina/o national origins. The terms are not exclusive to the United States, as activists of African descent in Latin America and the Caribbean have also begun to use them (Whitten and Torres 1998; Seelke 2008). As the Latina/o population has grown in the United States, so has the number of Latinas/os of African descent (López and Gonzalez-Barrera 2016). According to the 2010 U.S. census, the 50.4 million Latinas/os in the United States (the nation's largest panethnic group) account for 16.3 percent of the country's population. About 2.5 percent of those Latinas/os also identified themselves as "Black" on the 2010 census. That compares with close to 53 percent who said they were also "White" and the 36.7 percent who described themselves as "some other race." (The 2010 census permitted Latinas/os to select a "Hispanic/Latino" ethnic origin category in addition to selecting any number of the racial categories of black, white, Asian, or "some other race.") Most Afro-Latinas/os in the United States can trace their origins to Colombia, Cuba, the Dominican Republic, Panama (among other Central American countries), and Puerto Rico, though over a quarter of a million people of Mexican heritage also defined themselves as "Black" in the 2010 census; many Mexicans are of African descent (Vinson and Restall 2009). As compared to other Latinas/os, Afro-Latinas/os are much less likely to be immigrants and are more likely to speak English in their homes.

Despite the small percentage of Latinas/os who officially acknowledge their African ancestry on U.S. census forms, the academic study of their complex identities predates the origins of Latina/o studies as a field. Indeed, the Afro–Puerto Rican bibliophile Arturo Alfonso Schomburg added his collection of more than 5,000 books, 3,000 manuscripts, 2,000 etchings and paintings, and several thousand pamphlets concerning Afro-Latinas/os and other African diaspora descendants to the New York Public Library Division of Negro Literature, History and Prints back in 1926; this division was the forerunner to the presently named Schomburg Center for Research in Black Culture (Sinnette 1989; Valdés 2017). Today, the Schomburg Center is one of the world's leading research facilities devoted to the preservation of materials on the global African and African diaspora experiences.

Yet in spite of the richness of the existing material regarding the Afro-Latina/o experience (Jiménez Román and Flores 2010), this area of research is often overlooked in Latina/o studies. Silvio Torres-Saillant (2003) has noted that many Latina/o studies scholars have thus far been content to treat the racial mixture of Latinas/os as eviscerating any racial differences. In fact, Latina/o studies extends the Latin American studies concept of *mestizaje* (the notion that racial mixture in a population is emblematic of racial harmony and insulated from racial discord and inequality) into the belief that Latinas/os in the United States are racially enlightened because of their racial mixture (Dzidzienyo and Oboler 2005). At the same time, Torres-Saillant (2003) has noted that many Latina/o scholars have been content to focus on *mestizaje*-pride without thoroughly interrogating its subtext of white supremacy.

Some examples of the *mestizaje*-pride element surface in the work of Victor Valle and Rodolfo D. Torres (1995), along with the more famous example of Gloria Anzaldúa (1987). Anzaldúa was so enamored of *mestizaje* as a concept that she went so far as to refer favorably to Mexican philosopher José Vasconcelos's (1925) "cosmic race" theory of Latin American racial superiority through racial mixing, without mentioning the strong white supremacist aspects of his theory. According to Vasconcelos, the benefits of the cosmic race mixture occur as "the lower types of the species will be absorbed by the superior. In this manner, for example, the blacks could be redeemed, and step by step, by voluntary extinction, the uglier stocks will give way to the more handsome" (1997 [1925], 32). Anzaldúa's endorsement characterizes the cosmic race theory as being "opposite to the theory of the pure Aryan, and to the policy of racial purity that white America practices"; she adds that "his theory is one of inclusivity" (1987, 77). Despite the fundamental racism of Vasconcelos's theory, Anzaldúa goes on to posit that a Latina/o "mestiza consciousness" breaks down paradigms and is thus more progressive about race relations and thereby allows mestizas (read "Chicanas") to act as mediators linking different groups of people together. This fascination with a benevolent *mestizaje* is also echoed by Victor Valle and Rodolfo D. Torres when they characterize it as an "outlaw discourse" which is "radically inclusive" and a "response to Western imperialism" (1995, 148–49). Unfortunately,

Latina/o celebrations of *mestizaje* leave little room for acknowledging the particularities of more pronounced African ancestry in facial appearance, skin shade, or hair texture.

As Afro-Cuban author Evelio Grillo has noted in his memoir about growing up in Tampa, Florida, in the 1920s and 1930s, Afro-Latinas/os are often "too black to be Hispanic" (2000, xiii). This coincides with Piri Thomas's (1967) experiences as described in his memoir of growing up in New York City in the 1930s and 1940s, as well as with observations of the contemporary Afro-Latina/o context (Bonilla-Silva 2010). Latina/o studies as a discipline has traditionally reflected this invisibility of Afro-Latina/o identity (Hernández 2003).

What is most disturbing about the dearth of Afro-Latina/o research in Latina/o studies is the way in which it obscures the complexity of the socioeconomic racial hierarchy that exists across Latina/o communities. Indeed, Afro-Latinas/os in the United States consistently report receiving racist treatment at the hands of other Latinas/os in addition to being perceived as outsiders to the construction of Latina/o identity. For example, Afro-Latinas/os are frequently mistaken for African Americans in their own communities and upon identifying themselves as Afro-Latinas/os are told, "But you don't look Latina!" (Comas-Díaz 1996, 168). Indeed the *2002 National Survey of Latinos* sponsored by the Pew Hispanic Center and the Kaiser Family Foundation indicated that Latinas/os with more pronounced African ancestry, such as many Dominicans, more readily identify color discrimination as an explanation for the bias they experience from other Latinas/os (Pew Research Center 2002). Moreover, the *2010 National Survey of Latinos* found that after immigrant status, skin color discrimination is the most prevalent perceived form of discrimination for Latinas/os (Pew Research Center 2013). In turn such experiences of bias within the U.S. culture of racial consciousness motivate Latinas/os of African descent to begin self-identifying as Afro-Latinas/os.

In addition, studies suggest that the socioeconomic status of Afro-Latinas/os in the United States is more akin to that of African Americans than to other Latinas/os or white Americans. According to *How Race Counts for Hispanic Americans* (Logan 2003), a study by the State University of New York at Albany released in July 2003, Latinas/os who define themselves as "black" have lower incomes, higher unemployment rates, higher rates of poverty, less education, and fewer opportunities and are more likely to reside in segregated neighborhoods than those who identify themselves as "white" or "other." Based on such data, the study concluded that there are stark differences between the standard of living for Afro-Latinas/os and that of all other Latinas/os in the United States. For this reason, the U.S. Census Bureau's suggestion for modifying the census demographic questions so as to remove the Hispanic/Latino option as an ethnic choice and instead have it presented as a racial category distinct from black and all others has been viewed with alarm by Afro-Latina/o activists (Reyes 2014). Collapsing Latina/o and Hispanic ethnic identity into the list of racial categories risks obscuring the number of Afro-Latinas/os and rendering invisible the socioeconomic status differences of Latinas/os across race that exist.

The disparities in living standards among Latinas/os of different races may thus also account for the increased willingness to identify as Afro-Latina/o in the United States (Darity Jr., Hamilton, and Dietrich 2010). Furthermore the segregated residential patterns of Afro-Latinas/os in areas of African American settlement provide Afro-Latina/o youth with an exposure to African American culture and racial consciousness that also influences their choice to identify as Afro-Latinas/os (Golash-Boza and Darity Jr. 2008). Indeed, one study of Afro-Dominicans found that the longer Afro-Dominicans resided in the United States, the more likely they were to identify with African Americans (Bailey 2001). These are all issues that warrant much closer examination in the field of Latina/o studies.

There are notable exceptions to the disregard for Afro-Latina/o subjects in Latina/o studies. Latina/o scholars Miriam Jiménez Román and Juan Flores made a significant contribution to the field when they published *The Afro-Latin@ Reader: History and Culture in the United States* in 2010. The anthology is a rich compilation of texts regarding Afro-Latina/o identity, history, culture and politics.

In addition to making a significant contribution to Latina/o studies, the burgeoning work on Afro-Latinas/os also enriches other related fields such as Black studies and African diaspora studies. Frank Guridy's (2010) work examining the cross-national relationships between Afro-Cubans and African-Americans is a prime example of the production of knowledge in this area, along with Antonio López's (2012) distillation of a century-long archive of Afro-Cuban / African American experiences in the United States. Nancy Raquel Mirabal (2017) has focused on Afro-Cubans in New York City in the nineteenth and twentieth centuries. In addition, the intersectional positions of Afro-Latina women (Jorge 1979; Comas-Diaz 1996; Vega, Alba, and Modestin 2012) and Afro-Latino gays and Afro-Latina lesbians (Lara 2010; Johnson and Rivera-Servera 2016) are also beginning to be researched. It is to be hoped that with the growth of knowledge of Afro-Latinas/os, the discipline of Latina/o studies will continue to expand and move beyond representations of Latinas/os as racially homogenous.

2

Americas

Alexandra T. Vazquez

Imagine carrying a gargantuan landmass, capped by glaciers, across your shoulders, the way people pose with reptiles at Coney Island. "Americas" is an impossible wonder to take on. This heavy expanse of a sign has the tendency to weigh down even the most ebullient. It means nothing and everything. America is named and narrated after the Florentine navigator Amerigo Vespucci—a figure whose unverifiable itineraries continue to stump historians across the centuries (Lush, date unknown; Arciniegas 2002; de las Casas 2010). Although he was not the first to encounter all that lay west of Europe, nor are his voyages fully substantiated or substantiatable, the ancient continents were made his attribute by the German cartographer Martin Waldseemüller, who imposed it on his 1507 in utero rendering of the world, the *Universalis Cosmographia* (Hébert 2003). The naming, a grandest of prizes given to this grandest instance of fronting, carries in it a mystifying credit, a grotesque trophy, a cartographer's stamp. Americas has tried hard to shorthand and eradicate vast and dynamic Indigenous conceptions of space and time. As a catch-all, it supports a lazy and willful forgetting of Tawantinsuyu (Quechua for the four regions of the Inca Empire) and Anáhuac (Nahuatl for the Aztec's "land by the waters"). Why these names don't roll off all our tongues suggests the unfamiliar and unrelenting consonants roiling under our collective surface. This imposition of the Old World and all its diseased baggage atop the New, the actual and discursive annihilation of what and who was here before,

is just one method in the genocidal repertoire enabled by what Walter Mignolo calls the "two entangled concepts" of "modernity and coloniality" (Mignolo 2005, 2011; Quijano 2007). Americas is a utility for the making-vague and making-available of history and all its submerged players so that the New World can be easily wedged into the Old World's narrative of progress, within which we'll include area studies. In other fields that hold up the North American academy, "The Americas" is what the field of English, and English discipline, will do just about anything to repress, or make a special issue of, even and especially when it allows for "American Literature" (Saldívar 1991; Brady 2002; Gruesz 2002).

And yet, Americas is one of the dozens, if not hundreds of New World signs (like the "New World") that require an "and yet" after an acknowledgment of its ferocious development and usages. The "and yet" turns up voluminous, insurgent actions that have long been prepared for any annihilating project. It is a creative holding place for that which takes in and moves in the words of Sylvia Wynter (1995, 7), "beyond the premises of both celebrants and the dissidents." And yet, although the term's ambiguity has facilitated violence, its very ambiguity can and has made possible the wondrous availability of Americas for other means. It is warranted and needed when there is a clear line between the us and the them (Martí 2002; Montero 2004). It can be a baroque altar for study that insists on all the racial, ethnic, gendered, and classed histories that have been lived, danced, and sounded across national paradigms; a way of retaining the complications and unpredictable effects of the "coloniality of modernity" without leaving anyone or anything out. There are as many senses of Americas as there are Americans. There is no way to take singular possession of it, even if that is the shared and singular aim of many. Americas suggests all parts north, central, south, and the archipelagos that spindle out from its corners. It is an ongoing, collective process that reveals just how the New World formed and forms the Old. Take the posthumous rebellion by the artist Felix Gonzalez-Torres and his generous minimalist experiments in world-making that shook up the America pavilion at the 2007 Venice Biennale (Spector et al. 2007). Evoked in whatever language or paralanguage, Americas can hold a mangrove tangle of Afro/Hispano/Luso/Franco/Indo/Sino/Creole phonics and accompaniments. To use "Americas" or "Américas" might not matter as it can't ever be fixed or made into a satisfactory pronoun with orthographic correctives. Regardless of whether one wants the word to represent and make legible its internal differences (or not), there is still the fact of all the unfamiliar and unrelenting accents roiling above our collective surface. Americas rustles the singular and plural at once.

And yet, how to take all this in? And just as hard, how can we ever hope to notate all that Americas retains and refrains? Herein lies the possible transformative power of approaching and reproaching the keyword. "Dance to the hurt!" as Earl Lovelace (1998, 14) once wrote. Americas requires the setting up of ghetto blasters on every corner of every sentence. All that makes it and is made up by it in music expands the repertoire of theory and theorists we associate with the Americas in Latina/o studies. Music allows for us to pick up the ends of the hemisphere's vertical lines and work them into a helix, double-dutch style, where all, but especially girls, have made beautiful movements. Hear a most palpable instance in Rita Moreno's version of "América," after and through Chita Rivera, in that standard penned by Bernstein and Sondheim for *West Side Story*. This song, an overheard castaway that deserves and requires further listening, is mistakenly shrugged off—via its women's chorus—as assimilatory fodder. In Moreno's telling, after Rivera, there is a palpable aesthetics developed by immigrant women who make do and find ways to *stay*

alive despite all that works against them. They set us up, to sample the great phrase by Frances R. Aparicio, for "listening to the listeners" (Aparicio 1998). This song is performative anticipation of and feminist trouble for *El Plan de Santa Bárbara* that followed (Chicano Coordinating Council 1969). Several decades later, this "América" is made the primary sample and activist grounds for an anthem that marked the conquest's quincentenary: Los Fabulosos Cadillacs' 1992 "Quinto Centenario" (*Play it!*). Their version of this brutal anniversary occupies the Broadway standard version of "América" so that we may listen to the volatile marrow established by some of its past performers. The song leans on this primary songtext as a rumbic invocation, uses it as a suitcase to carry the ska bomba that jumps out of it several bars later. And when the song shows most of its cards, one will need to jump up and down, hard. The anthem reveals how Americas can't help its myriad punk anti-assimilationisms.

Americas is a sound system: its components, tangled wiring, and conch shells conspire to make immersion the only way in. "Do It Properly," instructs the house super group 2 Puerto Ricans, a Blackman, and a Dominican— just a few of the company members who turn our ears to the inter-American grounds that are always in search of a vocal. To tend to and aerate these grounds, Americas demands that its scholars (whether musician, balloon seller, professor, nurse) be ready for anything; to do Americas properly means always keeping the dance circle flexible enough for all and any kinds of exits and entries. It insists that we change direction, if not give up on the idea of direction once and for all, as Louise Bennett's (2008) "Colonisation in Reverse" has for so long taught us. Americas might denote a particular geography, but it is also the kind of anti-cartographic object, curricular and aesthetic and alive, that gets us toward a more expansive sense of place and time and people.

3

Art
Rita Gonzalez

Latina/o art is the shaping, iterating, and/or interrogating of the cultural expressions of one's relationship—even if contested—to *latinidad*. This definition speaks to the concerns of artists who may choose to directly or indirectly address *latinidad*, as well as to the reception and interpretation of the work of Latina/o artists. When art is used with a qualifier such as the point of origin or gender of an artist, questions arise about whether such a designation implies a uniform or identifiable aesthetic outcome. Just as "Latina/o" and "Latin American" are heavily contested terms, so too is "Latina/o art" in that it can be used as an umbrella term to encompass diverse artistic practices from geometric abstraction to activist driven social practice art.

Adriana Zavala (2015) has addressed the shortcomings of the term "Latin@ art," in particular in its emphasis on immigrant cultures and the ways it does not account for particular histories like the Hispano experience in the Southwest, as well as its elision of class and race differences. Zavala ultimately argues for the importance of Latina/o art as a category worth defining, studying, and supporting so as not to further marginalize the practices of artists who have been relegated to the periphery of attention in American and Latin American art historical accounts.

As a term, "Latina/o" should be considered fluid and similar to the constructed identities of American and Latin American. Latina/o artworks range from the didactic to the diffuse, with some employing the use of clear and succinct iconography to celebrate a cultural knowledge, and others questioning the very framework of nationality, belonging, and authenticity. Guillermo Gómez-Peña (1986) once described as proto-postmodern the hybrid tactics and syncretic aesthetics of Chicano and Latino art. Latina/o art has often been site driven by and critical of institutions, long before site-specific installation art or institutional critique. Muralism has been considered a didactic project bound to the walls, but it has a performative dimension that feminist artists such as Judith Baca and the artist group Asco have elaborated (Cockcroft and Barnet-Sánchez 1993; Latorre 2008; Chavoya and Gonzalez 2011). A deconstruction of language and a problematizing of the role of translation have been key thematics of Latina/o art, as demonstrated by the work of Celia Alvarez Muñoz, Freddy Rodríguez, Coco Fusco, and Ester Hernandez, to name a few.

The term "Latina/o art," like "Latin American art," is increasingly being considered necessary for diversifying the production and critical reception of art histories. Practically speaking, "Latina/o art" can be used to define, in E. Carmen Ramos's (2014) broad term, "a field of production" by Chicanas/os, Puerto Ricans, Cuban Americans, or those of Caribbean or Latin American descent. This "field of production," and the critical apparatus that is being defined by a multidisciplinary group of scholars and curators, emerged out of multiculturalism and the slow but important growth in numbers of Latinas/os in the arts.

While the institutional framing of Latina/o art within art history is important, it is essential to acknowledge the key role of this designation as always having been shaped by distinct communities and audiences. Amalia Mesa-Bains (1989) has called for a criticism that is attentive to the concept of nutrient sources. Mesa-Bains uses the term "nutrient" to describe how culture feeds "sensibility" and "intention." As a scholar and artist, Mesa-Bains describes an intertextual approach to Latina/o art practices, which acknowledges the specificities of place and circumstance. Art historian Jennifer A. González has modeled what she describes as a "historical and dialogic" methodology aligned with this ethos (2008, 17).

The critical task of contextualizing Latina/o art involves not only an intertextual approach but one that acknowledges and promotes a broader history of art spaces and spaces of reception. As a field of study, Latina/o art and cultural history is a recent response born out of civil rights activism, interdisciplinarity, and the growth of institutional support structures. There is a shared sense of belatedness that the category of Latina/o art shares with Latin American art but also with American art. Just as the field of American art had to fight the tendency of equivalencies (American artists are just as good as European), so too do Latin American and Latina/o artists bear the burden of proving themselves worthy of being considered for integration into the canon.

As has been said before in a variety of contexts, the histories of Latina/o art have yet to be fully documented. This focus on documentation of Latina/o art derives from systemic and structural erasures that exclude its importance to the overarching history of art in the United States. Interdisciplinarity has been key to collection, documentation, and assessment as the formation of a critical discourse on Latina/o art has come chiefly from fields outside of art history, in particular literature, ethnic studies, and anthropology (Bishop 2006; Artistic Research 2011).

Whether Latina/o art is always understood as politically engaged depends upon the artist's practice and critical framing of the work. However, there are shared historical conditions, as well as common experiences of erasure and exclusion from the cultural mainstream, that must be considered. Latina/o civil rights movements have shared aesthetic, community-based strategies, with strong print cultures connecting struggles of Puerto Ricans and Chicanas/os, for example. At the same time, U.S.-based Latina/o artists have responded to government interventions in Central America. In this sense, Latina/o art is a strategic means to identify affinities, whether those are shared historical legacies or similar political and aesthetic modalities.

In *Resisting Categories: Latin American and/or Latino?*, Héctor Olea, Mari Carmen Ramírez, and Tomás Ybarra-Frausto, scholars and architects of a major art historical documentation project on Latina/o and Latin American art, describe Latina/o and Latin American art as an "intellectual field," focusing on how grassroots, activist, and academic print cultures have been key in "defining" and "defying" these terms (2012, 40–49). They also subscribe to a majority opinion in the field of art history, which has taken Latin American and Latina/o art to be an "operative concept" or "construct"—that is to say, one that is problematic yet necessary to make an argument for the inclusion, qualification, and appreciation of this art.

The critical reception of Latina/o art has also of late been defined by a certain refusal on behalf of mainstream art critics to acknowledge the need for identity-based frameworks, with the argument being that grouping artists together according to cultural affiliation is no longer necessary or desirable. Ironically, this has been an argument that has also been fostered by Latina/o artists who want their work to be judged on aesthetic merits or demand that their work be shown within a variety of art historical considerations. Exhibitions such as El Museo's Bienal *The S Files* (Museo del Barrio, New York, 2000–ongoing), *Phantom Sightings: Art After the Chicano Movement* (LACMA 2008), and *The Question Is Known:*

(W)here Is Latin American/Latino Art (Mission Cultural Center for Latino Arts, San Francisco, 2008) used a variety of curatorial frameworks to present Latina/o art forms as a multitude of conceptual and formal approaches, at times at odds with each other (Gonzalez, Fox, and Noriega 2008).

Criticism and reflections on Latina/o art have to negotiate a dual (or even multiple) reality of transnational identity while still understanding how the local or regional inform the works of many artists. There have been numerous critiques of the overemphasis on Latina/o artists and movements in California, New York, Texas, and Florida, leaving under-acknowledged the role of Latinas/os in the Midwest, Pacific Northwest, and even the South (Herrera 2008).

Art is by and large a creative expression, but the arbiters of meaning and value oftentimes delineate what is deemed to be art. When art is formally codified, or recognized and identified, as such, in general, determining factors are "funding sources, public exhibitions, art collection, and critical discourse" (Noriega 1999, 187). While both Latina/o and Latin American artists as well as those who investigate their work have fought for inclusion and representation, the outcome for each field has differed dramatically. There are concerns and struggles in both the Latin American and Latina/o art historical fields that overlap, as reflected in the title for the aforementioned ICAA's critical anthology *Resisting Categories: Latin American and/or Latino?*, but there are also differences in vantage point. Structures of validation and legitimization will function differently because, as Tomás Ybarra-Frausto (2013) articulates, "Latino Arts have been mainly created and disseminated apart from official cultural patronage and institutions." This points to an apparent paradox concerning the presence of Latina/o artists, especially those whose practices are not easily integrated into the mainstream.

4

Assimilation

Catherine S. Ramírez

Assimilation has long functioned as the *telos* in narratives about the American experience and as an organizing rubric in U.S. immigration history, the social sciences, particularly sociology, and public policy (Alba and Nee 2007). Immigrants and their U.S.-born descendants are expected to blend into and to find acceptance, if not success, in the mainstream. Indeed, assimilation is often linked to the American dream. Those who do not assimilate or who are deemed inassimilable are generally regarded and treated as outsiders or failed citizens.

Assimilation is the process whereby the boundary between mainstream and margin blurs, disappears, or paradoxically, is reinforced. While the term is commonly used in the United States in relation to immigrants, it may also be applied to any group not deemed part of the mainstream, such as religious, linguistic, and sexual minorities, and to the production, circulation, and consumption of cultural practices and products (for example, Mexican food, such as burritos and guacamole). In this latter sense, "to assimilate" is synonymous with "to mainstream" or "to cross over." In many instances of assimilation, formerly distinguishable groups, practices, or products eradicate, blend into, or transform one another, becoming more similar in the process. However, in others, the dominant group absorbs a minority or minoritized group as its distinct, constitutive, and subordinate other.

The paradoxical process by which a person or group assimilates or is assimilated as an outsider is known as differential inclusion (De Genova, Mezzadra, and Pickles 2015). Examples of differential inclusion can be found in the U.S. Supreme Court cases of *Cherokee Nation v. Georgia* (1831), *Dred Scott v. Sandford* (1857), and *Downes v. Bidwell* (1901), which respectively saw the incorporation of the Cherokee as "wards" of a "guardian" state (*Cherokee Nation v. Georgia* 30 U. S. 2), African Americans as members of "a subordinate and inferior class of beings" (*Dred Scott v. Sandford* 60 U. S. 404–405) and the island of Puerto Rico as "foreign . . . in a domestic sense" (*Downes v. Bidwell* 182 U. S. 341). The figure of the model minority also exemplifies differential inclusion. Lisa Sun-Hee Park argues that the model minority does not enjoy "full citizenship rights . . . but rather, a secondary set of rights reserved for particular minorities who 'behave' appropriately and stay in their designated subsidiary space without complaint" (2015, 17). In his memoir *Hunger of Memory* (1982), Richard Rodriguez, the son of Spanish-speaking Mexican immigrants, rails against bilingual education, affirmative action, and identity politics in a plea for assimilation and colorblindness. Yet this former Berkeley PhD student and expert in British Renaissance literature enters the mainstream not as a bona fide American writer, but as a model minority and, paradoxically, a "representative 'Hispanic' subject" (Schmidt Camacho 2008, 206).

The sociologist Robert E. Park and his colleagues at the University of Chicago have been credited with theorizing the concept of assimilation in the early twentieth century. While the Chicago School's influence on American social sciences is apparent, the concept predates its members' publications and is implicit in earlier practices, policies, institutions, and narratives, such as proposals to deport putatively unassimilable African Americans in the eighteenth and nineteenth centuries and efforts to "civilize" Native Americans in the nineteenth and twentieth. In the early twenty-first century,

"assimilation," "acculturation," "incorporation," and "integration" are often used interchangeably. However, a number of scholars are careful to distinguish those terms from one another. For example, acculturation (the minority's adoption of the dominant language, dress, diet, habitus, and so on), incorporation (for example, through naturalization), and integration (the opposite of exclusion or segregation) may be stages in the assimilation process and are not necessarily the same as assimilation in and of itself.

During the first half of the twentieth century, "assimilation" in the United States was synonymous with "Americanization" and "Anglo-conformity," terms that signaled the dissolution of the immigrant's or minority group's culture within and by an Anglo-Protestant mainstream. With the civil rights and Black Power movements and surge in ethnic revivalism among Americans of all stripes, the imperative to assimilate into a dominant Anglo-Protestant culture appeared to wane in the last decades of the twentieth century. Scholars questioned what had come to be known as the "assimilation model" (Morawska 1994) and proffered instead the "bumpy line" (Gans 1992) theory of assimilation, foregrounding the retention of the immigrant group's native language and customs in the host society. In "Is Assimilation Dead?," the sociologist Nathan Glazer (1993) declared assimilation a failure, not only because the ideologies of pluralism and multiculturalism had eclipsed it, he argued, but because African Americans remained socially and economically marginalized.

The title of Glazer's article notwithstanding, Americans never abandoned the concept of assimilation altogether. Since the 1940s, the ideologies of pluralism and multiculturalism have allowed many to assimilate into the mainstream as so-called ethnic or hyphenated Americans (Roediger 2005; Jacobson 2008). As scholars in critical whiteness studies have demonstrated, one way "provisional whites," like the Irish in the nineteenth century and Italians in the twentieth, became bona fide Americans was by actively distancing themselves from blacks and other groups branded "colored," such as the Chinese and Mexicans (Hochschild 1995; Jacobson 1998; Roediger 1999).

Assertions that a group is unable or unwilling to assimilate bring into relief assimilation's relationship to citizenship and race. For example, some Americans opposed extending citizenship to Mexicans domiciled in the Mexican Cession and to Puerto Ricans because they considered those groups physically, culturally, and morally unfit for the responsibilities of U.S. democracy during the nineteenth and early twentieth centuries. In short, they considered Mexicans and Puerto Ricans non-white. As a number of laws—from the 1790 Naturalization Act on—stressed, U.S. citizenship was supposed to be the purview and property of whites. Ultimately, Article VIII of the Treaty of Guadalupe Hidalgo, the 1848 treaty that ended the Mexican American War, made Mexicans eligible for U.S. citizenship, while the Jones Act of 1917 conferred U.S. citizenship on Puerto Ricans. The extension of citizenship to these groups rendered them whites, if only in name and not in practice. It also prompted a generation of Latina/o activists to fight for full citizenship by claiming whiteness during the first half of the twentieth century (Foley 1997; Guglielmo 2006; Haney López 2006).

Despite their nominal whiteness, Latinas/os have long been seen and treated as foreigners in the United States. For example, many Mexican Americans were derided as "greasers" or "beaners" by white Americans and as *pochos* by Mexicans throughout the twentieth century. *Pocho* originally meant faded, overripe, or expired, but in Mexican Spanish, it came to refer to an Americanized Mexican or Mexican American. Historically, it has been pejorative. Rather than highlight biculturalism, cultural hybridity, or transculturation—the last a term coined by the Cuban anthropologist Fernando Ortiz (1995) to signify the merging and converging of cultures—the label has been associated with alienation and cultural and linguistic loss and degradation on both sides of the U.S.-Mexico border. However, in the last decades of the twentieth century, Latina/o cultural workers began to ascribe new, affirmative meaning to *pocho*, just as an earlier generation had reclaimed the erstwhile invective *Chicano*.

In the early twenty-first century, doubts about Latina/o immigrants' ability to be good Americans have resurfaced, with some immigration restrictionists insisting that those who enter or remain in the United States without authorization are undeserving of regularization (whether it be through permanent residency or naturalization) and that the U.S.-born children of undocumented immigrants, so-called anchor babies, should not be eligible for birthright citizenship as provided by the Fourteenth Amendment. Because they have long been associated with undocumented migration and temporary labor and because of the proximity of their homeland to the United States, Mexicans are deemed especially unassimilable. They are also seen as a threat to Anglo-Protestant culture and institutions, with some cultural commentators lamenting the "browning" of the United States and warning about a *reconquista* of the lands once held by Mexico (Hanson 2003; Huntington 2004b). The political scientist Adrián Félix (2008) has labeled Mexicans' perceived inability and/or unwillingness to assimilate "Mexican exceptionalism."

Concepts like differential inclusion and Mexican exceptionalism signal that assimilation in the United States can be a partial and contradictory process. Social actors are frequently assimilated in or by one social arena, but excluded from or by another. For instance, undocumented workers are, by and large, well

ASSIMILATION CATHERINE S. RAMÍREZ

integrated in the U.S. economy in the early twenty-first century. At the same time, those workers are not formally assimilated by the state. In many cases, they are actively excluded and persecuted by the state. Often, undocumented workers' inclusion in the market depends on and derives from their exclusion in other social arenas.

Similarly, some undocumented individuals, especially those who arrived in the United States at a young age, have acculturated. They speak English without a foreign accent, generally do not wear distinctive signs of foreignness, such as turbans or *huipiles*, and participate in mainstream society—for example, as students or soldiers. Many of these immigrants call themselves and are called "undocumented Americans" and/or "DREAMers," a reference to the Development, Relief, and Education for Alien Minors Act, which was first introduced in 2001 in the United States legislature but has not been passed (Vargas 2013). Especially if they grew up in the United States unaware of their undocumented status, many pass as Americans and feel American, signaling the performative and affective aspects of assimilation. Yet as "illegal aliens," they are marginalized, particularly in the market, and are vulnerable to exploitation and deportation.

Where DREAMers have been upheld as valuable and vital members of American society who lack formal citizenship, the alien citizen is a U.S. citizen by virtue of her/his birth in that country, but is presumed to be and is treated as foreign (Ngai 2004). The concept of alien citizenship points to the simultaneity of formal membership in the polity and de facto or de jure marginalization or exclusion. The historian Mae M. Ngai maintains that Mexican Americans' association with temporary labor in the United States—a tradition going back to the Bracero Program—has rendered them alien citizens.

The figures of the undocumented American, DREAMer, alien citizen, and bracero expose the discrepancy between economic and social integration and membership in the polity, between citizenship as process or practice (what some scholars call "cultural citizenship") and citizenship as legal status (Rosaldo 1994; Coll 2010; Glenn 2011). Moreover, they point to intersectionality (the nexus of social identities, categories, and relationships, such as race, class, gender, and sexuality) and show that inclusion at one level of society can reinforce and even be predicated on marginalization in or exclusion at another.

Like differential inclusion, the concepts of segmented assimilation and racial naturalization draw attention to assimilation as a vexed process. Segmented assimilation, as theorized by the sociologists Alejandro Portes and Min Zhou (1993), posits that individuals and groups assimilate into a particular segment of society, not necessarily the mainstream. While some individuals and groups have assimilated and continue to assimilate into the white mainstream in the United States, others are barred from it due to differences that are perceived as insurmountable. These individuals and groups may be incorporated into other segments of the population, such as "ethnic niches" and "enclaves" or racial minority groups (Kasinitz, Battle, and Miyares 2001). For example, black immigrants from Africa, the Caribbean, and Latin America and their descendants may assimilate and be assimilated as African Americans, a process the critical race scholar Devon W. Carbado (2005) terms "racial naturalization." His concept highlights the ways in which some groups are violently included in the United States via racial subordination and exclusion from the white mainstream.

"Assimilation" is an important term in Latina/o studies, but not so much because it should function as a lens for narrating and interpreting Latina/o history or the so-called Latina/o experience. Nor should assimilation be dismissed as a force to be resisted so that a beleaguered, static, or enduring cultural identity can be uncovered and rescued. Rather, assimilation merits critical attention because of the ways in which it points to differential inclusion, segmented assimilation, and racial naturalization—in short, inclusion in a tiered society rife with inequalities. Assimilation illuminates belonging just as much as it sheds lights on marginalization and exclusion. Finally, assimilation allows us to understand the dynamism of culture and society and the complex relationship between social structures and social agents. Assimilation is often a two-way process, albeit an uneven one (Zolberg and Woon 1999). Latinas/os will continue to transform the United States just as the United States continues to transform Latinas/os.

5

Barrio
Gina M. Pérez

At its most basic level, "barrio" refers to a place—a neighborhood, community, enclave, and/or region—that is familiar to many and evokes a range of affective responses. Unlike the term *colonia*, which conjures ideas of semi-rural spatial formations, barrios are often imagined as decidedly urban spaces—as dense enclaves, which are familiar features of American cities (Sánchez Korrol 1994; D. Diaz 2005; Vigil 2008; Ward 2010). They are places born out of histories of segregation, uneven development, conflict, and marginalization; but they are also the precious spaces that affirm cultural identities, nurture popular cultural production, and provide sanctuary for people with long histories of displacement, land loss, repression, and collective struggle. In this way, barrios share a great deal in common with African American ghettos. According to Diego Vigil, both spaces derived from people's experiences of having to "settle in inferior places that were spatially separate and socially distanced from the dominant majority group" (2008, 366; also see D. Diaz 2005). This spatial and social isolation exacerbated economic, political, and social marginalization and contributed to powerful narratives of racial and cultural difference, which both stigmatized residents and justified their continued marginalization. But as many scholars, artists, and activists have noted, "There is another side of this view of segregation" (Beveridge 2008, 358). This involves individuals making a conscious choice to live in spaces that circumvent, as much as possible, their stigmatization by whites and to pursue opportunities to "develop on their own in their own communities" (Beveridge 2008, 358; also see Jackson 2001). It is precisely this other side of barrio life—as a space for cultural affirmation, ethnic solidarity, collective determination, and nostalgia—that leads its residents to defend and preserve these spaces in the face of powerful stigmatizing forces. As Raúl Villa notes, the barrio is "a complex and contradictory social space" (2000, 8). In short, *el barrio* is simultaneously a place, space, and metaphor with a range of meanings for scholars, policy makers, residents, and artists (Pérez, Guridy, and Burgos 2011).

Cities like New York, Los Angeles, and Chicago have long histories of barrio formation, which share important structural similarities as well as notable differences. As with African American ghettos and Chinese enclaves, racism, residential segregation, poverty, and social marginalization were structural forces giving shape to barrios beginning in the late nineteenth century. In Los Angeles, for example, Mexican residents were relegated to "ecologically inferior neighborhoods" like East Los Angeles as a result of land loss, demographic shifts, and public policy measures, which racially marked and socially isolated Mexican residents in the city (Vigil 2008, 366; Villa 2000; D. Diaz 2005). Similar histories of dispossession and displacement also led to the formation of El Barrio (also known as East Harlem or Spanish Harlem) in New York City, with the initial arrival of thousands of Puerto Rican migrants in the early twentieth century; in the post–World War II era, the barrio grew rapidly as a result of U.S-led industrialization and economic and social displacement in Puerto Rico (Sánchez Korrol 1994; Dávila 2004). While specific geopolitical and economic forces set populations in motion to U.S. cities, barrios developed as a result of specific policies on the local, state, and federal levels, which not only caused and codified racial segregation, but also reflected patterns of unequal urban development that contributed to the proliferation of substandard and limited housing stock and poor schooling, as well as severely circumscribing people's economic mobility (Logan and Molotch 1987; Fernández 2011; Pérez, Guridy, and Burgos 2011). In the popular imagination, early twentieth-century barrios were replete with social pathologies, disorder, and disease. Similarly stigmatized, their residents were the object of policy interventions aimed at ameliorating social ills through, for example, public health campaigns and Americanization efforts. These efforts often focused on women as potential agents of change in the name of protecting the broader public from social and physical ills originating in barrios and their residents (Ruiz 1998; Briggs 2002b; Molina 2006; Mckiernan-González 2012). Thus, while the specific plans and policies that led to the creation of diminished social and economic mobility were increasingly invisible to the broader public, barrio residents were increasingly visible, stigmatized, and regarded as a problem that needed to be solved.

Despite negative characterizations, barrios are spaces where meaningful communities, social networks, cultural institutions, businesses, and social organizations are created and sustained. They are places that offer "some security in the midst of the city's social and economic turmoil" (Griswold del Castillo 1979, 150) and "preserve the integrity of [people's] cultural place-identity within and against the often hostile space regulation of dominant urbanism" (Villa 2000, 5). As Arlene Dávila observes, places like El Barrio (Spanish Harlem) in New York City have a kind of preciousness not only because they are the spaces where people have worked, engaged in collective struggles, and built communities, but also because through these efforts, residents have "imbued space with meanings and memories" (2004, 64). For many scholars, *el barrio* is a unique and critical space to nurture distinctive forms of cultural production, political organizing, and solidarity (Ybarra-Frausto 1989; Muñiz 1998; J. Flores 2000; Villa 2000; Gaspar de Alba 2003; Rivera 2003; Nabhan-Warren 2005; Treviño 2006; Iber and Regalado 2007; Cordova 2011). Creative writers have also focused on *el barrio* as a way to explore issues of individual and collective survival, violence, assimilation, resistance, and self-discovery (Thomas 1967; Galarza 1971; Cofer 1980, 1995; Cisneros 1984; L. Rodriguez 1993). And still others have directed their efforts at providing historical context and critical analysis in order to address and ameliorate the criminalization, marginalization, and social dislocation of barrios and their residents (Dohan 2003; Díaz-Cotto 2006; Vigil 2007; Rios 2011).

Although barrios often tend to be conceptualized in homogenous terms, they have always been far more heterogeneous, serving as home to a range of people from different national origins, class positions, and distinct racial, gender, and sexual identities. Historic barrios in urban centers serve as important settlement communities for newcomers from different Latin American and Caribbean nations, who have often significantly transformed the cultural landscape. The changing demographics of barrios, along with urban development policies upscaling formerly marginal barrios, has had a dramatic impact on many communities and has ushered in community organizing efforts to preserve the use value of working-class neighborhoods (Villa 2000; Dávila 2004; G. Pérez 2004; Rúa 2012). These efforts have also been buttressed by powerful narratives of uplift that provide yet another way of conceptualizing barrio: it is a metaphor used to capture spatial, social, and economic mobility. From prominent U.S. congressional representatives (Gutiérrez 2013) to well-regarded businessmen, narratives of leaving barrios for boardrooms (Rentería 2011), Capitol Hill, and the Supreme Court (Sotomayor 2013) provide poignant insight into the unique struggles Latina/o communities face in their efforts to gain access to quality education, housing, health care, social services, and public recognition not only for their own self-improvement, but also their commitments to improve the lives of the communities from which they come. As sociologist Jody Agius Vallejo observes, upward mobility for middle-class Mexican Americans leaving "barrios for burbs" defies the conventional wisdom that presupposes assimilation and integration into white middle-class society by the ways their middle-class aspirations include familial obligation, a desire to give back to one's community, racial and ethnic identity, and civic participation (2012a).

Over the course of the twentieth and early twenty-first century, barrios have become ubiquitous features of American cities, a reality that underscores the enduring legacies of spatialized inequalities in urban America. Neoliberal urban development policies beginning in the 1990s not only hardened of the contours of some barrios in cities like Chicago and New York, but also opened up new development strategies that relied on the commodification of cultural spaces as entities to be marketed and sold (Dávila 2004). Sometimes, as in Chicago's Puerto Rican neighborhood of Humboldt Park, community activists have successfully harnessed municipal resources to revitalize urban spaces in culturally significant ways, to resist the negative consequences of gentrification, and to preserve cultural institutions, practices, organizations, and identities. In other instances, as in Union City, New Jersey, the Latinization of urban spaces is contested, undermined, and dismantled in the name of revitalization and urban redevelopment, processes that increasingly rely on private investment and reflect racial and class hierarchies (Londoño 2012). Thus, while some scholars have pointed to the curious ways that the New Urbanism—with its emphasis on live-work spaces, walkable neighborhoods, face-to-face encounters, and communal public space—is, in fact, what David R. Diaz and Rodolfo D. Torres (2012) refer to as "barrio urbanism," they also emphasize how these trends often do very little to ameliorate the political and economic forces that continue to generate and sustain spatialized inequality based on class, ethnicity, and race. Barrios, therefore, remain complex and complicated spaces that play an important role in Latina/o social, political, and scholarly work. They are enduring reminders of dire material conditions in which many Latinas/os live, work, and build meaningful lives; yet they also highlight *el barrio*'s deep cultural, material, and symbolic meanings for so many who seek not only to ameliorate economic and social conditions, but also to preserve them as precious spaces that nurture and sustain cultural identities and ways of living and being and as spaces of hope, resistance, and radical possibility.

6

Borderlands
Nicole M. Guidotti-Hernández

Borders are fictions of material consequence, created by empires and fortified with the invention of the modern nation-state. They restrict the limits of territory and mark the transition between kingdoms, colonies, and private land holdings in advanced capitalist societies. Where national territory or private property begin and end, borders signal the essence of power relations. The actual geographic spaces of borders tend to be highly contested. Particular to Latina/o studies, the boundaries of Spanish and Anglophone empires and of the nation-state pervade how we theorize borders and borderlands in the field. While some borders are highly privileged and centralized, others are just as contested.

The subfield of borderlands theory emerged in the late 1980s. Part theory of language, part theory of subjectivity, and part theory of geography, it accounts for the relationship between the centers and margins of power, which are in dialectic tension for Latina/o populations. As Juan Flores and George Yúdice have stated, the "border houses the power of the outrageous, the imagination needed to turn the historical and cultural tables. The view from the border enables us to apprehend the ultimate arbitrariness of the border itself, of forced separations and inferiorizations. Latino expression forces the issue, which tops the agenda of American culture" (1990, 80). A generative site of theory, the study of borders and the borderlands subfield are essential to understanding of communities, self, and subject-formation.

We cannot know borderlands theories or geographies in Latina/o studies without considering how the colonization of the New World impacted the categorical formation "Latina/o" as an identity and subject position in the making. An expanded definition of borderlands would argue that an ocean can be a border, especially if we consider the history of Chinese migration to the Americas in the fomenting of a diaspora. So, too, can a river be a border, as in the case of the Rio Grande dividing Mexico and Texas. Intensifying the geopolitics of borderlands to include water as a defense line, especially in the case of the divide between Cuba and the United States, has created much of the discourse that dominates Latina/o studies today. Militarized *fronteras* infiltrate how we understand what it means to be Latina/o in the Américas. Moreover, the abstract concept of "border" becomes materialized through policing, inclusion, exile, and permitted passage, setting the stage for how the creation of a "border" morphs into a borderlands imaginary.

In this spatial ordering of the world, travel pathways, water, and mobility are privileged, not strict community and national boundaries. Borderlands theories come into being precisely because with the advent of British and Spanish Empires, contact contributed to a gradual and more intensified demarcation of territory over time. Porous psychic and spatial collisions of value and an expansive imagining territory as localized created the groundwork for the borderlands theories and histories we have come to know today. A multi-border perspective in Latina/o studies cites myriad international and psychic boundaries that acknowledge conflicts with Indigenous and Afro-descendent populations because these communities are at odds with their mestizo and Anglo contemporaries in the maintenance of territory and freedom. But we must also remember that the context of such communities historically pits civilization against barbarism. Violence represents a desire to at once

stabilize borders and boundaries and track their fluidity. Fully steeped in militarized rhetoric, barbarism stays with us as a means of empire's self-justification. An offshoot of borderlands theory is a discussion of mestizaje, the racial mixing of European, black, and Indigenous peoples. While many contemporary critics celebrate mestizaje as a form of cultural hybridity that will save us from domination, it is not a panacea. Similarly, native peoples and immigrants described with hostility and/or barbarity contextualize militarism as the basis of borderlands theories.

And yet, when we think of borderlands in Latina/o studies, we should also localize our conversation in Central American America (Arias 2003). Scholars like Ana Patricia Rodríguez (2009) and Claudia Milian (2013) deconstruct the configuration of the isthmus by pointing to the hierarchical nature of the north-south continuum as an uninterrupted cartographic binary. Their multi-nodal approach claims and reorients spatial dynamics of power and borderlands discourse in the Americas by turning our attention to El Salvador, Honduras, Guatemala, and their respective diasporas wrought by U.S.-backed military interventionist wars in these nations. The view from the center, that which is Centroamérica, or what Kristen Silva Gruesz (2012) has called "Centrocéntrico," is an intervention into current time-space continuums that dominate the field of Latina/o studies. By reorienting reading practices, we see that historical recovery becomes one of the fundamental methodological modes for redress by charting the isthmus as a U.S. Latina/o borderland.

The Haiti–Dominican Republic dividing line is also central to borderlands theory. Silvio Torres-Saillant (1997), Sibylle Fischer (2004), David Scott (2004), Ginetta E. B. Candelario (2007), Susan Buck-Morss (2009), Lauren Derby (2009), and Lorgia García-Peña (2016) all examine Hispanic Caribbean racial imaginaries to demonstrate how racial identification for the Dominican subject has historically been shaped by the actual and imaginary borders between the Dominican Republic and Haiti. The Murder of the Galindo Virgins on May 30, 1822, is one foundational narrative for Haiti-Dominican borderlands discourses. Of the three men who were convicted of killing the young girls, only one, Pedro Covial, was Haitian, and yet this event was used to mobilize the nascent Dominican nation against a vile black Haitian enemy. In addition, a notion of Hispanic culture became the means by which to identify Dominican nationals, while Indigeneity was the mechanism for explaining the racial mix that made Dominicans not black (García-Peña 2016). Haiti–Dominican Republic borderlands buttress Caribbean Latina/o studies' theorizations of racialization—blackness and Indigeneity through spatiality—and extend U.S. land borders by influencing and constructing liminality, psychic spaces of conflict, and forced migration histories for Dominicans and Haitians on the mainland because of U.S. military interventions.

The U.S.-Mexico border dominates field-based borderlands theories, especially in early work by Américo Paredes (1995a), who examined the complex relationships that ethnic Mexicans had with Mexico and with the United States, as well as the dialectic tension between Spanish and English, cultural and political citizenship, and modernity and tradition in "Greater Mexico." There is no doubt that the U.S.-Mexico border is "the" border in Latina/o studies, despite the fact that the very same border is more primary to Chicana/o studies. The fact that the United States and Mexico physically touch each other signals intimacy, conflict, and marginality. That intimacy has become the basis for the institutionalization of regionalism and nationalism in Chicana/o and borderlands studies and their preoccupation with that border as a site of violence and conflict where cooperation and collusion of state powers deport migrants regularly and allow drugs to flow with ease.

For diverse reasons, Gloria Anzaldúa's *Borderlands / La Frontera: The New Mestiza* (1987) is a hallmark of the field. A strong and unapologetic humanistic theory of the violence embodied in spatial and cultural clashes, Anzaldúa's work addresses intimacy as a shrunken space between two individuals and two nations. Borderlands intimacy can be applied to any space of conflict, including the inner psyche of subject formation. In theorizing plural intimacies and sexual difference, she provides a template for how intersectionality (simultaneous compounding forces of race, class, gender, disability, sexuality, and generation) marks subjects for discipline and discovery. Clashes of culture and nations delimit how we cannot have the one object without the other (the United States without Mexico), as they are co-constitutive. And while the United States and Mexico have clearly maintained an uncomfortable intimacy for hundreds of years, the culture of injury and renewal harkens to racial mixing as much as it does to the flowing waters of the Rio Grande that separate the two nations geographically. Vague, undetermined, and fixed through an international border that determines the safe and unsafe, borderlands are everywhere and nowhere, and can impact the subject at any time. Norma Alarcón argues that "formations of violence are continuously in the making" (1996, 44), and the U.S.-Mexico border and the subjects who live along, around, or on it make the process possible. Borderlands theories of intimacy and violence are a means of reckoning with the "use of space to naturalize violent racial, gender, sexual and class ideologies," as Mary Pat Brady has argued (2002, 6). Overall, borderlands theories provide intellectual and actual mobility that is often denied to those non-normative sexual or racialized individuals who live at the margins of society.

According to Antonio Viego's understanding of the border subject via both Anzaldúa and Frances R. Aparicio (2003b), "Prior to living between two cultures, the transmovement of the human subject is reflected in its movement between two or more signifiers. . . . Whatever split, whatever breech, or division implied by the term *border* is ultimately explained by social, cultural, and historical determinants" (2007, 128). Here, it is the borders of language and the use of psychoanalytic theory that form border subjects, not the actual U.S.-Mexico border. The middle land of *nepantla* is breech and rupture, and transmovement of the subject, which preexists contact with a physical border, even if a border shapes the psychobiography of a people. Metaphorically charged in nature, *nepantla* (a concept from the Nahuatl language extensively employed by Anzaldúa) and the ideas of border as signifier shape psychic borderlands. When Aparicio argues that "the theorization and development of the concept of a border subject and hybrid identity has been one of the most significant contributions of Latino studies to cultural studies" (2003b, 20), she dislodges the border subject and borderlands from a strictly Chicana/o and/or U.S.-Mexico paradigm. The concept instead demonstrates theoretical and geographic flexibility. The appeal for a Latina/o studies genealogy is not about authenticity (who gets to claim borderlands as their concept), but rather how we create our own narratives to challenge authority, document existence, and name the subject as a subject. Hence, borderlands theory is just as much about explaining the cutting up of lands, bodies, and psyches as it is about territorial disputes and disparate geographies of Latina/o studies.

While pivotal, decentering the U.S.-Mexico borderlands as "the border" reveals that the assumed cartographies of Latina/o studies are suspect and that when we evoke borders or borderlands, we need to provide our students myriad models of particular Caribbean, Central American, or Pacific flashpoints. This suggests that in addition to stressing 1848 (the signing of the Treaty of Guadalupe Hidalgo that established the U.S./Mexico border), we must recognize 1822 (the Haitian invasion of the Dominican Republic), 1898 (the Spanish-American War involving Cuba, Puerto Rico, and the Filipinas), and U.S. military interventions in Central America during the 1980s. With these particular time-space imperial referents, the middle, Central America and the Caribbean, disrupt the U.S./Mexico binary. That middle would suggest that Central Americans, Puerto Ricans, Dominicans, and even Filipinos are not the newest Latina/o groups but rather, as Gruesz points out, "a newly visible subgroup" (2012).

The very real geography of borders and borderlands, and the kinds of violent racist regimes they produce, is, thus, not just a fiction on the page but in fact the cleaner version of lived and embodied experiences. The Latina/o multi-border perspective can both reorient the narrative history of the Americas and account for the ways in which particular racial or sexual formations such as those of queer, Afro-descendant, or Indigenous populations tend to be erased from the Latina/o United States. The multi-border analytic can guide us to consider comparatively or synchronically, the historic relational and distinct experiences of Spanish colonial spatial organization (the specificities of Spanish empire in the Americas and elsewhere, in relation and conflict with American imperialism), or borderlands as mutually constitutive. Perhaps a multi-border perspective on borderlands is the rubric Latina/o studies needs to unseat particular kinds of celebratory and recuperative nationalisms, mestizajes, and epistemologies that stake their claims in land, essentialism, or authenticity. Borderlands, then, should always be hemispheric, plural, and multi-sited. The Latina/o studies scholar and student must not take for granted the definitions of borders or borderlands. We must question why certain borders are privileged as sites of intellectual inquiry over others. The hemisphere is our borderland.

7

Brown

Joshua Javier Guzmán

Brown is not an identity. Brown, along with its nominal form, *brownness*, are also not objects of knowledge in the ways that identity markers such as "Latina/o" or "Chicana/o" are in the late twentieth and early twenty-first centuries. The more popularly used ethnic marker aligned with a certain hue or accent of brownness, "Latina/o" is widely understood as designating a population historically displaced from Latin America and living in the United States. Other identity variants exist within the Latina/o population that are assigned to people from specific national and cultural heritages; the most widely used of these is the politically charged banner of Chicana/o, which signifies a person of Mexican descent or origin living in the U.S. Southwest. The definitional incoherence of Latina/o—let alone Chicana/o, Cuban American, Nuyorican, and so on—reveals how not all identities capture the people, lives, and experiences they seek to demarcate. As a result, the aesthetic realm, particularly colors such as white, black, yellow, red, and brown, points to the impossible collection of people under one racial or ethnic category in the United States.

The categorical crisis within race and ethnicity in the United States from which brown gains its political importance reveals how brown is hard to categorize as well, and especially when one tries to make sense of brown as a temporal phenomenon. Sometimes brownness evokes an eerie anticipation for what José Vasconcelos (1925) termed *la raza cósmica*. The cosmic race might be understood as

a speculative fiction describing a future wherein an agglomeration of all the races will yield a Universópolis, a new civilization formed without respect to color since all will be a part of *la raza de bronce*. The alloyed components in bronze seem to promise, like Vasconcelos, the successful outcome of mixture and thus of a unified *polis* to come. On the one hand, brown tells a story of the ongoing mixing of all races, driven by a postracial ideology that then ignores the incommensurable differences of those singular beings organized and managed by oppressive regimes. In her essay "La Güera," the Chicana lesbian thinker Cherríe Moraga has warned that in the United States "lesbianism is a poverty—as is being brown, as is being a woman, as is being just plain poor. . . . The danger lies in failing to acknowledge the specificity of the oppression" (Moraga 1983a, 29). "Brown" ambiguously signals unity and distinction. This makes brownness hard to ignore since it terrifies those who attempt to whitewash history. White supremacist America flails in anxiety at the imminent threat of immigrant bodies, consequently revealing *his* logic within the artificial naming of brown people as *his-panic*. Brown folks are coming, goes the idea, in droves as displaced labor and thus browning *nuestra América*—a very different America than the Cuban poet José Martí might have imagined. What color was the United States before, one might ask? Was it not already brown? Indigenous peoples of the Americas have always *been here*, is also how the logic goes. Contrapuntally, brown people are either on their way or have always been here. But this paradox of recent arrival and simultaneous long presence reveals the very logic of brownness in the contemporary moment: that is, the United States must *become* what it already *is*. In this way, we might even ask, what karmic, though not necessarily punitive, logic discloses itself in brownness?

This question begins to ask how brownness might evoke some form of depressive or antiestablishment pedagogy, in the sense that even when considered in a political vein, brown remains highly ambiguous if not capacious in its meaning. For example, *The Karma of Brown Folk* tells us how brown as a racial signifier is capacious enough in its reach not only to signal Latinas/os or Indigenous peoples within the United States, but also to move transnationally and mark what some call the "global South" (Prashad 2000). From Latin America across South Asia to Frantz Fanon writing in Algeria and up to the present day occupation of Palestine, the karma of brownness runs, on the one hand, as the ongoing if not ubiquitous struggle of anticolonial resistance, while on the other hand, always mysteriously symbolizing what Prashad calls "a fantasy of redemption for the trials of the world" (2000, 2). It can be said that brown—even in the harrowing irony of Hugo Ferdinand Boss's famously designing and manufacturing the SS uniforms in black and brown—stands as the very color of displacement and also the color of fascism. These displaced bodies are signs of displaced futures. After all, any white fantasy of redemption must cover over the loss of the future for some within the here-and-now. It does this by negating brownness, while demanding more labor, more capital, and more care from those it exploits and seeks to put in constant deferral.

Meanwhile, brownness reminds us that this world is never really enough. The loss constituting brownness is not nothing. Far from figuring as lack, brownness stages the smoldering indention of its own vulnerability by exposing itself to erasure in the very act of longing, such as in the brown art work of Ana Mendieta and Felix Gonzalez-Torres. If brownness tells a story of dispossession, then it is this history of divestment that gives back to brownness its own meaning, modifying a field of possibility often dominated by white colonial forces. The brown struggle recalibrates the political dimensions in which it finds itself entangled and opens itself onto the ontological possibilities of its emergence. Such maneuvers showcase how brownness possesses its own ontology and how this ontology is first and foremost a doing (an action). No better example showcases the vulnerable longing structuring brownness than the far-reaching lyrics of the popular bolero "Sabor a mí," written by the late Afro-Mexican singer Álvaro Carrillo. The song is noted for its migratory stretch across Latin America's sonic landscape, iterated in many covers including Luis Miguel, Olga Guillot, and the late 1990s Chicana lesbian punk band Las Cucas. The lyrical nuance undergirding the haunting, if not maledictive refrain, "sabor a mí," outlines the arrested development of a seemingly healthy codependent contract between the singing subject and the object of desire. "Sabor a mí" rewrites the relationship between Latin America and the United States into a narrative about an ongoing harvesting of the U.S. Empire from an unrequited longing to be loved (González 2011). However, the forlorn hope swelling the present tense of the lyrics only exacerbates, like brownness, the future tense as always carrying a remainder/reminder of a persistent past that, however vulnerable, refuses its own negation: *pero allá tal como aquí / en la boca llevarás / sabor a mí* (for there as well as here / in your mouth you will carry / the taste of me).

Similarly, "brown" carries a delectable etymology. Beyond an adjective that just names the rich color, the word "brown" can describe something as dark or dusky. As a verb, it marks the process of something cooking, or someone becoming upset. In Old English, "brown" connoted duskiness in color yet brightness in polish, the latter still being operative in the contemporary use of the word "burnish." Indeed, the interplay between opacity and clarity, darkness and light, is the study, as in the *room*, for brownness. "Brown study," an idiom referring to a state of deep thought or abstraction, might be thought of in tandem with the subfield of academic research known as "brown studies," which usually focuses on the histories, politics, and cultures of "brown people." More interestingly, the potential for brown as an object of study anticipates brown as a methodology and a mode of reading. Swati Rana has argued that the future of what she calls "brownness study" depends on a certain formalist literary hermeneutic attuned to the "ideological manifestations of the millennial discourse of race, and also the inconsistencies within them, thereby opening a critique from the inside out" (2015, 299).

José Esteban Muñoz also understood how brownness moves from the inside out, enabling a critique that opens and shares outward to the world rather than shutting down and closing off the world's prospects. In "Feeling Brown," Muñoz begins by thinking of brown as a bridge between ethnicity and affect, a bridge where those Latina/o citizen-subjects congregate in exile from the majoritarian sphere since they are performatively and affectively blocked from accessing normativity (Muñoz 2000). Feeling brown for Muñoz then takes on a choreography addressing not only social and affective norms, but also the psychic life of the historically displaced subject. "Feeling brown, feeling down" becomes a way to translate Melanie Klein's psychoanalytic notion of the depressive position into a brown vernacular that most importantly "link[s] position with feeling," thereby making positions "provisional and flexible demarcations, practices of being" (Muñoz 2006, 681). Much like Klein's depressive position, the underbridge known as brownness survives in the face of heavy pressure from corrective regimes, because it is malleable to change and seeks to rework the world from the position of the problem. In other words, just like a bridge, brownness works as an avenue of feelings aiding in the seemingly impossible project of belonging in difference. This project/projection requires empathy, and Muñoz was most attuned to this vital sense. In "'Chico, What Does

It Feel Like to Be a Problem?,'" Muñoz argues: "There is something emphatic about this shared affective construct I am calling Brownness, this response to a certain negation within the social that corresponds to this question of feeling like a problem" (2007, 445–46). Feeling like a problem describes a situation where excusing oneself from the coercive mimetic demands built in to what it means to be Latina/o in the United States—hot, spicy, over-the-top, unaware, unwavering—means producing a certain knowledge that exists outside of knowledge itself. Here is what Muñoz called a brown otherwiseness, a particular rerouting of knowledge into "imagining a provisional de-universalizing of reason for the express purpose of imagining and describing multiple modes of being, feeling, and knowing in the world" (2014, 250).

Belonging in difference sometimes feels impossible in a world that threatens to correct the mistakes of brownness. However, it is precisely the act of sharing this impossibility with others that helps Muñoz re-understand brownness as a *sense*. Moving beyond what Raymond Williams calls the "structure of feeling" (1977, 128–35), Muñoz argues that the sense of a cultural object and one's *manera de ser* (way of being) does not necessitate knowledge to do the work of explaining their respective value. Similarly, brownness exists outside of value, and as a historical form persisting within the here-and-now, yet radiating—from the inside out—as something incalculable, like "art, friendship, love, thought, [and minoritarian] knowledge" (Muñoz 2011, 197). Muñoz's rigorous work on brown mirrors the vital trajectory of brown's own dedication at remaining unfinished, an intellectual itch refusing satisfaction. These incommensurable, impure, and "arduous modes of relationality" are what constitute brown's vital resistance to mere identification (Muñoz 2015). In fact, lingering within a brown study and refusing cathartic determination—"I cannot reconcile"—is how the writer Richard

Rodriguez closes his ruminations on brownness in his collection of essays, *Brown: The Last Discovery of America* (2002, 224). Perhaps like Rodriguez's last discovery of Anglo-America, Muñoz will too discover in his still unpublished *The Sense of Brown* the failure of reconciliation to be the onto-poetic ground in which we find our contemporary United States of America.

It is precisely because brown fails to reconcile itself as an identity-knowledge project that the study of brownness is always an investigative process into the vital phenomena of mixture and immiscibility. This failure of mixing unmixable things comes to figure, quite ironically and much like the act of burnishing a table, as the refinement of knowledge in the face of an increasing anti-intellectual United States. Such refinement in thought is far from the purported apoliticism of aesthetic theory, since the rub, as it were, lies within the production of friction often negatively misrecognized as inciting the *feeling* of irritation or depression, as in the English phrase "browned off." This political irritation is part-and-parcel of what Ronald Sundstrom (2008) has called the "browning of America" and more recognizable in the shrill remarks of Samuel Huntington's (2004a) response to the browning of America as the "Hispanic Challenge." To brown America is to bring it down, depress what is notably and nobly understood as White America, thereby staining it and dragging it to its limits. Even the philosopher of colors, Goethe, associated brown, a color he did not necessarily enjoy, with seriousness and melancholy. The sobering intensity of the disenfranchisement of minoritarian people in the United States is nothing less than browning the way we understand the misapplication and abuses of those suspended realities known as justice, democracy, and freedom. Here is the drama within the color brown: it is itself a mixture of yellow, red, and black—the iridescent reminder that we are in brownness and of brownness, here and now.

8

Capitalism
Ramona Hernández

The first use of the word "capitalism" has been credited to an 1855 British novel, *The Newcomes*, which narrates the story of an English family who became wealthy through business and marrying into money (Thackeray 1996). While the term retained associations with wealth, "capitalism" is commonly linked to Adam Smith and Karl Marx, two political economists whose writings about society were published one hundred years apart and who held opposing views regarding capitalism. These views became schools of thought and have influenced and divided the world in opposing camps until today. What follows briefly describes (a) key elements of Smith's and Marx's views; (b) the roots of capitalism in the Latin American region; and (c) the nexus between capitalism and migration from the Dominican Republic to the United States.

Capitalism is a mode of production that stimulates the private ownership of the means of production, the use of free labor, and the increasing accumulation of capital. It also generates capitalist ideology, a system of beliefs that justifies the system's existence. Capitalist ideology is maintained and reproduced by the sword if needed; it permeates society's institutions and people, ensuring the reproduction and development of capitalism.

Many scholars link the rise and spread of capitalism to the European discovery and colonization of the Americas. In 1492, Spain took possession of a new world loaded with land, minerals, and peoples. José Carlos Mariátegui describes Spain's penetration into South and

Central America as follows: the Spaniards "plundered the treasures of temples and palaces; they allotted land and men with no thought of their future use as forces and means of production" (1971, 1). Other European empires followed suit, particularly Portugal. Soon, England, France, and Holland, armed with cannons, also demanded to share in the treasures uncovered in the new lands. By the end of the seventeenth century, the continent had been totally transformed: from masters of their own destinies, the aboriginal populations became the property of a few European warfare nations; the immense wealth of the New World landed in the coffers of the invading nations. Ways of life and thinking were profoundly altered forever. The discovery of America by Spain created the nexus between capitalism and the new lands and their people.

European nations competed for primacy and control of the transatlantic market. The massive wealth appropriated by each provided abundant capital to solidify a European capitalist class that invested in the economic development of these nations. The raw and unprocessed cotton brought from the New World, for instance, nurtured a manufacturing industry that transformed this fiber into textiles and then into wares that were sold everywhere, including among aboriginal populations and African slaves who were forced to cover their tropical bodies in the name of European decency. This transformation alone changed the world forever and created a lasting garment market that extended almost throughout the world. In the end, the rise of capitalism was intrinsically connected to the growth of mercantile-maritime cities; to transatlantic routes that interconnected a rich new land to a wealth-seeker Old World, and to a commercial nexus and exchange of commodities, all made possible through the conquistadores, whether Spanish preachers, Portuguese missionaries, or English Pilgrims.

In *An Inquiry into The Wealth of Nations*, first published in 1776, Adam Smith described the essential components of capitalism, one of which is the pursuit of individual wealth. Smith relates the desire for personal wealth to a man's particular self-interest. A man can expect to have returns from others, Smith said, when he shows them "that it is for their own advantage to do for him what he requires of them" (1937, 14). During Smith's time, wealth and capital were synonymous, and capital, which Smith defines as that part of a man's possession that is used to generate his wealth (1937, 262), was in his view available to all people. Smith believed that man's self-regard motivated him to accumulate capital. Rooted then in an innate attribute—man's self-interest—the creation of wealth is, in the end, cumulative and generates *the wealth of a nation* because "by pursuing his own interest [man] frequently promotes that of the society more effectually than when he really intends to promote it" (1937, 423).

In *Capital: A Critique of Political Economy*, first published in 1867, Karl Marx challenged Smith's generalized view about the relationship between capital and people's intrinsic aspiration. Marx argued that "capital comes dripping from head to foot, from every pore, with blood and dirt" (1984, 712). Man's self-interest is not a noble attribute that culminates in collective wealth. Quite the contrary. Marx pointed out that "at the historical dawn of capitalist production . . . avarice, and desire to get rich, are the ruling passions" (1984, 556) and that pursuing personal interest causes the misery of others since "the capitalist gets rich . . . at the same rate as he squeezes out the labour-power of others, and enforces on the labourer abstinence from all life's enjoyment" (1984, 557). Accumulation of wealth is in this view, not a human trait, but rather a characteristic of capitalism.

If the peoples and the lands of the Americas were transformed into colonies by mercantile-imperialist capitalism in the age of Spanish, Portuguese, British, French, and Dutch conquest, the era of independence and the establishment of republics in the Americas brought a socioeconomic and political realignment of the world in which the United States emerged as the new empire. The nascent United States grew up equipped with a capitalist ideology that, as Christianity in the hands of Spain, became a powerful platform to rationalize its way of life and its imposition upon all others on earth. The United States penetrated the lands of their neighbors and through their mighty economic power and war armaments ensured its hegemony in the region and created the infrastructure to geometrically increase the wealth in its coffers. Primary accumulation, the appropriation of enormous economic resources by a group in a given society, served the United States well, as it became, speedily, the decision-maker for the nations, peoples, and places under its boots (Harvey 2003).

In capitalism, the need to accumulate is constant and shadows capitalists everywhere. Latin America's largest neighbor, "el coloso del Norte," began to expand its territory and capital right after its declaration of independence in 1776. Mexico, for instance, lost much land to the United States in 1848 after capitulating in a war that the United States declared in the name of its presumed rights to such lands. Moreover, the Progressive Era, a period roughly between 1898 and 1924, characterized by increasing economic prosperity in the United States, is also the time when the United States intensified its presence and dominion in Latin America through military invasions in Puerto Rico (1898), Cuba (1898 and 1906), Panama (1903), the Dominican Republic (1907 and 1916), Nicaragua (1909), and Haiti (1915). The 1916 U.S. military occupation of the Dominican Republic provides a clear example of modern capitalism on its imperialist stage.

Countries engaged in war do not engage in much agricultural production. Europe had long been the world's largest producer of sugar, but World War I hindered European countries' ability to produce sugar during that time, or other agricultural products for that matter. But while the production of sugar, mostly from sugar beets, declined drastically—along with that of coffee, tobacco, and cacao—demand for it had not. Meanwhile, the Dominican Republic had the historical capacity to abundantly produce those commodities. Indeed, it is there that the sugar industry was born in the New World (Bosch 2016).

The United States presumably feared an intervention in the Dominican Republic by European nations and used this fear to justify the 1916 U.S. military invasion of the island; the U.S. Marines stayed in the country until 1924. The Dominican government owed money to European countries and could not make payments. Similarly, various factions of the Dominican elite were engaged in struggles for power, keeping Dominican society politically unstable. As the war continued, the demands for sugar increased and so did its price. Between 1905 and 1914, the price of 100 pounds of sugar remained roughly at $5.50. By 1920, the price had increased to $22.50 (Moya Pons 2013). The production of agricultural commodities was so lucrative during the war years that Latin American countries that produced such goods experienced a moment of economic boom popularly known as "la danza de los milliones" (Moya Pons 2013). Many of these millions, however, went into the coffers of the United States, which controlled the economies of various countries in the region.

Indeed, in the Dominican Republic, the U.S. occupying forces put into motion a primary accumulation process that permanently impoverished thousands of Dominican people who once owned their lands. Such primary accumulation also provided the United States with abundant labor and capital at once, readily available to generate profit. It is having control of a large quantity of both labor and capital, the two most important factors of production, which undergirded the enormous amount of wealth found in the hands of some people or in the arks of some nations and not their investment in resources or in sweat.

The U.S. government implemented legislation that benefited its own capitalists: it reduced the taxes on U.S. imports to the Dominican Republic, thereby inundating the Dominican market with American products, sending local producers who could not compete into bankruptcy. A new agrarian law required Dominican peasants to present the titles of ownership of their lands. But very few had such titles: Dominican land tenure was based on communal ownership, making individual titles unnecessary. The state, represented by the U.S. military government, appropriated all lands from those who could not present the newly required documentation. Thus, many Dominicans became landless and unable to sell their products. Landless peasants and former producers joined the ranks of the proletariat, or those who must sell their labor to earn a living. Eventually, part of the dispossessed, impoverished, working Dominicans, unable to make a living at home, would find their way to the United States in a forced migration process that put them, ironically, in the same society that had effected their uprooting in the first place.

U.S. capitalists involved in sugar plantations bought Dominican lands sold by the U.S. military government on behalf of the Dominican State. In 1924, when the U.S. Marines left the Dominican Republic, there were twenty-one sugar plantations. Of these, eleven belonged to two American corporations: the West India Sugar Finance Corporation and the Central Romana Corporation, Ltd. Of the remaining ten plantations, five had dependent relations with the Central Romana Corporation. When the Central Romana Corporation was established in the country, it had a declared capital of $450,000 and a territorial extension of 17,486 *tareas*, equivalent to almost 2,717 acres. However, in 1925, the value of this corporation increased to $9,961,349 and its territorial extension to 931,792 *tareas*, equivalent to almost 144,781 acres. In other words, its original capital had multiplied 21.5 times and its territory 53 times (Bosch 1981).

The occupying American military government built roads connecting the country from north to south and from east to west. As horses and carriages were replaced by automobiles and became obsolete, all inputs, including the asphalt for the resplendent roads, the gas for the cars, and the cars themselves, had to be imported. In the end, U.S. capitalism transformed Dominican society into one that produced what it did not consume and consumed what it did not produce.

Marx believed that workers follow capital. Indeed, 1.5 million Dominicans live today in the United States, the majority of whom came seeking a better life. However, migration represents just a change of geography for many of them. They live in a capitalist society not too different from the one they left behind. Poor at home, the majority of them, now transformed into Hispanics or Latinas/os, continue to be poor in the new abode. How their future will evolve, depends as much on them as on the socioeconomic system they will partake in.

9

Chicana, Chicano, Chican@, Chicanx

Sheila Marie Contreras

Self-naming is political, ideological, and resistant. "Chicano" remains thus inflected, true to its emergence in activist communities of the 1960s and 1970s to signify self-determination, working-class origins, and a critique of social relations of power. Although not entirely clear who first appropriated "Chicano" for this usage, it is generally accepted that at one time the word circulated in Mexican Spanish as a negative reference to the "lower classes." Its appropriation by students and activists transformed it into an empowering alternative to "Mexican," "Mexican American," or "Hispanic." To name oneself as "Chicana" or "Chicano" is to assert a gendered, racial, ethnic, class, and cultural identity in opposition to Anglo-American hegemony and state-sanctioned practices of representing people of Mexican descent in the United States. As it evokes the "radical" politics of cultural nationalism, "Chicano" stands against the institutionally normative "Hispanic," as well as the linguistically insistent "Latino" (Alcoff 2005). Always associated by Chicanas and Chicanos with State attempts to classify, homogenize, and deracinate, "Hispanic" is typically linked to conservative political values, even as it is often the name chosen in English by many in the U.S. Southwest who in Spanish might call themselves *tejana* or *mejicano*. In the U.S. Southwest, "Mexican American" most often appears in academic program names and Chicana and Chicano studies scholars tend to use "Mexican American" and "Chicana/Chicano" interchangeably.

Conventional wisdom holds that a "Chicana" or "Chicano" is a Mexican American who knows their own history. "Mexican American" is understood to refer to a person of Mexican descent born in the United States, while "history" refers both to the sixteenth-century Spanish conquest of Mexico and to the nineteenth-century Anglo-American colonization and settlement of the southwestern United States. The meaning is expanded to include those who may have migrated from Mexico as children, but were socialized and educated in the United States. Journalist Rubén Salazar, in an article published after his death in 1970, wrote that "a Chicano is a Mexican-American with a non-Anglo image of himself" (1970, B7). His definition establishes the specificity of Chicana and Chicano identity in relation to other Spanish-speaking communities, and also implies that most people of Mexican descent in the U.S. do *not* know their own history. Salazar's emphasis on historical knowledge is a commentary on the absence of Mexican American content across the K-12 curriculum, which is again being recognized in the U.S. popular media (Rich 2012). This suppression of historical and cultural knowledge enforced what Salazar and others would call "Anglo images" of Mexicans that exist in popular culture. Neither positive nor uplifting, the representations have been simplistic and narrow, focusing on impoverished workers, lawless gangsters, and female vixens, to name a few (Berg 2002). Consequently, the structuring and packaging of curricular material throughout the U.S. education system, in which people of Mexican descent have had little input, has assured the alienation of Mexican Americans.

Chicano educational activists began focusing on curricular content during a period of U.S. political activism from the 1960s to the early 1980s known as "the Chicano movement," or "el movimiento." The ideological base was cultural nationalism, modulated at times by Marxist social critiques of capitalist class systems or new appreciations for Indigenous ancestry and history. The Indigenist forms of Chicano nationalism, originally influenced by post-revolutionary Mexican cultural politics, have been most enduring. In art, literature, and cultural practices such as *danza*, activists and artists reclaimed Indigenous influences on the historical mestizaje, or mixture, that produced present-day Mexicans and Mexican Americans, or mestizas/os (mixed-race or mixed-blood people). Filmmaker Moctesuma Esparza elaborates in the "Pride and Prejudice" episode of the PBS television series *Latino Americans* (2013): "When we identified with the word 'Chicano,' our understanding was that it was the same word that is the root word for 'Mexico,' which is the name of the Aztec Indians, and their name was 'Mexica.' . . . And when you drop off the first syllable, 'Me,' you get 'Xica,' which becomes 'Chicano.' MeXICANO. And that's what we were." The "X" is here pronounced "sh," a feature of Mexican Spanish that documents the impact of the Indigenous language of Nahuatl on the European language of the colonizers.

Los Angeles high school teacher Sal Castro became a formative influence on Esparza and other students when he started to integrate educational material that affirmed Mexican cultural identity. He was instrumental in the 1968 Chicano student walkouts, or "blowouts," modeled on the *huelgas*, or labor strikes, used as a negotiation tactic by the United Farm Workers. Students walked out of class in protest of treatment by schoolteachers and administrators, curricula that did not include Mexican American history, art, or literature, and the school-to-military and school-to-prison pipelines. Their demands included more Mexican American content in classes and the hiring of Mexican American teachers and administrators. Their efforts also impacted higher education as Chicano studies programs and departments were established, primarily in the U.S.

Southwest, and especially at the community college level in California (Acuña 2011). But "Chicano studies" was never the term of choice on the East Coast of the United States, where Latina/o communites had origins throughout the Caribbean and Latin America. And as political conflict and military repression forced the migration of thousands of Central and other Latin Americans in the 1980s, Latina/o communities throughout the United States became more diverse. In California, however, the demographic reality had already been uniquely acknowledged and documented in San Francisco State University's early decision to forgo "Chicano Studies" in favor of "Raza Studies" and, later, "Latino Studies." Similarly, in Detroit, Wayne State University's 1972 program began as the "Center for Chicano/Boricua Studies." Other Chicano studies programs in California and the Midwest have made recent name changes to reflect more accurately the populations they serve and to move beyond narrow definitions of the field. Over the last decade, we have seen a preference for "Latino" (or Latina/o) in academic program names in recognition of the diversity of Spanish-speaking people in the United States (U.S. Census Bureau 2015). This reconfiguring of Chicana/o studies to Latina/o studies has broadened the scope of scholarly activity, transforming teaching content and enriching the experiences of students, faculty, staff, and community engaged in and by the study of U.S. Latinas/os.

The blowouts show the transformative potential of positive curricular intervention and the significance of formal education as a site of identity-formation and politicization. It is true that many Mexican Americans "become" Chicana or Chicano in college, but these identity shifts have been made possible by social movements. The political activism of the Chicano movement created academic communities of students and faculty and resulted in curricular material that included U.S.

Mexicans. Nevertheless, most academic knowledge continues to emanate from a perspective that is decidedly European, heterosexual, and male.

As a term of self-identification, "Chicano" is not accepted by all who could claim it. There is considerable debate about the extent to which the larger Mexican-descent community ever adopted "Chicano." Some scholars hold that it was popular primarily among students, with little acceptance outside of academic activist circles, as Albert Camarillo wrote in 2013. Maurilio Vigil (1977) argues that older, more conservative Mexican Americans did not accept the radical political ideology associated with "Chicano," while Juan Gómez-Quiñones contends that the term was "rejected as pejorative on the political right and by middle class people while at the grass roots it was questioned because Mexicano was preferred" (1978, 13). José Limón (1979) dismisses the notion that Mexican Americans were simply political conservatives who did not like the "radical" ideology of "Chicano." Instead, he writes, the broader range of Mexican-descent people did not identify with the "style" of its usage, which was "fundamentally a rejection of a performance context judged as inappropriate for this essentially folkloric term" (1979, 20). But Martha Cotera, in her introduction to her 1976 *Diosa y Hembra* (Goddess and Woman), announces that "the term Mexicana, Chicana, Mexican American and Hispana woman is used throughout interchangeably simply because the author and the Central Texas community she lives within does exactly this" (1976, 2).

Membership in the group of those who would call themselves "Chicano" was thus self-regulated by individual choice, but it was also regulated by the collective. Not all Mexican-descent subjects were readily incorporated into these nationalist, activist communities; women and those who were gay, lesbian, bisexual, or trans* tended to be excluded. Richard T. Rodríguez

reminds us that "gay, lesbian, and feminist struggles were often seen as antithetical to Chicano liberation" (2011, 113). Dominant Chicano political and activist critique of social relations of power did not willingly or easily extend to analyses of how gender and sexuality inflected power, a reality exposed by Cotera and other Chicana feminists. And when it appears here, the use of the masculine form of the noun "Chicano" is intentional, meant to reflect the truth of *el movimiento*: it was heteronormative, male-dominated, and male-centered. Language purists may argue that the use of the masculine "Chicano" is simply the correct standard Spanish grammar for mixed-gender groups of people. Early Chicana feminists never accepted this logic, and were critical of masculinist politics from the beginnings of movement activism (A. García 1997; Blackwell 2011). Angie Chabram said it brilliantly: "And she enters movement discourse with her own name, a name which constructs her both as Chican-a and a woman and subverts the twin myths of malinchismo and assimilation" (Chabram-Dernersesian 1992, 86). Chabram, like many Chicana feminists, critiques nationalism while still claiming national belonging. She speaks to the power of self-naming, while also countering misogynist interpretations of the life of one of Mexico's most significant female historical figures, La Malinche / Doña Marina, interpreter and advisor to Hernán Cortés. Inserting this feminine form of the noun—ChicanA—into Chicano movement discourse demanded inclusion and challenged sexism in the movement, while at the same time refusing to negate community.

This Chicana critique of Chicano politics circulated through verbal interventions at local, regional, and national conferences, as well as in publishing venues (Cotera 1976; Martínez 1998). Adelaida del Castillo's groundbreaking 1974 essay on La Malinche was especially transformative (1977). Poetic challenges to movement patriarchy have existed since the 1970s period of Chicana literary history; examples include Lorna Dee Cervantes's 1975 "Para un Revolucionario" (1993) and Carmen Tafolla's 1978 "La Malinche" (1993). The choice of whether or not to align with feminist principles, however, was a topic of intense debate among women in the movement (Longeaux y Vásquez 1997). In 1982, women created Mujeres Activas en Letras y Cambio Social (MALCS) to provide space for initiatives and agendas that they were at that time unable to pursue in the National Association for Chicana and Chicano Studies (NACCS).

Over time, these critiques have become more central to the field as scholars have refused to forget Chicana feminist interventions, acknowledging their foundational impact on contemporary scholarship and research. This recognition became evident as academic convention shifted, for the sake of brevity, to "Chicana/o" in place of the longer "Chicana and Chicano." Around the turn of the last century, a new iteration emerged, "Chican@," part aesthetic response to the cumbersome punctuation of the former abbreviation, part recognition of emergent digital identities, and part as an instance of queering or making queer. Another variation, which has been in use since at least the 1980s, is "Xicana" or "Xicano," a reference to the Indigenous origins of Mexican-descent people. Poets Alurista (1981) and Cherríe Moraga (2011) have used this spelling in work that spans thirty years.

More recently, language and letters have again shifted. A new iteration gaining acceptance and usage recenters the exploration of race, class, gender, sexuality, and relations of power: "Chicanx." The "x" signifies fluidity and mobility, setting aside the conventions of ideological, philosophical, and medical binaries that assign humans to one gender identity out of two when they are born. The "x" in "Chicanx" is nonbinary; it

acknowledges self-determinations that refuse immovable assignments of identity. This transformation of "Chicano," from its beginnings in narrow understandings of subjectivity and experience, contains within it these histories of internal critique and oppositional struggle. The "x," now at the end, rather than the beginning, urges us onward, advancing a social analysis that honors mobile, uncategorized ways of being and expression.

10

Citizenship

Nicholas De Genova

Citizenship, as we know it, is a technology of modern state power. It is the elementary political form by which people—embodied persons embedded in dense and complex webs of social relations—are reduced to "individuals" who may be abstractly figured as "equals" before the law. The modernity of this form of power derives precisely from the notion that the rule of man (as in a monarchy or an aristocracy) has been irreversibly replaced by the rule of law. As abstract individuals, therefore, all citizens are ostensibly equal, commensurable, effectively interchangeable, as the law is supposed to apply uniformly to all, and no one is supposed to be enduringly subjected to personalistic and hierarchical forms of domination and dependency. Citizenship therefore corresponds to a social order in which everyone is presumed to voluntarily and "freely" engage in exchange, whether it be the exchange of goods for money, or much more commonly, the exchange of the capacity to labor for money wages. In short, citizenship is a political form that abides by the abstract rules that govern the capitalist marketplace.

The legitimacy of modern state power, furthermore, is presented as originating from a mythical covenant, a "social contract," among naturally free and equal individuals. Thus, the power of the state is purported to derive from the natural-born power for self-government that is said to reside within each and every individual. Once people are gathered together into some sort of political "community," the effective freedom and equality that are considered to be everyone's birthright become not an individual power of self-government but a collective one. Citizenship, then, is necessary to translate this wild, "natural" freedom into the sort of politically and juridically defined liberty that can be used to justify the authority of the state as the "democratic" expression of a popular will. The state's sovereignty now appears to be legitimate, ostensibly derived from the innate and natural sovereignty of "the people."

In the name of freedom and equality, in other words, citizenship serves to subject people as "individuals" to state power. Simultaneously, citizenship inscribes people as proper "members" belonging to an imaginary, abstract, and artificial political community of equals, usually called "the nation." This is how citizenship serves to stitch together such exalted notions as "freedom," "equality," "democracy," and "human rights" with state power and nationalism.

As citizens, we are fashioned as the supposedly free and equal subjects of "democratic" self-government, while in fact citizenship is how we are made the *objects* of modern state power. Likewise, despite its broadly inclusive and egalitarian mystique, once we locate citizenship as a kind of legal personhood within a polity defined by the territorial borders and juridical boundaries of a state, it becomes clearer that citizenship is always an inherently exclusionary and divisive framework for the production of various degrees of non-citizenship and thus, legal non-personhood. In this respect, we can only properly assess the true meaning of citizenship from a global perspective that is not confined within the borders of any particular state formation. Nonetheless, each citizenship tends to be configured at precisely the "national" scale of a particular (territorially defined) state, and can be properly examined only in the context of the sociopolitical history that has been shaped and disciplined—indeed, *bordered*—by that particular (nation-)state.

In the United States, citizenship was never originally intended to include people who were not considered to be "white." The very first Congress enacted the newly independent nation's very first law explicitly dealing with citizenship through the Naturalization Act of 1790, in which no immigrant would be permitted to become a citizen unless he were "a free, white person." Just three years earlier, in 1787, the Constitution had already been proclaimed on the basis of upholding the notion that enslaved Africans and African Americans were not persons in any substantive sense, that they were merely property. Similarly, the Constitution treated the Indigenous peoples of North America as entirely "outside" the U.S. "nation" and beyond the pale of "civilization." Because Blacks and Native Americans were deemed to be inherently and irreversibly inferior, they were judged to be incapable of self-control and thus incompetent for self-government, and hence disqualified from any prospect of citizenship. By a cruel and twisted logic, those who were enslaved were likewise presumed to have somehow found themselves in that condition because of a "natural" weakness, a "slavishness" that was alleged to be inherent in their racial non-whiteness. It followed by the same merciless logic that citizenship, associated with the capacity for self-government, would be guarded as the preserve of so-called whites—even if the law never troubled itself with providing a definition of this commonsense category of the social regime of white supremacy. The racial whiteness of these prospective migrants, furthermore, was coupled with their status as "free," meaning that even if they were considered to be "white," they could not become U.S. citizens if they were indentured laborers or otherwise dependent upon and dominated by the rule of a master. Their citizenship—their equality before the law—would have to correspond to their social condition as "free" labor, able to sell their capacity to work for a wage in the marketplace. From its inception, therefore, U.S. "democracy" had white supremacy as its defining bedrock, and U.S. nationhood was forged through an unabashed white nationalism.

The problem of Latina/o citizenship consequently always turned on the question of race. The first major historical episode in the encounter between Latinas/os and citizenship in the United States ensued from the war of conquest through which the United States invaded and militarily occupied Mexico. After having debated whether or not to take the whole country and herd the majority of Mexicans onto the equivalent of Indian reservations, the view that prevailed was that the United States wanted as much Mexican land as possible inhabited by as few Mexicans as possible. Thus, with the conclusion of the war in 1848, the Treaty of Guadalupe Hidalgo established a new border roughly corresponding to the Rio Grande (Río Bravo), by which roughly half of Mexico's national territory was annexed. The newly colonized Mexicans who already resided in the occupied territories of what has since come to be known as the U.S. Southwest were given the choice to leave, to retain their Mexican citizenship and thus become "foreigners" in their native land, or to do nothing and automatically become subjects of the United States, to "be admitted, at the proper time (to be judged of by the Congress of the United States) to the enjoyment of all the rights of citizens of the United States according to the principles of the Constitution" (Griswold del Castillo 1990, 189–90). This language is sometimes mistakenly interpreted to mean that the Mexican inhabitants of the newly conquered territories were assured U.S. citizenship. In fact, this language subtly deferred the decision about citizenship to the adoption of the respective state constitutions, which eventually instituted white supremacist provisions for the citizenship of "white Mexicans" only (Griswold del Castillo 1990; De Genova

2005, 215–21). The great majority of former Mexican citizens who might have been entitled under the treaty's apparent protections saw their putative citizenship systematically subverted. Most were despoiled of their land, and their ostensible civil rights were routinely violated, often through outright racist terror.

The very limited extent to which the treaty genuinely enabled citizenship status for Mexicans, however unstable and insecure, came only with the compulsory requirement that citizenship be racialized as the preserve of "white" men. This was put to the test in a racial prerequisite case for the Naturalization Act of 1790—*In re Rodriguez* (1897). In that case, a federal court in Texas considered the application for citizenship of Ricardo Rodríguez, a migrant from Mexico, whose petition for naturalization was initially rejected on the grounds, simply enough, that he was "not a white person," that he was "one of the six million [Mexican] Indians of unmixed blood." For his part, Rodríguez declared that he was a descendant of neither Indigenous nor Spanish ancestors, and identified himself racially, quite frankly, to be a "pure-blooded Mexican." Rodríguez's legal defense was formulated by T. M. Paschal. Notably, Paschal concurred that Rodríguez was truly an undesirable candidate for naturalization and could rightly be denied eligibility for citizenship on the basis that he was indeed racially an Indian, and otherwise an ignorant Mexican, illiterate in both English and Spanish. However, the racial prerequisite cases for naturalization simply did not apply to Mexicans, Paschal contended, because the Treaty of Guadalupe Hidalgo had extended to Mexicans the same rights and privileges enjoyed by whites and therefore had treated Mexicans, de facto, as virtual "whites." Mexican migrants, he reasoned, had therefore to be granted the right to apply for citizenship as an exception to the racial rule, out of respect for federal law. Positing the absurd legal fiction that Rodríguez was "white" according

to the treaty's provisions of citizenship for Mexicans, the court concluded that the applicant was indeed eligible for naturalization (De León 1979; Haney López 1996, 61–62; Martinez 1997b; Menchaca 2001, 215–76, 282–85; Gómez 2007, 139–41; Molina 2010). Apart from these legal casuistries, the *In re Rodriguez* decision became the basis, for a time, for a special exception made for Mexicans within the U.S. immigration and naturalization regime during the early twentieth century. The incorporation of Mexican/migrant labor nonetheless relied precisely upon the racial subjugation of Mexicans in order to secure their subordination as labor. Thus, by 1930, in the wake of mass migration from Mexico during the first decades of the twentieth century, the U.S. Census Bureau had come to officially designate "Mexican" as a separate and distinct "racial" category (Gómez 2007, 152; Molina 2010, 197). In 1933, furthermore, the U.S. Supreme Court revisited the issue of Mexicans' putative whiteness by treaty, and called the *Rodriguez* precedent into question (Haney López 1996, 242n37).

The other major formative encounter of Latinas/os with the regime of U.S. citizenship, historically, was the colonization of Puerto Rico following the Spanish-American War of 1898. In an echo of the Treaty of Guadalupe Hidalgo, the Treaty of Paris, which concluded the war with Spain, declared, "The civil rights and political status of the native inhabitants of the territories hereby ceded to the United States shall be determined by the Congress." Whereas Spanish inhabitants of the newly annexed colonies could choose to retain their Spanish citizenship, the "natives" were stripped of any former citizenship and summarily reduced to colonial subjects of the United States (Perea 2001, 156). The fact that U.S. political and legal authorities considered Puerto Ricans to be an "alien race" was the recurrent justification for excluding them from U.S. citizenship (Perea 2001, 155–61).

Then, two decades later, the Jones Act of 1917 unilaterally conferred U.S. citizenship upon Puerto Ricans, collectively, and legally abolished their prior quasi-status as "citizens of Puerto Rico." Without the consent or participation of the Puerto Rican people in the change of their juridical status, and in flagrant disregard for any organized expression of their political desires, the grant of U.S. citizenship was an unequivocal affront to Puerto Rican sovereignty and independence aspirations (Cabranes 1979; Cabán 1999; Burnett and Marshall 2001). In effect, the extension of citizenship to Puerto Ricans irrevocably tied the fate of Puerto Rico to the United States (Carr 1984; Cabán 1999). Furthermore, the law's passage in 1917, on the eve of the U.S. entry into World War I, ensured for many Puerto Ricans that the most palpable significance of their newfound citizenship status was that it made Puerto Rican men eligible to be drafted into the U.S. military. Approximately sixty thousand Puerto Ricans—more than 12 percent of the island's adult male population—were conscripted into military service during the First World War (Carr 1984, 65). Puerto Ricans' citizenship, while expanding their legal "duties" to the U.S. nation-state, did not even safeguard for them the full protection of the Bill of Rights or other constitutional guarantees of the presumed "rights" of citizens (Smith 1997, 433; 2001). In the 1922 decision of *Balzac v. Porto Rico*, the U.S. Supreme Court ruled, for example, that in an officially "unincorporated territory" such as Puerto Rico, the constitutional right to trial by jury did not apply (Cabranes 1979, 49; Burnett and Marshall 2001; Rivera Ramos 2001; Thornburgh 2001). In addition to the extension of U.S. citizenship, the Jones Act established that the island's governor would continue to be imposed from the mainland and thus would be a federally appointed (non-Puerto Rican) U.S. official. Likewise, the U.S. president and Congress would retain veto powers over any act of the new Puerto Rican legislature, and thus would never be beholden to any legislative expression of the Puerto Rican people (Carr 1984, 54–55). Meanwhile, Puerto Rico would have no representation in the U.S. Congress, and the island's inhabitants would not be permitted to vote in U.S. national elections. This restriction on Puerto Rican citizenship remains in force today, such that the mainland-versus-island residence distinction sustains an unequal two-tier structure for Puerto Rican political rights. Inasmuch as they were denied equal rights to political participation, Puerto Ricans were thus bestowed with a decidedly "second-class" citizenship as the juridical expression of their colonial subordination.

Hence, rather than the presumptive ideal of inclusion and belonging, citizenship for Latinas/os has long been a technology for their racial subordination, deployed as a means for their unequal, contradictory, and differential inclusion/exclusion within the legal regime of the U.S. state (De Genova and Ramos-Zayas 2003; De Genova 2005). In this light, rather than the customary liberal plea for the belated realization of the egalitarian promises of citizenship, our greatest challenge is to cultivate a radically open-ended imagination about how to enact various forms of political struggle beyond and against the treacherous allure of citizenship (De Genova 2010).

II

Culture

Arlene Dávila

Culture is one of the most contested concepts for students and scholars to handle, and even more so when approaching it from a Latina/o studies perspective. The word has different meanings and manifestations whether it is defined in terms of values, objectified in terms of material representations, or equated with "civilization." Yet when thinking about the concept of culture from a Latina/o perspective, matters of power and hierarchies of value come immediately to the forefront. In particular, a Latina/o studies perspective challenges common assumptions of homogeneity, consensus, authenticity, and ahistoricity that are continuously associated with the term while also foregrounding the political reverberations and deployments of more static definitions of "culture" in a variety of social movements. In other words, Latina/o studies highlights the concept of culture in some of its most contested deployments and manifestations, first by foregrounding the diversity of culture(s) entailed in the very concept of Latinas/os, alongside the many political and strategic mobilizations that are also being carried through and in the name of a single or objectified Latina/o "culture." After all, Latina/o is a panethnic identity made up of diverse racial, ethnic, and national constituents, each of which could be simultaneously recognized as having its own "identifiable" culture.

Indeed, classical and anthropological definitions of culture have differentially equated it with civilization (as in "Culture" with capital C—often associated with Western and modernist culture), or alternatively with the ethos of a people, or a folk tradition that emanates authentically from a "People" and is linked to a particular location, for instance, with a politically or geographically bounded group, region, or nation-state. This last definition has tended to link definitions of culture with "bounded" collectivities in ways that inhibit understandings of culture as fluid and shared by groups that may be diasporically spread and not bounded in time and space, as are Latinas/os (Gupta and Ferguson 1997). In this way, Latina/o studies, which is neither limited to a single identifiable "culture" nor spans a specifically bounded location, represents a direct challenge to dominant conceptualizations of culture as static, homogenous, and unchanging by prompting us to analyze Latinas/os as historically constituted and fed by immigration and transnational processes.

A Latina/o studies perspective also sheds light on the abiding tension between particularizing and universalizing definitions of culture—the former evoking plurality and difference and the latter a homogeneous (Western) civilizing project—which have preoccupied anthropologists for decades. Within this framework, marginal cultures have often been identified as "too particular" and "lacking culture" or civilization or alternatively as having "too much culture" and hence little civilization. This evokes the tension between culture and citizenship at the heart of the concept of cultural citizenship (Flores and Benmayor 1998). This idea is fed by the recognition that national state projects work by equating citizenship with normativity in ways that make dominant cultures "invisible" while racial and ethnic minorities are rendered hyper-visible (Rosaldo 1993). In this way, visible culture (or ethnicity) is best understood as being constituted by those positioned "at the border of empire," that is, by subjects whose visibility is defined in relation to whatever dominant definition of normativity obtains for a particular national culture, for instance in regards to religion, race, language, and so on (B. Williams 1989).

This tension between the ways in which culture and citizenship have been oppositionally conceived within modernist/nationalist projects is a key reason why Latina/o culture-based movements are historically linked to anticolonial/anti-imperial projects challenging Eurocentric and dominant U.S. Anglo-Saxon nationalist projects around which proper North American citizenship has been narrowly defined. Against such conceptualizations, Latina/o culture is consistently deemed as faulty, foreign, and/or a threat to the "purity" of the dominant U.S. national community (Santa Ana 2002). This positioning informs a range of antihegemonic movements of cultural assertion and reevaluation launched in response and as a challenge and aimed at reevaluating the value of aspects of Latina/o culture that are consistently denigrated in mainstream culture, with the rise of Latina/o studies and ethnic studies as valuable epistemological spaces for knowledge production providing good examples of this trend. The hierarchies embedded in the culture/civilization dyad are also a reason why many Latina/o cultural movements—the Nuyorican and Chicano movements, for instance—have tended to focus on the reevaluation of some of the most debased elements of Latinidad, for instance, by rescuing its African and Indigenous roots or elements of popular culture (Ybarra-Frausto 1991; Y. Ramírez 2005; Pulido 2006). Most powerfully, particularistic definitions of culture can lead to the equation of "culture" with manifestations of ethnic or racial identity, such as nationalist identifications, be it Mexican, Colombian, or Puerto Rican, or more Pan-Latino identifications. These become one (or more) among other identities that are treated as a goal or an end in itself that can and should be safeguarded, promoted, marketed, or undermined in regards to specific interests. This is culture as articulation and "boundary of difference" (Appadurai 1996) among other accounts of culture that treat it not as a given but as socially constituted, objectified, and mobilized for a variety of political ends. A variety of Latina/o cultural and social movements is predicated on this treatment of culture, as is a variety of corporate-sponsored "Latino" identified industries, products, or projects.

Latina/o studies scholars must be vigilant about how these cultural politics can also engage in processes of cultural objectification wherein culture is linked and defined in relation to material objects, expressions, and traditions that can be contained, studied, or exhibited. While this tendency helps to identify and demarcate culture for political purposes, it can also contribute to ahistorical and essentialist definitions that limit culture to particularized material objects or embodiments that can in turn serve as bases of exclusion and discrimination according to judgments about the greater or lesser value and authenticity of different expressions or elaborations that do not fit more sanctioned definitions of culture. One example is when we reduce Latina/o culture to a particular language be it English or Spanish or Spanglish, or to a particular whitened "Latin look" that excludes Latinas/os who are Indigenous or Afro-Latinas/os, or belong to a particular location or class, as in the tendency to think of urban Latinas/os as more "authentic" than suburban ones. In contrast, there is the impetus to recognize culture through more "ideological" and "behavioral" approximations, as beliefs, worldviews, or ways of being, or as ever-changing forms of everyday life and popular culture that are alive and resistant to identification and "objectification." Yet, when elaborating these definitions, we also need to be aware of how these treatments can also be used to reproduce exclusions, as in the association of Latina/o culture with particular values that reproduce sexism or heteronormativity.

Additionally elaborations of culture as "ways of life," beliefs, or affective states can also lead to more celebratory and sometimes naïve conceptualizations of culture as always resistant, in ways that veil culture's constant engagement with power and the ways in which culture in all of its expressions—be they discursive, ideological, emotive, or material—can become the subject of appropriations, transformations, and articulations with different political projects and interests.

Indeed, Latina/o studies scholars must be especially attentive to all the different central treatments of culture, which are constituted and deployed materially and discursively to frame particular politics. This is one of the reasons why Gramscian conceptualizations of processes of cultural hegemony have been so useful and popular in Latina/o studies analysis, especially in approaches that highlight the centrality of cultural politics as a defining element for assessing power and politics (Morley and Chen 1996; Álvarez, Dagnino, and Escobar 1998).

Foremost, Latina/o studies scholars must be vigilant about the relationship between culture and capital, and the ways in which in our present neoliberal and mass-mediated societies, culture industries are always involved in the appropriation, shaping, and dissemination of more mainstream and sanitized definitions of culture. In other words, our analyses necessitate engagements that incorporate the appropriations, circulations, and transformations of Latina/o culture(s), and the particular trajectories involved in any cultural product or creation in order to resist more static definitions of culture. Careful consideration also needs to be paid to projects that insist on treating culture as a conduit of progress and development devoid of distinct identifications—"culture" masked in attending discourses of globalization and treated as a medium of uplift, industry, entrepreneurship, and progress, or as involving projects of uplift and elitization. In my work, I have contrasted the different goals and objectives of marketing culture for economic development, which favors definitions of culture cleansed from ethnic memories and politics, with those that are part of larger assertions of identity, place, belonging, and inclusion. These political deployments remind us that peoples and cultures are never easily reducible into commodities, even in a heightened privatizing context.

In sum, to fully understand the stakes involved in definitions of "culture," we must engage in the production, circulation, and consumption of culture, as well as in matters of political economy, alongside an understanding of the different political projects involved in its making. This is not in opposition to appreciating the "intangible values" that are also associated with the concept of culture, be it as a reservoir of identity or as the realm of the aesthetic or of affective values. The issue is the importance of appreciating the complexities involved with the term and the need for interdisciplinary approaches that fully grapple with all that culture evidences, but also with all that it can also help to hide.

One final consideration is that in our neoliberal and colorblind society, culture is also increasingly used as synonym for difference, and as a veil for discussions of race and difference. This context beckons us to place race and racialization processes at the heart of the concept of culture to expose the hierarchies that may be reproduced or veiled through this term. One example is when appeals to Latina/o culture are deployed to erase racial heterogeneity, or when ethnic unity is summoned to avoid engagements with intra-Latina/o and interethnic racisms. Important keywords that are closely and sometimes mutually related to the concept of culture include art, citizenship, folklore, food, race, cultural politics, hegemony, values, and worldviews.

12

Decolonial

María Lugones

"Decolonial" is a central term in the conversation among theorists who think from the place of the oppressed. Many women of color in the United States theorized racial and gender oppression from within in resistant relationality with people of color without necessarily using the term "decolonial." The uses of the word considered here are interestingly connected, but importantly different in terms of where and why it is used. I will characterize these uses so that controversies around the decolonial, when they are about meaning, become clearer. In the case of Chela Sandoval (1991, 2000) and Emma Pérez (1999), as well as in my own work (Lugones 2007, 2010, 2012), liminality figures centrally as an in-between space where those who have been denied humanity and voice have a diminished agency—what I call "active subjectivity"—and exercise resistance. For us, the possibility of decoloniality is tied to those intersticial spaces, both unseen and hidden by coloniality. In each case there is a relation to colonization. In each case, "decolonial" marks or forms sites and methods of resistance to the colonization that dehumanized most of the people in the world. Aníbal Quijano (2000a, 2000b, 2007), Walter Mignolo (2007, 2011), and I share the idea that the dehumanization produced by the modern/colonial system of power is the from-within-which decoloniality is conceived and theorized.

Emma Pérez, who is Chicana, focuses on Chicanas within Aztlán—the territory from where the Mexica moved to Tenochtitlan—rejecting the U.S.-Mexico border as a legitimate division of a people. Born in Argentina, and living in the U.S. since I was twenty, I have focused on Abya Yala, the name that the Puna of Panama have given to the territories that the colonizers called "America." Chela Sandoval, who is Chicana, thinks of global colonization. The uses of "decolonial" by Aníbal Quijano (who is Peruvian) and Walter Mignolo (who is an Argentinian residing in the United States) are tied to the larger and longer global history, including the present of the coloniality of power.

Emma Pérez thinks of the "decolonial imaginary" in relation to third-world feminism as a genealogical tool "for recovering the hidden voices of Chicanas that have been relegated to silence, passivity" (1999, xvi). Within a Chicana feminist historical imagination, Pérez seeks and listens to the interstices and gaps where "the different, fragmented, imagined, non-linear, non-teleological" find their place in the stories we tell about Chicanas (1999, xiv)—that is, where agency is exercised and where the historian hears the unheard, the unthought, the shadows. The interstices constitute a third space that is nonlinear, heterogeneous, discontinuous, cotemporaneous with and parallel to the eventual discourses of the seen. The interstices are where the decolonial imaginary is at work. As Pérez reviews Chicano historiography, she "sexes" the colonial imaginary looking for and finding women's agency under colonization. She proposes "diasporic subjectivity" as "the oppositional and transformative identity that allowed these women to weave through the power of cultures, to infuse and be infused, to create and re-create newness" (1999, 81). For Pérez, "decolonial" is not a liberatory term but a term of transition between the colonial and the postcolonial. The decolonial imaginary is "a rupturing space, the alternative to that which is written in history" (1999, 6). It is a way, a method, of doing history.

Chela Sandoval (2000) locates her creation of a decolonial theory and method in the mid-twentieth century's battles for self-determination of colonized and marginalized people in Africa, the United States, and elsewhere and their disavowal of Western rationality, seeing Western rationality as an "ethnophilosophy" rather than as a universal rationality. Sandoval seeks the forces and affinities within the undercurrent of oppositional consciousness in the twentieth century and articulates them methodologically, shaping a singular tool for "forging twenty-first century modes of decolonizing globalization" (2000, 2). She seeks the junction where the thinking of decolonial theorists such as Frantz Fanon, Gloria Anzaldúa, Donna Haraway, Roland Barthes, Angela Davis, Audre Lorde, Michel Foucault, Julia Kristeva, Cherríe Moraga, and many others aligns and links. She emphasizes the importance of seeing the work of poststructuralist theorists, "lesbian and gay theorists, the alienated, the marginalized, the disenfranchised" (2000, 11) as decolonial in nature. She creates a methodology of consciousness that gathers up means of opposition within liberation movements into a consciousness that is differential, one that links the strategies and central oppositional moves into one decolonial consciousness. U.S. third-world feminism is understood as having developed such a form of consciousness, one that is historical and can align social movements with each other toward decolonization and thus be coalitional.

Importantly, Sandoval theorizes this alignment not only in its subordinated but in its oppositional form. That is, she is not overwhelmed by the power of power as she takes up active beings in resistance to it. One central form of activity lies in the resistance to Western culture's division of meaning into binaries as a powerful way of repressing those who do not fit. Those who live in the in-between have politicized the "shattering of binaries." Third-world feminism's politicization of the in-between in the 1980s and 1990s incarnates this rejection of binaries, transforming the in-between into a third force. Importantly, the in-between incarnates a rejection of the sex-gender binary. It posits a tactical subjectivity, being "women without a line," an intimate face of struggle, which is coalitional.

Sandoval theorizes U.S. people of color having survived "in the in-between (silent) space" within domination; once the in-between is made visible within a nondominant making of sense, "the nature of social affinity must change" (2000, 152). This "third space" is where a politicized oppositional consciousness arises. As oppositional consciousness moves tactically through different forms, it becomes a "differential" and coalitional consciousness. Thus, differential consciousness goes farther than oppositional consciousness. It is the consciousness that experiences "the meanings that lie at the zero degree of power" (2000, 147), relinquishing the hold of dominant consciousness. What constitutes it as differential is the listening to, taking up of, and being receptive to the technologies, strategies, and creations of those who resist domination and dominant sense, to third meanings, meanings that go beyond revealing the meaning structure of domination. It is coalitional because it is receptive to "obtuse third meaning," to meaning that has to be hidden, that cannot make dominant sense, to meanings created in the spaces of survival and struggle. Sandoval detects a new country people struggling for egalitarian social relations, "activists for a new decolonial global terrain" (2000, 184), welcoming others to a new homeland. What is decolonial in Sandoval's methodology is that it lives in the third space, comes from it; it is attentive to what takes place in it and what it can make possible.

Aníbal Quijano (2000a, 2000b, 2007) introduces the analytical concept of the "coloniality of power" and understands decoloniality as tightly related to this concept. With the coloniality of power, Quijano theorizes the coming into being in colonial modernity of the idea of race, the classification of peoples into superior and inferior by nature, the very idea of society as articulated in a hierarchical order. Coloniality and modernity are two axes of what Quijano calls the "Modern Colonial Capitalist System of Power." That is, the reduction of the colonized to nonhuman beings is inseparable from the denial of value to any of their practices, knowledges, and understandings of the universe. That denial, which gives meaning to the exclusion from humanity, constitutes and is constituted by an understanding of knowledge, knowledge production, and of the very nature of the human as a being of reason that creates a non-heterogeneous totality that is enclosed, without an outside, as uncovering and creating, universal truth. Dehumanization of the colonized and the enslaved Africans reconstituted capitalism as a racialized system of production. Racialization and Eurocentrism continue to constitute that "Modern Colonial Capitalist System of Power."

Quijano also introduced the term "delinking" to think about decoloniality, to think about delinking from the linkages between rationality/modernity and coloniality, from the distorted paradigms of knowledge produced by colonial power, from instrumental reason and its tie to power. He uses the concept of "heterogeneous totalities" to characterize all cultures other than the one that takes its own specific cosmic vision as universal rationality. "Outside the 'West,' virtually in all known cultures, every cosmic vision, every image, all systematic production of knowledge is associated with a perspective of totality. But in those cultures, the perspective of totality in knowledge includes the acknowledgement of the heterogeneity of all reality" (2007, 177). The decolonial alternative is "the destruction of the coloniality of world power" (2007, 177). Epistemological decolonization is needed for decoloniality "to clear the way for new intercultural communication, for an interchange of experiences and meanings as the basis of another rationality" (2007, 177).

Walter Mignolo's proposal for decoloniality begins with Quijano's understanding of "delinking." He elaborates and enacts delinking as an epistemic shift from the logic and grammar of modernity, from the coloniality of knowledge, thus bringing to the "foreground other epistemologies, other principles of knowledge and understanding and, consequently, other economies" (2007, 453), other knowledges from the exteriority of modern colonial epistemic domination, or from what was to be conquered, colonized, and dominated. This double shift is what Mignolo proposes as decoloniality, a shift from what he calls "theo-" and "ego-" politics of knowledge to "geo-" and "body-" politics of knowledge. The hegemony of Christian theology from the sixteenth to the eighteenth century tightly controlled knowledge and subjectivities in Europe and the Americas. The ego-politics of knowledge displaces the hegemony of the theological politics of knowledge as the sovereignty of the subject becomes central to the politics of knowledge production. The decolonial epistemic shift affirms what has been denied by the spatial organization of the modern world in the theological and ego-politics of knowledge, making possible "the re-emergence of the reason that has been denied as reason" (2007, 463), naming the historical location of the loci of enunciation of those who have been denied. Asking who, when, where—a shift from the enunciated to the act of enunciation—are central questions to the geopolitics of knowledge. The body politics of knowledge is the decolonial response to the marking of the body racially inferior. The body and geo-politics of knowledge create a fracture in the hegemony of colonial politics, opening the doors "to all forms and principles of knowledge that have been colonized, silenced, repressed, and denigrated by the totalitarian march of the genocidal dimension of modernity" (2007, 494). Mignolo understands this fracture as a move from universality to pluri-versality, a "universal project of a world in which many worlds can co-exist" (2007, 499). The local epistemological shifts meet through "border thinking," a decolonial method that is the spatial connector between local knowledges with a history of colonial subjection. The border "lies where . . . Western knowledge and subjectivity, control of land and labor, of authority, and ways of living gender and sexuality have been 'contacting' other languages, memories, principles of knowledge and belief, forms of government and economic organization since 1500" (2007, 497). The decolonial shift of border thinking enacts intercultural dialogue. Mignolo understands decoloniality, enacted through the geo and body politics of knowledge, as placing all lives, including human lives, first.

I have asked myself the question: Why do many men of color, colonized, and/or enslaved men treat women of color as subordinated and/or with violence? I want to understand the indifference that men who have been racialized as inferior "exhibit to the systematic violences inflicted upon women of color. I want to understand the construction of this indifference so as to make it unavoidably recognizable by those claiming to be involved in liberatory struggles" (Lugones 2010, 369). I came to understand that they are loyal to the symbiosis of modernity and coloniality, its logic, its conflation of humanity with whiteness. That question led me to what I call the "coloniality of gender" (Lugones 2010). The spatio-temporality of the coloniality of gender and decoloniality places me in relations among the dehumanized by Eurocentered modernity, moving from their reduction to animality and thus the impossibility of being

gendered, to seeking decolonial possibilities. Gender, in my understanding, is both a mark of the modern conception of the human and a colonial imposition. Gender marks what the colonized are not. This negation requires a rejection of the very understanding of the human, an understanding that created a man, a gendered being who hid his own gender away from reason under the bloomers of the semi-human European woman and violently asserted it over the bodies of Indigenous and African peoples of Abya Yala in the sixteenth century. Assimilation to the Eurocentered ideal of masculinity and the aspiration to reach it become a form of my answer to my initial question, though I think it is important to investigate the conditions under which Indigenous people and Africans affirmed, internalized, and accepted the subordination of non-white women, even when they themselves remained powerless in the coloniality of power. The denial of gender does not lead me to affirm the use of the gender category to analyze relations among the contemporary peoples of Abya Yala, precisely because of its tie to the modern understanding of the human, an oppressive concept charged with the values, norms, and ideology of modernity/coloniality, including heterosexuality. To struggle against "coloniality," the dehumanization of most of the people in the world through a racialized system of production of goods, knowledge, and politics, is to engage in a double struggle. One aspect of the struggle engages the inseparability between the dehumanized people of the world and the coloniality of gender. In the second moment we reject the disappearance of Indigenous and Afro women through a reduction to labor and sexual organs, enacting a decolonial feminism that seeks to transform and rethink their embodied sensual, spirited, sexual, intelligent, *acorazonada* relations in continuity with their universes of sense active during their history of resistance to dehumanization. A decolonial reconception and transformation of the human requires that the body reduced to labor and/or reproductive organs, and thus disappeared, become, be lived, related to, valued as a sentient, sensual, intelligent body as within, immersed in, habitats where interrelation with what there is takes the whole sentient body as permeable, seeking and providing inter-relational integrity and reciprocity in all aspects of living in connection. The coloniality of gender is centrally tied to the destruction or attempt at destruction of community. In my understanding of decolonial feminism, the communal is central, with communal intentionality and complex communality constituting the human.

Race, colonization, the colonial wound, and the coloniality of power, of knowledge, of being, and of gender are central to a politicized Latina/o and Chicana/o historicized analysis of oppression for our present. The decolonial imaginary, the season of decoloniality, delinking, borderlands, border thinking, differential oppositional consciousness, social erotics, and inhabiting interstices are the decolonial creative Latina/o and Chicana/o responses to this condition. When thinking of colonization and decolonization, of coloniality and decoloniality, we think in conversation, with an attention that is much larger than the confines of the United States or of national borders. Borders stand for colonial markers.

13

Diaspora
Ricardo L. Ortíz

The following discussion tests out the viability and even pliability of "diaspora" as both critical concept and descriptive category for a decidedly varied set of historical formations, especially as they appear at this moment in the material and intellectual unfolding of the field of U.S. Latina/o studies, a field that appears finally to be experiencing a kind of institutional consolidation and stabilization. The fluid volatility of economic, political, and social conditions in the inter-American scene in the middle of the second decade of the twenty-first century both complicates and challenges the efforts of the field of U.S. Latina/o studies to make coherent historical and cultural sense of all of the processes of mass movement and settlement from Latin America and the Caribbean to the United States since the nineteenth century, and in whatever collections of formations the field takes to be its primary object(s) of knowledge. From its early history as a field, from the 1960s and into the early 1990s, U.S. Latina/o studies could divide its attention between work on historic communities of Latin American and Caribbean descent annexed by the United States in the course of its project of imperial expansion from the early 1800s on, and immigrant communities from a small collection of sending countries or spaces that seemed to account for the vast majority of Latina/o immigrant communities in the United States, including in order of prominence: Mexican Americans, mainland Puerto Ricans, and Cuban Americans. In these decades, the majority of

U.S. Latina/o studies work conformed fairly readily to the methodologies and practices of immigrant studies. By the 1990s, it found itself both expanding its scope to include more newly arrived immigrant populations from the Dominican Republic, Haiti, El Salvador, and Guatemala, and complicating its analytical work on immigration by deploying newly activated critical concepts such as the borderlands, mestizaje, and (multi)cultural hybridity. And, thanks to the contributions of many scholars and theorists of diaspora working in the course of the early 1990s (Hall 1990; Safran 1991; Boyarin and Boyarin 1993; Clifford 1994), what Juan Flores (2009) has called "the explosion of diaspora-speak" began in that decade to exert its own critical conceptual influence on the work of the field.

"Diaspora" as a concept took hold in part because it could complicate and deepen modes of analysis that comparable categories such as immigrant, exile, refugee, expatriate, and even guest worker too often kept within narrower, more restrictive scopes. First, "diaspora" insists on a mass and collective experience of displacement, scattering, and relocation: an individual could call herself an exile or immigrant or refugee or ex-pat or guest worker and no one would blink; calling oneself a "diasporic," however, necessarily suggests identification with a group, however scattered, committed to the same work of cultural retention, reproduction, and revival of a home culture in an alien, foreign, "host" setting. Second, "diaspora" insists on the expansion of the temporal range of study to include at least two, often multiple, sometimes numerous, even countless, generations committed to that work, living potentially indefinitely beyond the singular experience of displacement that only an originating or otherwise discrete generation of immigrant-"diasporics" can undergo. Third, "diaspora" also insists on the role that extreme necessity or even violence can play in forcing such displacement on

a mass scale (and these causes can range from forcible capture and transportation into slavery, to the threat of genocidal extermination, to extreme forms of structural economic privation, to mass expulsion following political upheaval, to flight from acute conditions of state failure that render whole sectors of a society vulnerable to extreme, even life-threatening, precarity); diasporic communities evince their lack of choice in migrating precisely by at least resisting if not entirely rejecting the often common, and for some understandable, "immigrant" impulse to assimilate fully into the host country and its culture. Finally, for the purposes of this discussion, "diaspora" also insists on naming a set of living human practices that inhabit a specifically *cultural* field; while "immigrant/exile/refugee/ex-pat/guest worker" all primarily denote forms of official legal, political, or economic status, "diasporic" retains an entirely informal, unofficial, ambiguous, even improvisatory, undocumentable (and for this reason often expressive, imaginative, creative, *critical*) sense. To put it bluntly, no one can ever ask for, and no one could ever produce, official "papers" or documentation proving "diasporic" status (Edwards 2001; Gopinath 2005; Flores 2009).

Of the major national groups arguably contributing in the greatest numbers to the unfolding of the diverse processes of diasporic life in the multicultural United States, those hailing from Latin America and the Caribbean pose a distinctly heterogeneous and uneven set of examples, resulting mostly from the distinct effects of the United States' complex history of colonial and imperial ambition in the region, and the varying effects of two centuries of shifting terms in trade policy, labor policy, immigration policy, and foreign policy across the states in question. Because the large plurality of Latina/o Americans are people of Mexican descent, and because the formation of a hybrid and widespread Mexican American world predates even the 1848 Treaty of

Guadalupe Hidalgo, which settled the terms of the U.S.-Mexican War, any description of a Mexican "diaspora" in the United States would have to concede an intense internal complexity and heterogeneity, one that would have to reconcile the centuries-long, fully hybridized mode of "Mexican American" life on the actual territorial border with the more explicitly conscious, intentional, and activist modes of, say, "Chicana/o" cultural and political practice since the 1960s, and with the proliferation since the 1980s of multiple new outposts of Mexican immigrant settlement in the United States in locations as widespread as the Great Northwest, Midwestern cities like Chicago and Detroit, and the American South.

Dynamics of Puerto Rican migration from the island to the mainland, especially since the 1898 annexation of the island after the Spanish-American War, might as readily avail itself of an insistent set of internal complexities. In the Puerto Rican case, that different set of complexities comes in part from the island's neocolonial status in relation to the U.S. state (rendering all Puerto Ricans U.S. citizens, for starters), the more focused bilateral formation of immigrant movement between the island and locations of settlement closely collected around New York City and its surrounding tristate area, the perhaps more constant movement of whole populations back and forth between island and mainland, and the distinctly different racial challenges that especially Puerto Ricans of African descent encountered across a twentieth-century United States transitioning from Jim Crow to the civil rights movement to a more complex mode of "multicultural" racial consciousness that finally understood that Latina/o and black were not actually mutually exclusive states of existence.

Cuban Americans in turn also arrived into their own modes of diasporic life and practice in a manner that reflects their country of origin's irreducibly distinct geopolitical relationship with the United States. While Cubans had also been leaving the island and moving to mainland North America since the early 1800s for both political and economic reasons, the mass exodus of almost a million people who fled the island after the 1959 Castro Revolution came to determine the defining characteristics of whatever formation could call itself "Cuban America": more politically conservative than the other major Latina/o groups, more readily ascending to "model minority" status thanks to favorable immigration policies in the United States and the cultural if not political capital it brought with it as a primarily displaced elite class, likelier in its earlier waves of migration to be whiter, and likelier too to reflect the attitudes and values of the dominant, vocal political class that settled in Miami and in a few short decades converted that city into as important and influential a Latina/o American metropolis as New York or Los Angeles or San Antonio. Similar kinds of historical accounts of this complexity and heterogeneity could also be offered for the other national groupings settling into their American diasporic life in as large numbers, if more recently, especially from the Dominican Republic, Haiti, Guatemala, and El Salvador (Flores 2009; Ortíz 2009a, 2009b; A. P. Rodríguez 2009; Zavella 2011; López 2012).

For the remainder of this discussion, however, we will need to take a step back and consider some larger, more amorphous but perhaps more viable diasporic formations that demand as much if not even more attention from the field of Latina/o studies, especially going forward, than those organized around the more conventional and always problematic logics of the nation-state. One of these formations is regional, or perhaps in other ways alternatively geographical: this means, for example, studying diasporic formations coming not from Cuba, Puerto Rico, or the Dominican Republic specifically, but from the Caribbean more generally, or even specifically from the "Spanish" Caribbean, or from the island of Hispaniola; it also means studying a more general Central American transnational diasporic formation, one including all the significant sending nations in the region (Nicaragua, Honduras, Guatemala, El Salvador, Panama) and tracking thereby a decidedly transnational political exodus driven by the threats to life and livelihood of an intensely violent several decades of civil war, gang war, drug war, and genocide. Such "regional" analysis would in turn take shape in North American sites of diasporic settlement mostly by looking specifically at forms of trans-diasporic interaction and exchange: for example, when increasing numbers of Central Americans modify to the point of transforming the Mexican-dominant Latina/o character of Los Angeles, or the Caribbean-dominant Latina/o character of New York City, or when the intensifying Latina/o diversity occasioned by increasing numbers of Colombians, Venezuelans, and Haitians overwhelm and recast the once Cuban-dominant Latina/o character of Miami.

Certainly other alternative logics of diasporic formation can be as fruitfully studied; these include racial logics that would, for example, focus on the African (or American, Indigenous, or mestiz@) diasporic dimensions of the U.S. Latina/o diaspora; they could also include economic logics that distinguish between the practices of displaced elites fleeing dictatorships in countries like Cuba, Haiti, or the Dominican Republic from the practices of more conventional, working-, under-, and subaltern-class "economic" migrants primarily responding to the push-and-pull forces of a fully globalized transnational labor market. In addition, these also might include the "logics" of family, gender, sexuality, and physical ability, wherein conditions forcing mass displacement and enabling stable-enough resettlement and cultural reproduction elsewhere might differently impact men and women (especially but not exclusively depending on their parental status and the citizenship status of their children), sexual minorities forced to confront queer- and trans-phobic violence in both home- and host-lands, and the growing number of "medical" migrants seeking access to health benefits and services.

In the mid-2010s, the most telling indicators of how future mass movements of peoples from a variety of Latin American and Caribbean locations might grow from or redirect the course of such movements from the past include: the viral and incipient growth of extreme criminal violence related to the drug trade and the cartels and street gangs that manage that trade in countries like Mexico, which struggle with effects of government corruption so pervasive that politically they operate emphatically as narco-states, and where, in countries like El Salvador, Guatemala and Honduras, already vulnerable and unstable national states are literally ceding aspects of direct political and social control to gangs; the Puerto Rican government's failure to meet its mounting debts, threatening to plunge the island's economy into a deep and perhaps irreversible depression; the intensifying racist, anti-immigrant legal initiatives on the Dominican side of Hispaniola to displace and depatriate hundreds of thousands of people of Haitian descent born in the Dominican Republic as far back as the early twentieth century but never acquiring official documentation of Dominican citizenship; the reestablishment of diplomatic relations between the United States and Cuba after nearly fifty-five years of animosity, stalemate, and blockade; and, finally, the epochal state failure of the United States' federal legislature itself to pass the kind of comprehensive immigration reform that would meaningfully transform the character and the promise of the U.S. Latina/o diaspora writ large by incorporating into the nation's political, economic, social, and cultural life the many millions of undocumented Americans hoping to remain, and to rise as, Americans.

14

Education

Angela Valenzuela

Because of its generally positive impact on the life chances of individuals, and because it engenders greater social equality, education in the United States is more frequently characterized by what it accomplishes (outcomes) than by the knowledge that is actually taught in schools (content) or by the way it is delivered (process). Hence, education as a means to socially desired ends is a focus herein, although the content and process—frequently cast as policy alternatives in the education of Latinas/os—are also addressed. The growing demand for ethnic studies by the Latina/o community across the country is a testament to the currency that debates over content and process have. A shift from outcome to content and process draws on a civil rights frame that positions the Latina/o not as an object of study, but rather as a subject of personal and social transformation. Accordingly, this shift permits greater understanding of relation of self to society, root causes of oppression, positive cultural identity, and a sense of place in history in a democracy where a powerful sense of rights and responsibilities gets nurtured.

Despite the relation of education to mobility, education is, at best, a vexed proposition for most U.S. Latinas/os. Low levels of educational attainment and academic failure persist as a defining feature of their U.S. educational experience. Explanations for this tend to look either to cultural or to structural factors. With respect to the former, individual background characteristics, as well as institutional and historical circumstances are examined. With respect to the latter, although arguments about cultural and genetic inferiority have been largely discredited, the dominant culture of measurement embodied in our systems of high-stakes testing and educational accountability is influential in reinscribing a worldview of deficit thinking because of its embedded assumption of Anglo cultural superiority (Padilla 2005). Since the power to measure is an extension of the power to rank and assign value to humans on continua related to educational competencies, where Latinas/os systematically come up short, the silence on this by mainstream models of achievement allows myths like individualism, meritocracy, and Anglo cultural superiority to flourish (Steinberg 1996; Ochoa 2007).

Mainstream models of achievement ignore unearned privilege as a factor in mobility and begin instead with the premise that education in U.S. society is based primarily on individual merit and effort. In this view, personal income, occupational status, and educational attainment levels result from one's personal investment in these. In his classic comparative analysis of the U.S. and British secondary educational systems, Ralph H. Turner characterizes the U.S. educational system as one of "contest mobility," as opposed to "sponsored mobility" (1960, 855). Otherwise termed a "meritocracy," elite status goes to those that earn it through their efforts. The popular meritocratic myth—better known as the "American Dream"—aligns to a larger conceptual framework that sociologists term the "immigrant analogy," whereby the incorporation experiences of all other racial and ethnic groups in U.S. society are likened to that of their European-origin counterparts (Steinberg 1996).

Turner's (1960) sponsored mobility thesis outlines how entrance into elite society is contingent on one's sponsorship by elite members already located within the circle in order to gain access. Anticipating what later became scholarship in the area of cultural capital and social reproduction frameworks (see, for example, Bourdieu and Passeron 1977), this thesis posits that those who are already members of the elite judge potential entrants on the extent to which they possess characteristics that they wish to see in their future peers.

Persistent correlations of race/ethnicity, class, and gender with academic achievement and educational attainment, however, not only cast doubt on the view that the United States is a meritocracy, but also point to historical and institutional factors that both illuminate the role of sponsorship mobility in the United States and explain Latinas/os' overwhelming social location as members of our society's lowest classes. Historically, the concept of "mode of incorporation" has explanatory power. It differentiates the European-origin experience of coming to this country and continent in a voluntary manner, as opposed to other groups like Latinas/os that become part of this country involuntarily as a result of conquest, slavery, or colonization (Blauner 1972; Ogbu 1978; Leiberson 1980; Ignatiev 1995; Steinberg 2001). These historical facts of minorities' forceful incorporation experiences into the U.S. political economy is not mitigated by the presence of recent Latina/o immigrants on a putatively voluntary basis since they inherit the legacy of social, cultural, political, and economic oppression and disenfranchisement experienced by their racial and ethnic forerunners.

Turning now to institutional factors with this historical backdrop in mind, a defining feature of U.S. education is "majority-minority relations." The word "minority" is not a numerical term. Rather, it references both power and its relational aspect. One cannot have a minority without a majority or vice versa. Hence, societies can have a demographic majority like Latinas/os that is simultaneously a social, cultural, political, and economic minority.

Robert Blauner (1972) and Joel Spring (1997) maintain that because of their modes of incorporation, Latinas/os and other minority groups are forced to shed their languages, cultures, and community-based identities and adopt cultural ways of speaking, behaving, and interacting that mirror the mores, values, and interaction styles of the dominant, Anglo majority group. I refer to this as "subtractive schooling" (Valenzuela 1999). Moreover, drawing from educational philosopher Nel Noddings's (1992) work on caring and education, I acknowledge the presence of aesthetic or superficial ways of caring that most Anglo teachers possess as a result of their culture and preparation and that have the effect of objectifying Latina/o youth. Reduced to objects—especially test scores—they get treated in a bureaucratic manner whereby teachers teach subjects, not students (McNeil and Valenzuela 2001).

Noddings (1992), in contrast, advocates for authentic caring toward youth by school functionaries in a manner that respects the totality of who they are and what they bring to educational contexts. I acknowledge both the transformative potential and politics of authentic caring and further posit that the youth I studied in a three-year ethnography of an urban, inner-city high school reject not education, but *schooling* (Valenzuela 1999). That is, they reject being objectified and having precious little if anything about their histories, stories, languages, communities, or cultures deemed worthy of inclusion into the school curriculum or learning experience. Worse yet, youth's resistance to this objectification places them at risk within educational settings (Valenzuela 1999; Ochoa 2007).

Ser bien educada/o, or being well educated in the Latina/o sense, emanates from a set of cultural values based on respect, reciprocity, and relation. Despite Noddings's (1992) assertion that all educational experience should be premised on relation, Latinas/os' lack of power in institutional settings render them—and consequently, this important value—not only different from, but invisible to, the dominant group. In his participatory action research study among high school youth in San Bernardino, California, Louie Rodriguez (2012) extends this analysis of caring to the "politics of recognition," wherein youth seek acknowledgment in different ways. For some, this consisted of simple, relational recognition, whereas others desire that the curriculum and learning experience, as well as deeper levels of recognition, be related to the historical, social, psychological, cultural, and political realities of their communities.

Blauner (1972) indicates that while many ethnic groups that migrate to the United States similarly face discrimination and begin life at the proverbial "bottom," the insistence of the dominant group that the subordinate group subscribe to its language, culture, values, and norms is particularly humiliating to U.S. minorities. Latinas/os' minority status is evident in numerous ways, including the underrepresentation of Latina/o teachers in public schools (7.1 percent, nationally according to Villegas [2007]); the lack of books and curricula that speak to Latinas/os' history, culture, and experience; hyper-segregation in underfunded schools—particularly among English learners within large, inner-city districts; an uneven commitment to bilingual education; curricular tracking coupled with Latinas/os' concentrations in the lower, non-college-bound tracks; excessive standardized testing; high retention rates; over- as well as under-identification of special education needs; low teacher expectations; and lack of access to quality teaching, advanced placement courses, tutorial support, after-school programs, and public schools themselves, particularly in the wake of school closures that are taking place throughout the country (for instance, see de la Torre and Gwynne's [2009] analysis of Chicago public schools).

Defying the notion of a meritocracy, institutionalized discrimination overwhelmingly defines the educational experiences of Latinas/os in the United States such that even if Latinas/os make progress, the gap relative to Anglos remains constant (Gándara and Contreras 2009; Madrid 2011). Moreover, this culturally chauvinist posture of U.S. schooling is layered over a long history of de-indigenization not only in the United States but also in public schools in Mexico and Latin America from which many of our immigrant youth emanate. Consequently, Latina/o students have endured a long history of educational neglect and lack of recognition that further attaches to a widely shared experience of alienation from schools (Carter 1970; Valenzuela 1999; Ochoa 2007; L. Rodriguez 2012).

Latina/o studies' education scholars have endeavored to identify means for overcoming the social stigma of being Mexican or Latina/o in the United States, generally. The most promising directions are in the areas of bilingual education (Bartlett and Garcia 2011); culturally relevant teachers and teaching (Villegas and Irvine 2010); improving teacher recruitment and teacher preparation (Ochoa 2007); sociocultural and sociopolitical curricula and instruction (Bartolomé and Balderrama 2001; Nieto et al. 2012); respecting and affirming cultural difference and incorporating the cultural wealth that exists in Latina/o communities (Yosso 2005; Palmer 2008); making use of students' funds of knowledge (González, Moll, and Amanti 2005); countering stereotypes and deficit thinking (Valencia 2010); increasing parent involvement by reframing it as bicultural parent engagement (Olivos, Jiménez-Castellanos, and Ochoa 2011); developing parents' interpersonal networks of support that include teachers (Stanton-Salazar 1997); and advocating for research-based policies that address the structural and organizational features of school, including tracking (Flores-González 2002), retention

(Valencia and Villarreal 2005), high-stakes standardized testing (Valenzuela 2005), and disciplinary policies and school culture (L. Rodriguez 2012).

Drawing from scholars like the late Paulo Freire (1970, 1998) and Daniel Solórzano and Dolores Delgado Bernal (2001), among the most significant, current theoretical preoccupations in Latina/o education scholarship pertain to the relationship of identity and acculturation to the development of positive orientations toward schools and students' transformational consciousness. To this end, the mediating role of a culturally relevant Latina/o studies curriculum and a critical bicultural pedagogy in the classroom holds promise. Responding, in effect, to the above-mentioned concerns related to the politics of recognition and caring (Valenzuela 1999; L. Rodriguez 2012), these approaches would mean not only that students are taught in their native tongues, but that critical bicultural educators interrogate, along with their students, the ideologies, policies, practices, and structures of domination that shape their lives and their communities. Such a curriculum encourages them to consider the ways that they seek emancipation for themselves, as well as for their communities, while simultaneously considering the ways that they themselves are colonized and contradictory (Darder 1991).

Scholarship on community-university-school partnerships (e.g., Valenzuela and López 2014), together with participatory action research, makes this pedagogy actionable by equipping youth with the intellectual, scholarly, policy, and political tools they need in order to become agents of change in their own respective contexts. In the process, they secure preparedness for college (Cammarota and Fine 2008; L. Rodriguez 2012). Hence, college preparedness is a byproduct of an otherwise meaningful engagement with education, which considers student's desires, need for recognition, and quest for fairness and equity.

Chicana feminism and critical race theory—through their shared intellectual preoccupation with power relations, identity, and consciousness—acknowledge the broader power relationships in institutions and society and how their priorities, policies, and practices shape Latinas/os' educational experiences. Chicana and Latina scholars' separate and combined intellectual preoccupation with epistemology, spirituality, and indigeneity (e.g., Facio and Lara 2014) illuminates other ways of knowing and being in the world that further align to notions of well-being and being well educated from a Latina/o perspective (*ser bien educada/o*). This is not a call to a new orthodoxy, but rather a call for epistemological freedom in a form of education that is inclusive, enriching, culturally resonant, and humane as part and parcel of a progressive social-justice agenda.

15
Empire
Lázaro Lima

It is a commonplace in American studies to consider the nation's founders as progenitors of the conception of the United States as an "exceptional" empire such that Thomas Paine's oft-cited aphorism "We have it in our power to begin the world all over again" begets Thomas Jefferson's call for an "Empire of Liberty," which, in turn, would spread freedom across the globe in the name of the equally pithy and consecrated Declaration of Independence's "life, liberty and the pursuit of happiness." What then is particular and theoretically constitutive of the keyword "empire" for the field of Latina/o studies? "Empire" is the keyword that frames both the field of Latina/o studies and what Latina/o studies projects interrogate in order to make visible how empire's scattered remains throughout the Americas cross national borders as well as affective states of being. In so doing, Latina/o studies' methodological recourse to and critique of empire seeks to apprehend empire's legacies beyond the singular historical actor model of the exceptional nation-state in order to engage how empire saturates and conditions affects across space, time, and bodies. This is particularly significant when we consider that Latinas/os are the nation's largest "minority" at over 55 million strong yet the most underrepresented in national institutions, circuits of power, and political blocks. Yet despite this daunting demographic reality, the absence of Latinas/os from circuits of power largely render this expansive demographic of multitudes of variegated *latinidades*

invisible. As Kirsten Silva Gruesz (2003, 56) succinctly diagnosed the vagaries of the Latina/o question, "as Marx said of capital, Latinos seem to be everywhere and nowhere at once." What are the mechanisms that both delimit Latina/o political emergence and sustain Latina/o invisibility despite the demographic evidence to the contrary?

Latina/o studies' critique of empire insists on making this multitude historically manifest as well as laying bare the imperial logics that occlude historical cause and effect relations: there is no Latina/o migration or immigration to the United States that was not first occasioned by either U.S. intervention throughout the Americas or as a result of U.S. corporate interventions into nationally or culturally sovereign states (as is the case with Puerto Rico). If Latinas/os are cast as interlopers feeding on the national body politic's ever-shrinking largesse, then Latina/o studies' relation to empire provides the scaffolding to examine and explicate empire's historical erasures. As Fredric Jameson puts it, "history is what hurts" (1981, 102), but it hurts Latinas/os disproportionately, and beyond corporal abjection and death. That "hurt"—what Gloria Anzaldúa (1987) once called the "1,950 mile-long open wound"— bleeds into the realm of epistemological impossibility: Latina/o knowledge projects that attempt to document the Latina/o experience are as susceptible to the same crisis of legitimation in the academy as Latina/o bodies are in the political sphere. Countering such imperial violence requires theoretical and methodological acuity, which can archive and render visible how and why Latinas/os did not come as immigrants or migrants to the United States, but rather "the United States came to them in the form of colonial enterprises" (Stavans 2011, iiii). More than a decolonial gesture, such a reframing of imperial logics is an epistemological investment that seeks to reap the dividends of Latina/o futures through the agencies of a nimble Latina/o studies project that unsettles empire's founding conceits premised on freedom. Such a project insists on untangling Jefferson's "Empire of Liberty" from the imperial mechanisms that delimit freedoms and cast liberty's others as literally and figuratively invisible. The promise of economic freedom, freedom from unjust harm, and the freedom to achieve affective states of fulfillment are counterfactuals in the face of the brutal and illegitimate appropriation of space, time, and bodies that inveigh against democratic egalitarianism's promise. It is in this sense that Latina/o studies' engagement with empire seeks an accounting that would make visible how and why "the gift of freedom" is empire's principle calumny—the impossible promise that, beyond redress, requires the necessary correctives to set past "odious debts" afire through historical visibility and the theoretical armor to guard against those future "deaths to come" (Nguyen 2012, xii).

The liberal left conception of empire was radically altered in the field of American studies after the publication of Amy Kaplan and Donald E. Pease's *Cultures of United States Imperialism* (1993). Kaplan and Pease's major contribution resided in their collection's methodological and theoretical rejection of the intellectual strictures of the disciplinarily bound field of "diplomatic history" and its well-known founding insistence in understanding the "age of empire" as neatly and temporally bookmarked between 1898 and 1917 and, to stress the obvious, ensconced in the past. Kaplan and Pease's volume conceived of empire largely as a process of critique requiring the interrogation of how U.S. capital incursions, or "Pecunia Americana," motivated imperial interventions in the Américas and the world with the concomitant but ever elusive promise of freedom held in abeyance from freedom's always future colonial subjects. However, perhaps it was Antonio Benítez Rojo

(1931–2005) in his influential *La isla que se repite: El Caribe y la perspectiva posmoderna* (1989), translated in 1996 as *The Repeating Island*, who most cogently anticipated what we might consider a critique of empire from the vantage point of the global South. Following Colombian historian Germán Arciniegas (1900–1999) and his monumental study, *La biografía del Caribe* ([1945] 1966; translated as *Caribbean, Sea of the New Word* [1946]), Benítez Rojo succinctly summarized the inter-American origins of empires' logics beyond the historical strictures of the modern nation-state when he centered the critique of empire on "Pecunia Americana"—that is, on a critique of capital and how liberty's others have become exchangeable commodities under capital. Benítez Rojo makes the connection between world-systems theory and capital critiques from the epistemic anchor of the global South when he writes, "The Atlantic is today the Atlantic (NATO, World Bank, New York Stock Exchange, European Economic Community, etc.) because it was the painfully conceived child of the Caribbean. . . . It is possible to defend successfully the hypothesis that without deliveries from the Caribbean womb Western capital accumulation would not have been sufficient to effect a move . . . from the so-called Mercantilist Revolution to the Industrial Revolution" (1996, 5). The "American" legacies of this Atlantic and inter-American history of empire's circum-Caribbean emergence condition the field of Latina/o studies' relation to and critiques of empire from the vantage point of a "Latina/o studies of the global South" model of capital economic and historical critique. It is in this sense that Michael Hardt and Antonio Negri could be said to elaborate—however unwittingly—Benítez Rojo's critique of capital in their book *Empire* (2000) vis-à-vis what I am calling "Pecunia Americana" in my critical short-hand.

Hardt and Negri argue in *Empire* that we live in a U.S.-dominated imperial world order wherein the nation-state has so lost its geographically determined specificity that temporal and spatial limits of domination are enacted across space and time through the agencies of capital. Where Negri and Hardt recenter the United States as the locus of critical sense-making for a critique of the "empire of liberty," Benítez Rojo's intervention has the advantage of naming, not the most recent iteration of empire's manifestation, but the origin of a structured world-system that has historically achieved military, economic, and psychic domination through racialization and by attempting to convince the colonized that they have been colonized for their own good. Both reconstituting and extending the disciplinary blinders of diplomatic history's bookmarks for empire (1898 and 1917), the emerging field paradigm of Latina/o studies of the global South insists on an accounting capable of moving beyond the historical and interpretive blinders of Jefferson's "Empire of Liberty."

It is to this end that scholars in ethnic studies, American studies, and Latina/o studies have extended Michael Paul Rogin's (1983) coinage of the term "the American 1848" in order to map the emergence of post-industrial racialization as the precondition for denying freedom to liberty's others: Amerindians, blacks, Asians and Southeast Asian Americans, and Latinas/os as the racialized confluence of these "legally" and socially disenfranchised others. For Rogin, the Mexican American War (1846–1848), along with "the eruption and apparent pacification of the slavery crisis, between 1846 and 1851, defines the American 1848" and anticipates the Civil War (1983, 103). In pursuing his analysis, Rogin elaborates what Marx termed the "beautiful revolution," the French Revolution of 1848, in order to distinguish it from its Mexico-U.S. analogue in 1848. While the French Revolution had social inequality as its principal object for correction, the latter was ultimately about establishing racial inequality as the structural

precondition for the post-industrial incarnation of the empire of liberty as Arciniegas and Benítez-Rojo would have understood it. As I have summarized elsewhere, it is under these conditions that the epistemologically violent appropriation of territories and bodies emerge so that, for example, the national signifier "Mexican" can be appropriated as a term of racial identification and as a synonym for racialized blackness after the American 1848 (Lima 2007).

Methodologically speaking, Latina/o studies of the global South's critique of empire necessarily reframes familiar *grand récits* in order to defamiliarize their naturalization as givens guarded against epistemological reflection and critique. While the familiar narrative arc of the Monroe Doctrine (1823), for example, had it that any efforts by European nations to interfere in the Americas would be met by U.S. military aggression, it ignores generative Latina/o studies work that goes against the grain of such historical amnesias. Raúl Coronado's *A World Not to Come: A History of Latino Writing and Print Culture* (2013) reminds us that the Monroe Doctrine was ultimately the co-creation of U.S. diplomats as well as of radical republican Latin American agents who wished to oust Spain from both Cuba and Puerto Rico after the French Restoration's invasion of liberal Spain in 1823. As Jorge Cañizares-Esguerra has reminded us, "For every fictional Berrian ready to liberate Mexico and create empire, there was a nonfictional Latino Lafayette helping Philadelphia and Washington find their republican selves" (2016, 200).

Such key reframings of historical master narratives—from the American 1848's prehistory vis-à-vis the Monroe Doctrine, to the U.S.-Mexico War of 1848—characterize Latina/o studies' investments in critiques of empire above and against American studies' field critique of empire. Beyond diplomatic history's bookends of 1898 and 1917, the Spanish American War

(1898) is understood not as a U.S imperial exception that ends in 1917, but rather as a continuation of Arciniegas' and Benítez-Rojo's structural reframing, which privileges not state actors but Pecunia Americana's evacuation of cause-effect relations and its corresponding historical amnesias. It is in this sense that the Foraker Act of 1900, which made Puerto Rico a protectorate of the United States, begets the truncated citizenship imposed on Puerto Ricans in 1917 through the Jones Act after the U.S. colonization of the island in 1898.

Read from this generative framing proposed by a Latina/o studies of the global South and its critique of empire, the gift of freedom can no longer be understood through Jefferson's "Empire of Liberty" as a deferred promise for Pecunia Americana's others but rather as empire's principal epistemological trap from which critiques of empire can emerge to fortify democratic practice rather than delimiting it through historical amnesias. Such an investment in methodological anchors from the vantage point of the global South have the potential to revise what stories count beyond their conditions of reception and the vicissitudes of historical archiving in order to safeguard deaths to come as well as the odious debts that must be rescinded on ethical grounds. The prehistories of empire's occluded remains, its temporal present, as well as its related futures, are Latina/o studies' signal contribution to the reframing of single-actor model understandings of empire. In the process, Latina/o studies of the global South's reframing of empire foregrounds a capacious method that can account for the historical, affective, and corporeal hauntings of empire's remains.

16

Exile
José Quiroga

"Exile" names a condition as it has been inflicted upon subjects (exiles) by some form of state bureaucracy giving itself the power to allow, deny, or otherwise define life, movement, and being. As a condition, its essence is narrative: there is a before and after the exiled subject came to be. Temporality is also intrinsic to the term when it refers to a subject, for it describes a timeless waiting for a resolution that will end the state that it names. Anchored to its context because of its decisively political nature, "exile" refers to culture and society but it also resonates (perhaps from the onset) as a religious term: a profoundly unnatural state that separates human beings from all other sentient creatures and that became—at least since European Enlightenment philosophy and then Romantic aesthetics reflected on its implications—one of the defining elements for modern thought. Arguably, some notion related to what we now call "exile" was constitutive to the social lives of Indigenous populations of the Americas, though the "castaway" or the "banished" who appear in many surviving pre-Columbian accounts may not have always been exactly a political subject in the modern sense of the term. It is clear that the establishment or consequent abandoning of Mayan or Aztec urban centers involved some idea of wandering and return; this is evident in the Popul Vuh, and also embedded onto the notion of Aztlán as originary site, or the founding of Tenochtitlán as preordained city-state, or of political narratives such as that of Quetzalcoatl's departure and future return.

We could call these "exilic narratives," though the precise understanding of the concept for us is inevitably occluded by these cultures' forceful encounter with Europeans. While exile also appears in African religious thought brought onto the Americas, the horrors of enslavement, forced dislocation, and uprootedness were key elements for much of the exilic content of African American poetics, religion, and aesthetics, as these were understood and practiced by women and men in the various sites to which they were forcibly displaced.

For Latin Americans or Latinas/os, the historical precision of exile in modern terms originates within the Spanish colonial state bureaucracy and its political (social, and hierarchical) distinctions between European-born Spaniards and their American-born offspring. A complex resentment accounts for the growing rift between colonial administrators and the native-born *criollos*, as the former benefited politically and commercially from Spanish royal policies, while the latter increasingly felt politically distant from, and unappreciated by, a monarchy to which they had been bound by a common language, culture, and worldview. *Criollos* understood themselves partly as European "exiles," though this soon led to an "organic" or "nativist" appreciation for their immediate surroundings that was crucial for the "imagined communities" that created concepts such as brotherhood, citizen, or nation (Anderson 1983; Castro-Klarén and Chasteen 2003). The Latin American wars of independence can be partly understood as anticolonial struggles that pitted the foreign versus the native, the autochthonous as opposed to the imported, radical difference as opposed to copied models. *Criollos* engaged these oppositions as politically expedient for the task at hand: assuming control of the land that they understood as their right and inheritance, having been born out of the transplanted European culture that nurtured in them a sense of difference.

Arguably, "exile" or the "exilic" condition serves as the phantasmatic "Other" producing or giving ideological weight to the political break that caused *criollos* at the *cabildos* to fight the Spaniards. At the same time, exile marked subjects along the literary axes that define expression in the Americas since colonial times, with the "exile" understood as the subject whom it was necessary to cast out in order for the proper functioning of government to take place. From the onset, the disputes around the proper form of government for Latin America produced strong-armed *caudillos* as well as those who opposed them. Some *caudillos* themselves were forced into exile only to come back when the chaos left by their departure produced unsustainable situations that only they themselves could maneuver. The exile of political figures, however, also included their scribes—Latin American intellectuals who first collaborated and then opposed *caudillos*' power, or those who opposed it from the beginning; those betrayed by the promise of national peace and progress that *caudillos* offered to a poor and weary population, or those who never believed in the promise in the first place (Rama 1996; J. Ramos 2001; Lomas 2008).

The roster of the exilic in Latin/o America is long and distinguished—too long, too distinguished, perhaps: the Latin American short story, it is said, was created by the exiled writer Esteban Echeverría, who crafted the allegory of "El matadero" in order to comment on the horrific life of Argentines under the dictatorship of Rosas; the Latin American novel is born out of the encounter of Juan Domingo Sarmiento with the same dictatorship in the River Plate in his *Facundo*; the Romantic tradition in Latin America has as one of its foremost exponents José María de Heredia, who lived exiled in Mexico from his native Cuba, while the memoirs of the exiled priest Fray Servando Teresa de Mier in the nineteenth century inspired the work in Cuba by Reinaldo

Arenas, one of the island's best known writers, exiled due to persecution by the Cuban Revolution after 1980. Many of the heroes of the Latin American wars of independence themselves later became exiles in Europe (José de San Martín is one example), while the Portuguese court as a whole exiled itself to Brazil upon the Napoleonic invasions of the Iberian Peninsula. At the end of the nineteenth century, the last two remaining Spanish colonial outposts in the Americas, Cuba and Puerto Rico, produced their share of exiles throughout their long struggle for a political pact with the metropolitan power of Spain. It is to one of those exiles, José Martí, who in turn did political work among exiles in the United States, to whom we generally turn in order to talk about the origins of modern Latin American literature. One could also consider Martí himself the last literary exile of the nineteenth century and the first modern exile of the twentieth.

Given the political history of the Americas and given the relation between politics and claims, it would be hard to arrive at an understanding of this term in ways that would not simplify its complex usage for the past two centuries. The political events in Latin America during the second part of the twentieth century, which resulted in major displacements of populations, are at the root of the tensions inherent in the word "exile" with respect to when and how it is used, and in reference to what segments of the population.

It is important, then, to return to our point of departure: as a political term—which it always is—"exile" names a condition and a subject, it defines a community and every single member of it. Who defines the exile is less important than the condition of their residence—whether they are granted or whether they regain the rights, privileges, and obligations of their previous state. Sometimes these opinions conflict because of the very nature of bureaucracy to complicate things.

The varieties of exilic experience in the United States are many, but it is important to distinguish, if only in terms of usage, exile from migrant or immigrant, not only in terms of the "host" country (the United States) but also in terms of the countries of origin.

Belonging—which can also allude or refer to possession, perhaps ownership (though one doesn't necessarily own what is possessed, nor does belonging necessarily mark solely a site, but rather can be understood as a multiplicity of sites, or the here and now of a community)—can be fictive or real, or it can even be posited as something beyond those oppositions. For example, Benedict Anderson (1983) brilliantly conceived belonging as an "imagined"—a desire whose site was in the past or is in the future—source of pleasure or agony (for which one can sacrifice oneself or others). Belonging can also be seen as the result of a sense of community (an exile is a singular subject insofar as s/he is or represents something beyond the singular, to the extent of practically abolishing and re-instating the community). Exile is to community the sign of a non-place, which obversely states (defines) the community as such. Bearing the weight of the absolute, the exile constitutes the community; and just as a community has its dead, it also has its exiles, sometimes as if a living-dead.

Utopia is not the counterpoint to exile, but the exile faces utopia unsure of whether to be a cynic or a servant—a docile subject who sees in utopia the possibility of self-abolishing. It is, sadly, true, that we have more experience with exile than with utopia; but then again, perhaps the same road leads from one to the other.

EXILE JOSÉ QUIROGA

17

Family

Richard T. Rodríguez

If one were to identify the single attribute most politicians incessantly assign Latinas/os—and assume and emphasize as a point of solidarity for the sake of vote procurement for their campaigns—it would indisputably be the salutary possession of "family values." Although what counts as "values" in the electoral context tends to rely on ethnic and religious typecasting and ideological supposition, the family is nonetheless crucial for Latinas/os as it has long functioned as a "crucial symbol and organizing principle" for collective mobilization and quotidian affairs (R. T. Rodríguez 2009). Indeed, as politicians and others are astutely aware, the family is almost impossible to disentangle from how we understand Latina/o cultures, histories, and politics.

Notwithstanding the intermittent praiseworthy family qualities granted to them, the "problems" ailing Latina/o communities are routinely held responsible for maladjusted relations. Contrasting with a family values ideal that conforms to a nuclear kinship network—one that historian Stephanie Coontz (1993) argues is animated by an unfeasible nostalgic longing—Latina/o family dynamics have long been subjected to derision and pathology. Foundational scholars in the social sciences (particularly in the fields of anthropology and sociology) who investigated Mexican and Puerto Rican families, for example, were instrumental in attributing factors such as poverty and machismo to reputed cultural beliefs and habits fueling familial dysfunction.

Writing about the work of William Madsen and Arthur J. Rubel, sociologist Norma Williams maintains that such early scholarship on Chicano families "adopted the stereotypical definitions of the majority society in describing Mexican Americans" (1990, 2). Because many Latina/o family practices did not correspond with those of the dominant culture, the value of moving beyond nuclear models of household formation would be lost on those invested in upholding normative perceptions of family arrangement. Indeed, fictive kinship practices like *compadrazgo* and *comadrazgo* exceeded the ties between immediate blood relations by counting extended relations and unrelated community members as family.

Responding to social science distortions and emphasizing the distinct modes of fashioning family in light of the various forms of discrimination experienced by Latinas/os in the United States, scholars like Octavio Ignacio Romano-V., Virginia E. Sánchez Korrol, Miguel Montiel, Patricia Zavella, and José Hernández aimed to set the record straight by showing the plethora of familial experiences that do not subscribe to hard and fast notions of gender relations and inflexible ideas of tradition. Recently, anthropologist Brian Montes (2005) has shown how the work of anthropologist Oscar Lewis—whose books *Five Families: Mexican Case Studies in the Culture of Poverty* (1959) and *La Vida: A Puerto Rican Family in the Culture of Poverty—San Juan and New York* (1966b) are representative—holds persistent sway in some quarters of the academy as his "culture of poverty" thesis continues to be lauded despite the critiques of it made by Latina/o scholars.

With many scholars studying Latina/o communities intimately connected to emergent social movements, the reclamation of the family took on symbolic significance for galvanization purposes. Various segments of the Chicano civil rights movements of the 1960s and

1970s—from student activists to the United Farm Workers, for example—deployed the family (or *la familia*) as an organizing principle to bond unrelated yet similarly disenfranchised individuals as a community. Writer and activist José Armas self-published a manifesto in 1972 whose title alone, *La Familia de La Raza*, signaled the importance of casting "the people" as an extended family. The impulse behind Armas's call to mobilization was also at the heart of "El Plan Espiritual de Aztlán." Also known as the Chicano Movement Manifesto, "El Plan" was drafted at the historic Chicano Youth Liberation Conference in 1969 and identified Chicano culture as that which "unites and educates the family of La Raza towards liberation with one heart and one mind" (Chicano Youth Liberation Conference 1972, 405). Exemplifying what sociologist Maxine Baca Zinn designated "political familism" (1975), la familia de la raza functioned as the fundamental cultural nationalist beckoning for collective empowerment and action.

Yet well before Chicanas/os would reclaim the family for nationalist self-determination, the linkage between family and nation that materialized in Puerto Rico during the late nineteenth and early twentieth centuries was emblematized as "la gran familia jíbara" (or the great *jíbaro* family). Like the mestizo who stood at the center of Chicano cultural nationalist ideology, the mytho-historical figure of the *jíbaro*, or the peasant, served as a decisive symbol for Puerto Rican nationalist ideology given its adaptability within a range of historical, social, and political contexts. Identifying a recharged significance of la gran familia jíbara as an organizing strategy in the early twentieth century by the creole elite to oppose the colonial authority of the United States, Arlene Torres (1998) notes how blacks and mulatos surprisingly found themselves integrated into the Puerto Rican national family despite past and enduring marginalization based on racial difference.

Whereas Latinas/os might be said, in the words of Chicana lesbian writer Cherríe Moraga, to "fight back with the family" (1993b), the nationalist impetus to conflate the nation or the community with the family tends to overlook the hierarchies that exist among those comprising a presumably cohesive constituency. To be sure, racialized, poor, gendered, disabled, and non–sexually normative subjects are granted secondary status if not excluded entirely from cultural nationalist constructions of the family. Tallying the affirmative attributes of cultural nationalism and extolling its upholding of familiar principles, Moraga also names institutionalized heterosexism, inbred machismo, and a lack of cohesive national strategy as pitfalls that always foreclose the possibility of unity.

Despite the heteronormative and homophobic renderings of the family in Latina/o cultural politics and in the everyday lives of Latinas/os, struggles have been waged by queers (particularly gay men, lesbians, bisexuals, and transgender individuals) to gain acceptance by families into which they were born as well as to forge kinship relations extending beyond biological ties. During the 1970s the San Francisco-based Gay Latino Alliance (GALA) was formed by gay and lesbian Latinos and Latinas seeking to forge an alternative family with others who shared not only a nonheterosexual identity but similar political sensibilities. In spite of the factors that brought them together, for some, belonging in GALA proved difficult, with women in particular feeling disrespected and silenced by male members. Thus the organization did not fulfill its goal of achieving a sense of kinship rooted in democratic egalitarianism (Roque Ramírez 2003; R. T. Rodríguez 2009). While queer Latinas/os hold no other option but to create family with strangers given their banishment from their biological families, sociologist Katie L. Acosta (2013) has shown how "sexually nonconforming Latinas" both create and negotiate their families of origin. According to a report released by the Williams Institute at the University of California at Los Angeles (Kastanis and Gates 2013), an estimated 1.4 million Latinas/os in the United States identified as lesbian, gay, bisexual, or transgender (LGBT). Detailing an estimated 146,000 Latinas/os living in same-sex households, the report further notes that same-sex Latina/o couples are 1.7 times more likely than white same-sex couples to be raising children. Just as they choose those with whom they make family, many LGBT Latinas/os simultaneously hold on to relationships with their biological kin as a means of economic, social, or emotional sustenance.

The family is nothing short of central to scholarship on migration, which has long remained a vital strand of Latina/o studies. And an unabashedly visible and influential undocumented rights movement emerging in the early twenty-first century in cities like Chicago, Los Angeles, and New York (Gonzales 2013) has shifted the terms of debate as immigration policies and laws have changed in tandem with more recent waves of migration from Latin American and the Caribbean. The current embrace of the family as an organizing principle by undocumented justice advocates, however, remarkably mirrors the efforts of Chicanas/os in the 1960s and 1970s. Identified by political scientist Amalia Pallares as "family activism" (2015), the move toward politicizing the family—in large part due to enforced laws dividing and displacing relatives—has enabled immigrant rights activists to make compelling claims for family reunification in order to supersede legal notions of citizenship that rigidly fix familial belonging in a narrowly conceived national frame.

From another trajectory, Latina/o immigrants living and working in the United States have forged and struggled to sustain cross-border family ties amid economic struggle. Examining the circumstances of transnational Salvadoran families, sociologist Leisy J. Abrego (2014) has noted the complications stemming from the severed family ties generated by the need to provide monetary support for an extended familial support network. Indeed, remittances are what solidify the transnational kinship networks that are equally maintained and tested, given the overwhelming political economic circumstances experience by those providing them. As part of an increased awareness and concern for undocumented people who are positioned differently with respect to gender and sexuality, younger activists in an "undocuqueer" movement (which extends the goals of DREAMer actions that seek to grant rights to undocumented youths brought to the United States at an early age) embraced the notion of "queer familia" to rally undocumented LGBT Latinas/os. Fittingly, an organization named Familia: Trans Queer Liberation Movement took flight in 2014 in order, as its website announces, to "address, organize, educate and advocate for the issues that are important to the LGBTQ Latin@ community."

Although scholarship on the Latina/o family has emerged chiefly from the province of the social sciences, the humanities and creative forms like literature and film have generated a stunning range of family representations that either complement or complicate the important work in, for example, sociology, anthropology, or political science. Cultural expressions, although sometimes discounted as fictional or said to be lacking empirical evidence, often broach a wide array of issues and concerns that may escape the purview of scholarly work.

Novels by Sandra Cisneros (*Caramelo*), Arturo Islas (*The Rain God* and *Migrant Souls*), and Loida Maritza Pérez (*Geographies of Home*); short story collections by Helena María Viramontes (*The Moths and Other Stories*), Manuel Muñoz (*Zigzagger* and *The Faith Healer of Olive Avenue*), and Junot Díaz (*Drown*); plays by Cherríe Moraga (*Giving Up the Ghost* and *The Hungry Woman: A Mexican Medea*); and memoirs by Piri Thomas (*Down These Mean Streets*),

Judith Ortiz Cofer (*Silent Dancing: A Partial Remembrance of a Puerto Rican Childhood*), and Sandra and Sheila Ortiz Taylor (*Imaginary Parents: A Family Autobiography*)—all elegantly represent Latina/o families from a kaleidoscopic perspective. A number of films and videos—from narrative shorts to documentaries, and from feature-length to experimental productions—highlight the complexities of family dynamics in Latina/o cultural contexts. León Ichaso's *El Súper* (1979), Harry Gamboa Jr.'s *Baby Kake* (1984), Darnell Martin's *I Like It Like That* (1994), Gregory Nava's *My Family* (1995), Laura Simón's *Fear and Learning at Hoover Elementary* (1997), Aaron Matthews's *My American Girls: A Dominican Story* (2001), Patricia Riggen's *Under the Same Moon* (2007), Gloria La Morte and Paola Mendoza's *Entre Nos* (2009), and Fro Rojas's *Tio Papi* (2013) illustrate how a focus on the family necessarily encompasses deep concerns with immigration, gender, citizenship, sexuality, blackness, and economic disenfranchisement particular to transnational and translocal Latina/o communities whose origins stem from the United States, Mexico, the Caribbean, and Central and South America.

Some scholars have expressed frustration with constantly equating Latina/o issues with family issues, insisting that the seemingly inextricable bond Latinas/os share with the family is an exaggeration bordering on stereotyping. There is no denying that the family persists across decades as a symbol and principle to which Latinas/os have turned for support or necessary reinvention. Yet the crucial function of the family for Latinas/os cannot be understated. And despite calls by white queer theorists to forget the family (a call that evidences an unfamiliarity with or disregard of a decades-long history of writing emphasizing the vital meanings of familial ties for queers of color), the family will persist as a means to subvert racism, homophobia, sexism, and class discrepancies, while always running the risk of reproducing those very inequalities in its uncritical adaptations.

18

Feminisms
María Eugenia Cotera

Latina feminism offers an intersectional approach to understanding and combating the relations of domination and subordination that structurally disenfranchise Latina/o communities, broadly conceived. Like the Latinas who developed its primary conceptualizations, theories, and practices, Latina feminism has been shaped as much by experiences of colonization and U.S. imperialism and of diaspora and border-crossing, as it has been by day-to-day lived experiences of heterosexism, racism, and classism in the United States. Indeed, contemporary Latina feminists—from academics to community organizers— have charted a genealogy of praxis that reaches beyond national borders and deep into history, recuperating a set of feminist practices that articulate the complex intersections of identity and subjectivity.

Figures like La Malinche / Malintzin Tenepal (Hernán Cortés's translator in the Conquest of Mexico) and Sor Juana Inés de la Cruz (a seventeenth-century Mexican nun and author of "Hombres necios," a poem that exposes the contradictions of colonial patriarchy) offer key articulations in this feminist genealogy, as do the writings of women like Sara Estela Ramírez (a Mexican revolutionary feminist, who organized on both sides of the U.S.-Mexico border) and Puerto Rican anarchist feminist Luisa Capetillo (an advocate of gender and class equality who worked as a labor organizer in Puerto Rico, New York, and Florida), both of whom produced numerous tracts that proposed a political imaginary at the intersection of gender, race, and class. More recent figures, like Emma Tenayuca (leader of the 1930s Pecan Sheller's strike in San Antonio, Texas) and Luisa Moreno (a Guatemalan feminist and labor organizer, who became a key advocate for the "Spanish Speaking" in the 1930s and 1940s) anticipate the strategies and tactics that postwar Latinas would later adopt to articulate their experience of gender, race, and class subordination and combat the power structures of capitalism, imperialism, white supremacy, and heteropatriarchy.

A key conceptual linkage point in this genealogy is found in the meanings of community. Because Latina feminists (like other women of color feminists) understand feminism in relationship to other struggles for liberation and decolonization, their approach to "women's liberation" necessarily moves beyond gender, just as their commitment to end racism and colonialism moves beyond race and nation. This distinguishing factor shaped the relationships that Latina feminists developed within the social movements that came into prominence after the passage of the Civil Rights Act (1965) and in the wake of the Vietnam War. Latinas participated widely in the women's liberation movement, the Chicano movement, the Young Lords Party, and other movements in the 1960s and 1970s. While they often led key organizing initiatives and projects within movement spaces, their participation was frequently complicated by the tendency of identity-based movements to frame their praxis around a singular or monocausal vision of oppression, as Audre Lorde (2007) and others have observed. Partly in response to these limitations, and partly as a result of their need to find a political language that could address the particular ways in which the oppressions of class, race, gender, and imperialism impacted their lives, Latinas began to conceptualize an oppositional praxis at the crossroads of race, class, and sex—one that resonated with the theories of third-world and black feminism developing in New York

and the Bay Area activist circles (Angela Davis, the Third World Women's Alliance, among others). As Argentine-born socialist feminist Mirta Vidal observed: "Raza women suffer a triple form of oppression: as members of an oppressed nationality, as workers, *and* as women" (1971, 3–11). Vidal noted that this "triple oppression" suggested an important distinction between the "problems of the Chicana and those of other women," one that called for a new perspective on revolutionary struggle. This notion of a "triple oppression" has developed over time into a somewhat more diffuse and nuanced formulation of intersectional feminism, an oppositional praxis that unpacks the structural effects of multiple and compounding oppressions and explores how new feminist epistemologies and new political imaginaries are produced in the interstices of those multiple oppressions.

Over the 1970s and 1980s Latinas developed their particular understanding of intersectionality in response to their social condition as members of a broader Latina/o community that had experienced five hundred years of colonialism, U.S. imperialism, state violence, and labor exploitation. Pointing out that this collective experience of oppression had particular (compounding) effects on women and sexual minorities—just as the arc of patriarchal oppression expressed itself differentially across the lines of class and race—these early articulations of the race/class/sex nexus signal a "third space" critique of dominant oppositional ideologies. In this sense, the historical emergence of late twentieth-century Latina feminist praxis can be seen not only as a continuation of a much longer feminist tradition in Mexico, Latin America, and the Caribbean, but also as a response to the masculinist symbolic order of dominant nationalisms (which sought to incorporate women as "helpmeets" of revolution) and dominant forms of white, hegemonic feminism, which too often relegated Latinas to the margins or treated them as second-order tokens.

One can see this critique clearly delineated in the challenges to hegemonic feminisms and nationalisms of Chicana feminists like Martha P. Cotera and Anna Nieto Gómez, the rejection of patriarchal nationalisms (and heterosexism) by women in the Young Lords Party of New York, and the critique of a reductive reproductive rights discourse in the "Pro-Choice" movement by Puerto Rican and Chicana welfare rights advocates, all of which highlighted a profound "disidentification" with singular frames for understanding oppression, and especially with the political practices and agendas that such frames supported (Alarcón 1990). These critical rearticulations of the nature of oppression as intersectional—coupled with their calls for greater attention to "difference" within collective movements— opened the way for an overlapping generation of Latina feminist writers and theorists to take up the insights of intersectional praxis in their critical theory, personal essays, and creative work. This intergenerational shift was to have a deep (though still largely underexamined) impact on the nature of feminist theorizing more broadly.

Looming particularly large in this 1980s and 1990s critical constellation are creative nonfiction writers like Gloria Anzaldúa, Aurora Levins Morales, and Cherríe Moraga, who explored the subjective nexus of race, class, gender, and sexuality in both their creative and their critical work. A child of the "borderlands," Anzaldúa (1987) theorized from her particular location as a Mexicana/Chicana, queer, poet/critic. Drawing theoretical insights from her experience of growing up working class and racially marked on the U.S.-Mexico border, as well as her experience within Chicana/o, feminist, and queer movements, Anzaldúa articulated a feminist voice from the borders of multiple activist imaginaries. Moving that voice from margin to center was her activation of the "borderlands" as both a concrete place and a theoretical space. Her foundational work, *Borderlands / La Frontera: The New Mestiza*, an assemblage of poetry, essays, and critical anthropology, embodied the borderlands space in its very form even as it offered an example of theorizing from the intersections. Articulating "a new mestiza consciousness" at the crossroads of multiple oppressions, Anzaldúa pointed out how reductive conceptualizations of oppression often lead to reactionary thinking. "It is not enough to stand on the opposite river bank, shouting questions, challenging patriarchal, white conventions," she argued, because this "counterstance" ultimately locked one into a binary vision of "oppressor" and "oppressed," reducing both to a "common denominator of violence" and erasing the differences and heterogeneities that shape experiences of oppression (1987, 78). Instead, Anzaldúa proposed a path of *conocimiento* to a "new consciousness" that could heal the split "between the two mortal combatants" and thus enable the "new mestiza" to "see through serpent and eagle eyes" at once (1987, 100–01).

Anzaldúa's "new mestiza consciousness" proposed both an understanding of identity as multiple and shifting and a radical revisioning of the "oppressor and oppressed" binary that Latinas adopted in their theorizations of feminism beyond the race/sex/class nexus. Puerto Rican writer Aurora Levins Morales (2001) illuminates this consciousness in her own historical autoethnography, *Remedios: Stories of Earth and Iron from the Histories of Puertorriqueñas*. A recuperative genealogy of Puerto Rican women, *Remedios* draws from the multiple histories and knowledges (Indigenous, African, European, and beyond) that have shaped identity in the Caribbean to reconstruct a feminist subjectivity at the crossroads and thereby "heal the split" enacted by centuries of colonialism, imperialism, and heteropatriarchy.

Aurora Levins Morales and her mother, Rosario Morales, were key contributors to the foundational feminist anthology *This Bridge Called My Back* (Moraga and Anzaldúa 1981), which brought the writing of (primarily queer) Latinas, black, Asian American, and Native American women into dialogue to articulate the "unexplored affinities inside difference" that could "attract, combine and relate new constituencies into a coalition of resistance" (Sandoval 1998, 362). As co-editor of that volume and in her later publications, Cherríe Moraga echoed and concretized Anzaldúa's interventions in her "theory in the flesh," a mode of critical feminist analysis that excavated the commonality of oppression while remaining attentive to the complexities of our particular social locations within systems of domination and subordination. In *Loving in the War Years*, her own compendium of essays, critical theory, and poetry, Moraga observed that "no authentic, non-hierarchical connection among oppressed groups can take place" without a "grappling with the source of our own oppression, without naming the enemy within ourselves and outside of us" (1983b, 52–53). That she made this observation from the standpoint of her personal experience as a biracial, working-class, queer woman does not undermine the theoretical relevance of her intervention. On the contrary, Moraga's "theory in the flesh" challenged the borders between "experience" and "theory" and demanded a critical reframing of the boundaries that delimit and hierarchize feminist knowledge practices. Moraga's "theory in the flesh" proposed a theoretical process through which "the physical realities of our lives—our skin color, the land or concrete we grew up on, our sexual longings—all fuse to create a politic born out of necessity" (Moraga and Anzaldúa 1981, 23).

Like Anzaldúa's *concientización*, Moraga's "theory in the flesh" was, at its heart, a deeply political praxis that highlighted the relevance of personal experience to the development of theories of resistance and, conversely, the importance of theory for understanding the "oppressor within." Most importantly, it envisioned a model of feminist theory that could not only describe but also substantively transform the lives of Latinas and other women of color. As Anzaldúa would later argue in *"Haciendo Teorías,"* a part of her introduction to *Making Face, Making Soul*, our task as feminist theorists is to "de-academize theory and . . . connect the community to the academy" by envisioning "new kinds of theories with new theorizing methods" that could cross borders, blur boundaries, and "rewrite history using race, class, gender and ethnicity as categories of analysis" (Anzaldúa 1990, xxv). Other Chicana/Latina contributors to *This Bridge Called My Back* developed their own "theories in the flesh," which centered on their particular experiences as Latinas. In their essays for the anthology and in their later writing, research, and organizing, contributors like Cuban American lesbian feminist Mirtha Quintanales, Puerto Rican feminist writer Rosario Morales, and her daughter, Aurora Levins Morales, explored the ways in which multiple and intersecting experiences of oppression had shaped the identities and histories of Latinas of Caribbean origin. In centering "difference" as a point of coalition, and calling attention to the multiple and shifting nature of identity (a conception of identity that was nevertheless grounded in lived experience), the Latinas who contributed to *This Bridge Called My Back* and the feminist of color anthologies that followed it proposed a revolutionary oppositional optic that shifted the axis of contemporary feminist theory, one that Latina feminists still deploy in their theoretical, creative, and activist work.

Notwithstanding the profound implications of this important revisioning of the practices and aims of feminist theory, the theoretical insights of *This Bridge Called My Back*—particularly the centrality of "difference" to its comparative optic and its praxis of "theory in the flesh"—have been consistently misapprehended and even rendered illegible by mainstream feminist theory. Misread as a call for cultural pluralism, or still worse, as the villain in the declension narrative of the women's movement, the attention to "difference" that Chicanas, Latinas, and other women of color saw as the necessary center for any coalitional praxis presented a serious epistemic challenge to dominant modes of thinking about identity, oppression, and political struggle—a challenge that goes far beyond the additive model of "diversity of women" promoted in (neo)liberal modes of multiculturalism. Indeed, as Norma Alarcón, Chela Sandoval, and others have observed, this attention to difference among, difference within, and difference as a site of alliance suggests an epistemological orientation that refuses to maintain a static understanding of "woman," "nation," or "other," even as it challenges us to revision revolutionary struggle and the very logics through which we imagine oppositional praxis.

Likewise "theory in the flesh," which highlights the dialectical entanglement of experience and theory and foregrounds feminist theory's potential as praxis, has been consistently misread through the lens of "identity politics." Such reductive readings actively erase the long history of Latina disidentification with the logics of identitarian political movements and suggest a reading of "experience" as necessarily unmediated by "theory." "Theory in the flesh" demands that we examine how theories "matter" both personally and politically, and that we remain attentive to the ways in which the hidden theories of identity that subtend relations of domination and subordination structure not only our lived experience as women of color, but also our understanding of those experiences, and even our gestures toward alliance. Drawing from our lived experience to deconstruct those hidden theories of identity and to craft "a politic born out of necessity" remains a central praxis of Latina feminisms today.

19

Film
Sergio de la Mora

Latina/o film names the cinematic histories, practices, and institutions of U.S. Latinas/os. Stemming in particular from the 1960s civil rights movement, Chicana/o and Puerto Rican activists demanded access to the means of production to ensure self-representation, correct negative and damaging images in the media, and replace these with positive, empowering, and more authentic representations (Noriega 1992, 2000; L. Jiménez 1996). Media activists and artists saw the urgency of struggling against the ways the media stereotyped Latinas/os, arguing that access to the means of representation was critical for full political and cultural citizenship. As leading scholars Chon Noriega and Ana M. López state, Latina/o media "no longer marks the site of simple oppositional practice vis-à-vis Hollywood, but must be seen through the filter of a number of competing disciplines, traditions, histories" (Noriega and López 1996, ix). This is the "matrix of differential histories" (xiii) through which they argue Latina/o films should be read.

The history of Latinas/os in front and behind the screen has been traced back to the earliest U.S. cinema (Reyes and Rubie 1994; Ríos-Bustamante and Bravo 2005). Using the lens of stereotypes, the documentary *The Bronze Screen: 100 Years of the Latino Image in Film* (Dominguez, de los Santos, and Racho 2002) constructs a genealogy of the transformation and stasis of said stereotypes. Scholars such as Charles Ramírez Berg (2002) have also taken up the role played in Hollywood's racial imaginary by looking at their role as Others: from greasers/bandits/gangsters to the Latin lover and his female counterpart the Spitfire to Anglos playing Latinas/os in brown-face, such as Natalie Wood in *West Side Story* and Marlon Brando in *Zapata*. Anxiety around Latinas/os, a mix of fear and desire, is partially a product of colonialism and U.S. imperial expansionism. How are Latinas/os framed in the U.S. racial imaginary? Why do Latinas and Latinos consistently appear as the racial Other (Barrueto 2014)?

Scholars, including Clara E. Rodriguez (2004), have examined the production and reception of films with Latina/o actors in order to gauge the sociocultural conditions shaping the representation of Latinas/os in Hollywood. Focusing on stars from the silent period to roughly the present, Rodriguez "uncovers" and "give[s] voice" to those who have been marginalized, silenced, and written out of official Hollywood histories. Revealing this suppressed history is important to creating a richer and more complex history of racial diversity in the United States that by far exceeds the outdated black and white racial paradigm. Mary Beltrán (2009), in turn, focuses on Latinas/os on and off screen, notably U.S. Latina/o stars. Others have focused on pan-Latina/o and Latin American approaches (Woll 1977; Keller 1994; Noriega and López 1996; C. Rodriguez 1997, 2004; Baugh 2012) and on questions of distribution (Puente 2011).

Taking a cue from the radical revolutionary aesthetics and politics of the 1960s and 1970s, practitioners of the new Latin American cinema—notably Cuban cinema and the theories and practices of Third Cinema—and Latina/o filmmakers, theorists, and historians have frequently positioned Latina/o film as oppositional (Fregoso 1993; Noriega and López 1996). Chicana/o cinema has been located "in opposition to Hollywood and in alliance with Latin American cinema" (Noriega 1992, 2000), and as a cinema defined as by, for, and about Chicanas/os (Keller 1985; Johansen 1992; List 1996). A problem with this model is that it overlooks early (1960s and 1970s) experimental and avant-garde film practices such as those of Ernie Palomino, Willie Varela, and Harry Gamboa Jr. and art collectives such as Asco (Chavoya and Gonzalez 2011). Furthermore, the aforementioned statement evinces an anxiety over Hollywood's influence on Chicana/o film practices, and does not fully account for early Mexican American film viewing practices (Gunckel 2015). Rosa-Linda Fregoso (1993, 2001, 2003) moves the debate from questions of authenticity and realistic, positive representations to ones that look at the construction of identities that speak to representation and power. She has focused much of her scholarship on Chicana and Latina filmmakers, particularly on the work of Lourdes Portillo.

Queer, feminist, and cultural studies have taken up the racialization and sexualization of Latina/o stars from big butts (Jennifer López) to sassy hips (Ricky Martin) to skin color and accents and explosive personalities (Lupe Vélez) (Negrón-Muntaner 1994; Fregoso 2003; D. Vargas 2009). Queer readings offer varied strategies that can range from the analysis of independent, low-budget films, as in José Esteban Muñoz's (1996) discussion of Cuban American Ela Troyano's *Carmelita Tropicana: Your Kunst Is Your Waffen*; Luz Calvo's (2002) appraisal of masculine lesbian figures in Orson Welles's *Touch of Evil*; Frances Negrón-Muntaner's (2004) discussion of the Puerto Rican drag performer Holly Woodlawn; and Daniel Enrique Pérez's (2009) reexamination of the Latin lover, among other queer tropes.

Two lesbian Latina directors, the aforementioned Chicana Lourdes Portillo and Puerto Rican Frances Negrón-Muntaner, clearly insert themselves into the practice of blending, interrogating, and expanding discourses of documentary and fiction films. This occurs in Portillo's *Después del terremoto / After the Earthquake*

(1979) and *The Devil Never Sleeps / El diablo nunca duerme* (1994) (discussed by Fregoso 2001) and Negrón-Muntaner's 1994 *Brincando el charco: Portrait of a Puerto Rican* (analyzed by La Fountain-Stokes 2009).

Within Cuban American film production, which Ana M. López (1996) calls "greater Cuba," León Ichaso is the most successful director, who, after the critical success of the exile drama-comedy *El Súper* (1979), went on to achieve audience crossover with Latina/o focused films such as *Crossover Dreams* (1985), *Piñero* (2001), and *El Cantante* (2006). *El Súper* was based on an off-Broadway play and gained national attention for being one of the few works by Cuban-Americans to look at the experiences of Cuban immigrants in New York City; *Crossover Dreams* looked at multiple Latina/o communities. Both films have been categorized as Latina/o films, while Ichaso's *Azúcar Amarga* (1995), a Spanish-language film that focused on a disaffected supporter of the Communist Revolution in Cuba, has been labeled a foreign film. Ichaso's next work, *Piñero*, a well-received account of the Nuyorican poet and playwright Miguel Piñero's life, is often considered an independent film.

The films of Cuban filmmakers that were produced in the 1960s and 1970s and had a significant impact on U.S. Latina/o audiences, include those by Tomás Gutiérrez Alea, Humberto Solás, Sara Gómez, and Santiago Álvarez. Cuban national cinema's influence, albeit largely carried out through the official channel of the Cuban Film Institute (Instituto Cubano del Arte e Industria Cinematográficos, ICAIC), was also highly influential through the circulation of film theory linked to the new Latin American cinema movement, the most important being Julio García Espinosa's "For an Imperfect Cinema" ([1969] 1997), a polemical essay that advocated for the democratization of film production and called for film productions to be attuned to the necessities of the historical context and location of where they are made.

To what degree does Latina/o cinema exist as a genre or subnational cinema? Most U.S. Latina/o film festivals include Spain in their purview, largely a result of seeking to reach as broad an audience as possible. What about new modes of production and distribution (Dávila and Rivero 2014)? One example of an issue Latina/o cinema scholars will need to contend with are the transnational Mexican-U.S. co-productions by Pantelion Films, a joint venture between Lions Gate Entertainment and Mexico's Televisa originating in 2010, which are made primarily for entertainment and do not have pedagogical concerns, unlike Diego Luna's 2014 biopic *Cesar Chavez*. I'm thinking of Eugenio Derbez's underwhelming light comedy *Instructions Not Included* (2013), which grossed $45 million dollars in the United States at the box office and $99 million dollars worldwide. What is to be said of the scant interest in *Cesar Chavez*, which grossed only $5,571,497 domestically, in spite of boasting leading actors such as Michael Peña, America Ferrera, and Rosario Dawson? *Instructions Not Included* is now the highest grossing Spanish language film and the fourth highest foreign language film of all time.

Are films made by Mexicans in the United States, which have no Latina/o content and feature an all-Anglo cast, such as Alfonso Cuarón's *Gravity* (2013) and Alejandro González Iñárritu's *Birdman* (2014) and *The Revenant* (2015), to be considered Latina/o films? Why or why not? What about Chilean director Pablo Larraín's *Jackie* (2016)? Are we supposed to consider Spanish actors such as Penélope Cruz and Oscar-winner Javier Bardem as Latinas/os? What about the generally entertaining cinema of Robert Rodriguez (Ingle 2012; F. Aldama 2015a)?

These issues will continue to be of concern as the Latina/o population continues to increase in a commercial film landscape that for the most part ignores Latinas/os (Negrón-Muntaner 2014). Statistics should convince leading studios to think otherwise: while Latinas/os make up 17 percent of the population, they make up 26 percent of the box office. As studies show, "Latinos are the 'heaviest moviegoers' of any demographic, according to the MPAA's recent survey. As of 2012, African-Americans make up 12 percent of the population but only account for 11 percent of North American ticket sales. Hispanics make up 17 percent of the population but account for a whopping 26 percent of sales at the box office" (Gittell 2014). This scenario should warrant more attention to Latinas/os.

20

Food
Zilkia Janer

Descartes's enduring separation of mind and body resulted in the disqualification of food and eating as objects of intellectual inquiry because they belong to the realm of sensory experience and bodily functions. Nevertheless, in the past few decades there has been a veritable explosion of interdisciplinary scholarship on food related issues. Human beings need to eat to live, so it should not come as a surprise that food is intertwined with all aspects of human culture. In the field of Latina/o studies, food has received increased attention both as material and nonmaterial culture (Janer 2008). As material culture, food is an indispensable object of study given that Latinas/os are the backbone of the food industries in the United States. As nonmaterial culture, food is equally significant for Latina/o studies since food-centric discourses have been instrumental both in the marginalization and in the self-assertion of Latinas/os.

Food has been at the center of Latina/o sociopolitical struggles. The United Farm Workers, a union of agricultural workers, has been one of the most important organizations in the Latina/o civil rights movement. Latinas/os are a major labor force in farms, processing factories, and restaurants. In spite of their central role in food production and preparation, 23.7 percent of Latina/o households were food insecure in 2013 (Coleman-Jensen, Gregory, and Singh 2014). The food insecurity problem is often compounded by the lack of access to nutritious food, which results in a high incidence of diet-related health problems like obesity, diabetes, and heart disease. The lack of justice in the current food system could not be more clear.

Latina/o labor in the food industry is not only underpaid; it is also undervalued. Beyond physical labor, food work involves knowledge and creativity. Indeed, Latina/o food workers have played an important role in the shaping of the palate of the mainstream American consumer who enjoys Latina/o and Latina/o-accented foods on a daily basis. Latina/o cooks work in restaurants of all varieties, leaving their imprint on how foods from all over the world are being interpreted and prepared in restaurant kitchens in the United States. The plight of Latina/o cooks is not unlike that of Remy, the talented rat chef in the Disney movie *Ratatouille* (Bird and Pinkava 2007), who produced sublime food but remained hidden because his physical presence was considered unacceptable.

There are some signs of change for the better. There have always been few Latina/o farm owners, but their number increased by 21 percent between 2007 and 2013 (National Agricultural Statistics Service 2014). Farms with Latinas/os as principal farm operators are located mostly in southern and western states, and they are dedicated primarily to beef cattle and to combination crops. Latina/o farmers still constitute only 3.2 percent of all farmers in the United States, and their farms tend to be smaller than the national average. Nevertheless, having more Latinas/os as principal farm operators could bring significant changes in coming years, especially in terms of farm labor conditions and production practices.

There is a renewed interest in Indigenous ways of growing and cooking food. Some Latina/o activists have found the exploration of Indigenous diets empowering. They are connecting alternative food movements to Indigenous and Latina/o decolonial practices (C. Rodriguez 2013). Websites and books like *Decolonial Food*

for Thought and *Decolonize Your Diet* (Calvo and Esquibel 2015) have taken on the mission of publishing Indigenous recipes as a way of revitalizing cultural knowledges that were suppressed and discredited by colonialism. The recipes are vegetarian and highlight local ingredients and Indigenous techniques. Food knowledges that were devalued as "traditional" are presented as a way of combating the ill effects of modern diets on health, society, and the environment. Latina/o food activism has many shared concerns with the broader local and sustainable food movements. However, these movements continue to be predominantly white and middle class. The local food movement in the United States so far has not been very inclusive and culturally responsive. Immigrant and other Latinas/os, many of whom are endowed with agricultural knowledge that is increasingly scarce in the United States, could play a decisive role in the direction and success of alternative food movements (Mares 2014).

For many immigrant Latinas/os, maintaining culturally meaningful food practices is related to broader claims to space and place, community membership, and the reshaping of cultural identity (Mares 2012). Latina/o families and communities make it a point to collectively prepare and consume dishes that distinguish their respective groups. For example, while Mexican Latinas/os get together to prepare tamales, Ecuadorian Latinas/os organize gatherings to roast guinea pigs. But food can be used both to maintain cultural continuity and to articulate change. In Latina/o homes, food has been at the center of the reformulation of subjectivities and the construction of space. Meredith Abarca has showed how Mexican American women have transformed the kitchen from a space of female subordination and drudgery into a feminist space where they assert their agency as creators and thinkers (2006). This is consistent with the argument of feminist scholars who are challenging the separation between thinking and doing and asserting that cooking is a thoughtful practice (Curtin and Heldke 1992). The recognition of the epistemic dimension of food work enables a revalorization of food laborers, both inside and outside the domestic realm.

Beyond material culture, discourses about food have been instrumental in the racialization and marginalization of Latinas/os. Racial slurs often use food as a marker of difference: "beaners," "hot tamales," "berry pickers." Even where Latina/o foods are part of the mainstream American diet, its acceptance has been framed by what Frances R. Aparicio and Susana Chávez-Silverman have called "tropicalization" (1997, 8), which is a way of defining peoples and places through stereotypical representations and narratives. The tropicalized incorporation of Latina/o food was built on the gentrifying "Hispanic fantasy legacy" discourse (Valle and Torres 2000) that allowed Southwestern cuisine to claim a "Hispanic" heritage that highlights the white and European aspects of Mexican culture while romanticizing the history of violence of the frontier. Latinas/os and their food have generally been represented as hot, exciting, and somehow dangerous. These representations have been mobilized both by hegemonic American culture and by Latinas/os themselves, particularly in the context of restaurants.

The trajectory of Mexican restaurants and of Mexican food in the United States illustrates the precarious and contradictory character of the process of identity negotiation. Scholarly work on Mexican food in the United States, by far the most studied Latina/o culinary culture, has strived to explain its process of transformation from marginal to mainstream (Pilcher 2012; Arellano 2013). This process has involved the appropriation of Mexican and Mexican American culinary knowledge by celebrity chefs, cookbook authors, and food industry entrepreneurs, who were in a better socioeconomic position to take the lead in the mass commercialization of Mexican food. Mexican American food is popular all over the world, but Mexican Americans have not been the main agents or economic beneficiaries of its spread. Nevertheless, it is important to stress the agency of Mexican Americans in the creation of a new culinary culture. Popularly, Mexican Americans are still widely perceived as a people who have failed to protect a cultural heritage—imagined as singular and fixed—rather than as creators of their own culture.

The history of Cuban and Caribbean restaurants also allows us to explore the contradictions of the process of construction of Latina/o identities. Lisa Maya Knauer (2001) has analyzed the different ways in which Cuban identity has been constructed, performed, and negotiated in Cuban restaurants. In the Nuevo Latino trend, Latina/o chefs have used tropicalizing discourses to their personal advantage. Some of them have become celebrities, and they have elevated the status of Latina/o food above the stereotype of being cheap, greasy, and plentiful. Nuevo Latino restaurants are able to charge much higher prices than the vast majority of Latina/o restaurants. However, this success was achieved by submitting Caribbean and Latin American culinary cultures to the techniques of French cooking, downgrading them to the level of being providers of ingredients and inspiration without recognizing them as producers of culinary theory and technique on their own right (Janer 2007).

The generalized view of Latinas/os as physical laborers without intellect or creativity was dramatized by the controversy over the "Cultivating Thought" campaign of the Chipotle Mexican Grill restaurant. This campaign features excerpts of stories by famous writers on the restaurant's paper goods, but in its 2014 launch, it did not include a single Mexican American or Latina/o writer. Intense criticism made the company correct its course, but their initial exclusion of Latina/o writers made it clear that while the company depends on Mexican American cuisine and on Latina/o laborers, it did not consider that Latinas/os belong in the category of thinkers and artists.

The restaurants of relatively recent Latina/o populations have not received enough scholarly attention. An exploration of a pan-Latina/o neighborhood suggests that these restaurants perform and negotiate their national differences, while collectively challenging the dominant restrained sensory culture with an aesthetics of excess (Lee-Pérez and Audant 2009). In the last two decades there has been a considerable expansion of the varieties of Latina/o foods that are commercially available in small restaurants, trucks, and grocery shops. These establishments give visibility and vitality to the foods of smaller Latina/o communities, which were for a long time subsumed under the larger and more established ones. The smaller food venues have also allowed us to witness the development of connections between Latina/o and other culinary cultures, as exemplified by the Korean taco truck phenomenon in Los Angeles (Gelt 2009).

Food has always had an important role in Latina/o literature. Tomás Rivera's classic 1971 novel, . . . *And the Earth Did Not Devour Him*, portrayed the life and struggles of migrant farm workers (Rivera 1995). Food in literature often constitutes an alternate language. As can be expected, food in Latina/o literature has been used to articulate cultural identity and difference in the context of constant change and hybridization. Literary scholars who have followed the tracks of food references in Latina/o literature have found that it illuminates the relationships that the characters have with themselves and with the multiple places that they inhabit. In Esmeralda Santiago's texts, for example, food reveals feelings of personal shame and pride (Marshall 2007), as well as nostalgia and ambivalence toward Puerto Rico

(Fellner 2013). In Cristina García's *Dreaming in Cuban* the characters use food to define themselves and their politics regarding Cuba and the United States (Skinazi 2003). Food has also served to explore gender power relationships. Latina writers like Esmeralda Santiago and Julia Alvarez use food to talk about feminist resistance and empowerment (Zeff 2008). Furthermore, the language of food in literature has been instrumental in the articulation of new theories of Latina/o subjectivity. Scholars of Chicana/o literature have used a food lens to recognize the emergence of a postnational sensibility that redefines authenticity as compatible with change and difference (Pascual Soler and Abarca 2013). Meredith Abarca (2014) has found in Latina/o literature a holistic approach to food and identity that allows for change while still honoring tradition.

The complexity of the sociopolitical and economic web of the food system, along with the undeniable affective power of food, warrant an increased focus on food in Latina/o studies. Scholarly interest in food helps to abolish the Cartesian mind/body divide. It also allows for the understanding of the complexity and fluidity of identity. We are not only what we eat, but also what we ate and what we would like to eat.

21

Gender

Sandra K. Soto

"Gender" is difficult. Like the terms with which it most often travels ("race," "sex," and "sexuality"), gender is a complex and contested concept that, although used quite widely and more and more frequently in both academic and nonacademic contexts, means significantly different things to different people and across different institutional locations. Does it name an essential part of what it means to be a (*particular*) human being, a fundamental attribute that directs our sense of self and our outward presentation of that self, and that guides our interactions with others, especially our sexual attractions, encounters, and relationships? Does that description underestimate our agency, failing to allow for the possibility that *we* direct, guide, and perform gender, or that at the very least gender is malleable and fluid enough that our presentation of "it" is a combination of willfulness and inheritance (whether from the biological or the social/cultural or both)? And if much of the feminist scholarship produced by women of color over the past forty years has encouraged an intersectional approach to power, knowledge, embodiment, and subjectivity, what tools and collaborations are most conducive to approaching gender not monologically but as mutually constitutive with other categories of difference?

These are just a few of the epistemological and ontological questions generated by our efforts to apprehend, theorize, historicize, and denaturalize gender. While the questions may be unanswerable, at least in any precise

way, there is great value in pushing at and experimenting with them. Indeed, some of the most exciting and generative work produced in Latina/o studies as a field—and as the rubric we often use to name a constellation of individual but related fields such as Chicana/o studies and Puerto Rican studies—indexes the importance and politics of racialized gender (Alarcón 1990; Saldívar-Hull 1991; E. Pérez 1999; Fiol-Matta 2002, 2017; J. M. Rodríguez 2003, 2014b; E. Torres 2003; Lima 2007; R. T. Rodríguez 2009). Because the frequent objects of analysis that drive Latina/o studies—including, but not limited to, nation(alism), migration, culture, racial formation, and racialized embodiment—necessarily require facility with gender as a category, Latina/o studies has much to teach women's studies and gender studies about gender's imbrication with other processes productive of difference and power, and about the different vocabularies and cultural registers through which gender and sex travel and signify.

As Chicana feminist poststructuralist theorist Norma Alarcón argued some twenty-five years ago in her path-breaking essay, "The Theoretical Subject(s) of *This Bridge Called My Back* and Anglo-American Feminism" (1990), intersectional approaches to power, language, knowledge, and subjectivity have the potential to fundamentally challenge the persistence of the "gendered standpoint epistemology" undergirding "Anglo-American feminism." As the title of her essay suggests, Alarcón was speaking not directly about Latina/o studies but about the kind of experiential and experimental "theory in the flesh" reflected in the watershed anthology *This Bridge Called My Back: Radical Writings by Women of Color*, co-edited by Cherríe Moraga and Gloria Anzaldúa (1981, 23). However, because of that anthology's utmost importance for feminist scholars working in what we now call Latina/o studies, and because Alarcón herself can be considered a key theorist in Latina/o studies, that essay's interventions are relevant to this discussion of how gender has been taken up in the field.

For Alarcón, *Bridge* powerfully exemplifies that we do not become women in the same way: there is much variation in relation to the scripts, codes, experiences— including "psychic and material violence"—and processes that lead some to the category of "woman" (1990, 359). That difference compels more precise identifications, such as "woman of color," and suggests that "one should not step into that category [of woman] nor that of man that easily or simply" (1990, 360). Such easy, simple identification ignores the epistemological and ontological lessons that *Bridge* offers us about difference, intersectionality, (dis)identification, and complex alliances that exceed the terms of binary oppositions. And if Alarcón complicates *identification* in this way—even posing the provocation, "But what is a 'woman,' or a 'man' for that matter?" (1990, 361)—she also complicates the *subject* of feminist theory (gender) and its related commitment to "gendered standpoint epistemology"—a system that emphasizes women's supposed "sexual difference" from men through a logic of oppositional counteridentification. One of the many effects of taking women as "the common denominator" across difference, she argues, is that "since the subject of feminist theory and its single theme—gender—go largely unquestioned, its point of view tends to suppress and repress voices that question its authority" (1990, 359–60). This is why, according to Alarcón, in its first decade of circulation, *This Bridge Called My Back* had only a "cosmetic" impact on Anglo-American feminism (1990, 357).

Interestingly, the term "gender" that Alarcón used in her 1990 essay to name the counteridentificatory limitations of feminist studies and its form of standpoint epistemology is the very same term that has been used optimistically by some feminist scholars and women's studies (now "gender studies") departments in their attempts to address those same, and related, limitations. That is, where Alarcón understands "gender" as a category of analysis to be structured through and through by a binary opposition (men versus women), with all of the homogenizing that entails, other feminist theorists have looked to "gender" as a *flexible* category of analysis—one that can better attend to the insistence by women of color on an intersectional approach to embodiment, subjectivity, and power, and one that can help challenge the primacy of "women" in the field of "women's studies." This optimistic and quite-familiar account of gender as the (newer) key term of feminist studies would situate it in contra-relation to the categories "women" (seen as at once too universalizing and narrow) and "sex" (conceptualized as the biological stuff of the body). In that women-to-gender progress narrative, gender functions as a corrective—one that is more capacious than "women," encapsulating as it does masculinity, femininity, androgyny, butch, and femme, to name a few gendered forms, especially as those embodied forms are differently racialized (e.g. cha-cha femme, homeboy masculinity); more fluid than "sex" and thus more interesting as a site of transgression; and more available to the kind of intersectional analysis called for by many of the scholars traveling and traversing the interdisciplinary fields of "identity knowledges." That narrative might also celebrate the much-deliberated and publicized name-changes over the past two dozen years that saw many "women's studies" courses and units (whether centers, programs, or departments) become some variation of "gender studies." However, as Alarcón's 1990 essay suggests, and as Robyn Wiegman persuasively argues in *Object Lessons*, that progressive self-narrative might be too quick to laud the political and knowledge transformations that the newer object "gender" is capable of bringing about:

GENDER SANDRA K. SOTO

the "well-rehearsed failure [of the category 'women'] to remain conceptually coherent and universally referential for *all* women within the field domain of Women's Studies has inaugurated a turn toward a host of new investments organized increasingly under the sign of *gender*. . . . [T]he term has come to collate much of what the category of *women* is said to exclude: from men, masculinity, and queer sexualities to trans and intersex identities and analysis" (2012, 38).

Likewise, the denaturalizing and destabilizing efforts to illuminate the ways that gender is *produced* by the repeated things we say, do, and perform may meanwhile unwittingly help *stabilize* sex as an indisputable fact of biology (Fausto-Sterling 1999). And even those attempts to unglue gender from binaries must recognize that we are increasingly expected to provide our "gender" on the countless bureaucratic forms we fill out—from medical intake forms to airline ticket purchases—by selecting one of two options ("Male" or "Female"). Moreover, gender can be harnessed institutionally in disciplining ways as something that we can be considered to *fail* at and as something that can be *corrected*. In 1973, the *Diagnostic and Statistical Manual of Mental Disorders* (DSM-3) infamously replaced the homosexual "disorder" with the gender identity disorder (GID). And the DSM-5 (2013) has replaced GID with "gender dysphoria," to diagnose "individuals who see and feel themselves to be a different gender than their assigned gender" (American Psychiatric Association 2013).

That Alarcón, Wiegman, and Fausto-Sterling—together with the DSM-5 example—remind us that there is nothing inherently liberating about "gender" means that we must continue to find ways of experimenting with and contesting its disciplining effects and how it relates to other categories—probably most especially to "sex," a term with which it is variously conflated, used interchangeably, distinguished, or, in

the case of Gayle Rubin (1975), positioned as two parts of the same "system." One of the most important early explorations of the relationship between gender and sex was Rubin's (1975) essay "The Traffic in Women: Notes on the 'Political Economy' of Sex." Suturing gender to sex as a "sex/gender system," Rubin captures the ways in which the natural and the biological were intervened upon by human activity in order to produce gender. Brilliantly weaving Lévi-Strauss's anthropological work on kinship with Freudian and Lacanian psychoanalysis, Rubin argues that while psychoanalysis may be maddening in its failure to call for new arrangements in light of its strong acknowledgment about the shame, humiliation, and pain of girlhood and womanhood (the shattering of the female ego), it is not only open to intervention by feminists, but indispensable to the study of gender. Likewise, Rubin's work should be seen as a resource for Latina/o studies, indispensable *and* open to intervention, and vice-versa. Even the interrogation of the perplexing positioning of sex in relation to gender, a question to which I will return shortly, can be enriched by considering the ways that Latina/o studies and other bodies of critical ethnic studies scholarship negotiate the shifting meanings of—and relationship between—"race" and "ethnicity," terms that are variously (and confusingly) deployed as either interchangeable synonyms or as coupled terms whose differentiation depends on an inherited notion that race is more associated with skin color, biology, and power relations (just as sex is associated with genitalia, chromosomes, and other received criteria of supposedly measurable embodied difference), while, in contradistinction, ethnicity (like gender) would appear to be associated more with the social and cultural. While race/ethnicity by no means operates analogously to sex/gender, the shared historical and political entanglements of signification of those two sets of terms remains unexplored.

From the vantage point of the mid-1970s, when Rubin wrote "The Traffic in Women" (first as part of an undergraduate thesis), these proposals were radical. She had essentially appropriated some of the vocabulary and insights from Marxist thought—historical conditions, human intervention—and called for a theory of sex-gender, one that would neither subsume sex/gender to economic conditions, nor divorce it from those conditions; one that had the historical breadth to investigate why the oppression of women predated capitalism; and one that offered some conclusions about how to change the social relations that (re)generate the oppression of women. Rubin's own radical dream was "of an androgynous and genderless (though not sexless) society, in which one's sexual anatomy is irrelevant to who one is, what one does, and with whom one makes love" (1975, 204).

Whether one agreed with Rubin's call for a genderless society (and many feminists did and do), her essay helped encourage the continued critical exploration of the relationship between sex and gender within the fields of feminist studies and (critical) gender studies. Such exploration has generated, especially since the 1980s, a rich archive of immanent critique, a practice that Judith Butler describes as "seek[ing] to provoke critical examination of the basic vocabulary of the movement of thought to which it belongs" (1999, vii). That self-reflexive process of experimentation has sharpened our understanding of identity, subjectivity, embodiment, power, performativity, intersectionality, and social relations—all of which are particularly apt sites from which to consider gender's influence and influences. Aiming not at the "Truth" of gender, immanent critique approaches gender as a contested and dynamic construct because, as Joan W. Scott cautions in the opening to her influential essay, "Gender: A Useful Category of Analysis," "Those who would codify the

meanings of words fight a losing battle, for words, like the ideas and things they are meant to signify, have a history" (1986, 1053).

Given the incredibly rich body of primary cultural productions by Latin@ artists, writers, and performers who innovatively experiment with the complexity of various racialized forms of femininity, gender fucking, masculinity, trans*, and gender policing, Latina/o studies scholars who analyze that material have much to teach us about the kind of history for which Scott calls. Largely because of the momentum created by *This Bridge Called My Back*, and together with the growth of independent publishing houses geared toward feminist and/or Latin@ publications, the 1980s was a particularly productive decade for culturally specific literary representations of Latin@ gender. One of the most important of these treatments is arguably Sandra Cisneros's *The House on Mango Street* (1984), a collection of vignettes that reads as a novel and that in the most nuanced and three-dimensional ways depicts gendered curtailment of mobility in the lives of girls and women—as well as the burdens of racialized masculinity for boys and men. What makes this book a classic is Cisneros's artful narrative technique: we learn about the world of Mango Street through the point of view of a young woman, Esperanza, who has not yet developed the critical tools and vocabulary for critically reflecting on the pleasures, injuries, threats, and desires that are everywhere across the book saturated with gender codes, policing, and hierarchies. This limited point of view allows Cisneros to hint at gendered violence, rendering it suggestively rather than explicitly. The upshot of this technique is that we, the readers, must fill in the missing details of stories, but also, more significantly, Esperanza's youth—her naïveté and innocence—is clearly meant to bring into sharper (affective) relief the disempowering and confusing network of social norms and emotional and

GENDER SANDRA K. SOTO

physical violations that circumscribe gendered life on Mango Street.

In closing, I want to reverse the usual direction of primary/secondary material by suggesting that Latina/o studies might approach the form and content of *The House on Mango Street* not only as a rich collection of vignettes about gender, but as a model for how we might attend to some of the limitations I've been addressing in relation to the disciplining effects of gender. That is, Cisneros's capaciousness—her refreshing willingness to refute the "Truth" of gender, her remarkable ability to allow gender as a category to be three-dimensional and unpredictable as a source of *both* pain *and* pleasure, her respect for her readers' agency in inviting them to fill in where the narrator does not go—all of these can help us learn from the lessons that Alarcón is right to say we have been missing.

22

Health

John Mckiernan-González

In 1984, Paul Castro sued ABC News affiliate KGO after the film crew refused to touch him, even to place a microphone on his person, because of their alleged fear of AIDS. In his press release and subsequent interviews, Paul Castro repeatedly emphasized, "I am not a disease, I am a person" (Roque Ramírez 2010, 118). His statement openly challenged disease stigma, as he obstinately refused to accept his expulsion from middle-class America (Moraga and Anzaldúa 1981; Hames-García 2011b). This queer Tejano migrant Reagan-era civil rights strategy at the dawn of the AIDS pandemic brings out the interweaving of health and citizenship, of illness and national expulsion. Defending health and fighting disease in the United States has often implied expelling foreign bodies; Latinas/os—too often visibly foreign bodies in the American body politic—vividly demonstrate the biopolitics of assimilation and exclusion in the racial history of the United States. Latina/o health matters bring out three broad ways American health concerns shape Latina/o and minority communities in the United States (Dubos 1987; Rosenberg 1992, xi; Grob 2002). First, scholars work to expose the medical dimension of racial scripts, denoting the bodies and labor that are valued, devalued, and disposable (Farmer 2006; Brier 2009; Molina 2014). Second, research into health policies and health status bring out the ways "health" provides a measure of critique and a means for social reform. Third, health has been a key analysis in social movements that challenge established and normative—and in 1984 California, homophobic and racist—social mores. These three broad rubrics for health—a racial script, a measure of belonging, a point of volatile contestation—animate scholarly work in Latina/o studies.

Latina/o studies scholars repeatedly emphasize that medical anxieties over white futures have long shaped American efforts in policing the presence of Latinas/os in the United States. Medical historians Mariola Espinosa and John Mckiernan-González, among others, argue that the first wave of federal quarantines invoked the medical and financial threat posed by transnational Latina/o communities linked to the Mexican Gulf Coast, Cuba, and the northern Caribbean (Kraut 1995; Molina 2006; Espinosa 2009; Mckiernan-González 2012). These medical measures regulating the passage of Latinas/os across U.S. borders predate the germ theory in the United States. Medical historian Natalia Molina and legal scholar Sam Erman have used Latina/o challenges to this medical policing to trace out their popular claim on belonging in the United States (Molina 2006; Erman 2008). As Erman has shown, in 1899, when Isabella González challenged her "likely to become a public charge" detention after her arrival from "disease-wracked Puerto Rico" (which conjoined medical and labor concerns), the ensuing Supreme Court decision in *Gonzales v. Williams* made movement between Puerto Rico and the United States an emphatically domestic, and not a foreign matter (2008, 5–17). Although Puerto Ricans' colonial status provided entry to the United States, the national burden of being a possible medical and financial threat lay heavier on the shoulders of women (Romo 2005, 223–9; Stern 2005a; Mckiernan-González 2012). These two Progressive Era policies—medical quarantine and "likely to become a public charge"—provided the template for Latina/o passage across medical borders.

While nineteenth-century policymakers in the United States feared transnational Latina/o communities, they also assumed working-class Mexicans, African Americans, and Native Americans would disappear in the face of American progress, and that any medical intervention would only delay their ultimate extinction (Roberts 2011; Kunitz 2015). When Mexican communities persisted in the United States, state authorities argued for medical interventions that insulated Mexican disease conditions from white communities, keeping them from "involving some of the rest of us" (Mckiernan-González 2012, 39). Once policymakers understood Latina/o communities were a permanent part of the American landscape, reproductive containment shaped the broad substance of policy (E. Gutiérrez 2008). Alexandra Minna Stern and Natalie Lira (2014) demonstrated a rise in the coerced sterilization of Latinas/os in state schools, juvenile detention, and prisons in California. Natalia Molina traced how Los Angeles County public health officials went from building separate maternal and child clinics for Mexican families to expelling Mexicans in the 1920s (Molina 2006, 75–150). Best demonstrated by California and Puerto Rico, this broad, multilayered, and complicated push to control the number of children born to Latinas illustrates the political dimensions of American health improvement (Ramírez de Arellano 1983; Briggs 2002b; E. Gutiérrez 2008; I. Lopez 2008; Mcquade-Salzfass 2014).

Access to medical services has become a key site for analyzing American racial scripts. Anthropologists Leo Chavez (1997) and Jonathan Inda (2005) point out the ways doctors and nurses across Orange County, California, have been "targeting immigrants," transforming Latina/o use of and right to basic health services as evidence of immigrants' drain on public resources. The accompanying underutilization of hostile health services by working-class Latinas/os is the situation analyzed as a "Hispanic Paradox" by Ruben Rumbaut (1997). As Rumbaut shows, long-term immigrants lived relatively longer lives than their black or white neighbors. Even when scholars took neighborhood effects and socio-economic status (SES) into account, varied studies documented lower infant and maternal mortality rates relative to white and African American residents (Rumbaut 1997; Hayes-Bautista 2004; Gálvez 2011). Finally, the growing approximation over time to comparatively low American health outcomes (Rumbaut 1997; Viruell-Fuentes 2007; Kunitz 2015, 57–70, 191–210) raised broad questions regarding the negative impact of American culture and American life on Latina/o health. In emphasizing that medical discourse and official medical policy on Latina/o communities focus more on controlling Latina/o communities than changing health outcomes, Latina/o studies scholars point to the colonial dimensions of the American body politic.

Health provided a measure of critique and political authority—a deeply ambiguous and highly potent model of trans-American authority—in Latina/o communities. In late nineteenth-century Puerto Rico and Cuba, physicians broke ranks early with Spanish rule, using the devastation in slave quarters and haciendas to indict the sickness of Spanish rule and emphasize their role in the new body politic (Amador 2014). Ramón Emeterio Betances is one example of this liberal ideal; Drs. José Celso Barbosa and Juan Guiteras embodied a republican version of this form of authority, with the Afro-Puerto Rican Barbosa ascending to the Executive Cabinet during the first phase of the U.S. occupation of Puerto Rico, and the Cuban liberal Guiteras to the head of the Board of Health under the Maximato (Mckiernan-González 2013). Mutual aid associations provided nationally inflected primary care under gender-specific lines. The Club Asturiano, a cigar-worker-based mutual aid association in Ybor City, the Cuban majority

neighborhood in Tampa, Florida, initially provided syphilis treatments, eventually branching into tuberculosis and family medical care for its members (Mormino and Pozzetta 1987). In the Southwest, the Woodmen of the World and the Alianza Hispanoamericana provided unemployment insurance and workplace injury–associated assistance for emergency surgery (Zamora 2000). The Woodmen did not include the provision of medical care for women or non-workplace associated illnesses. After World War II, doctors like Daniel Saenz from the League of United Latin American Citizens (LULAC), Hector P. Garcia (American GI Forum), and Jorge Prieto (Catholic Interracial Council) translated conditions their patients faced into policy prescriptions, arguing for meager measures to help them be "fit to become citizens" (Prieto 1989; D. Gutiérrez 1995, 154; Oropeza 2005, 11–45; I. García 2003; Molina 2006). Ana Minian (2013), in a path-breaking analysis, charted the ways United Farm Workers' medical services officially forbade birth-control and sexual health services to women in their clinics. The measure of critique enabled by an embrace of official medicine pushed the medical ambitions and realities of women and LGBTIQ Latina/os to the margin (Cohen 1999).

By bringing women into the sphere of analysis, Latina/o studies scholars point to a far more volatile America, where conflicts over medical matters raise interlocked questions about structural inequality and cultural hegemony. Organizing for healthy conditions for women and men on the margins of Latina/o communities challenges norms that support patriarchy, heteronormativity, and class privilege (Viruell-Fuentes, Miranda, and Abdulrahim 2012; Wanzer-Serrano 2015). By focusing on these points of conflict over medical norms, gender-inflected Latina studies have done much to explain the workings of gender inequality in class-stratified Latina/o communities. The typhus bath riot in 1917 El Paso is a key example. For three days, commuting domestics and laundresses based in Ciudad Juárez used their bodies to physically stop traffic across the Santa Fe Bridge and challenge the intrusion of medical inspection and daily fumigation. This riot—lost to public memory until historian Alexandra Minna Stern's article appeared in 1999—was a moment when working women openly challenged the assumption that white security and health must be paid for by the work and indignity suffered by Latina workers (Stern 1999; Mckiernan-González 2012, 165–96).

This, however, was not the only time women's medical matters challenged the taken-for-granted nature of federal medical policy. The medical detention and certification of women walking on working-class streets in Ponce, Puerto Rico, and San Antonio, Texas, led to protests against military sexual privileges outside U.S. Army bases and to prevention of sexually transmitted diseases in the Progressive Era (Findlay 1999; Rosas 2012). In New York, the death by botched abortion procedure of a young Puerto Rican woman at Lincoln Hospital led the Young Lords, a decolonial Nuyorican political organization, to challenge the reproductive necropolitics of medicine and take over Lincoln Hospital (Young Lords Party 2011; Wanzer-Serrano 2015, 115). In *Madrigal v. Quilligan*, Mexican immigrant women sued to challenge the sterilizing of young immigrant Latinas without their consent (E. Gutiérrez 2008). The settlement provided grounds for enhanced Spanish-language materials and the presence of interpreters to help guarantee informed consent; it did not help create ways for the claimants or young Latina workers to wield more control over their lives and their bodies (Schmidt Camacho 2008; Tajima-Peña 2015).

The focus on sexuality in Latina/o studies weaves medical matters into a far wider web of social relationships. Returning to the 1980s and 1990s, Frances Negrón-Muntaner's film *Brincando el Charco* (1994) highlights the unofficial death sentence imposed by homophobic authorities in the midst of the HIV/AIDS crisis on Puerto Rican LGBTQ communities in the United States and Puerto Rico, prominently featuring queer activist Moisés Agosto (La Fountain-Stokes 2009). Cherríe Moraga and Gloria Anzaldúa, in bringing together *This Bridge Called my Back* in 1981, exposed and challenged the intersecting ways race, colonialism, and patriarchy make early death and disabled lives an American way of health for women of color across the United States. Even current work on AIDS and Mexican migrants demonstrates the way silence about sex cuts access to life-extending medication and affirming communities across borders (Cantú 2009; Hames-García and Martínez 2011; Ramirez-Valles 2011). Latina feminist analysis and LGBTIQ critique have consistently put "health" on notice for its normative exclusions and colonial ideals.

23

History
Gerald E. Poyo

History requires considering the particular and the universal (Ryn 2003). A distinguished body of writing has interpreted many aspects of the particular experiences of the history of persons of Latin American descent in the United States, utilizing a variety of analytical categories including national origin, class, race, gender, culture, and region, to name a few. Only recently are historians taking up the challenge of thinking about Latina/o history with broad and integrative strokes, including crossing national group boundaries to consider the connections and affinities necessary to produce holistic approaches. If the danger of focusing on the affinities is over-generalization and homogenization of particular experiences, understanding the various groups as mutually exclusive is equally problematic. Insofar as affinity may be understood as a continuum from particular group experiences to related or shared experiences, then comprehensive Latina/o historical narratives are surely possible (Goizueta 1992; Gracia 2000).

The idea of a distinct and enduring Latina/o history challenges the traditional assimilation paradigm in United States history, which has been premised on the assumption of a linear cultural movement toward a distinctly white Euro-American culture (Dinnerstein and Reimers 1975). Ironically, the dominant society's discriminatory and exclusionist attitudes and policies undermined this assimilation paradigm from the nation's very origin and encouraged the development of ethnic and minority perspectives among non-whites, including Hispanics, African Americans, Native Americans, and Asian Americans. For Latinas/os, the integration process in the United States did not follow a linear course, but rather produced enduring ethnic cultures that maintained their distinctiveness over generations; these include Mexican Americans since colonial times and Cubans and Puerto Ricans since the late nineteenth century. This contrasted with European immigrants who in some cases maintained a sense of their cultural origins and participated in the pluralist resurgence of the 1960s and 1970s, but in the end identified with a dominant white Euro-American society.

Latina/o history is found in the intricate textures and layers of political, socioeconomic, and cultural intersections over time. This history spans at least five centuries, challenges strictly drawn historiographic boundaries, and includes many common themes, as well as involving questions of historical methodology, incorporating interdisciplinary approaches, providing chronologies and historical timelines, and creating dialogue among pertinent and diverse historiographic traditions. Latina/o history includes Latin American history, U.S. Borderlands history, Mexican American history, Cuban American history, Puerto Rican history, and the history of many other national groups and, of course, the relationship and impact of Latinas/os on the general trajectory of United States history writ large, especially immigration and ethnic history.

Themes central to Latina/o history include the legacy of violent confrontations of Iberian and Native American civilizations in the sixteenth century and the incorporation of African slaves into new colonial societies. Whether they were settlers in eighteenth-century Texas or twentieth-century Latin American immigrants in New York City, all descended from people formed in the political, economic, racial, gender, and social legacies of

Iberian colonialism. These racially and ethnically heterogeneous communities included not only people with strong cultural attachments to their Indigenous, European, African, or Asian ethnic and cultural backgrounds, but also people who identified with some amalgam of these backgrounds as a result of centuries of mestizaje, or mixing of races and cultures (Gruzinski 2002).

St. Augustine (1564), Santa Fe (1607), and later places like San Antonio (1718) and San Diego (1769) reflected this mestizaje and were among the earliest European-inspired settlements in what eventually became the United States (Jones 1979; Weber 1992). United States territorial conquest during 1803–1848, known benignly as "Manifest Destiny" and "Westward Expansion," beginning with the Louisiana Purchase and culminating in the Mexican War, resulted in the wholesale annexation of fully formed Hispanic communities in territories from Florida to California. The annexed communities held well-established traditions and strong regional identities that originated the U.S. Latina/o experience (Weber 1982).

During the late nineteenth and twentieth centuries, Latin Americans fled oppressive social, political, and economic systems that privileged the few at the expense of the larger societies. Efforts in Latin America to transform the region's long-standing colonial legacy resulted in periodic upheavals and displacements, including the Latin American wars of independence (1810–1824), Caribbean revolutionary movements (1860s–1890s), the Mexican Revolution of 1910, industrialization policies in Puerto Rico during the 1950s, the Cuban Revolution of 1959, and the political-economic chaos in South and Central America during the 1960s through the 1980s. Forces of displacement and out-migration grew even stronger with United States demand for agricultural and industrial labor and economic imperial expansion first into Mexico, Cuba, and Puerto Rico and then the rest of Latin America. These long-term push and pull factors that drove immigration produced new communities in the United States.

Immigrants forged Latina/o communities within the historical tension between the defensive posture needed to combat the essentially hostile attitudes of the Euro-American mainstream society and the affirmative process of adapting specific Latin American national group cultural forms to a new environment. Latinas/os grappled with the consequences of racism and a long-standing British-inspired Black Legend that assumed an inherent collective inferiority of Iberians when compared with northern European civilizations (Powell 1971; DeGuzmán 2005). In the nineteenth century, Mexican Americans faced oppression and loss of lands and status in the Southwest, while Cuban working-class immigrants in Florida were often considered an interloping, exotic, and inferior class of people. In the early twentieth century, Puerto Ricans endured racism in New York as they fled their U.S. occupied and economically transformed country. These experiences set the pattern for the subsequent treatment of Latina/o peoples migrating from other areas of Latin America (Pitt 1966; De León 1983; Vega 1984; Montejano 1987; Ingalls 1988). The racist assumptions of United States society imposed on Latinas/os a sense of shared exclusion, but they also shared creative experiences and patterns steeped in the practices of maintaining and adapting cultural heritage in order to coexist with and conform to life and customs in the United States (Mormino and Pozzetta 1987; G. Sánchez 1993; Sánchez Korrol 1994; Romero, Hondagneu-Sotelo, and Ortiz 1997; Torres-Saillant and Hernández 1998). Over time, these same processes pointed the way for imagining Latina/o history.

At first, destinations for Latin Americans in the United States had a generally regional pattern—Mexicans in the Southwest, Cubans in Florida, and

Puerto Ricans in New York—but a variety of forces eventually forged the way toward integrated Latina/o experiences. Traditional regional destinations based on nationality broadened, producing a diversity of groups in major cities like New York, Chicago, Miami, Houston, Los Angeles, and others (Reimers 1992; M. García 1996; Bergad and Klein 2010). Many lived their lives as ethnic and/or exile subjects interacting socially, economically, politically, and culturally. Intermarriage blended and mixed similar Latin American cultures into Latina/o expressions. Newspapers and later radio and television disseminated vibrant journalistic and literary traditions. Resistance, civil rights activism, and coalition politics produced Latina/o political identities of national proportions. The emergence of an intellectual class with an interest in affirming Latina/o affinities, engagement with labor movements, complex language politics, and rich and varied religious traditions all contributed to an affirmative consciousness about the existence of Latina/o experiences, identity, and history in the United States.

The enduring nature of Latina/o communities has also had much to do with the proximity of the Latin American homelands. Geography has provided Latinas/os the opportunity for constant transnational connections to their countries of origin through ongoing immigration, circular migration, remittances, familial relationships, visits home, and globalization generally. Not only are Mexican, Puerto Rican, Cuban, Central American, and other Latin American identities in the United States not disappearing, but they are growing stronger and also becoming deeply embedded in a collective Latina/o identity that influences the United States and even the entire Western Hemisphere as places like Miami, San Antonio, and Los Angeles deepen their ties to the South (F. Padilla 1985; Matovina and Poyo 2000; J. García 2016).

Latina/o history speaks to "American" history in the broadest sense of the word. It lies at the intersection of Euro-American and Hispanic worlds and brings visibility to themes that challenge the United States' traditional self-image as exceptional. The study of the Latina/o experience in the United States invokes, in often uncomfortable ways, shared and overlapping themes and patterns in the history of the Western Hemisphere. Whether of British, Iberian, or French extraction, Europeans conquered Indigenous people, enslaved Africans, had sexual relations with those whom they oppressed, and created colonial structures for their own economic benefit; eventually their descendants struggled for their independence and freer societies. An honest consideration of Latina/o history reminds us of this legacy of which Latin and North America were a part, despite narratives of exceptionalism to the contrary. Latina/o history offers one conduit for interpreting the broad and complex process that is American hemispheric history and requires historians always to keep in mind the imperative for considering the particular and universal dimensions of historical processes.

24

Housing

Zaire Z. Dinzey-Flores

Housing and home: two concepts that are often used interchangeably. The Universal Declaration of Human Rights (1948) states that housing is a fundamental *human right* (Article 25) and that "no one shall be subjected to arbitrary interference with his . . . home. . . . Everyone has the right to the protection of the law against such interference or attacks" (Article 12). Indeed, the physical, proverbial "roof over the head" is also metaphorical. A shelter is deemed to provide more than a place for lodging and dwelling; it provides security, safety, dignity, supports identity, and is a place for belonging, a home, a *casa*, and an *hogar*. The range of significations for a casa-hogar/housing-home is vast—personal, collective, social, material.

In the United States, housing/homes and the policies that model them have been a powerful historical tool for distributing racially defined social hierarchies that benefit and privilege dominant groups. Access to land ownership, discriminatory Federal Housing Authority (FHA) mortgages, redlining, blockbusting, suburbanization, the resulting residential segregation and the consequences for socioeconomic opportunity, including access to education and wealth-building, have revolved around the question of housing. Painted in black and white, Latinas/os have remained largely invisible in the accounting of this narrative. Yet Latinas/os have been, and are, ever present in the formulation of housing and its consequences.

Housing policies and trends in the United States cover a wide range of housing and neighborhood forms: low-income subsidized housing, a private market that incentivizes and support buying and owning homes, cooperatives, institutional housing, and urban and suburban neighborhoods. These housing types are mired with congealed social significations, particularly with regard to class and race and ethnicity. Even if incognito, Latinas/os have been part and parcel of these housing forms and their histories in the United States.

In 1937 the Wagner-Steagall Housing Act established the United States Housing Authority (USHA), the first agency to deal exclusively with low-income housing concerns. Prior to 1937, housing reform programs in the United States had been included in bills whose primary intentions were to reduce unemployment. Thus, the Public Works Administration (PWA) included a housing division, which built fifty-one public housing projects between 1933 and 1937. The USHA embraced its mission of providing affordable housing and between 1937 and 1942 had built 100,000 units in over 140 American cities, providing both mortgage assistance and subsidized public housing to tenants (von Hoffman 1996).

In its initial stages, public housing largely excluded populations of color. Latinas/os were especially vulnerable and overlooked due to housing discrimination, language barriers, failure to advertise programs in Latina/o communities, and the site selection of public housing developments (Alvarez 1996). The Gautreaux project in Chicago, a program in response to a successful lawsuit challenging the segregated placement of public housing sites in exclusively black communities, further highlights the gaps in which Latinas/os have fallen with regard to securing affordable housing (Alvarez 1996). A case cast in "black and white" and aimed at deconcentrating the poverty of African American communities, it overlooked how Latinas/os would be not only excluded but also affected by the Gautreaux's racial integrationist objectives (Polikoff 2007).

Largely unacknowledged in U.S.-mainland housing policy, there are numerous examples of how Latinas/os have been central in the formulation of housing in every iteration of U.S. history, and in every corner of the "mainland" United States, its territories, and the world. In the Southwest, for example, "barrios" are not simply residential agglomerations of Latinos; they are historical extensions of *colonias*, created from the very processes of southwestern colonial expansion and forced displacements (Vigil 2008).

Colonialism produced a network of other Latina/o housing developments. Propelled by financial and technocratic patronage from the United States, Puerto Rico became perhaps one of the largest laboratories for housing policies in the middle of the twentieth century. From the island, strategies for low-cost housing, including public housing and self-help housing programs, were being implemented (Dinzey-Flores 2007; Kwak 2015). The reach was global, and ideas for how to house the "tropical" world and "tropical populations" came from the housing strategies for colonial Latina/o populations (Kwak 2015).

During the height of imperial Cold War jostlings, Cuban migrants in Miami established ethnic enclaves in ways that altered the ethno-racial distribution and representation of the city (Portes and Stepick 1993). Ethnic enclaves reframed debates about residential integration and assimilation, and the conditions under which isolation and concentration resulted in limited access to opportunities or protective factors for community (Sanders and Nee 1987; Small 2004).

Even when the focus on enclaves and enclave economies has considered concentrated Latina/o communities, the question of ethnic agglomeration or clustering, racial segregation, and the prospects of residential agglomeration has not been cast in a Latina/o light. And yet, considering Latinas/os illuminates the questions from different and important vantage points. Mexican American Henry Cisneros was the secretary of Housing and Urban Development (HUD) between 1993 and 1997, precisely at the time where reframed questions of the adequacy of public housing and a push for greater access to homeownership resulted in radically altered urban housing landscape, including the flattening and displacement of public housing buildings and communities, as well as increased rates of homeownership among people of color. Subsequently, Cisneros's Bridges and Pathway organization, launched after his stint as secretary of HUD, promised pathways to integration, through housing, of new immigrants to the United States.

Residential integration has been cast as the vehicle to assimilation from the very early stages of social scientific thought in the United States, and also the mark of upward mobility. To purchase a home in suburbia represented the realization of the American Dream (Hayden 2002). In this regard, Latinas/os have been found to be less residentially segregated than African Americans and more segregated than Asian Americans (Massey and Bitterman 1985; Iceland 2004). However, Caribbean Latinas/os and Afro-Latinas/os tend to be as segregated as African Americans (Massey and Bitterman 1985). The greater proximity to white populations, often represented by suburbia, has suggested that Latinas/os have closer access to "assimilation" and the "American Dream" as these are consolidated in the suburban neighborhood and house. Nonetheless, Latina/o segregation has increased, with explanations pointing to continued immigration and enclave formation (Iceland 2004). Thus, while a portion of the Latina/o mobilization is approximating the suburban American Dream and its implied upward mobility, many Latinas/os remain urban.

Like African Americans, Latinas/os were left behind in underserved and disinvested "inner cities," spatially removed from employment opportunities, isolated in limited social networks, and subject to concentrated poverty. The burned Bronx in New York and East L.A. in California were the prototypes of concentrated poverty and violence. Resistance manifestos such as "El Plan Espiritual de Aztlán" and movements like the Young Lords had specific housing and neighborhood demands. Others resisted by creating community gardens, as well as by developing culturally infused vernacular designs for *casitas* (little houses used as cultural centers) that invoked the homeland and challenged the exclusions felt in the political-economic productions of urban jungles (J. Flores 1995). Still, for many, the options that remained were to keep a firm grasp of the housing that they were able to access and to stake claims on public housing, barrios, and their communities. Today, rapid gentrification in long-standing communities has displaced historically Latina/o communities and introduced a new set of housing and neighborhood challenges (G. Pérez 2004).

Latinas/os remain largely underserved in terms of gaining access to affordable housing. Moreover, with racial narratives failing to include Latina/o ethnicity within or intersecting the racial landscape, that failure in itself limits access to housing programs for Latinas/os. In some instances Latinas/os have been unable to secure the social safety benefit of housing programs due to their immigration experience, language barriers, or inability to meet continuously changing qualifying criteria, of which immigration status is central. In other instances, stereotypical, mythical, and racialized perceptual constructions have suggested that Latinas/os are averse to receiving certain safety-net programs and social service benefits like public housing due to a stereotyped work ethic and cultural values.

Still, garnering their foundational "human right" to housing in U.S. soils, and in some instances in Caribbean and Latin American soils, has placed Latinas/os at the center of housing struggles throughout U.S. housing history. Latinas/os fought for the access of communities of color to public housing, demanded that their communities be designed in ways that respected their histories and experiences, and have staged numerous fights demanding affordable housing. Still, Latinas/os have remained largely segregated, living in low-income neighborhoods, and suffering housing discrimination. The housing crisis of 2008 disproportionately affected Latinas/os, particularly because of predatory home mortgage loans and foreclosure. Majority-Latina/o neighborhoods in Southern California were "the epicenter of the foreclosure crisis" (Molina 2015, 82). Given that Latinas/os hold most of their wealth in homes, as do blacks, the corollary declines in Latina/o wealth have been massive (Taylor et al. 2011; Molina 2015). Stripped of their housing, Latinas/os of all generations saw not only their economic solvency stripped, but their communities and their potentials—their access to their American-dream-home—move farther away.

But the material realities, and challenges, of housing do not fully capture the texture of the Latina/o housing/home experience. Latinas/os have left a mark in U.S. housing and neighborhoods in many ways. Latinas/os have inflected the architecture and aesthetics of their surroundings with their histories, preferences, and experiences, staking claims to belonging in cities like Boston, Los Angeles, New York, and San Francisco. They have taken over the street and redefined its use by making their porches social areas and selling their goods on the sidewalk (Rojas 1991, 2010). They have formed enclaves and communities that honor their modes of life. They have occupied and infused an entrepreneurial spirit into previously depopulated cities, and given life to remote zones.

Latinas/os' influence in housing is not limited to the United States' "main"-landscape. U.S. Latina/o migrants have also changed the housing landscape of their home cities and towns in Latin America and the Caribbean, sending unparalleled quantities of "housing remittances" that take the form of improved shelters for their families, wealth investments, and new residential structures.

At issue, in both the challenge and the celebration of Latina/o housing/homes is the definition of what constitutes an adequate dwelling—what makes a house meritorious of the idea of "home." Politically, the concept of housing and dwelling space invokes social and hegemonic ideals of varying kinds, ones that partition and stratify land, property, community, and even memory with narrow social significations that recycle inequality and privilege white elites. In this sociopolitical configuration, Latinas/os have found themselves devising their sense of home against conquest "growth machine" forces (Molotch 1976) that emplace them in unfamiliar political or physical landscapes, making arguments in defense of organic communities like Chavez Ravine in the face of the L.A. Dodgers baseball stadium, and shuttling them between *colonias*, tenements, areas designated as "slums," barrios, ghettos, and trying to stave off the forces of capital that made their neighborhoods attractive to newcomers. Latinas/os have fought back earnestly to demand that their communities be preserved, that they fit their architectural demands, as in the case of the Villa Victoria public housing community in Boston (Small 2004); that they have access to public housing; and very recently, that their affordable public "projects" continue to house them and not be sold to the highest bidder. Perhaps most illustrative of these efforts to consolidate a Latina/o home in U.S. housing is the work of James Rojas (1991, 2010), which visually documents how Latinas/os aesthetically, and formally as well as informally, stamp/plan their spaces—home interiors, front yards, and neighborhood sidewalks and streets—with their presence, blending the house with a home.

25

Hyphen
Frederick Luis Aldama

Like many in the United States I identify as Latino. Yet, if we put slight pressure on this identity category, it falls short. I'm Mexican-American, Guatemalan-American, and Irish-American. I'm GuaMex-Irish U.S. American. I'm of the hyphen. I create the hyphen. I activate the hyphen—a hyphen that signals how Latinas/os actively and constantly transform U.S. American identity categories themselves.

Millions of Latinas/os in the United States are the product of multiple cultural identity categories (Allatson 2002; Caminero-Santangelo 2013). Whether one identifies as Latina/o, Hispana/o, Chicana/o, Nuyorican, Cubana/o, Juban (Jewish Cuban-American), and so on, one way or another Latinas/os inhabit in-between identity spaces. We inhabit the hyphen as Mexican-Americans, Dominican-Americans, Cuban-Americans, and as Central American-Americans, to use Arturo Arias's (2003) term. And these hyphens splinter and multiply: Porto-Mexes, Cubo-Bolivians, Mex-Pakistanis, Black-Latinos, Luso-Latinos, among others. Each has a seeming infinite number of further variations. Each has its own history as a term. Mexican-Americans who want to foreground a politicized identity silence and displace the hyphen. For self-proclaimed Chicanas/os or Xicanas/os, the Nahuatl root sound of "ch" celebrates a new hyphenated relationship—one with our Indigenous ancestral past. We see the same move happen with Boricua, but this time to embrace the Taino ancestral roots inhabiting

Borinquen, or what came to be known as Puerto Rico after the conquest.

The history of identity categories for the hyphenated and silently hyphenated Latina/o groups that make up the larger category of U.S. Latina/o is fluid. In each of the self-identified categories (and not those issued by the government or media), hyphenated Latinas/os try to represent the facts of our varied, deeply multicultural, multi-hyphenated history as Latinas/os. This history includes the people of the pre-conquest Indigenous hyphen that we've reclaimed as well as those of African and Arabic origin (Aguirre Beltran 1972).

Whether in the case of a term like "Porto-Mex" or "Luso-Latino," or any other mentioned above, we come back to the question of the hyphen. Older sociodemographic melting-pot models considered the hyphen as a kind of passageway of Latinas/os to become assimilated U.S. Americans (Rumbaut and Portes 2001; Golash-Boza 2006). Identity has traditionally been considered to be a key component of the assimilation process. The melting-pot model is based on the idea that immigrants and their children first identify as, say, "Mexican-Americans" and then as "American" *sans* the hyphen, whereby erasure of the "Mexican-" functions as the sign of total assimilation. For scholars who base their work on émigré populations that cross oceans—and that do not have proximate contact with homelands, as with the U.S.-Mexico border—the argument was that all émigrés would assimilate into U.S. society in a unidirectional manner, leaving behind the home country's culture and language (Gordon 1964; Gans 1979). That is, all immigrants would take the same path of assimilation.

Today, we see more and more how the hyphen for Latinas/os is not necessarily a directional sign toward assimilation. In fact, the hyphen functions as a sign that makes visible the parts that make up the whole, but not necessarily an assimilated whole. Indeed, the

hyphen has been used (and in some cases continues to be used) to identify the parts that exist in opposition to the whole. So, the hyphen in "Mexican-American" is not a directional sign that implies a *move* from Mexican *toward* American; instead, it signals where the Mexican stands firmly on its own two feet—and in clear opposition to the American. The *hyphen* reminds us both of our separateness (self-proclaimed and sovereign) and of the forced exclusions that have kept us apart within a dominant, xenophobic Anglo-America.

For Latinas/os, the hyphen is slippery. The hyphen might prompt us to unify disparate cultural, linguistic, and national identities; it might also trigger in our minds an opposition, conflict—*war*—between these identity categories. Thus when we Latinas/os encounter this grammatical marker, we bring our *hermeneutics of the hyphen* tool to decipher, discuss, debate, and critique its presence as situated in and given meaning within everyday experience.

Scholars of Latina/o literary and cultural studies bear this out. Many reject the second term in the equation, claiming that it implies assimilation from the first ethnic category to the greater one of American—and this in the face of those who state that hyphenated identities should always be subordinate to the category "American." We see an even more radical approach to the hyphen in the work of Juan Bruce-Novoa (1990). In *RetroSpace* he maintains that Latinos reside in a liminal space between Mexican and American—a space that is not the hyphen, Bruce-Novoa insists, and not "Mexican American," but "nothing"— the "intercultural *nothingness* of that space" between Mexican and U.S. relations (1990, 98; emphasis in original). He chooses for the wiping out altogether of categories like "Mexican American" and "Chicano," proposing instead that they remain undefined as nothingness; but not a "nothing in no negative way" but rather a nothing that "perversely resists final definition" (1990, 94).

For other scholars, the hyphen marks a space of creativity, improvisation, and active biculturalism. We see this in the work of Ilan Stavans (2003) and his celebration of code switching and Spanglish as diasporic, permeable like jazz, and influencing the mainstream. And for Juan Flores (2000, 167–90), the fact that Puerto Rican American lacks a hyphen leads him to declare this Latino group as existing *off the hyphen*—a safe space against prepackaged hyphenated Latina/o categories that one way or another privilege an American status; the trope is also taken up by José L. Torres-Padilla and Carmen Haydee Rivera (2008). More recently, scholars of early trans-American Latina/o cultural studies have recovered texts that exist within the hyphen. I think of Jesse Alemán (2003) and his work on biographical figures such as Cuban-born Loreta Janeta Velazquez, who troubled the hyphen between genders and nationalities by crossdressing as a man to fight as a Confederate soldier during the American Civil War (Velazquez 2003).

Other Latino author-intellectuals take slightly different positions concerning the hyphen. For instance, in *Life on the Hyphen*, Gustavo Pérez Firmat (1994) embraces the hyphen, but as a member of what he identifies as the "one-and-a-half generation" of Latinos. For him, the hyphen is "appositional rather than oppositional" so that it is "impossible to determine which side of the bicultural equation has more power or influence," according to Paul Allatson (2007, 127). Pérez Firmat is of that Cuban-American generation born in Cuba, but raised in the United States, who said of his hyphenated identity: "If all these years in North Carolina haven't quite made me a good ole boy, a *cubanazo* redneck, spic and hick in equal parts, they certainly have colored my tastes and my values. By now, American sights and sounds are so embedded within me that I know I would find it difficult to spend the rest of my life only among Cubans" (1994, 6). And, we see how author-intellectuals like Richard Rodriguez shift their position concerning the hyphen. In *Hunger of Memory* (1982), Rodriguez distances himself from Chicanos and sees himself as Mexican-American, but where the hyphen signals a one-way flow away from Mexican toward mainstream American. In *Brown* (R. Rodriguez 2002), however, he sees the hyphen more as a multidirectional category of celebrated and self-affirmed impurity; it's the hyphen whereby Latinos are actively transforming—*browning*—America. And, fiction author and essayist Dagoberto Gilb recounts how he "was born and raised *pocho*—Americanized—and I didn't know much more about Mexico than most. . . . Mexico was a story to me, one that I knew not like a Mexican novella but like an American comic book: adventure, love, honor, pride, betrayal, *güero y moreno*" (2003, 12).

The hermeneutics of the hyphen is omnipresent in our cultural productions. In the early 1970s we had several authors at once solidifying and troubling the category of the hyphen. For Luis Valdez the hyphen meant assimilation. For example, the narrator of his 1968 one-act play *La Conquista de México* introduces La Malinche, saying, "This woman was to become infamous in the history of Mexico. Not only did she turn her back on her own people, she joined the white men and became *assimilated*, serving as their guide and interpreter and generally assisting in the conquest. She was the first Mexican-American" (1990, 59). But, in the work of author and lawyer Oscar "Zeta" Acosta, the hyphen is rejected altogether. We see at the end of his *The Autobiography of a Brown Buffalo* (1972) the declaration that he is neither Mexican nor American nor Mexican-American, but rather something entirely new, self-fashioned, and self-affirming as a Brown Buffalo. In Héctor Tobar's *Translation Nation* (2005), readers learn of his experience growing up in the United States as a Guatemalan-American in the 1960s. While his cultural heritage was forcefully present at home, basketball and baseball players became his heroes: "I was becoming an American, another species, different from all my ancestors" (2005, 5). In the end, Tobar considers himself neither Guatemalan nor U.S. American, but a new citizen of the "Latin Republic of the United States" (2005, 30). In *Their Dogs Came with Them* (2007), Helena María Viramontes creates several Mexican-American protagonists living in L.A. during the Vietnam War. As the Mexican-American neighborhood is destroyed (to make room for a freeway), the past percolates to the surface, and one of the main characters, Ermila, learns from her grandmother how her mother *"vanished in the hyphen of the Mexican-Guatemalan border"* (2007, 305, emphasis in original). And in *American Chica*, Peruvian-American author Marie Arana self-identifies as a "north-south collision, a New World fusion. An American *chica*. A bridge" (2001, 147). In Achy Obejas's *Memory Mambo* (1996), we see how the hyphen for her Cuban-born American lesbian character, Juani Casas, identifies her sense of both apartness from and connection to other peoples and their respective identities in the United States. Finally, in *The Dirty Girls Social Club* (2003) Alisa Valdes shows how an upper-middle-class materialist worldview can and does dissolve any and all presence of one's Latino culture of origin. The various parts that make up the whole in their hyphenated identities (Cuban-Irish-American, Afro-Puerto Rican, Afro-Colombian, Mexican-American, and Jewish Cuban-American) are lost and only a global (consumerist) identity remains.

In comics, Latinas/os create hyphenated characters to identify various identity categories (Aldama 2009). They create empowered superheroes like Javier Hernandez's Weapon Tex-Mex—a Texan who sports bullhorns and a Zorro mask. Weapon Tex-Mex is a hyphenated superhero who troubles what it means to be Texan in territories that used to belong to Mexico and Mexicans, as well as troubling macho gender identities.

And in creating his comic book *East Metropolis*, Alex Olivas (2014) wanted to be sure that his protagonist was a three-tier hyphenated identity: Mexican, Indigenous, and African, as he discusses in an interview featured in *Latinx Comic Book Storytelling* (Aldama 2016).

It is this reality of Latinas/os that is often reflected in the creating of our cultural objects. It is the reality of living in the hyphen as Latinas/os and the hyphen's cultural and linguistic impact on the mainstream, which Latina/o creators like Acosta, Hernandez, Obejas, Tobar, Arana, Viramontes, Olivas, along with many others, capture. This two-way influence and flow between Latina/o culture and the mainstream that Tobar and others write about is very much a contemporary phenomenon, as I discuss in the *Routledge Concise History of Latino/a Literature* (Aldama 2013).

We live in a country where we encounter the hyphen everywhere. The people who make up the United States come from many different cultures. Our mainstream is decisively multiethnic, multicultural—*hyphenated*. It is a country where hyphenated-identity creators and consumers make up the general population, developing a diverse appetite for a wide variety of cultural products. Satisfying the multiply hyphenated appetites creates new social, political, and cultural needs and demands, implying the education of all our senses: tastes, smells, touch, sounds, sights. It also implies the education of the multiply hyphenated cultural needs with respect to these appetites. It implies the education of aesthetic capabilities and interpretations. To be creating and consuming from the hyphen transforms the mainstream just as that Latino-fied mainstream transforms us Latinas/os. The hyphen is a two-way flow where nothing is lost, and all is gained.

26

Illegality

Cecilia Menjívar

The term "illegality" is often used uncritically and in facile fashion in public discourses of immigration to refer to the condition in which several million undocumented immigrants live today. As the political debate and public discourse show, language matters a great deal. People often think that they know exactly to what immigrants this term refers, as the term itself has become closely linked to the lives of Latina/o immigrants. Indeed, given the focus of the enforcement side of the immigration regime today, this term has become almost synonymous with Latina/o immigrants. And popular usage of the term "illegality" connotes association with criminality, with violation of the legal order, and, as such, it is often used to undermine the moral character of certain immigrant groups, as Peter Nyers (2010) notes. Thus, the popular use of this term does not simply reflect its technical legal meaning (Menjívar and Kanstroom 2014), and politicized debates frequently ignore the historical permeability of the line between "legality" and "illegality," obfuscating the distinction between illegality and crime. In immigration matters, unauthorized or undocumented presence is a civil offense and not a crime, but re-entering the country without documentation has recently been redefined as a felony. However, since the act of entering the country undocumented does not produce victims, it has been defined as a victimless crime.

Debates and popular discourses leave out the fundamental point that the law has moved to encompass increasingly more immigrants under the category of "illegality," which today is predicated on the construction of certain immigrant behaviors as criminal. Rather than assuming that individuals break laws when they are pushed into illegality, a more fruitful approach would be to begin by examining how this category is created and which immigrants have been moved into it—in short, how certain immigrants become illegalized. As Étienne Balibar (2000) notes, the state makes certain bodies illegal, and as a project of the state the illegalization of immigrants is deeply political and can serve many objectives. In recent years, the political project of merging immigration matters with criminal law (Stumpf 2006) has led individuals living in this category to have altogether different experiences than before, when this merger had not been made. The slew of Executive Orders that the newly-elected president signed in early 2017 attests to the harmful consequences of using law to construct immigrants as criminals and as threats to the nation.

Legal structures produce categories of illegality, and thus a useful avenue to examine this concept is to move away from the individuals who are presumed to be the bearers of this condition to the laws that produce it (Ngai 2004). In this light, it is important to bear in mind the constructed nature of the category of "illegality" (De Genova 2004; Ackerman 2012) and to consider how this category is created by laws, how it affects Latinas/os in particular, and how it intersects with other systems of inequality and oppression, as well as how this category has been transformed as a site of resistance in recent years.

Illegality is historically and legally produced and therefore malleable and changeable (Menjívar 2006; Moloney 2012). With the stroke of a pen, entire groups of immigrants have been moved from illegality to legality and vice versa. For instance, the government can pass law to grant legalization to certain individuals who meet a set of requirements; however, it can also end certain admissions that were previously lawful. Thus, it is critical to examine the sociopolitical contexts in which such categories are created and allegations of illegality are constructed (Massey, Durand, and Malone 2002).

Perhaps nowhere is the constructedness of the category of illegality more evident than in the comingling of immigrant illegality and criminality. The Illegal Immigration Reform and Immigrant Responsibility Act (IIRIRA) of 1996 expanded the list of crimes for which immigrants (undocumented and permanent legal residents alike) can be deported. Before this law, there were several civil offenses that would not lead to a deportation, but by expanding the category of "aggravated felonies" and thus deportable offenses, the law created the conditions for the removal (and inadmissibility) of thousands of immigrants. This change in law has had the consequence of illegalizing thousands, moving even immigrants who were legal permanent residents into the category of illegality. At this historical junction—characterized by the merging of criminal with immigration law and new enforcement practices that rely on vast technological networks, and by fears of security threats and a widening and deeper securitization regime—the "illegalization" of immigrants through law acquires new meaning (and multiple consequences) and must be examined critically.

One example of the process of illegalization and criminalization is the creation of a new category of "unlawful reentry." If an individual is deported from the United States and reenters the country, this "unlawful reentry" is categorized as a federal crime and counts as a criminal offense. Research has found that when deported migrants leave close family members in the United States, they will have a higher likelihood to remigrate to reunite with their loved ones (Rodríguez and

Hagan 2004). With such attempts to reenter the country now being categorized as felonies, the result has been a dramatic increase in the alleged criminal offenses committed by immigrants. Indeed, "unlawful reentries" represent a significant proportion of the crimes that immigrants supposedly commit. A recent analysis (Light, Lopez, and Gonzalez-Barrera 2014) shows that between 1992 and 2012, unlawful reentry convictions accounted for 48 percent of the growth in the total number of offenders sentenced in federal courts, which increased 28 times in this time period. Not all immigrant groups living in illegality experience this enforcement practice in the same way, as Latinas/os have become overwhelmingly targeted. For instance, whereas in 1992 Latinas/os constituted 23 percent of offenders charged with unlawful entry, in 2012 they made up 48 percent of these offenses.

A key aspect of today's enforcement practices is that the same behavior—for example, reentering the country after a deportation or using fake documents to work—was not classified as a felonious offense in the past nor would it count as a criminal offense in other contexts today. Furthermore, the immigration regime has created a situation in which the same act, such as shoplifting or driving over the speed limit, has enormously different consequences when it is carried out by someone who is classified as undocumented or by someone who is a citizen. And given that Latina/o immigrants are so overwhelmingly pushed into punitive spaces when they live in illegality, the intersection of illegality and race has acquired particular significance.

The racialized nature of the system in which the category of illegality operates today is evident in the demographics of the deportation regime. For instance, it is estimated that 52 percent of the approximately 11.4 million undocumented immigrants in the country in 2012 were of Mexican origin (Passel, Cohn, and

Gonzalez-Barrera 2013); however, they accounted for 73 percent of total deportations. The same pattern was observed for Guatemalans, who made up 9 percent of the deported even though they constituted 5 percent of the undocumented population; Hondurans, who constituted 8 percent of the deported, made up only 3 percent of the undocumented population; and Salvadorans, who constituted 4 percent of the deported made up 6 percent of the undocumented (Menjívar, Abrego, and Schmalzbauer 2016). Thus, even though immigrants from these four countries made up 64 percent of the undocumented population in 2012, they represented 96 percent of all deportations in that same year.

Another component of the enforcement system, border apprehensions, mirrors the composition of deportations, with 96 percent of apprehensions at the border made up of migrants from these four countries (*CBP Border Security Report Fiscal Year 2014*). And there is a significant difference in how individuals who become undocumented are treated in the system, with particularly negative consequences for Latinas/os. Immigrants who overstay their visas (that is, who came into the country with a visa but stayed past their allowed time) are not subject to the three-year or, more often, ten-year, bar to readmission if they leave the country (or are deported). However, those who come in without inspection (and more likely to have crossed the border) are barred from reentering the country for three to ten years. These patterns point to a profoundly lopsided enforcement system, embedded in law, which targets primarily Latinas/os. At the same time, the legislative side of the immigration regime continues to push these immigrants into illegality and significantly narrows their paths for admission and legalization.

The category of illegality is also classed and gendered. The overwhelming majority of Latinas/os in detention and those who are deported are poor immigrant workers, and, as research has noted (Golash-Boza and Hondagneu-Sotelo 2013), men are more likely to be deported; in 2014, 93 percent of those deported were men (TRAC Immigration 2014). Moreover, their deportation affects entire families left behind and can significantly alter gender dynamics and generational relations within families living in the United States and across borders. Furthermore, research has found that for Latinas/os, the combination of skin color and gender significantly increases the odds of police stops (K. M. White 2014). Therefore, the category of illegality is at present lived with particular intensity by poor Latinos.

Significantly, constructed social categories, even when unfounded or created in the context of political agendas, have real consequences for those who have been classified into them. Noteworthy, by its very nature the construct of illegality evolves over time and it is not static; it can change and encompass new groups of immigrants, as well as their descendants. One recent example comes from efforts to strip U.S.-born citizens of undocumented parents of their citizenship or even to rescind the citizenship of naturalized citizens who are found to have made even a minor mistake on their naturalization application. Permanent legal residents ("green card" holders) who are documented are now also at risk of losing their status due to the expanded and retroactive reach of new laws. Thus, the category changes and expands and contracts depending largely on the political currents at a particular historical moment.

As the category of illegality intersects with other social vectors of oppression, the experiences of those who have been pushed into illegality will differ. Thus, for instance, even though living in illegality constrains people's rights and limits access to social benefits, gender and sexuality create varying experiences in this already marginalized position. Since gender ideologies position women, even full-time workers, as caretakers of their families, women must interact with the institutions that dispense the social benefits that are often denied to those living in illegality. In these situations, women may experience illegality in particularly acute fashion. On the other hand, in their socially ascribed role of breadwinners, men may experience heightened forms of illegality when they work in jobs that must be performed in public spaces, as their mere presence may elicit suspicion and even trigger an enforcement action.

The category of illegality has multiple meanings and consequences for those who live in it, beyond the denial of social welfare rights and the push to increasingly more marginalized spaces. Often the social, economic, and cultural contributions of illegalized immigrants are devalued, regardless of how much these immigrants' labor contributes to the economy or how their social and cultural practices remake and revitalize communities. But just as often, the category of illegality has been vigorously contested and resisted. Immigrants have mobilized with diverse allies to challenge the ideological underpinnings of illegality and the stereotypes and constructions on which it is based. Examples of these mobilizations include the DREAMers, the National Day Laborer Organizing Network, and the UndocuQueer movement, among others. At a more personal level, in their everyday lives, immigrants who live in this category actively create spaces and practices that give them comfort and hope and through which they confront and produce alternative forms of belonging even as the dominant regime pushes them to the margins. While the immigration regime effectively forecloses paths to membership through expanding the category of illegality, immigrants continue to make a living, support families—here and there—and contribute to reshape the vibrant communities in which they live.

27

Incarceration
Michael Hames-García

Incarceration in the United States is geographically distinctive, historically unprecedented, and racially disproportionate. It is geographically distinctive because the United States incarcerates both more people and a larger percentage of its population than any other country in the world—by far. It has only 5 percent of the world's population, but 25 percent of the world's prisoners, and just under seven million people, or one in thirty-five, in the United States were incarcerated, on parole, or on probation in 2012 (more than the entire population of Chicago and Los Angeles combined). It is historically unprecedented because the U.S. incarceration rate fluctuated only mildly from the late nineteenth century until the 1970s and then increased 500 percent in thirty years. No modern democracy has ever imprisoned so many. It is racially disproportionate because people of color make up 36 percent of the nation's population, but 60 percent of those in prison. One in three African American men and one in six Latino men in the United States will spend time in prison during his lifetime (Hartney 2006; Mauer 2006; Public Safety Performance Project 2008; Wacquant 2009; Hames-García 2011a; Tonry 2011; Sentencing Project 2014).

From the medieval Latin *incarcerare* (literally "to put into confinement"), "incarceration" implies a forced removal from society and a limitation of physical freedom or mobility. There is an important distinction to be made between incarceration and slavery. While historically either one could result from military defeat, criminal conviction, or unpaid debts, modern slavery in the Americas was characterized by complex and varying social and legal relationships between enslaved people and their masters. One could be born into slavery or fall into it, be emancipated from or purchased out of it, but one was typically not sentenced to it for a set period of time. Furthermore, even when slavery in the Americas was justified by the presumption of biological inferiority, it was by and large not understood as a result of a person's immoral or criminal behavior. Abolitionist movements thus did not need to challenge justifications for slavery that were based on scientific racism in order to make the case that innocent slaves suffered unjustifiably under it. They could instead argue that the institution was unjustifiably cruel. Prison abolitionists, by contrast, are often accused of defending immorality, supporting harmful behaviors, or believing that wrongdoers should not face consequences. While many scholars in critical prison studies advocate the abolition of prisons, this has been a hard position to draw popular support for, even in the wake of a growing consensus that prison populations should be reduced. Immigrants with criminal histories, for example, were excluded from discussions at the national level about the DREAM Act, a proposal to create a pathway to permanent residency for some undocumented immigrants who arrived as minors. In order to pass this proposal, proponents sought to exclude those not of "good moral character," meaning primarily those with felony convictions. Missing from this approach is an understanding of all immigrants, including convicted felons, as deserving of the rights and opportunities available to citizens.

This view of criminals and prisoners as morally unworthy is relatively new, and has evolved in tandem with the racialization of prisons. In much of European history incarceration was used as a form of pretrial detention rather than a punishment in itself. Punishments were mostly financial or corporal, with the move to measuring retribution in units of time spent in confinement (days, months, years) becoming widespread throughout Western Europe and the Americas only in the wake of the Enlightenment (Morris and Rothman 1998). (An exception was the debtor's prison in which one would be confined until one's debts were paid off, but even here the length of time was not conflated with an inmate's punishment.) The expanded use of incarceration thus coincided roughly with the birth of the United States and the French Republic, and incarceration as punishment for crime further spread throughout the new Latin American republics as a key symbol of "modernization" in the decades following their independence from Spain (Salvatore and Aguirre 1996). In explaining the coincidence of modern democracy and the prison, scholars have argued that in a society in which all citizens are understood to have inalienable rights, including liberty, punishment for crimes against the state or "the people" are most appropriately punished through a proportionate loss of liberty. It is thus unsurprising that imprisonment in the United States was primarily restricted early on to white men. This reflected the absence of full citizenship (and hence, liberty) accorded to women and people of color (Davis 2003). For example, women could suffer corporal punishment or confinement in the home, often at the whim of their husbands, fathers, and brothers. They were typically punished by the state only when their transgressions were public. Public crimes associated with women (for example, infanticide, mariticide [murder of one's husband], prostitution, or theft) were nearly always construed simultaneously as transgressions of the law and violations of the ideals of proper womanhood (Freedman 1981). Despite the relative absence of women from early prisons, women, those regarded as sexual transgressors, and gender nonconformists have been objects of police and criminal-legal scrutiny since colonial times (Mogul, Ritchie, and Whitlock 2011).

Following Reconstruction, the nature of incarceration in the United States changed dramatically in the South. Southern prisons went from almost exclusively white to almost entirely black, and incarcerated blacks were put to work, often on the very plantations on which they and their ancestors had been enslaved (Davis 2003). In the wake of the civil rights era, a political realignment of conservative Republicans and southern Democrats forged the post-Goldwater Republican Party, successfully campaigning for "law and order" and greatly expanding the role of incarceration during the Nixon and Reagan-Bush eras. Most scholars understand this expansion—which escalated under Clinton, continued under the second Bush, and began to taper only slightly under Obama—as a use of formally colorblind, but racially coded policies to mobilize white voters while writing off poor black communities. What the late twentieth century thus saw was a spread of the post-Reconstruction Southern practice of racialized mass incarceration into a national practice implemented without direct reference to race but in such a way as to overwhelmingly target blacks (Weaver 2007; Parenti 2008; Tonry 2011).

According to the dominant explanation of late twentieth-century incarceration in the United States, the disproportionate effect of incarceration on Native Americans, Latinas/os, Native Hawaiians, and Southeast Asians is merely collateral damage in an undeclared war on urban African American communities (Tonry 2011; Alexander 2012). The explanation is strengthened by the fact that all of these populations have considerably lower rates of incarceration than African Americans, although much higher rates than whites. While understandable, the explanation of racialized mass incarceration as being primarily a strategy for African American subordination misses the specificities of other forms of racism, genocide, colonialism, and xenophobia that target Native peoples, Asians, and Latinas/os in specific ways (Grobsmith 1994; Rumbaut et al. 2006). Chicana/o and Puerto Rican communities have dealt with high rates of incarceration for most of the twentieth century, as the police and criminal legal system regularly served as a means to curb social unrest and political activism in these communities (Mirandé 1987). This historical relationship to policing and incarceration, in turn, has resulted in the prison being an important space of intellectual and cultural production as well as politicization for many Latinas/os (Díaz-Cotto 1996; Hames-García 2004; Olguín 2010). Notably, the incarceration of Latinas/os in the United States expanded the most dramatically not under the Reagan-era unrolling of disproportionate sentencing guidelines for crack and powder cocaine (when African American incarceration spiked dramatically), but rather under the one-two punch of Clinton's Violent Crime Control and Law Enforcement Act of 1994 and Illegal Immigration Reform and Immigration Responsibility Act of 1996. Further combined with the Personal Responsibility and Work Opportunity Act of 1996, this set of policies formed part of a concerted scapegoating of immigrants, both "legal" and "illegal" (read: "criminal") and resulted in rapidly accelerating rates of incarceration for Mexicans, Central Americans, Caribbean people, and Southeast Asians. These acts had devastating effects on poor and immigrant communities: reducing government assistance to the poor; restricting the ability of people convicted of drug and immigration crimes to receive assistance; reducing work and educational opportunities for undocumented immigrants, prisoners, and former prisoners; creating fifty new kinds of federal crimes (including new and enhanced penalties for crimes committed by "gang" members and crimes related to immigration); and establishing mandatory life sentences without possibility of parole for many repeat offenders, including drug traffickers.

This generalized assault, along with contemporaneous three-strikes and mandatory minimum sentencing provisions in states like California, should not be separated from the larger anti-immigrant fervor that swept the country in the 1990s, as exemplified by California's Proposition 187, which would have denied health care, education, and social services to undocumented immigrants in the state had it not been declared unconstitutional. Throughout the 1990s, the war on drugs combined with heightened xenophobia and helped to shift the focus of racialized mass incarceration toward Latina/o and immigrant communities (Díaz-Cotto 2006). The result has been a ballooning Latina/o presence in state and federal prisons. Due to the increased criminalization of undocumented immigration and the trafficking of people and illegal substances across the border, the federal prison system (including Immigration and Customs Enforcement [ICE] detention centers) has seen substantial increases in Latina/o prisoners. In 2012, Latinas/os accounted for nearly half of all federal felony convictions (Light, López, and González-Barrera 2014).

The Latina/o experience with incarceration in the United States allows us to see that the story of gradual transformation of prisons from places of pretrial detention to places of racialized mass incarceration following the end of segregation is insufficient and incomplete. In the 150 years since the Civil War, the Enlightenment prison concept has been adapted to a colonial prison concept, with subordinate racialized populations targeted and imprisoned at hugely disproportionate rates. Under this new form of population management, racialized groups understood as both undesirable and unreformable are disproportionately targeted and imprisoned with increasing blatancy, as incarceration becomes the accepted and expected method for dealing with every social problem from unemployment and homelessness to drug addiction and domestic violence. Not only does the story of incarceration as simply the new slavery or the new "Jim Crow" fail to account for the specificities of Latina/o incarceration; it masks them, making them that much more difficult to see, understand, and explain.

28

Indigeneity

Maylei Blackwell

Given the complex, and overlapping, histories of indigeneity and coloniality in the Americas, as well as the multiple ways indigeneity is deployed in Latina/o studies, the discussion that follows is as much about the parameters of indigeneity in the field as what it has been mistaken for. Indigeneity has best been described as a field of power by Aida Hernández Castillo (2010) to name how Indigenous peoples negotiate an array of power relationships (within nation-states or with social scientists, for example) in a struggle over meaning that delegitimizes their forms of knowledge and ways of being. As the original inhabitants of the Americas, most identify first as tribal nations or pueblos (peoples, communities, towns, following Lynn Stephen [2007]), as well as embracing the broader constructions of First Nations, American Indian, Native American, or Indigenous peoples to articulate a diplomatic and legal framework for their survivance, self-determination, and territorial integrity in relation to colonial powers and settler states. The political, spiritual, social, and discursive practices of original (aboriginal) peoples are embedded in cultural continuity within the living, transforming (and intervened upon) cultures of their ancestors. Many government officials and policymakers have tied this definition of continuity to a territorial framework, which fails to acknowledge that many Indigenous groups had territorial bases that included seasonal settlement and migrations based on hunting, social and ceremonial gatherings, and

trade. Further, many tribes and Indigenous peoples have been forcibly removed for purposes of colonial settlement and its aftermath, including policies of relocation, termination, and urbanization. Other Indigenous pueblos and nations have been falsely divided by colonial borders. Relationships to land are at the heart of Indigenous political and spiritual beliefs and practices, and yet, there is a growing recognition of how even when Indigenous communities are deterritorialized, they retain their cosmovisions, civic and political structures, and relationships to their ancestral homelands.

Who and what is Indigenous has been highly regulated and monitored by colonial systems of management that have been incorporated by modernist state projects, often through racializing processes. Chickasaw scholar Jodi Byrd (2011) has argued that homogenizing over five hundred Indigenous nations by U.S. settler colonialism, not to mention the 634 first nations in what is now Canada, is a process of minoritization that has made racial what is truly international. While the state has attempted to manage indigeneity via racial/ethnic categories (Barker 2005), others have argued that Indigenous people have radically different goals than a civil rights agenda or pluralist discourses of inclusion that misconstrue Indigenous claims as race-based (Kauanui 2008). In Latin America and the Caribbean, these strategies can be seen in the ways Indigenous pueblos have routinely been categorized as ethnicities in a minoritizing discourse that equalizes Indigenous peoples with all other minorities, potentially stripping away their specific claims toward self-determination and territory as original inhabitants of the Americas.

After years of struggle within the United Nations Permanent Forum on Indigenous Issues, the international Indigenous rights movement was able to get the UN Declaration of Indigenous People (UNDRIP) passed in

2007. The characteristics of Indigenous peoples within that document are:

- Self-identification as Indigenous peoples at the individual level and accepted by the community as their member;
- Historical continuity with pre-colonial and/or pre-settler societies;
- Strong link to territories and surrounding natural resources;
- Distinct social, economic or political systems;
- Distinct language, culture and beliefs;
- Form non-dominant groups of society;
- Resolve to maintain and reproduce their ancestral environments and systems as distinctive peoples and communities.

While the UNDRIP creates a shared international legal framework, one of the historic challenges within Latina/o studies is the often obscured fact that in any given space, there may be multiple colonialities at play and that these colonial projects are not isolated from one another but have historically colluded to create the power relationships we currently see.

The multiple colonialities at play between U.S. and Latin American coloniality and settler colonialism are critical to note. While the two forms of colonialism are often conflated, the distinction between the two systems is important and can be broadly understood as one intends to deindianize and the other to eliminate. Latin American colonialism, and later forms of state coloniality, aimed to erase Indigenous peoples through incorporation (Christianization, mestizaje, indigenismo, and so on). Settler colonialism, on the other hand, is a structure based on land expropriation through a logic of elimination (removal, relocation, termination, and the like). This does not mean one system

did not use the means of the other. In Latin America, extractive industries—what activists call "extractive capitalism/colonialism"—often require the elimination and removal of Indigenous communities for the exploitation of their land, water, labor or minerals. In the United States, elimination by means of sterilization, for example, has often been accompanied by strategies of violent incorporation, which include child theft, boarding schools, and/or adoption to white families on a mass scale. The differences and collusions have created a layered, multiple colonial system in California, Texas, New Mexico, and Florida, where settler colonial structures are built on a prior Spanish/Mexican colonial structure of power that include missions, haciendas, and a ruling-class elite. These layers of coloniality are not just historic strata but are constitutive of contemporary relations of power. These colonialities have produced the Hispanization (and later Mexicanization) of Indigenous peoples in the region. These multiple colonial layers also function elsewhere in the Americas with Russian, French, and Portuguese colonial powers. Indigenous survivance (understood as presence and continuance) (Vizenor 1994) has meant that Indigenous peoples, cultures, and languages have survived multiple colonialities and settler logics. In the Caribbean, the Taino have been erased through the vanishing Indian trope, a myth of the American frontier that romanticizes the savage nobility of the "last" remaining Indigenous peoples and becomes so ingrained in the American psyche that many believe there are no "real" Indians left. This myth is embedded in multiple colonial systems, meaning that U.S. imperial or neo-colonial relations in the Caribbean build on Spanish colonization.

These multiple, and divergent, colonialities have produced conflicting notions of indigeneity. Indigenismo was part of a mestizo intellectual and cultural movement in Latin America in which national elites imagined and constructed the nation by discursively locking Indigenous civilizations eternally in the past. For example, indigenismo was central to the nation-building project of post-revolutionary Mexico, with the largest Indigenous population in the hemisphere, by celebrating the grandeur of an Aztec past, while treating the present and future of the sixty-three Indigenous pueblos as something to be overcome through biological erasure, through mestizaje, and cultural incorporation. In *Bloodlines*, Sheila Contreras undertakes an exploration of Chicana/o indigenism and its usage of a symbolic archive that "draws from preceding traditions of Mexican indigenism and European primitivism" (2008, 6). She defines "indigenismo" as "the stylistic appropriation of Indigenous cultural forms and traditions by non-Indigenous artists and intellectuals" (2008, 24). As part of her critical reevaluation of *Borderlands / La Frontera* by Gloria Anzaldúa, Contreras argues that "less recognized, perhaps, is the degree to which *Borderlands* and other Chicana/o indigenist texts are deeply indebted to language and images first disseminated by European writers as part of colonialist endeavors and, later, as critical reevaluations of the Western social order" (2008, 114).

While recognizing the power of Mesoamerican Indigenous civilizations may seem like a positive development, it was tied with cultural projects of modernism and state projects of modernity. In the hands of state institutions, indigenismo as an ideology and set of policies allowed mestizo elites to regulate the meaning of indigeneity and determine which cultures were worth preserving. Portraying Indigenous people as being only of the past is part of a genocidal logic that fixes Indigenous people in a temporal frame of extinction and disappearance.

In Latina/o studies, mestizaje has been understood as the mixture of Indigenous, African, and European roots yet its historical origins have not been so innocently void of a racial project of whitening in Latin America, especially in countries like Brazil and Mexico. José Vasconcelos, minister of education in 1920s Mexico, imagined indigeneity and Africanness to be eradicated via whiteness (Saldaña-Portillo 2001). Uncritical deployments of mestizaje in the Chicano movement and by Chicana feminisms have recycled the Mexican state project of eugenics based on whitening and Indigenous/African erasure (Guidotti-Hernández 2011). The Chicano movement came into being by rejecting the hyphenated Mexican-American identities of prior generations, along with their logics of assimilation and liberal approaches to inclusion in the American Dream. Reclaiming the pejorative word "Chicano" was about reclaiming working-class origins and, for some, Indigenous roots. The adoption of Alurista's indigenista poetics into "El Plan Espiritual de Aztlán" (Anaya and Lomelí 1991, 1–5) claimed that bloodlines of the noble Aztecs and their mythic homeland of Aztlán in the Southwest were eternal. While this vision of Aztlán problematically overlays many other Indigenous nations (Chabram-Dernersesian 1992), it was an early attempt by Chicanos to decolonize themselves, even if their means of doing so echoed Mexican state politics of indigenismo and mestizaje. In effect, then, one of the foundational tenets of the Chicano movement conflated indigeneity with indigenismo. By occupying the space of the mythological or the indigenist, Xicana/o scholars not only replicate the Mexican state project of indigenismo, but also fail to name the powerful loss of their indigeneity that is itself a product of coloniality and mestizaje, what María Eugenia Cotera and María Josefina Saldaña-Portillo (2015) call "mestizo mourning." It is ironic that Chicanos would seek their way "home" to Indigenous roots on the very road of indigenismo and mestizaje that deindianized them in the first place. Further, by going

Aztec, indigenists, rather than grapple with the painful recovery from colonization and the historical trauma of loss, occupy a mythologized indigeneity that forecloses settler and arrivant forms of analysis and solidarity with the Indigenous peoples of the lands they now live and work on (Wolfe 2006; Veracini 2010; Byrd 2011).

The editors of the groundbreaking volume *Comparative Indigeneities* (Castellanos, Gutiérrez Nájera, and Aldama 2012) turn from colonial and state-sponsored forms of mestizaje to consider what they call "decolonizing mestizaje," arguing that authors like Gloria Anzaldúa have used mestizaje strategically as a way to resist racial hierarchies in the United States. When asked about her relationship to indigeneity, Anzaldúa precisely names this loss: "To have an Indian ancestry means to fear that la India in me that has been killed for centuries is being killed. It means to suffer psychic fragmentation. It means to mourn the losses—loss of land, loss of language, loss of heritage, loss of trust that all Indigenous people in this country, in Mexico, in the entire planet suffer on a daily basis" (Castellanos, Gutiérrez Nájera, and Aldama 2012, 9). Because of this loss, Anzaldúa proposes the term "new tribalism" as a "social identity that could motivate subordinated communities to work together in coalition" (2012, 9). Anzaldúa reflects, "tengo miedo que, in pushing for mestizaje and a new tribalism, I will 'detribalize' them. Yet I also feel it's imperative we participate in this dialogue no matter how risky" (2012, 12). Finally, she concludes, "the mestizaje and the new tribalism I envision adds to but does not dispossess Indians (or others) from their own history, culture, or home-ethnic identities" (2012, 13). In this tradition, other Chicana and Chicano scholars are standing in the contradictions of what it means to be detribalized but not entirely deindianized and searching out decolonial strategies and life ways, which are most pronounced in the recovery of ancestral

Indigenous knowledges in the realms of healing and spiritual knowledge, as well as in agriculture, food ways, and seed autonomy.

María Josefina Saldaña-Portillo famously asked, "Who is the Indian in Aztlán?" (2001). When I ask my students in Chicana/o studies classes if they consider themselves Indigenous, they often say that their ancestors or grandparents (and some parents) are Indigenous, but that they are not. I probe further, asking how is it that they are Indigenous in the past but not Indigenous in the present? Some say they do not identify as Indigenous because it erases those who are "currently" Indigenous. What going "Aztec" obscures is how "Chicano" can cover a diverse range of Indigenous identities, communities, histories, and practices, especially in the Southwest, where many Mexican Indigenous and American Indians were folded into Chicano urban communities during relocation days, and many others were told by family to just say they were Mexican to avoid anti-Indian hatred by Anglos and mestizos (Tamez 2013). Many families made the decision to not teach their children their Indigenous language to protect them from discrimination, stigma, or violence. While Chicana/o identity can cover over Indigenous identities, it can also, as the underside to mestizaje, mean being detribalized or made vaguely, formerly Indigenous. While Chicana/o indigenismo speaks to the desire to reclaim indigeneity, one issue that has not been addressed fully is the idea that Chicana/o claims to indigeneity are a way of grappling with Indigenous loss—a kind of Chicana/o melancholy or mourning for what appears to no longer exist but is often felt, known, and embodied in other undercover ways of being or subaltern knowledges. Cultural memory through ancestral knowledge is never quite eradicated, as many Chicanas and Chicanos live with Indigenous knowledge systems, whether partial or intact. This is the most common within the realm of spirituality and the realm of healing and medicinal knowledge (P. Gonzales 2012; Facio and Lara 2014).

In addition to reproducing a colonial temporal logic that places indigeneity in the past, within Chicana/o cultural production there is often a tendency to reduce "lo indio" to the ephemeral or to the realm of the spiritual. While reclaiming these knowledges is part of recovering from historical trauma, and ultimately decolonization, this slippage aligns with the "magical negro" trope in signaling what was lost to European enlightenment and is now only possible through the Other in the realm of the magical or nonmaterial. While Emma Pérez (1999) introduced a paradigm shift in the field with the publication of *The Decolonial Imaginary*, the critical work is to enact decolonial imaginaries linked not only to addressing cultural loss, but to current, nonmetaphoric projects of decolonization (Tuck and Yang 2012). A new generation of scholars is challenging the ways in which the Chicano movement and Chicana feminists have uncritically adopted Aztec imaginaries to reclaim their Indigenous roots by focusing on other Mexican American indigeneities (Alberto 2012, forthcoming). Indigenous artists and intellectuals are challenging other narratives of erasure such as the narrative of disappearance in El Salvador, or the way that Hispanic or Ladino identity is applied to Indigenous people who have migrated or urbanized. For example, the Mayan diaspora fled genocidal policies of war in Guatemala but retain their cultures in migration (Boj Lopez 2017; Estrada 2017). Similarly, Taino activists are challenging the colonial logic that Indigenous people of the Caribbean no longer exist (Barreiro 2006; Castanha 2011; Feliciano-Santos 2011).

Migration from Mexico and Central America to the United States has become increasingly Indigenous over the past thirty years, with links many decades prior to the Bracero Program. There are estimates that hundreds of thousands of Indigenous Oaxacans, largely Zapotecs, live and work in Los Angeles, and 30 percent of the California farmworker population are Indigenous, mostly Mixtec and Triqui (Fox and Rivera-Salgado 2004; Ramirez 2007; Stephen 2007; Mines, Nichols, and Runsten 2010). There is also a considerable Mayan migration to Los Angeles, the San Francisco Bay Area, and Houston, Texas (Jonas and Rodriguez 2015), as well as Garifuna migrations to New York and Los Angeles. Hokulani Aikau (2010) argues for the Kanaka Maoli concept of *kuleana* to name the responsibilities Indigenous migrants have to the Indigenous nations and lands they live and work on. A growing Indigenous diaspora from Latin America and the Caribbean raises the question of the role of Indigenous migrants in settler colonial projects. Jodi Byrd (2011) complicates both the settler/Indigenous dichotomy and Veracini's (2010) triad of Indigenous, settler, and immigrant with the idea of the arrivant, indicating that some migration occurs through forced displacement/enslavement. There is still much work to do to understand how Indigenous migrants interact with settler colonial projects. For example, if we take Patrick Wolfe's (2006) mantra that settler colonialism is a structure and not an event, we can complicate Wolfe, by seeing that someone still needs to clean that structure. In the current system of capitalism, since settler colonialism does not operate in a vacuum, those who are the surplus labor are often those dislocated by imperialist projects and neoliberal policies. While Indigenous migrants cannot (yet?) access settler privilege, it is not clear what work the positionality of arrivant (as a subject position) does and how this positionality might make possible the kind of responsibility (or *kuleana*) that Aikau speaks of in relation to the Tongva, Tativium, the Chumash, or Ohlone as Indigenous people of California, for example, many of whom are not federally recognized.

Some of these issues have been addressed by the long-term participation of scholars such as Inés Hernández-Ávila and Inés Talamantez and the formation of the Women's Indigenous Caucus (WINC) within Mujeres Activas en Letras y Cambio Social (MALCS) and in the Indigenous Caucus of the National Association of Chicana and Chicano Studies (NAACS). Within the Native American Indigenous Studies Association, Indigenous scholars have worked to make the association an inclusive space for global Indigenous peoples, while the Abya Yala working group worked to ensure the organization is inclusive of Indigenous scholars from throughout the Americas. Finally, a working group on Critical Latino Indigeneities has been concerned with how Indigenous migration from Latin America, largely Mayan, Mixtec, and Zapotec, is shifting ideas of indigeneity and Latinidad.

29

Labor

Shannon Gleeson

Latina/o studies scholars have looked to "labor" as a central theme for theorizing class inequality, spurring questions about exploitation, alienation, and potential for solidarity (Smith 2013). Operationalizing labor, however, is a complicated matter. Official estimates of the labor force include those who are either "available to work," looking for paid labor, employed, or waiting to be called back to their job (Bureau of Labor Statistics 2014). As such, Latina/o workers (referred to as "Hispanic" by the U.S. government), constitute over 15 percent of the labor force in the United States, and nearly half of the immigrant workforce (U.S. Department of Labor 2012). They are over-represented in traditionally low-wage occupations such as food preparation, building maintenance, farming, and construction. In 2011, Latina/o immigrant workers earned only 77 percent of what their native-born counterparts earned (Bureau of Labor Statistics 2012). These inequities are in part explained by lower levels of human capital, including low levels of English proficiency and educational attainment, in particular for those of Mexican origin (Duncan, Hotz, and Trejo 2006). Institutional barriers have further multiplied the disadvantage that Mexican Americans face, creating what Edward Telles and Vilma Ortiz (2008) refer to as "generations of exclusion." This disadvantage contrasts starkly with the positive selection of much smaller groups of other professional Latinas/os, such as Colombian and Puerto Rican engineers, who nonetheless have contradictory experiences as "privileged marginal migrants" (Rincón 2015, 213).

The predominant conditions of low-wage work for Latinas/os in the United States reveal striking disadvantages. For example, a national study of low-wage workers in the nation's three largest cities found that foreign-born Latinas/os had the highest rate of minimum-wage violations (35 percent), six times that of U.S.-born whites. Latina workers fared worse than their male counterparts (40 versus 24 percent) (Bernhardt et al. 2009). Research on Mexican and Central American immigrants confirm that undocumented workers face more hazardous workplace conditions and are less likely to be compensated for their risk exposure (Orrenius and Zavodny 2009; Hall and Greenman 2014). Foreign-born Latinas/os also represent a disproportionate share of fatal occupational injuries (Loh and Richardson 2004). Sexual harassment and assault on the job have been a major problem for Latinas, compounding what is already a violent journey for those who clandestinely migrated (Southern Poverty Law Center 2009). Indigenous migrants have become an increasingly significant component of migrant labor flows across the southern U.S. border. These workers face particular linguistic challenges and are targets for racial exclusion from both within and beyond the Latina/o community (Holmes 2013).

The range of industries in which Latina/o workers are concentrated often fall outside the law. For example, Latinas/os are over-represented in day labor and other sectors of the informal economy. Abel Valenzuela and colleagues' (2006) survey found that nationwide, 87 percent of day laborers hailed from Mexico and Central America. These workers face an epidemic of being misclassified as *independent contractors*, who by definition do not qualify for employee protections under key federal and state law (NELP 2009; Mukhija and Loukaitou-Sideris 2014). Nearly half of domestic workers are

women of color, and over half of housecleaners are Latinas (Burnham and Theodore 2012). In most states, these domestic workers lack the same enforceable protections as other workers do for wage and hour standards, workers' compensation in the event of injury, and against employer retaliation. In the fields, where Latina/o workers also predominate, most states also exclude farmworkers from the same provisions for overtime and collective bargaining (Perea 2011). In sum, Latina/o labor provides a direct lens for understanding the two-tiered system of labor protection and rights access.

These inequities have been a flashpoint when considering undocumented immigrants in the United States, the largest portions of whom hail from Latin America, including Mexico (59 percent), Central America (11 percent), and South America (7 percent) (Passel and Cohn 2009). While undocumented legal status is not the only factor driving workplace exploitation (Narro 2013), it does act as a "precarity multiplier" (Gleeson 2014). In 1986 the Immigration Reform and Control Act provided amnesty for nearly three million individuals, while also instituting a policy of employer sanctions. While initially supportive of the policy, the AFL-CIO ultimately rejected employer sanctions, in part given employer's frequent use of them as a tool to retaliate against employees (Hamlin 2008). Although undocumented workers qualify for a range of protections, they also "face numerous practical impediments to accessing these rights" (Gordon 2014, 137). Some workers who can show that they are victims of crime may qualify for a U or T visa, which were created by the Victims of Trafficking and Violence Protection Act (VTVPA) in 2000. However, unequivocally proving eligibility and gaining certification from a law enforcement agency can be extremely difficult (Lakhani 2013). Temporary Protected Status has provided short-term deportation relief and work authorization to 340,000 individuals, including significant numbers of Salvadorans (212,000), Hondurans (64,000) and Nicaraguans (3,000) (Messick and Bergeron 2014). This six to eighteen-month-long status, however, can negatively affect the labor market outcomes of these workers and the well-being of their families and broader communities (Menjívar and Abrego 2012).

The challenges facing Latina/o workers have been at the center of the evolving U.S. labor movement. Latina/o immigrant workers (alongside their Filipina/o brothers and sisters) formed the basis of the iconic United Farmworkers movement, and Cesar Chavez has been the enduring (in some ways reimagined) face of immigrant worker rights for years. However, the U.S. labor movement delayed formally accepting the full rights and inclusion of immigrant workers, including Latinas/os. Aside from their place in farmworker struggles, Latinas/os came to be recognized as core elements of the service industry (such as the Service Employees International Union [SEIU]'s Justice for Janitors campaign) and the building trades (as in the National Day Labor Organizing Network) (Milkman 2006). Latina/o leaders such as Enrique Fernandez (UNITE-HERE!), Esther López (UFCW), Eliseo Medina (SEIU), Ana Avendaño (AFL-CIO), and many others have ascended in the labor movement flanks. The swelling strength of the Latina/o labor movement both within traditional labor unions and through newly formed worker centers and coalitions (including the new Change to Win federation), as well as other migrant-led organizations (Fine 2006; Pallares and Flores-González 2010; Voss and Bloemraad 2011), was a key factor in driving the iconic protests that erupted in 2006 in response to the proposed Border Protection, Antiterrorism and Illegal Immigration Control Act of 2005 (HR 4437), which would have further criminalized undocumented migrants.

The labor struggles of Latina/o workers have also been an important aspect of the broader immigrant rights movement, as well as being at the heart of calls for deportation relief and a path to citizenship. Popular rationales of immigrant rights often point to the labor value of migrants and the costly nature of enforcement (Bosniak 2002; Baker-Cristales 2009; Gleeson 2015). Common slogans such as "they come here to work" and "we are workers, not criminals" focus on immigrants as economic producers, rather than felons, purported terrorists, and the unemployed. The DREAM Act, first introduced in 2001, failed to garner significant congressional support. Had it passed, the act would have provided a path to citizenship for high school graduates seeking higher education. In the wake of failed attempts at broader comprehensive immigration reform, President Obama issued an executive action, the Deferred Action for Childhood Arrivals (DACA), which called for the inclusion of undocumented immigrant youth in large part due to the economic boon these educated workers would provide the ailing economy (American Immigration Council 2013; National Immigration Law Center 2014). The proposed Deferred Action for Parental Accountability (DAPA) would have provided eligible formerly undocumented immigrants with work authorization and was billed as an "economic development" strategy for the nation (Oakford 2014). DAPA, though limited in its reach, was blocked by the courts along with an expanded version of DACA. These policies, however, would have left out millions of ineligible undocumented workers. Economic rationales for reform are politically salient and critically necessary to achieve legislative success. They also resonate strongly with the U.S. tradition of neoliberal citizenship, which is tightly tied to the market, and thus valorize the "self-reliant, independent *homo economicus* underlying the ideal model of the worthy citizen" (Volpp 2014, 82).

Intersectional scholars have for decades inserted critical questions into our understanding of labor and power, especially as they relate to women, racial and sexual minorities, and immigrants (Zavella 1987; Glenn 1992; Manalansan 2006). For example, the official focus on "workers, not criminals," as many campaigns emphasize, obscures the ways in which the penal system exacerbates wage and employment inequality, especially for African American and Latino men of color (Western and Pettit 2005). Welfare reform policies of the mid-1990s tied work to social provisions and removed many legal permanent residents (many of whom were Latina women) from eligibility. In conjunction with the Illegal Immigration Reform and Immigrant Responsibility Act and the Antiterrorism and Effective Death Penalty Act (both of 1996), the Personal Responsibility and Work Opportunity Reconciliation Acts (PRWORA) (also of 1996) brought together the ideals of punitive immigration and welfare reform. PRWORA solidified the supremacy of paid wage work over other forms of labor in the private sphere and excised noncitizen immigrant women entirely from the social safety net. Critics argue that by pushing women with little support for childcare or with little training into "workfare" in order to qualify for public assistance, Latinas/os were blocked from pathways for social mobility (Marchevsky and Theoharis 2006). In parallel fashion, the sweeping changes in immigration policy at this time paved the way for local interior enforcement programs such as 287(g) of the Immigration and Nationality Act (which created voluntary agreements with local jurisdictions) and later the Secure Communities program, which made this cooperation more compulsory. Both policies, which have seen a revival under the Trump presidency despite previous legal challenges, are not officially focused on workplace policy. However, their impact has immersed the day to day lives of Latina/o immigrant workers in racialized

surveillance and fear that a mundane traffic infraction en route to work would result in certain deportation (Lacayo 2010). These policies, alongside mass media constructions of Latinas/os as a demographic, political, and economic threat, further marginalizes Latinas/os in the United States (Santa Ana 2002; Chavez 2008).

Amidst these contested struggles for recognition, no perspective on Latina/o labor is complete without a global and transnational lens to understand the causes and consequences of migrant labor. For example, Saskia Sassen (1988) points to the export of global labor capital from the United States to Latin America and its impact on subsequent migration flows. This foreign direct investment came with a cost. For example, the proliferation of maquiladoras at Mexico's northern border largely employed young females, many of whom would become victims of *feminicidio* (Fregoso and Bejarano 2009). Meanwhile, the wages of Latina/o labor in the United States frequently support extended households here and in sending communities of origin. The United States is the primary sender of remittances, with $22 billion sent to Mexico in 2012, and another $5.4 billion to Guatemala, $4.6 billion to Colombia, and $4.2 billion to El Salvador (Cohn, Gonzalez-Barrera, and Cuddington 2013; Migration Policy Institute 2014).

Globalization has shaped labor-organizing efforts across Latin America. For example, in Central America, transnational activist campaigns led largely by student groups became critical to the anti-sweatshop movement (Anner 2011). Transnational resistance was also crucial to opposing U.S. foreign policy during the civil war in El Salvador, and migrant workers continue to play a major role in the current political scene, often mixing their civic engagement here and afar (COHA 2014). Today, transnational advocacy for the rights of Latina/o workers in the United States has implicated a range of institutional targets, including efforts to hold the sending state accountable for the rights of their co-nationals working abroad. The Mexican government's move into a realm of "active engagement" (Délano 2011) was prompted in large part by the work of grass-roots migrant-led organizations and unions with a strong immigrant worker presence, such as the United Food and Commercial Workers. They have demanded protection for Mexican immigrant workers in the United States, as well as increased accountability on the part of the Mexican government for non-migrant workers working for multinational corporations such as Wal-Mart (Bada and Gleeson 2015).

In sum, as the field of Latina/o studies considers the role of "labor," it will need to grapple with questions of whose labor counts, what it is worth, and the relationship of work to political and social membership. Non-economic forms of labor, including reproductive and emotional labor, should be valued, just as its commodification should be critiqued. As the Latina/o diaspora grows, it will also become imperative to consider labor across the borders of identity, the law, and the nation. Traditional forms of labor relations, and labor representation, will continue to be provide inadequate paradigms for understanding the reality of Latina/o work in the twenty-first century.

30
Language
John Nieto-Phillips

Among Latinas and Latinos, language is a complex and sometimes vexing matter. Inextricably bound up in notions of identity and civic belonging, language lies at the center of contemporary discourse about immigration, education, and citizenship; as such, it is inherently a political subject. But language usage is also intensely personal, often grounded in intimate contexts and choices. While both public and private dilemmas over language arise from the pressures of the present day, they might also be understood as the product of historical forces spanning oceans and continents.

For centuries, states have utilized language, variously, to amalgamate, colonize, coopt, or marginalize groups of people. In the Western world, Latin was the Roman Empire's lingua franca, enabling the administration of vast domains composed of disparate societies and tongues. In the modern age, the French, English, Portuguese, and Spanish empires used language to strengthen and expand their imperial domains (Lodares 2007).

The Spanish Crown, for example, came to view the language of Castile as foundational to its peninsular and, eventually, global ambitions. During the fifteenth century, *castellano* eclipsed other Iberian vernaculars and aided the "Catholic Monarchs," Ferdinand and Isabella, in their consolidation of their Iberian dominions. During the sixteenth century, it enabled a succession of Spanish kings to manage a vast empire that extended from Africa to Oceania, and from the Philippines to the Americas. Spain's global deployment of *castellano* was, by some accounts, strategic, aided in no small part by the codification of the language in 1492. In that momentous year, the Spanish scholar Antonio de Nebrija authored the first-ever compendium of Castilian grammar, which he dedicated to Queen Isabella. It is said that when Nebrija presented the book to the queen, she asked, "Why should I wish to read such a book, when I already know the language?" To this, Nebrija famously replied, "Your Majesty, language is the perfect instrument of empire." During more than four centuries, language proved one of Spain's most effective tools in extending its global reach (Elliott 2002; Nadeau and Barlow 2013).

In Spain's colonies, Castilian was the language of power, privilege, and education. But language was not a totalizing force, as Nebrija's statement might suggest. Millions who were subjected to Spain's exploits spoke a multitude of Indigenous languages and continued to do so even as their numbers plummeted through the use of violence, the introduction of disease, and exploitation at the hands of colonial officials. Indeed, Indigenous linguistic resistance, as well as accommodation and syncretism, are evident throughout the historical record. As Castilian spread throughout the Americas, it gave rise to new forms, prompting King Phillip V, in 1714, to consecrate the Real Academia Española (RAE). Founded a year earlier and modeled on institutions in Italy and France, the RAE sought to standardize the Spanish language and to guarantee its "purity" in the face of "errors" and "ignorance." That pretense was indicative of the extent to which the language had already been influenced by other tongues, including French, Nahuatl, Arawak, and any number of other Indigenous languages in the Americas (Medina, del Valle, and Monteagudo 2013; Nadeau and Barlow 2013).

Nebrija's association of language with empire becomes more compelling when one asks, "What happens when empires decline?" "Do imperial languages follow their demise?" Hardly. History is replete with examples to the contrary. In Francophone, Lusophone, and Anglophone lands, imperial languages became living emblems of new national identities—even as they remained enduring echoes of empire. When Spain lost its American colonies to independence during the early nineteenth century and to U.S. intervention in 1898, the Spanish language remained the most durable vestige of Spain's former glory, one imbued with ideological and geopolitical power. Moreover, the RAE continued to hold sway over matters of language in the Americas by way of its publications and the rise of affiliated *academias* between the 1870s and the 1940s (del Valle 2013; Nadeau and Barlow 2013).

During the early years of the twentieth century, Spanish linguists and intellectuals championed a global cultural movement known as "Hispanism," which involved the study of Spanish language, history, and culture. Hispanism served to reclaim some degree of Spain's influence in the Americas by way of "soft power," a concept coined by political scientist Joseph Nye (1990) to denote a nation's use of cultural persuasion rather than political or economic coercion. Within the United States, Hispanists generated broad interest in the study of the Spanish language and newfound appreciation for Spanish history and culture; within a generation, a transatlantic network of U.S. and Spanish scholars managed to transform centuries-old U.S. prejudice against Spain into admiration. They did that with institutional support.

From the 1910s through midcentury, universities and organizations invested heavily in Hispanic studies. Stanford, Columbia, Harvard, Berkeley, New Mexico, Illinois, and Wisconsin became nodes within a Hispanist network that had enveloped the Americas. University presidents actively recruited Spaniards to develop their Romance Languages departments, spawning collaborations between U.S. and Spanish scholars. Concurrently, wealthy patrons—most notably Archer Milton Huntington, heir to an industrialist fortune—invested heavily in Spanish art, language, and culture. It was Huntington who in 1909 founded the Hispanic Society of America in New York City, housed in a museum that would become a hub of exhibitions and events drawing public attention to Spain's cultural splendor; and it was Huntington who bankrolled the new Hispanic Studies program at Columbia University in 1916, as well as the nascent American Association of Teachers of Spanish (AATS) a year later. Thanks, in part, to the AATS's promotional efforts, Spanish language and literature courses become staple offerings at universities and secondary schools. As early as the 1920s, high school enrollments in Spanish language courses exceeded enrollments in French, German, and Latin combined. For generations, the U.S. public had been raised on "Black Legend" tales of Spanish despotism and depravity. What Hispanism offered, then, was a fresh and positive appraisal of Spanish history, culture, and language, and one that enhanced Spain's global standing following the loss of its empire.

Just as Spanish was an implement of Spain's empire, English became a tool of U.S. global expansion and imperialism dating from the nineteenth century. Adoption of the English language by Spanish speakers in the United States was commonly cited as a prerequisite for the enjoyment of "full" citizenship, including the right to vote or to participate in self-government. For Spanish-speaking individuals in lands taken by the United States—and for emigrants to the United States, more broadly—the pathway to inclusion in the body politic, many officials insisted, involved their Americanization; and the key to Americanization was the adoption of the English language.

For example, when the United States acquired New Mexico in 1848 following the two-year war with Mexico, Congress denied the territory's request for admission into the Union for more than six decades, citing the population's tenacious use of Spanish in public realms, insufficient literacy in English, and large non-white (Mexican and Native American) population (Nieto-Phillips 1999; Lozano 2013). When statehood was finally granted in 1912, New Mexico adopted both languages for use in government and education. By 1940, however, Spanish had been largely relegated to a subject of study in secondary schools, despite ongoing efforts to preserve bilingual instruction on the grounds that, among other things, it would bridge the family-school divide while promoting pan-Americanism. Although the state remained officially bilingual, English had become the principal language of public education.

In the territory of Puerto Rico, seized by the United States in 1898 during the Spanish-American War, language policy was also hotly contested as U.S. officials sought to Americanize the island, ostensibly as a necessary step to statehood, which itself was deeply divisive (Nieto-Phillips 1999; Lozano 2013). The outcome, however, differed markedly from that of New Mexico's struggles. In 1948, following a half-century of policies prioritizing English language in the schools, Puerto Rico reinstated Spanish as the official language of public instruction. Educators and lawmakers on the island pointed to Spanish as a symbol of their Puerto Rican national identity and political autonomy (Nieto-Phillips 1999; Lozano 2013). The language histories of New Mexico and Puerto Rico reveal the complex and often competing ideologies that fueled Hispanism, Americanization, nationalism, and pan-Americanism. They also suggest ways that Spanish-speakers living in the United States navigated the politics of language in post-imperial and neocolonial contexts.

By the 1950s, both English and Spanish had come to define the public and personal worlds of U.S. Latinas/os.

Politicians, educators, and parents, alike, tended to view English as instrumental to their civic and economic ambitions, though they remained divided over the value of Spanish. Assimilationists eschewed Spanish and adopted English, believing that the fight against their discrimination, segregation, and exclusion necessitated cultural and linguistic sacrifices. Some civic organizations, including the League of United Latin American Citizens (LULAC), founded in 1929, declared English as their official language, though in practice they operated in both languages. Pluralists espoused a more adaptive strategy to advance their interests, viewing home culture and language as an asset, rather than a liability. Many parents insisted on the preservation of Spanish as a home language, even as they fought for their children to be educated in English.

For their part, Spanish-speaking schoolchildren during the 1940s and 1950s often became caught in the vortex of adults' conflicting ideologies and agendas. Latina/o autobiographies are replete with coming-of-age predicaments over language and identity. Some accounts, like that of Frances Esquibel Tywoniak (Tywoniak and García 2000), describe feeling caught between two worlds (home and school) and two languages (Spanish and English). Like many of her bilingual contemporaries, Tywoniak acculturated by selectively adopting elements of Anglo-American culture while remaining grounded in her Mexican and New Mexican heritage. Perhaps more notably, Richard Rodriguez (1982), in his autobiography, *Hunger of Memory*, captured the painful dilemma of a child afflicted with shame regarding his family's Mexican heritage, dark physical (racial) appearance, and Spanish language, and torn between public and private identities. When the book appeared in 1982, it drew criticism for Rodriguez's embrace of English as a central feature of his assimilation and "public self" and his unflinching denunciation of bilingual education and affirmative action (Portes and Rumbaut 2001).

Widespread contempt for Rodriguez's assimilationism reflected a major shift in popular politics of language. During the civil rights movements of the 1960s and 1970s, Spanish had become a symbol of ethnic identity and pride. In many cities, Latina/o students and parents mobilized to demand more language resources, respect for and study of their culture and history, more equitable education, and more opportunities for higher education. Numerous states and localities implemented bilingual education programs that were partially funded by the federal Bilingual Education Act of 1968. While the federal law drew attention and resources to challenges faced by Spanish-speaking schoolchildren, it sought to transition those students into English-speaking classrooms, rather than fully develop their proficiency in both languages. Such programs were modeled on subtractive bilingualism, whose ultimate objective is to mainstream students into English. In recent years, educators have developed dual-language, two-way, and immersion programs modeled on additive bilingualism, which advances multilingual capacity (O. García 2009). The dichotomous premise of bilingual programs, whether subtractive or additive by design, tends to ignore the complex language practices that define daily life for multilingual Latinas and Latinos. Those practices, known as "translanguaging," may include code-switching, selective borrowing of words, lexical shifts, word play, neologisms, or other moves that defy easy categorization, but that sometimes are collectively referred to as "Spanglish." The English-Spanish dichotomy further obscures the growing number of Latinas/os who are speakers of Indigenous languages, such as Yucatec Maya or Quechua, for example. That said, Latinas and Latinos tend to view both Spanish and English as useful in their daily lives and as important to their sense of identity. The Pew Hispanic Research Center (Taylor et al. 2012) reports that nine in ten Latinas/os believe Latina/o immigrants need to learn English to succeed in the United States, but fully 95 percent believe that future Latina/o generations need to be able to speak Spanish. As the progeny of two empires, Latinas and Latinos are keen to possess English as well as Spanish—two instruments of global power.

31

Latinidad/es

Frances R. Aparicio

The question "How is it possible to know Latinidad?," posed by late queer Latino critic José Esteban Muñoz (2000), reveals the semantic messiness and the multiple layers of meanings that the term "Latinidad" suggests in its numerous and contradictory iterations. Yet, rather than indulge in skepticism about this term, I exhort Latina/o studies scholars to reclaim it and deploy it in ways that allow our communities and others to exert agency and more control over the public definitions of who we are. If the term "Latinidad" emerged most strongly in literary studies as an abstract signifier that remitted us to the condition of being Latina/o, today it is more strongly anchored in the social, everyday realities of our diasporic communities and in the spaces populated by Latinas/os of various nationalities, generations, immigrant statuses, and racial and gender identities. It now signals the mutual transculturations and horizontal hierarchies that emerge in these spaces. In this essay, I will trace some of the semantic shifts in the ways Latina/o studies scholars have deployed the term. If umbrella terms have been appropriated by the market, by media, and by activists, as G. Cristina Mora (2014) has examined in *Making Hispanics*, the term "Latinidad" has also been claimed as a hemispheric framework for the study of the Americas, as well as critiqued and rejected as a label that homogenizes the rich heterogeneity of our communities and inadequately, if at all, recognizes the inclusion of Afro-Latinas/os and mixed-race Latinas/os.

Since the 1980s most of the popular debates around labels of identity have centered on Hispanic versus Latino/a (Oboler 1995). Yet now most scholars deploy the terms "Latina/o" and "Latinidad" in generalizing ways. There are underlying tensions, however, that reveal our anxieties about umbrella terms. Marta Caminero-Santangelo (2007), in *On Latinidad*, summarizes the multiple scholarly voices that have resisted the term "Latina/o" as a reference to our collective identity. While it is the preferred term in academic circles and in many community organizations and groups, it is still suspect for its homogenizing potential. This effect is evident in the many scholarly works that include the word "Latina/o" in their title in order to sell, yet ironically tend to caution against the "homogenizing" effects of this term, which "elides historical specificity, ethnic and racial differences, sexual preference, and varying class perspectives into a monolithic conception" (McCracken 1999, 5). Chicana/o scholars have denounced Latinidad as a challenge and threat to the institutional spaces for which Chicanas/os have struggled (I. García 1996; Chabram-Dernersesian 2003). In 1987, Gloria Anzaldúa's *Borderlands / La Frontera* positioned the immigrant Mexicanos and the "Latinos from Central and South America" (1987, 87) as groups that needed to learn about Chicanas/os in order to create a truly strong front against Anglo domination. She critiqued the separatism that the dominant society imposes on people of color in order to "weaken" them. Instead, Anzaldúa proposes mutual knowledge about and among minorities, which will allow a stronger sense of an oppositional community. While she urges her readers to learn about each other, the fact that she separates Chicanas/os from undocumented immigrants, from Mexicanas/os, and from other Latina/o immigrants suggests her own personal awareness that these groups are not the "same" as hers. This suspicion is articulated earlier in "How to Tame a Wild Tongue," where she acknowledges her own anxiety about speaking Spanish in front of other Latinas (1987, 58). Much later, in 1996, Ignacio García denounced "a militant form of Latinidad" as a challenge to Chicano studies, arguing that other Latina/o immigrants claim "racism" and "poverty" as a common experience with Chicanas/os and thus demand inclusion into the academic spaces originally fought for by the latter. Despite the significant apertures of many Chicana/o spaces, institutions, and scholars vis-à-vis the larger Latina/o community in the United States—for instance, the changes in the names of programs and departments that include the term "Latina/o"; the curricular inclusion of Central Americans in the United States and of other ethnicities in teaching; the central participation of Chicana/o scholars in the Latina/o Studies Association (LSA)—even today there exist significant anxieties that the increasing strength and visibility of this "Latina/o" presence will ultimately destroy the institutions and resources that Chicanas/os have fought for in decades. This defensive posture on behalf of Chicana/o studies is also shared by Puerto Rican studies on the East Coast, which by the late 1990s was facing the challenges of how to represent and include Colombianas/os, Dominicanas/os, and the more recent Mexican immigrants in New York, where the proportion of Puerto Ricans in the Latina/o population decreased from 80 percent to 30 percent (Fritz 2003).

The discourses of exceptionalism that continue to emerge from each of the three historically major Latina/o groups—Mexican American, U.S. Puerto Rican, and Cuban American—constitute strong obstacles to engaging in comparative work. The Hispanic Trends Project conducted by the Pew Hispanic Center in 2012 revealed that 69 percent of Latinas/os questioned believed that Hispanics from different countries all have separate and distinct cultures, while 29 percent believe they "share one Hispanic/Latino culture" (Taylor et al. 2012). This suggests that among U.S. Latinas/os, there is a strong, commonsense knowledge that, despite post- and trans-nationalism, national identities are still strong values in our lives. Writing about the demographic diversification of a global New York, Juan Flores (1996) consistently argued for the need to recognize the historical primacy of Puerto Ricans in the city as the "original" Latina/o group, which all other more recent newcomers must recognize as a model. For him, Puerto Ricans are to be seen as "the historical touchstone against which much else that follows must be tested" (Flores 1996, 147). This argument leads to primordial hierarchies among U.S. Latinas/os. The grassroots origins of Chicana/o studies and Puerto Rican studies, informed by imaginaries of cultural nationalism, have historically fueled the resistance to acknowledge similarities and shared experiences. For colonized communities, one of the strategies of resistance has been precisely performing nationalism in the public space. Thus, there is a need to examine further the slippages between justified cultural specificity and exceptionalism.

In 2003, Angie Chabram mapped the contradictory meanings and social and political locations of the term "Latina/o" as it has been deployed by a variety of scholars, highlighting its close association with an increasing globalized world as well as its continued risks as a potentially homogenizing label: "If it is true that the promise of 'Latino/a' lies in its ability to access multiple social identities and their realities in political study, it is equally true that these aspects of its articulation remain difficult to access within global articulations of Latino Studies that do not allow us to see 'the differentiation along the lines of gender and sexuality,' 'the specific identity positions of Black Latinos' and 'mixed Latino backgrounds,' 'the critical understandings of translocality,' and the no less important and often obscured differences of social class" (Chabram-Dernersesian 2003, 116). The MexiRican feminist scholar states that this is in part due to "what might be construed as a settling down of semantics and poetics in the language of many emergent Latino studies" (2003, 116).

In the spirit of Chabram's critique, I have examined the more recent deployments of Latina/o and Latinidad as the basis for new scholarly conceptualizations. Unlike Chabram, I have found a more dynamic semantic field around these terms, which has allowed critics to modify and rewrite them. I have described the term "Latina/o" as a site of "competing authenticities and paradigms of identity that, together, and in conflict with each other, constitute the heterogeneous experiences of various Latina/o national groups" (Aparicio 1999b, 10). Thus, it is important to highlight the mobile, nomadic nature of this signifier, for it allows the field and its practitioners to rewrite, transform, and reclaim the term, even if, and precisely because, the signified, its referential content, the Latin American descent population in the United States, is constantly changing.

The plural term "Latinidades" has been preferred by many scholars to refer to the shared experiences of subordination, resistance, and agency of the various national groups of Latin American in the United States. "Latinidad" has been highly contested and defined in various ways. While for some it is still a problematic term, seen as "dangerously essentializing and rigidly identitarian . . . primarily functioning on literary, often elite realms" (Roque Ramírez 2007, 8), the plural form of the term has allowed other scholars to embrace it as an index of the diverse geocultural profiles of Latinas/os across the United States. The terms "Latino" and "Latinidad," as Marta Caminero-Santangelo writes, are of a dual nature: while they risk homogenization, they also allow scholars to produce the comparative work that "undermines the category's homogenizing tendencies"

(2007, 219). In other words, only under the rubric of "Latina/o" can we do the comparative work that highlights the differences, specificities, and commonalities among the diverse national groups.

"Latinidades" as a conceptual framework allows me to document, analyze, and theorize the processes by which diverse Latinas/os interact with, dominate, and transculturate each other. While the analysis of vertical power differentials between the Anglo-dominant society and Latina/o racial, ethnic, and sexual minorities is still much needed, given state ideologies of border security and anti-immigrant anxieties in these neoliberal and global times, I have suggested that we also need to begin to examine the horizontal scope of power differences, conflicts, tensions, and affinities between and among Latinas/os of diverse national identities, or what I call "horizontal hierarchies" (Aparicio 2014). These power differentials, in turn, are closely linked to geocultural regions and territories, each of which is producing unique Latina/o profiles. Chicago itself includes nineteen different Latin American national groups, from the Mexicano population that represents 79 percent, to Dominicanos at 4,000 or less than 1 percent. In New York, Mexicanos are now the third-largest Latino group in the city, forcing Puerto Ricans to reconsider their own privileged position as the "original" Latina/o minority in this region. In the Southeast, Mexicanos and Central Americans are now settling down in many small towns, radically transforming black-white relations in the region. In California, on the West Coast, and in the Northwest, Central Americans, particularly Guatemalans, Salvadorans, and Indigenous groups, are transculturating Chicana/o spaces, opening them up to the historical memories and traumas of the Central American populations. Karina Alvarado has approached these liminal positionalities as the result of the "anxieties of transculturation" on the part of dominant Latina/o groups in the region (2013, 367).

The term "Latinidades," in this regard, has been open to transformations and rewritings. It has been consistently modified by additional labels of identity that anchor it in a particular subgroup within the U.S. Latina/o sector. A group of scholars in Amherst, Massachusetts, are deploying the term "translatinidades" to refer to the translocal migrations of Latinas/os and Latin Americans, not only within the United States but also in Asia, Europe, and Africa. In terms of gender and sexuality, Jennifer Rudolph (2012) has proposed the term "masculatinidad" in her eponymous book as she examines the intersectionality of race, class, and masculinity among U.S. Latinas/os. Horacio Roque Ramírez has highlighted the term "Latinaje" to foreground the "always already plural process of making Latino worlds from below" and the "collectivist character in the creation of public cultures" (2007, 8), thus queering the term, as Juana María Rodríguez (2003), Alicia Arrizón (2006), and Ramón Rivera-Servera (2012) have done as well. The term has also been given gender modifiers such as Latinidades feministas in the *Telling to Live* anthology (Latina Feminist Group 2001). Deborah Pacini Hernandez (2010) has recently referred to "cosmopolatino" in the context of the musical flows and border crossings of the Colombian *cumbia*. Likewise, "Latinidad" has also been modified by a national identity, as in "Puerto Rican Latinidades" (Rúa and García 2007), in order to transcend the exhausted binaries that have been erected between national spaces and the sites of Latinidad (Rúa 2012).

Mérida Rúa and Lorena García's (2007) article, entitled "Processing Latinidad," highlights how Latinidad emerges from within nationalist spaces. They describe "complex moments of convergence" as they point to the Mexicanized version of the Puerto Rican plena "Qué bonita bandera / es la bandera mexicana," performed on a float sponsored by Puerto Rican politicians during the Mexican Independence Parade in Chicago. Local politicians, such as Luis Gutiérrez, have continued to make public overtures aimed at consolidating the political power of Latinas/os in the city, producing a strategic form of Latinidad. The ways in which Latinidad in Chicago brings into the public sphere the convergence of different national identities, as in this example, makes it an ideal site for exploring the power dynamics, interactions, and potential transculturations among Latin-American descent populations, which could be termed "interlatina/o" social dynamics. Latinidad has traveled from a semiotics of suspicion in which modifiers anchor it to a particular identity or community to one of plurality that recognizes the heterogeneity from within.

Moreover, the morphological shift of the term "Latinidad" from a label of identity to a doing, a political and liberatory action, is significant and illustrative of these semantic transformations in the scholarship. Marta Caminero-Santangelo, for instance, concludes her book *On Latinidad* by emphasizing the affiliative texture, the relational identities, and the "solidarity" that the terms "Latino" and "Latinidad" evoke (2007, 213–19). Contesting the numerous instances in which Latina/o identifications are deemed "strategic," Caminero-Santangelo argues that identifying as Latina/o "also allows us to express, to ourselves and to others, our commitment to attending to the historical and present differences among Latinos" (2007, 219), thereby speaking to the self-fulfilling effect of the term. The more we use it, the more we construct spaces and discourses of Latinidad. The equation of Latinidad with "solidarity" continues to engage with the activist, oppositional, and politicized deployments of this term. From the different disciplinary frame of political science, Cristina Beltrán echoes Caminero's postmodern approach to Latinidad—"the category . . . produces what it claims to represent" (2010, 9)—as well as exhorting scholars to reconsider Latinidad "as a site of permanent political contestation, as a site

of ongoing resignifiability—as a political rather than merely descriptive category" (2010, 9). Examining civic Latinidad as a "commitment to unity" and as illustrated through "mass participation and innovative performativity" (2010, 16), Beltrán adds another semantic layer to our understandings of Latinidad, one that tweaks the dominant homogenizations that we have all challenged for decades. Finally, Michael Rodríguez-Muñiz (2010), in "Grappling with Latinidad," discusses the participation of Puerto Ricans in Chicago in the struggles on behalf of their undocumented Mexican counterparts. He lucidly examines the ways in which U.S. Puerto Ricans deploy their citizenship—a privilege that traditionally marks this colonized sector as different from other Latinas/os—precisely "into a responsibility to act" (2010, 252). Thus, Latinidad sheds its homogenizing effects to become a signifier and label of collective identity that propels U.S. Latinas/os to become political agents and to have a public voice—hence, the term "liberatory Latinidad" (2010, 253), as Rodríguez-Muñiz proposes. By now, the signifier deserves our close attention as a semantic field rich with possibilities for empowerment.

32

Law

Enid Trucios-Haynes

The current public image of Latinas/os in the United States is that of the foreign, racialized outsider, too often labeled by the pejorative term of "illegal immigrant" or "illegal alien" (Brimelow 1995; Johnson 1996; C. García 2012). This matters because such perceptions influence policy makers and can affect Latina/o rights under U.S. law, particularly within the immigration system (Johnson 2009; Lopez, Morin, and Taylor 2010). This negative image persists although three in four Latinas/os are either U.S.-born (65 percent) or naturalized U.S. citizens (11 percent) (Krogstad and Lopez 2014). It is also true that immigration law and policy disproportionately impacts Latinas/os, who are the largest segment of the foreign-born group population in the United States (55 percent) and who represent 77 percent of the undocumented population. In 2012, Latinas/os were the largest minority group, totaling 54 million.

Critical Latina/o legal theory (LatCrit) analyzes issues of race and civil rights with a distinct emphasis on U.S. immigration law and policy (Johnson 2013). The LatCrit focus reveals the anti-Latina/o bias, couched in anti-immigrant sentiments, which often obscures the nature of the discrimination experienced by many (American Immigration Council 2008). Immigration law and policy concerns about national security overshadow the excessively restrictive impact of these laws on Latinas/os. The public's understanding of this context is limited by the legal construction of Latinas/os as an indeterminate racial group (G. Martinez 1997a; Gross 2007). LatCrit scholars examine the historic patterns of inequality and discrimination, exposing the link between past discrimination and current conditions, as well as demonstrating connections to the experiences of other historically marginalized groups (Haney López 1996, 2003). Over the past two decades, this history has been concealed by virulent anti-immigrant rhetoric that targets all Latinas/os. Immigration opponents encouraged state and local laws hostile to Latina/o undocumented people in the 2000s, and have thwarted recent federal immigration reform efforts.

The fact that Latinas/os are situated outside the dominant black-white racial paradigm leads to their indeterminate racial identification. Eighteenth-century racial group theories, premised on the biology of white supremacy, formed the foundation of immigration law and continue to impact it today. Racial concepts and identities, embedded in U.S. law, are integral to civil rights protection and are used to enforce civil rights laws and to monitor equal access in housing, education, employment, and other areas for populations that historically experienced discrimination and differential treatment because of race or ethnicity. The term "Hispanic" was implemented in 1977 by the Office of Budget Statistics and added to the U.S. census in 1980 to recognize this historic discrimination, although designating it as an "ethnicity" marginalizes Latina/o discrimination. While Latinas/os are protected under civil rights laws from national-origin discrimination, evidence of this discrimination is often very difficult to establish and is not based on a Latina/o group identification. The Supreme Court also has been unclear about the racial status of Latinas/os when it has invalidated discriminatory practices.

This indeterminate racial group identification no longer reflects the reality of Latina/o life in the United States. Bias, prejudice, and negative stereotypes affect daily lives, as well as law and policy. A majority of Latinas/os understand their identity in the United States in racial terms, regardless of their racial identity in their countries of origin or ancestry (Pew Research Center 2015b). This emerging Latina/o racial identity does not fit neatly within the traditional black-white racial paradigm. LatCrit scholars embrace this disruption of traditional racial identity hierarchies and suggest that equality and justice must include a multidimensional and comparative understanding of racial concepts (Matambanadzo, Valdes, and Vélez Martínez 2016).

Latina/o-centered scholarship has documented long-standing discrimination, which includes twentieth-century lynchings and other violence against Latinas/os, harmful and degrading stereotypes, and a lack of representation in the media and other areas of U.S. life. Foreign-sounding names, immigration status, accent, or inability to speak English are contributing factors.

Legal strategies to combat this discrimination included challenges to segregated schools, in Arizona, California, and Texas, both before and after the landmark case of *Brown v. Board of Education* (1954). In *Mendez v. Westminster School District of Orange County* (1947), the Ninth Circuit Court of Appeals invalidated the school district's segregation policy. It noted that the harms of segregation "foster antagonisms in the children and suggest an inferiority among them where none exists." The court's rationale was reiterated by the Supreme Court in *Brown v. Board of Education* when it noted that the segregation of black schoolchildren "generates feelings of inferiority as to their status in the community that may affect their hearts and minds in a way unlikely to be undone."

In *Hernandez v. Texas* (1954), a Supreme Court case decided two weeks before *Brown v. Board of Education*, the Court found pervasive discrimination against Mexicans in terms of education, public accommodations, and bathroom facilities in one local community (Crook 2008). The challengers argued that the selection process for juries was applied in a discriminatory manner, and the discrimination in education and facilities established the intent to harm Mexicans as a group. The Court found the jury selection practice was unconstitutional and recognized that "differences in race and color have defined easily identifiable groups which have at times required the aid of the courts in securing equal treatment." The Court did not recognize Latinas/os as a racial group, but instead noted that the Constitution protects more than two classes and is directed at more than the differences between blacks and whites.

Some legal challenges to Latina/o segregation relied on the indeterminate racial identification. Before segregation was declared unconstitutional in *Brown v. Board of Education*, discrimination targeting Latinas/os was justified by government officials who argued that Mexicans were white and that therefore the Fourteenth Amendment Equal Protection Clause, which provides that no state shall deny to any person within its jurisdiction "the equal protection of the laws," provided no protection. Later government officials argued that schools attended by blacks and Latinas/os were desegregated because Mexicans should be classified as white. Latinas/os in some cases argued that they were white as a litigation strategy.

Some LatCrit scholars have advocated a racial group identification, or a pan-Latina/o political identity (Oquendo 1995; Haney López 1996). Nearly all reject the rigid black-white paradigm as insufficient to recognize the multidimensional Latina/o experience. Scholars rely on theories of racial identity-formation based on internal (self) and external (public) identification. The U.S. census also currently relies on self-identification (U.S. Census Bureau 2013). This acknowledges that races and racial differences are socially constructed, yet also recognizes that "the concept of race continues to play a fundamental role in structuring and representing the social world" (Omi and Winant 1994). Although the biological "science" of race has been rejected, race is "a concept which signifies and symbolizes social conflicts and interests by referring to different types of human bodies" (Omi and Winant 1994). The U.S. racial hierarchy, relying on the concept of biological race, is described as a form of "racial stratification," built upon the model of a "hierarchical structure" of communities of color, instead of a model that "emphasizes the subordinate position of all racial and ethnic minorities" (Gotanda 1996). Latinas/os occupy a "position" within this entrenched racial hierarchy (Trucios-Haynes 1997, 2001).

It is obvious that Latinas/os have been the target of racism—of policies, law, and public perceptions based on stereotypes, bias, and prejudice. A 2012 Associated Press (AP) poll showed that most Americans expressed anti-Latina/o sentiments. A 2011 AP survey found that 52 percent of whites expressed explicit anti-Latina/o attitudes. A corresponding poll in 2012 found that 57 percent of whites had an implicit bias against Latinas/os. To compare, the poll established similar explicit (51 percent) and implicit (56 percent) anti-Black prejudice.

Latinas/os are perceived as a racial group. News media report on "black" and "brown" concerns regarding discrimination, educational achievement, and other issues. The term "illegal immigrant" is a racially coded term referring to Latinas/os generally, and more recently to Mexicans (C. Garcia 2012). As of April 2013, the AP no longer uses "illegal" to describe a person, and the *New York Times* announcement of new guidance for its editors was followed by other major newspapers (Colford 2013; Guskin 2013; Haughney 2013).

State and local anti-immigrant laws after 2010 discriminated against Latinas/os and were designed to limit access to housing and work (McKanders 2010). These laws targeted anyone perceived to be undocumented, including U.S. citizens and long-term permanent residents. The Arizona law, invalidated by the U.S. Supreme Court in *Arizona v. United States* (2012), required local law enforcement to identify those they believed to be deportable, primarily those viewed as undocumented.

Anti-immigrant laws after 2010 in Alabama, Georgia, Indiana, Pennsylvania, South Carolina, and Utah were similar to Jim Crow laws that excluded African Americans from communities and legally enforced segregation from the end of the Civil War in 1865 until 1954 (McKanders 2010). State and local legislators supported the anti-immigrant laws as necessary to address the failure of the federal government to restrict undocumented immigration. Opponents charged that the intent was to enable discrimination and exclude all Latinas/os, regardless of immigration status, especially in the South where no Latina/o or immigrant communities existed two decades ago (McKanders 2010).

Latinas/os understand that this discrimination is directed toward them as a group. A growing majority of Latinas/os say that discrimination is a major problem preventing them from succeeding in the United States, and this sentiment is most strongly expressed by Latinas/os born outside the United States (Pew Research Center 2010). In 2010, Americans viewed Latinas/os as more targeted for discrimination than African Americans.

The corrosive effect of anti-immigrant laws includes triggering negative racial attitudes, increasing people's implicit and explicit bias against Latinas/os, and supporting the view that Latinas/os are unintelligent and prone to break the law (Ryo 2016). Increased hate crimes against Latinas/os, linked to these laws, were reported by the Southern Poverty Law Center. A 2007 report found that "vicious public denunciation . . . of undocumented, brown-skinned immigrants—once limited to hard-core white supremacists and a handful of border-state extremists—[was] increasingly common among supposedly mainstream anti-immigration activists, radio hosts, and politicians. . . . Much of [this denunciation] implicitly encourages or even endorses violence by characterizing immigrants from Mexico and Central America as 'invaders,' 'criminal aliens,' and 'cockroaches'" (Mock 2007).

The anti-Latina/o, anti-immigrant rhetoric of the 2000s was exacerbated by 2016 U.S. presidential politics. Republican candidates scapegoated all Mexicans, and Latinas/os generally, as undocumented lawbreakers who commit crimes and take away jobs, despite the lack of factual support. Donald Trump announced his candidacy in June 2015 using inflammatory rhetoric linking stereotypes about Latinas/os to immigration status and criminal activity: "When Mexico sends its people, they're not sending their best. They're not sending you. They're not sending you. They're sending people that have lots of problems, and they're bringing those problems with us. They're bringing drugs. They're bringing crime. They're rapists. And some, I assume, are good people." The speech was criticized as racist, and as a form of hate speech against Latinas/os generally (Vasquez 2015). Among Trump supporters, anti-immigrant groups have joined forces with white supremacy neo-Nazi nationalist groups (Lee 2015; Smith 2016).

LatCrit scholars explicitly link this bias and prejudice to the history of legal subordination of marginalized groups (Mahmud, Mutua, and Valdes 2015). LatCrit inquiry reveals the limits of law. The racism directed toward Latinas/os cannot be challenged using traditional legal remedies. The 1964 Civil Rights Act recognizes national origin discrimination to the extent a claim is based on accent or a particular national origin (e.g., Puerto Rican or Cuban), but this does not include the broader recognition of discrimination against a Latina/o racial group. The equal protection principle of the U.S. Constitution permits government action that may disproportionately harm Latinas/os, unless there is ample evidence of intent to discriminate on the part of a government actor. The widespread discrimination found in *Hernandez v. Texas* (1954) illustrates the type of evidence required to establish intent to discriminate. State and local laws targeting undocumented people, and immigration laws with a disparate impact on Latinas/os are not viewed as unconstitutional discrimination.

The indeterminate racial identification of Latinas/os allowed the Supreme Court to evade the obvious racial implications of the SB 1070 Arizona law that targeted people for appearing to be undocumented immigrants. During oral argument for *Arizona v. United States* (2012), the answer to the first question from Chief Justice John Roberts to the solicitor general, who represented the federal government in its challenge to the Arizona law, confirmed that the case did not include a racial discrimination claim, which meant that an entire body of relevant law was dismissed. The Court invalidated three of the four sections of the law as infringements on the comprehensive federal power to regulate immigration.

Indeterminate racial group identification may also impede the development of genuine cross-cultural coalitions, as well as the pursuit of equality. Alliances are more likely when communities view their issues within a shared framework. For example, employment and hiring discrimination are issues experienced by Latinas/os and African Americans and could be a source of coalition-building but this has yet to flourish (McKanders 2010).

Latinas/os in the United States now share a racialized group identity, despite the tremendous diversity within the community (Pew Research Center 2015b). This internal self-identification coupled with the strong public perception creates this identity. The Census Bureau is considering a racial category question for Latinas/os in the 2020 decennial census, which has raised some concerns about ignoring Latina/o multidimensionality (Prewitt 2013; Gamboa 2014; Reyes 2014). This explicit racial group identification may lead to new ways to challenge seemingly neutral anti-immigrant legislation for what it is, a form of racial discrimination in the U.S. legal system. The indeterminate Latina/o racial group identification no longer reflects the current reality because Latinas/os are perceived as a racial group by others and are targeted by discriminatory rhetoric and practices. The law has constructed Latinas/os as the foreign, racialized, and undocumented "other" who fall outside of the familiar constructs that are an important feature of U.S. law and society. The emerging Latina/o racial identity, based on both internal and external identification, may be the final, necessary, and transformative step toward greater legal protections and full Latina/o participation in U.S. society. This change in the legal construction of Latina/o identity may be necessary, but it is also likely to be insufficient to achieve these goals.

33

Literature
Ana Patricia Rodríguez

In Loida Maritza Pérez's (1999) coming of age novel, *Geographies of Home*, the protagonist Iliana María seeks refuge from great personal, familial, and societal hardships by reading, telling, and writing stories. Early in the novel, readers learn that to overcome her harsh material conditions, Iliana María turns to literature: "*The Hobbit, Lord of the Rings, The Little Prince, The Chronicles of Narnia*—books whose content was alien to her reality had been best. She learned to make up stories of her own. In time these stories evolved from fantasy into plans. Excelling in classes became her immediate goal, her school, her venue for escape" (Pérez 1999, 127). Reading books "alien" to her own experiences permitted her to break through the walls of home and tradition and to imagine and pursue other courses in life, including college and writing. Like other works by Latina/o writers, Pérez's novel points to literature as a tool of empowerment and liberation, representation and storytelling as a space of identity and community formation, and Latina/o literary critical practice as a site of discursive struggle (Belsey 1990).

In *Critical Practice*, Catherine Belsey describes literature and literary criticism as "a self-conscious and deliberate practice, a method based on a reasoned theoretical position" (1990, 2), which inscribes, prescribes, and/or contests social norms, cultural assumptions, and "common sense" in dominant ideologies. Against these conventions, Latina/o literature offers a discursive space through which to articulate, represent, and negotiate issues of power, language, orality, ethnicity, community, migration, diaspora, struggle, social justice, home/land, and belonging, to name only a few. Thus, Latina/o literature can be read as a critical signifying and meaning-making practice, drawing from a myriad of formal and informal discursive strategies, forms, and languages deployed in creative ways to represent the many stories of its subjects and their struggles and worldviews. Contemporary Latina/o writers like Pérez, Julia Alvarez, Gloria Anzaldúa, Maya Chinchilla, Sandra Cisneros, Junot Díaz, Cristina García, Francisco Goldman, Cristina Henríquez, Nicholas Mohr, Cherríe Moraga, Tomás Rivera, Sandra Rodriguez Barron, Sylvia Sellers-García, Héctor Tobar, among too many others to name, contribute to a critical literary practice drawing from the diverse histories, genealogies, and thematics of Latinidades (see Bost and Aparicio 2013; Aldama 2015b).

Seen in this light, Latina/o literature is "a very complex phenomenon," representing the "multifarious practices, identities, and experiences of Latinos[/as] in the U.S." (Aldama 2013, xii, xvi). Projected to make up at least 30 percent of the total U.S. population by 2050, if not sooner, Latinas/os are associated with more than twenty countries and dependent territories in Latin America, Brazil, the Caribbean, and the Iberian Peninsula as well as generations of U.S.-born Latinas/os inhabiting U.S. territories, including Puerto Rico. How to tell their many varied stories and histories, in different languages and through diverse forms, is the subject and practice of Latina/o literature. While Spanish and "Hispanic" cultural markers have been used historically to denominate Latinas/os, the wide diversity and historicity of Latina/o presence in the United States makes any singular classification, as Aldama puts it, an "unmanageable category" (2013, ix), whether it be "Latina/o" or "Hispanic." Like other critics of U.S. Latina/o literature and culture, Frederick Luis Aldama interrogates a Latina/o "demographic

presence generationally and linguistically rooted in a common Hispanic ancestral heritage" (2013, x), though this may continue to be one of the many commonplace signifiers of U.S. Latina/o cultures in the United States.

Along these lines, Paul Allatson explains that "Latino[/a] is the preferred term of many Latino/as when adopting a panethnic identification or speaking of the self and community in national terms; it thus circulates as a self-adopted alternative to the government-imposed and media-preferred Hispanic" (2007, 140). As such, the term "provides the nominal base for the panethnic sensibility, imaginary and potential vector of community affiliation," as well as the basis for constructing and speaking about Latinidades (2007, 141). In adopting the term "Latina/o," this New York University Press volume of keywords follows up on Allatson's suggestion that we speak "against the gender power of the noun's masculine form to signify all Latinos, irrespective of gender, and to acknowledge Latinas as an essential component of the panethnic designation" (2007, 141). In this spirit of troubling gender and other normative designations in the analysis of Latina/o or Latinx literature, I began this keyword by referencing Loida Maritza Pérez's Latina storyteller, who rewrites the story of Latinidad from her own particular subjective contexts and positions.

Latina/o literature, thus, must be read as an in situ intersectional critical practice addressing issues of gender, sexuality, race, class, nationality, migration, generation, and age, among others, where discourses cross and are crossed to create what Gloria Anzaldúa calls the "third country—a border culture" (1987, 25). In this in-between space produced where and when multiple cultures, countries, and worldviews meet and often clash, new forms, practices, cultures, and subjectivities are produced, which are "nideaquínideallá" (neither from here or there), as the Nuyorican poet Tato Laviera puts it (2008). Anzaldúa reminds us that while "borders are set up to define the places that are safe and unsafe, to distinguish *us* from *them* . . . a borderland is a vague and undetermined place created by the emotional residue of an unnatural boundary. It is in a constant state of transition. The prohibited and forbidden are its inhabitants. *Los atravesados* live here: the squint-eyed, the perverse, the queer, the troublesome, the mongrel, the mulatto, the half-breed, the half-dead; in short, those who cross over, pass over, or go through the confines of the 'normal'" (1987, 25). Like borderland imaginary spaces, Latina/o literatures are ambiguous and differential material, symbolic, and affective sites in constant elaboration and signification. Latina/o literatures are also third spaces of *différance*, difference, and resignification, allowing for in-process subject formation, overlapping identities, coalition- and alliance-building, and complicated Latina/o crossings (De Genova and Ramos-Zayas 2003). Through multiple forms, genres, and practices, Latina/o literatures are suited to tell the stories of past, present, and future Latinidades.

To that end, numerous literary critics have dedicated precious time, resources, and research to excavate Latina/o texts, chart multiple genealogies, and rethink the histories of Latina/o writing (Padilla 1994; Gruesz 2002; Kanellos 2011; Coronado 2013). The "Recovering the U.S. Hispanic Literary Heritage Project" of Arte Público Press based at the University of Houston has been at the forefront of recuperating, archiving, and publishing a growing corpus of literary texts and criticism, covering a wide range of genres including chronicles, memoirs, letters, periodicals, plays, poetry, short stories, and novels, among others. The recovery of such texts has pushed back the deep genealogy of Latina/o literature to the pre-Columbian era, through Spanish conquest and colonization (Núñez Cabeza de Vaca 1993) and U.S. imperialist expansion in the Western Hemisphere, into the present era of globalization and diaspora. In essence, the genealogical project has enabled the remapping of the roots and routes reconfiguring Latinidades through various migratory flows, primarily from the Luso-Hispanophone worlds but also embracing Indigenous, African, and other origins. The continuous remaking of Latina/o literatures has also permitted fruitful discussions on the writing, reception, and canonization of U.S. Latina/o texts, resulting in the production of numerous anthologies and collections, including the voluminous *Norton Anthology of Latino Literature* (Stavans 2011). With these genealogical projects, Latina/o literature continues to be reconstituted not only historically but also spatially to include writers and texts from various periods and sites outside and inside of the United States, thus expanding spatially, topically, and discursively the field of literature (A. P. Rodríguez 2009).

In the 1960s and 1970s, with the rise of the civil rights movements and the demands of readers for wider representation in ethnic studies programs, classes, and texts, a market for Latina/o literature began to develop, and then began increasing with the Latina/o demographic upsurge in the 1980s and the Latina/o cultural boom in the 1990s (Machado Sáez 2015). According to Aldama, "It is only when the socioeconomic and political conditions begin to change, and when the population begins to increase and diversify socioeconomically, that we can begin to see a series of authors writing for a growing body of Latino[/a] readers who, over time, develop a very varied taste for all kinds of literature" (2013, xiii). Examining the work of post-1960s New York-based Latino-Caribbean writers, Raphael Dalleo and Elena Machado Sáez reconsider the "anticolonial" lens of a Latina/o literature associated with the civil rights movements and discuss the canonization, institutionalization, and consumption of a multiculturalist Latina/o literature produced at the turn of the twenty-first century (2007, 3). They suggest that the "market success" of multicultural Latina/o literature is due, in part, to the "reading of Latina/o texts as embodiments of linguistic hybridity and individual self-construction" and as cultural translations of Latinidades for the mainstream (2007, 4–5). In their critique, Dalleo and Machado Sáez encourage readers to reassess the critical practices and political projects of contemporary Latina/o literature in the twenty-first century (2007, 7–11) beyond prescriptive criteria, norms, and facile readings.

In the highly mediated era of globalization, mass migrations, and transnational financial, material, cultural, and technological flows and linkages, Latina/o literature may be rethought as a transnational, if not transglobal, critical practice, inclusive of diverse Latinidades. Along these lines, I have proposed that we examine the discursive shifts, reconfigurations, and reassemblages of Latina/o literature across geographies and study Latina/o literature as part of larger discursive circuits across the world (such as diasporic, postcolonial, transnational, and global South) (A. P. Rodríguez 2009). Reading Latina/o literature as reterritorialized discursive practices situated in local sites opens possibilities of reading across conventions, traditions, languages, cultural locations, geographies, geopolitics, and borders. In this context, U.S. Central American literature, for example, operates as an expanded notion of Central America that transcends national territories and borders, what I have called a "transisthmus," in which the diaspora is key to understanding reterritorialized expanded cultural identities and imaginaries (A. P. Rodríguez 2009). Thus, with the mass migration of Central Americans to the United States and elsewhere in the twentieth and twenty-first centuries, we see the production and reception of an attendant literary work that seeks to tell the story of those subjects of Latinidad. Latina/o literature, it is suggested here, must be theorized as an ever-transformative cultural field, taking shape in particular sites of dispersion and within the scope of larger histories, social dynamics, communities, and other geographies of home.

34
Maquiladoras
Norma Iglesias-Prieto

In the last fifty years, two linked phenomena have become more evident. On the one hand, there is an unprecedented massive migration from the global South to the global North in search of jobs and better salaries in the strong economies; on the other hand, there is the north-south movement of multinational companies (offshoring) in search of cheap and abundant labor markets in the weaker economies. The establishment of maquiladoras in countries like Mexico results from the fragmentation and transfer of production processes looking to cheapen production costs. This transfer affects workers in the countries of origin of capital because they lose employment sources and their labor is indirectly cheapened. It also affects workers in the destination countries because when jobs are created, migration needs are reduced.

The maquiladora or maquila is a type of industrialization model that generates foreign exchange, is cheap labor-intensive, and exports. Export Processing Zones (EPZ) were conceived as a new international division of labor in the late 1970s. Measured by its expansion, this industrial model has been a success, since in 1975 it included the participation of 25 countries, 79 zones, and 750,000 workers (Fröbel, Heinrichs, and Kreye 1981). By the early 2000s, there were 109 countries with more than 3,000 EPZs, and approximately 40 million employees, most of them in China (Mercier 2003). Asia, Africa, and Latin America have participated from the beginning to the present day in this world concert of production. Although they are not known as maquilas in other countries (except in Central America and the Caribbean countries), this industrialization model began the processes of productive globalization and international outsourcing.

Maquiladoras are assembly plants that have operated in Mexico since 1965, when the "Border Industrialization Program" was established by government decree. The rationale for creating this program was based on two premises: first, to provide jobs for those returning to Mexico due to the end of the Bracero Program in 1964; and, second, to take advantage of the need of U.S. companies to reduce costs in response to the wave of Asian imports and the establishment of Japanese companies on U.S. soil.

A maquiladora is a company that temporarily imports raw materials, components, technology, and even labor for assembly, manufacturing, repair, or service processes in the destination country. Upon completion of these activities, the end products and waste materials are exported back to the global North or elsewhere. In some cases, however, toxic waste has remained in Mexico and, upon its improper disposal, has generated environmental problems. Precisely environmental issues are also why some production processes are moved to Mexico, since the intent is to escape their stricter environmental laws in the United States.

Maquiladoras do not pay trade taxes (importing or exporting), but they do pay taxes on the process of manufacture (utility services, salaries, profit sharing, and so forth). The term "maquila" (regarding exports) originated in Mexico. Since January 2007, the Maquiladora Program (IME, Maquiladora Export Industry) was modified to include other Mexican programs of manufacture and service that also export to the United States. This new program was denominated Industria de Manufactura, Maquiladora y Servicios para la Exportación,

(IMMEX, Manufacturing, Maquiladora, and Export Services Industry); it accounted for 85 percent of manufacturing exports by 2013 (Secretaría de Economía [Ministry of Economy] 2013).

Since the Maquiladora Program's inception, all exports go to the United States, and in general, there is a clear dependency of maquiladoras on the U.S. economy. Economic crises in the United States—particularly the decline in industrial production—impact maquiladoras directly and negatively. By contrast, the economic boom in the United States and Mexican currency devaluations positively impact the volume of employment, establishments, and value added in Mexico. Today, assembly products and services in Mexico are directed to many diverse countries, but first touch U.S. soil (physically or virtually).

Whereas in 1980 there were 620 maquiladora plants that employed 120,000 workers (Carrillo and Hernández 1985), in April 2006 there were 2,820 factories with 1.2 million workers (INEGI 2006). By December 2013, under the IMMEX program, the number of manufacturing establishments significantly increased to a total of 5,049, but employment increased only by .9 million people (INEGI 2014).

At the beginning of their formation, maquiladoras could be located only in the municipalities of the northern border of Mexico, given that the Border Industrialization Program was a program of "exception" that was precisely against Mexico's economic policies of "import substitution." By the 1970s, the government authorized their location throughout the country; nonetheless, most of these factories are still located in the north because of the benefits that this brings to the companies. In general terms, foreign companies settled in Mexico for several reasons: the geographical proximity to the U.S. market, the low-skilled workforce, and lower costs (lower relative wages, labor peace, logistics, and so on).

In the 1980–1989 period maquiladora plants in the border municipalities accounted for 89 percent of the national total; in the 1990–1999 period they fell to 69 percent; and in the 2000–2006 period, they rose again to 78 percent (CIEMEX-WEFA 1991 and 2000; Christman 2005). Three border states stand out: Baja California, Chihuahua, and Tamaulipas; while 72 percent of plants in Mexico were concentrated there in the 1980s, and 64 percent were there in the 1990s, the concentration continued to drop to 58 percent in 2000–2006 period (CIEMEX-WEFA 1991, 2000; Christman 2005) and then to 35 percent by January 2010. (INEGI 2010). Ciudad Juárez and Tijuana continue to be the main locations where maquiladoras operate. If the cities of Reynosa, Chihuahua, Querétaro, Mexicali, and Matamoros are added, then these have a significant portion of the maquiladoras in Mexico.

The country of origin of the maquiladoras varies. Although there are Mexican companies, most are foreign, mainly North American. However, there are important Asian (Japanese, Korean, Taiwanese, and Chinese) and European (German and French, among others) companies. There are no restrictions for countries to open companies under the IMMEX decree in Mexico.

Since their inception, maquiladoras have implemented a wide range of activities in different industrial sectors, both manufacturing and services. They produce anything from broomsticks to military torpedoes, in addition to televisions, shirts, and electrical switches. They also offer services such as counting and classifying discount coupons used by American retailers. Today, the number of products and services that are carried out has increased dramatically. However, during the 1970s, most companies concentrated on the electrical and electronics sectors and, to a lesser extent, on garment manufacturing. At that time, most production processes were very simple, involving monotonous and repetitive tasks that did not stimulate the workers' creativity, and the vast majority of workers were female (80 percent), young (16–24 years), with only elementary school education, no employment or trade-union experiences, and little seniority in the workplace (Carrillo and Hernández 1985; Iglesias-Prieto 1985, 1997). It is estimated that the hiring of so many women in the maquiladora sector not only had an impact on labor relations within the industry, but also within homes, since many women became heads of households and breadwinners (Iglesias-Prieto 1985, 1997).

Although the argument for female hiring by companies focused on the delicacy of their hands, which allowed them to do a better job, companies reaped considerable benefits because women could be paid lower wages, were docile, and were less critical of their poor working conditions due to their lack of experience. In addition, companies developed control mechanisms that stressed and promoted traditional gender roles through events such as beauty pageants and fiestas. Another mechanism for the control and cheapening of labor is linked to the type of unions that exist in Mexico (*sindicato de protección* or *sindicato patronal*, a type of company union), which neither represent nor protect the interests of workers, but rather work on behalf of the company.

Over time, maquiladora production processes became sophisticated and expansive, and this demanded much more qualified labor. By the 1980s, the auto parts industry made its entrance and, in the 1990s, the aerospace industry and medical products made theirs. In the 1981–1989 period, the electronics, auto parts, and garment industries accounted for 80 percent of employment and 65 percent of the plants. In the 1990–1999 period they account for 71 percent and 48 percent, respectively (CIEMEX-WEFA 1991, 2000). And for the 2007–2010 period, it was 70 percent of employment and 50 percent of the plants (INEGI 2014). From 1998 to 2007 these three sectors represented more than 80 percent of gross value of production (Christman 2003). With these sectorial changes, the worker profiles did as well, with female participation decreasing to 60 percent in the mid-1990s (Carrillo and Santibañez Romellón 2001) and 50 percent by the beginning of the new century (Carrillo and Gomis 2013). The education average increased to secondary school. Similarly, previous work experience and seniority in the workplace increased considerably, as did the employment of men. The latter was due not only to the establishment of sectors such as the automotive one, but also to the shortage of female labor (for over ten years, the monthly turnover rate was more than 10 percent), and the increase of young unemployed men. The change in the gender profile of workers was called the "masculinization" of the maquiladora.

The product specialization of maquiladoras has been accompanied by territorial concentrations. Building on the experience of important companies that were already established, other companies in the same field of activity located themselves nearby to take advantage of the benefits that the regions offer. As competing businesses, supplier companies, export services, support institutions, and increased capabilities of academic institutions were established, various types of clusters began to form. These include, for example, the garment cluster (the world capital of jeans is in Torreón) and electronics cluster (the mecca of televisions is in Tijuana). Recently, other clusters, such as aerospace (Baja California and Chihuahua), automotive (Ciudad Juárez), and medical products (Tijuana), have developed. Some have seen their importance diminish (the garment cluster, for instance), while others have gained presence (for example, aerospace), and others have disappeared (toys, for one). The advantage of border cities—initially, it was mainly their geographical location (that is, proximity to the United States)—began to extend upon improvement of technological, organizational, and labor capabilities within companies and their locales. Another advantage was the reduction of lead time by joining research-development-design and manufacture in the same city and increasing access to human talent in the form of technicians and professionals.

Maquiladoras have followed a process of industrial upgrading, defined as the ability of firms to innovate and increase the added value of their products and processes (Pietrobelli and Rabellotti 2006). During the 1960s and 1970s, maquiladoras were dedicated mainly to simple assembly of parts and components. With some exceptions, they were small local businesses. The use of unskilled labor and low wages provoked strong criticisms of the maquila program, and this feeling intensified with the 1974 economic crisis in the United States. By the mid-1980s, some companies began to undertake increasingly complex production processes and technologies; expand the number and kinds of products made; incorporate process innovations and international certifications of quality (such as ISO 9000); and adopt best practices in areas such as manufacturing, among others. By the mid-1990s, design activities and product engineering began to develop, performance in quality, environment, and safety improved, and the managements of foreign companies were Mexicanized.

Another way of looking at the evolution of the maquila is in terms of generations of maquiladoras (Carrillo and Hualde 1996). The first generation involved the intensification of manual labor and simple assembly ("assembled in Mexico"). The second generation was characterized by the rationalization of work, growth in manufacturing, and adoption of new technologies ("made in Mexico"). The third generation featured an intensification of knowledge, research, development, and design activities ("created in Mexico"). And the fourth generation has come to involve the work of professionals in the coordination of different activities associated with regional corporate functions (productive, logistics, labor, financial, and so on) ("coordinated in Mexico").

Regardless of whether production processes are simple or complex, that workers are men or women, with basic education or a master's degree, at the border or in the center of a country, in isolated plants or in industrial clusters, maquiladoras will exist as long as there is a tremendous wage disparity in the world, which is the result of the incredible concentration of wealth under capitalism.

35

Media
Mari Castañeda

In the late 1970s, Latina/o scholars began to examine the forgotten history of Spanish-language newspapers and radio in the United States, and the differences in purpose and content that these media outlets demonstrated as compared to their English-language counterparts. Latina/o media scholar-activists such as Jorge Reina Schement and Ricardo Flores (1977), Felix Gutiérrez (1977, 1981), and Federico Subervi-Vélez (1979) were some of the first to recognize that the lack of media coverage of Latina/o issues in mainstream outlets both created invisibility and placed a highly contested responsibility on Spanish-language and bilingual media. Additionally, this tension often did not mesh with the advertiser-supported structure that underpinned the broader mass media system in the United States. Although media outlets oriented toward Latina/o audiences viewed their readers, listeners, and viewers as cultural citizens who were attempting to claim a visible position within the American social landscape, the pressure for profits created an imagined Latina/o public that was dynamic only as consumers. This assimilation has consistently affected the political potential of Spanish-language and Latina/o commercial media in the United States. Yet despite the capitalist drive to utilize media outlets as corporate tools for Latina/o consumer marketing, the ongoing practices of Spanish-language media, especially community newspapers and radio outlets, is to highlight the injustices Latina/o individuals and communities encounter locally and across the United States.

The propensity to use media as forms of public service was in fact present in newspapers dating back to 1850, after the Treaty of Guadalupe Hidalgo placed Mexicans in a precarious position as the United States sought to build the nation. Media as a tool for social justice was also extant in the 1950s during Latina/o resistance against "Operation Wetback" and the forced deportations of thousands of Mexican Americans. Today, media continues to operate as a mouthpiece and point of connection, as evident by the many Spanish-language newspaper and broadcast workers and cultural interlocutors who aim to tell their story about the impact Latina/o immigrants are having across the United States and Canada. Furthermore, Chicana feminist scholars such as Dionne Espinoza (2001) and Maylei Blackwell (2011) have also conducted research documenting how Chicana and Latina activists utilized newsprint as a political tool for developing counternarratives regarding the principles and values of the Chicano movement and moratorium that took place in late 1960s and early 1970s. In this regard, nonprofit communication outlets have historically operated as productive mediascapes— virtual spaces of symbolic communicative and cultural flows—which have the potential to challenge dominant narratives while also creating audiovisual voices for Latina/o public spheres that are generally invisible and silent in mainstream media (A. Rodriguez 1999). The debate over the role that media plays in Latina/o communities in fact continues today as political pundits decry Spanish-language and Latina/o community and commercial media as participating in (as opposed to simply reporting about) social justice movements and mobilizations for immigration reforms, for instance, particularly during high-stakes presidential election cycles.

Media are powerful social forces that are highly contested because they are pervasive and persuasive sites of cultural expression, political discourse, and lamentably, racist, sexist, and homophobic audiovisual representations that have the potential to reinforce, shift, and/or undermine our understanding of the world. The word "media" was originally extracted from the broader term "mass media." Scholarly examinations of media histories, media representations, media activisms, and media theories, to name a few, along with intersections between them, have pointed to the significant roles that radio, television, print, film, and now the Internet play in the cultural, political, economic, and social ways of life across different local and global populations, including Latina/o communities. The early part of the twentieth century marked the moment when electronic forms of communication such as radio and film were viewed as technologies that had the potential to not only reach multiple audiences simultaneously, but also reinterpret conceptual understandings, especially of our increasingly globally networked societies. Numerous scholarly projects have noted how media (a plural word but increasingly used as a singular word as well) play a considerable role in the ways in which Latina/o communities are imagined and treated in material and discursive contexts (Noriega and López 1996; Valdivia 2000; Mayer 2003; Amaya 2013). For example, Juan González and Joseph Torres (2011) argue that the American media system has played a central role in reinforcing racial oppression, both through its coverage and its efforts to delegitimize ethnic media, particularly those with transnational roots in the Caribbean and Latin America.

Much of the work by Latina/o (media) studies scholars has aimed to uncover the historical and contemporary ways in which Latina/o communities have engaged with media and how English-language outlets in particular have visually and discursively wounded this perpetually attacked community. Relatedly, Latina/o studies scholars have made key insights, especially in the area of media representations that have furthered our discernment of media as a powerful social force that can influence people and affect cultural change (Negrón-Muntaner 2004). For instance, forms of resistance, such as the reconceptualization of Latinidades, not only are present in popular culture and entertainment content, but are also represented by transnational media celebrities such as Selena, Shakira, Jennifer Lopez, and Eva Longoria. Through them, we are able to analytically examine the embodied intersections of gender, race, sexuality, class, and citizenship in Latina/o communities and media imaginaries. Additionally, scholarly insights have pointed to how audiences themselves interpret the cultural, personal, and political significance of media texts such as telenovelas, radio programming, newspaper reporting, and filmic representations (Paredez 2009; Cepeda 2010; Molina-Guzmán 2010; Rios and Castañeda 2011). In this sense, media—as a site of critical analysis in Latina/o studies—has benefited from theorizations from other disciplines such as feminist studies, critical cultural studies, ethnic studies, global studies, Chicana/o studies, and American studies, as well as sociology, anthropology, and communication. Media are more than communication technologies: they are material and cultural embodiments of historical and contemporary practices that map the terrain of meaning surrounding the production, distribution, and consumption of mass-mediated popular content.

Additionally, media—as sets of practices and institutions—circulate today in what are no longer simply information and entertainment modes. As Douglas Kellner and Meenakshi Gigi Durham (2009) note, media "is both a space of interpretation and debate as well as a subject matter and domain of inquiry." It is also a domain of social movement activism, ranging from petitions to increase access to commercial and community-based media outlets to utilizing digital circuits of expression to challenge normative interpretations of undocumented LGBTQIA youth. Latina/o studies scholars have asked questions such as: How do government and industry policies and economic structural conditions shape access to media outlets? Who is left out? And how have communities responded by developing their own forms of media access through grassroots activism and outlets? Accordingly, examinations of the political economy of Latina/o radio, for instance, have shown that regulatory changes in the last decade have consolidated the sector and reorganized the broader Spanish-language media industry (Castañeda 2014). Currently, the ownership of broadcast media properties by Latinas/os is nearly non-existent and the Federal Communications Commission (FCC)—the U.S. regulatory body that oversees communication systems and media content across the country—lacks Spanish-speaking and Latina/o staff. Such political-economic structures matter because they affect programming by constricting the broadcast airwaves for pro-immigrant rights organizing, for example, or by imposing a pervasive cultural politics that privileges patriarchal and homophobic radio humor (Casillas 2014).

Yet Latina/o media activists and media justice organizations such as the Hispanic Media Coalition are consistently advocating for changes to mass media access and equitable representation, while also recognizing that the U.S. communication system is based on capitalist, racist, and sexist principles that have historically excluded Latinas/os and communities of color from gaining access to the airwaves. The media policy debates in the 1970s between the FCC and minority activists groups, for instance, were attempts to rectify the media injustice that pervaded the communications landscape prior to and after the civil rights movement. In this vein, recent Latina/o studies research that analyzes electronic media history is also questioning assumptions about how and why Spanish-language print, radio, and television outlets emerged in the United States. Scholarship by Dolores Inés Casillas (2014) and G. Cristina Mora (2014), for example, points to the need for specific examinations of media history, representation, and access in conjunction with policy, economics, gender, and race, rather than as separate issues and processes in the making of Latina/o media culture, citizens, and consumers.

By the same token, the role of (digital) media in Latina/o social movements, particularly in the most recent DREAMers movement, challenges notions of Latina/o communities as technologically oblivious and in fact highlights the multiple ways in which Latinas/os engage in the questions of cultural citizenship through the transnational audiovisual and discursive spaces that globalized media embody, particularly the Internet and digital devices. The DREAMers' strategic use of social media, for instance, has created international awareness of the issues, and in some cases, the viral nature of digitalization has led to the suspension of deportation proceedings for some youth activists. Such activism has created a globally connected online support network that is able to crowdsource information and action for immigrant rights. Thus, the emergence of digital media scholarship in relationship to Latinas/os reveals not only the ways in which media technology is changing, but also how Latinas/os are also investing in, engaging, and expanding new technologies. In this regard, digital media will increasingly become critical sites of investigation as Latina/o communities become an influential demographic group in the twenty-first-century media environment.

Lastly, media literacy is an area within Latina/o studies that has much potential, but more research is needed to more adequately comprehend how Latina/o media users critically assess and produce audiovisual texts as well as how they conceptualize the social, cultural, economic, and self-expressive forces of media. Given the media circulation of hate speech against Latinas/os and their migratory lived experiences, it is increasingly urgent to reflect on how media is imagined, taught, and discussed in communities and schools in our highly connected mediated societies. It is imperative that Latina/o studies scholars continue to develop and expand media literacy investigations since they can help create school programming that inspire youth or community social engagement (Yosso 2002; Báez 2008; L. Vargas 2009).

Thus, media are more than simply venues for news and entertainment. As Laurie Ouellette notes, "To approach the study of media critically involves situating media within economic, political, cultural and social context and addressing its relations to capitalism, labor, citizenship, gender, race and class dynamics, inequalities, sexuality, globalization and other issues that are both larger than media, and intertwined within the production, circulation, and use of media texts, images, sounds, spaces, artifacts, technologies and discourses" (2013, 3). Media do not exist in a vacuum outside of social and power relations; they partake of a larger cultural framework. Hence the importance of critical examinations of the relations between these audiovisual and print institutions and practices and material and affective experiences within Latina/o communities. Just as we analyze education, religion, economics, public policies, and their influence on the contested formations of Latinidades, so we must treat media as meaningful sites and modes of engagement that help constitute multiple lived realities (Aparicio 1998). Latina/o scholars have successfully argued for this recognition but there is more at stake with the continuously changing contours of communities and the dynamic role of (digital) media in contesting, negotiating, resisting, silencing, and creating the historical and contemporary imaginary of Latinidad. Indeed, the imperative to evaluate, interpret, and produce media in all its formations is more important than ever.

36

Mestizaje

Alicia Arrizón

"Mestizaje," which is associated with the word "mixed," can be understood as the product of mixing two distinct cultures—that is, Spanish and Indigenous American. While it is etymologically connected to the French *métis* (a person of mixed ancestry, similar to *mestiza/o* in Spanish) and *métissage* (the cultural process that leads to this) and to the Portuguese *mestiço* (a person of mixed ancestry), it is an unstable signifier that has different meanings depending on its context. Referring to the biological and cultural mixing of European and Indigenous peoples in the Americas, mestizaje can be understood as the effect caused by the impact of colonization. In North America, the closest approximation to "mestizaje" is the word *métis*, indicating a person of mixed aboriginal and European ancestry. For example, in western Canada the term is used in reference to people of Caucasian and Native Indigenous ancestry. However, both *métissage* and *métis* are used primarily in Francophone culture and literature. English, on the other hand, has no equivalent for "mestizaje," although in theory, it has been identified as synonymous with cultural hybridization or hybridity, as both represent the space-in-between (Anzaldúa 1987; Bhabha 1994; García Canclini 1995). Epistemologically, however, mestizaje and hybridity need to be differentiated in postcolonial inquiries, because the colonial experience in the Americas is distinct from other forms of colonization in the regions of the global South (such as Asia and Africa).

Another form of "mixing" is expressed by "mulatez" or "mulataje" (mulatto-ness), terms that refer to the black hybrid body and the biological and cultural mixing of European and African heritage (Buscaglia-Salgado 2003, 79). Both "mestizaje" and "mulataje" can be associated with relations of power, racial mixing, and the postcolonial imagination; conversely, they can also be seen as forms of transculturation. As understood by Cuban anthropologist Fernando Ortiz (1940, 1995), transculturation is fundamental to the different stages and results of cultural contact among people brought together by European colonial expansion into the Americas. While the concept of mestizaje is itself the result of cultural contact(s), it has also served to disguise blackness within processes of national homogenization and the reality of racism. Before and after the independence wars in Latin American and Caribbean countries, nationalist regulations of mestizaje by the *criollo* elite (Europeans born in the Americas) served to eradicate not only indigeneity but also African heritage. In addition, the effects of *blanqueamiento* (or whitening) were encouraged in the late nineteenth and early twentieth centuries to improve and "purify" the race, meaning the general national racial composition or the Hispanic race. Clearly, the ideology of *blanqueamiento* arose from the legacies of European colonial domination, including a caste system in which Spaniards were ranked at the top and the conquered "other" at the bottom (Quijano 2000b; Wade 2003; Lugones 2007). Since mestizaje was linked with illegitimacy (bastardy) and connoted "impurity" from early on in the colonial period, mestizos and African-descended phenotypes were often stigmatized and referred to as *la mancha* or "the stain" of the race. The Spanish phrase "mejorar la raza" (to better or improve the race) became an undergirding theme, permeating every area of life while diluting the African and Indigenous characteristics from Latin America.

Elsewhere, I have suggested that European colonization of Indigenous peoples and the subsequent transatlantic slave trade have played important roles in the processes of racialization by which mestizaje acquired social and historical significance. In *Queering Mestizaje: Writings on Transculturation and Performance* (2006), I examined how mestizaje has manifested itself in three geographically diverse spaces—the United States, the Hispanic Caribbean, and the Philippines—with a shared history of Spanish colonialism and U.S. imperialism. As demonstrated in the book, the meaning of "mestizaje" varies within and across time and locations. Significantly, the multiple categories that can be used to express the meaning embedded in mestizaje, the mixed-racialized body, are not fixed. From the conceptual knowledge embedded in hybridity to creolization, or the process through which Creole cultures emerge in the New World, the notion of "intermixture" emphasizes the plural "mestizajes" as a polyvalent signifier.

Thus it is imperative to understand mestizaje as the product of a history formed by cultural encounters, colonial difference, and the "whitening" of the Indigenous/black subordinated colonial subject. Whether in the Caribbean or in Latin America, the development of mestizaje goes back to the conquistadores' easy sexual access to Indigenous women, especially in the first colonial period (the first half of the sixteenth century), when racial mixing became a significant phenomenon. Massive miscegenation was facilitated not only by the social condition of the Indigenous peoples, but also by the conquistadores' position of power, which made it possible for them to exploit women at will. Moreover, Indigenous women of important status and lineage were offered to Spanish officers by their families for the purpose of developing connections and kinship lines with the conquistadores. The Spanish and Portuguese colonizers who demonstrated an insatiable appetite for Indigenous women resulted in the rapid formation of a mestizo people; by the end of the sixteenth century, mestizos were a near majority. While the mestizos became the majority in the postcolonial Americas, the mixed Spanish-Malay population in the Philippines has remained comparatively small. Nevertheless, the influences and contributions of the mestizo people in the Philippines are distinct, and their presence is linked to the creation of the modern nation in the nineteenth century. On the other hand, during that time in Latin America, the majority of mestizos were poor and uneducated, and constituted an inferior socioeconomic class. For every mestizo who gained a comfortable place in society, there were a hundred others who remained in miserable circumstances. In contrast, the mestizo population in the Philippines became associated with ownership and prosperity, and the term "mestizaje" was equivalent to socioeconomic potential gained by a disassociation from Indigenous people. And whereas for most of the colonial period in Latin America, mestizos were grouped socially with Indigenous peoples, blacks, and mulattos (persons of African and European descent), in the Philippines, they were socially comparable to the Peninsulares (Iberian-born Spaniards).

In Latin America, "mestizaje" came to be used more broadly during the independence movements, from the early nineteenth century to the early twentieth. Although it partially helped to organize the diverse ethno-racial groups in a common struggle against the colonial power of the Spanish conquistadores, the ideology of mestizaje developed within the search for national self-definition and self-affirmation. Intellectuals and independentists like José Martí, who coined the notion of "nuestra América mestiza," envisioned a positive continental identity by means of an empowered mestizaje. This view of mestizaje, according to Amaryll Chanady

(2003), contributed to the development of ideals during the nineteenth-century period of national consolidation, following movements of independence against coloniality. Thus, whereas in the colonial period mestizaje was as an instrument supporting Hispanization and European hegemony, in the nineteenth century, mestizaje paradoxically affirmed cultural difference from the United States and Europe through the consolidation of nation-states.

The ideology of mestizaje gained strength after the Mexican Revolution (1910–1924) and after the philosopher José Vasconcelos popularized it in his writings on *La raza cósmica* ([1925] 1997). As expressed in his "manifesto," Vasconcelos's reading of mestizaje predicted the birth of a fully mixed "cosmic race" capable of solving ethnic and racial obstacles of colonized nations. Although his idea of "cosmic race" tends to view the melting-pot theory as a necessary solution to racial discrimination, ironically, his notion of mestizaje—a positive process of miscegenation—also promoted the idea that blackness would vanish from the social fabric of Mexico and elsewhere in Latin America. Vasconcelos's ideas of mestizaje are still considered revolutionary, but his proposed manifesto of equality through mixing can ultimately be seen as an endorsement of *blanqueamiento* or of a broader project of whitening. In general, Vasconcelos's ideology of mestizaje was imagined in terms of the voluntary extinction of the "negative" traits of the "inferior" races and proposed that through assimilation and intermixing, a cosmic race would develop in Latin America.

From seventeenth-century colonial Spanish America, when "mestizaje" implied a mixture of animal species, to the nineteenth- and twentieth-century independence movements that linked mestizaje to the search for national identity (Mexican, Peruvian, Cuban, and so on), the historical trajectory of the concept is complex and heterogeneous. More recently, in the late twentieth and early twenty-first centuries, mestizaje has been treated as an act of resistance striving to seek agency through postmodern rewriting and retextualization. Here, Gloria Anzaldúa's (1987) politicization of a "new" mestizaje came to play an important role in marking feminist intersectionalities and border thinking in Chicana/o culture. For Anzaldúa, the shaping of the "new mestiza consciousness" in the theorization of the border becomes an attempt to reclaim mestizaje for the use of a counterhegemonic struggle. The author links mestizaje, or what she calls "mestiza consciousness" to U.S. third-world feminist criticism to demonstrate how both have embodied a transnational politics of resistance. Mestizaje as a "method" in Chicana feminism, to use Chela Sandoval's (1998) perception of Anzaldúa's epistemological inquiries, is a transcultural form of consciousness, constantly traveling back and forth between race, gender, sexuality, language, and nations. Conceptualized as key site of intervention and resistance in the narratives of U.S. hegemony and racism and in the context of the urgent need for social justice, Anzaldúa's borderland consciousness breaks down dualities, furthers the critique of essentialism, and has an ongoing effect on the contemporary notion of mestizaje.

In particular, Anzaldúa's "border feminism" and queer epistemologies of alterity invoke a kind of mestizaje that transcended Vasconcelos's notion of "cosmic race" or the idea of "la raza," as adopted in the nationalist Chicano movement. For Anzaldúa, the theorization of "the new mestiza consciousness" involves a redefinition of mestizaje in terms of gender and sexuality and a plurality of languages (Spanish-American, Aztec-Náhuatl, and Anglo-American) through which women literally speak and define their identities. Thus Anzaldúa's mestizaje can be conceived only as the result of the "plurilanguaging" system that requires an understanding of history and the epistemology of Chicana feminism. While her conceptualization of mestizaje is the result of a polyvalent mode, it reclaims what has been lost through the shackles of colonization (Alarcón 2002). Anzaldúa's theorizations of "nepantla" (middle place, in-between-ness, or place of passage) are linked to her understanding of mestizaje: both can be described as "liminal" spaces, where multiple forms of reality are viewed at the same time.

37

Militarism

Manuel G. Avilés-Santiago

Militarism is an ideology that sees society, politics, and culture as ultimately defined by war and allots the highest value to those activities that either prepare for or facilitate the waging of war. As a cultural ethos, this default value set is the result of and a participant in public opinion and its discourses, models, and metaphors (Ekirch 1956; Sherry 1995; Mundey 2012). The historical dynamic of militarism in the unfolding of the United States as a nation and its rise to the status of global hegemony has had a broad impact on Latina/o populations, since militarism has partly defined the mechanism for deciding who does and does not belong to the nation. In particular, given the marked violence that has characterized relations between Latin America and the United States, militarism includes either direct U.S. military intervention or the threat of U.S. military intervention, as well as U.S. alliances with the militaries and security forces of other nations. On the other hand, given the way the U.S. military has operated as a social program allowing upward social mobility to minority populations, Latina/o communities have also been targeted successfully for recruitment in the military machine. Against this background of intervention, militarism has reshaped the kinds of possibilities for inclusion and exclusion that have befallen the Latina/o community in the United States from World War I to the years leading to the War on Terror.

Even before the gigantic surge of military spending that came about as a result of World War II, the United

States was an aggressive player throughout the Americas. After it carved out and swallowed huge chunks of territory from Mexico as a result of the Mexican-American War of 1848, expansionists called for further military conquest in the Caribbean. It was then, according to Alan McPherson (2013), after the Spanish-American War of 1898, that the United States became a constant military interventionist in Latin America, taking control of Puerto Rico and maintaining a strong military presence in countries like Mexico, Cuba, Panama, Nicaragua, Haiti, and the Dominican Republic. However, those interventions were the tip of the iceberg, as U.S. economic and ideological hegemony generated a collaborationist cultural, political, and social apparatus among Latin American and Caribbean elites. Subsequently, the U.S. involvement in World War I marked a new stage in military mobilization, wherein the U.S. military first began recruiting in the Latina/o population for soldiers.

Hector Amaya (2013) argues that, historically, military service and national identity have been constitutive of one another. After the breakup of mercenary forces characteristic of the seventeenth and eighteenth centuries, military service was a pathway to membership in a national community. This was born out of the concept of the citizen soldier, which emerged in the American and French Revolutions. However, this tendency of obtaining an automatic pathway to citizenship is less uniform than is presented in official histories.

Maggie Rivas-Rodriguez (2005) observes that historical accounts of U.S. wars generally exclude Latinas/os. Notwithstanding the fact that their active involvement dates back to the War of 1812, it was not until World War I that Latina/o soldiers were mentioned explicitly (Wilmoth 2013). For many Latinas/os in the Southwest, that war represented their first experience with assimilation into mainstream U.S. society. For others, it represented their legal admission to the nation.

For example, Puerto Ricans were granted U.S. citizenship as a result of the 1917 Jones Act and the need for military manpower. According to Harry Franqui (2010), that admission to the nation entailed a paternalistic stance whereby the military establishment took the island's peasants as wards to be protected and reshaped before being drafted into the military. Yet, just as with African Americans, Latino military service did not bring equal rights to the servicemen. Instead, the segregation that ruled in the civilian sphere was imposed as a set of ethno-racial exclusions in the military sphere. Afro-Puerto Ricans were assigned to black units. Other Puerto Ricans served in separate Puerto Rican units. Yet the extended mobilization for World War I and the Wilsonian justification for the war in terms of defending national self-recognition combined to create a civil rights consciousness among the troops that contributed to the struggle for equal rights throughout the rest of the twentieth century. While some Latinas/os on the home front refused to register for the draft, either out of anarchist or pacifist inclinations or to protest second-class citizenship, most complied. There was some hope that active participation in the war effort would translate into a fairer peacetime social order.

While those hopes came to naught, World War II and a greatly increased military formed the logic of postwar American liberalism. Estimates of the total number of Latina/o soldiers who fought in the war range from 250,000 to 500,000 or about 2.5 to 5 percent of soldiers overall (Ruiz and Sánchez Korrol 2006). Out of these numbers emerged the American G.I. Forum (AGIF), a civil rights organization dedicated to addressing problems of discrimination and inequities endured by Mexican American veterans. Groups like AGIF showed that the military was one of the great theaters in which the struggle for Latina/o civil rights played itself out, a struggle that was not confined to the troops, but extended to those working in the manufacturing sector that supplied the military machine.

After 1941 and the United States' official entrance into World War II, demand for additional workers to replace those who left their jobs to serve grew. Initiatives like the Bracero Program brought Mexican contract laborers to work in U.S. agricultural jobs. In the postwar years, liberal policymakers would see the military culture as a vector through which they could effect social change. The idea of the military as a positive catalyst for social change came to a head in the 1960s, when Lyndon B. Johnson's Great Society programs promised civil and economic opportunity to marginalized groups, while the Vietnam War seemed, to many leaders of these groups, to show America's endemic racism and imperialist mindset.

During the first fifteen years of the Cold War era (1945–1960), when the U.S. military or the CIA staged interventions in places like Cuba, the Dominican Republic, and Guatemala, there was not much protest. When Fidel Castro seized power in Cuba and turned to the Left, however, this intervention became more violent. The 1960s seemed to be a turning point in U.S. history as anti-military politics briefly melded with American liberalism, identifying the fight against the Pentagon with the fight for equal rights. In sharp contrast to the Cold War celebration of the military, the New Left coalition sought to capitalize on the unpopularity of the Vietnam War; the draft of thousands of Latinos into the jungles of Vietnam added Latina/o voices to the antiwar protests at the same time that Chicana/o political movements sought more power for Chicana/o workers and communities. For example, groups like the Young Lords, a Puerto Rican nationalist group militant in several U.S. cities, and the Chicano Moratorium, a Chicano activist movement, organized anti–Vietnam War demonstrations in cities like Chicago, Los Angeles, and New York.

The conservative turn that came with the election of Ronald Reagan in 1980 shut down the lively discourse about American militarism, at least in establishment circles. The heavy military motif and celebration of U.S. military force, which was spread in the popular media, eclipsed the anti-military movement. Although more than one million people protested in the early 1980s against nuclear weapons, the movement was essentially shut out in Washington, DC. The end of the Cold War in the early 1990s seemed, at first, to promise a return to a less militaristic era. Military spending was, in fact, cut back, but the military still occupied a dominant position in the American political culture. Significantly, the first Gulf War (1990–1991) seemed to prove that the United States could fight wars without a "price." At the same time, the militarization of criminal activity, particularly smuggling drugs, allowed the military to intervene in Latin America in an increasingly heavy way—from the invasion of Panama in 1989 to the supplying of military equipment to governments in Colombia and Peru.

It is inherent in the logic of sustaining an imperial military presence that more and more issues are caught in the web of military concepts and "solutions." The criminal becomes an "enemy," and the enemy is dealt with by an increasingly militarized police force and a vast increase in incarceration. Although the military was never a major factor in enforcing Prohibition in the 1920s—when the criminals were mainly white Americans—drugs, associated with African Americans, Latinos, and "foreigners" became the object of militarized control. This, too, was a consequence of the conservative turn of the Reagan years, when legislation and investment in favor of military surveillance arose, keeping government spending high even as the prevailing ideology was about "shrinking" government. With this increase came the emergence of a discourse of invasion

MILITARISM   MANUEL G. AVILÉS-SANTIAGO

and loss of sovereignty, as well as an articulation of Latina/o immigrants and their communities as a threat to the nation. For example, in 1986, the Immigration Reform and Control Act (IRCA) intended to toughen U.S. immigration law by enforcing border security and requiring employers to monitor the immigration status of their employees. Subsequently, according to Leo Chavez (2013), the increasing levels of surveillance and militarization of the border have turned the border into a war zone. Here, the Minuteman Project, started in April 2005 by a group of private U.S. individuals in Arizona to monitor the U.S.-Mexico border's flow of immigrants, is telling. This armed vigilante subculture was fed by a nationalistic fervor: their slogan "Defending our Borders" complemented the spectacle presented by the mostly white, middle-aged male volunteers who favored military-style clothing, bore arms, and used military-style communication equipment. In response, groups like NotiMore and No Más Muertes (No More Deaths), along with the National Council of La Raza, have worked to demilitarize the border. Even so, it is not only on the border that we see the effects of the easy descent into military thinking: in many U.S. urban areas, policing has become more militaristic, with a proliferation of military gadgets and SWAT teams.

The events of September 11, 2001, reactivated and accentuated the dichotomy of us versus them and revived politics of militarism that had languished after the end of the Cold War. Under the terms of this new nationalism, dark-skinned people were both the enemy and the objects of oppression, who needed to be eliminated and "liberated," respectively, by military means. Latina/o bodies and communities fell within the penumbra of this national threat paradigm as subjects of the discourses that emerged from 9/11 in what Luz Gordillo (2009) refers to as "migraphobia." In that regard, the concurrent War on Terror (WOT) was exhibiting the paradoxical complexities of militarism while becoming a platform for fulfilling what George Bush referred to as "the ultimate act of patriotism" in reference to non-citizen U.S. soldiers, also known as "green card soldiers."

In an early assessment of the WOT in 2003, when the occupation of Iraq was still being presented as a success in the media, Jorge Mariscal (2003) pointed out that the renewal of militarism was not antipathetic to many Latina/o immigrants in the United States. The volunteer military at this point was finding some success in recruiting in the Latina/o community, who joined with mixed motives—patriotism, economic advantages in a recession, and a path to affordable higher education. In fact, during the ongoing WOT, Latinas/os have been targeted at twice the rate of the general population, including through public school programs such as the Junior Reserve Officers' Training Corps (JROTC) and Troops to Teachers (Maira 2009; G. Pérez 2015). Both of these initiatives aim to disseminate information about military values to high school students. Spanish-language advertising, such as the TV and radio recruitment campaign "Yo Soy el Army," has been another strategy.

Meanwhile, as Mariscal (2003) observes, "green card soldiers" represented many of the early casualties during the Iraq invasion of March 2003. Jocelyn Pacleb (2009) has gone on to argue that by granting posthumous citizenship and by celebrating the service of green card soldiers, the U.S. military is overshadowing the economic, social, and political disenfranchisement of Latina/o communities—a disenfranchisement that goes beyond the civic life and has extended to the absence or lack of recognition of Latinas/os in the configuration of U.S. military history.

If it is true that U.S. militarism, the traditional form by which a liberal society both marginalizes populations and ritually includes them, has shaped the civil experience of Latinas/os, it is also true that historical accounts and the most prominent media narratives have traditionally excluded mention of their part in American history, creating, in effect, a representational second-class citizenship (Avilés-Santiago 2014). During the last decade, Latina/o organizations have fought for the inclusion of the Latina/o military experiences in history books, documentaries, and films. Oral history has become primary source material aiding writers, historians, and filmmakers not only to better understand the stories, but also to include them in future accounts of the history of militarism and U.S. Latinas/os. In addition, Latinas/os are taking their representational history into their own hands and using digital social media to reproduce, circulate, and archive their military experience.

38

Modernity
José F. Aranda Jr.

In the context of Latinidad in the United States, modernity is a concept, ethos, and social and cultural border that supports and promotes the differences between a global North and a global South. As such, modernity cannot be easily divorced from its companion Latin American versions like *modernidad, lo moderno, modernismo,* and so on, or from the successes and failures associated with the wars of independence in the nineteenth century, or from the idealism and excesses associated with the revolutions of the twentieth century, or from the abuses of dictators and the incursions of U.S. imperialism especially. Modernity for Latinas/os is necessarily already hybrid, fluid, and contradictory, as well as a place and space in the material, cultural, and ontological registers that Néstor García Canclini (1995) understands individuals as always in the process of entering or leaving. In essence, living under the sign of modernity has a phantasmagorical quality, not unlike the confusion one intuits when Alice walks through the "looking glass," and realities and fantasies cease to have reliable differences. Modernity for U.S. Latinas/os is the accumulation of both fact and fiction, a combination of impulses that can be understood only in terms of powers that continually seek to reinforce what European settler colonialism instituted globally over five hundred years ago.

Therefore, the term "modernity" has its origins in the series of economic processes, technologies, linguistic, visual, and textual communication systems, and philosophical traditions that began in 1492 with the exploration and subsequent colonization of the lands later referred to as "India," the "New World," and the Americas and of their native peoples, who were termed "indios." Because modernity marks the moment when Europe begins to assert itself as a global power, this term often corresponds and collapses with other terms that evolved in an attempt to define, periodize, and categorize the significance of Europe beyond its own local perimeters. Philosophy, history, literature, the arts, science, and technology become venues and vehicles for asserting the supremacy and primacy of European civilization over all others. Thus, modernity is also coloniality, the first world-system, as Aníbal Quijano has demonstrated (Quijano and Wallerstein 1992); in its first phase, it gives rise to nation-states and capitalism, by way of large-scale slavery, the development of haciendas and plantation labor systems; in its second phase, it gives rise to the Enlightenment and contingent concepts like "the rights of man" and property as the basis of individual identity and agency. By the end of its second phase, modernity marks the transition of the European social order governed by monarchies to one governed under the premise of a representative government and a judiciary ruled by reason and precedent.

Because of its relationship to coloniality, modernity is also the source for the eruption of racial and gendered classifications of peoples, flora, and fauna encountered by Europeans in their conquest, subjugation, extraction, and conversion of "terra incognita" into wealth on behalf of and for the betterment of Europe. The imposition of these classifications on the colonized resulted in the institutionalization through official and unofficial means of what is popularly understood as racism, sexism, and patriarchy, as well as the imposition and regulation of gendered differences through sexuality, sexual identities, and reproduction, as María Lugones (2007)

argues. In short order, a caste system emerges out of conquest and slavery, which positions "el español" (the Spanish man) at the head of a complex hierarchy of racial and gendered categories that include *indio/a, negro/a, mulato/a, mestizo/a, castizo/a, morisco/a,* and so forth. The creation and maintenance of such classifications were aided and abetted by the imposition of Christianity on Indigenous peoples and slaves of African descent, with the concept of "soul" being introduced as a kind of spiritual landscape where conversion to the faith could be legitimized but also actualized, through force if need be. In the end, modernity structured the eventual merging of the Spanish Catholic "gente sin razón" in North America with the Protestant mandate of forwarding the "city on the hill" for the chosen elect with devastating and ongoing consequences. Hence, one of modernity's core processes is the production of the Other. According to Nelson Maldonado-Torres (2007), it is through the production of the Other that modernity as coloniality and coloniality as modernity sutures together the conquest of land, peoples, and extractable wealth into one unassailable and continuous project.

Thus, for Latina/o communities in the United States, modernity both reveals and occludes the histories and processes that have produced them. On the one hand, there is no way to understand Latinas/os without engaging the logic of coloniality, which transformed the hemisphere of the "New World" into outposts of European design. In this context, modernity reflects the promise of liberation that Enrique Dussel (2000) identifies as the major outcome of the Enlightenment: the fantasy of becoming modern, becoming human, becoming subjects of rather than objects of history. While Latina/o communities have strived to enact the promise of an autonomous coherent subjectivity in the United States, there have also been great hurdles and contradictions inherent in this project, including everything from racism to class warfare, from linguistic oppression—English-only movements—to nativist demonizations of the undocumented as alien, dangerous, unworthy of citizenship. Despite the civil rights movement and its successes, disenfranchisement returns precisely in those moments and spaces when Latinas/os are on the brink of redefining the terms of power that have underwritten modernity for centuries. The current nativist, anti-immigrant, and mainstream fear of the "browning of America" comes just when Latinas/os, the new "majority minority," threaten to destabilize the status quo through electoral politics.

On the other hand, if electoral representation is one of the rewards of modernity, then what are the costs of full citizenship given the European, white, patriarchal, Christian, exceptionalist origins of the U.S. Constitution? Another way of phrasing this question might be: What happens when those "DREAMers," those children of undocumented parents who have lived most of their lives in the United States, finally become "documented"? Then what? The absence of a clear response to either question above actually underscores the precarity of living under the sign of modernity for women and men and people of non-European descent.

Furthermore, the racial, religious, linguistic, sexual, political, and class diversity of U.S. Latinas/os precludes any totalizing attempt to critique modernity (or coloniality). From what subject position does one critique modernity if even the terms "Latinidad" and "Latina/o" are historically steeped in France's 1860s attempt to establish an empire in Mexico? The French architects of this invasion sought to make an empire based on shared Latin roots of language, Catholicism, and culture. These French architects of war invented the term "Latin America" to hail themselves as the saviors of Mexico and beyond.

Nonetheless, the invasiveness and pervasiveness of modernity in the Americas has never gone unchallenged by those marked as victims or objects of European or European-American settler colonialisms. This challenge is what Walter Mignolo (2000) calls "colonial difference," the recorded places and spaces where local people contested the global designs of coloniality. For instance, despite the inherent compromise in losing native languages in favor of Spanish, Portuguese, French, Dutch, and English, those languages have evolved away from their supposed purer versions in Europe. Nor have all native languages disappeared. In fact, some of those native speakers, like Zapotecas/os in Los Angeles, are among our newest Latina/o communities in the United States. Similarly with place names—Europe may have carved up and invented New Spain, New England, New Netherland, and New France, but since then, well after the colonization of the Americas and in the shadow of its continued punitive legacies, the majority of Latinas/os have lived, worked, and made their own places, referred to as "barrios" or "colonias," or in regional terms such as "Spanish Harlem," "Segundo Barrio," or "La Pequeña Habana." They gather in places of worship like iglesias, shop in bodegas, and practice santería or curanderismo. Likewise ethnic identification since the nineteenth century has evidenced an uneven multiplicity to be sure, but one inflected with the political conditions of its own social construction. Thus, derogatory terms like "greasers" or "spiks" are confronted and denounced in favor of self-identifications like Chicana/o or Nuyorican. Although the U.S. Census Bureau over time has adopted "Hispanic" and then "Latina/o" for identifying people of Latin American and Spanish origin, regional communities have signaled their local preferences and resistances. In Texas alone, people of Mexican descent have a range of choices, from "Hispanic" to "Tejano," "Chicano," "Mexicano," "Norteño," and "Mexican American" (with and without a hyphen). The multiplicity of such terms is no doubt a response to increased immigration from Mexico to Texas, but is also connected to the unprecedented militarization of the border since the North American Free Trade Agreement (NAFTA) and increased state-sponsored xenophobia since 9/11. This increased policing of the border has nonetheless provoked diffused but consistent resistance—a resistance that is often located in the very language used to describe a relationship to place or region under state surveillance. Thus, in the same period of nativist hostility that accompanied the implementation of NAFTA, Latina/o communities in California have increasingly favored referring to the state as "Califas."

Although evidence of "colonial difference" in the past, as in the present, is legion, where "local histories" reveal not only the imperial designs of Europe but also the ingenuity of the local non-European to resist, to adapt, and to re-assert agency, nonetheless, one should always be alert to the occluding powers of modernity, for the products of modernity are the products of coloniality. If modernity has evolved to be a series of horizons of "enlightenment" for Europe and its settler colonies, it has been structured to forget, hide, minimize, and distance itself from the blight it has created elsewhere. The means of creating this blight has been and remains violence, writ small and large, physical and spiritual, epistemological and ontological. For Nelson Maldonado-Torres, the goal of the "decolonial turn" in criticism is one of consistent opposition to what has driven and fueled modernity: war (2007, 262). Accordingly, for over five hundred years, the European justification of war in conquest of lands has permeated every aspect of human society. Unmasking the darker sides of modernity will always reveal the inherent violence of coloniality. By contrast, decoloniality presents itself as an ethical choice to move away from and against the imperial violence of Europe. The call for the end of imperial violence here is not utopian, but rather a concession to the need

for constant intervention wherever power and knowledge are linked in service of modernity (Maldonado-Torres 2007, 262). Invariably such interventions are the basis for the acts of justice Chela Sandoval refers to as "decolonial love" (2000, 140).

In years to come, the intricacies of understanding the historic role and function of modernity will come to dominate the field of Latina/o studies in unprecedented ways. This is not to say that the field has not already paid attention to this critical site of study. Rather, because of the demographic growth and changing political clout of Latinas/os in the United States modernity/coloniality as a site of critical inquiry will evolve over time. In other words, modernity/coloniality is continuously evolving with those in power and the instruments of their authority, as well as with those who aspire and achieve power, however belatedly. Indeed, already the social, cultural, and political status of Latinas/os waxes and wanes with each new electoral season, especially so with the presidential election. The moment that Latinas/os come to define the course of U.S. history will inevitably also mark the moment that ideological and class differences take on dimensions once reserved for white, Anglo, mainstreamed communities. Likewise, because of immigration and global economics, the field of Latina/o studies will increasingly need to account for the overlapping and competing modernities with Latin America. Alliances and collaborations with Latin American "theories of liberation" (Dussel 1985), which have been ongoing, will only strengthen and change because of the increased adoption and adaptation of these decolonial theories by Latina/o studies scholars.

39

Music

María Elena Cepeda

Music has long served as an essential conduit of Latina/o self-expression and social organization within the United States, and a primary vehicle through which Latinas/os are sonically, visually, and kinesthetically registered within the U.S. popular imagination. It constitutes a cultural vector through which Latinidad is rendered legible to both non-Latinas/os and Latinas/os alike, albeit not always in the most nuanced of terms. These processes possess demonstrable historical roots not only in more contemporary phenomena such as the most recent Latin(o) music "boom" of the late twentieth and early twenty-first centuries, but also in earlier moments such as the rumba craze of the 1930s and the mambo fad of the late 1940s and 1950s, among others. Significantly, these historical junctures are best understood not necessarily as signs of an increased acceptance of the Latina/o presence within the United States, but rather as market-driven responses to shifting demographics and political conditions throughout the hemisphere, such as the enhanced (although not unprecedented) incidence of transnational activity prompted by greater Latina/o (im)migration throughout the twentieth century. The latest Latin(o) music "boom" is thus in part a market-driven media phenomenon predicated upon the commodification of Latinidad and Latina/o audiences, or an attempt to capitalize on the monetary resources of Latina/o consumers and engage in the management of social identities (Levine 2001). Current market environments and genre categorizations notwithstanding, Latin(o) musical forms may be conceptualized as incisive social mirrors that lend greater insight into the communal values and practices of a given moment, particularly with respect to normative notions of ethno-racial identity, gender, sexuality, class, and nation.

In contemporary scholarship, the term "Latin(o) music" has been used to underscore the tensions between the designators "Latin" (the label that much mainstream U.S. media employs) and "Latina/o" (a grassroots designator utilized by many Latinas/os themselves), without privileging either. This terminological approach emphasizes the symbolic gaps between the category of "Latin music" and the social groups that presumably produce and consume these forms (Aparicio and Jáquez 2003). Indeed, the divergent messages reflected in this overlapping yet conflicting nomenclature echo the underlying character of the transnational Latin(o) music industry, which has long been dominated by crossover narratives and their attendant discourses of discovery. While cutting across all categories of difference, the dynamics of crossover have particularly reflected a black/white ethno-racial binary and the rigid understandings of "American" identity adhered to within the U.S. popular music industry, which has traditionally catalogued Latin(o) genres and Latina/o performers under "foreign," "ethnic," or "World" musics. Crossover, or the movement by Latina/o artists into the coveted Anglo market (wherein even veteran Latina/o performers are "discovered" by and in turn packaged as novel entities for mainstream consumption), demands considerable critical reflection. Crossover is not simply a question of assimilated Latina/o performers entering new markets because they now perform in English, reside in the United States, and record music that incorporates genres more widely associated with the Anglo/English-speaking world, such as rock or pop (D. Vargas 2012). To adhere to such logic is to ignore the realities of Latina/o musical production over time, during which hybridity has constituted the norm as opposed to the exception, and "hybrids of musical hybrids" such as bugalú, bachatón, salsatón, vallenato moderno, and crunkiao (to cite but a few examples) have been constantly surfacing under the expanding influence of globalization's time-space compression. Moreover, to question the logic of crossover is to challenge the highly gendered, raced association of rock and pop in particular with the musical production of Anglo males, a critical stance that ultimately reaffirms Latinas/os' well-documented historical contributions to global genres not typically associated with Latin(o) musical production.

The workings of the Latin(o) music industry further reveal the markedly gendered structural elements of its modes of production, representation, and dissemination. While numerous women such as Victoria Hernández, Celia Cruz, and Gloria Estefan have played pivotal roles as promoters, business owners, composers, and musicians (Glasser 1995; Aparicio 1999a, 2002; Guevara 2003; Cepeda 2010), most often the popular vision of Latinas in the industry has been exclusively limited to that of lead vocalist or back-up singer/dancer. The very notion of what constitutes Latin(o) music in the United States has also been historically informed by class, as the initial samplings of Latin American genres deemed fit for production in the United States (such as the European-inflected Puerto Rican danza and the Colombian bambuco) were selected by more privileged Latin American industry executives who generally had little contact with the local musicians whose talents were featured on these early recordings. Finally, inter-Latina/o tensions, lack of Latina/o upper management or ownership within the U.S. recording industry, and regional rivalries have also shaped the character and distribution of Latin(o) music across time, as witnessed throughout the brief, conflict-ridden history of the Latin Grammys (Cepeda 2010; Pacini Hernandez 2010).

Despite its often vexed relationship with the transnational recording industry, Latin(o) music has also long served as a productive site for the exercise of Latina/o political and artistic agency. Key periods such as the lively jazz scene of wartime and post–World War II Los Angeles, the heyday of politically oriented salsa in the New York City barrios of the 1970s, and the rise of hip-hop culture in the same city during the late 1970s and 1980s underscore the frequency and depth of these communal artistic efforts (Rondón 1980; R. Rivera 2003; Macías 2008). For example, the emergence of Latin jazz in the 1940s and 1950s under figures such as Machito and his Afro-Cubans and Chico O'Farrill demonstrates the intimate relationship between broader structural factors and the development of Latina/o artistic movements. In the case of Latin jazz, inequitable New York housing policies such as redlining fomented the musical social ties and cultural practices that arose as both a product of and a response to institutional discrimination (Valentín-Escobar, forthcoming). Throughout the United States, Latin(o) musics have thus contributed to vital place-making processes within and across various Latina/o communities. However, until recently these movements have passed with little acknowledgement of the multifaceted artistic collaborations forged between Latinas/os and other ethno-racial minorities, particularly African Americans, throughout their trajectories. That said, much like Latinas/os themselves, Latin(o) musical genres cannot be read exclusively through the lens of African, Indigenous, and Spanish hybridity. To the contrary, (im)migration from around the globe has contributed to the transculturated sonic and dance forms that have emerged with Latina/o communities, as noted in genres such as the wide-ranging norteño, whose accordion-based instrumentation can be traced to the arrival of Polish immigrants in northern Mexico during the nineteenth century.

Just as Latin(o) musical forms are most accurately conceptualized as inter- and multi-ethnic creations, so must they be understood as direct products of vibrant transnationalisms. Indeed, the genres themselves, much like their modes of production and distribution, clearly illustrate the impacts of transborder flows. The extensive mobility of genres such as the cumbia (originally of the Colombian Caribbean, but now existing in myriad localized versions around the globe) epitomizes the impact that the movement of bodies, the long arm of global media, and the introduction of new technologies in general often have on once distinctly regional expressive forms (Pacini Hernandez 2010; Fernández L'Hoeste and Vila 2013). Nevertheless, the singular sonic qualities, visual vocabulary, and kinesthetic character of now globalized Latin(o) musical genres cannot be entirely divorced from the socioeconomic, political, and cultural conditions from which they originally arose, which inevitably encompass colonialism proper as well as internal colonialism. Shaped by the interracial and class tensions that have long defined life for those of Mexican descent in the U.S.-Mexico borderlands, the conjunto music of Texas of artists such as Lydia Mendoza and Leonardo (Flaco) Jiménez offers a prime example of how many Latin(o) musical forms have arisen in direct response to the material circumstances of internal colonialism (M. Peña 1985).

Reflecting the hybrid underpinnings of the genres themselves, current scholarly investigations into Latin(o) music have largely been interdisciplinary. Much of this work has borrowed from the cultural studies tradition, and specifically its tendency to celebrate the more agential and/or transgressive facets of Latin(o) musical production, performance, and reception. Latin(o) musical genres more readily recognized as "ethnic" contribute to the bulk of the scholarly corpus, although in recent years research on more so-called commercial forms such as hip-hop, reggaetón, pop, punk, and rock has also materialized (R. Rivera 2003; Pacini Hernandez, Fernández L'Hoeste, and Zolov 2004; Habell Pallán 2005; Rivera, Marshall, and Pacini Hernandez 2009; Cepeda 2010; Pacini Hernandez 2010). These latter studies acknowledge the impossibility of truly extricating economic concerns from any type of musical production, regardless of genre; the fact that ethnic forms and the communities from which they arise do not exist as static entities; and the error of treating ethnic genres as somehow more aesthetically "Latina/o" or "authentic" in character, a move that ultimately erases the multiple historic contributions of Latinas/os to mainstream musical forms and bypasses the intrinsically hybrid foundations of Latin(o) music as a whole. In sum, the growing scholarly emphasis on commercial forms and/or the commercialization of ethnic genres underscores the arbitrary nature of such strict categorizations.

While much of the existing scholarship focuses primarily on the question of Latina/o ethno-racial identity, some scholars have opted to engage in more comprehensive approaches to categories of difference within Latin(o) music, and to examine the intersecting roles of gender, sexuality, class, nation, and language. Major (inter)disciplinary influences on the contemporary analysis of Latin(o) musics in addition to cultural studies include ethnic studies, ethnomusicology, gender studies, history, literary studies, media studies, performance studies, and queer studies. Relying on a blend of these critical approaches, recent scholarship in the field has at times explicitly embraced a transnational perspective on musical production and performance, just as it has rejected traditional categorizations of Latin(o) music as that which is solely performed in Spanish by Latin

American (im)migrants; as forms that have experienced parallel yet separate trajectories vis-à-vis Anglo music; or as genres possessing neatly defined, irrefutable cultural origins. Increasingly, some scholars have also highlighted the vital musical contributions of lesser-studied Latina/o populations, a perspective that illuminates pan-Latina/o cultural practices just as it expands the parameters of Latinidad writ large (Cepeda 2010; Pacini Hernandez 2010; Vargas 2012). Research exploring the embodied elements of Latina/o musical spaces as vital sites of queer place-making has also emerged as of late (Paredez 2009; Rivera-Servera 2012; Vargas 2012). With few exceptions (Fiol-Matta 2017), however, the scholarship on gender and sexuality in Latin(o) music has centered on heterosexual women. The symbiotic relationship between dance and Latin(o) music constitutes another frequent gap in the scholarly literature.

Given the rapid demographic growth of the various Latina/o populations and the subsequent increased visibility and audibility of Latina/o musical practices in the United States and around the globe, Latin(o) musical forms will certainly persist as one of the more readily identifiable markers of Latina/o identity. As the contradictory site of tropicalized presentations of Latinidad as well as their contestations, Latin(o) music lays bare the frequent conflicts between musical production on the ground as well as the transnational market forces and more localized circumstances that inform its creation, dissemination, and reception. The multifarious genres that fall under the category of "Latin(o) music" thus serve as intensely hybrid sensorial texts that exemplify the complex dynamics of Latina/o cultural production in response to globalization.

40

Nationalism
Raúl Coronado

Is the nation—that famed "imagined community" Benedict Anderson theorized back in 1983—the best way we have to imagine belonging to something greater than ourselves? Notwithstanding Anderson's grave historical inaccuracies in accounting for nationalism in the Americas or his over-reliance on print culture as the means by which nationalism was promulgated (Chatterjee 1993; Lomnitz-Adler 2001; Castro-Klarén and Chasteen 2003), what continues to make his anthropological theory compelling is its emphasis on the discursive nature of the nation (it is imagined) and its profoundly affective orientation (it causes people to feel and act on a wide array of emotions). It's a way of imagining oneself belonging to a community where one will never meet everyone in that community, where that community is limited and not universal. Born of necessity, out of pain, in coming together as a nation, the imagined community redeems itself and that painful past, cementing the cathartic, emotional bonds even further. Thus, the imagined community "invents" an imagined past with its origins in antiquity, narrating its history of travails leading to the redeeming moment of the nation's coming into being.

The powerful, centrifugal force in his anthropological theory hovers across the spiritual-transcendence spectrum: the nation serves as the community's ontological foundation. Religion, argues Anderson (1983), was one of the great affective sources from which the nation drew its seductive power. For millennia,

Christianity had offered humanity in the West an "imaginative response to the overwhelming burden of human suffering" (10). The power of religion, Anderson claims, was in its "attempt to explain" loss, grief, and pain. Likewise, Christianity "responds to the obscure intimations of immortality, generally by transforming fatality into continuity. In this way, it concerns itself with the links between the dead and the yet unborn, the mystery of re-generation" (10–11). Religion provides ontological meaning, certainty, and truth, akin to Jacques Derrida's concept of metaphysics of presence, as "that which makes possible an absolutely pure and absolutely self-present self knowledge. . . . God's infinite understanding is the other name for the logos as self-presence" (1997, 98). Thus, where Christianity had offered access to transcendence, a buoyed sense of fullness and belonging, to the eternal for millennia, that relationship began to fracture, collapsing ever more with each succeeding wave of thought that chipped away at Christianity's hegemony: the Protestant Reformation, the Renaissance, the Enlightenment, and, finally, the demise of monarchical rule and rise of republican government (C. Taylor 2007). In the process—and to be very clear, through no tautological causation, only pure accident—this universal human need to access transcendence cathected itself to the nation as an alternate source of ontological certainty. The nation was imagined, constructed, narrated into existence, as Homi Bhabha famously riffed on Anderson's thesis (Bhabha 1990). It became what is true, authentic, real, undeniable, something to be fought for and, if necessary, to die for. It is elusive, emotional; it inspires and unites; it divides and causes unspeakable, unpardonable sins.

During the wars of Spanish-American independence, revolutionary creoles sought to shift the people's loyalty from Catholic monarchical rule to newly imagined republican nations. Their task, far from easy, required a reworking of a Spanish-American imaginary that had constructed their world on a concentric model of belonging that paralleled Catholic political philosophy's account of sovereignty (Annino and Guerra 2003). If the secularization thesis offered above—the one beginning with the Reformation and ending with the Enlightenment—holds for the northern Atlantic Protestant world, it certainly did not for the southern Atlantic Catholic world, which remained resolutely Catholic, not admitting of Cartesian, Baconian, or Lockean thought until the late eighteenth century (Lanning 1940; Herr 1958; Lavrin 1996). To be clear, the Spanish-American road to a disenchanted world was not a belated one, but an alternate, divergent road to modernity, as *Divergent Modernities: Culture and Politics in Nineteenth-Century Latin America,* the translation of Julio Ramos's foundational book *Desencuentros de la modernidad en América Latina: Literatura y política en el siglo XIX* declares (2001). At the outer realm of this Spanish American cosmos was the universal Catholic-Christian Hispanic imaginary, consisting of all members of the Hispanic monarchy, from Spain to Spanish America to the Philippines (Rafael 2010). Next were the various kingdoms or viceroyalties comprising the global Hispanic monarchy, followed by regional imaginaries, what may be associated with the *patria chica.* It was these layered, concentric, and at times competing loyalties, at different affective levels, that had to be reconfigured into the love of *the* nation (Annino and Guerra 2003).

This legacy of belonging to multiple, related communities can be traced throughout the nineteenth century and, arguably, the present. It helps explain the profound solidarity between revolutionaries from throughout Spanish America, each finding common cause in their struggle against Spain even as they sought to construct their particular nationally imagined community. And yet the struggle was not always against Spain. As Jaime

E. Rodríguez O. (1998) has persuasively argued, the wars of Spanish-American independence erupted, first, as a global civil war. Grievances and radical calls for reform defined these early struggles. But as it became clear that reform would not come soon, Mexico and other countries on the American mainland shifted their sight toward independence. Meanwhile, in Cuba and Puerto Rico, planters and merchants prospered from the unfolding sugar boom and lucrative slave trade, thus thwarting the cause of national independence (Poyo 1989; Schmidt-Nowara 1999; Figueroa 2005).

Indeed, nineteenth-century Spanish American nationalisms sought with desperation—as all nationalisms do—the hearts of their citizens (Brading 1985; Franco 1999; Chiaramonte 2004; Chiaramonte, Marichal, and Granados García 2008; Rodríguez O. 2008). The absence of a free press during the colonial period, which had stymied the cultivation of consensus across large swaths of Spanish America, explains, in part, the difficulty of nation-states to congeal (Mexico, for example, experienced a coup virtually every two years for the first fifty years of its existence) (Guerra and Lempérière 1998). But nationalism (distinct from the apparatus of the state), as a nostalgic desire to bring into being a community, would continue to fuel efforts throughout the Americas.

In what is today the United States, nineteenth-century Mexican communities in the Southwest were only beginning to turn their hearts to the newly formed Mexican state when U.S. conquest and colonization disrupted and discombobulated those efforts (Z. Vargas 2010). The East Coast, on the other hand, received waves of revolutionary expatriates, especially from the Caribbean, who settled in communities in Philadelphia, New York, and Florida (Vega 1984; Poyo 1989; Mirabal 2017). From there, they created liberal to revolutionary organizations, all with an eye to produce change at a variety of levels, from the local to hemispheric. They also produced vibrant print cultures, all writing to and, simultaneously, producing imagined communities that spanned the Hispanic Atlantic world (Lazo 2008; Almeida 2011; Vogeley 2011; Coronado 2013). We see, then, the Ecuadorian Vicente Rocafuerte in the early nineteenth century, the Cuban José Martí at century's end, and the Puerto Rican Bernardo Vega in the early twentieth century writing from the U.S. East Coast about the national liberation struggles of Ecuador, Cuba, and Puerto Rico, respectively, and yet being simultaneously wedded to the liberation of the rest of their Spanish American brethren. It is this affective concept of nationalism that fueled the radical social movements of the 1960s and 1970s. If the Spanish American nationalism of the nineteenth century sought independence from Spain and territorial consolidation of their respective nations, the Chicana/o and Puerto Rican nationalisms of the 1960s and 1970s were inspired more by a desire to undo the racial ideologies that had denigrated anything and everything Latina/o by paramilitary designs to actually secede from the United States (Klor de Alva 1989). This is not to say that they were fruitless. What they sought to accomplish was a complete reversal of racist discourses (which had had very real material consequences) that had debased and deracinated Chicanas/os and Puerto Ricans. Political and cultural activists celebrated their cultures and advocated self-determination. They organized festivals, political rallies, and all kinds of electoral and equitable-labor campaigns. Thus, in his 1969 "Plan Espiritual de Aztlán" (Valdez and Steiner 1972, 402–6), Alurista vividly brought to life the long-lost mythic Chicana/o homeland of Aztlán, borrowing the concept from the fortuitous midcentury flourishing of scholarship on Mesoamerica. Mainland Puerto Ricans turned to the similarly romantic concept of Borinquen, the name of the island given by its original inhabitants (Klor de Alva 1989). They wrote odes to their homelands, producing yarns that would come to serve as spiritual foundations for their communities' cultural renaissance (Valdez and Steiner 1972; Babín and Steiner 1974; Anaya and Lomelí 1989; Santiago 1995). Within the academy, where racist social scientists had long blamed Latinas/os' culture for their socioeconomic position, a new wave of Latina/o scholars used their pens as weapons, firing off critiques and offering new conceptual models for Chicana/o and Puerto Rican history, which were influenced by the prevailing cultural nationalism of the period (Romano-V. 1968; Bonilla and González 1973; Almaguer 1989).

The case of Puerto Rican nationalism, however, most certainly remains distinct, given the virtual colonial status of the island where pro-independence groups have long sought and fought for independence from the United States, the most memorable being the 1950s Nationalist Party's armed insurrection and the subsequent unleashing of U.S. troops and bombs on the island (Denis 2015). Mainland Puerto Rican nationalism has long been fueled by the continuous, circular migration to and from the island, enriching and producing a diasporic sense of Puerto Ricanness (Duany 2002; Flores 2009). The process is somewhat similar for Mexican American communities (the key defining difference being that all Puerto Ricans were granted U.S. citizenship in 1917, making migration easier), where the contact between recent Mexican immigrants continues to feed a sense of a Mexican American imagined community (T. Jiménez 2010).

The social movements of the 1960s and 1970s produced regional networks of communication that did not solidify in the way they had before. For the first time, Mexican Americans from Texas, New Mexico, California, and other parts of the Southwest and Midwest came together, most clearly in the 1969 Denver National Chicano Youth Liberation conference, which saw as many as 1,500 participants (Ontiveros 2013; Gómez-Quiñones

and Vásquez 2014). And yet because of limited technological and financial means, there was little communication between the large, settled communities of Chicanas/os in the Southwest and Puerto Ricans on the East Coast, notwithstanding the well-known though smaller integrated community of Chicanas/os and Puerto Ricans in Chicago (F. Padilla 1985). It is in part for these reasons that Latina/o studies would develop along more national lines of Chicana/o studies and Puerto Rican studies, though the East Coast, because of demographic numbers, would see an expansion of Puerto Rican studies to Caribbean studies as well (Cabán 2003a).

By the early 1970s, we begin to see a small though robust number of Latina/o scholars, the first generation to enter universities beyond the handful that had arrived in the early to mid-twentieth century, come together and advocate for the creation of Chicana/o and Puerto Rican studies, all in the name of their people (Cabán 2003b). Nationalism, then, has served as a crucial antidote to the crushing, painful conditions that racism had imposed on these peoples; the nation offered redemption, brought the people into being, revealing to them their long lost history rooted as it was in Aztlán and Borinquen. But, to return to Anderson's definition, the nation is also limited: it xenophobically demarcates those who are of the nation and those who are not. And, quickly, by the late 1970s and early 1980s, those who had been relegated to the margins of the marginalized—specifically, women and queers—began to speak back to the heteropatriarchal male leaders of these communities who sought to demean and dominate them (Moraga and Anzaldúa 1981; Moraga 1983b). The nation began to crumble, even as some, like Cherríe Moraga, continued to seek to invigorate Chicana/o nationalism through her vision of Queer Aztlán (1993a).

Given this complex, moving history of cultural and political renaissance, we can see how Chicana/o studies and Puerto Rican studies can be so wedded to the idea of their respective nations, their imagined communities. Cultural nationalism had offered solace against a painful history of conquest, colonization, and racism; and it had offered cause for celebration. Remove that and what would be left? Thus, the shift to pan-Latina/o studies since the 1990s has often been seen as an attempt to erase or diminish this history (I. García 1997). Which returns us to our original question: Is the nation the only conceptual tool we have at our disposal to imagine our communities? What would it mean to imagine ourselves as comprised of the diverse, diasporic Latina/o communities that now inhabit the United States, including Mexican Americans, Puerto Ricans, Cubans, Dominicans, and Central Americans? This question is far from being restricted to abstract academic hand-wringing. Scholars have turned to the material, social emergence of a pan-Latina/o community, where Latinas/os of various national origins not only socialize with one another, but, indeed, are intermarrying and producing a much more heterogeneous sense of community (J. Flores 2000; Suárez-Orozco and Páez 2009). If the nation's power emerges from its ability to offer ontological certainty, redemption from a painful past, and an affectively powerful sense of belonging, how might a sense of Latinidad offer something comparable, especially given that being "Latina/o" correlates with no particular nation?

Here, we may take a cue from Juan González's (2011) *Harvest of Empire: A History of Latinos in America*, in which the lesson "we are here because you were there" emerges as the predominant leitmotif. The history of U.S. intervention in Latin America becomes the central cathartic unifying thread. If the "painful" thesis is U.S. conquest, colonization, and on-going imperialism, then the antithesis would be a sense of Latinidad that seeks to redress that history.

The concentric model of belonging that had defined the Hispanic monarchical world may be of use here. Indeed, we may be witnessing a reconfiguration of that model out in the social world, as the many examples of social-political interaction between Latinas/os of various national origins reveals (De Genova and Ramos-Zayas 2003; Aparicio 2007; Rocco 2014). As webs of communication continue to expand, bringing, for example, Latinas/os from south Florida in contact (even if virtual) on a more regular basis with those from northern New Mexico or those from Connecticut with those from California, we could begin to see a less nation-based imagined community for Latinas/os and a more concentric one, rooted in the histories of more local, national-origin communities, expanding further out to diverse regional communities, then out to a more national level, and, perhaps indeed, to the hemispheric. Far from homogenous, these concentric communities of Latinidad may already be in formation, producing not staid accounts of commonality but of productive, at times conflictive if not contradictory accounts of belonging and the public sphere (C. Beltrán 2010).

41

Performance

Ramón H. Rivera-Servera

"Performance" and "Latina/o" gained popularity as critical keywords designating objects of study and critical optics for the analysis and theorization of Latina/o life and culture in the United States during the 1990s. The coincidence between the gradual eclipsing of "Hispanic" by "Latina/o"—as the umbrella designator for interethnic and pan-ethnic social interactions, imaginaries, and coalitions of Latin American–descent populations in the United States—and the rise of performance—as a cultural unit and as a theoretical approach to identity as iterative effort rather than stable truth—led to the emergence of *latinidad* as a term that more accurately renders the dynamic, processual nature of the ethno-national range and crossings "Latina/o" as a concept sought to encompass. This shift to performance and *latinidad* also avoids the settler-colonialist assumptions behind the privileging of Spanish or Hispanic as the primary unifying feature of Latin American–descent populations by extending the repertoires of cultural practice central to Latina/o studies beyond those centered on linguistic genealogies, especially writing, and moving beyond Spanish European heritage and colonial history into an engagement with the plurality of the region and its traveled histories, including African, Asian, and Indigenous routes and communities. Moreover, this shift, a critical performative feat in and of itself, also anchored an increasingly comparative and inter-Latina/o focus for Latina/o studies, which, while maintaining the significant legacy and current value of

the varying ethno-national specificities within Latina/o culture (Cuban, Puerto Rican, Mexican, Dominican, and so on), sought to understand the promises and frictions of constituting an amalgamated ethno-racial category within the national and international spheres. Performance offers an object of study and an analytic for understating *latinidad*.

"Performance," as a keyword in critical cultural analysis, can refer to presentational aesthetics and their execution in formal artistic practice (such as music, theater, dance, and performance art). Scholarly attention to theater has perhaps been the most influential to early conversations about Latinas/os. Especially significant have been the historical accounts authored by Nicolás Kanellos since the 1970s, but especially his 1990 historical survey; thematic and formal analysis of Chicano drama by Jorge Huerta (1982, 2000) and Jon Rossini (2008); feminist critique of Chicano theater by Yolanda Broyles-González (1994) and Yvonne Yarbro-Bejarano (2001); Tomás Ybarra-Frausto's critical examination of humor and *rasquachismo* in the *carpa* tradition in the Southwest United States (1989); and Alberto Sandoval-Sánchez's critical engagement with Latina/o representation on Broadway as well as on community stages across the United States (1999). Emergent from the scholarship on Latina/o theater is the formulation of a public culture built in relation to dominant (to varying degrees) institutions and cultural traditions: from the historical assumptions of Broadway's whiteness to Latina/o culture's patriarchal and heteronormative orientations. Also evidenced in this scholarship are long traditions of artistic practice drawing from the cultural specificities of Latina/o experience and resulting in a discernable cultural formation specific to *latinidad*.

Performance can also approximate other communicative acts that deploy embodied aesthetic frameworks (such as ritual, festivity, and political rallies) as well as quotidian practices that recur to or can be analyzed as activating performance codes and conventions in social exchange (as in speech, dress, and gesture). In its most basic definition, "performance" concerns communicative events that present aesthetically framed and rehearsed behavior with varying degrees of intention before an audience, be it human or nonhuman, real or imagined. Key to this version of performance was the scholarship of theorist and theater director Richard Schechner, who expanded the criteria of cultural practice we could understand as performance by applying the aesthetic analytics previously focused on formal theater and casting an anthropological frame on performance as a social arrangement that organizes performers and audiences alike. Schechner pinpointed intention as the key component in rehearsal and presentation, which together structure all performance as "twice behaved behavior" (1985). Also influential, especially in the approach to quotidian performances, was the work of communication scholar and ethnographer Dwight Conquergood, who saw in performance repertoires embodied alternatives to what he labeled the "scriptocentrism" of Western culture (2002).

In all three of the frameworks outlined above (artistic, cultural, quotidian), performance constitutes an object of study; it is a discernible cultural unit with established scholarly engagements from academic disciplines in the humanities and humanistic social sciences. All three frameworks allow for approaches to Latina/o cultural and social life that attend to the role of aesthetic communication in the formulation of *latinidad*. Thus, performance serves as a key object of study in the development of Latina/o studies as an academic field. Along with language, literature, and the visual arts, performance—from artistic to cultural to quotidian—offers a catalogue of traits that evidences Latina/o culture, much the way that theater does, relative to the nationalist construct of USAmerican culture. As theater and performance scholar David Román (1997) observed, "Latino performance—from its earliest manifestations in the religious and secular cultural rituals of the indigenous people of the Southwest to the incorporation of many of these rituals into the nascent theater conventions of the mid-nineteenth century—has primarily functioned to rehearse and enact various Latino cultural beliefs and customs" (152).

In their foundational studies of Mexican American folklore, Tejano scholars Américo Paredes (1958, 1995b) and Jovita González (1997, 2006) found in the performance cultures of the *corrido* and *vaquero* customs, respectively, a bordered, often contrapuntal position to the narrative of USAmerican exceptionalism. Performance confirms and extends the definitional model of "beliefs and customs" into a relational subaltern position to serve as an agentive platform/tactic for articulating a minoritarian position and intervention relative to a majoritarian Anglo-American culture. Both scholars transformed the direction of the field of folklore studies from a tradition in which Mexican culture had been documented within a paternalistic or intentionally objectifying framework in terms of what literary scholar Ramón Saldívar (2006) has aptly characterized as the interrelated paradigms and agendas of "entertainment" and "colonization" (33). Their inaugural venture into Mexican American performance culture founded what could be identified as the Texas school of performance studies, grounded in folklore studies and using an anthropological methodology. Their approach was taken up and expanded in the important ethnographic works of anthropologists José E. Limón (1992, 1994) on subaltern aesthetics and Richard Flores (1995) on performance practices of gifting, among others, which furthered the critical optics for approximating the creative force of marginalized communities, especially in the Texas region. This scholarship became foundational for a new generation of scholars in Latina/o studies for whom performance similarly offered a grounding of the political promise of *latinidad*.

In other Latina/o ethno-national contexts, musical and dance performance have played similarly central roles in the definition of and affirmative claim to a Latina/o cultural position and legacy relative to USAmerican national culture. Bomba, salsa, and hip-hop, for example, have been central to the development of a Puerto Rican cultural studies that attends to the history and politico-economic coordinates of diaspora. Juan Flores (2000) and Frances R. Aparicio (1998), both scholars who have focused on Puerto Rican popular music and its relationship to Latina/o culture, have developed key entry points into an analysis of performance that invests in both the mobile, transnational nature of cultural forms and the contextual specificities of the practice in local communities. Juan Flores introduced a healthy dose of suspicion over the rubric of *latinidad*, evidenced by the differential regard with which performance practices and their attendant labor are approached in a mainstream where musical genres and practices come to be regarded simplistically as amalgamated commodities of *latinidad*, by warning against the potential loss of critical politico-economic specificity and history. He ultimately invites an analysis that prioritizes ethno-national specificity. In contrast, Frances R. Aparicio (2003a) understands the critiques of *latinidad* as both a top-down homogenizing amalgamation of Latina/o difference and as bottom-up shallow utopias of cohesion that ignore tension. Nonetheless, she insists on the increased significance of *latinidad* and labors to introduce a more complex and grounded approach that attends to both "convergences and divergences" of *latinidad*.

It is no coincidence that the scene that prompts Aparicio (2007) to "(re)construct" *latinidad* in light of its dynamic incorporation of Latina/o difference is a concert she attended with a heterogeneous group of Latinas/os with differing ethno-national, racial, class, migratory, and educational backgrounds. In the shared experience of a Latina/o concert, she argues, a version of *latinidad* emerges in which ethno-national specificity is not simply substituted; rather, this specificity can complement it, exceed it, or challenge it in promising ways. In this scene, *interlatinidad* emerges as a paradigm oriented toward the dynamics of performance and animated in its assembled audience. This is an important move for the analysis of *latinidad* and one that orients analysis away from the close reading and decoding of meaning of specific performance phenomena and toward an engagement with it as social phenomena. Scholars in Latina/o dance studies have followed this approach. In my work, I look at movement-based performance practices that assemble Latina/o queer collectives into proto-political and at times explicitly political units resulting from the "convivencias diarias" or quotidian social interactions facilitated by performance (Rivera-Servera 2012). In her study of salsa dancing in Los Angeles, Cindy García (2013) turns her ethnographic eye not just to the specificities of choreography and technique but also to the quotidian negotiations undertaken by club patrons in getting to, affording, and experiencing the economic and social hierarchies of salsa networks.

Other scholars have advanced significant theorizations of Latina/o culture by focusing on the constitution of a Latina/o audience in popular cultural dynamics, especially fan cultures since the 1999 Latin music explosion. For example, in an important study of the fan cultures and the collective mourning of Tejana pop star Selena Quintanilla, which is much like Aparicio's engagement with the heterogeneous assembly of fans before the homogenously packaged sign of *latinidad*, Deborah Paredez (2009) demonstrates how popular performance may open up the space for the emergence of

Latina/o publics. Similarly, Laura G. Gutiérrez (2010) pursues the assumptions of these publics to transnational scales where *mexicanidad*, like *latinidad*, circulates as feminist and queer texts and animates social networks.

Ultimately, the most commonly deployed approach to Latina/o performance has focused on the labor of the performer as agentive cultural force. The work of queer feminist Chicana scholar Alicia Arrizón has been foundational here. Focusing on the tactics of performance as intervention, Arrizón (1999) launched both an archival and contemporary critical project seeking to outline ways Latina feminist and queer positions resulted from the creative critical actions enacted by performers in the public sphere. Scholars such as Lawrence La Fountain-Stokes (2011) and Deborah Vargas (2012) have followed suit, attending to cross-dressing/transloca and voice performances, respectively, to identify alternatively queer and feminist genealogies of practice attentive to the dynamism of *latinidad* as/in performance.

The analytical frameworks developed to understand the vast range of communication and cultural practices we classify as performance have been similarly influential in developing understandings of the iterative nature of subjectivity under the rubric of performativity. Here performance anchors an anti-essentialist position that advances a cultural theory reliant on the rehearsed, repeated enactments of conventions, be they gender, race, or others. Performance unsettles the assumed certainty of cultural and social coordinates by highlighting them as effects of performative enactment and thus dependent on continuous repetition to sustain their force and apparent constancy. Originally developed out of the speech act theories of J. L. Austin as adapted to the theorization of gender by feminist queer studies scholar Judith Butler and sexuality by queer literary scholar and theorist Eve Kosofsky Sedgwick, performativity has journeyed from a primarily discursive orientation into an increasingly embodied one. The introduced and often productive (but not reproductive) uncertainty of the performative has opened avenues for a range of minoritarian critiques that rely on the gaps created by the iterative model to identify alternatives to the previously assumed incorruptibility of social truths.

Feminist and queer approaches to Latina/o performance have tended to interrelate performance and performativity. José Esteban Muñoz is the most widely cited scholar of Latina/o queer performance studies in the field. Beginning with his work on disidentification, or the strategic distancing and engagement with dominant cultural forms by minoritarian performers (1999), and extending to his understanding of the utopian politics of performance as always in the horizon (2009), Muñoz modeled an approach that pursued the formal practices of Latina/o performance art or the quotidian aesthetics of queer subjects as discernible cultural units worthy of analysis and capable of political intervention but also as points of departure for the understanding and theorization of performativity and its governing of both discursive and embodied orientations to and interventions in the world, as lived and as imagined. The work of feminist and queer theorist Juana María Rodríguez (2003, 2014b) follows a similar trajectory in pursuing Latina/o queer practices as performative discursive formations that in their repetition at once outline the emergence of *latinidad* as a discursive field and pursue its iterative constitution as a queer openness with promising destabilizing features.

In sum, performance—in its various approximations as cultural unit of analysis or discursive iterative formation; as formal aesthetic practice or social convention; as assertive of or challenging to *latinidad*—has become foundational to Latina/o cultural studies and allied disciplines concerned with and invested in the ways *latinidad* emerges from social interaction, communicative exchanges, aesthetic expression, and political action.

42

Philosophy

Linda Martín Alcoff and Rolando Pérez

Philosophy is generally understood as consisting of ancient Greek and modern European figures such as Plato, Aristotle, Kant, and Nietzsche. The work of such figures is presented as a decontextualized search for truth, as if philosophical discourse was delinked from the place or the people that gave rise to it. In reality, philosophy has always been a tool of intervention in the specific life-world of communities and individuals, providing a meta-level analysis that both reveals and shifts conventional assumptions. Hence, all philosophies bear the trace of different periods and localities.

The concept of Latina/o philosophy is, today, an intervention in dominant assumptions about philosophy itself. It is a conscious move to expand the imaginary geography of philosophical thought and to expose the Eurocentrism of the standard philosophical categories. Generally, the term is not used simply to describe philosophy written by Latinas/os; rather, it is used in a more delimited yet robust way to refer to philosophies that are grounded in, and responsive to, a Latina/o context, whether or not written by Latinas/os. This is similar to the way in which "American" pragmatism is often understood, that is, as a philosophical trend that bears the marks of its historical and national genealogy.

Latina/o philosophy tends toward certain topics such as immigration justice, hybrid identities, liberation theology and philosophy, citizenship, and race (Valadez 2000; Lugones 2003; Mendieta 2007; Nascimento 2013;

Rocco 2014). Although the field spans diverse philosophical traditions (analytic, continental, pragmatism), one can discern distinctive patterns in the approach taken to these topics, such as a non-ideal and contextual approach to doing ethics and political philosophy, and a broadly culturalist or particularist approach against pure proceduralisms or formalisms that would minimize the relevance of context. There is also a focus on unearthing and interpreting the distinct traditions of Latin American philosophy. This has offered a grounding as well as an orientation for Latina/o approaches to philosophy in ways we describe below (Gracia and Millán-Zaibert 2004; Nuccetelli, Schutte, and Bueno 2010; Dussel, Mendieta, and Bohórquez 2011).

Just as one often refers to ancient Greek philosophy as the fountainhead of the Western philosophical tradition, one can claim a similar tradition of ancient or proto-Latin American philosophy in Nahua (or Aztec), Mayan, Incan, Quechua, Mapuche, and Guaraní philosophy. Influences such as Yoruba thought also impacted the colonial cultures of the Caribbean and countries like Brazil as a result of the slave trade. As contemporary Mexican philosopher Miguel León-Portilla (1988, 1990) has pointed out, Mayan and Aztec philosophers did not passively accept their mythologies, but questioned them and the place of human beings in the world. Hence, it is important to understand that Mesoamerica had not just a wisdom tradition, unquestioned and relatively undeveloped, but a sophisticated and complex metaphysics with an associated ethics.

Nahua metaphysics, for example, is a process-based form of ontological monism (the idea that there is one basic kind of element in the universe) in which the fundamental element is motion (Maffie 2014). *Teotl* is the dynamic, self-generating sacred force, and all existing things are its varied manifestations. The struggles of regeneration occur in specific forms of motion, such as *nepantla,* or intermixing, and *malinalli,* or spiraling. These ideas are influential in how some Latina feminist philosophy conceptualizes hybrid identity and cultural formations, in which mixing and movement are taken as the norm rather than a special situation.

The concept of hybridity became a central focus from the beginning of the Conquest in the work of one of the first published mestizo writers, known as El Inca Garcilaso de la Vega (1536–1616). He is often considered the first Latin American writer, since, in his *Royal Commentaries*, he reflected on his mixed cultural and ethnic identity and affirmed it without apology (Vega 2014). He argued that the Incas had a civilization equal to that of the Spaniards and that they were just as capable of reasoning as any European, so his life was not one of becoming assimilated to civilization but of melding two distinct forms. His positive articulation of "mestizaje" inspired the work of other Latin American and Latina/o philosophers like José Vasconcelos (1882–1959), author of *The Cosmic Race* ([1925] 1997), as well as Octavio Paz (1914–1998) in *The Labyrinth of Solitude* (1950, 1985), and more recently Gloria Anzaldúa (1942–2004) in *Borderlands / La Frontera: The New Mestiza* (1987, 2007). Garcilaso de la Vega instigated a tradition that brought questions about identity, purity, and hybridity into social and political philosophy.

Against the European tendency to value cultural integrity and unity against cultural intermingling and difference, this Latin American work on hybridity provided an alternative tradition for Latina/o philosophy. The status of "mestizaje" was also, of course, the subject of fierce debate. For example, the Argentine writer and one-time president of Argentina, Domingo Faustino Sarmiento (1811–1888), found it a source of cultural regression. Debate centered not only on hybridity itself but also on the particular kind of mix that occurred, including Indigenous and African cultures alongside European ones.

Some, such as Vasconcelos, celebrated hybridity but only between certain groups, while others, such as José Martí (1853–1895), argued that Latin America's institutions and forms of government must incorporate all of its peoples and cultures, without mimicking Europe's disdain for the African and the Indigenous (Martí 2002).

Martí gave a philosophical articulation of national sovereignty based on the unique conditions of a post-colonial Latin America facing ongoing colonial and neocolonial threats. He took sovereignty to be integral to the development of a Latin American modernity that would articulate its own conception of progress. This required achieving ideological sovereignty and hence a critique of Eurocentrism as well as a philosophical exploration into the social constructions of Latin American identity that had underemphasized the full range of influences. Martí's arguments effectively intervened in the nationalist discourses circulating throughout Latin America, criticizing their colonialist mimicry, and inspired new thinking about the multiple meanings of modernity and the mixed legacy of the European Enlightenment.

A further important link between Latin American and Latina/o philosophy concerns the idea of human rights in relation to cultural differences. The very concept of universal human rights was first articulated in the famous Valladolid debates of 1550–1551 between Ginés de Sepúlveda, a doctor of theology, and Bartolomé de Las Casas, a Dominican monk, concerning the cruel Spanish treatment of the Indigenous peoples. Sepúlveda argued that the Indigenous peoples could not be conceived as having equal human status to the Europeans because of their barbaric pagan practices of human sacrifice, and thus the Spaniards were in the right to subjugate them and convert them by force. Las Casas, who had lived among the native peoples in Chiapas, argued that their complex city-states and belief systems were proof of their capacity for reason, and hence that they were not barbarians. Their beliefs were *different* from the Spanish, but this did not justify treating them as "natural slaves" (an Aristotelian concept). A true barbarian, he held, would be a person with *no* beliefs, or one who acts on impulse, as many of the Spanish tyrants were doing in Mexico. This debate inaugurated the concept of universal humanism, and it also inspired Latin American philosophy to become primarily practical and concerned with morality. Thus, ethics and politics, rather than metaphysics, took the place of "First Philosophy," and here again one can discern a link to Latina/o philosophy with its focus on practical questions and the political treatment of Latinas/os in North America. Current debates over the need for assimilation involve assumptions about "backward" cultural practices similar to Sepúlveda's arguments. Las Casas's approach allowed for the idea of a cultural diversity that did not need to be hierarchically ranked.

The exchange between Las Casas and Sepúlveda also opened up ongoing debates about the role of religious belief in political policy. Against assumptions that only secularism can provide a basis for rational moral and political values, liberation theology, influenced by Las Casas, held that Christianity has resources to support the expansion of human rights. Liberation theology was a mixture of a Marxist approach to social justice and the rights of labor with a Christian ethics of love, and it became a central influence in the development of both African American and Latina/o theologies as well as considerations of political theology in general. This also led to the development throughout the Americas of a more secular liberation philosophy offering new interpretations of the Marxist tradition.

Hence, Latin American philosophy has been a useful source for Latina/o philosophy given its long engagement with transnational hybridity, with colonialism as

it is manifested in the sphere of ideas, and with the analysis of oppression and racial inequality. It has also provided an alternative understanding of philosophy's role in society as well as the nature of philosophical methodology. Far from a disengaged conversation among social elites, philosophy in Latin America has often been on the front lines of social conflict.

Today, Latina/o philosophy is emerging as a distinctive field not only because of the topics it explores, but also because of the methodological approach it takes toward those topics. An important feature of this is the non-ideal approach to normative argument, one that aims not for abstract claims with universal scope but for contextual claims with reparative efficacy. In Latin America, this approach began with Simón Bolívar (1783–1830). Bolívar's vision of an independent and unified Latin America inspired many anticolonial movements because it grappled directly with the hybrid character of the continent's political constituency and culture. Bolívar's political thought does not imagine an ideal just society that can then provide a model for institutional development, but takes the current conditions of recently liberated nations as setting out the criteria for developing the conditions of political justice and democracy. He saw himself as creating a form of transitional democracy. In the twentieth century, the work of José Carlos Mariátegui (1894–1930) also took a contextual and nondoctrinaire approach to the application of Marxism in the Americas. In his 1927 book, *Seven Interpretive Essays on Peruvian Reality*, Mariátegui (1971) employed Marx's thought as a tool to analyze the economic conditions of his country, which he likened to the feudalism of czarist Russia, yet took creative license to imagine a socialism in Peru grounded in Incan pre-Columbian communalism.

Recent work in Latina/o political philosophy in particular has taken up this sort of contextual, non-ideal approach to addressing normative and political issues as well as questions of social ontology. Ideal concepts of the citizen and of citizenship rights are revealed to harbor ethnic exclusions, and idealized approaches to national or transnational formations are shown to underestimate colonial dangers. Cosmopolitan aspirations are reinterpreted through cultural specificity. Social identity in the context of Latin America has never been imagined to contain pure kernels of bounded essences; it has always been understood as a fluid amalgam of diverse and conflicting influences. In the midst of such diversity and oppression, there is much work on the political challenges to effective communication and democratic deliberation.

Grounded in its connection to the particular tradition of Latin American philosophy, Latina/o philosophy is not simply distinct from Anglo-American and European philosophy but provides a critique of essentialist, idealized abstractions that pursue a decontextualized truth. Still, the possibility of universalism emerges from the fact that Latina/o conditions of transnational, cultural, and racial hybridity as well as colonial oppression have a global resonance and relevance. Looking not simply to Europe but also to the rest of the world will undoubtedly provide better interlocutors for the philosophical development of this field.

43
Poetry
Urayoán Noel

In a U.S. Latina/o context, poetry can be thought of in terms of both literary texts and expressive cultural practices, and the tension between these two understandings of poetry has been integral to the evolution of Latina/o literary and cultural studies.

In the context of literary studies, we tend to think of poems as more or less stable texts whose relative formal difficulty requires certain modes of formal analysis, such as the "close reading" advocated by the New Critics, who found poetry central to their project of institutionalizing literary study as a field demanding a quasi-scientific rigor. In cultural studies, by contrast, we eschew the hermeticism of close reading, and we seek instead to understand poetry in and along a broader textual field and in the context of everyday practices and evolving Latina/o histories.

Poets and poetry were at the forefront of the Chicano and Puerto Rican movements of the 1960s and 1970s that helped shape the interdisciplinary academic field of Latina/o studies, with epic poems such as Rodolfo "Corky" Gonzales's "Yo soy Joaquín" (1967) and Pedro Pietri's "Puerto Rican Obituary" (1969) epitomizing this socially engaged and oppositional *movimiento* poetics. Such poems were at once blueprints for a movement, extensions of a movement, and an eccentric movement all its own: Gonzales helped spearhead the First National Chicano Liberation Youth Conference in Denver in 1969, while Pietri performed his poem during the 1969 takeover of the People's Church in East Harlem by the

Young Lords Party, which published his poem in its journal *Palante*. These 1969 events gave us two foundational political documents from the movimiento era: "El Plan Espiritual de Aztlán" (featuring a poem-prologue by the poet Alurista) (Anaya and Lomelí 1991, 1–5) and the Young Lords' "13 Point Program and Platform" (Enck-Wanzer 2010, 9–10). Movement-identified poets such as Alurista and Louis Reyes Rivera were also instrumental to the development of Chicano, African American, Puerto Rican, and ethnic studies departments and programs in the late 1960s and early 1970s.

As Chicana/o and Puerto Rican studies sought national visibility and legitimacy and then evolved into or alongside Latina/o studies in the 1980s and early 1990s, many scholars writing on poetry sought to negotiate an institutionally appropriate focus on Latina/o poems as literary texts while echoing the socially engaged (or even outright decolonial and oppositional) politics of the *movimiento* era. Perhaps unsurprisingly then, many scholars emphasized poetry's intimate relationship to expressive cultures and vernacular practices, from "interlingual" poetics (Bruce-Novoa 1982) and the use of Spanglish (Aparicio 1988) to song and oral poetry traditions such as *declamación* (Kanellos 1985), salsa improvisation (Aparicio 1988), and border *corridos* (Limón 1992). Some scholars connected the textual difficulty of these Latina/o poems to the difficult social and cultural situations that inspired them, reading them as "a response to chaos" (Bruce-Novoa 1982) or as performances that resisted linguistic (and thereby political) assimilation (J. Flores 1993).

There is a tension, though, between these scholars' (and our own) nods to the embodied histories of Latina/o poetry and its *movimiento* legacies and the institutionalizing imperative that drove the rise of Latina/o studies in the late 1980s and 1990s, in the shadow of the canon wars that brought these institutional politics to the academic foreground. To use Diana Taylor's terms, we might say that while Latina/o studies has long celebrated the repertoire that "enacts embodied memory—performances, gestures, orality, movement, dance, singing—in short, all those acts usually thought of as ephemeral, non-reproducible knowledge," it does so firmly from the regulatory space of the archive, and of an "archival memory" that is "supposedly resistant to change" and that "sustains power" (2003, 19). The publication of the *Norton Anthology of Latino Literature* (Stavans 2011) has only made this tension more explicit. While the anthology does not shy away from its archival imprimatur, it makes some praiseworthy efforts to bring breadth to the archive by including a section called "Popular Dimensions" that features everything from jokes and corridos to cartoons—or as the book's description puts it, the anthology "traces four centuries of writing, from letters to the Spanish crown by sixteenth-century conquistadors to the cutting-edge expressions of twenty-first-century cartoonistas and artists of reggaeton."

Notwithstanding the irony of selling the anthology's cool inclusiveness by mashing up conquistadores and cartoonists, the *Norton*'s archival moves are worth taking seriously. By opening with a section called "Colonization" (Stavans 2011, 1–158), which includes translated stanzas from conquest epics such as Juan de Castellanos's *Elegías de varones ilustres de Indias* (1589) and Gaspar Pérez de Villagrá's *Historia de la Nueva México* (1610), the *Norton* challenges us to consider the decolonial legacies of Gonzales's and Pietri's 1960s movimiento epics in the broader colonial history in which the archive is inevitably enmeshed: What would it mean to frame U.S. Latina/o poetry as starting with the conquest, and how would the problem of the archive (of whose story gets told and how) be central to this reframing? Similarly, its inclusion of non-U.S.-born nineteenth-century poets and political figures such as José Martí and Fabio Fiallo brings to the foreground the complex question of canonicity and its relationship to transnational cultural and political networks explored by Kirsten Silva Gruesz in her classic book, *Ambassadors of Culture: The Transamerican Origins of Latino Writing* (2002).

Seeking an alternative to both the standoff between a *Norton*-worthy colonizing archive and a decolonial *movimiento* repertoire, we might instead argue for a genealogy of U.S. Latina/o poetry that begins in the modernist period, when the primacy of print begins to be called into question, and when the wider availability of newspapers and little magazines allows for a range of regional and transnational poetics to circulate: the *Norton* helpfully includes a section called "Southwestern Newspaper Poetry" (Stavans 2011, 218–228), which features work from the late-nineteenth and early-twentieth centuries, when U.S. Latina/o modernists such as William Carlos Williams (who is included in the *Norton*) and Salomón de la Selva (who is not) were published in early issues of *Poetry* and other iconic modernist journals. One might argue whether a term such as "Latino modernist" has any meaning when applied to poets as different as the New Jersey-born Williams (who wrote in English, although incorporating Spanish, as in 1917's *Al que quiere!*) and the Nicaragua-born de la Selva (whose famed 1918 debut *Tropical Town and Other Poems* was in English but who later turned toward Spanish), but that is precisely the point: both poets were non-monolingual in life and on the page, and both wrote works that, while steeped in and well received by Anglo-American modernism, were also attuned to Latin American modernismo, in a tangle of global Souths that U.S. Latina/o literary studies is only slowly beginning to investigate.

Williams is particularly resonant not only for his stature but also for his fusion of Spanish with a range of U.S. English vernaculars, his identification with both the cosmopolitan and the peripheral, and his ambivalence regarding the archive. As I have argued elsewhere (Noel 2013), in his 1930s poem "The Defective Record," Williams hints that a poem might be an impossible archive "killing whatever / was there before" (Williams 1991) and in a 1942 reading for the National Council of Teachers of English and Columbia University Press Contemporary Poets series posted on the online archive PennSound, Williams performs the poem with a mixture of jittery energy and plainspoken understatedness that matches the eccentric vernaculars of his classic *Paterson* but that also works as an ironic meditation on the poet in the age of mechanical reproduction (Williams 2006).

The *movimiento* poets of the 1960s were explicitly anti-technocratic (Roszak 1969)—as in Pietri's at once wistful, funny, and angry "If only they / had turned off the television / and tune [sic] into their own imaginations" near the end of "Puerto Rican Obituary" (1973). But Pietri's irony echoes Williams's in that both understand poetry as a series of remediations across and along print and performance, sound and visuality, the institution and the street, in a flow of damaged vernaculars. From a culturalist perspective, our tendency might be to align U.S. Latina/o poetry with the living repertoire, with the community-centered culture of poetry readings and performances epitomized by the Floricanto festivals and the Nuyorican Poets Cafe in the 1970s, and to be sure, such performance cultures were central to the *movimiento*, and their role as engines and laboratories for generations of U.S. Latina/o poets should not be underestimated. Yet, we should keep in mind all the ways in which these poets were invested in both critiques of the archive and in the development of what I call in my book, following Charles Bernstein, "provisional institutions" such as small presses, little magazines, community readings, independent radio, and so on (Noel 2014). As John Alba Cutler suggests in *Ends of*

Assimilation (2015), the complex institutional and community history of a publisher such as Quinto Sol, the iconic Chicano movement press, is its own movement, its own alternative history that might complement but also complicate our understanding of Latina/o literary history and poetics.

Given that mainstream publishers have largely moved away from publishing poetry, the health and evolution of Latina/o poetry remains largely in the hands of small and/or independent publishers, from legacy publishers emerging in the context of the *movimiento* effervescence of the 1970s—among them Bilingual Press, Arte Público Press, and Norma Alarcón's recently revived Third Woman Press— to regional publishers such as San Antonio's Wings Press and California's Floricanto Press, with a few notable exceptions such as the University of Arizona Press's Camino del Sol series.

Cutler is part of a new generation of Latina/o studies scholars who are revisiting *movimiento* poetics with archival rigor but also with an appreciation of embodied histories. This leveraging of archive and repertoire seems essential to Latina/o poetics scholarship moving forward, given the regulatory force of the *Norton*, the institutionalization of Latina/o studies in the corporate university, and, as Michael Dowdy argues in his landmark study *Broken Souths* (2013), the precariousness of Latina/o bodies in the context of neoliberalism and globalization.

Still, Latina/o poetry and poetics are largely invisible in this post-*Norton* panorama. Despite the naming of Juan Felipe Herrera as the first Latina/o poet laureate of the United States in 2015, the national visibility of younger poets as engaging as Aracelis Girmay (2011) and Eduardo C. Corral (2012), the continued richness and diversity of Latina/o performance poetry, the rise of innovative poets such as those included in Carmen

Giménez Smith and John Chávez's *Angels of the Americlypse: An Anthology of New Latin@ Writing* (2014), and the attention generated by Richard Blanco's reading of his poem "One Today" at Barack Obama's second inauguration in January 2013, few scholars write on contemporary poetry, and there is no equivalent to the *movimiento*-era synergy between poets, publishers, activists, and scholars at a time when such synergy is desperately needed. (Blanco has yet to receive the critical attention befitting his cultural stature, to say nothing of the poets published alongside him in the 2007 anthology *The Wind Shifts: New Latino Poetry* edited by Francisco Aragón.)

It is ironic that in a globalized and neoliberal moment when humanities scholars are struggling to redefine what they do (as digital humanities, alternative-academics, and so on) poetry has seemingly dropped out of the picture. I am thinking of the stunning, challenging, wonderfully weird yet profound poems that make up much of Gloria Anzaldúa's classic *Borderlands / La Frontera: the New Mestiza* (1987); while the essayistic portions of the book are widely read and anthologized (including in the *Norton*, where Anzaldúa appears after Isabel Allende in a section called "Into the Mainstream"), the poems remain wondrous oddities, as if independent of the book and somehow resistant to the galvanizing force of the archive.

Of course, the idea of a poetics of embodied knowledge is central to Chicana/Latina feminism, but even Williams (decidedly not a feminist) has a curious posthumous book of notes and short essays called *The Embodiment of Knowledge* (1974). While the disappearance of poetry from the mainstream of Latina/o studies is alarming, the playful, painful auto-ethnographic mode of Anzaldúa's poems (and with it, the promise of a poetics inspired by the *movimiento* but also positioned against its certainties and hegemonic moves) is alive and well in books as important and as wonderfully different from one another as Corral's *Slow Lightning* (2012), María Meléndez's *How Long She'll Last in This World* (2006), and J. Michael Martinez's *Heredities* (2010).

More recently, groups such as the Undocupoets and the Mongrel Coalition Against Gringpo have taken to social media in a spirit of activism and institutional critique around issues of immigration and racism, while projects such as the online journal *Acentos Review* and the poetry organization and workshop CantoMundo (founded in 2008 and 2009, respectively) have sought to rebuild and sustain national (and transnational) coalitions. At the same time, poets such as Jennifer Tamayo have begun producing (net)works that bridge print, performance, and digital spaces, urging us to intersectionally rethink embodied politics and the coordinates of Latinidad in the age of social media. The promise of U.S. Latina/o poetry is the promise of a culturalist form, an embodied archive, a record as defective as the bodies it purports to map.

44

Politics

John A. García

"La política" or politics can envelop one's life, encompass a significant set of experiences, and color one's worldview. Yet while one can portray politics as all-pervasive and omnipresent, how does one relate that notion for Latinas/os in a way that can convey power, influence, and community for such a dynamic and growing population? Harold Lasswell (2011) defined politics as "who gets what, when and how." Within that broad definition, there are the notions of expressions, needs, will, impact, outcomes, affect, and change. How are these relevant to the over 55 million Latinas/os residing in the United States (Stepler and Brown 2016)?

While democratic principles place emphasis on an individual who expresses and seeks responsiveness from our "democratic institutions," group interests and collective voices resonate more loudly and effectively. For this reason, establishing a community of interests is vital to connecting politics to Latinas/os. Much has been written about the distinctiveness and commonalities among persons whose ancestry and culture come geographically from Mexico, Central and South America, the Caribbean, and the Iberian Peninsula. Historical experiences and traditions, colonialism, language, and cultural beliefs and practices can be antecedents to the lived experiences, interactions, and objects of American public policies for those Latinas/os living in the United States (and those who have and/or expect to live here). As a result, the politics of the Latina/o community incorporates both what experiences, values, and skills Latinas/

os bring with them (for the foreign-born segment) and the experiences, desires, interests, and knowledge, which are accumulated while living in the United States (J. García 2016). To examine and understand the politics of Latinas/os (as well as any other specific community), you cannot look only to the group members; you need to understand the sociopolitical institutions and representatives that impact this community; the policies of the different levels of governments; the larger sociopolitical climate; and other group interests that may challenge or compete with Latinas/os' concerns and issues (Affigne, Hu-DeHart, and Orr 2014; Baretto and Segura 2014; García Bedolla 2014; J. García 2016).

For example, the area of immigration reform, especially as related to undocumented migration to the United States, has been framed as major problem, with Latinas/os being targeted as the main body of undocumented immigrants and creating negative consequences of such migration (Bada, Fox, and Selee 2006; Navarro 2009; Voss and Bloemraad 2011). Images of "hordes of people" crossing the southern U.S. border, pushing Americans out of jobs, importing a culture that is less desirable than American values and norms, and tapping social welfare benefits circulate in public sentiments, rhetoric, and policy debates. Key elements of politics—community, power and influence, expressions and impact—are well represented in this policy domain. Generationally, Latinas/os are linked to the immigrant experience; hostilities toward undocumented Latinas/os impact naturalized and native-born Latinas/os, who are being "tagged" as part of a negative, "less desirable" segment of society (Navarro 2009; Massey and Sánchez 2010; Magaña and Lee 2013; García Bedolla 2014). Thus community for Latinas/os incorporates culture, common origins, both self-identified commonalities and linked fate, and externally perceived stereotypes, images, and targeted public policies.

The expression of community concerns, issues, and policy preferences is also relevant to Latinas/os and immigration reform. For example, during the 1990s several statewide initiatives that focused on immigration and affirmative action reached the electorate in California and were met with strong (at times varied) Latina/o community reaction (Armbruster, Geron, and Bonacich 1995; Alvarez and Butterfield 2000; Pantoja and Segura 2003). Proposition 187 (1994) sought to deny undocumented immigrants access to social services. Proposition 227 (1998), also known as the English Language in Public Schools Statute, was sponsored by the wealthy businessman Ron Unz and sought to eliminate bilingual education programs. In general, the political climate was highly charged, with Latinas/os (both immigrant and native-born "sectors") targeted for restrictive and punitive action. Similarly, repressive and criminalizing policies like the Border Protection, Antiterrorism and Illegal Immigration Control Act of 2005 (better known as the Sensenbrenner bill) also sparked Latinas/os and others to voice, in collective settings, their concerns and their belief in the need to redirect immigration reform so that it is not repressive, but rather facilitates immigrants to regularize their status and set up pathways toward eventual citizenship (Bada, Fox, and Selee 2006; Bloemraad 2006). Participants in mass marches and demonstrations throughout the United States chanted: "Today we march, tomorrow we vote!" (Barreto et al. 2009; Rim 2009; E. Pérez 2015). The size of these demonstrations, their extensive organizational coordination, and their heightened group consciousness are good indicators of the expanding realm of Latina/o politics (Mohamed 2006; T. Jiménez 2010). They reflect the coming together of a broad base community around a culturally and organizationally focused set of concerns and the prioritization of certain concerns in a way that can impact the policy-making process.

Characterizing the factors and circumstances of what it means to be Latina/o and live in the United States is central to identifying how this community can help to establish a political force in American politics. Latinas/os in the United States can accent, moderate, eliminate, and/or influence and adapt their sense of common circumstances and experiences into distinguishable concerns and public expressions (Fraga et al. 2010, 2012; J. García 2016). The contemporary Latina/o community is vibrant, interconnected, and quite identifiable: the essentials of what constitute a community are present, and these recognizable shared spaces—geographical, cultural, affective, and collective—are found throughout all regions of this country. Regardless of whether the presence of Latinas/os in neighborhoods, towns, and cities is short- or long-term, such presence serves as a foundation for establishing a collective community life. This is true across the twenty-plus countries of origin that Latinas/os come from or are linked with. It is this "living in the USA," along with externalities such as non-Latinas/os' attitudes, stereotypes, and behaviors, governmental policies and implementations, mass media portrayals or omissions, and so on, that play a major role in shaping and defining Latinas/os as a community.

Part of this community development is related to the reality of treating persons of various Latina/o national origins as, more or less, a singular racial/ethnic group (Beltrán 2010; J. García 2016). It is clear that the popular media, the general public, and governmental agencies and officials have incorporated the terms "Hispanic" and "Latino" in the everyday general vernacular. Within Latina/o communities, some have taken the perspective that national origin (Peruvian, Honduran, Mexican, and so on) is a more salient and primary identification than a broader "pan-ethnic" cluster (López and Espiritu 1990; Taylor et al. 2012). It is clear, from extant research, that Latinas/os think of themselves according to a variety of identities (such as racial, ethnic, and linguistic, and in terms of national origin, including being American), and that the concept of Latino/Hispanic has become an integral part of Latinas/os' lives (Keefe and Padilla 1989; Benitez 2007; Fraga et al. 2010, 2012). But while it has become an American identity for Latinas/os, this identity does not supplant national origin identity, or other relevant social identities.

The increase in Central and South American and Caribbean migrants in established Latina/o areas (among Mexicans, Puerto Rican, and Cuban communities), as well as in regions in which there has been much less Latina/o presence (such as the South and the central Midwest), has also contributed to community development. Along with continued population growth, greater diversity among Latina/o national-origin groups, wider geographic dispersion, and Latina/o-based national organizations and leaders cultivating a broad sense of community, the relevance and viability of Latinas/os as a community is very much a daily reality (Fraga et al. 2012; Affigne, Hu-DeHart, and Orr 2014; Barreto and Segura 2014).

Thus, I am suggesting that elements associated with constituting a vibrant and dynamic Latina/o community are alive and functioning in the United States. At the same time, this notion of a Latina/o community does not require unanimity or absolute consensus; it can include a diversity of cultures and practices, as well as multiple identities and allegiances (Beltrán 2010; J. García 2016). The dialectic of differences and commonalities is a coexisting dynamic among members of the Latina/o community.

What are the bases for politically relevant thoughts, arenas, and substance for political engagement? What are Latinas/os' expectations? One can think of concepts such as freedom, rights, fairness, opportunities, equality, enjoying the fruits of one's labor, representation, and responsiveness (Garcia and Sanchez 2007; J. García 2016). While these are fundamental principles or values for a democratic system, their articulation and activation for Latinas/os are more specific. That is, there have been major efforts for Latina/o organizations and leaders to put forth a Latina/o policy agenda so that the community's concerns, experiences, and status are addressed (Baretto, Segura, and Woods 2004; Baretto, Nuno, and Sanchez 2007; Fraga et al. 2012). More importantly, the "what of politics" requires the Latina/o community to define and translate their own realities into issues, concerns, policy proposals, and actions. That process has been ongoing, and at times, groups coalescing around national origins, sexual orientation, gender, undocumented status, and so forth have developed their own movements and pushed for social and political change. For the most part, the more prevalent policy foci for Latinas/os have been educational opportunities and quality schooling; rights and fair treatment of immigrants; political representation and responsiveness by governmental officials; immigration reform; labor market opportunities and workers' rights; and basic civil and voting rights (Crawford 2000; Espenshade and Ramakrishnan 2001; Bloemraad, Korteweg, and Yurdakul 2008; Bloemraad and Trost 2008; Alvarado and Jaret 2009).

Latina/o organizations and leaders, as well as Latina/o media and research/policy centers have expressed concerns and conducted analyses regarding: (1) human rights and positive immigrant reforms (as opposed to punitive and criminalizing measures) (Hagan, Eschbach, and Rodriguez 2008; Hagan, Rodriguez, and Castro 2011); (2) improved and more culturally sensitive educational policies (including equal financing across school districts, curriculum reforms, improvement of facilities, greater parental input, and so on) (Lopez 2009; Leal and Meier 2010; Zambrana and Hurtado 2015); (3)

dismantling discriminatory practices in the workplace, housing, social services, and the criminal justice system, and many other areas of daily life for Latinas/os (García and Sanchez 2007; García Bedolla 2014); and (4) ensuring access to and equal participation in our political system, especially through voting and thus representation (Pantoja and Segura 2003; García and Sanchez 2004; Hopkins 2011; Zepeda-Millan and Wallace 2013; Sanchez et al. 2015). One could argue that these considerations are applicable beyond Latina/o communities, but "la política latina" focuses upon the greater effects of these policy areas on this community, and the need to seek reform and redress in various areas. This focus is manifested primarily in local grass-roots work to improve their schools, neighborhoods, and pressure governmental entities to commit funding and effective policy implementation to ensure better outcomes (Gonzales and Bautista-Chavez 2014; Abascal 2015).

The rise of the public face of the undocumented communities though massive protests that began in 2006 showed this community not only coming out of the shadows, but also engaging the federal government to be responsive to the interests and needs of undocumented persons and families (Suro and Escobar 2006; Zlolniski 2008; Barreto et al. 2009; López, Morin, and Taylor 2010; Affigne, Hu-DeHart, and Orr 2014). While a negative backlash occurred within some segments of this nation and among conservative politicians, the corresponding punitive policies activated the second generation and beyond Latinas/os, labor unions, human rights activists, and other progressives to broaden the scope and base of Latinas/os' political engagement (García Bedolla 2014; J. García 2016). This policy area illustrates the accented development of a Latina/o policy agenda (operating at different political "levels" and issues) as well as the community's ability to collaborate with other like-minded ones.

As a community connected by private spaces and expanding into public spheres of daily life, Latinas/os have become critical players in the American political landscape. In this intersection of Latina/o public and private lives, the struggles for and challenges to the realization of full and open opportunity structures are negotiated, and the persistence to overcome significant obstacles and achieve victories is sustained. For Latinas/os, politics embodies building and maintaining a viable community and advancing the betterment of its members through the enhancement of its human resources and its power to influence the public actions and conversations of the body politic. What constitutes those expressions and how the goals are achieved need to be driven, as much as possible, by Latinas/os themselves.

45
Popular Culture
Curtis Marez

Latina/o popular culture is not a thing or a discrete object of analysis but in Raymond Williams's (1958) famous formulation, "a whole way of life." Williams's work resonates with scholars of Latina/o popular culture because his definition foregrounded culture as everyday material relations in opposition to an imperial Anglo culture. Latina/o popular culture includes bottom-up cultural productions and practices as well as popular appropriations of top-down forms of mass culture. Tomás Ybarra-Frausto's famous claim in "Rasquachismo: A Chicano Sensibility" (1989) that Chicana/o popular culture inverts hierarchies of power and brings the high low is true of Latina/o popular culture more broadly. At the same time, however, popular culture can encourage and express Latina/o incorporation into dominant state and capitalist formations. Like black popular culture as analyzed by Stuart Hall (1998), Latina/o popular culture is at one and the same time responsive to the everyday needs and desires of working-class brown people *and* vulnerable to appropriation, commodification, and co-optation. The field of Latina/o popular culture studies has thus been partly defined by critical attention to these contradictory dynamics, focusing alternatively or simultaneously on Latina/o popular culture as opposition and as incorporation. Additionally, Latina/o popular culture studies brings a critical perspective to bear on patriarchal white supremacy in dominant popular culture.

While the longer history of Latina/o popular culture studies remains to be written, here I offer a brief and partial genealogy, starting with Jose Martí's late nineteenth-century writings about Coney Island and Buffalo Bill Cody's "Wild West" shows. As Laura Lomas argues, in his writing on Coney Island Martí references "the peculiar difficulty of Latino alterity within the space of New York's mass culture of entertainment and consumption" (2008, 138). She suggests that Martí articulates the double consciousness of a Latino migratory subject marginalized "by the frenetic, almost freakish consumption at Coney Island" (139), including racist sideshows. Whereas such entertainments enlisted working-class European immigrants into U.S. forms of anti-blackness, Martí articulates a Latino migrant distance from what he interprets as part of a popular culture of white supremacist imperialism. Similarly, in his chronicle "¡Magnífico espectáculo!" Martí observes that for European immigrants, "Cody's show channeled class, racial and even international tensions into the unifying project of Anglo imperial modernity." In response, Martí attempts to imagine the audience from the perspective of the Indigenous performers and present an opposing vision of the show (Lomas 2008, 138, 254–255).

A genealogy of Latina/o popular cultural studies must also recognize the theories and practices of labor organizers, starting with the work of Communist organizers Emma Tenayuca and Homer Brooks (1939), who argued in "The Mexican Question in the Southwest," that the exploitation of Mexican workers was made possible by official attacks on their popular culture, including English-only public schools that denigrated Spanish and the segregation of public spaces and sites of popular entertainment such as schools, parks, dance halls, and restaurants. In response, they proposed a "democratic people's front movement" and demanded resources to support autonomous spaces for Mexican popular culture.

Américo Paredes's work on borderlands music, especially corridos of masculine border conflict such as "El Corrido de Gregorio Cortez," represents another important point in this genealogy. Recalling Martí, Paredes (1958) analyzed corridos as a kind of musical double consciousness in conflict with a white supremacist popular culture that celebrated Texas Ranger terrorism while demonizing working-class Mexicans.

A vital but underappreciated contribution to Latina/o popular cultural studies, Mauricio Mazón's *The Zoot Suit Riots: The Psychology of Symbolic Annihilation* (1988) brings psychoanalysis to bear upon the social history of Mexican immigrants and U.S. militarism. Whereas subsequent critical accounts have foregrounded Pachuca/o popular culture (L. Alvarez 2009; C. Ramírez 2009), Mazón focuses on the popular culture of wartime white nationalism as represented in the tabloid press, comic strips, and the popular practices of "symbolic annihilation" directed at zoot suiters. While Mazón and the other authors in my provisional genealogy all analyze Latina/o popular culture, they also often draw upon and develop analytic frameworks about white nativism and nation-building from Latina/o popular cultural studies and use these frameworks for the interpretation of white supremacist popular cultures, with Mazón in particular addressing how anti-Mexican racism historically intersected with white masculinity and xenophobic militarism.

The 1990s witnessed an explosion of research in popular culture, partly sparked by the broader cultural studies turn represented by a special issue of the journal *Cultural Studies* on "Chicana/o Cultural Studies" edited by Angie Chabram and Rosa-Linda Fregoso (1990). The issue emerged from a 1989 National Association for Chicana and Chicano Studies (NACCS) panel that deconstructed the conference theme of "Community Empowerment and Chicano Scholarship." Contributors focused on the contradictions of efforts to represent the people and the popular, which, while oppositional in many ways, also served, like the spectacles analyzed by Martí, to hail Latinas/os for incorporation into state nationalisms.

The cultural studies moment in Chicana/o studies questioned unitary and hence exclusionary constructions of the subject of nationalism, "community," "the people," and "the popular" in ways that rearticulated similar moves in British cultural studies (Chabram and Fregoso 1990, 203). Chicana/o cultural studies constitutes an improvement over its British precursors by presenting a rigorous theorization of culture and power based in intersections of race, nation, gender, and sexuality. Chicana/o cultural studies in many ways thus overlapped with women of color feminism, especially popular intellectual texts like *This Bridge Called My Back* (Moraga and Anzaldúa 1981) and others.

That 1990 special issue of *Cultural Studies* was followed up almost a decade later with a second entitled "Chicana/o Latina/o Cultural Studies: Transnational and Transdisciplinary Movements" edited by Chabram-Dernersesian (1999). Of particular note is its focus on music, including essays by Michelle Habell-Pallán on El Vez's popularity in Europe; Frances R. Aparicio on Celia Cruz's transnational performance of her Cuban blackness; and Lisa Sánchez González on how salsa supports critical "organic intelligence" and "liberatory desire" among the Puerto Rican diaspora. The 1990s and shortly thereafter also witnessed the publication of a host of important works by Chon Noriega (1992), Rosa-Linda Fregoso (1993), George Sanchez (1993), Yolanda Broyles-González (1994), José E. Limón (1994), Ruth Glasser (1995), Coco Fusco (1995), Arlene Dávila (1997), José David Saldívar (1997), Frances R. Aparicio (1998), José Esteban Muñoz (1999), Juan Flores (2000), Michelle Habell-Pallán and Mary Romero (2002), and Alicia Gaspar de Alba (2003).

Why did the 1990s witness the emergence of a new critical mass of scholarship on Latina/o popular culture? The cultural studies turn in general, and the turn to popular culture in particular, was partly a response to neoliberalism and its ideological and material attacks on public spaces including schools, museums, arts programs, community centers, and public access media. Chon Noriega's *Shot in America: Television, the State, and the Rise of Chicano Cinema* (2000) marks this cultural studies turn by historicizing Chicana/o film in relationship to forms of public-access TV that had largely disappeared by the time the book was published. Meanwhile Arlene Dávila's work (2008) demonstrates how in neoliberal contexts Latina/o advertisers attempt to hail consumers by colonizing Latina/o popular cultures and identities. We could also understand Latina/o popular culture studies in this period as response to the privatization in the early 1990s of what had previously been a publicly supported communications project—the Internet. While subsequent scholarship has made visible both new problems and new kinds of network-based popular cultures, I recall there being great skepticism over the commercial cooptation of the Internet, which, in turn, helped reinforce a turn toward critical popular spaces.

The literature on Latina/o popular culture in the new millennium is varied and vast, resisting an exhaustive explication, but I conclude by outlining two promising trajectories in current and future research. I call the first trajectory "critical synesthesia," which involves analysis of the combination or interaction of multiple sensory registers in the production and reception of popular culture. Finding inspiration in the neurological term for people who experience one sensation in the mode of another (most commonly, when the sight of particular images triggers the sensation of hearing a particular sound), critical synesthesia focuses not on individual sensations in isolation but on their interactions or larger economies, what Michael Taussig (1993) refers to as the entire "sensorium" engaged by modern popular culture. Historically Western philosophical and political theories have privileged vision over other senses, creating a hierarchy of sensory registers that supports what critics have called a "male gaze" or an "imperial gaze," as well as fascist mass political spectacles (Mulvey 1975; Jay 1993; Pratt 2007). Work in critical synesthesia challenges these tendencies by analyzing sound, vision, and power together. Accordingly, in *Sounds of Belonging: U.S. Spanish Language Radio and Public Advocacy*, Dolores Inés Casillas (2014) studies how undocumented immigrants engage the politics of public (in)visibility, including police surveillance, via radio. Similarly, in *Dissonant Divas: The Limits of La Onda in Chicana Music*, Deborah Vargas (2012) constructs an archive out of multiple sensory registers, including not only musical style, genre, qualities of voice and phrasing, "oral fragments of memories," and *chisme* (gossip), but also performance, costumes and sartorial styles, dance styles, album covers and publicity photos, films, performance spaces, monumental architecture, and the gendered visual symbolism of musical instruments. Vargas thus reconstructs what she theorizes as a "sonic imaginary," a concept that nicely represents what I've called critical synesthesia in its combined reference to sound and sight.

The second trajectory for emergent research can be described as "making popular culture out of popular culture studies." Employing elements of popular performance and modes of appropriating Internet culture, a number of contemporary cultural workers straddle the line between scholars and producers of popular culture. Coco Fusco, for instance, has long combined scholarship and performance, but in "Observations of Predation in Humans" (2013), she borrows the character of Dr. Zira, the feminist/pacifist ape scientist from the popular *Planet of the Apes* films. In full ape makeup, Fusco as Dr. Zira presents a lecture, based on observations of human behavior on TV and other forms of visual culture, about the role of raced and gendered "human aggression and predatory behavior" in the accumulation of wealth and the production of inequality. Fusco borrows from B-movies to produce a lecture on neoliberal violence in the form of a popular "TED talk." My own contribution to this practice is called "Cesar Chavez's Video Collection," a digital essay built out of a multimedia archive of popular images and viewing practices. "Cesar Chavez's Video Collection" evidences farmworkers' appropriation of visual technologies to project social alternatives to the patriarchal white capitalism of agribusiness corporations (Marez 2013).

Finally, performance studies scholar Ricardo Dominguez has recently popularized forms of "electronic civil disobedience" (ECD). Working with a group of activist artists and software designers called the Electronic Disturbance Theater, Dominguez developed and deployed "FloodNet," an Internet application that enables hundreds and often thousands of users to request large servers to provide information they do not hold, thus triggering the servers to repeatedly post error messages that both slow down their functioning while at the same time lodging symbolic protests in the heart of power.

One of Dominguez's best known applications of FloodNet was in 1998, in support of the Zapatista movement in Chiapas, Mexico, in its efforts to draw attention to the dispossession and displacement of Indigenous peoples that resulted from the North American Free Trade Agreement (NAFTA). In one gesture, FloodNet users were able to upload messages to the server logs of the Mexican government's website by asking for a nonexistent URL titled "justice" or "human rights," leading the server to repeatedly return messages like "justice_not found" or "human rights_not found." In another gesture, FloodNet users uploaded to the Mexican state server the names of Indigenous people who had been massacred by the military. Like so many of the great twentieth-century movements for social justice, Dominguez's theory and practice of ECD dramatizes inequality for the digital age, drawing attention to the disparity between powerful institutions and the everyday and popular forms of resistance wielded by the relatively powerless.

46

Poverty

Patricia Zavella

Poverty is highly politicized by how it is defined as well as by programs designed to help the poor. Further, the explanations of forces said to lead to poverty come from widely divergent perspectives, and politicized notions about the poor are sometimes embedded in scholarly work.

On one end of the political spectrum are structuralist explanations for poverty, as seen in the United Nations Special Rapporteur's report on extreme poverty and human rights. Magdalena Sepúlveda Carmona (2011) suggests that states and social forces that penalize those living in poverty are interconnected and include legislation, regulations, and practices that unduly restrict the performance of life-sustaining behaviors in public spaces by people living in poverty. Further, excessive and arbitrary use of detention and incarceration threatens the liberty and personal security of people living in poverty.

Structuralist perspectives gained prominence through the concept of the "precariat," millions of people around the world "without an anchor of stability," constructed through neoliberal economic models dependent on global competitiveness and labor market flexibility that transfers risks onto workers and their families (Standing 2011, 1). The precariat, a "class-in-the-making," do not know their employers or fellow employees and have unstable salaries, statuses, benefits, and/or trust in the state. This controversial perspective on the precariat views them as lacking in consciousness of themselves as a class and therefore regards their demonstrations as inchoate.

There is a long history of conservative views that categorize those on the downside of advantage as deserving or undeserving of state or private sources of support or suggesting that the poor abuse social welfare. In the nineteenth century, the "deserving poor," who included widows with young children, were provided support, whereas paupers, who were seen as indolent, were left to their "vicious habits" (Katz 1986, 19). The discourse that receiving state support rather than working was shameful was directed particularly at men, assumed to be primary breadwinners for their families. However, the idea that accepting state support is shameful endures, even to the contemporary period since those who receive social benefits must justify their need in relation to whether or not they are employed and to their marital status (Halpern-Meekin et al. 2014).

The conservative concept of the "culture of poverty" became prominent during the mid-twentieth century. This perspective views poverty as the product of poor decision-making, orientation to the present time, lack of personal responsibility in securing educational degrees or vocational training, and as enduring through values, norms, and patterns of behavior related to "gaming the system," which are passed through generations of those living in poverty (Lewis 1965, 1966a). This view, while critiqued by scholars (Leacock 1971; Small, Harding, and Lamont 2010), gained popularity when Ronald Reagan accused a woman from south Chicago of abusing welfare, and even though he did not use the term "welfare queen," the notion that the poor, especially women of color, are undeserving of state support for their fraudulent behavior still circulates (Briggs 2002a; Kohler-Hausmann 2007).

Similarly, the phrase "urban underclass," which originated in the early twentieth century and is still in use today, focuses on the poverty of African Americans, Puerto Ricans, and Mexicans (Neckerman 1993). Underclass theory suggests that economic restructuring in inner cities, middle-class flight from poor neighborhoods, high male unemployment, and the isolation of the poor from mainstream norms and behavior lead to more female-headed households and social disorganization within families and communities (Wilson 1987, 1993). As such, underclass theory has been critiqued for blaming the victims and paying insufficient attention to structural inequalities as well as to creative adaptation by the poor (Katz 1986; Reed 1992; Moore and Pinderhughes 1993). Scholars have also noted how underclass theory was codified in the Personal Responsibility and Work Opportunity Reconciliation Act (1996), commonly known as "welfare reform," which requires extraordinary efforts on the part of welfare recipients to "improve" themselves and has detrimental effects on poor women (Collins 2008; Collins, di Leonardo, and Williams 2008), including Latinas, who endure travails with insensitive, punitive welfare agencies and poor labor markets (Edin and Lein 1997; Edin and Kefalas 2005; Marchevsky and Theoharis 2006).

The federal poverty level, established in 1965, is based on the annual cost of buying basic groceries (adjusted for inflation), assuming families spend one third of their income on food. Yet critics point out that this poverty measure is a political compromise. It discounts regional differences in cost of living and seasonal labor markets, and ignores the fact that many of those deemed officially poor are actually working for wages. The official poverty level also overlooks the ways in which the U.S. economy increasingly relies on part-time workers who receive few benefits. Thus, Manuel Pastor and Justin Scoggins (2007, 3) suggest that we should also count the working poor and that an appropriate measure of working poverty is equivalent to one full-time worker per family based on total annual hours completed by all working aged adults in the family and equal to 150 percent of the federal poverty level, adjusting for regional variations in the cost of living. They suggest that significant work includes twenty-five hours per week for a minimum of thirty-five weeks during the year as a standard that also incorporates those who have seasonal downtimes.

When considering the working poor, scholars often attend to those working in the informal sector with irregular hours and payments in cash or who run their own informal businesses. These include day laborers, gardeners, or landscape workers who often face wage theft, few benefits, and violence in their worksites (Valenzuela, Kawachi, and Marr 2002; Valenzuela 2003, 2009). Women in the informal sector often work in their own homes so they can continue their reproductive labors—caring for family members and maintaining homes—while garnering an income (Ibarra 2000, 2002, 2003). Immigrants are more likely to work in the informal sector and often must rely on their own limited social networks when seeking jobs, which may offer a modicum of protection against exploitative or abusive employers (Castañeda and Zavella 2003), but can also direct them to jobs likely to keep them in poverty (Pastor and Marcelli 2000; Gomberg-Muñoz 2010). The forces that funnel Latinas and Latinos into particular sectors and occupations often include gendered notions of "women's work" and "men's work," which for immigrants originate in other countries, as well as structural barriers to women entering higher paying jobs traditionally performed by men (Zavella 2011).

In 2011, responding to debates about measuring poverty, the U.S. Census Bureau developed the Supplemental Poverty Measure (SPM), which uses a wider range of factors than the official federal measure to determine poverty status. These include medical expenses, tax credits, non-cash government benefits—such as food stamps, housing subsidies, and school lunch programs—and cost-of-living adjustments for different geographic areas. Using the SPM in 2010, the overall poverty rate was 16 percent, yet there were significant differences among racial groups. The supplemental poverty measure was 11 percent for whites, 17 percent for Asians, 25 percent for blacks, and 28 percent for Hispanics (Lopez and Cohn 2011, 1). Furthermore, during economic downturns such as the recession of 2007–2009, Latinas/os were affected more than other racial and ethnic groups and the poverty rate for immigrants was higher than for U.S. citizens (Lopez and Cohn 2011, 3). There were also remarkable differences in poverty rates among Latinas/os. In 2013, when the total U.S. poverty rate was 16 percent, Guatemalans, Hondurans, and Dominicans had the highest rates (28 percent each) and Argentineans had the lowest rate (11 percent) (Pew Research Center 2015c, 1). In between, the percentages were Puerto Ricans 27, Mexicans 26, Cubans and Salvadorans 20 each, Ecuadorians 19, Venezuelans 18, Nicaraguans 17, Colombians 16, Spaniards 13, and Peruvians 13.

There is a long history in the United States of attempting to ameliorate poverty, yet these policies and their implementation are highly politicized and disproportionally affect Latinas/os. Cybelle Fox (2012) demonstrates that welfare policies during the Progressive Era and the New Deal were shaped by race and immigration in such a way that European immigrants received generous access to social welfare programs while blacks and Mexicans did not. During the Great Depression, more than 400,000 Mexicans were repatriated after the Immigration and Naturalization Service conducted raids demanding to see passports, creating a climate of racial animus in which relief workers pressured Mexicans to depart "voluntarily" and thus avoid state dependency (Hoffman 1974; Arredondo 2008). An estimated 60 percent of those deported were U.S. citizens, and the majority spoke English (Telles and Ortiz 2008, 83). During the Bracero Program (1946–1964), Mexican migrant men were deployed as the reserve army of labor par excellence—brought in to perform labor in agriculture, the railroads, and some factories with the assumption that they would return to homes in Mexico after a work season (Galarza 1964; Calavita 1992).

In the contemporary era under neoliberalism, with its emphasis on free market fundamentalism, individualism, limited government, and flexible labor, state support for social programs and education is curtailed while support for capital accumulation and globalization persists (Harvey 2005; Martínez 2016; Martínez and Rocco 2016). Particularly after NAFTA's displacement of millions of rural families and industrial workers in Mexico, there has been increased migration to the United States (Massey, Durand, and Malone 2002; A. López 2007). Many of these workers face long hours in unhealthy conditions for below-subsistence wages (Zlolniski 2005; Gomberg-Muñoz and Nussbaum-Barberena 2011). Simultaneously, outsourcing and deindustrialization, an enduring gender pay gap, and recessionary fluctuations in unemployment have led to slippage of the middle class into tenuous circumstances and debt in the United States (Goode and Maskovsky 2001; B. Williams 2001, 2008; American Association of University Women 2017). Thus, even as more Latinas/os are entering the middle class (Agius Vallejo 2012b), overall the American middle class is declining in size as the wealthy are gaining larger portions of income (Pew Research Center 2015a).

Questions of poverty also raise questions of class. Regardless of whether it is a Marxian notion of class in which reserve armies of labor are mobilized or displaced according to the logics of capital, or a more sociological definition of class related to occupation, education, and income, the poor are often marginalized economically, socially excluded, and subject to blaming discourses. Those living in poverty often internalize the stigma of receiving social benefits or articulate their desire to work, even if in sectors not matched to their skills or professional training (Quesada 2011; Dávila 2012). Scholars working in Latina/o studies further emphasize the importance of internal differentiation among the poor. Alejandro Lugo (2008), for example, argues that within classes there are border zones—based on differences related to gender, sexuality, nationality, race, age, or ability—in which there are diverse circumstances or experiences within social classes. Such "class borderlands" should be "regarded as creative sites of culture and class making and unmaking, both of which demand additional investigation within and beyond officially recognized borderlands" (Lugo 2008, 226). Similarly Patricia Zavella (2011) and Lynn Stephen (2007) point out key differences in the experience of poverty on the part of women, queers, the unauthorized, and Indigenous peoples, who must struggle to overcome multiple barriers to accessing employment and health and social services. Others analyze exclusionary policies or practices that lead to persistent poverty by state entities, employers, or landlords (G. Pérez 2004; Holmes 2013). Finally, some analysts point out that region or location is key to understanding poverty. Carlos Vélez-Ibáñez (1996, 2010) and Pablo Vila (2003) point out that the U.S-Mexico border region is a site where the absence of basic infrastructure and services in *colonias* (unincorporated settlements) makes daily life a constant struggle. Further, residents of *colonias* are subject to crass objectification and prejudice (Hill 2003), and as Victor Talavera and colleagues (2010) have found, the presence of so many unauthorized migrants can erode a sense of community and create palpable anxiety among the low-income residents who fear detention and deportation. The sensitivity of poor Latinas/os to changes in policies can be seen in a recent study of those who qualified for the 2012 Executive Order on Deferred Action for Childhood Arrivals (DACA), which allows those who were brought as children to the United States to apply for work authorization and other benefits such as drivers' licenses. On average, DACA recipients experienced a 150 percent increase in wages after they were able to secure better jobs (Hinojosa and Wynn 2014).

Scholars working in poverty studies increasingly find those living in poverty demonstrate remarkable flexibility, creativity, and resiliency (Edin and Lein 1997; Ibarra 2000, 2002, 2003; Edin and Kefalas 2005; López 2007; Marchevsky and Theoharis 2006; Stephen 2007; Zavella 2011; Holmes 2013). The poor seek better employment, housing, and/or privately funded resources such as food banks, often migrating in the process and constructing households with multiple wage earners. The poor articulate their dignity and contest blaming discourses, sometimes joining public demonstrations in favor of reforms related to immigration, health care access, wage increases, or other policies that would benefit their lives and advance social justice.

47

Race

Silvio Torres-Saillant and Nancy Kang

The term "race" as used in contemporary discourse, whether academic or demotic, purportedly refers to the distinct ancestry of a differentiated human population. Exactly what specific collection of features in a person's ancestry determines his or her race seems less easy to discern from current usage. Nor can we always tell whether the elements involved in assigning a racial label to one group will correspond identically to the characteristics used in classifying another group under a different racial category. For instance, on May 12, 1977, the Office of Budget Statistics issued "Directive 15: Race and Ethnicity Standards for Federal Statistics and Administrative Reporting," which classifies the U.S. population into five segments according to origins. Unlike the Asian, Black, Native American, and White subdivisions, when it came to the "Hispanic" segment, which encompassed people of "Mexican, Puerto Rican, Cuban, Central or South American or other Spanish culture or origin," the classification brought together various subgroups "regardless of race" ("Background: Development of Directive 15," 1994). U.S. Hispanics thus became an "ethnicity" as opposed to the other four subdivisions that consisted of "races" in the official taxonomy that the U.S. Census Bureau would recognize. Yet, one wonders how Asian Americans can constitute a single "race" given that the configuration of ancestries and phenotypes in their midst appears at least equally diverse.

While speakers in general, from specialists to laypeople, tend to proceed as if a consensus exists as to what race is, the extent to which they share a common frame of reference seems unclear (Hannaford 1996, 3). Based on the state of scientific knowledge at the time, in 1951 UNESCO issued a statement disavowing race as a reliable marker of biological differences among branches of the human population. Over half a century ago, biological anthropologist Frank B. Livingstone argued persuasively that the concept of race had been "overworked" as a measure of "human variability," noting that "many characteristics which were thought to be racial have been found in many widely separated populations" (1962, 279–81). With the spread of information prompted by geneticists like Luigi Luca Cavalli-Sforza (2000) about the migration of genes as our species populated the globe starting from a common point of departure in Africa, the biological commonality of humans has become uncontroversial—hence the currency of the mantra "Race is socially constructed." Oddly, even while repeating this mantra, learned observers may still be found to reproach particular individuals or groups for failing to identify themselves racially in a manner that is supposedly more accurate or authentic. Dominicans, for instance, may find themselves admonished by other "people of color" for insufficiently stressing blackness as part of their identity. The simultaneous tendency to deny and yet affirm the existence of race corresponds to the peculiar developments that brought the word into the lexicons of modern European languages less than five centuries ago. A nebulous term for a set of discursive practices as well as lived experiences, "race" remains ubiquitous and contentious. In the contemporary United States, for instance, it crops up in discussions of national politics, law enforcement, educational standards, immigration, employment, popular culture, and entertainment, among other areas of prevailing social concern.

As a field that tackles the histories, cultures, politics, arts, social developments, and overall experience of people of Hispanic descent, Latina/o studies connects inexorably with racial matters. This branch of ethnic studies owes its birth to the racialized rendition of the U.S. experience, which, until the 1960s, had largely omitted the words and deeds of the non-white sectors of the country's population from the conventional founding narratives of the nation. Additionally, those in the demography that Latina/o studies encompasses—namely, people ancestrally linked to Latin America, the Caribbean, and the Iberian Peninsula—hail precisely from the regions of the world where race first acquired its social significance. People of Hispanic descent inherit, as victims and perpetrators, equally virulent Spanish and English traditions of racial aggression. In view of this composite heritage, Latina/o studies offers a suitable platform for undertaking the sort of meditation that might one day help us transcend the cul-de-sac that racial conversations have reached in the United States at a prematurely announced "post-racial" moment. For instance, 2014, a year characterized by much lethal police brutality against unarmed minority males, closed with the killing of two New York City police officers, Asian American Wenjian Liu and Latino Rafael Ramos, at the hands of a vengeful African American civilian angered by the prior police killings of Michael Brown and Eric Garner, black males from Missouri and New York, respectively. Former New York City mayor Rudolph Giuliani and other right-wing militants used the occasion to blame concerned citizens who had protested unjustified lethal force by law-enforcement officers for presumably creating the "anti-police" environment that led to the deaths of the two officers.

In light of this conceptually and emotionally muddled climate, with influential voices venting antipathies instead of aiming for clarity, National Institute for Latino Policy (NiLP) president Angelo Falcón (2014) decried the "broken discourse, the loss of a language adequate enough to connect racially discordant voices." He noted how, in the absence of a meaningful racial vocabulary, we "desperately try to connect via the simplicity of the hashtag." Falcón appealed to sobriety and reason, urging observers on all sides to find a way of speaking that might "bring us to a better understanding of the bigger picture within which we will all thrive or, ultimately, destroy ourselves." Perhaps it behooves Latina/o studies scholars more than colleagues in any other field to act upon Falcón's appeal with the hope of formulating and securing a salutary, inclusive language that enlightens rather than obscures. This language ought to overcome the temptation to refry the clichés that inevitably arise when speaking from the midst of the social pathologies that racial matters generate without attempting to unearth the cause of the pathologies in the first place.

A dogma begotten by the colonial transaction nearly five centuries ago, racism emerged to address the moral transgressions that Christian nations incurred when they claimed leadership roles in imperial domination. The conquest and colonization of the Americas involved depriving overseas populations of their lands, destroying their societies, reducing Indigenous peoples to backbreaking, coerced toil in labor camps, inclemently punishing whoever did not satisfy the production quota expected of the captives, and perpetrating genocide against any group that opposed the colonial order. In other words, the colonial transaction put conquering Christians in the position of having to do unto others much that their creed forbade them to do. Because of that moral quandary, Christians ushered in a new chapter in the history of imperial domination. Unlike previous stages in the history of conquest based on social domination and enslavement, the one marshaled by

Christians insisted on representing their violent plundering of foreign societies as charitable, often depicting the injured parties as heathens rescued from the evil of their ancestral beliefs and customs. This new domination required conquerors to dehumanize the subject peoples so as to render them ineligible for Christian piety, thereby ennobling or, at the very least, justifying, the aggression perpetrated against them. The conquerors waged psychological warfare daily against the vanquished, while the apologists of the new economy assembled a colonial epistemology that construed the conquered as debased beings deserving of their plight due to moral, mental, spiritual, aesthetic, and physical inferiorities. Construing the vanquished as specimens of a lesser form of humanity persisted even after many adopted the religion of their masters and relinquished the presumed heathenism of their forebears. For instance, African-descended San Martín de Porres (1579–1639), a lay brother of the Dominican Order in the Viceroyalty of Peru, occupied a second tier in his religious order. His race barred him from full membership. This reason was also the impediment that stymied the ascent of many Indigenous servants of the Lord, regardless of the strength of their faith or holiness of their actions.

In more recent times, when trying to express the indignation and malaise produced by the racially motivated murder of nine black parishioners at Mother Emmanuel AME Church in Charleston, South Carolina, during a Bible study session on June 17, 2015, then U.S. Attorney General Loretta Lynch called the killings a "barbaric crime" with "no place in our country . . . no place in a civilized society" (Office of the Attorney General 2015). One wonders whether the attorney general subscribes to too benign a view of civilized society. Different kinds of ingredients contribute to different civilizations. The idea that people from certain ancestral origins, when not used for slave labor, constitute an obstacle to society's advancement was a core ingredient to the colonial civilizations that emerged in the Americas. Racial disparagement and the extreme violence that has often accompanied it have not only had a "place in our country" for centuries, but have also figured as a building block of virtually every "civilized society" that emerged in the Western Hemisphere in the wake of the colonial transaction. Twenty-one-year-old Dylann Roof, the white man who perpetrated the killings, did not target his victims randomly but did so with a clear sense of who belonged legitimately in the United States and who did not (Apuzzo 2015). When, prior to pulling the trigger so many times, he voiced the belief that blacks were "taking over our country" and "raping our [white] women," he drew from the body of negrophobic thought to which many of the most cultivated minds of Europe and the Americas had continuously subscribed for more than four centuries. The deaths of these nine African Americans proved shocking because of the juxtaposition of violence with prayer in a supposedly safe space: the church.

It shocks no less to see the 2013 law issued by the Dominican Republic's Constitutional Court to suspend the citizenship status of nearly 250,000 Dominicans of Haitian ancestry. Looking at the Court's ruling, one easily discerns Dominican justices under the spell of negrophobic ideology that has pervaded the discourse of nationality and cultural identity in the region since the colonial period. These justices—irrespective of their phenotype—were most likely identifying with the Hispanic component of their mixed ancestry. They feared the exponential growth of a segment of the population that, according to consensus at home and abroad, is supposedly "blacker" than Dominicans. The cultural instincts of the judges seem to have been influenced by notions of race and nation promoted by former president Joaquín Balaguer, who, from 1930 to 1961,

uninterruptedly served the tyrant Rafael Leónidas Trujillo. Trujillo's regime had instituted white supremacy as central to Dominican identity. Apart from just doing his job as an ideologue of the dictatorship, the negrophobic Balaguer had valid intellectual grounds for embracing the Caucasian ideal. As a man of letters who looked to the great thinkers of Latin America and the Iberian cultural tradition as a whole, he had learned the white supremacist creed taught by such seminal nineteenth-century authors as Juan Bautista Alberdi (1966) and Domingo Faustino Sarmiento (1915). These thinkers had equated Latin American progress with the prevalence of whiteness. The civil death experienced by the denationalized Haitian-descended Dominicans did not come from overt violence; it emerged from the pens of well-groomed, mostly mixed-race (mulatto) jurists worried about Dominicans of a despised ancestry supposedly "taking over" the country. They differ from Dylann Roof simply in that their weapons do not spew bullets yet still leave behind a legacy of despair, trauma, fear, and alienation.

Racism has been and remains one of the core constituents of American civilization. We must own up to that reality and be aware of its endemic presence in our lives. Doing so is a prerequisite for taking the first steps in the quest toward achieving a post-racial society—if that is indeed what is desired. Without admitting to the horror of our beginnings as a civilization (namely the theft, destruction, murder, and mistreatment that it took to build our modern societies in the hemisphere), we will go nowhere. We will continue to restrict the field of our social action to responding to *individual* expressions of the problem rather than to addressing its root causes. Punishing racist acts may satisfy the dictates of the law and perhaps offers partial consolation to victims and their loved ones, but it does not address the problem that triggers the acts in the first place. Latina/o studies scholars working specifically on racial matters are uniquely poised to debate and understand the genesis of racism, as well as dissect its forms of implementation. The onus is on us to help interrupt and disable the psychological and social mechanisms that have trained vast groups of people to withhold empathy and stanch a sense of commonality across ancestral difference in their rapport with others.

Racism does not cease the moment the government of a state or nation withdraws its support for, or even criminalizes, the abuse of a racialized other. Abuse often occured under the law and received sanction by leaders and the institutions they represented. The racist who has internalized as "natural" the social superiority and ability to control people of other ancestries will most likely react with confusion or rage when confronted with the loss of such capacities. The ensuing backlash will most likely increase the vulnerability of those enjoying only *de jure* equality. Given that the specter of racism is persistent and intergenerational in the United States, we should not permit ourselves the folly of recognizing it only when invoking a racial lexicon or other sets of discursive practices that allude to ancestral difference in a transparent, familiar, or easy way. We should attend to its lurking presence in policies that may have a noxious daily effect, especially on people of color; these can include the closing of public schools, continued income inequality, and the practice of "stop and frisk" championed by former New York City Mayor Michael Bloomberg. In 2015, for instance, roughly a year after completing his term as the top city official, Bloomberg could not possibly have forgotten the court order that demanded the cessation of the policy given its multiple flaws and transgressions. It had violated the law by racially profiling city residents; the overwhelming majority of the people stopped were minority males (read: African Americans and Latinos). It had squandered public

funds in its failure to reduce crime since the people of color arbitrarily searched by the police usually showed no sign of involvement in any criminal activity. No less important, Bloomberg's policy further corroded the relationship between non-white communities and the police; this atmosphere of distrust worsened racial relations in the city overall. On February 5, 2015, Bloomberg offered an audience of over four hundred people at the Aspen Institute his solution to the problem of gun violence in the country: have law enforcement focus on the actions of minority males, aged fifteen through twenty-five (Herchenroeder 2015). It is as if he had learned nothing at all from the contrary evidence offered in the policy's aftermath.

In a similar way, new awareness of voter ID laws gained currency in U.S. politics when Barack Obama, the son of a white Midwestern woman and a black Kenyan man, rose to political prominence as a credible presidential hopeful. His ascent to that top leadership role energized unprecedented numbers of citizens from communities of color to exercise their right to vote and participate in other civic processes like campaigning and fundraising. In 2008 and 2012, however, it became clear that the new laws had acted to suppress voter turnout, an eerie parallel to the poll taxes and literacy test requirements of the segregated South. This was the same vociferous racism that had kept Strom Thurmond, the ardent negrophobe who fathered a child by a young black domestic working for his family, reelected as a U.S. senator for South Carolina until the age of one hundred. More recently, the anti-immigrant, anti-Mexican, anti-Muslim, and broadly Hispanophobic rhetoric displayed by celebrity business tycoon Donald Trump invigorated his campaign as he vied for (and eventually won) the Republican Party's presidential nomination in 2015–16.

Many Latina/o scholars have tackled the thorny issue of racism within and among U.S. Hispanic populations, pointing to internalized negrophobia, anti-Indigenous sentiments, tensions with other groups, and white supremacist tendencies that inform everything from slang to hairstyling. Their findings shore up crucial areas that require further investigation. Racism, for example, operates as a pedagogy that informs the thoughts, feelings, and actions of whole societies, not just individuals. Extricating it from these societies requires an effort at least equivalent to that which racial pedagogues invested in its conception, inculcation, and maintenance. While prejudices tend to originate in the master class, which is also the primary beneficiary of their existence, nothing bars them from trickling down to the marginal and subaltern groups, since structures of socialization and schooling almost invariably come from above. The oppressed are not immune to the logic and ethos of the oppressors; nor can they assume that their manner of fighting racism will automatically be free of the danger of replicating racist paradigms and practices.

Overall, inquiries that privilege racism as the occasion wherein the abstraction of race achieves materiality, approached from the perspectives of political economy and intellectual history, have the best potential for fleshing out the subject in a manner that can advance the conversation broadly and contribute to the empowerment of diverse populations. Unlearning intolerance, especially by discarding automatic assumptions and deconstructing stereotypes, may help restore empathy and compassion across stark categories of difference. People whose ancestors have suffered dehumanization must find ways of shaking off the presumption that they are racially on the "right side" simply by virtue of their descent from victims rather than perpetrators of barbarity and destruction. As a body of knowledge, a dogma, and a set of social practices, racism pervades the atmosphere of entire societies, enveloping the vanquished no less pervasively than the vanquishers. It therefore behooves those historically inhabiting the victim's side to remain alert to their own potential for disempowering others as well as themselves. They ought to delink from internalized racism while affirming their ability and willingness to refrain from doing unto others as has been done unto them. Only with the humility and the forbearance that these existential exercises entail can we hope to envision an eventual post-racial society.

With this goal in mind, one could argue that the United States can epitomize greatness writ large only if it musters up the humility to be honest about its racist past. To be able to work toward the amelioration of social relations requires a recognition that awful events took place in the process of creating this grand civilization, and that the ascent and well-being of some occurred at the expense and suffering of many. Finding a way to own up to that past and create a climate of respect for the descendants of victims and perpetrators alike remains both an imperative and a challenge for inhabitants of this country and the rest of the Americas.

48

Radio

Dolores Inés Casillas

Scholars of Chicana/o and Latina/o studies have long stressed the archival and political role of the oral—testimonios, storytelling, songtelling, and even *chisme* (gossip)—for communities of color left out of the pages of U.S. histories (Paredes 1958; Herrera-Sobek 1990; Schmidt Camacho 2008; D. Vargas 2012). The voice, either lyrically or narratively, stands in as "flesh" for Latina/o bodies and as sound evidence of past and continued injustices. Oral practices help circulate stories, archive experiences, and strengthen emotional ties for Latinas/os with allegiances to more than one culture, language, or nation. Radio, with its audio feature, is an extension of such oral traditions, modernizing them by playing music from homelands and islands left behind; by broadcasting politics and news updates; by offering a public space for listeners to engage each other; and/or by helping listeners learn how to navigate newfound political structures in the United States. In many ways, whether musically or through talk shows, radio serves as an acoustic ally to a legion of Latina/o listeners. Latina/o radio, broadcast in Spanish, English, or code-switching between the two, brings a sense of political recognition to a listenership long neglected by English-language media and defined by class, race, language, and/or legal status.

The broader field of media and communications privileges topics related to televisual media, the Internet, and other forms of digital media, but gives inconsistent attention to race and language and much less to legal status and its influence on media representations, choices, and practices (Dávila 2001; Nakamura 2008). Indeed, even radio scholars have some culpability. The majority of radio studies focuses on the historical significance of radio between the 1920s to the early 1950s, dubbed as the "Golden Age of Radio;" or before television's arrival purportedly killed radio (Douglas 1999; Russo 2010; Hilmes and Loviglio 2013). Moreover, Latina/o studies thus far have also favored television and film, yet show more inspiring strides in the area of music (Aparicio 1998; Zolov 1999; Habell-Pallán 2005; Cepeda 2010; D. Vargas 2012). Taken together, these exceptions, combined with both Latina/o population growth and a cultural affinity for oral traditions, position radio as a creative lens for looking at citizenship, consumerism, identity, and immigration.

Radio's technological transformations throughout the twentieth century have been influenced, in part, by the economic, political, and racial moment. Physically, the radio set itself has evolved from its initial big box form with a static (poor) sound quality, controlled by a manual dial to its contemporary pocket sized, sonic (crisp) features, now often managed remotely. Radio's pricey 1930s introduction to U.S. and Latin American households coupled with its stationary living-room location created a culture of familial, group listening. Today, radio's affordability and mobility make it possible for radio listening to take place virtually anywhere. These transitions have helped shape how Latina/o listeners make sense of their diverse, transnational lives over the airwaves.

Early 1920s to 1940s radio provided English-speaking Americans the opportunity to "travel" to Latin America via radio. A precursor to the motion picture films funded by the-then Good Neighbor policies, the radio waves enticed American listeners with shows dedicated to boasting the beauty of all things Latin American.

Good Neighbor policies were recognized as collaborative, hemispheric campaigns meant to befriend our southern, Latin American neighbors by presenting them as charming, exotic, and business-worthy allies. Government-sponsored and generously funded, several hundreds of radio shows were involved in these cross-border public relations tactics. Spanish-speaking musicians, Latin American dance styles, and on-air "tours" of ancient ruins and natural landscapes were featured, for instance, on CBS's *La Cadena de las Américas* and NBC's *Radio Panamericana*, while the show *Calling Pan America* focused on a different Latin American capital each week, posing as a radio infomercial for cosmopolitan Latin American cultures. Spanish-speaking communities were imagined, thanks to radio, as living *over there*, far away and across our geographical U.S. borders, rather than in booming numbers in urban America. As a result, American English-language listeners assigned these "different" voices to distant communities while cultivating a romantic if not exotic attraction to Spanish and Spanish accented voices.

Not imagined within these Pan-American radio shows were the growing Mexican and Mexican American communities in Los Angeles or San Antonio, Puerto Ricans in New York City, or Cubans in Miami—all cities known for their early radio broadcasts directed at local Spanish-speaking listeners. For instance, the popular Los Angeles–based radio host Pedro González used his early morning show as an on-air community bulletin board; he publicized local employment opportunities, advertised ethnic-run businesses, played heartfelt rancheras and corridos about immigrant injustices, and denounced the unlawful repatriations of Mexicans during the Great Depression. He was adored as a hero by Angeleno listeners but known as a "rabble-rouser" by law enforcement agencies for his politically charged messages. González's 4 a.m. radio show attracted

sponsorships, a rarity for the few radio programs at that time targeting Latinas/os in the United States. Despite his commercial success, González was falsely convicted of a crime, sent to prison, and then eventually deported to Tijuana before returning to southern California decades later. His storied career was detailed in the 1984 documentary *Ballad of an Unsung Hero* (Artenstein 2006) and later became the basis of a Hollywood film, *Break of Dawn* in 1989 (Artenstein 2002).

Pedro González's early vocal advocacy on behalf of a legally vulnerable listenership set the stage for the kind of activism heard on Latina/o radio today. His work calls to mind the local community groups and religious congregations that coordinated the pro-immigrant marches of 2006 in Los Angeles, followed soon after by marches in a dozen other U.S. cities. Spanish-speaking radio hosts are largely credited for using their microphones as bullhorns to rouse a record-setting turnout. Decades later, immigrants continue to seek radio as their transnational ally, an audible medium for learning about shifts in immigration legislation and labor policies, rumored sightings of Immigration and Customs Enforcement (ICE) raids, and/or the campaign goals of both U.S. and Latin American political candidates.

Even in conservative-leaning Florida, *Radio Martí*, considered a Cold War staple for its prolific anti-Fidel Castro broadcasts, has been used for decades to influence conservative Cuban exile listeners. Funded, in part, with federal funds, thanks to then-President Ronald Reagan, *Radio Martí* plays a similar, transnational advocacy role for Cubans nostalgic for a pre-embargo Cuba. Despite Cuba's President Raul Castro's public disdain for and blocking of *Radio Martí* from airing on the island, DVDs and flash drives of the show are routinely shipped to Cuba, serving as an audible, emotional, and political connection for Cubans displaced by ninety miles of sea and a chilly political relationship between the United

States and Cuba. Because most Cubans on the island do not have Internet access, radio even in a prerecorded format functions as a critical oral link for the Cuban diaspora.

Applauded for its ability to unify listeners, and in an effort to rally around all-things-American, listening to baseball on the radio became a popular post–World War II pastime. Arguably, the sport's geometric diamond design and its steady rhythm of long pauses between pitches made mentally following along easy. Sports broadcasters helped their primary male listening base envision a hit to right field, an outfielder diving for a ball, or someone attempting to steal second base. Radio also made it possible to "attend" a baseball game without purchasing a costly ticket or sitting in a racially segregated section. Instead, Latina/o communities would congregate in public around a radio, listening keenly for the broadcast of a Spanish-surnamed baseball player, at a time when baseball players from Mexico, Cuba, and Puerto Rico were recruited to Major League Baseball (MLB) (Burgos 2007). Listening to baseball, recognized intrinsically as American, while cheering in Spanish, spoke to a unique U.S. Latina/o experience: listening *here* yet rooting for those from over *there* or those like *me*.

Today, listening to sports over the radio has fast become a lucrative, busy format on Spanish-language radio. Case in point: the Los Angeles Dodgers, affectionately known as Los Doyers, earmark the bulk of their Latino-directed marketing to their Spanish-language radio announcer, Jaime Jarrín, who has been announcing Doyer games since 1959. To cite another example, ESPN Deportes (ESPN Sports) is the most popular U.S.-based radio streaming and podcast site, an indication of both the increase of Latin American and Latino players as professional athletes and the loyalty of Latina/o fans who tune in. Then, too, the football Superbowl Champions of 2016, the Carolina Panthers, made headlines for

their popular Spanish and Spanglish broadcasters, Jaime Moreno and Luis Moreno Jr., an uncle and nephew duo. Their signature line, "Touchdooooooown!," a familiar vocal nod toward the Latin American tradition of shouting "Goooool" during soccer matches, amused English-language sports broadcasters and helped attract Latina/o listeners to tune in via radio rather than English-language television. The attention Moreno and Moreno Jr. received focused on their on-air charisma but arguably had much more to do with the mounting presence of Latinas/os since the mid-1990s in North and South Carolina and the surprising vocal, brown allegiance to American-style football.

The installation of radio sets within vehicles during the 1950s and 1960s changed how Latina/o youth cruised around town—mainly at leisure paces and in circles, while listening to music, and for hours as a pastime. By 1965, not only were nearly 60 percent of all automobiles outfitted with a car radio, but also used-car sales gave Latina/o car ownership a marked boost. On the West Coast, specifically, cruising in low riders, or vehicles purposely rebuilt to sit lower (Calvo-Quirós 2007), propelled Mexican American youth to drive slowly and to turn the radio up. Listening to the radio became mobile, noticeably public, and, at times, racially charged depending on the song style or level of volume.

The arrival decades later of satellite radio, Pandora, iTunes radio, podcasts, and more has challenged how we define radio as listeners gravitate toward earbuds and other more private and arguably, "whiter" modes of listening (Casillas 2014). Latina/o listeners tend to be more working class and immigrant-based, and much more likely to listen to broadcast radio than an online radio station. Listening figures alone confirm that Latina/o listeners, regardless of their preference to speak English or Spanish, tune in to radio an average of three hours longer than the general, English-dominant radio listener. Their annual household earnings, averaging approximately $35,000 a year, are among the lowest in the country. In many ways, the browning of radio and often public sounds of broadcast radio from laborers and workers themselves—for instance, booming from the back of restaurant kitchens or outside construction sites—challenge public norms (Casillas 2014) and have made Latina/o labor and their presence, at times during tense moments of anti-immigrant sentiment, publically audible.

The courting of Latina/o listeners has become starkly evident in radio ratings, especially since the 1990s. Media companies clamored to satellite and online radio opportunities, and, in turn, Spanish-language and bilingual commercial radio seized the broadcast airwaves. Each of the five principal radio markets in the United States—New York City, Los Angeles, Houston, Chicago, and Miami—routinely lists a Spanish-language or bilingual radio station in one of its top three positions. Even areas in the new Latino South such as North Carolina, Arkansas, and Georgia have welcomed new Latino-targeted radio stations. Latina/o radio serves as a political ally for those recently arrived in U.S. communities by making politicized statements over the airways and serving as a transnational audible link between here and back "home." A rechristening of the present state of broadcast radio as the "Bronze Age of Radio" best captures the zeitgeist.

49

Rasquachismo
Laura G. Gutiérrez

Rasquachismo, a critical concept in Chicana/o cultural and visual studies, came into academic usage over two decades ago and is used to explicate a resourceful, working-class, neo-baroque aesthetic sensibility present(ed) in the productions of some Chicana/o artists. Within the larger field of Latina/o studies, "rasquachismo" exists alongside a cluster of terms that have been used to describe representational strategies, mass-produced material culture, and ways of relating to and undermining forms of power; these include *chusmería*, *cursi* or *cursilería*, *choteo*, and *chuchería*, which are used mainly, though not exclusively, in the Caribbean and the Caribbean diaspora. If we continue to expand farther outward, the much-written about concepts of camp and kitsch would be part of this constellation of signifiers that denote a style (or lack thereof) and/or sensibility. In this brief essay I focus on rasquachismo, but relate it to these other keywords since they all function similarly to denote an attitude that can be perceived in material, visual, and performance cultural practices produced by Latinas/os.

"Rasquachismo" is derived from the word "rasquache," a distorted Spanish term from the Nahuatl that connotes anything that lacks style or good taste and indexes—in most contexts beyond academic or artistic circles—the socially scripted practice in Chicana/o and Latina/o circles of distinguishing oneself from others in terms of class status. As the Chicano cultural critic Tomás Ybarra-Frausto writes in the opening of his seminal essay, "Rasquachismo: A Chicano Sensibility," "One is never *rasquache*, it is always someone else of a lower status who is judged outside of the demarcators of approved taste and decorum" (1989, 5). Thus, in the long-standing social practice of reproducing hierarchies and maintaining a certain status quo through injurious speech acts, rasquache is used to keep certain sectors of society in an inferior position. However, as with other concepts that have undergone resignification, to self-consciously self-name as "rasquache" has been instrumental in Chicana/o and Latina/o critical practices.

This vernacular use of "rasquache"—also spelled "rascuache"—is used to describe something vulgar, poor, or of a lower quality, status, or value and is associated with a person who has some of these characteristics and who is resourceful and creatively inventive out of a necessity to make do. Examples of this working-class resourcefulness are wide and vary (and may or may not involve duct tape), but here I will provide just two: (1) instead of throwing away the used tin cans of salsa, jalapeños, or coffee, in some instances folks use them to pot a plant or flower; (2) others might cut up larger and flatter tin cans into rectangles to use as "canvases" as in the vernacular Catholic tradition of painting *retablo ex-votos* to give thanks to a divine power for a miraculous intervention. These practices can be and are also extended to describe an attitude and underdog sensibility, exemplified most directly by the *pelado* or *peladito* character/type that was featured in many of the itinerant tent (*carpa*) theater sketches of the beginning of the twentieth century and some of the early films starring the great comedic actor Mario Moreno, better known as "Cantinflas." "*Pelado*" and its diminutive form "*peladito*" both translate as "the bald-headed one"; both refer to the down-trodden urban pariah that must make do with what's available, even if by trickery and undermining the system. However, while we often associate

Cantinflas with the *pelado* as the prototypical rasquache figure, it is important to note that this figure straddled gender lines, as well as geopolitical ones and that it was very popular on both sides of the border, as Rita Urquijo-Ruiz (2013) has demonstrated. In Ybarra-Frausto's own words, "Mexican vernacular traditions form the base of rasquachismo, but it has evolved as a bicultural sensibility among Mexican Americans. On both sides of the border, it retains an underclass perspective" (1989, 5). This attitude and sensibility, as well as associated practices, form the basis for conceptualizations of the term "rasquachismo" in Chicana/o and Latina/o critical studies examining the artistic practices and productions particularly that began to proliferate during the post–civil rights era.

One of the first, if not the first, Chicana/o cultural uses of the concept of rasquache for artistic ends was El Teatro Campesino's *La Carpa de los Rasquachis*, first staged in 1974, and thereafter revived several times. With a script written by Luis Valdez, the play reworks the tradition of early twentieth-century Mexican itinerant *carpa* theater to tell the story of the trials and tribulations of Jesús Pelado Rasquachi, a farmworker who has migrated from Mexico to the United States. According to Ybarra-Frausto, the *carpa* tradition, along with *tandas de variedad* (variety theater) were the "standard bearers of rasquache aesthetic," and the peladita/o was the embodiment of a rasquache sensibility, "remind[ing] us to draw sustenance from fundamental life processes and to use them for surmounting adversity" (1989, 7).

It is precisely these characteristics of the peladita/o that have made the figure appropriate for post-*movimiento* Chicana/o re-elaboration and recontextualization. With *La Carpa de los Rasquachi* specifically, as well as their work in general, both Luis Valdez and El Teatro Campesino were "articulating and validating the rasquache sensibility in dramatic form" (Ybarra-Frausto

1989, 7). Ybarra-Frausto further contextualizes this notion, writing that "the very essence of a bicultural lived reality was scorned as un-American by the dominant culture. A necessary response was to disown imposed categories of culture and identity and to create a Chicano self-vision of wholeness and completion. Signs and symbols which those in power manipulated to signal unworthiness and deficiencies were mobilized and turned about as markers of pride and affirmation" (1989, 7). Moreover, as the Chicana artist and curator Amalia Mesa-Bains emphasizes, rasquachismo is both material and attitudinal: "In its broadest sense it is a combination of resistant and resilient attitudes devised to allow the Chicano to survive and persevere with a sense of dignity. The capacity to hold life together with bits of string, old coffee cans, and broken mirrors in a dazzling gesture of aesthetic bravado is at the heart of rasquachismo" (1999, 158).

This vernacular sensibility that is at once resourceful, validating, and aesthetically replete and pleasurable is associated with the work of a number of well-known Chicana/o and Latina/o artists, including the visual artists Rudy Martínez, Amalia Mesa-Bains, Patricia Rodríguez, David Avalos, Pepón Osorio, and Franco Mondini Ruiz and the poet José Montoya. However, I would also include here the performance work of the East Los Angeles collective Asco (active in the 1970s and 1980s), the Lower East Side of New York's Carmelita Tropicana (a.k.a. Alina Troyano), and the Bay Area-based "border brujo" Guillermo Gómez-Peña, who expanded the meaning of rasquachismo beyond El Teatro Campesino's expression of it. By expanding rasquachismo, I aim to bring forth the specific ways in which materials that are often associated with Latina/o everyday life are some of the primary objects repurposed in the process of making visual art, including installations, which results in baroque and heavily ornate products.

But, as was suggested above, these rasquache aesthetics have been in direct conversation with traditional forms of performance, most specifically carpa and Teatro Campesino plays. Thus it should be of no surprise that some of these strategies of excessiveness and, crucially, of conscious positioning against the oppressive systems of power have been integrated into recent performances produced by Latinas/os, most specifically queer Latina/o solo performances (as in Carmelita Tropicana) and border performance (as in Guillermo Gómez-Peña). Thus, regardless of whether rasquachismo takes the form of a painting or an installation or a staged performance, it is precisely the creative inventiveness in repurposing and using given materials in ways that leave very little visual or aural empty space that contributes to the principal characteristics of rasquache aesthetics, a sort of neo-baroque, if you will.

The above-mentioned forms of excess and their subversive relationship to power have been described as raquachismo's oppositional capabilities and differ widely from the apolitical nature and sparse aesthetics of other artistic movements such as Minimalism (Gaspar de Alba 1998, 12). The visual differences that I have been mentioning are important to highlight for several reasons: Chicana/o and Latina/o artists insert themselves within vernacular traditions to recycle not just material, but also techniques. Drawing from the popular culture of Latina/o neighborhoods across the United States, whether in the form of the inner-city *botánica* (herb or folk medicine store), with all of its mass-produced candles and other religious paraphernalia, or home altars set up during the Days of the Dead, they emphasize texture, color, and excessive ornamentation, such that there is seldom any space to spare. This reveling in the pleasure of going against dominant artistic forms of expression, which are often ensconced within modern art and can be identified as having more

European or Europeanized sensibilities, is only one part of the work that Latina/o artists do. In a rasquache aesthetic and sensibility, paying homage to traditions, practices, icons, and iconography is just as important, if not more. For example, Mesa-Bains's use of the vernacular tradition of home altars to create *An Ofrenda for Dolores del Río* (first created in 1984 and then recreated in 1991)—a beautifully constructed and ostentatiously ornate installation devoted to the Mexican film icon Dolores del Río, which has been featured in various exhibitions since its creation, most recently in *Our America: The Latino Presence in Latino Art* (Smithsonian American Art Museum, 2013)—brings the private practice of paying homage to loved ones who have passed away to the public sphere (or museum space) in a way that subverts dominant paradigms of artistic production, value, and exhibition; not only are Latina/o artists taking up space in the museums and galleries that have often discriminated against them (and to a large extent still do), they are also challenging perceptions that see their work as "lesser than," deficient, or inferior. The work of artists such as Pepón Osorio, Franco Mondini-Ruiz, and Carmelita Tropicana function similarly: they are often re-workings of everyday objects, languages, and performance traditions, and the artists politicize their expressions through the filters of queer, feminist, and/or anti-racist discourses.

Other terms associated and sometimes conflated with "rasquachismo" are "kitsch" and "camp," both of which have been theorized from an academic or critical perspective and used in certain artistic production and/or practices (Olalquiaga 1992; Gaspar de Alba 1998; Muñoz 1999). "Domesticana" is another term used by the artist-curator Mesa-Bains to describe a particular Chicana rasquache and feminist sensibility and aesthetic practice. Additionally, related concepts include *cursi* (used to describe an excessive form of

sentimentality, as Monsiváis [1970] and Valis [2002] discuss), *choteo* (a verbal strategy that involves playful opposition), *chusmería* (the ways in which the so-called unwanted perform excessiveness—being loud, effusive, melodramatic—which is what marks them as unwanted), and *chuchería* (used to describe an object of little value). These vernacular practices, all of which register excessiveness, can serve critical purposes for Latina/o visual and performance artists. For example, as José Esteban Muñoz (1999) has pointed out, Carmelita Tropicana's performances purposefully embody *chusmería* in their tackiness and loudness and deploy *choteo* verbal tactics as Latina/o queer modes of being. Meanwhile, the excessiveness of Puerto Rican-born, Philadelphia-based Pepón Osorio's artwork, as exemplified in his three-dimensional piece *El Chandelier* (1988, also exhibited in the aforementioned *Our America*) immediately signals a repurposing of *chucherías* (Indych 2001). Adorned with cheap, yet meaningful objects for the Puerto Rican and Latina/o communities (dolls, cake decorations, frogs), this functioning chandelier high*lights* the strategies of making do with what's readily and cheaply available.

All of these practices have been used in Latina/o cultural productions in a variety of ways, at different times. Thus, whereas Ybarra-Frausto conceives of rasquachismo as a phenomenon of the post–civil rights era, others place it, and its related forms, in a postmodern context, as well as seeing connections with notions of kitsch and understanding it in terms of Susan Sontag's (1983) influential "Notes on Camp." Together, "rasquachismo" and its related terms serve to describe specific Latina/o vernacular working-class and affective modes of practicing art and engendering an affirmative stance amidst a hostile environment that is mostly classist, racist, homophobic, and misogynist; they need to be theorized further by Latina/o cultural studies scholars.

50

Raza

B. V. Olguín

There is lingering dissent, and outright confusion, over the etymology of the term "raza." Indeed, as a noun and as an adjective, it conceals and effaces as much as it reveals and illuminates. The Real Academia Española traces the term to the Latin *radía* or *radíus* (rod, spoke, or ray), and offers such disparate definitions as *casta* (caste), *grieta* (crack in a horse's hoof), and *raya de luz* (ray of sunlight). All of these etymological touchstones involve the vocabulary of cartography, race, zoology, and even refracted light, that is, color. The term thus invites postcolonial, ethnic, and critical race studies appropriations of its Spanish medieval resonances and early modern inflections, particularly the colonialist *castas* taxonomy depicted in the infamous sixteenth-century series of images from "New Spain," or the Americas.

Castas refers to eugenicist hierarchical mappings of genealogy based on early modern notions of race in which the Renaissance idea of "fair beauty" came to carry increasingly more currency in direct proportion to the growth of European empires. In their colonial Latin American iterations, there were sixteen general codifications of *castas*, several of which had their own subcategories that exponentially increased the number of racialized permutations. These ranged from *criollos* (who were born to a Spaniard and another European person who was born in the Americas); *mestizos* (of Amerindian and Spanish parents); *pardos* (having Spanish, African, and Amerindian roots); *mulato* (from "mule," referring to people of Spanish and African heritage); *lobo* (or "wolf," formed by offspring of Spanish and Moor [*albino*] paired with offspring of Spanish and African [*mulato*]); and even *chino* (from *cochino*, or "pig," born of *mulato* and Amerindian parents).

These convoluted value-laden depictions of race were inextricably related to the discourses of *limpieza de sangre* (cleansing of blood), *mejorando la raza* (improving the race), and racialized religious hierarchies that informed Christian proselytizing in the medieval and early modern periods. In this reified taxonomy, which lingers today, opportunities and presumed virtues were sought through the progressive generational whitening or lightening of one's offspring through unions with lighter-skinned people, cosmetics, and cultural strategies such as religious conversion. These notions are related to the more contemporary trope of "passing" in the African American and Afro-Latina/o communities. Significantly, the dogmatic binary notion of a *vendido*, or "sell out," is a critique levied against Latinas/os accused of trying to "pass," as they are perceived as effacing their cultural heritage as members of La Raza for personal or political gain. All these negotiations of power remain highly problematic, reified colonialist models of race, even as these coping mechanisms are undergirded by a materialist gnosis, that is, the awareness that Western European lineages offer improved life choices in the West.

As an alternative to the *casta* signifiers of subordination, contrapuntal readings of raza have come to predominate in postcolonial, Latin American, and Latina/o studies. Yet, raza's earlier traces of racial-darkness-as-pathology and racial-darkness-as-bestiality remain. A comparative intellectual historiography of the poetics of raza underscores the term's limited use value as a floating signifier of power relations, identity, and agency in the Americas.

William Shakespeare's 1611 tragicomic play, *The Tempest*, offers one of the earliest touchstones for the vexed notion of race in the Americas, and informs other syntheses of raza. This play focuses on a group of Europeans shipwrecked on a Caribbean island. Aided by a spirit named Ariel whom he freed from captivity, the tyrannical patriarch Prospero, who is a bookish magician, enslaves the native character Caliban (related to "cannibal"), who is described as a half-man and half-fish creature born of an Algerian "witch."

Early twentieth-century Latin American intellectuals such as Uruguayan José Enrique Rodó (1900) adopted Ariel as a metonym for Latin America's presumed European genealogy in opposition to the cultural, economic, and military threat posed by the United States, a threat also denounced by intellectuals such as the exiled Cuban José Martí. In contrast to Rodó, Cuban Roberto Fernández Retamar ([1971] 1989), writing in the context of the Cuban Revolution, adopted Caliban—despite his attempts to rape Prospero's daughter to "populate the island with Calibans"—as a paradigmatic figure in postcolonial studies and related anti-colonial political struggles. Chicano scholar José David Saldívar's (1991) formulation of the "School of Caliban"—his term for a multiracial, subaltern global cadre of contrapuntal intellectuals—underscores Caliban's salience as a racialized archetype for Latin American, Latina/o, and subaltern studies despite this figure's masculinist, violent contradictions. At the same time, feminist scholars such as Jamaican Sylvia Wynter (1990) offer a pointed critique of Caliban and tried to envision a space for women of color.

In succeeding periods of Latin American, Latina/o, and U.S. intellectual history, various figures sought to transcend or skirt the binaries embodied in the opposition between Ariel and Caliban by further troping raza as a new epistemology and ontology. Mexican intellectual José Vasconcelos ([1925] 1997) is renowned for synthesizing the idea of a "Raza Cósmica," or "cosmic race," which presumably consists of the best of all peoples in a new amalgamated race for which Mexican *mestizas* and *mestizos* serve as his paradigmatic model, though he apparently harbored antipathies toward indigenous and especially black people. Chicano poet Alurista (1971) adapted Vasconcelos's poetics of amalgamation to celebrate Chicanas and Chicanos as "La Raza de Bronce," or the Bronze Race. Privileging the Indigenous heritage of *mestizas* and *mestizos*, Alurista's intervention had a symbiotic relationship to the mass mobilizations known as the Chicana/o movement. This social movement and its accompanying discursive component had a profound impact in opening new spaces for Chicana/o political agency, which ranged from various cultural nationalisms such as Alurista's, to revolutionary Marxist paradigms.

For all its potential, however, Alurista's notion of La Raza de Bronze was burdened by profound internal contradictions. In his 1969 preface to "El Plan Espiritual de Aztlán," for instance, Alurista sought to thicken the idea of La Raza de Bronce, later fully articulated in his first book of poetry *Floricanto en Aztlán* (1971), by proclaiming a "bronze people," "bronze culture," and "bronze continent" (Anaya and Lomelí 1991). However, his use of raza to recuperate the Aztec diasporic story of Aztlán is articulated through masculinist metaphors (such as "Brotherhood unites us"), as well as other nostalgic allusions to an idyllic Aztec past that fetishize Aztec warrior heroes, in what Curtis Marez (2001) has called an *"indigenismo* of the antique." Further, Sheila Contreras (2008) points to the irony that the nostalgic models of indigeneity and mestizaje operative in Chicana/o nationalist cultural discourses are drawn from European and Eurocentric sources, discourses, and caricatures, which render these terms highly problematic and contradictory.

Despite some critiques of Gloria Anzaldúa's (1987) neo-Indigenous discourses on *mestizaje*, which María Josefina Saldaña-Portillo (2003) claims efface specific Indigenous tribes, and which Taunya Lovell Banks (2006) critiques for effacing the African legacies of Mesoamerica, Anzaldúa nonetheless is most successful in synthesizing raza as both a metaphysical and corporeal epistemology and ontology. Anzaldúa's synthesis of mestizaje extends far beyond the term's superficial allusion to racial mixtures that animated *casta* discourses. Instead, she moves toward a much broader conceptual space that can accommodate interstitial subjectivities and gnosis—her borderlands paradigm—and thus her deployment of raza is less burdened by Alurista's overt fetishizing of skin tone and phenotype. Indeed, Anzaldúa's intertwining of raza (she alludes to Vasconcelos throughout *Borderlands / La Frontera*) with mestizaje in the U.S.-Mexico borderlands in her explication of the "new mestiza" affords a revolutionary recovery and recentering of the margins of Chicana/o discourse through her autobiographical poetic persona: a dark-brown-skinned Indigenous mestiza, who is a rural working-class, multilingual, multicultural, Chicana lesbian. While Anzaldúa's "outing" of Chicana/o studies, as it were, is enabled more by her metaphor of the new mestiza, Vasconcelos's and Alurista's syntheses of the term "raza" informs her revolutionary intervention both as a touchstone and as an antithesis. It must be noted, however, that outside of Anzaldúa's usage of "raza," the term offers little latitude for accounting for the complexities of uniquely racialized and gendered Chicana/o subjectivities, which Sandra K. Soto (2010) insists must not be disarticulated in Chicana/o theories of being, knowing, and doing.

As a racialized gendered metaphor for "my people," the etymological legacy of "raza" is continually engaged, challenged, and synthesized in a multiplicity of ways throughout various Latina/o groups. Theories of Puerto Rican ontology involve unique permutations of "raza" that account for the African heritage that oftentimes is effaced in Chicana/o theories of La Raza. In a retort to Antonio S. Pedreira's ([1934] 2002) Eurocentric paradigm of racial "fusion" leading to "confusion," theorists such as José Luis González (1980, 1990) made important attempts to recognize the Spanish, Indigenous Taíno, and African heritage of Puerto Ricans, which were followed by myriad theorists such as Juan Flores (1993), as well as Frances R. Aparicio and Susana Chavez-Silverman (1997), in addition to myriad performers who variously emphasized mulataje (Buscaglia-Salgado 2003) or the racial mixture of Europeans and Africans with an expansive vocabulary. For instance, Nuyorican poet Willie Perdomo's (1996) dramatic dialogue "Nigger Reecan Blues" addresses the vexed notion of phenotype and the trope of "passing" through a poetic persona who is fully actualized and proud yet nonetheless becomes angst-ridden after encountering other people's anxieties about his mixed-race heritage—including Puerto Ricans'. Perdomo's use of the vernacular term of endearment "pana mía" (my good friend) as well as "brother" (with its deep meaning in African American culture) illuminates the insufficiency of "raza" as an ontological signifier. In Puerto Rican contexts, other terms such as "Boricua"—from the Indigenous Taíno term "Borikén," which roughly means "Land of the Valiant"—offer more precision, in addition to the productive ambiguity that Perdomo privileges.

Similar alternatives to "raza" exist throughout the Americas in a dynamic that involves continual renovation of nomenclature, rendering "raza" and related terms, *sous rature* (under erasure). Indeed, various syntheses of "raza" reveal that its hegemonic and proposed counterhegemonic syntheses remain inseparable, with "raza" ultimately illuminating its own radical insufficiency as a term for interrogating real power relations. As is the case with Native American studies scholar Ward Churchill's (1999) antipathies to Marxism as a prism for mapping indigeneity, Latina/o studies' renderings of "raza" also frequently are antithetical to materialist, and particularly Marxist, theories of race, and related political programs that investigate class and other social formations. Like the equally slippery term "subaltern," "raza" effaces a wide range of class conflicts among the very population the term seeks to identify. For instance, as a core component of Chicano cultural nationalism, theories of praxis predicated upon various syntheses of La Raza, or the Chicano people, run the danger of animating a capitalist political agenda as much as they offer the promise of a Marxist one. The wide ideological range that existed within the Chicana/o Raza Unida Party in the 1960s and 1970s underscores this point. Similar to the term "subaltern," which has gone out of vogue for its obfuscation of the class privileges some postcolonial intellectuals continue to possess in their diaspora, the term "raza" can easily degenerate as an adjective to the point where it can accommodate Raza capitalists, Raza imperialists, and even Raza fascists.

Moreover, the etymological roots of "raza" in masculinist Chicano cultural nationalist discourse leave little room for the complexities of gendered racialized Latina/o subjectivities and equally complex relationships to ideology. Other terms, which also have their limits, are far more productive in creating a space for unexpurgated ontologies. These include "mestiza/o" (with the limits noted above), "Xican@" (still burdened by its filiation with Chicano cultural nationalism), and "Nepantler@" (a variation of "mestizaje" and "borderlands," which is undergoing a continual thickening since its seventeenth-century Nahuatl resonance as a signifier of the anomie arising from cultural hybridity).

Ellie Hernández's (2009) call for new postnational (and especially post-heteropatriarchal Chicano nationalist) mappings of Chicana/o subjectivity even more productively segues with the decolonial search for new vocabularies.

This ongoing search for new vocabularies seeks to address how terms such as "raza" and "subaltern" fail to transcend another limit: androcentrism. Ironically, given that one of the etymological threads of "raza" (that is, *grieta*) alludes to the cracks in a horse's hoof, "raza" fails to shed its androcentric dimensions—or harness its *casta* bestial allusions—to offer a space for new theories of what presently are still referred to as "cyborgs" (though "post-human" is gaining traction). "Raza" simply offers little room for proactive reclamations of interstitial interspecies ontologies. Significantly, Susana Ramírez's (2015) new archaeologies of Gloria Anzaldua's science fiction and fantasy writing offer promising insights on how Anzaldúa's use of *nepantla* as a trans-temporal, trans-species, and trans-spatial category transcends the androcentric limits of mestizaje. Sonia Valencia (2016) further shows how Chicana lesbian performance artist Adelina Anthony offers equally provocative renderings of trans-species ontologies in her plays and performance art featuring animals. These new scholars illustrate how "raza" has failed to live up to its potential as a term that can facilitate theories of new ontological realities in a post-postmodern world in which prostheses take multiple forms, from mechanical limbs to cell phones to Internet avatars. That is, Latinas/os have, for some time, been conditioned by various simulacra to understand race, and La Raza, in ways that have moved far beyond the earlier androcentric and racially solipsistic iterations.

So what is the use value of "raza" for Latina/o studies today? Any answer to this question must not efface the important kinetic force this root metaphor had in particular times and places, from *castas* and corresponding apartheid societies, to 1960s and 1970s radical social movements that included problematic masculinist and homophobic cultural nationalisms, to revolutionary theories of praxis that involved complex historical materialist understanding of race. Mario Barrera's (1989) critical race synthesis of class segmentation is but one Marxist synthesis of "raza" that reveals the term's radical potential as the root of a counterhegemonic gnosis. While Raza studies programs and paradigms have long since been assimilated and contained as mainstream academic (and no longer primarily counterhegemonic) fields and practices, the potential remains for a reclamation of this term. Indeed, new, and newly discovered, racial, religious, and cultural fusions among Latinas/os may tempt scholars to reclaim "raza" as an operative term in the field. These include the multigenerational Mexican American Punjabi community that Karen Leonard (1994) has illuminated, the growing Latina/o Muslim population, and every possible "interracial" union imaginable, not to mention the specter of genetic engineering afforded by current technologies. The question that arises, of course, is what we lose when we attempt to rehabilitate such a problematic term vis-à-vis what it enables.

51

Religion

Anne M. Martínez

As numerous scholars have noted, there is long-standing resistance in Latina/o and Chicana/o studies, in particular, to writing about religion (Espinosa and García 2008). Some of this resistance derives from the origins of Chicana/o and Boricua studies, which were deeply imbued with Marxist trends and influences, but it also has to do with the historical stigmatization of Indigenous and African traditions in the Americas. Further, the association between Christianity and colonialism leads some scholars to regard Catholicism as a tool for the oppression of Latina/o communities by colonial forces. Such perspectives minimize the contemporary centrality of religion to Latina/o populations, as well as the ways Latinas/os have used religion to resist oppression in a variety of settings.

The majority of Latinas/os in the United States are Catholic (55 percent), often with an infusion of Indigenous and African practices and devotions. However, the Catholic share of the Latina/o population is rapidly declining, as the Pew Research Center (2014) report on *The Shifting Religious Identity of Latinos in the United States* indicates. In 2014, one quarter of the Latina/o population identified as former Catholics who had become Evangelical Protestants or unaffiliated with a religious tradition. The largest growth in the twenty-first century has been among unaffiliated Latinas/os (18 percent) followed by Evangelical Protestants (16 percent). Mainline Protestants make up 5 percent of the Latina/o population (Pew Research Center 2014).

The experiences of Latinas/os in the United States are shaped by historical legacies that marked Catholics as backward, lazy, and primitive. This American narrative of "Latin" slovenliness has deep roots, dating back to British antipathy toward Spanish culture and Catholicism during the Enlightenment and the era of colonial expansion. The American understanding of the Spanish past is shaped by ideas of colonial Spain in the U.S. historical imagination. Richard Kagan coined the term "Prescott's paradigm" to describe "the juxtaposition of Spanish decadence and American progress," a perspective that dominated U.S. discourses of Spain throughout the nineteenth century and into the twentieth century (1996, 425). William Hickling Prescott (1837, 1853) and his nineteenth-century contemporaries advocated the "Black Legend," based on details described by Spanish friar Bartolomé de las Casas in his *Brevísima relación de la destrucción de las Indias* ([1552] 1994), which was widely promoted by Dutch and English Protestant writers from the sixteenth century onward. The "Black Legend" cast the Spanish as exceptionally cruel and intolerant in their interactions with Indigenous peoples in the New World. Spain was characterized as outside of the European Protestant mainstream in its interactions both within Europe and in the Americas.

Colonialism and Catholicism are inseparable, as Spanish Catholic missionaries did significant work among Indigenous peoples on assorted New World frontiers in ways that were at times more akin to slavery than to evangelization. As Jorge Cañizares-Esguerra (2006) has shown, Spanish, British, and Dutch colonial rule was similarly damaging to Indigenous populations and cultures, regardless of the religious background of the colonizer. However, the historical legacy of Catholic cruelty has had more rhetorical force in U.S. historical narratives.

Prescott's paradigm haunted U.S. interaction with Mexico during their mid-nineteenth-century war, when there was still widespread antagonism toward Catholics in the United States. Likewise, Prescott's paradigm was reinforced by the Spanish-American War in 1898, after which the United States gained the last of Spain's colonial territories. Despite efforts like Herbert Bolton's (1933) to paint a "White Legend" of Spanish friars on the frontier civilizing Mexicans and Indians, rather than exterminating them, the historiographical habit of seeing Spain—and the fruit of its conquest, Mexico—in a villainous light persisted. This, of course, erased early American interactions of the British, Dutch, and French with Indigenous populations, which more often led to elimination or forced migration than integration. American exceptionalism was confirmed by U.S. interactions with Spain and Mexico. As destined as the United States was to prosper, Spain and Mexico were destined to fail. Mexico's independence from Spain did nothing to free it from the Black Legend, and Mexico was cemented into a permanent past in reference to the United States. Catholicism, superstitious and secretive, was the foil to the religious ethos of the United States, which promoted individualism and progress, ordained by God through Protestantism.

Latina/o Catholic practice was often cast as idolatrous by Euro-American priests within the U.S. Catholic Church in the late nineteenth and early twentieth centuries. Mexicans in the United States faced efforts to reform their expressions of the faith, including the worship of patron saints and the Virgin of Guadalupe. Through mission churches and at times served by Spanish priests, Mexicans were able to establish parishes in cities like Chicago, San Antonio, San Francisco, and Los Angeles. As Mexicans became more established in many areas, their Catholic faith served as a focal point in their communities, and often a refuge from their sometimes hostile surroundings. Mexicans and Puerto Ricans also faced Americanization campaigns in cities throughout the United States in the early twentieth century, which often included conversion to a Protestant denomination.

U.S. Catholic leaders saw ways to exploit the religious unrest in Mexico, caused by the Mexican Revolution, in rallying American Catholics to support missionaries in the U.S. Southwest and in newly acquired U.S. territories around the world (A. Martínez 2014). Father Francis Kelley, president of the Catholic Church Extension Society, befriended Mexican bishops in exile in the United States and orchestrated a U.S. Catholic campaign to save the Mexican Catholic Church in the 1910s. This U.S. Catholic fervor was revived during the Cristero Rebellion (1926–1929), a Catholic uprising against an anticlerical government bent on limiting the role of the Catholic Church in Mexican society. Kelley used *Extension Magazine* to reach Catholics across the Northeast and Midwest and invoked the Spanish Catholic past in the Philippine Islands, Puerto Rico, and the U.S. Southwest to urge American Catholics to support mission work amongst "our Catholics." Kelley exploited the fact that these were American territories, but sought to counter the classic Americanization projects that included Protestant evangelization. Kelley reminded American Catholics that these lands and peoples had already been civilized by the Spanish friars, and that it was the responsibility of U.S. Catholics to sustain the faith among these peoples. This narrative of Catholic uplift also reinforced the notion that Mexicans and Puerto Ricans needed the help of Americans to sustain democracy, as expressed through religious liberty in this case.

During the *segundo mestizaje*, as Virgilio Elizondo (1983) calls the Mexican presence in the United States, the Virgin of Guadalupe, in particular, has served as a source of pride and strength—both national and religious—for generations of Mexican-descent men and women in the United States. Jeannette Rodríguez (1994) argues that Mexican American women experience *la virgen* as a role model for survival of the self, family, and community, and as a source of empowerment. Since the 1970s, Chicana artists have also embraced the Virgin of Guadalupe as a source of empowerment. Yolanda M. López, for example, painted a series of three generations of Mexican women as *la virgen*, portraying them as strong, independent women. These extra-religious images were not always welcomed by traditionalists and the Catholic hierarchy. In 2001, Chicana artist Alma López created a digital image referencing *la virgen*, which provoked a significant backlash from conservative Catholics who saw the likeness of the Virgin of Guadalupe in a bikini made of roses as sacrilegious. Alicia Gaspar de Alba (Gaspar de Alba and López 2011, 1–12) documents the ways Latina artists envision the Virgin of Guadalupe as a national, cultural, and spiritual source of inspiration that is not dependent on the sanctioning of the Roman Catholic Church. This Chicana spirituality is a source of empowerment for Mexican American women who grew up with the presence of *la virgen*, but did not see the institutional church itself as supportive (Sendejo 2014).

Religious sanctuary was a tool used as part of an interfaith movement to shelter Central American refugees in the 1980s, who were escaping civil wars in their home countries, largely driven by U.S. foreign policy. American Catholic, Protestant, and Jewish congregations provided food, shelter, jobs, and protection from law enforcement to Salvadoran and other Central American families who fled political persecution in their homelands. The assassinations of American Catholic nuns and Catholic Archbishop Oscar Romero in El Salvador in 1980 by forces supported by U.S. foreign aid provoked those of many faiths, in addition to some progressive cities and universities, to attempt to counter American foreign policy. Sanctuary challenged this policy by offering humanitarian aid to those escaping U.S. government-sanctioned violence and repression. At the same time, however, the Catholic Church often supported repressive regimes in Latin American countries. Romero initially did so, but eventually came to embrace Liberation Theology, a Latin American theology of the poor. Pope Francis (Jorge Mario Bergoglio, elected pope in 2012) was scrutinized by Argentinians for his alleged role in defending the authoritarian regime against the poor during the dictatorship, accusations that have been largely discredited.

The twenty-first century has seen an increase in Latina/o evangelicals throughout Latin America, the Caribbean, and the United States. Among the 22 percent of U.S. Latinas/os who identify as Protestant, approximately three-quarters are part of evangelical denominations. Latinas/os between thirty and fifty years of age are leaving the Catholic Church for evangelical churches while younger Latinas/os (aged eighteen to twenty-nine), are becoming unaffiliated with religious institutions. This overall shift away from Catholicism has been occurring quite rapidly. As recently as 2010, Pew research showed that 67 percent of Latinas/os identified as Catholic. Latina/o former Catholics have been drawn to charismatic movements within the United States, such as Victory Outreach and Vineyard, which have sought to appeal to Latina/o youth, in particular (Sánchez-Walsh 2003). More traditional groups such as Mennonites and Mormons have also made special appeals to Latinas/os in the United States.

Some Catholic organizations have moved toward more charismatic and varied practices to attempt to attract Latinas/os. For example, the Valley Missionary Program in the Coachella Valley built a shrine with a pyramid topped by a statue of the Virgin of Guadalupe as part of its outreach to Latina/o immigrants, carving out a space within Catholic practice for Indigenous symbolism and the patroness of the Americas (Groody 2002, 88–89).

As dramatically as the Latina/o Catholic landscape has been shifting, so has the Latina/o presence within the Catholic Church in the United States (Matovina 2012). As of 2013, Latinas/os made up one-third of the U.S. Catholic population. While younger Latinas/os are less likely to be Catholic, younger Catholics are more likely to be Latina/o. Since Latinas/os are a statistically young population, and are growing faster than the white population, their presence in the Catholic Church is likely to grow.

Mexico and the United States have both seen a revival of Indigenous religious expression. Historically, Indigenous religions resisted, coopted, and transformed Catholicism in Mexico. Many Indigenous faiths were believed to have died out but are being revived or becoming more openly practiced by Indigenous communities throughout Mexico. In some cases, this revival is tied to efforts to promote the use of Indigenous languages. Among the Huichol, Mazatec, and other Indigenous groups, language, religion, and culture are not easily separable. In many cases, Catholicism has become part of this spiritual practice, along with rituals that predate the Spanish invasion (Foudree 2013). In the United States, *calpulli* and *danzante* groups have embraced Indigenous Mexican dances and rituals in an effort to express resistance to the Spanish colonization of the sixteenth century and the American neocolonization from the mid-nineteenth century to the present.

Puerto Ricans are overwhelmingly Catholic, but their religious practice, like that of Mexicans, is often considered to be outside the Catholic mainstream (Díaz-Stevens 1993). Caribbean Catholic culture was shaped not only by Indigenous cultures, but also by the traditions of Africans who were brought to the islands as slaves. Cubans and Cuban Americans have a wider range of spiritual practice with a stronger presence of non-European religions, especially among non-elites. Santería (Way of Saints), or Regla de Ocha (Rule of Osha), has deep roots in Cuba, dating to the slave trade. This Yoruba-origin religion has incorporated elements of Catholicism into its New World practice. Miguel De La Torre (2003) documents Santería in the Cuban American population and its interaction with Catholic and other religions in the Miami area. Michelle A. González (2006) argues that regardless of race, Afro-Cuban culture is integral to Cuban culture and religion. Others have highlighted the role of Judaism among Cubans and Cuban Americans (Behar 2007).

Latina/o religious expression and identification is as diverse as the Latina/o population itself. It draws on the distinct historical legacies of Latin American national origins, and their specific relations with, and arrival in, the United States. Though still predominantly Catholic, Latinas/os are becoming more religiously diverse in the twenty-first century.

52
Sexuality
Juana María Rodríguez

Generally imagined as referring to who you are or what you do sexually, the word "sexuality" is used to name a wide range of social identifications predicated on sexual object choice, romantic desires, political identifications, social affinities, and/or erotic proclivities. Discursively linked to activities of procreation, reproduction, and social organization, sexuality also functions to name nonreproductive sensory pleasures and modes of erotic and amorous expression that exceed gender or genitals and are not reducible to sexual identities such as heterosexual, bisexual, lesbian, or gay. Formed through its relationship to other categories of social difference and forms of embodiments, Latinx sexuality is best understood by probing the ways it is mobilized, encountered, and sensed in the body and in the world. Rather than a precise codification of sexual practices, communities, or forms of erotic expression, the histories, politics, and scholarship that surround Latinx sexuality register the ongoing exchanges of power that instantiate and trigger multiple forms of social control. That the delights of corporeal exploration, fantasy, and sexual joy might persist despite these mechanisms of sexual regulation suggests the unruly ways desire disrupts and reroutes these disciplinary flows.

In dominant discourse, rather than being aligned with pleasure, Latinx sexuality has long been framed as pathological and a menace to Anglo civil society. Historicized accounts demonstrate how embodied understandings of Latinidad predicated on nationality, color, class, physical and cognitive norms, gender, age, immigration status, and other registers of difference impact understandings of Latinx bodies, desires, and sexual practices. In the late nineteenth century, racist nativist impulses fed directly into the burgeoning eugenics movements that swept through the United States and lasted well into the twentieth century, resulting in a range of efforts to control the sexuality and reproduction of newly conquered and colonized subjects. These racialized discourses that rendered Latinx bodies and sexualities as dirty, deviant, and diseased continued to be marshaled throughout the twentieth century and were forcefully activated during the Bracero Program that brought millions of male migrant workers, many of whom were Indigenous Mexicans, to the United States (Loza 2011). On the East Coast, early sociological accounts, such as Oscar Lewis's *La Vida: A Puerto Rican Family in the Culture of Poverty—San Juan and New York* (1966b), specifically linked what Lewis termed "cultures of poverty" to aberrant forms of sexuality and gendered deviance. These immigrant waves had significant and lasting effects on both the perceived and the practiced sexual realities of migrant communities, disrupting kinship patterns and sexual practices, while also creating new sexual opportunities for those who no longer felt bound to the inherited sexual norms of their communities of origin.

The characterizations of Latinx culture as sexually deviant and dangerous that emerged as a result of immigration, forced annexation, and colonial occupation have remained central to depictions of Latinxs within U.S. popular culture. While a select few light-skinned men ascended to the status of "Latin Lover" in early Hollywood, most were depicted as drunken brutes who sexually abused women, or as desexualized or feminized (and therefore abject) comic figures (Berg 2002). These associations transformed over time, ebbing and flowing in relation to labor demands and other social factors, while depictions of sexualized Latino masculinities continue to draw on images of the patriarchal macho, a racialized term used to script Latino men as abusive and sexually threatening. Latinas have been represented in a similarly stereotypical manner as either sinners or saints, emphasizing the implied cultural and sexual difference of Catholicism from Anglo-American Protestant norms. The result has been images of Latinas as virginal martyrs who are victims of the machismo of their culture; as "spitfires" who are wild, untamed, and exude uncontrolled sexuality; or as mothers whose excessive reproduction mark them as aberrant or manipulative agents intent on planting "anchor babies" in an effort to secure U.S. state resources. These characterizations are also racially coded, impacting those Latinxs who visually register as Indigenous or black in ways that align with the perverse particularities of those racial stereotypes. These sexualized associations have become foundational to Latinxs' ethnic, racial, and gendered identities as (non)citizen subjects of the United States, marking Latinx sexuality as wholly excessive, yet always lacking.

Early scholarship in the fields of Chicano and Puerto Rican studies—academic initiatives that emerged as part of activist movements—responded to these sexualized characterizations with sanitized patriarchal images of the *familia* that supported heteronormative nationalist projects. Organized around a politics of "traditional" values and political unity, these representations of cultural nationalisms actively erased other historically and socially significant sexual practices and forms of gendered expression from public view, or else portrayed them as manifestations of corrupt influences brought about through migration or association with Anglos (R. T. Rodríguez 2009; C. Beltrán 2010). However, Latinas engaged within the various social movements of the 1970s and 1980s quickly pushed back against masculinist formulations of ethnic nationalism to forge more dynamic understandings of the cultural significance of sexuality. On the West Coast, Chicanas formed their own organizations such as Las Hijas de Cuauhtémoc and Las Adelitas de Aztlán, and on the East Coast, specific caucuses within the Young Lords were organized to address the impact of sexism on both men and women, eventually leading that group to speak out in early support of the gay liberation movement (C. Beltrán 2010; Blackwell 2011).

During the 1970s and 1980s, Latinas also joined with other women of color to counter the Eurocentrism within U.S. feminist and gay and lesbian movements, and discussions of sexuality and sexual practices were often a central feature of these consciousness-raising efforts (Blackwell 2011). The ground-breaking anthology edited by Cherríe Moraga and Gloria Anzaldúa (1981), *This Bridge Called My Back*, specifically addressed the cultural and political necessity of analyzing how race, gender, and sexuality were mutually constructed, and became a foundational text for an emerging women of color feminism. Many of the feminist and queer writers of that generation wrote of the pain of feeling ostracized by their families and cultural communities of origin for expressing a sexual identity that was not predicated on heterosexuality or traditionally defined gendered roles (Moraga 1983b; Anzaldúa 1987). Latina lesbians were particularly active in forging spaces that considered the impact of sexuality and sexual identities, forming newsletters, editing anthologies, and creating local and international groups through the Encuentros de Lesbianas Feministas de América Latina y el Caribe (J. Ramos 1987; Trujillo 1991; Pérez 1998; de la tierra 2002; J. M. Rodríguez 2003). Within these circles, Latinas actively debated the cultural significance of sexual practices such as pornography, bisexuality, sex-work, sadomasochism, transgender identity, and gender roles such as butch and femme. At times, these discussions resulted in the exclusion or censorship of those who did not conform to imagined community standards of sexuality (Hollibaugh and Moraga 1983; de la tierra 2002; J. M. Rodríguez 2003, 2014b). The advent of AIDS in the 1980s brought an urgency to activist efforts to respond to the crisis with explicit and culturally relevant discussions of sex (J.M. Rodríguez 2003; Roque Ramírez 2010, 2011). LGBT Latinx groups in California, Texas, New York, and elsewhere formed volunteer community organizations to meet the physical, psychic, and spiritual devastation that surrounds the AIDS pandemic, and some groups later succeeded in securing funds and increased legitimacy to continue those efforts. As new medical interventions have emerged—interventions that benefit only some—the funding and political energy surrounding community sexual health projects has dwindled even as new cases of AIDS continue to impact the most vulnerable members of the Latinx community: youth, transgender women, sex workers, and others impacted by poverty, racial discrimination, and social precarity.

While different constellations of queer Latinx community groups have dealt quite explicitly with the politics and passions surrounding sex and sexuality, these attempts to impact Latinx representation remain marginalized. In most Latinx-produced forms of cultural representation, particularly films intended for "crossover" (that is, for non-Latinx) audiences, depictions of idealized Latinx families have served as a way to counter mainstream associations of Latinx sexual deviance, even as they often promote sanitized images of self-sacrificing mothers and strict hardworking fathers. Efforts at cinematic representation generally ignore issues of domestic violence, socially authorized forms of male promiscuity and dominance, the cultural shaming of sexually active women, nonheterosexual practices and identities, and those who do not conform to gendered norms. Independent films remain the most robust visual medium for depictions of transgender, queer, and nonheteronormative Latinx sexualities, with some notable films including *La Mission, Gun Hill Road, Mosquita y Mari, Tangerine,* and *Mala Mala.*

Given the centrality of sexuality to representations of Latinx populations within dominant society, and its pivotal role in the long history of political and social engagement within the activist and academic practices, it is no wonder that questions of sexuality have become a central feature of Latinx studies. Latinx sexuality, specifically the cultural associations attached to our multiply-coded bodies, has been investigated through art (L. E. Pérez 2007; Gaspar de Alba and López 2011), music (Aparicio 1998; D. Vargas 2012; Vazquez 2013), dance (Ovalle 2010; Rivera-Servera 2012; C. García 2013), ethnography (Roque Ramírez 2007; Decena 2011; S. Peña 2013), literature (Chávez-Silverman and Hernández 2000; Esquibel 2006; Lima 2007; R. Ortíz 2007; Soto 2010), film and media (Noriega and López 1996; Fregoso 2003; C. E. Rodriguez 2008), performance (J. Muñoz 1999, 2009; Negrón-Muntaner 2004; Paredez 2009; L. Gutiérrez 2010), and cultural criticism that cuts across these various genres (E. Pérez 1998; Quiroga 2000; J. M. Rodríguez 2003, 2014b; Asencio 2009a; La Fountain-Stokes 2009; Hames-García and Martínez 2011).

Reflecting cultural and racial identities formed through colonialism, enslavement, state policies of incarceration and detention, and the day-to-day precarity of low-wage labor, racial hostility, and sexual violence and harassment, much of the discourse on Latinx sexuality, particularly female sexuality, has been tied to narratives of survival and resistance. These accounts often elide more complex questions of how sexual pleasure might endure or the multiple ways that sexual subjects might engage racialized abjection or sexual violence on their own terms. Despite the seeming abundance of critical work on Latinx sexuality, specific work that presents more explicit depictions of Latinx sexual pleasures and erotic practices remains less widely circulated, albeit with notable exceptions. Graphic accounts of Latinx sexuality include the literature of gay Chicano writer John Rechy (1963), an early chronicler of underground homosexual sexual culture in Los Angeles and elsewhere; Arnaldo Cruz-Malavé's (2007) account of the tempestuous life of Juanito Xtravaganza, a Puerto Rican hustler in the 1970s; Jaime Cortez's (2004) bilingual graphic novel *Sexilio/Sexile* about the life of trans activist and former sex-worker Adela Vázquez; the many irreverent comics of openly bisexual Erika Lopez (1997); and the salaciously rich "as-told-to" autobiography of porn legend Vanessa del Rio (2010). In the performance arena, Xandra Ibarra, who performs under the name La Chica Boom, draws on hypersexualized and racialized references in what she terms "*spic*tacles"; Elizabeth Marrero performs as drag king "Macha"; the queer collective Butchlalis de Panochtitlan explores butch intimacies; and April Flores, a self-identified "fat-girl," has made a name for herself in queer and BBW (big, beautiful women) pornography. Increasingly some academics are becoming bolder in addressing topics such as online sexual practices, BDSM, bisexuality, pornography, sexwork, and other more socially charged articulations of Latinx sexuality (Decena 2011; I. Ramos 2015; J. M. Rodríguez 2014b; D. Vargas 2014; González-López 2015).

While certain inroads have been made in portraying more diverse and nuanced forms of Latinx sexuality in the media, the arts, and the academy, the same cannot be said of the Latinx political arena, where monogamy, marriage, and romanticized versions of family continue to dominate discussions of immigration reform, reproductive rights, the criminal (in)justice system, and labor policies. Sexual realities such as bisexuality, polygamy, under-age sexual activity, multiple families, and the multifaceted sex industry are rarely discussed as relevant to Latinx politics, or, if so, are depicted as problems to be solved, not social actualities that need to be addressed. In response to representations within both mainstream Anglo and Latina/o political agendas that depict Latinx sexuality as dirty, Deborah R. Vargas has reappropriated the term *sucio* (dirty, dishonest, and impure), as a queer Latinx analytic "in relation to contemporary neoliberal projects that disappear the most vulnerable and disenfranchised by cleaning up spaces and populations deemed dirty and wasteful" (2014, 715). This racialized sexualized excess that refuses to disappear at times operates locally under the names *chusma*, *chola*, or *chonga* as a means to censor and shame those who refuse to perform normative Anglo sexuality (J. Hernandez 2009). This ongoing tension between attempts to sanitize Latinx sexuality by reducing it to the sphere of the private in the service of social acceptance and more radical and capacious manifestations that reject the politics of respectability, and the shame, censorship, and social stigmatization upon which it is based, remains at the heart of attempts to bring discussions of Latinx sexuality into greater view. While the discourses that surround sexuality can only be understood at the nexus between various historically situated forms of social discipline and articulations of individual and collective expression, the willful and wayward corporeal and psychic pleasures that sexuality also ignites, more often than not, elude the traps of linguistic capture to hover in the vapor of memory, feeling, and the sensorial.

53

Social Movements

Randy J. Ontiveros

Ricardo Falcón was killed on August 30, 1972, at a gas station along a lonely stretch of highway in southern New Mexico. The twenty-seven–year-old activist was caravanning to El Paso for a convention of the La Raza Unida Party (LRUP). When the group pulled over to cool a broken radiator, Perry Brunson, the white owner of the station, insisted they pay for water. An argument ensued, and Brunson shot Falcón twice. According to Falcón's colleagues, locals refused medical help or the use of a telephone (Castro 1972). Brunson, later discovered to belong to the segregationist American Independent Party, was released from jail without bail. In December 1972, he was acquitted of manslaughter (E. Vigil 1999).

Falcón's death is the sort of event that sometimes sparks a wave of protests and launches a movement. His didn't. Activists with LRUP organized press conferences and filed legal motions, but Falcón's murder went ignored by the public. Stories like his raise hard questions about political life: Why do some injustices ignite collective action, but not others? What conditions must exist on the ground for organizing and mobilizing to be effective? How do waves of protest start and end? These are just some of the questions posed by scholars of social movements, a term first used in 1850 by the German sociologist Lorenz Von Stein (Tilly and Wood 2009). Herbert Blumer (1949), an early authority, defines them as "collective enterprises to establish a new order of life." The phrase is most often associated with leftism, and within Latina/o studies it has been used to analyze labor movements of the 1930s and 1940s, the Chicano movement (Ontiveros 2013), the U.S. Central American sanctuary movement, and the immigrant-rights movement. However, scholarship on social movements also helps understand conservative campaigns. The Cuban American National Foundation (CANF) was formed in 1981 with the stated goal of supporting anti-Castro policies in Washington, but it operated during the 1980s and 1990s as a vehicle among segments of the Latina/o population for right-leaning, "free-market" activism, even becoming party to Reagan's interventions in Angola and Nicaragua. Whether liberal or conservative, progressive or reactionary, the two threads uniting social movements are (1) their collectivism and (2) their desire for sweeping social change.

Latinas/os are underrepresented in the literature, but research on social movements has considerable explanatory power when it comes to Latina/o history, politics, and culture. Take the question of what ignites a social movement. Developed in the first half of the twentieth century, the earliest answers held that individuals form collectives only at the point of desperation. This "collective behavior" approach took seriously the role of grassroots activity in a political system, but it tended to dismiss protesters as hysterical mobs (Crossley 2002). In the 1970s, scholars responded with a "rational-actor theory" that framed participants in the political process as self-interested individuals who join movements only after a careful cost/benefit analysis. Rational-actor theory didn't condescend to activists. However, it introduced a new wrinkle: the free rider. Why would someone sacrifice time, money, and health when he or she could do nothing and still benefit from the sacrifice of others? Recent scholarship has addressed the problem of the free rider in several ways: by arguing that participants garner feelings of satisfaction; through a "resource mobilization approach" that sees activists as entrepreneurs taking advantage of structural opportunities; and by investigating "new social movements," a phrase popularized by European Marxists to describe post-1960s leftist campaigns organized principally around identity rather than class.

This latter concept holds particular importance within Latina/o studies. Social scientists categorize many of the diverse campaigns that make up contemporary Latina/o politics as new social movements. This categorization is useful in that it situates Latina/o campaigns as collective efforts to assert the existence and dignity of social differences that have long been devalued by the dominant society. It also historicizes Latina/o struggles within a broader field of leftist activism. The National Latina/o Lesbian, Gay, Bisexual, and Transgender Organization (LLEGÓ) was founded in 1987 and operated for nearly twenty years as a prominent leader in LGBTQ activism in the United States and Puerto Rico. LLEGÓ formed part of a broad movement aimed not only at changing federal, state, and local policy, but also at transforming the dominant "frames" (another keyword in social-movement scholarship) used in Latina/o activism (Goffman 1974). During the 1960s and 1970s, nationalist organizations like the Young Lords and the Brown Berets often used patriarchal and heteronormative metaphors of family and tradition to forge collective identity. Queer activists for their part demanded and often won sexually inclusive frameworks for organization and mobilization. Some on the left have criticized new social movements for undermining the class struggle. Such criticisms ignore the fact that identity politics have long been a part of the labor movement, particularly in the ugly history of union segregation. They also ignore the powerful role that culturally specific organizations have played in revitalizing the labor movement in the United States and abroad.

The "DREAMers" campaign offers a useful case study for thinking about social movements. DREAMers are young people who arrived in the United States without legal authorization when they were small children and who are fighting for passage of the Development, Relief, and Education for Alien Minors Act, a piece of legislation first introduced in Congress in 2001, which would grant them legal status. The story of their struggle gives weight to the theory that social movements take shape when the material conditions of everyday life deteriorate for a sizable segment of the population. DREAMers came of age during a volatile era in American politics when immigrants—especially, but not exclusively, immigrants from Latin America and the Caribbean—were scapegoated for unemployment, crime, failing schools, and terrorism. Their very existence became criminalized as local, state, and federal authorities passed laws that blocked access to medical care, housing, transportation, jobs, language, and family.

When DREAMers were young, they were shielded from some of the worst abuses their parents faced because of the 1982 Supreme Court decision *Plyler v. Doe*, which recognized the constitutional right of undocumented children to attend public schools. Schools became places of "relative refuge" (Nicholls 2013). However, as DREAMers grew older, they were increasingly vulnerable to police harassment, labor exploitation, and ultimately deportation. The threat drove many of them into the fold of movement organizations such as United We Dream, the Coalition for Humane Immigrant Rights of Los Angeles (CHIRLA), AB 540 student groups, and a host of allied organizations that together exerted enormous grassroots pressure on lawmakers. The trajectory their activism took was an example of what social-movement theorists call "cycles of protest," or the rhythms of beginning, ending, and evolving that all social movements undergo. Organizations like CHIRLA in

California or CASA de Maryland on the East Coast, were formed during the 1980s by U.S. Central Americans and their allies to oppose U.S. military interventions and to aid those displaced by the violence. The civil wars in the region came to a formal end in the 1990s, but these organizations continue to help with the aftermath and have become infrastructure for other social movements within Latina/o communities, including the DREAMers campaign.

The anti-immigrant and anti-Latina/o climate that has dominated American politics for the last several decades is an essential element of the story of the DREAMer movement. It's not the whole story, though. Political theorists have argued that "rising expectations" can do as much to spark a social movement as deprivation, and maybe more. Their reasoning is that individuals must first be able to imagine a better world and to believe that better world is attainable—at least in part—before they are willing to risk life or property. Sociologist James C. Davies puts it this way: "It is when the chains have been loosened somewhat, so that they can be cast off without a high probability of losing life, that people are put in a condition of proto-rebelliousness" (1962, 7). The "rising expectations" model is overlooked today because it rests more on psychology than structure, but it illuminates an important aspect of the DREAMer struggle. DREAMers often identify with their nation of birth, but they also see themselves as Americans, and they believe themselves entitled to the same rights and protections given to others in the United States. Their courageous claim to cultural citizenship even when denied legal citizenship was made tenable by decades of civil rights struggle (Rosaldo 1997).

There were, however, structural opportunities that combined with rising expectations and deteriorating conditions to give rise to the DREAMer movement. During the Clinton and Bush presidencies, in particular, police agencies complained they lacked resources to enforce immigration law, and business leaders in agriculture, retail, and hospitality lobbied for immigration reform because they wanted a reliable source of low-wage labor. Eager to win a growing segment of the electorate, leaders in the Democratic and Republican Parties also called for reform. The DREAMer movement found a responsive audience and won important victories—including the 2012 Deferred Action for Childhood Arrivals (DACA) program—because it was able to tie its outsider demands to what Walter Nicholls calls "niche openings" within the political system (2013). The DREAMers movement evidences a truth that history confirms time and time again: for social movements to transform society, they must be able to work both inside and outside the system. To borrow a keyword from Latina/o studies, they must be able to code-switch.

If the causes of social movements are complex, so too are the methods they use to achieve their goals. Scholars use a variety of frameworks to explain social-movement strategy, but the leading one is sociologist Charles Tilly's "repertoires of contention." According to Tilly, the strategies and tactics that social movements employ are shaped by the historical conditions. "On the whole," he writes, "when people make collective claims they innovate within limits set by the repertoire already established for their place, time, and pair," the latter word referring to a "claimant" and an "object of claims," such as an employee and her boss, or a citizen and his government (2006, 35). Tilly says that in Europe during the 1700s and before, repertoires of contention tended to be local in scope and targeted directly at the culprit. He gives as examples "the destruction of tollgates, invasions of enclosed land, and disruptions of ceremonies and festivals." During the 1800s and after, as the bureaucracies of nation-state widened and

as capitalism's global division of labor deepened, repertoires of contention increasingly revolved around symbolic displays of "worthiness," "unity," "numbers," and "commitment." Importantly, these displays were aimed not at local constituencies but at a broad and abstract public, and one usually defined by national boundaries. Of course, in recent years the most significant development in social-movement repertoires has been digital technologies. The early years of the Internet brought enthusiastic pronouncements about how "hypertext" would revolutionize everything, including activism. The pervasive commercialization of the Internet and its mainstreaming have tempered this euphoria, but campaigns like UndocuQueer and #BlackLivesMatter—a movement that includes black Latinas/os and Latina/o allies—have shown the capacity of digital technologies to educate, inform, and inspire.

Social movements end in different ways. Some are sometimes sabotaged by the state or by opposition. They can be wrecked by infighting or by dependence on a figurehead. Others fail to adjust their tactics to changed social and political realities. These endings bring mourning, but social movements are impermanent by nature. When they realize their "new order of life," or when new opportunities or crises emerge, they metamorphose. The mutability of social movements is their greatest vulnerability, but it is also their greatest strength because it allows them to react to conditions on the ground, to recruit new participants, and to be reinvented. Ricardo Falcón illustrates this reality. His death didn't make front-page news, but his life's purpose endured and expanded through his wife Priscilla. An impressive activist in her own right, Priscilla Falcón distinguished herself in the decades after her husband's killing as a grassroots educator and organizer in Colorado (Falcón 2011). Stories like theirs capture the true power of social movements.

Because it emerged out of grassroots activism, the discipline of Latina/o studies has long been interested in social movements. Some of the earliest literature in the field dealt directly or indirectly with questions posed today by scholars in social movement studies. In recent years, Horacio N. Roque Ramírez (2011), Sonia Song-Ha Lee (2014), Maylei Blackwell (2011), and many other Latina/o studies scholars have joined this tradition and made powerful contributions to our understanding of collective action, its history, its complexity, and its potential. At this moment when our communities are under siege, their insights are as urgent as ever.

54
Sovereignty
Nelson Maldonado-Torres

Whether implicity or explicity, questions of sovereignty haunt Latina/o consciousness, Latina/o identity, and Latina/o studies. The same is arguably true of all other colonized and racialized forms of consciousness, identities, and studies. The reason is that part of what it means to be a colonial and/or racial subject is to lack the conditions of possibility to successfully achieve full recognition and full participation as a member of a sovereign people and of a sovereign state in the modern world. Being sovereign is considered to be, in turn, a central feature of what is to be modern, which means that belonging to or exclusion from modernity is at stake in the claim to be sovereign.

Latinas/os lack the possibility of claiming (modern Western) sovereignty because, among other considerations, they overwhelmingly experience forms of second-class citizenship or are not U.S. citizens while living, working, and having families in the United States. They are perceived as perpetual foreigners whose "real" habitat or place of origin is seen as a kind of failed state in a region of the world where people lack the capacity to govern themselves. And it is not the case that living in the United States overwhelmingly gives Latinas/os some kind of privileged position in those other communities or countries. Being a Latina/o often involves the experience of being as excluded in the United States as in whatever other land one is perceived to belong.

Latinas/os therefore appear to be condemned to non-sovereignty; they seem to belong to the category of the *damnés*, or condemned (Fanon 2004), rather than to that of the "people" or the "multitude" (Maldonado-Torres 2004). Frantz Fanon proposes the concept of "damnation" as a way to understand, not so much the plight of the working classes in a presumed dialectical revolutionary struggle with capitalism, but the conditions of subjects and communities who are conceived to be below the category of the human. Fanon's ideas were very influential in multiple social and political movements in the 1960s and 1970s, including what we would today call Latina/o movements in the United States, which were concerned with the challenge to their humanity and their aspirations to one or more forms of sovereignty. Fanon's ideas arguably continue to be relevant for the analysis of dehumanization and sovereignty, and his account of damnation can help to complement, if not correct, analyses of sovereignty—and exclusion from it—based on other categories, including important ones such as the Foucauldian concepts of biopolitics and of sovereign power (Foucault 2003) as well as Giorgio Agamben's (1998) elaboration of the categories of "bare life" and "homo sacer." In this essay, I will use the Fanonian concept of damnation and the analysis of modernity as intrinsically connected to coloniality (Mignolo 2000; Quijano 2000b) as a guide to critically address the potential and limits of the modern idea of sovereignty. My main thesis here is that reflecting about sovereignty in light of damnation, modernity/coloniality, and Latina/o culture, history, philosophy, and socio-political formations leads to a critical genealogy and an analytics of sovereignty that reveals both the coloniality of sovereignty and the importance of efforts to decolonize it.

According to Robert Jackson, "Sovereignty is an idea of authority embodied in those bordered territorial organizations we refer to as 'states' or 'nations' and expressed in their various relations and activities, both domestic and foreign" (2007, ix). It is "a fundamental idea of authority of the modern era, arguably the most fundamental" (2007, ix). For Daniel Philpott (2001), the modern Western idea of sovereignty emerged and developed not only through practices, but most fundamentally by virtue of the ideas produced to address practical and intellectual challenges. For Philpott these challenges have led to two revolutions: the first is "the shift in Europe from the medieval world to the modern international system, which took full shape at the peace of Westphalia in 1648," and the second one is the period of colonial independence after the Second World War (2001, 4). If the first revolution, that of Westphalia, created the first formal set of states that claimed sovereignty, the second, that of colonial independence, led to the most significant expansion of the sovereign state system to the point that, as Jackson points out, "There is no inhabited territory anywhere on the planet that is outside" (2007, 10).

Theorizing sovereignty with particular consideration for Latina/o positionalities, including Latin American and Caribbean perspectives, involves an exploration of the significance of colonization, as colonization has been traditionally understood as the absence or usurpation of sovereignty. In the case of Latinas/os, the experience with colonization comes typically through the relation with the Spanish Empire and later, in some cases, with U.S. expansionism. One could also consider the impact of neoimperialism and neoliberalism in Latin America and the Caribbean and their effects in Latina/o communities in the United States. When approaching the matter from this perspective, one has to consider the idea that both the Protestant Reformation and the Peace of Westphalia were preceded by the "discovery" and conquest of the Americas and that, as Enrique Dussel (1998) has pointed out, Martin Luther's call for reform may not have had the impact that it had had it not taken place in central Europe right in the aftermath of the "discovery" and conquest of the "New World."

The "discovery" made a significant difference for Europe and arguably played a major role in the transition from "medieval" forms of authority to modern ones (Dussel 1995; Wynter 1995; Maldonado-Torres 2014). Not only did such discovery give access to riches that would fuel the divisions between European kingdoms, but it also served as a bedrock for the new conceptions of subjectivity, identity, and authority that emerged in the sixteenth and seventeenth centuries. The sovereign, in Europe, had supreme powers over his territory and increasingly defined and brought "religion" under the control of the state, while simultaneously employing secular and religious ideas in the domination of colonial peoples across the world.

In short, while sovereignty is "a constituent idea of the modern age" (Jackson 2007, 6), coloniality is both constitutive of modernity and of sovereignty. To understand the emergence of sovereignty, one needs to engage not only "religious difference," as in the conflicts between Catholicism and Protestantism in the sixteenth and seventeenth centuries, but also colonial and imperial difference in that period (Mignolo 2000). This "decolonial turn" has implications both for approaching questions about the emergence of Western ideas of sovereignty and for understanding the second major revolution of sovereignty: the anti-colonial search for independence. The revolutionary character of the search for independence may reside less in the expansion of modern sovereignty, and more in its decolonization. If so, this would mean that approaching Western modernity as intrinsically connected to coloniality would lead to a critique of ideas of modern sovereignty and of independence, both of which fall short of the idea(l) of decoloniality.

A focus on Latinas/os demands attention not only to the emergence of modernity and to the relationship between Europe and its colonies around the world, but also to the United States, its process of state formation, and its form of imperial expansion. This would lead to a close study of the significance of the American-Indian Wars in the settlement of the colonies, slavery, and expansion over the continental United States and abroad, as well as to a consideration of the multiple forms of contestation before and after the anti-colonial revolutions for independence in the twentieth century. Also significant is that the wave of those revolutions, along with the multiple forms of critical thinking about modernity and colonization that were inspired by them, coincided with the rise of the United States as a world power. A specific U.S. mode of sovereignty, based on the creation of a largely segregated nation dependent on slave labor and built over lands that were taken from other peoples, rises to an unparalleled level of influence. The formation of the U.S. state arguably represents yet another revolution in sovereignty. Latinas/os are of course very much part of this story.

Since modern state sovereignty depends on the creation of borders, one place where to begin a critical reflection of U.S. sovereignty is the U.S.-Mexico border. Borders are not natural lines of division, but designs of sovereignty. In the case of the U.S.-Mexico border, it included and includes not only territorial considerations, but also anthropological and ontological ones in the sense that they mark spaces where different kinds of (human) beings are believed to exist. It also involves, as Gloria Anzaldúa (1987) dramatizes in her classic *Borderlands / La Frontera*, dynamics of conquest in terms of Spanish settlement, Mexican governance, and U.S. expansion. All of this combined makes the U.S.-Mexico border a paradigmatic case for understanding the ideologies and technologies of sovereign control in the age of modernity/coloniality.

The dividing line that constitutes the U.S.-Mexico border was established, "after less than transparent negotiations," in the Treaty of Guadalupe Hidalgo of 1848 when about half of Mexico became part of the United States (Rincón and Oboler 2012, 134). This created a large border zone where Mexicans and colonized Indigenous peoples who had been living in territory claimed by the Mexican state suddenly became part of the United States. The treaty established the property rights of individuals regardless of citizenship and offered the option of acquiring U.S. citizenship (Rincón and Oboler 2012). In addition to the already existing problems created by Spanish colonialism and Mexican state formation, which severely limited property rights and preserved colonial relations with indigenous peoples, another problem was that U.S. citizenship was the province of white people, which led to the exclusion of many, as well as to the effort by Mexican elites to present themselves as white. However, even "white" Mexicans faced attempts to recategorize them as "colored" (Overmyer-Velázquez 2013).

The U.S.-Mexico border is not only a specific territory, but more amply, a zone of damnation that has served as a paradigm for the exercise of sovereignty in border zones and beyond. In that sense, the forms of damnation at the border inform the exercise of sovereignty in multiple other spaces. The U.S.-Mexico border extends to the border between different neighborhoods, communities, and subjects inside the United States. And it is not only Mexicans and Mexican Americans who are affected. Everyone who is perceived as coming from the other side of the border or as a border crosser faces the dynamics of violence that exist in the border zones. This violence often comes in the form of housing segregation, challenges in the job market, and deportation (De Genova 2004; D. M. Hernández 2008), but it is also manifested in multiple other ways. Consider

that sovereignty is conceived to be primordially a white, male, and heterosexual attribute and that it also depends on a hierarchical separation from various other categories, which involves violence. That is why, for example, as Ana Alonso notes, the sexual molestation and rape of women has been part of the increased militarization of the U.S.-Mexico border and why similar dynamics are present in the U.S. "war on terror" (Alonso 2005, 44).

Damnation at border zones, including communities who live in the border and those who are perceived as passing through it (considered by the sovereign state either as legal or illegal) from lands perceived as inferior and dominated with violence (Arias and Milian 2013), is not the only way in which Latinas/os are subjected to modern state sovereignty. If the Treaty of Guadalupe Hidalgo in 1848 represents the formation of the border under the state of U.S. modern/colonial sovereignty, the Treaty of Paris in 1898 between the United States and Spain inaugurates a new way of handling colonies. These treaties should be carefully considered, alongside the Treaty of Westphalia, when trying to understand state sovereignty and its coloniality in the twentieth and twenty-first centuries.

Currently, Puerto Rico is the most populous of all the United States' unincorporated territories obtained under the Treaty of Paris. Puerto Ricans constitute a nation spread between the Caribbean and the entire United States, without a corresponding traditional sovereign state (Duany 2002, 2003). Puerto Ricans in Puerto Rico and those in the rest of the United States participate in colonial relations that are, to some extent, increasingly familiar in the global neoliberal age (Grosfoguel 2003). The model of the sovereign state poses two main options for Puerto Ricans in Puerto Rico: either obtaining independence, or fully becoming part of another independent and sovereign nation-state. That Puerto Ricans as a whole have traditionally supported a third alternative—that of the "Estado Libre Asociado," or resisted selecting independence or statehood—indicates their skepticism about the traditional options (Negrón-Muntaner 2007). The skepticism sometimes turns into cynicism, but sometimes becomes productive as when those who defend independence do it while embracing subaltern forms of internationalism, such as pan-Africanism, and those who defend statehood do it as a form of evading more menacing forms of neocolonialism and of joining the struggle for the expansion of liberties and rights in the United States. Puerto Ricans have been voicing these more critical and selective uses of independence and statehood since early in the twentieth century, and they continue to do so today (Negrón-Muntaner and Grosfoguel 1997; Fusté 2014). These options can be understood as ways to decolonize sovereignty.

Decolonizing sovereignty is a mode of critical and creative engagement with the idea and practice of sovereignty, which seeks to undo its colonizing dimensions and to open up politics beyond sovereignty itself. Puerto Ricans are not the only ones who have engaged in efforts to decolonize sovereignty. The ethnic power movements of the 1960s in the United States adopted ideologies of nationalism that included claims of sovereignty. For example, "El Plan Espiritual de Aztlán," considered the founding document of Chicano nationalism in the 1960s, called for "the independence of our mestizo nation" (Gonzales and Urista 1969, 5). The call for independence reflects an awareness of a double form of colonization (Spanish and Anglo) as well as of a double form of exclusion (from the United States and from Mexico). It is also a decisive move away from efforts to claim whiteness, which was an explicit goal of a number of Mexican American organizations in face of the negative racialization of Mexicans in Texas and other territories that became part of the United States

(Rincón and Oboler 2012, 133). To be sure, Chicano nationalism was more cultural and intellectual than territorial, and Aztlán was more an attempt to revalue the relationship between people of Mexican descent and Indigenous peoples than a political project of reconquest (Miner 2014). In that sense, Aztlán called for a consideration of Indigenous conceptions of sovereignty and for exchanges and coalitions with Indigenous peoples in the United States and Mexico. Therefore, the call for "independence" was not simply a replication of modern conceptions of the state and of sovereignty. It was rather an attempt to decolonize sovereignty. To be sure, these efforts were limited to the extent that they reproduced sexism and homophobia (A. García 1989; Barker 2006; Asencio 2009b). More consistent forms of decolonizing sovereignty are found in the corpus of Chicana feminism and feminisms of color (Moraga and Anzaldúa 1981; A. García 1997). Concepts such as the body as bridge, mestiza consciousness, and decolonial love provide the basic elements of an-*other* understanding of identity, politics, and conviviality (Anzaldúa 1987; Sandoval 2000) different from practices based on independence, supremacy, and the segregationist use of borders. These perspectives can be combined with calls for building on emerging forms of "shared sovereignty" in order to address the increased migration and the formation of transnational communities in places like the United States (Rocco 2004, 2014).

55

Spanglish

Ana Celia Zentella

Ever since the word "Espanglish" first appeared in print, on October 28, 1948, both the style of speaking that it refers to and, more recently, the label itself, have been mired in debates enmeshed in the language politics of the day, with critical implications for the reproduction or interruption of social inequality in Latina/o communities. Salvador Tió (1948), former president of the Puerto Rican Academy of the Spanish Language, published his definition fifty years after the U.S. occupation of Puerto Rico in 1898 imposed English as the language of instruction, amidst a debate about reinstating Spanish. Tió's definition included notions that remain popular: that Spanglish is a new language consisting of parts of English and Spanish words, that it reflects confusion and ambivalence and represents a death knell for Spanish via English/U.S. imperialism: "This new language will be called 'Espanglish.' . . . It is an ambivalent language. It is a real fusion. Bilingualism is a confusion. It is implanted with the goal of making us dominant in a language that hopes to dominate us" (Tió 1948; translation mine). These themes persist in definitions like Wikipedia's—"Spanglish is informal due to the lack of structure and set rules"—and the Urban Dictionary's—"Urban American language. Not quite English, Not quite Spanish." In a *New York Times* op-ed, a Yale University professor said Spanglish is "an invasion of Spanish by English" that is spoken mainly by "poor Hispanics, many barely literate in either language," and that it represents "a grave danger to Hispanic culture and to the advancement of Hispanics in mainstream America" (González Echevarría 1997). These comments reflect various aspects of "*chiquita*fication" (Zentella 1995)—that is, the trivialization of Latinas/os' use of varieties of Spanish (as non-authentic and non-European), the disparagement of their knowledge of English (as non-standard), and the bashing of their bilingual skills, particularly Spanglish (by referring to them as a-linguals or semi-linguals). As Latinas/os became the largest minority, language discrimination intensified, along with anti-Latina/o violence (Zentella 2014).

Attacks on Spanglish reflect the ways in which negative attitudes toward diverse ways of speaking perpetuate inequities: the "standard language" of the elite is considered superior to the disparaged ways of speaking of the working masses, and many believe that those who speak "correctly" are better prepared for life, even better people. Many insulting definitions of Spanglish are couched in a kind of "I'm only saying this for your own good" rhetoric. For example, Ilan Stavans (2003) praises Spanglish as "creative" and "democratic," but also refers to it as "a hodgepodge" of "barbarisms . . . deformed, perverted," and as "the tongue of the un-educated," which does not "pay attention to the rules of syntax. But does it matter?" Stavans fails to cite any linguists who have long studied the rules of Spanglish shared by varied U.S. Latina/o groups, such as Shana Poplack (1980), John Lipski (1985), Almeida Jacqueline Toribio (2001), Carmen Silva-Corvalán and Kim Potowski (2009), and I (Zentella 1997). In a study of ninety-four Spanglish speakers (Zentella 2016), respondents had heard or used only 16 percent of the 2,073 entries in Stavan's dictionary, which was published under the name *Spanglish: The Making of a New American Language* (2003); 23 percent were rejected completely—that is, respondents had never heard of or used those words. Nor is the number of borrowings from English into Spanish and Spanish into English a threat to the English or Spanish lexicons.

Moreover, proclaiming Spanglish a new language distorts the linguistic facts. Most switches occur at sentence boundaries, and those that occur within sentences follow English rules in the English part and Spanish rules in the Spanish part. Even young children on a New York Puerto Rican *bloque*, or "block," honored Spanish and English syntax in 95 percent of their 1,685 switches (Zentella 1997); anyone who spoke both languages understood them without recourse to a third grammar. Finally, "defending" Spanglish as a new language masks the nature of linguistic prejudice and its harmful repercussions. Many Spanglish speakers, including *el bloque*'s children, are on their way to losing Spanish, not creating a new language, because they are made to feel ashamed of their bilingual skills. A Latina/o studies scholar who acknowledges that "many Spanglish speakers are fluent in both English and Spanish," concludes that "for many Latino/as whose first and only language is a form of Spanglish, their linguistic world reflects their socioeconomic status: limited, marginalized, lacking mobility, and unlikely to be valued or heard beyond their immediate communities" (Allatson 2007, 215). Refuting these assumptions requires an anthro-political linguistics (Zentella 1995).

At the macro level, anthro-political linguistics sees through the language smokescreen that obscures ideological, structural, and political impediments to equality and, at the local level, actively challenges the practices and policies that construct a group's ways of speaking or raising children as inferior, and thereby benefiting the continued domination of a powerful class. Employing the methods of linguistic anthropology, it advocates studying language use in context to reveal the rule-governed nature of nonstandard dialects and challenge damaging ideas about "pure" languages. Above all, we reject ideologies that produce rigid linguistic, cultural,

and national boundaries, recognizing instead that "different types of identity are neither exclusive nor singular" (Kroskrity 2001, 107). Years of ethnographic studies and careful analyses of its structure reveal that Spanglish is best defined as a rule-governed, in-group, and informal style of speaking among bilingual Latinas/os, an act of "doing being bilingual" that reflects our dual worlds and challenges static notions of "Latina/o identity." It consists primarily of some phonologically adapted (e.g., roof > *rufo*) and un-adapted (e.g., dime) English loan words inserted in Spanish, some Spanish loans in English, loan translations, a few borrowed structures, and switches between Spanish and English, usually at sentence boundaries, but also within sentences.

The disparaging of Spanglish and its speakers reveals how race has been remapped from the body onto language, as a way of avoiding racist comments about hair texture, skin color, or the shape of lips, eyes, or noses, while allowing comments about language to do the work of racist stereotyping (Urciuoli 2011). This remapping is facilitated by notions of purity, hierarchy, and boundaries in the construction of both race and language: both are deemed to consist of superior and inferior varieties and as having inherent qualities that require strict separation, or boundary patrolling, to prevent pollution. Consequently, Spanglish is often denounced as a contamination of both English and Spanish. The similarities between the construction of race and language end with a jarring difference: whereas race is viewed as unchangeable and therefore beyond an individual's control, language ideologues insist that non-standard speakers change their ways of speaking. The racialization of Spanglish speakers has profound implications for "non-white" Latinas/os because both their bodies and their ways of speaking are perceived as contaminated.

In southern California, Mexican American students who crisscross the San Diego-Tijuana border to live and work or study learn that standard bearers in both countries demand keeping Spanish and English separate. Half of the college students I interviewed (n=40) (Zentella 2013 [forthcoming 2017]) honored Uriel Weinreich's view that "the ideal bilingual" switches according to changes in the speech situation, but "certainly not within a single sentence" (1953, 73). They defined Spanglish as destructive, and emblematic of undesirable *pochos* who speak *pocho* or *mocho* (Mexican-Americans who speak in a chopped up way), even when their Spanglish critique caused laughter: "*Pochos* are people who speak Spanish and English together *y no deben hablar así* [and they shouldn't talk that way]." Like La Migra, the feared federal agents who pursue the undocumented, these adamant critics have become La Migra Bilingüe, the Bilingual Border Patrol, policing the boundaries between Spanish and English. These future educators, social service workers, health personnel, and managers—or gatekeepers—are likely to perpetuate views of linguistic deficiency, even as others see it as natural border talk: "I don't know if it's weird but it's just the way, *yo pienso que es una dinámica ya de vivir aqui en la frontera de que se te sale el inglés o se te sale el español* [I think it's already a dynamic of living here on the border, that English comes out and Spanish comes out]."

La Migra Bilingüe can count on the support of the Royal Academy of the Spanish Language (RAE), the arbiter of Spanish norms for over three hundred years, whose dictionary initially defined "espanglish" as: "From Eng. Spanglish, fusion of 'Spanish' and 'English.' n. Way of speaking of some Hispanic groups in the United States, in which lexical and grammatical elements of Spanish and English are mixed, deforming them" (Real Academia Española n.d., translation mine). Hundreds of signatures on petitions demanded a revised definition (del Valle and Zentella 2014), which resulted in the removal of *deformándolos* (deforming them) in late 2014, although the online definition took longer to be changed.

The views of the RAE and others who have not done any research on the topic are not surprising, but it is dismaying to find scholars who have documented and defended the forms and functions of Spanglish waging war against the term itself. Also couching their criticism in "helping hand" rhetoric, they maintain that the word "Spanglish" is "as out of place in promoting Latino language and culture as are the words crazy, lunatic, crackpot, or nut case in mental health, or bum, slob, misfit, and loser in social work" (Lipski 2008, 72). Similarly, Ricardo Otheguy (2009) insists that by combining parts of "Spanish" and "English," the term "Spanglish" erroneously communicates a merging or mess because it merges or meshes parts of the names of two languages, just as any word that ends with "-cide" implies murder or killing. Inappropriate analogies aside, no mental health or social work advocates have adopted any insulting label with pride, whereas many speakers embrace "Spanglish." Likewise, the adoption of "queer" and "black" is proof that vilified communities can invert negative appellations. Spanglish can be, and is for many, a proud label for bilingual skills and identities. When 115 Latinas/os across the country were asked if they favored the label or not, most (71 percent) approved of it, including the majority of non-Spanglish speakers and equal percentages of males and females; the remaining 25 percent were against, and 4 percent were indifferent (Zentella 2016). More research along these lines is needed.

Some linguists insist that the word "Spanglish" suggests a mish-mashed variety and/or semi-lingual speakers who know only half a language, when in fact, they point out similar patterns of lexical borrowing, semantic bleaching, and syntactic transfers exist in many national varieties of Spanish (Otheguy 2009; Otheguy and Stern 2010; Potowski 2011). They prefer "popular Spanish of the U.S." to place this way of speaking in the Spanish fold, to salvage its prestige. But "popular Spanish of the U.S."

ignores the inequality, domination, and oppression of Spanish speakers by English speakers in the United States, which distinguishes them from speakers in Latin America or Spain. The "Spanglish" label forces us to confront the way language is used to impose national and cultural boundaries and to disguise racial and ethnic prejudices; it invites us to discuss the specific sociohistorical, cultural, economic, and racial contexts that give rise to Spanglish. The detractors of the "Spanglish" label stand outside the speakers, looking in at them, not at language in its context, and not respecting the profound—albeit sometimes problematic—relationship that speakers have with this way of speaking. To deny that conflicted relationship does a disservice to Spanglish speakers and their struggle to be recognized as authentic members of both the dominant and subjugated groups, and to connect proudly with both.

When Tato Laviera (2008, 26) writes "spanglish is *cara-holy inteligencia*," he invites fellow Spanglish speakers to enjoy the pun that juxtaposes the curse *carajo* with "holy" reverence/reference. In addition to puns, jokes, and double entendres, Spanglish speakers perform acts of bilingual identity while deploying more than two dozen discourse strategies, such as topic and role shifting, quoting, translation, mitigation and aggravation of requests, and so on (Zentella 1997). Ultimately, Spanglish is a graphic way of saying, "We speak both because we are both." Despite widespread condemnation and formidable opponents, our Spanglish rejects linguistic border patrolling that reinforces monoglot imperialism; the label itself proclaims its border crossing nature. Precisely because "Spanglish" is a label misused by the enemies of U.S. Latinas/os, we must wrest it from them, insisting that it is not our way of speaking or the label that is holding us back, but the power imbalances that language enforcers end up concealing. We embrace Spanglish with open and frank appraisals of its roots and structure.

56

Spirituality
Theresa Delgadillo

In religious studies, including Latina/o religious studies, "spirituality" traditionally refers to the faith and understanding fostered by the practices, ceremonies, rituals, and training of individuals and groups participating in religious denominations or groups (de Luna 2002; MacDonald 2005; Nabhan-Warren 2013; Tirres 2014). Latinas/os of all denominations embrace spirituality in this traditional sense, including Christians, Muslims, Buddhists, Jews, and others (Aponte 2012). Even though some Latina/o religions have not always enjoyed acceptance as a religion—such as Santería, Lucumí, Yoruba, Orisha, Regla de Ocha, or Candomblé— their adherents similarly describe the process of growing in belief, knowledge, and understanding through religious activities as the spiritual (M. Vega 2000). Alternately, in contemporary usage, "spirituality" may also refer to a relationship to a realm larger than the self—such as the cosmos, the whole of creation, or a nonmaterial sphere (MacDonald 2005).

In Latina/o studies, "spirituality" best describes the cultivation and expression of one's relationship to the sacred as a way of life. Among Latinas/os, conceptions of the sacred often flow from sources outside of traditional religions, such as Indigenous or diasporan worldviews, mythic knowledge systems, varied cultural traditions, popular or home-centered religiosities, or social, cultural, and arts formations (Carrasco 1982; Delgadillo 2000, 2011; León 2003; Cadena and Medina 2004; Acosta-Belén and Santiago 2006; L. E. Pérez 2007;

Espinosa 2013). Among the multiracial, multiethnic Latina/o population of the United States, perspectives on the sacred are diverse, and Latina/o spirituality is often hybrid in that it incorporates or embraces diverse traditions (Delgadillo 1998). For example, some describe Espiritismo or Mesa Blanca as the "official folk religion of Puerto Rico," recognizing how those who embrace it might also be adherents of other, more "official" religious communities but also underscoring how much of a cultural influence it exerts and reflects throughout the island. As a religious practice, it embodies the cultural identity of Puerto Ricans as descendants of Indigenous peoples, Africans, and Spaniards (Flores-Peña 2004).

Latina/o studies research encompasses these multiple arenas for the spiritual among Latinas/os, and often centers on the interrelationship between the spiritual and the cultural realms. The study of both everyday forms of popular religiosity and cultural expressions of spirituality has been at the forefront of Latina/o studies research, which explores how Latinas/os have created unique practices and rituals born of both their religious and their national/ethnic/racial formations, sometimes but not always extra-institutional ones (J. Rodriguez 1994; Davalos 2002; Matovina and Riebe-Estrella 2002; Gonzalez 2006). Scholars have also explored the development of Latina/o theology rooted in Latina/o experiences that are gendered and racially, culturally, and religiously diverse in ways that have sought to amplify the space for Latinas/os in distinct religious traditions (Isasi-Díaz 1996; Aquino 2002; Gonzalez 2006), while others have explored the history and experience of Latinas/os within religious denominations such as Catholicism, Anabaptism, and Pentecostalism, including how denominations responded to the social and political issues around them and how these issues influenced the shape of religious and spiritual life (M. Sandoval 1990;

Espinosa 2002; L. Medina 2005; Hinojosa 2014). Social justice, civil rights, and feminist movements became spiritual concerns in some denominations, and this has shaped church involvement in social issues. Yet other denominations, such as Pentecostalism, with large numbers of Latina/o members and 1,200 Latina clergy, focus on transforming lives through participation in a "Spirit-filled relationship with Jesus" but have generally eschewed involvement in feminist and political concerns (Espinosa 2002), instead embracing an appreciation for spiritual gifts and submission to a divinity in a way that is also reflected in the embrace of traditional family structures and norms, though some newer Pentecostal communities are less traditionalist (Sánchez Walsh 2003). Pentecostals cultivate recovery and rehabilitation through religion, and have and continue to do significant work among addict communities and in service to Latina/o communities (Sánchez Walsh 2003). Archaeologists, historians, and religious studies scholars have examined centuries of diverse religious practices as well as the power of Latina/o religious creativity in melding together colonial and Indigenous systems of belief both in the past and in the present (Carrasco 1990; León 2003, 2004). And spirituality has emerged as a central concern of Latina/o art in the twentieth and twenty-first century (Lindsay 1996; C. Ramírez 2004; L. E. Pérez 2007; T. Romo 2011).

Worldviews that do not fit neatly into the Western category of religion and were thus historically suppressed and vilified in the violence of colonialism and empire endure in varied forms among Latinas/os (Anzaldúa 1987; Carrasco 1990; Hernández-Ávila 2008). African diaspora spiritualities have a long history in the Americas despite the fact that in earlier periods they often existed at the margins of acceptable religious behavior or community and were practiced in secret lest adherents suffer punishment or persecution (M. Vega

2000). Mesoamerican and Indigenous worldviews have long been of interest to Chicanas/os and Latinas/os, either because some are members of Indigenous communities in the present or because many in these groups have participated in the decolonial project of re-learning about the Indigenous peoples they count as forebears (often, in contrast to an exclusively Spanish/Hispanic identification). When these views are not compartmentalized as a separate, organized religion, they are often named as "spiritual" in the contemporary and Latina/o studies usages of this term. As a people's knowledge about themselves in the world, these worldviews are communicated through socialization, enacted in cultural and artistic practices, and embodied in social relations (Castillo 1995; Harris et al. 2004). For example, some women practitioners of Santería have, through the construction of altars, aspired to remember the history of Afro-Caribbean women. In notable cases, they also ensured that others documented their religious artistic practices, both as a means of cultural preservation and an assertion of acceptance amidst efforts to discredit these non-mainstream religious communities (De La Torre 2009; Juncker 2014).

Spiritism, Santería or Lucumí, and Curanderismo, have gained greater currency and study as religions proper, philosophical systems, or medicinal systems, yet elements of these and other worldviews that circulate commonly among Latinas/os are often embraced under the rubric of "spirituality" (Rodriguez, Sánchez Korrol, and Alers 1984). For these "alternative" spiritualities and similar formations, the symbiotic relationship between healing/medicinal systems and engagement with worlds larger than the self appears to be much stronger than in traditional religious denominations. This defining feature of these practices, which address the needs of individuals and groups who both historically and contemporarily confront racism, sexism, homophobia, and the enduring legacies of coloniality, also, importantly, enacts communal formation and reaffirmation.

Shamanic traditions such as Curanderismo operate on a spiritual level as well as material and mental level (Trotter and Chavira 1997), and their efficacy in treating ailments has been increasingly recognized as modern medicine deepens its knowledge of varied Indigenous healing systems and its interest in holistic healing systems (Cervantes and McNeill 2008). Curanderismo is now recognized as a "legitimate belief system with its own history and systematics" in which a healer accesses divine energy through ritual and prayer, working to envision a cure with a patient, while also employing curative substances to benefit the patient (de la Portilla 2009). Curanderos and shamans are viewed as spiritual or sacred specialists who are initiated into a practice of spiritual, psychic, and material healing through their own "ecstatic acquisition of knowledge" (Carrasco 1982). This form of spirituality emerges from and reflects shared cultural traditions and beliefs but is not necessarily tied to any particular religious denomination or formation; as such, it is an example of the spiritual in the cultural rather than in the religious domain, often with partial roots in Indigenous worldviews (de la Portilla 2009, 62–63). Spiritism and Santería/Lucumí can also be viewed as spiritual systems of healing, and the work of Spiritist priests in healing adherents/clients has been compared to the healing effected through psychoanalysis (F. Sánchez 1996).

The relationship between the spiritual and the expressive arts is not a new one, but analyses of it in Latina/o literature, art, and performance are. Religious participants and scholars alike have long been attentive to the aesthetic dimensions of faith practices. In Santería, for example, a selective and communal curatorial practice exists with respect to vessels and artifacts employed in altar-making. This, in turn, has influenced artists who engage with this Afro-Caribbean religious imagery in creating contemporary art (Juncker 2014). Recent research examines how Latina/o literature and art—works too numerous to list here—represents, engages, and reimagines religion and spirituality, often portraying hybrid spiritualities in hybrid visual languages and literary forms (Delgadillo 1998, 2011; L. E. Pérez 2007). New visions of spirituality linked to social justice have been powerfully present in Chicana/o and Latina/o literature, art, and culture of the late twentieth and early twenty-first century (Carrasco 1982; L. E. Pérez 2007). Views of the sacred derived from Amerindian or diaspora worldviews appear throughout Latina/o visual culture (Mesa-Bains 2001; Cullen, Garcia, and Nieves 2005–2006), while Latina/o spiritual formation in traditional denominations takes aesthetic form in home altars, the creation of ceremonial objects, tokens of popular religiosity, and elaborate ritual preparations (Kalb 1994; Lindsay 1996; Turner 1999; Fields and Zamudio-Taylor 2001; M. Vega 2004).

Chicanas and Latinas have been at the forefront of embracing and expanding upon redefinitions of spirituality in the ways described above, participating in new spiritual formations, engaging in spiritual aesthetics, and creating art and literature about spirituality in ways that contest traditional and limiting norms about gender and sexuality. Chicana feminist artists and Chicana lesbians have "made peace" with La Virgen de Guadalupe, a figure traditionally associated with submission and conservative religiosity, by humanizing her in images as an everyday woman who gets things done, a feminist fighter, a nonjudgmental mother, or an Indigenous woman linked to Indigenous goddesses. These revisions often lead to new spiritualities as a redefined Guadalupe becomes a potent cultural and spiritual symbol of nonconformity with oppressive ideologies, embrace of unconditional love for all, and a specifically Chicana cultural inheritance (Trujillo 1998; Esquibel 2006). Chicanas and Latinas have also joined together in new spiritual circles and communities that retain aspects of their religious cultural inheritance—whether Christian, Indigenous, or African—while also cultivating an ethos of recognizing interconnections, valuing the erotic as an aspect of spirituality, and respecting spiritual knowledge from multiple cultures (Medina 1998). For many feminist artists and writers, worldviews and religions of the Indigenous and African diaspora peoples of the Americas empower alternative understandings of the nexus of gender/race/sexuality and disrupt normative assumptions about race and ethnicity (Delgadillo 1998, 2011; L. E. Pérez 2007). The work of Latina/o artists on spirituality includes a spectrum that ranges from those, like Gloria Anzaldúa, who see the spiritual as a necessary component of the creative act, to those whose art is animated by engagement with religions or religious art forms, to those who enact healing through spiritwork that restores denigrated bodies, worldviews, and aesthetics (Anzaldúa 1987; L. E. Pérez 2007).

Understanding spirituality as the beliefs, practices, and performances through which individuals and peoples define and engage the sacred for themselves is also a way of tracking anti- and decolonial movements. Dominant ideologies and cultures in the Americas that sought to erase and marginalize Indigenous worldviews, cultures, and peoples led those same peoples to seek multiple and creative ways to continue to exist and to define their realities. In our more recent history, Latina/o civil rights movements demanded a right to an education about the history, cultures, languages, literatures, and arts of these groups in the United States. One of the founding documents of the Chicana/o Movement, "El Plan Espiritual de Aztlán," penned by the poet Alurista and read publicly for the first time at the Denver Youth Conference of 1969, mentions "religion" only once, as a kind of exclusive grouping or demarcation that it suggests Chicano nationalism transcends, yet it adopts "spiritual" in its title and with this term signifies both a shared relationship among those it appeals to and an ethos of commitment to anti-racism, social justice, compassion, and liberation that it asserts (Anaya and Lomelí 1989, 1–5). In this way, the call resignifies "sacred," ascribing to it a meaning that extends beyond that of monotheist traditions. The call's invocation of a sacred origin place was a reclamation of an Indigenous and spiritual identity (Mesa-Bains 2001). These values were also invoked by the United Farm Workers movement and by Cesar Chavez in the 1960s and 1970s struggles for farmworker rights, a struggle that sometimes took the form of spiritual ritual in fast, prayer, and pilgrimage (León 2014). For the young people gathered in Denver in 1969, "church" was named as one of the places where *El Plan Espiritual de Aztlán* must be distributed, but not viewed as the only home of the spiritual" (Anaya and Lomelí 1989). On the East Coast, Puerto Rican civil rights organizations also often developed new understandings of the spiritual, as for example, when the Philadelphia Young Lords, a Puerto Rican social and political organization, embraced liberation theology as it partnered with local religious groups to provide needed social services in Puerto Rican communities (Whalen 1998), thereby recentering community service as spiritual work. In the Latina/o context, "spiritual" no longer referred exclusively to one's formation in a traditional religion, with its emphasis on ritual and education in a specific denomination, and charitable work being seen as a reflection of one's commitment to the divine. Instead, Latinas/os reimagined the sacred within and among themselves, or as present in wider social, cultural, and material relations, adopting a decolonial stance that empowered their minority knowledge and culture. As many have observed, social movement and religious resurgence converged among Latinas/os in the 1960s and 1970s to impact traditional denominations (M. Sandoval 1990; Díaz-Stevens and Stevens-Arroyo 1998; L. Medina 2005).

The unique histories of Latinas/os in relation to multiple worldviews and belief systems may be the very reason that spirituality has long signified differently in these communities and in this field than in mainstream religious studies. That is, the Latina/o invocation of spirituality ascribes value to the knowledge and experience of worldviews that are devalued in the mainstream (Anzaldúa 1987; Delgadillo 2000; Anzaldúa and Keating 2002; L. E. Pérez 2007) and gestures toward a fuller understanding of the complexity of the interrelationship among experiences, histories, expressive cultures, and beliefs among varied Latina/o groups.

57

Sterilization

Alexandra Minna Stern

Latinas/os have a complex relationship to surgical sterilization as well as to related long-acting forms of birth control. For more than one hundred years, Latinas/os—above all Chicanas and puertorriqueñas—have been subjected episodically to unwanted sterilizations in state institutions and public clinics. At the same time, Latinas/os have struggled to obtain access to safe and affordable birth control, including sterilization, contraceptive technologies, and in recent years, long-acting reversible contraception (LARC). This dueling pattern of hypervigilant reproductive control and structural exclusion from reproductive health services has characterized, and continues to characterize, Latinas/os' fraught relationship to sterilization.

For much of the twentieth century, Latinas/os, like all Americans, faced tremendous barriers to obtaining elective sterilizations. Until 1969, women seeking the procedure at the doctor's office had to adhere to the American Congress of Obstetricians and Gynecologists' (ACOG) formula, in which age multiplied by number of children had to be greater than or equal to 120 before elective sterilization would be considered (E. Gutiérrez 2008). For example, to qualify for sterilization, a forty-year-old woman needed to be the biological mother of three children, and a twenty-year-old woman the biological mother of six children. In addition, two physicians and one psychiatrist had to approve the operation. Except for the privileged few who had access to a sympathetic private physician, Latinas were able to obtain reproductive surgery only through programs established under the auspices of population control and neo-eugenic policies.

Starting in the 1930s, the United States oversaw the initiation of such a program in Puerto Rico, whose goals were to "fix" the island's unemployment and development problems by regulating family size (Briggs 2002b). The regulation of sexuality and reproduction had a long history in Puerto Rico, connected to concerns about female "decency" that characterized both Spanish and U.S. colonialism on the island (Findlay 1999). Twentieth-century tubal ligation efforts, which affected women neighborhood by neighborhood, house by house, led to a situation in which approximately one-third of puertorriqueñas had been sterilized by the 1960s. This population policy extended to the diaspora on the East Coast as well, most notably at Lincoln Hospital in the Bronx, where high numbers of postpartum sterilizations, many nonconsensual, were performed on Puerto Rican women. Overall, the high rates of sterilization of Puerto Rican women reflected an incongruous convergence of imperialist neo-Malthusian population programs, feminist support of the expansion of sterilization as an important birth control option, and the constrained choices of women, many already mothers, for whom tubal ligation was an available and sometimes desired procedure (Lopez 2008).

Concurrent with the rise of sterilizations of Puerto Ricans on and off the island, Chicanas on the West Coast were subjected to sterilization abuse (E. Gutiérrez 2008). Hospitals in the Los Angeles area, supported by the Los Angeles Regional Family Planning Council, launched programs to sterilize Mexican-origin women using funds newly available through the Department of Health, Education, and Welfare (HEW) and emergent Medicaid programs. Although the clinics performing these sterilizations at no cost did adhere to basic consent protocols, they offered these procedures only to poor women, the vast majority of them Latinas. The most egregious violations occurred in the early 1970s at Los Angeles County-University of Southern California (USC) Hospital where over two hundred Mexican-origin and African American women were coerced into postpartum tubal ligations (E. Gutiérrez 2008; Stern 2005b). While under the duress of labor or sedated, women were falsely told by the obstetric staff that their husbands had already consented to the procedure, were communicated to only in English despite being monolingual Spanish speakers, or simply told nothing at all. Eventually two sets of plaintiffs, all sterilized nonconsensually at that hospital, sought justice. Ten women, represented by Antonia Hernández and Richard Navarette from the Model Cities Center for Law and Justice, filed a class-action lawsuit seeking punitive damages and the creation of federal safeguards for sterilization (Tajima-Peña 2015). Represented by the law firm Cruz, Díaz, and Durán, three other plaintiffs filed a civil suit for $6,000,000 in damages. Despite powerful testimonies and affidavits detailing an environment of coercion, the courts decided against the plaintiffs. In *Madrigal v. Quilligan*, the judge explained away this reproductive injustice as the product of cultural misunderstandings and asserted that the implicated physicians had not done anything wrong or unethical. Yet these trials, as well as legal and media attention to similar allegations involving African American and Native American women in several regions of the country, raised the visibility of the extensiveness of sterilization abuse (Nelson 2003). Within several years, HEW instituted and revamped regulations for women whose sterilizations were funded through Medicaid or federal programs.

In preceding decades, Latinas/os had been subjected to sterilizations in state institutions around the country (Lira and Stern 2014). From the early 1900s to the 1980s, thirty-two U.S. states maintained sterilization laws authorizing reproductive surgeries—for women, salpingectomies, and for men, vasectomies and sometimes castrations—for those deemed unfit to procreate. These eugenic sterilization laws impacted a wide cross-section of people, including European and Asian immigrants, people with intellectual disabilities and psychiatric conditions, as well as poor and minimally educated people who became entangled in the net of juvenile or county court systems (Chávez-García 2012). In most states, Latinas/os were not one of the primary groups affected, largely due to their low numbers in Virginia, North Carolina, and Michigan, three of the states with the highest absolute sterilization rates. However, in California, which had a considerable Latin American–origin population, Latinas/os were significantly impacted, if not explicitly targeted, by sterilization programs.

Review of recently obtained records from the state of California demonstrates that Spanish-surnamed patients were sterilized at over twice the rate of non-Spanish-surnamed patients, with Latinas under eighteen years of age bearing the brunt of disproportionate sterilization rates (Novak et al. 2016). Notably, Spanish-surnamed patients constituted 20 percent of those sterilized in the state's largest "feebleminded" home and 19 percent in the largest psychiatric home during the peak period of 1937 to 1948. At Pacific Colony, an institution established to house "morons," a class of "feebleminded" the state found particularly worrying, Spanish-surnamed patients were sterilized at an average rate of 25 percent from 1929 to 1952, with a peak of 36 percent in 1939. Records indicate that the vast majority of Spanish-surnamed patients were of Mexican origin; they were sterilized at rates that far surpassed their recorded census population, which never rose higher than 6.5 percent between 1920 and 1950 (Lira and Stern 2014).

Mexican-origin youth, both girls and boys, deemed incorrigible, delinquent, or promiscuous, regularly found themselves committed to the state's juvenile homes. It was not uncommon for them to be transferred temporarily or permanently to institutions, such as Sonoma, where they were sterilized (Chávez-García 2012). During the era of eugenic sterilization, both Latinos and Latinas, often entire sibling groups, overwhelmingly of Mexican origin, were sterilized in state hospitals and homes. Again and again, Chicanas/os were explicitly identified as degenerate and inferior by California eugenicists (L. Chavez 2004).

Yet Chicana/o families did not automatically accept or acquiesce to recommendations from superintendents that they or their family members be sterilized on account of mental, intellectual, or physical defects. Indeed, Chicana/o parents were the most vocal opponents of sterilization, protesting the operation for religious, legal, and moral reasons (Lira and Stern 2014). In 1930, in what appears to be the first instance of any challenge to the state's sterilization law, Concepción Ruíz and her guardian sued in district court for damages after her sterilization at Sonoma. In 1939, Sara Rosas García, the mother of a young woman named Andrea sterilized at Pacific Colony also sued the state, challenging the constitutionality of the sterilization law. García secured legal counsel from David C. Marcus, a Jewish American lawyer with strong ties to the Mexican Consulate and the National Association for the Advancement of Colored People (NAACP), who wrote a compelling criticism of Andrea's sterilization as a violation of the equal protection clause of the Fourteenth Amendment and of due process, given that there was no mechanism for patient appeal. Although these two lawsuits failed, they are small but salient illustrations of the resistance against sterilization waged by Chicana/o parents who contested juvenile court officers, wrote multiple letters refusing the operation for one or more children, and sought support from the Catholic Church, the Mexican Consulate, and local Mexican American civic organizations.

A sturdy thread of Latina/o resistance against nonconsensual sterilization runs from these early instances of protests in the 1930s across the twentieth century to the 1970s and 1980s, when Chicanas/os, puertorriqueñas, and their allies organized and marched against sterilization abuse. It is no coincidence that the legislator who spearheaded the repeal of California's eugenic sterilization law in 1979—after seventy years on the books—was Art Torres, a Mexican American state assemblyman from the very district where members of the community were misled into reproductive surgeries at Los Angeles County-USC hospital.

In the twenty-first century, the problem of sterilization abuse has not disappeared. In 2013, journalists and legal advocates uncovered approximately 150 cases of unauthorized sterilizations in two California women's prisons (Johnson 2013). Overwhelmingly affected were women of color and poor women incarcerated for minor offenses whose contact with their children was made contingent upon permanent birth control. Although there is limited information about most of these women, those who have spoken out about their experiences are African American and Latina. Echoing arguments from the eugenics era, in which fears of dysgenic offspring were coupled with concerns about protecting the public purse, the obstetrician contracted to perform these operations for the prison system justified them as cheaper "compared to what you save in welfare paying for these unwanted children—as they procreated more" (quoted in Johnson 2013).

For Latinas, sterilization abuse is not a relic of the past but a potential reality, particularly in institutional settings. Keen awareness of this possibility prompted a group of reproductive justice advocates to issue a strong statement in 2013 about the continued need for safe-guards, mostly established in the wake of the abuses that unfolded in the 1970s, to protect poor women and women of color (Reid 2014). These safeguards include a thirty-day waiting period for any Medicaid-funded sterilization, availability of bilingual consent forms, and a prohibition on operations on minors. However, this perspective is challenged by another group of feminists, working largely in women's health, who believe that Medicaid requirements severely limit women's access to wanted sterilizations (Borrero, Zite, and Creinin 2012). They argue that women of color and poor women are unduly harmed by the bureaucratic demands of these cumbersome requirements. Their recommendations are supported by recent research that strongly suggests that tubal ligation rates are higher among Latinas because sterilization is their preferred form of birth control and that Latinas face multiple obstacles to obtaining LARC (Potter et al. 2012; White et al. 2014). Notwithstanding, other studies show that Latinas are more likely to express regret after sterilization, indicating that undue pressure or significant miscommunication occurred at some point in the process (Shreffler et al. 2015).

Sterilization and oral contraception are the two most common forms of birth control, and tubal ligations and vasectomies are requested by millions of men and women across the demographic spectrum every year. It is much more than a simple medical procedure, however, since it has been caught up in struggles over reproductive control with multiple actors and stakeholders. For Latinas/os this dynamic is further complicated by cross-currents of colonialism, racism, and xenophobia, which sit at the core of stratified reproduction. Sometimes these dynamics have played out through tense gender politics. For example, when Chicanos propounded militant ethnic nationalism in the 1960s and 1970s, many Chicanas challenged their presumptive principal roles as mothers and breeders of la raza, and gendered fissures emerged in the Chicana/o movement. Largely because of strong female leadership among Puerto Rican activists, a more comprehensive understanding of reproductive control along feminist lines was incorporated into political platforms and movement politics (Nelson 2003).

Latinas/os have had a wide diversity of experiences with sterilization, ranging from being victims of coerced operations to overcoming significant economic and administrative barriers to obtain permanent birth control through reproductive surgery. These patterns are the most pronounced for Latinas, whose contact points with any form of birth control is likely to be constrained by racial biases, institutional inequities, and intransigent political wrangling about women's reproductive bodies. Given deep-seated historical patterns and the contemporary combative landscape of reproductive politics in the United States, sterilization will probably continue to be a troubled issue for Latinas/os, particularly for those reliant on public health systems or explicitly excluded from health coverage through the Affordable Care Act because of undocumented or tenuous immigrant status.

58

Television

Mary Beltrán

Television can be thought of as a conduit of creative and political expression, as a reflection of the national imaginary, and as a cultural forum that plays a role in uniting diverse Latinas/os as an imagined community. As a mass medium, it is a site where ideas about Latinas/os have been enacted on a national scale. Since the inception of English-language television in the late 1940s, series such as *I Love Lucy* (1951–1957), *Chico and the Man* (1974–1977), *Ugly Betty* (2006–2010), and more recently *Jane the Virgin* (2014–) have presented, reinforced, and occasionally challenged mainstream conceptions of what it means to be Latina/o in the United States. In addition, Spanish-language television, and in recent years, bilingual television have powerfully contributed to the Latina/o imaginary regarding notions of race, gender, class, citizenship, and other axes of identity and social politics.

Spanish-language television and radio serve as cultural forums for Latinas/os and Latin Americans in the United States, uniting diverse individuals from a wide variety of national origin groups under the rubric of "Latinidad," which has been defined by the Chilean American scholar of Latina/o media studies Angharad Valdivia as the experience of being Latina/o and "the assignment of Latina/o traits to people, culture, and habits" (2010, 4). News programs have played an important role in this regard, educating and rallying the Latina/o community to proactively respond in times of political challenge, as Mexican American scholar Mari Castañeda (2008) has documented. Television personalities such as Univision news anchor Jorge Ramos and talk-show host Cristina Saralegui also play major roles as community organizers through the medium of television. Moreover, Spanish-language entertainment programming, such as telenovelas and the variety show *Sábado Gigante*, provides familiar points of cultural reference for viewers within the Latina/o diaspora. Popular telenovelas on Univision and Telemundo, the two largest Spanish-language networks in the United States, now regularly compete with English-language series for a spot among the top-rated network shows in the nation each evening.

English-language television also has played a powerful role in the construction of Latinidad in the United States. It has had a particularly substantial impact, given the size of its national audience, the export of its programming around the world, and the way that it has reinforced and only occasionally challenged Latina/o racialization and American social norms. As this author's area of expertise, it will be the focus of the remainder of this essay.

Unfortunately, Latinas and Latinos have generally been marginalized in English-language television as part of a dynamic of *erasure* that reinforces cultural and linguistic hierarchies in the United States, as Christopher Chávez (2015) notes. While limited progress can be seen in recent years in the form of a few multidimensional and broadly appealing Latina/o roles, such as in the critically lauded *Jane the Virgin* and now-canceled *George Lopez* (2002–2007), Latina/o lead characters still are few and far between. Studies have long documented this invisibility and misrepresentation. The most recent study, led by Puerto Rican filmmaker and researcher Frances Negrón-Muntaner at Columbia University, found that while Latinas/os constituted 17 percent of the population in 2013, there were no Latina or Latino lead characters in prime-time series that year (Negrón-Muntaner et al. 2014). Furthermore, the dearth of Latina/o writers, producers, and executives in the television industry has contributed to depictions that have often failed to convey the complexity of Latina/o experience. Latinas/os did not hold creative positions in substantial numbers until the 1990s; from 2010 to 2013 they constituted only 1 percent of employed producers, 2 percent of writers, and 4 percent of directors (Negrón-Muntaner et al. 2014).

In this regard, English-language television has been viewed by some Latinas/os as a hopelessly demoralizing realm of popular culture. There have been a few exceptions, however, with respect to portrayals and series that have been a source of pride, among them *I Love Lucy*, Latina/o public affairs shows of the 1970s, *Chico and the Man*, and *Resurrection Blvd.* (2000–02). *I Love Lucy*, for instance, was an exception in the early years of television as a family sitcom starring a Latino and Anglo-American couple. As Cuban American researcher Gustavo Pérez Firmat (1994) aptly documents, Desi Arnaz, a Cuban-born actor and musician, and Lucille Ball, his Anglo-American wife in the series and in real life, became beloved stars when their series became a hit and then akin to America's "first family" when they integrated Ball's pregnancy and the birth of their son into the storyline. While Arnaz's role as Ricky Ricardo did demand that he exaggerate his accent, he was portrayed as a successful musician and businessman and "straight man" to Lucy, his unpredictable wife. Arnaz and Ball also maintained creative control of the series. Arnaz became executive producer of *I Love Lucy* and the first Latino television executive as president of Desilu Productions, which subsequently produced other popular series.

The 1970s also resulted in important developments for Latinas/os in television as the efforts of activists began to have an impact. During the peak of Chicana/o and Puerto Rican movements in the late 1960s and early 1970s, Latina/o advocates agitated for media industry reforms. As Chicano film studies scholar Chon Noriega

(2000) has underscored in his research, these activists fought for improvements in how Latinas/os were represented in film and television and for the hiring of Latinas/os in various roles in the media industries. Among their successes was the entrance of the first Latinas/os to entry-level television production positions and the launching of Latina/o public affairs series with names like *Ahora!*, *Acción Chicano*, and *Realidades*, at several public television stations around the country. Bilingual children's programs such as *Carrascolendas* (1970–1978), *Villa Alegre* (1973–1977), and *¿Qué Pasa, U.S.A.?* (1977–1980) also found homes on local and national public television in this period, spurred in part by educational legislation that supported bilingual programming. Puerto Rican television scholar Yeidy M. Rivero (2012) and Mexican American television producer Aída Barrera (2001) have documented how *¿Qué Pasa, U.S.A.?* and *Carrascolendas*, respectively, targeted Latina/o youth and supported the navigation of their bicultural identities.

In the realm of entertainment programming, the socially conscious climate of the 1970s motivated network interest in prime-time comedies that addressed racial diversity and social issues. While Mexican Americans and other Latinas/os seldom appeared in these narratives, NBC tried to fill this gap with *Chico and the Man* (1974–1977), the first U.S. television series to feature a Chicano lead character. It featured Freddie Prinze as Francisco "Chico" Rodriguez, a young Chicano who moved in with an embittered white auto shop owner in East Los Angeles; the two come to work together and care for each other over time despite their culture clash. As I note (Beltrán 2009) in research on the production of the series and the reception it received, it initially elicited complaints from both Latina/o and non-Latina/o viewers regarding Chico's depiction as subservient to Ed and the casting of Prinze, who was Hungarian and Puerto Rican, as Mexican American. Despite this, it proved to be a hit with audiences and made a star out of Freddie Prinze before his untimely death in 1976.

Shifts in later decades also encouraged television images and series that presented Latinas/os with more dimensionality. Among these shifts, misperceptions regarding Latinas/os' language preferences began to be cleared up for television professionals; it may have been a surprise to some that most U.S. Latinas/os consume both English-language and Spanish-language media and thus were not being served solely through Spanish-language television. Projected demographic changes also provided motivation for the television industry to improve its outreach to Latinas/os. In the 1990s, the U.S. Census Bureau projected that by 2000 Latinas/os would surpass African Americans, then 12.5 percent of the population, to become the nation's largest non-white ethnic group. Appeal to Latina/o viewers thus was becoming more integral to the success of series and to the networks more broadly. Latina/o advertising agencies also were instrumental in educating the public and the media industries regarding Latina/o buying power and growth as an American audience and consumer market, as Puerto Rican advertising scholar Arlene Dávila (2001) documents in her research.

In the late 1990s and early 2000s, Latina/o writers, producers, and executives began to have a substantial impact on television. Important milestones included the first series with a predominantly Latina/o cast and Latina/o production team, *Resurrection Blvd.* (2000–2002), about a Mexican American family with several brothers competing in the world of boxing. Writer-producer Dennis Leoni, of Mexican and Italian descent, was show runner for the Showtime series. Other Latina/o-led series have included *American Family* (2002–2004), created by Mexican American filmmaker Gregory Nava; *Ugly Betty* (2006–2010), helmed by Cuban American producer Silvio Horta and Mexican executive producer

Salma Hayek; *George Lopez* (2002–07), a family sitcom co-created and co-produced by Mexican American comedian George Lopez, who also starred in it; and most recently *Cristela* (2015), executive-produced and starring the first Latina show runner, Mexican American comedian and writer Cristela Alonzo.

Building on the foundational work of the early Chicana/o and Latina/o media activists, the National Hispanic Media Council and other advocacy organizations continue efforts directed at the networks regarding the employment and portrayals of Latinas/os on and behind the television screen. However, there are a number of conundrums when it comes to pushing for progress in this regard. One is that surveys of progress by advocacy groups and the networks themselves typically tally numbers of characters, actors, and creative professionals who are Latina/o, while the quality of portrayals is much more difficult to assess and often has gone without critique. In recent years we have also been witnessing what might be termed a "whitewashing" of Latina/o characters, as fair-skinned Latina/o actors of partial European heritage have increasingly come to be cast in various productions, and as Latina/o characters may be portrayed as having no connections to a Latina/o community (Beltrán 2009). These trends beg in-depth thought and discussion. While blatantly stereotypical Latina/o characters with exaggerated characteristics such as broken English, heavy accents, and wildly colorful costumes are less often included in television story worlds, we now seldom find any culturally marked Latina/o characters or see Latina/o communities depicted.

Debates regarding the definition of and impact of "positive" images of Latinas/os are also ongoing. Presenting Latinas/os as middle-class professionals has often been promoted by advocates as more desirable than presenting them as working class, in service positions, or as not fluent in English. However, given that many

Latina/o families still struggle with socioeconomic disadvantage and poverty, it is relevant to consider the impact of this advocacy; children from all socioeconomic backgrounds arguably benefit from seeing families like their own portrayed sensitively, as well as from viewing aspirational images. In classroom discussions, television series such as *George Lopez* and the more recent *Devious Maids* (2013–) demonstrate how Latina/o characters in "stereotypical" jobs can be still admirable protagonists possessing dignity and intelligence. The *diversity* of Latina/o images is of grave importance in these discussions, however; if the only images that we see of Latinas are of Latina maids, then that would be a clear problem.

As noted earlier, progress for Latinas/os in English-language television can be seen in the success of a few series with Latina/o leads and in the entrance of the first Latina/o writers, producers, and executives as working professionals in the industry. Some of these writers and producers are finding an entrée through producing Latina/o-oriented web series, such as *East WillyB* (2011–2013), *Ylse* (2008–2010), and *East Los High* (2013–). However, as Vittoria Rodriguez and I note (2017), the rise of Latina/o-oriented television series exhibited on streaming media sites raises new questions. Even the most successful online series have had a hard time continuing beyond a few seasons because of lack of sustained funding, pointing to an important topic of future discussion, that of financial support of Latina/o television production. During the height of the Chicana/o and Puerto Rican civil rights movements, there was a call for community-supported arts efforts, particularly for media productions that would take control of Latina/o representation away from Hollywood. Does a new call need to be sounded to ensure that Latina/o television will flourish as well? As more Latina/o writers and producers are taking up digital media tools to produce their own television programming, this will be a question of ongoing importance.

59

Territoriality

Mary Pat Brady

"Quisqueya," "Borinquen," "México de afuera," "Aztlán," "Greater Cuba": these richly evocative names describe and collate familiar topos and draw together felt affinities, carefully harbored histories, and methods of knowing that shift between institutional abstractions and more intimate articulations. These names and concepts produce territoriality—which is to say they provide opportunities to ascribe forms of belonging that reach across and away from national and imperial claims to a monopoly on violent control of a geospatial arena. These are terms that circulate with the currents of nationalism, but that also try to plumb the decolonial depths in order to undo the work that territoriality typically does in an imperial register.

"Territoriality" names a way of thinking about the world, space, ownership, and belonging. An old word, derived from the Latin for *terra* (*tierra*, earth), it suggests ontologically the condition of being a territory and also a stance, a practice of defending or guarding a resource and thus an epistemological practice of understanding. Its earliest and most common uses revolve around forms of management that splice power into a sociospatial register in order to enhance and coagulate power and domination.

For people interested in Latina/o or Latinx cultures and histories, the word has disciplinary resonances as well. It suggests a practice of demarking, of guarding resources (methodologies, archives, histories), and of delimiting access to material or to the opportunity to make claims. Beginning almost fifty years ago, for example, as students fought unceasingly for the opportunity to pursue formal study of Chicana/o and Puerto Rican literatures, they encountered disciplinary structures in which Latin American studies scholars eschewed their efforts as the work of distant cousins of the *true* Latin American culture and Americanists could not imagine a place within their field for *foreigners* (albeit in a "domestic sense").

Within academics and beyond this form of territoriality names a significant aspect of knowledge production: *scaling*. Latin/Americanists, in delimiting areas of canonicity, of importance and difficulty, and of scholarly and institutional value, veer toward a form of territorializing that instantiates author(itie)s as gatekeepers. In other words, the movement between belonging and possessing chugs along through territoriality toward violence. Could it not then be said that such scaling is also practiced when scholars narrate their work under the rubric of Chicana/o, Puerto Rican, or Cuban studies? Does "Latina/o" enable an escape? Or "hemispheric"? Or "decolonial"? These are not, ultimately the most generative of questions, although they are certainly ones that scholars moving around and among a form of hemispheric turnings implicitly and explicitly invoke. By and large the struggles scholars have had within U.S. institutions in insisting on the "validity," on the importance of studying Chicana novels or Nuyorican poetry, to take two examples, emerged in part because of the larger violence of nation-making within world systems. Area studies programs have been produced in the name of nation-making and territoriality. Fields like Latina/o studies can refute the templates established by area studies because they invoke an altogether different idea of territoriality, one that does not repeatedly give birth to the nation-state.

Lurking behind territoriality in these two senses is a particular way of imaging humanness and space. If territoriality marks a relationship of ownership, of possession, it also remarks the *possibility* that geos, cultures, and accounts can be guarded and possessed, and that such possessing means something about the guard and possessor as well as those who don't guard, who don't possess. But territoriality also suggests, within a national and disciplinary imaginary, the primacy of abstracted space, space as rationalized, made everywhere the same, emptied of specific content, abstracted from affective and cultural relations, mapped, surveyed, charted, folded into a world system, a globalized/capitalized imagination. As Sallie Marston and her collaborators argue (Marston, Jones, and Woodward 2005), this form of spatial imaginary relies on scale for its articulation (local, regional, national, global) and scaling (which is to say the habits and practices of slotting spaces, people, and capital into scaffolded relations with each other). By scaling, I mean not just the planetarily ascribed globality, which is understood through the lenses of local, regional, national, and global scales, but also the affective values that accrue to those scales as well as the technologies that narrate and enforce them such as visas, green cards, and advertising. As a vertical metric, scale reinforces hierarchies, assigns glamour and power to larger scales, and denigrates and dismisses the quotidian, gendered female, and parochial local practices by scaffolding meaning within relations of value. To territorialize is to scale and inevitably to privilege larger movements and to assign value for the movement of small to larger. Territoriality hierarchizes and privileges larger spaces (world systems, nation-states) as opposed to more immediately felt spaces. Implicit in territoriality is a concept of agency that links institutional forces (such as global capital, the state) together and further assigns agency only to those who may be said to embody them. This form of territoriality presumes a kind of agency that looks very much like the European colonial master *I*-cogito/*I* conquer and only *I* can claim all, can bound space, can vacuum power through remaking the meaning of the earth, turning the planet into the globe. To speak of territoriality as it has traditionally been understood is to land inside a senseless world in which so called agency lies mythically in the hands of a few, transcendence is the goal, and a spatial hierarchy of scalar force never gets questioned. Yet, if we dig around, there are other forms of imagining relationships, other kinds of territorialities—both those that start from critique but do not stay there and those that dwell in another possibility, in another territory altogether.

Such a vision emerges in the poetry of Martín Espada (2004), who writes of "a centipede of hands moving" and of "fierce" lives that navigate border patrol vans "snoring on the first hill / like a watchdog dreaming of meat." With these poems Espada eschews the boundedness that territoriality demarcates; he even jokes, "We remembered parking at the corner of La Revolución and La Constitución, two avenues that never intersect." The speaker moves about asking peddlers where to find the revolution, and each answers, "Más allá." *Allá* is an *abrazo*, arms enclosing and opening simultaneously. For, as his poem impishly suggests, the dominant territoriality (La Constitución) cannot produce a revolution in socio-spatial imaginaries (not when it has helped establish and cement them). The invocation of "allá" names the possible through a differential, horizontal movement within and beside rather than above and beyond.

"Allá" and "revolución" are haunted by the strategies of territoriality practiced by the state. They respond viscerally to the movements and practices that produce a territoriality signaled by the vituperative U.S. Supreme Court's determination to call Puerto Rico "foreign in a domestic sense" (Burnett and Marshall 2001). Juan Seguín, almost a half-century before that declaration, articulated the enmeshment of territoriality in racialism

and in that way prophesied the wording of U.S. Justice Henry Brown's 1901 decision when Seguín described his own experience as a "foreigner in my native land" (Seguín [1858] 1999, 358). "Foreign"/"native" describes Eurocentric state practices that, as Seguín predicted, produce a structure of living for Latinas/os that animates the experience of being made to feel both foreign and yet native—denied at any rate access even to full "nativity."

On the other hand, Aztlán, Quisqueya, Borinquen could be seen as modes of being together, of belonging to each other, that do not absolutely have to embrace the state's deployment of these (p)articulations. They reject in a vivid sense the state's recourse to foreign and native as emblems hung together to define and delimit and to produce the sense of territory and the regime of a spatial imaginary that enforces limitation. Such a rejection entails a different vision. When Martín Espada combats such territoriality, it is to move toward finding new forms of being together.

It may well have been this desire to understand relations differently that drew installation artist Felix Gonzalez-Torres to the musings of a very young Elizabeth Bishop. Toward the end of his life, he faxed Bishop's description of birds in flight to a gallerist as a gesture of description without comment: "The interspaces [between the birds] moved in pulsation too, catching up and continuing the motion of the wings in wakes, carrying it on, as the rest in music does—not blankness but a space as musical as all the sound" (Corrin 2000, 8). The sky is not background to the birds; they and the sky move together, creating one another. It may well have been this sense of pulsing engagement that captured Gonzalez-Torres's imagination and helped him feel his life's work to be to shift art from its status as object to a chance, an opportunity for interactions that are not temporally static or spatially sedimented, where meanings and objects and visual signals fold viscerally together indescribably. So with pieces like his 1995 "Untitled (Water)," a curtain of beautiful beads filling a doorway, he pursues, alongside Espada, a different sense of moving in space that shifts away from ownership and toward the perception of relation—movement. Or an absence. Most well known for a series of billboards placed around the New York metro area in 1991 showing the white sheets of an empty, unmade bed, Gonzalez-Torres, as bell hooks writes, "taunted us with remembered connection. . . . We confront an absence that is also a trace" (1994, 48). For Gonzalez-Torres, art can be a "virus." It can "work within the contradictions of the system . . . to try to create a better place" (quoted in Mc-Namara 2009, 256). To name a practice as viral and to get that it feeds on contradictions is to shift out of the binary register of foreign/native entirely and to unbraid the assimilative/individualist matrix, to remake territoriality as engagement, even orientation, but not conquest, as being together, next to each other, to shape the possible and shift from a territoriality of mapping abstraction to the particularity of being next to each other.

In *Their Dogs Came with Them*, Helena María Viramontes (2007) collapses together the corrosive effects of different forms of territoriality: corporate wealthmaking underwritten by the state in the form of community destruction and freeway construction, state policing in the form of blazing police violence, gang warfare in the form of drugs and entrapment, transnational colonizing in the form of World War II internment camps and Cold War proxy battles in Vietnam. All of these practitioners and practices collude together in habits of territoriality that terrorize. Viramontes illustrates that territoriality likes scales, likes organizing meaning through hierarchies, likes creating verticalities that squash and render lives into excess. Yet if this bleak sphere is the product of territoriality as a practice and orientation, of scaling ownership and control

and resources, Viramontes brings the reader not to the realm of nested hierarchies but within the place of detail, to the mesh bag that holds onions, and bakelite pay phones, to thinning time, and to PCP-enhanced music that slithers under flesh "like greenish larvae pupating." What Viramontes draws readers to is a practice Alex Vazquez (2013) calls "listening in detail," which moves together with a sense that there is no distinct object that is observed or heard but that the listener and the observed summon each other into being, engage and make real together meshed within pulsating interspaces: "Amá was part of the house, carelessly repaired with cardboard and duct tape like her cracked windows. Frank was part of the house, a loose, exposed wire ready to electrocute anyone who touched him" (Viramontes 2007, 161).

In the work of Viramontes, Espada, and Gonzalez-Torres, movements of all kinds do not initiate from conquest or in consequence, but together through a porosity, an indistinction that does not disperse a capacity to exchange meanings or shift relations, that undoes the bounding entailed by practices of exclusion and inclusion, in order to shift away from that other rooted cousin to territoriality—to terror, to frighten, to flee from fear, and to tremble.

60

Testimonio

Arnaldo Cruz-Malavé

Variously classified as a genre or subgenre of Latin American and Latina/o nonfictional writing, an activist pedagogical technique for the constitution of a subject that has undergone trauma or been marginalized and silenced by being placed in a "border" condition between official or hegemonic discourses, in the category, that is, of those who, as one of its practitioners ironically states (Barnet 1994, 203), have ostensibly "no history," as well as a method for the transformation of that condition into consciousness, collective memory, theory, and political action, testimonio is the resulting textual or visual product of an individual act of witnessing and/or experiencing an abject social state that is more than individual, that is indeed collective. Atrocity, genocide, extermination, torture, rape, and social abjection due to race, ethnicity, gender, sexuality, or some other politically or socially marked difference are never far from it. These are the unspeakable background or referents that haunt the witness or *testimonialista*'s (testimionio's narrator or speaking subject) act of "coming to voice," of truth-telling and "speaking back" to the social powers that be in order to transform his or her unspeakable experience of trauma into consciousness, collective memory, political action, and theory. Thus an overarching literary or rhetorical trope that structures the products of this otherwise nonfictional genre—where truth-telling, the presence of the other's voice, and the "effect of the real," however achieved, are most often privileged—is the figure of the speaker who narrates his or her story under the duress of the social order's threat of abjection, invisibility, or death, or what the New York Puerto Rican writer Manuel Ramos Otero, who wrote about social abjection and death and died of AIDS in 1990, called in his meta-testimonial tale, "Vivir del cuento," "the Scheherazade Complex" (1987, 55). Like Scheherazade, the female narrator of the *Arabian Nights*, who must tell a different story every night to stave off death and save herself and the women of Persia from the sultan's sword, the speakers of testimonio narrate under the threat of social invisibility and death their unspeakable tale to save themselves and their community by reconstituting their sense of self and their community's collective memory. This feminine trope for the production of testimonios has been especially generative in the United States where, as we shall see, testimonios have most often been deployed in Latina/o writing for the expression of gender and sexual dissidence.

Heir to a long tradition of Latin American writing that seeks to speak for others who cannot speak for themselves, to confront official European book learning with the words and oral histories of the defeated or subaltern, testimonio can trace its roots to the early Latin American colonial period, when writers such as the Inca Garcilaso de la Vega (1539–1616) subtly revised Spanish historians' versions of the conquest by supplementing or "augmenting" their "insufficient" accounts with the words and oral narratives of the history and customs of the Incas as told to him by his defeated relatives, Inca nobility, and his former schoolmates in his *Comentarios reales*, or *Royal Commentaries* of 1609 (Vega 2014).

Yet its modern form dates from the 1950s and 1960s, when, with the introduction of the tape recorder, progressive social historians began to incorporate the transcribed interviews and oral histories of people whose opinions and everyday experience had not been previously included in historical accounts: African Americans, Latinas/os, women, workers, rural folk, and the urban poor. This tendency to incorporate the everyday experiences of the socially marginalized other is further amplified in the Americas by the Cuban revolutionary process, which, in its various attempts (historical, literary, and cinematic) to revise the inherited official story of the development of the nation, sought to underscore the previously elided role of women, workers, and especially Afro-Cubans in the construction of the nation. Indeed the first modern text to self-consciously assume the genre of testimonio is the Cuban ethnographer and poet Miguel Barnet's *Biografía de un cimarrón* (1966; *Biography of a Runaway Slave* [1994]). Inspired by the historical revision fostered by the Cuban revolutionary process and the turn in the social sciences toward the everyday experience of marginalized peoples, which the anthropological work of Oscar Lewis exemplified, Barnet presented in his *Biografía de un cimarrón* the life story of Esteban Montejo, an illiterate, 103-year-old runaway slave who fought in Cuba's war of independence from Spain. Like Lewis in his ethnographies of the urban poor, including *The Children of Sanchez: Autobiography of a Mexican Family* (1961) and the polemical, even infamous *La Vida: A Puerto Rican Family in the Culture of Poverty—San Juan and New York* (1966b), Barnet presented Montejo's story in a first-person narrative as if Montejo were directly speaking to his audience and to him without the mediation of a context, an interviewer, or the interview questions normally prepared by oral historians, anthropologists, and sociologists. Thus, in presenting the life of a subaltern subject this way, this modern form of testimonio seemed to assume that long Latin American tradition of speaking for, or on behalf of, the subaltern other, what Alberto Moreiras has called "prosopopeic" representation (1996, 203), in order to revolutionize it by having the subaltern speak

for the first time for him- or herself without the mediating authority of a scholar or *letrado*, a "man of letters" or book learning, to validate that self. It is in this sense that critics have seen testimonio as "a fundamentally democratic and egalitarian form of narrative" (Beverley 2004, 75).

Testimonio's appeal to immediacy, presence, directness, authenticity, voice, its apparently unmediated access to subaltern others and their subjugated knowledge and vernacular languages, does not mean that it is an artless form. On the contrary, as Mary Louise Pratt (2001) suggests in her reading of the controversy about the veracity of Nobel Prize–winning Guatemalan activist Rigoberta Menchú's (1983) much-celebrated testimonio, set off by anthropologist David Stoll's (1999) book, the capacity of Menchú's testimonio "to enlighten and move metropolitan subjects does not derive from the fact that the book is the *testimonio* of a young Guatemalan indigenous woman who suffered many painful experiences" (Pratt 2001, 40). "It derives" instead "from the manner in which the text is made, its expressive power, its coarticulation of aesthetic, narrative, ethical, and emotional dimensions, its ability to evoke a history and a country, and also a cosmos" (40). Indeed, in what is the genre's most popular and widely read examples, such as Montejo's and Menchú's testimonios, the final product of *testimonio* is the result of a rhetorically mediated, negotiated collaboration among a scholar, critic, or professional literary writer, variously known as the author, editor, compiler, or *gestor* (activator or agent) of the text, who conducts interviews with the testimonial subject, transcribes, edits, organizes, and frames them, adding at times scholarly notes on content, context, and language; a speaking subject, or testimonialista, who is the direct, personal witness of a collective traumatic condition or event; and an addressee or audience who is considered metropolitan, middle class, and racially and ethnically different from the testimonial subject. And testimonio as such is the stage, locus, or site for what Jean Franco (1988) has called an intense "struggle for interpretative power" and authority across cultures, ethnicities, gender, race, and class, whose trace haunts its texts, even when it is dissimulated, attenuated, or denied by the author/editor's framing (as it is for instance in Elizabeth Burgos-Debray's editorial prologue to Menchú's testimonio), by the elimination of his or her word from the testimoniante's tale (as it is in almost all accounts), or by the complete disappearance of the author/editor from the text (as happens for instance in Elena Poniatowska's *Hasta no verte Jesús mío* [1969]). As Doris Sommer (1999) has noted, then, minoritarian or subaltern subjects in testimonio do in fact speak, but they do not do so in an unmediated manner. They speak through the creative deployment of rhetorical strategies or tropes whose inventiveness are a testament to the limits of both their agency and their ability to negotiate with hegemonic or dominant others, including their *letrado* editors and middle-class metropolitan readers.

Rather than an artless or transparently unmediated form, testimonio may be seen then as a border or *transculturated* genre, which, as Mary Louise Pratt (2001) has suggested, straddles the borders of fiction and nonfiction, literature and documentary evidence, writing and oral traditions, metropolitan and colonial or postcolonial life-worlds, canonical and hegemonic discourses and the corporal, the bodily, the unsaid, what Elzbieta Sklodowska (1996) and others have called, following Jean-Francois Lyotard (1988), the unrepresentable or "incommensurable" residue of the testimoniante's traumatic experience or "differend," and it is this border condition of testimonio that has proven most generative for U.S. Latina/o writing and cultural expressions.

While testimonial writing among Latinas/os in the United States can be traced to the testimonies of the subordinated or defeated Mexican or Californio elites, such as Eulalia Pérez de Guillén Mariné's "Una vieja y sus recuerdos" (1877), its extensive use as a genre, a trope for the production of texts in literature, history, theory, and social science research, and as an activist pedagogical method among U.S. Latinas/os dates most certainly from the development of oral history projects to reclaim the silenced histories of marginalized populations in the 1960s, the expansion of testimonio throughout the Americas under the auspices of the Cuban revolution's revisionist history, its use by Central American refugees in the North American Sanctuary movement of the 1980s (Westerman 1998), and its adoption by the American women's movement in college women's studies curricula and by Latina feminisms throughout the 1980s and 1990s.

Inspired by the new Latin American genre of testimonio, Latina writers such as Cherríe Moraga and Gloria Anzaldúa, among others, sought to articulate, in *This Bridge Called My Back* (1981) and *Borderlands / La Frontera* (1987), texts that have since become foundational for Latina/o studies, a new literature and theory that addressed the unspoken parts of their experience that both the discourses of Chicano nationalism and the American women's movement failed to express, a theory and a literature, that is, based on their embodied experience as Chicanas, women, and queer, what Moraga called in *This Bridge* "theory in the flesh" (1981, 23). Similarly, activist, community-oriented research centers such as the Centro de Estudios Puertorriqueños in New York aimed to empower Latinas through literacy projects that privileged testimonio as a self-writing, consciousness-raising, and community-building practice (Benmayor, Torruellas, and Juarbe 1997). And videos on women's health, domestic violence, ethnic identity, and AIDS, such as the ones curated by the New Museum of Contemporary Art in New York for its exhibit *Testimonio* (1993–1994), proliferated during this period. Despite a growing disappointment with what some critics have considered the increasing canonization and aestheticization of testimonio and subsequent skepticism about its political effectiveness (Nance 2006, 152–55), the 1990s and early 2000s saw the production of testimonios, especially among Latinas, that broadened the contours of Latina/o history, including Fran Leeper Buss's *Forged under the Sun: The Life of María Elena Lucas* (1993) and Mario García's story of Frances Esquibel Tywoniak, *Migrant Daughter: Coming of Age as a Mexican-American Woman* (Tywoniak and García 2000), and the emergence of new mixed genres that combined testimonio with family history, cultural criticism, photography, and music (N. Cantú 1995; Broyles-González 2003; Sandoval-Sánchez 2007).

It is also in this context of critical skepticism about the political efficacy of testimonio that a new, particularly self-conscious form of testimonio was developed by the Cuban American anthropologist Ruth Behar (1993) and the Latina Feminist Group (2001), and in my own *Queer Latino Testimonio, Keith Haring, and Juanito Xtravaganza: Hard Tails* (Cruz-Malavé 2007). In these new self-consciously crafted testimonios, instead of dissimulating the role of the editor to create an apparently unmediated, first-person, authentic narration, and muting the cultural and class differences between the testimonialista and the editor, and between the testimonialista and his or her projected metropolitan middle-class audience, the authors or editors open up the form and expose the genre's dissonance, tensions, and contradictions in order to foster the reader's self-conscious engagement with the testimonialista's tale and his or her ethical response.

Since then, testimonio has continued to expand to multiple media—video, television, and Internet—to express the especially unrepresented condition of certain Latina/o subjects, such as the return migrant (J. Flores 2009), the undocumented worker (Orner 2008), and the HIV-positive youth, as in the Internet videos of the Hispanic AIDS Forum. Retrospectively, too, testimonio has continued to grow, as critics now see its imprint on such founding texts of Latina/o studies as *Memoirs of Bernardo Vega* (1984) (M. Rodríguez 2012–2013) and Oscar Z. Acosta's *The Autobiography of a Brown Buffalo* (1972) (Hames-García 2000). We can also detect it in the pathos of the first-person accounts of traumatic experiences of authors such as the Dominican American Junot Díaz in his first book, *Drown* (1996), and in the equally compelling resistance of his characters in his award-winning novel, *The Brief Wondrous Life of Oscar Wao* (2007), to confess.

61

Theater

Lillian Manzor

Theater and theory are inextricably tied through a common etymology: both are derived from the Greek word *theastai* (θεάομαι), meaning to gaze at or contemplate. In addition to theory, theater is dramatic literature, that is, both published or unpublished texts and the staging or productions—the mise-en-scène—of those texts. But theater also includes the many artists involved in theater-making, along with spectators, theater festivals, and the communities of practice in which theater is immersed. The project of reconceiving Latina/o theater as communities of practice, like Ramón Rivera-Servera's notion of "curatorial framing," is vested in "the artists and audiences it convenes and the collective experience it creates—as the definitional locus for a theatrical practice that is as invested in cultivating Latina and Latino theater artists as it is in circulating their artistry to wider audiences" (2013, ix).

Theater within Latina/o studies has referred primarily to the theatrical and other performative practices produced by and for Latina/o communities in the United States. Traditional historiographical studies mark 1965 as the beginning of "modern" Latina/o theater. It is the year that Luis Valdez founded El Teatro Campesino on the Delano Grape Strike picket lines of Cesar Chavez's United Farmworkers Union. Along with El Teatro Campesino, other groups primarily in California and the U.S. Southwest became emblematic of El Movimiento, the Chicano Theater movement. Following the 1960s goals of El Movimiento and 1970s Nuyorican

Consciousness, analyses of Latina/o theater usually connect it to studies of identity or community politics. In addition, its origins are always set in community-based activism: this was a guerrilla theater for the times when it was still believed that "a revolution" was possible.

The historiographical teleology, based primarily on the Chicano theater movement, has three identifiable periods. The 1960s through the 1970s is the period of community-based theaters, which in the midst of sociopolitical upheavals, existed outside of major funding agencies. The 1980s and 1990s corresponds to a period of professionalization, when playwrights, that is, individuals, became more important than collectives. Some have argued that theater began to "sell out" to mainstream audiences in part due to funding from the National Endowment for the Arts (NEA), the Ford Foundation, and other institutions. As a result, Latina/o theater became less "nationalistic" by the 1990s (Rossini 2008). The beginning of the twenty-first century marks, finally, a period of "Latina/o arrival," as exemplified by Nilo Cruz's, Quiara Alegría Hudes's, and Lin-Manuel Miranda's Pulitzer Prizes, granted in 2003, 2012, and 2016, respectively.

The factual and historical inexactitudes of this periodization reflect both the challenges to and the possibilities of theater as a keyword for Latina/o studies in the twenty-first century. These challenges and possibilities include (1) the lack of and need for archival resources for Latina/o theater; (2) the lack of and need for cross-geographical, interdisciplinary, and transnational approaches to Latina/o theater studies; and (3) the need for the continued collaboration among four fundamental "actors" or cultural workers in the production of knowledge from within, for, and about Latina/o theater: the artist/researcher, the researcher/artist, the artist and researcher working together, and the participating researcher (not an artist) who produces knowledge based on the theatrical event itself (Dubatti 2014).

Latina/o theater archives are key to the preservation of this legacy, and their accessibility for research is crucial to a more nuanced historiography. The groundbreaking studies on Chicana/o theater and the early publications of anthologies began to create a canon that laid the foundation for what eventually would become Chicano/Latino and now Latina/o theater studies (Garza 1976; Huerta 1982; Kanellos 1989). However, since many of the characteristics identified are specific to Chicano theater, these do not necessarily cross the slash that brings together and demarcates Chicano and Latino. Research based on previously nonexistent collections such as the Jorge Huerta Papers at the University of California, San Diego, the Guadalupe Cultural Arts Center Records at the University of Texas, San Antonio, the Latino Theatre Initiative/Center Theatre Group Papers at the University of California, Los Angeles (UCLA) Chicano Studies Research Center Library, the Miriam Colón/Puerto Rican Traveling Theater Collection at the Hunter College Center for Puerto Rican Studies, or the INTAR Theater Records and the multiple theater collections at the University of Miami Cuban Heritage Collection demonstrates that before 1965, there was ample theatrical activity by Latinas/os in New York, Miami, and elsewhere: Miriam Colón was in René Marqués's *La Carreta* in 1953, and by 1964 she was acting in two traveling plays in Spanish directed by Osvaldo Riofrancos and produced by Joseph Papp in New York. Latina/o artists were nominated for and won important awards such as Obies since José Quintero's best director (1956), María Irene Fornes's distinguished play (1965), and El Teatro Campesino's special citation (1968). As a matter fact, between 1980 and 1999 Latinas/os won more awards than in the supposed later period of arrival.

Cross-geographical, interdisciplinary, and transnational approaches to Latina/o theater studies result in a more nuanced, comparative, and differentiated reading of our theaters. In addition, it moves theoretical discussion away from previous dichotomies such as political versus apolitical, community versus commercial, and national versus transnational. As Raphael Dalleo and Elena Machado Sáez have argued for literature, "rather than turning away from politics, contemporary Latino/a writers are renewing that political tradition by engaging with the triumphs and defeats of the past, formulating political projects that will mark our future horizons in substantial and creative ways" (2007, 7). An approach that takes funding into account, for example, proves that the differentiation between "community theater" and "professional" or "commercial theater" is inoperable for the theater produced in Spanish in Miami, New York, and Chicago during the 1960s and 1970s (Manzor and Rizk 2012). When you take into account financial support, as Jon Rossini and Patricia Ybarra (2012) have done, it is obvious that the relationship between cultural production and funding structure is extremely complicated, and that Latina/o theater does not fit neatly in the previous decade-based historiography. The National Endowment for the Arts, for example, had two major programs to which Latina/o theater companies could apply and the two established a marked distinction between theatrical practices that were community-based—these had to have an educational and social goal—from those "professional" theatrical practices that had to be measured solely by creativity and artistic standards. Interestingly enough, Latina/o theater studies followed the NEA division between "community-based" and "professional" and created a narrative in which Latina/o theater companies (operated by, for, about, and within their communities during the 1960s and 70s) began to receive funding in the early 1980s, became commercial, and started to produce for the mainstream (Rossini and Ybarra 2012). Research has demonstrated, however, that Teatro Campesino was funded by the NEA since the mid-1970s and that companies in New York—the Puerto Rican Traveling Theater and Mews Spanish Theater (Repertorio Español)—received funding since the 1960s. In Miami, the first theatrical institution to receive NEA funding (not the first Latina/o company, but the first theatrical company in the city) was Sociedad Pro Arte Grateli in 1974. Players Repertory Theater of Greater Miami, which would become the resident company of the regional Coconut Grove Playhouse, was eventually funded in 1976 and 1978 to produce work aimed at bringing the best of musical theater to a Latina/o community that had a long tradition of musical theater (Manzor and Rizk 2012). As a matter of fact, Miami predated and foreshadowed what occurred in the late 1980s and throughout the 1990s, when regional, professional theaters throughout the United States received massive funding in order to go "multicultural."

The 1990s are seen as the period when Latina/o theater begins to break away from stories about its different communities. At the same time, it is the period when we see "the emergence of a new form of transnational artistic citizenship" which, according to Rossini and Ybarra, "occurred as much because of legal reforms under neoliberalism as by an expanded consciousness in the face of said reforms" (2012, 168). Yet, collection-based research in archives and transregional approaches to theater allow us to recognize that in New York, Latina/o artists were part and parcel of the Off-Off Broadway movement and were creating stories that had a transnational artistic sensibility since at least the early 1970s (as in Manuel Martín Jr.'s *Rasputín* [1975] and *Francesco* [1973]). In Miami, much of the theater produced in Spanish by the Cuban communities since the 1960s also had a transnational artistic sensibility. As a matter of fact, that sensibility played an important role in the transformation of Miami into the "gateway of the Americas" and a global city by the end of the 1970s (Manzor 2013). Throughout the 1970s, theater programs, even those for light comedies such as *Luna de miel, 25 años después* (Martín 1979), appealed to and began to construct subliminally a Latina/o community with a cosmopolitan, primarily European, taste. Culture and creative industries, primarily those in Spanish, became an important source of economic as well as symbolic capital. Finally, it is important to remember that Teatro de la Esperanza's director Rodrigo Duarte Clark "attended the First Meeting of Latin American and Caribbean Theatre Artists in Havana in June of 1981 and along with Nuyorican theatre collective Teatro 4, Esperanza formed the East Coast-West Coast Theatre Brigade (Brigada Chicana-Latina) that went to Havana in August of 1981" (Mayer-García 2015). The ensuing exchanges between the Latinas/os of Teatro de la Esperanza and Teatro 4 and the Cubans of Teatro Escambray is another important example of transnational projects in Latina/o theater antedating the 1990s.

Theater festivals, different actors, audiences, and many other artistic and popular forms that belong to Latina/o theater as a community of practice also need to be taken into account in order to get a fuller picture of how Latina/o theatrical practices, whether in English or in Spanish, are the communities' gestures to safeguard their "home" culture, of the contradictory ways in which they inserted themselves into and transformed the cultural landscape of different cities in the United States, and of the multiple forms of dialogue in which they engage with theaters across the Americas, Europe, and other parts of the world. On the one hand, this new approach forces us to focus on a nuanced Latina/o theater history that goes beyond the Chicano theater movement and opens the stage for other Latin@s (Rizk 2009; Falconer and López 2011). On the other, it calls for a renewed acknowledgement that Chicana/o theatrical practice, community praxis, theory, and scholarship have been foundational to the field of Latina/o theater studies. Our Chicana colleagues left us a legacy of an embodied scholarly practice and praxis, a theorizing through the flesh that antedates performance studies (Moraga and Anzaldúa 1981; Alarcón 1990; Broyles-González 1994; Arrizón 1999; Gutiérrez and Núñez 2008). Their publications and productions laid the groundwork for artists and researchers working together, as well as encouraging other participating researchers to produce theater/theory and knowledge about that production. Throughout the years, many of us have redeployed Chicana strategies in our cultural work of building bridges between artistic and scholarly communities, as well as between academia and our different communities through theater and performance. Our focus on theatrical practices by women has also furthered the transgeographical approaches that moved the field from Chicana/o to Latina/o by focusing on the ways in which Latina/o theater is not anchored necessarily in one national or ethnic identity (Sandoval-Sánchez 1999; Arrizón and Manzor 2000; E. Ramírez 2000; Sandoval-Sánchez and Sternbach 2000, 2001; Svich and Marrero 2000; Ramos García 2002; C. Rodríguez 2010).

Since 2012, two parallel actions have been taking place within Latina/o theater. First, the Theater Communications Group (TCG) has curated several online salons in which Latina/o theater is part of the discussion of American and global theatrical practices (tcgcircle.org). Second, several Latina/o theater artists, propelled at first by Karen Zacarías, created the Latina/o (now Latinx) Theatre Commons (LTC) at HowlRound; this is "a fluid national platform that serves and connects diverse Latina/o theater artists throughout the United States" in order to facilitate "an ongoing national and regional arena for conversation live and online; and the production of more powerful, diverse Latina/o voices

in the American Theater" (B. Herrera 2015, 2). LTC met in 2013, created its online arm *Café Onda*, inspired the creation of several regional Latina/o theater alliances, and had its 2014 Encuentro in Los Angeles, and then its 2015 Carnaval in Chicago included a festival of Latina/o works. Both actions exemplify the present and future of Latina/o theater artistic practice and research: the need to foster the circulation of Latina/o theater artists and the analysis of the ways in which they are moving toward transethnic and transnational sociocultural formations, affects, and artistic sensibilities. Latina/o theater now is really part and parcel of the new transnational American theater. As Luis Valdez suggested at the closing of the 2013 LTC Convening, "we are the theater of New America—theater by, for and about the New Americans . . . and of the Americas" (Herrera 2015, 153).

62

Transnationalism

Ginetta E. B. Candelario

"Where are you from?" These four words, innocuous and friendly conversation starters when asked by whites of whites, are often experienced by Latinas/os in the United States not as innocent interrogations, but as thinly veiled intimations of foreignness and racial difference. Furthermore, for Latinas/os the answer is quite often far more complicated than a simple "Milwaukee" or "Mexico." What if we are from both Milwaukee and Mexico? What if we are from Milwaukee and Mexico while living in Massachusetts? Then where, indeed, are we from? Where is home now? Who are y/our people? Most important of all, where do y/our allegiances lie?

Latina/o immigrations to, migrations within, and return migrations from the United States are often the manifest or latent consequence of U.S. intervention in Latin America and the Caribbean, or as journalist Juan González (2001) put it, the "harvest of empire." That is, U.S. settler colonialism and imperialism trigger and create conditions in our heritage countries that, inevitably, make it impossible for some segment of our population to live out their lives in the countries of their birth. "We didn't cross the border; the border crossed us!" exclaimed Chicanos organizing against Anglo-American nativist racisms (Acuña 1987). Whether for putatively economic reasons, purportedly political reasons, or more often than not, some combination of geopolitical and economic forces, Latinas/os are driven to establish communities in the United States. "We're here because you were there" is thus a leitmotif of Latina/o migrations. Both

proximity and common—if ironic—patterns of colonial subjects' migrations to the metropole explain why Latinas/os end up in what José Martí called the "belly of the beast" that is the United States empire.

Not long after Martí's aphorism, social critic Randolph S. Bourne coined the term "*trans*-nationalism" in 1916 (my emphasis). Bourne called upon his fellow Americans to abandon the nationalist nativism that fueled the anti-immigrant violence and ideology of his day. As an alternative, he argued for embracing a cosmopolitan internationalism, legalizing dual citizenship, and allowing the "free and mobile passage of the immigrant between America and his native land" without prejudice. Bourne was nonetheless a man of his times; he considered U.S. society culturally superior to sending societies that had presumptively "inferior civilizations" (1916, 88) and reassured his countrymen that most (if not all) of the immigrants' "baser" cultural elements would eventually melt away (1916, 94). Still, he rejected the melting pot, Anglo-conformist model of assimilation. Instead, he argued that "America [was] coming to be, not a nationality but a trans-nationality, a weaving back and forth, with other lands, of many threads of all sizes and colors." For Bourne, "trans-nationalism" was "a trans-nationality of all the nations," "a wholly international nation" (1916, 95–96). In this formulation, transnationalism required tolerance and respect for diversity, and promised a cultural smorgasbord prepared in Israel Zangwill's (1908) famous "melting pot," which would necessarily expand yet satisfy the American palate. Given that the (im)migrants Bourne was concerned with were predominantly European, the famous huddled masses of Emma Lazarus's (2002) "New Colossus," this was largely a question of ethnic assimilation, rather than one of political, civil, and human rights.

By contrast, when cultural anthropologists Nina Glick Schiller, Linda Basch, and Cristina Blanc-Szanton (1992) re-coined the term "transnationalism" in the early 1990s, not only were they seemingly unaware of Bourne's earlier formulation, but they were describing and advocating a critical understanding of the superficially similar yet fundamentally different experiences of late twentieth-century migrants and migrations from what was once the third world. Whereas earlier immigrants came predominantly from Western and Southern Europe because of internal and continental dynamics, late twentieth-century immigrants come predominantly from "the global South"—Latin America and the Caribbean, Africa, Asia—from countries that Vijay Prashad (2013) has aptly denominated *The Poorer Nations* produced by colonialism, chattel slavery, and imperialism.

While early and late twentieth-century immigrants alike emigrated largely due to political and economic forces produced by industrial and finance capitalism's intensifying globalization, unlike their European predecessors, the "new immigrants" come increasingly from the United States' colonies, neocolonies, and societies unsettled by U.S. interventionism, particularly during the Cold War period. Moreover, despite the end of the Cold War, U.S. interventionism not only continues but is now amplified by international and extranational organizations such as the International Monetary Fund (IMF) and the World Bank. Emigration continues apace, and chain migration replenishes immigrant communities and families with new members so that first, second, third generation, and beyond interact regularly. Therefore, this new transnationalism is not simply a product of empire, but is an active, creative, and purposeful response to its fallout (Levitt and Khagram 2008).

While European immigrants were subject to nativist discrimination in policy, politics, and practice, they nonetheless were incorporated into white society. That is, although culture shock and nativism fostered transnational behaviors and identities in the first immigrant generation, by the second and third U.S.-born generation, those communities became increasingly less transnational, less ethnic, and more unhyphenated American. Theirs was a transnationalism fueled on the sending side by heritage ties and on the U.S. side by ethnocentrism, which eventually faded as their children and grandchildren were assimilated into whiteness. By contrast, for Latin American and Caribbean immigrants, ethnocentricism is coupled with racism not only for the first generation, but into the second and third generation as well. Considered both perpetually foreign and non-white, Latinas/os, by implication, are not assimilable as a group, even if "white" Latinas/os can assimilate individually.

If "transnationalism is a process by which migrants, through their daily life activities and social, economic, and political relations, create social fields that cross national boundaries" (Schiller, Basch, and Blanc-Szanton 1992, 23), then Latinas/os are citizens of those social fields because neither their nations nor their states have fully lived up to their respective promises. One of the earliest contemporary examples of the term "transnational" being used to describe—if not exactly theorize—the lived experiences of and relationships sustained between Latina/o emigrants and those who stayed in place was Eugenia Georges's (1990) book on how Dominican emigrants who migrated from rural to urban communities in their homelands and then from those urban centers to urban centers abroad such as New York City increasingly began to "take actions, make decisions, and develop subjectivities and identities embedded in networks of relationships that connect them simultaneously in two or more nation-states" (Basch, Schiller, and Szanton Blanc 1994, 8). They created and sustained a "single social field" of *dominicanidades*.

A single social field is a deterritorialized "space" between two or more nation-states, where people live in both at once, "speaking two languages, having homes in two countries, and making a living through continuous regular contact across national borders" (Portes,

Guarnizo, and Landolt 1999, 217). At the individual level, "livin' *la vida loca!*" (Child and Rosa 1999) transnationally requires both the economic resources (money) and the legal-juridical capacity (passport, residency, citizenship) to move freely, which only some have. At the community level, however, the fact that the phenomenon exists and is enacted by more highly resourced community members has effects and implications for the community overall. Only some may be travelers, but the social field as a whole is affected by the wake of their travels.

As "transmigrants," rather than simply "immigrants" or "migrants," Latinas/os living transnationally sustain an ongoing interest in and commitment to both their heritage societies and their current ones, so they make a life that transcends borders and oceans through their interests, affiliations, and actions. The actions include participating in the economies of several countries, whether paying taxes, privately financing public infrastructure development, sending person-to-person money transfers, or formally and informally importing and exporting consumer goods. They engage in sundry political behaviors, from securing dual citizenship where possible and voting in elections, to holding public office, to lobbying public officials and organizing in both countries, to claiming a stake in the foreign affairs of both nations. They trade in "social remittances," such as values and ideas that travel across the immigrant's societies and cultural production, in transformations of existing material culture and practices such as food, music, and dance, or the creation of new cultural products that are "of both places" (Levitt and Khagram 2008). And they communicate regularly and routinely across the geographical spans.

Since immigrants and migrants to the United States did most if not all of these things at the turn of the twentieth century—and indeed recent historiography of that period routinely deploys a transnational theory to frame the narrative—what, beyond the racial formation issue,

is distinctive about the late twentieth- and early twenty-first-century transnationalism of Latinas/os? Some scholars have argued that the difference lies in the "time and space compression" afforded by technological innovations of our era, which in turn have allowed for both more extensive and more intensive linking behaviors that create a more generalized transnational Latina/o social field. Low-cost communications technologies facilitate regular and increasingly routine contact with family "back home"; rather than the weekly or monthly phone call or "snail mail" letters, now there's instant dialogic communications. Whether via email, talking or texting, WhatsApp©, Skype©, Facebook©, Instagram© or Twitter©, it is possible instantly and constantly to know the details of daily life *allá* as well as *aquí*. Even the now quaint phone call can happen anywhere and anytime, thanks to the proliferation of cell phones throughout the hemisphere. Likewise, money transfers—quite often the most material form of communicating on-going connections and kinship ties—can happen with a few clicks of a keyboard or taps on an app.

Another distinguishing factor for Latina/o transnationalism and historically emerging transnationalism is proximity to the heritage countries. Simply stated, we are much closer geographically to our parents and grandparents' homelands than earlier immigrants from Europe or contemporary immigrants from Africa and Asia. And for those whose origins lie in Mexico, Central America, or South America, it is possible to rely solely or primarily on overland travel between destination points. But proximity alone does not account for the retention of active ties to the homeland and heritage country for the second and third generations.

I would argue further that the insistence on claiming and sustaining multiple ethno-racial and "national" identities, even when those identities are supposedly contradictory or mutually exclusive, as well as the refusal to hyphenate or even to choose among the available options, is also a product of twenty-first-century transnationalism. The 1998 plebiscite on the political status question in Puerto Rico yielded "None of the above" as the most preferred option over the Current Territory Status, Free Association, Statehood, and Independence vis-à-vis the United States (Negrón-Muntaner 2007); Latinas/os consistently choose "Other" on the U.S. census race question (Cobas, Duany, and Feagin 2009); and Latina/o spoken word performers such as Elizabeth Acevedo claim to be 100 percent of all their heritages at once.

In essence, transnationalism posits membership and belonging as a multilocal process and possibility. Not only do immigrants get to retain their "places" in their countries of origin while establishing a place in the new country, but their children and grandchildren born elsewhere get to claim a place in their heritage countries as well. As Peter Kivisto indicates, "Transnational migrants forge their sense of identity and their community, not out of a loss or mere replication, but as something that is at once new and familiar—a *bricolage* constructed of cultural elements from both the homeland and the receiving nation" (2001, 568).

Likewise, transnationalism in Latina/o studies implies a bricolage of ethnic studies and area studies, incorporating questions of assimilation and incorporation into U.S. civil society and culture, questions of maintenance of ties of heritage homelands as well as questions about U.S. foreign policy in the Americas and domestic politics in the heritage countries. As Silvio Torres-Saillant tells us, "The burden of citizenship usually weighs heavier for members of diasporic communities than for the regular citizenry, since they have more than one society to improve. Among ethnic minorities in the United States, Latinos face this civil overload with distinct acuity" (2005, 281). *Y en fín*, the empire always strikes back, transnationally if not quite yet intergalactically.

63

White

Julie A. Dowling

Whiteness in the United States is a social identity category that developed historically as a way of constructing boundaries to exclude certain groups from economic and political rights. Indeed, one had to be white in order to become a citizen, own property, and vote in this country (Haney López 1996). This history of racial exclusion in the United States is often depicted in popular culture as a division between European Americans and African Americans. Indeed, most Americans are quite familiar with pictures of separate drinking fountains and other images of racial segregation involving whites and blacks, but are frequently less aware that Latinas/os have an extensive history of racialization and exclusion in this country. In the Southwest, Mexican Americans faced similar practices of segregation, including being prohibited from living in certain areas and being barred from going to restaurants, schools, or public recreational facilities that were for "whites only" (Montejano 1987; Almaguer 1994). These practices extended beyond the Southwest, as Latinas/os on the East Coast and in the Midwest also faced discrimination in housing and other venues. In Chicago, for example, Mexican Americans and Puerto Ricans faced restrictive housing covenants that forbade them from living in some white neighborhoods (Betancur 1996).

Yet, while Latinas/os experienced these aspects of segregation that were similar to African Americans, the history of the racial classification of Latinas/os in relation to whiteness differs significantly from this group in that Latinas/os have been continually imagined as both inside and outside the category of "white," often legally defined as white while socially treated as non-white (Gómez 2007). For Mexican Americans specifically, the origins of this tenuous relationship to whiteness can be traced to the Treaty of Guadalupe Hidalgo in 1848. After the U.S. defeat of Mexico, the treaty stipulated that the United States would acquire a substantial portion of Mexico's land, including what is now the U.S. Southwest. In the treaty, the United States agreed to treat those Mexicans currently residing in the colonized territory as U.S. citizens. At the time, however, citizenship in the United States was afforded only to whites; hence, the treaty granted Mexican Americans the legal rights of whiteness. But the promises of the treaty were not honored, and Mexican Americans were typically regarded as non-white; they lost their land and livelihood; and a lengthy history of discrimination in education, housing, employment, and political participation ensued (Montejano 1987; Almaguer 1994; Foley 1997; Menchaca 2001; Gómez 2007).

Mexican Americans fought this treatment on multiple fronts including legal challenges against segregation and exclusion. A common strategy in such arguments for integration was the reliance on this legal definition of Mexican Americans as white, often referencing the Treaty of Guadalupe Hidalgo or emphasizing the Spanish ancestry of Mexican people. The League of United Latin Americans Citizens (LULAC), formed in Texas in 1929, frequently put forth this argument for whiteness in its fight against discrimination. LULAC even successfully petitioned for having a "Mexican" race removed from the U.S. census in 1930, arguing against the racial classification of Mexicans as being separate from whites (Foley 1998). But while some of these attempts at claiming whiteness were successful, social definitions of Mexican Americans as non-white prevailed, and notions of cultural or linguistic inferiority were often used to justify continued school segregation, for example, even when courts ruled against the separation of Mexican Americans from other "whites" (Montejano 1987; Foley 1998; Gómez 2007).

While claims to whiteness dominated much of the early rhetoric of Mexican American civil rights cases, there were many who disagreed with this strategy (Márquez 2003). Legal whiteness certainly posed challenges in the struggle for civil rights as it made claiming "racial" discrimination more difficult. For example, when Mexican Americans argued that a trial with an all-white jury represented a breach of their civil right to a jury of their peers, the legal definition of Mexicans Americans as white complicated their arguments (Gross 2003; Sheridan 2003). Moreover, the strategy of asking to be allowed to attend the white school or facility because they too are white did not challenge the underlying issue of white superiority, manifested in the continuing oppression of African Americans and other racialized groups.

Many Latinas/os would later abandon these claims to whiteness in favor of embracing pride in their Indigenous or mestizo roots. While these identity claims existed in some organizing efforts in the early twentieth century, during the 1960s and 1970s, calls for "brown power" and pride in racial difference became the central platform for racial justice organizing. The United Farm Workers and La Raza Unida political party, among others, implored Mexican Americans to assert their racial identity, working-class status, and cultural difference in the fight for economic and political recognition and power (Márquez 2003).

This history of these two competing strategies for civil rights organizing—one focused on claims to whiteness and the other on assertions of racial otherness—still influence constructions of Latina/o racial identity today as the ambiguous racial position of Latinas/os remains highly contested. According to the U.S. government, Latinas/os are currently considered an ethnic or cultural group composed of persons who may be of any "race." No Latina/o racial option has been on the census form since 1930, when the "Mexican" racial option was used for the first and only time. But since 1980, the U.S. Census Bureau has enumerated Latinas/os on all census forms by including a "Latino, Hispanic, or Spanish" ethnicity question that is separate from the race question. Approximately half of Latinas/os mark "white" for their race on the census, while most of the remaining half check "some other race" and write in a Latina/o identifier such as Latino/Hispanic, Mexican, or Puerto Rican. Additionally, small percentages of Latinas/os check black, American Indian, or Asian.

While some scholars have interpreted these Latina/o racial responses on the census as reflective of skin color and/or levels of assimilation (Denton and Massey 1989; Yancey 2003), interview research with Latinas/os reveals that Latina/o understandings of whiteness and racial otherness are far more complex than this. For example, in sociologist Clara E. Rodriguez's (2000) interviews with Latinas/os, primarily Puerto Ricans and Ecuadorians in New York, she found her respondents identified as racially "other" largely due to their perception of race as a cultural or political identity. She argues that this differs from the dominant narrative of race in the United States, which focuses primarily on notions of biology and skin color. Similarly, additional research on Puerto Ricans and Dominicans in New York has found that Latinas/os identified racially on the census in ways that did not match their skin color or experiences with discrimination (Roth 2010). Interviews with Mexican Americans in Texas further reveal that rather than reflecting skin color, "white" racial responses on the

census are more closely linked to ideologies of race and how the respondents interpreted their experiences with discrimination. Much like those who claimed whiteness to defend against discrimination in the past, Mexican Americans in Texas currently use whiteness defensively in trying to assert their Americanness in the face of racial profiling (Dowling 2014).

Yet, despite evidence that white racial responses on the census may not mean that Latinas/os either see themselves as white or are seen by others as white, these responses have continually been interpreted as evidence that Latinas/os are indeed becoming white and are no longer facing discrimination. Indeed, a 2014 *New York Times* piece that used census data to argue that Latinas/os are assimilating into whiteness sparked a firestorm of public debate in the media (Cohn 2014; Demby 2014). And questions regarding the racial status of Latinas/os have continued as additional cases in which Latinas/os have been defined as white for political purposes emerge.

In 2015, a controversy erupted in Texas as evidence was presented that Texas police officers code Latinas/os as "white" in traffic stops instead of as "Hispanic," thus evading possible charges of racial profiling (Collister and Ellis 2015). While the state of Texas includes a "Hispanic" option among race/ethnicity options on traffic tickets, the federal definition of Latinos as not being a separate racial group has allowed officers to feel justified in grouping them with whites. And without accurate numbers of how many Latinas/os are stopped and ticketed, documenting discrimination is particularly challenging. This situation highlights how the ambiguous racial position of Latinas/os in relation to whiteness can have adverse consequences for civil rights monitoring and enforcement.

Interestingly, in a 2016 case, a U.S. federal court ruled that Latinas/os constitute a racial group for the purposes of discrimination lawsuits. The twist in the case is that it is not a Latina/o who was claiming the discrimination. The case involved an Italian American, Christopher Barrella, who claimed he was passed up for promotion to police chief because the mayor appointed a less qualified Latino officer for the position. The defense argued that Latinos are not even a racial group so what happened cannot be racial discrimination against the white man because they are both "white." The federal court decided that Latinos are a racial group and that the white officer was indeed subjected to racial discrimination (Eustachewich 2016). This outcome is emblematic of how the courts use the racial versus ethnic classification in differing ways historically and currently—often to the detriment of Latinas/os. In the Texas example, "Latinos are white" is used to justify not monitoring discrimination against them. And yet, in this case "Latinos are not white" is used to document alleged discrimination against whites.

Given the legacy of and continued presence of discrimination, all of this begs the question, Should Latinas/os be counted as a "race" rather than a potentially white "ethnic" group? There have indeed been numerous proposals to create a "Latino/Hispanic" race, which have been considered by the U.S. Census Bureau over the years (C. Rodriguez 2000). However, there are two very important concerns with doing so. First, while Latinas/os are most often associated with a "brown" skin color, there are Latinas/os whose ancestry is primarily European, African, or Asian and who thus do not fit this image. If a Latino racial option were present, how would an Afro-Dominican identify racially, for example—as black, Latino or both? And how would a white Cuban respond? And if all Latinas/os identify solely with the Latino racial option, how would we examine important differences among Latinas/os such as how black or Indigenous Latinas/os fare economically compared to other Latinas/os? Second, considering that some Latinas/os identify defensively as white, there have been

concerns that making Latino a race might lead to an undercount as some would not check the box if it is a racial option because they are resisting the stigma attached to being defined as non-white. While these are both very valid points that challenge a proposed Latino racial option, the current over-inflation of the number of "white" Latinas/os in the census and the use of these numbers to dismiss continued discrimination against Latinas/os are grave concerns many have with the current racial options (Dowling 2014).

Recent experimental testing by the U.S. Census Bureau may have created an option that could both validate the racialized experiences many Latinas/os have while allowing for identification with other racial options such as white, black, or Asian. This combined race and ethnicity question allows respondents to "check all that apply" and includes options for Latino/Hispanic origin alongside various racial groups. Those who identify solely as Latino may do so without being asked to fill out a separate racial question, and those who identify as black, white, or any other racial group may do so in combination with Latino. Using this format, the number of "white" Latinas/os dropped significantly from half of Latinas/os to only 9–16 percent. Moreover, when interviewed, these white Latinas/os actually identified as such in their daily lives and not only as a defensive strategy on the form, meaning the data from the this new question format yielded a better count of white Latinas/os (Compton et al. 2012).

In conclusion, historically and currently, whiteness has been a strategy for gaining access while at the same time a detriment to making civil rights claims. We must work to balance the reality of varied racial experiences among Latinas/os with the dominant construction and treatment of Latinas/os as "brown" racial "others." The persistence of racial stereotyping and discrimination against Latinas/os still casts a shadow on the ability of Latinas/os to enter the category of whiteness in the United States.

Bibliography

Abarca, Meredith E. *Voices in the Kitchen: Views of Food and the World from Working-Class Mexican and Mexican American Women*. College Station: Texas A&M University Press, 2006.

———. "Culinary Encounters in Latino/a Literature." In *Routledge Companion to Latino/a Literature*, edited by Suzanne Bost and Frances R. Aparicio, 251–60. New York: Routledge, 2014.

Abascal, Maria. "Tu Casa, Mi Casa: Naturalization and Belonging among Latino Immigrants." *International Migration Review* 49, no. 3 (2015): 1–32.

Abrego, Leisy J. *Sacrificing Families: Navigating Laws, Labor, and Love across Borders*. Stanford, CA: Stanford University Press, 2014.

Ackerman, Edwin. "'What Part of Illegal Don't You Understand?' Bureaucracy and Civil Society in the Shaping of Illegality." *Ethnic and Racial Studies* 37, no. 2 (2012): 1–23.

Acosta, Katie L. *Amigas y Amantes: Sexually Nonconforming Latinas Negotiate Family*. New Brunswick, NJ: Rutgers University Press, 2013.

Acosta, Oscar Zeta. *The Autobiography of a Brown Buffalo*. San Francisco: Straight Arrow Books, 1972.

Acosta-Belén, Edna, and Carlos E. Santiago. *Puerto Ricans in the United States: A Contemporary Portrait*. Boulder, CO: Lynne Rienner, 2006.

Acuña, Rodolfo F. *Occupied America: A History of Chicanos*. New York: Harper Collins, 1987.

———. *The Making of Chicana/o Studies in the Trenches of Academe*. Piscataway, NJ: Rutgers University Press, 2011.

Affigne, Tony, Evelyn Hu-DeHart, and Marion Orr, eds. *Latino Politics en Ciencia Politica: The Search for Latino Identity and Racial Consciousness*. New York: New York University Press, 2014.

Agamben, Giorgio. *Homo Sacer: Sovereign Power and Bare Life*. Translated by Daniel Heller-Roazen. Stanford, CA: Stanford University Press, 1998.

Agius Vallejo, Jody. *Barrios to Burbs: The Making of the Mexican American Middle Class*. Stanford, CA: Stanford University Press, 2012a.

———. "Socially Mobile Mexican Americans and the Minority Culture of Mobility." *American Behavioral Scientist* 46 (2012b): 666–81.

Aguirre Beltrán, Gonzalo. *La población negra en México*. Mexico City: Fondo de Cultura Económica, 1972.

Aikau, Hokulani K. "Indigeneity in the Diaspora: The Case of Native Hawaiians in Iosepa, Utah." *American Quarterly* 62 (2010): 477–500.

Alarcón, Norma. "The Theoretical Subject(s) of *This Bridge Called My Back and Anglo-American Feminism*." In *Making Face, Making Soul / Haciendo Caras: Creative and Critical Perspectives by Women of Color*, edited by Gloria Anzaldúa, 356–69. San Francisco: Aunt Lute Books, 1990.

———, ed. *Chicana Critical Issues*. Berkeley, CA: Third Woman Press, 1993.

———. "Anzaldúa's Frontera: Inscribing Gynetics." In *Displacement, Diaspora, and Geographies of Identity*, edited by Smadar Lavie and Ted Swedenbug, 41–54. Durham, NC: Duke University Press, 1996.

———. "Anzaldúa's Frontera: Inscribing Gynetics." In *Decolonial Voices: Chicana and Chicano Cultural Studies in the 21st Century*, edited by Arturo J. Aldama and Naomi H. Quiñonez, 113–28. Bloomington: Indiana University Press, 2002.

Alba, Richard, and Victor Nee. "Assimilation." In *Blackwell Encyclopedia of Sociology*, vol. 1, edited by George Ritzer, 191–96. Malden: Blackwell, 2007.

Alberdi, Juan Bautista. *Bases y puntos de partida para la reorganización política de la República Argentina*. Buenos Aires: Editorial Universitaria, 1966.

Alberto, Lourdes. "Topographies of Indigenism: Mexico, Decolonial Indigenism, and the Chicana Transnational Subject in Ana Castillo's *Mixquiahuala Letters*." In *Comparative Indigeneities: Towards a Hemispheric Approach*, edited by M. Bianet Castellanos, Lourdes Gutiérrez Nájera, and Arturo J. Aldama, 38–52. Tucson: University of Arizona Press, 2012.

———. *Mexican American Indigeneities*. New York: New York University Press, forthcoming.

Alcoff, Linda Martín. "Latino vs. Hispanic: The Politics of Ethnic Names." *Philosophy and Social Criticism* 31, no. 4 (2005): 395–407.

Aldama, Frederick Luis. *Your Brain on Latino Comics: From Gus Arriola to Los Bros Hernandez*. Austin: University of Texas Press, 2009.

——. *The Routledge Concise History of Latino/a Literature*. New York: Routledge, 2013.

——, ed. *Critical Approaches to the Films of Robert Rodriguez*. Austin: University of Texas Press, 2015a.

——, ed. *Latino/a Literature in the Classroom: Twenty-First-Century Approaches to Teaching*. New York: Routledge, 2015b.

——. *Latinx Comic Book Storytelling: An Odyssey by Interview*. San Diego, CA: San Diego State University Press, 2016.

Alemán, Jesse. "Authenticity, Autobiography, and Identity: *The Woman in Battle* as a Civil War Narrative." In *The Woman in Battle: The Civil War Narrative of Loreta Janeta Velazquez, Cuban Woman and Confederate Soldier*, by Loreta Janeta Velazques, ix–xvi. Madison: University of Wisconsin Press, 2003.

Alexander, Michelle. *The New Jim Crow: Mass Incarceration in the Age of Colorblindness*. New York: New Press, 2012.

Allatson, Paul. *Latino Dreams: Transcultural Traffic and the U.S. National Imaginary*. Amsterdam: Rodopi, 2002.

——. *Key Terms in Latino/a Cultural and Literary Studies*. Malden: Blackwell, 2007.

Almaguer, Tomás. "Ideological Distortions in Recent Chicano Historiography: The Internal Model and Chicano Historical Interpretation." *Aztlán* 18, no. 1 (1989): 7–28.

——. *Racial Faultlines: The Historical Origins of White Supremacy in California*. Berkeley: University of California Press, 1994.

Almeida, Joselyn M. *Reimagining the Transatlantic, 1780–1890*. Burlington, VT: Ashgate, 2011.

Alonso, Ana M. "Sovereignty, the Spatial Politics of Security, and Gender: Looking North and South from the U.S.-Mexico Border." In *State Formation: Anthropological Perspectives*, edited by Christian Krohn-Hansen and Knut G. Nustad, 27–52. London: Pluto Press, 2005.

Alurista. *Floricanto en Aztlán*. Los Angeles: Chicano Studies Research Center, 1971.

——. "Cultural Nationalism and Xicano Literature during the Decade of 1965–1975." *MELUS* 8, no. 2 (1981): 22–34.

Alvarado, Joel, and Charles Jaret. *Building Black-Brown Coalitions in the Southeast: Four African American-Latino Collaborations*. Atlanta, GA: Southern Regional Council, 2009.

Alvarado, Karina Oliva. "An Interdisciplinary Reading of Chicana/o and (U.S.) Central American Cross-Cultural Narratives." *Latino Studies* 11, no. 3 (2013): 366–87.

Alvarez, Alicia. "Call for Fairness: The Historical and Continuing Exclusion of Latinos from Public Housing in Chicago." *Berkeley La Raza Law Journal* 9 (1996): 155–75.

Alvarez, Luis. *The Power of the Zoot: Youth Culture and Resistance during World War II*. Berkeley: University of California Press, 2009.

Alvarez, R. Michael, and Tara L. Butterfield. "The Resurgence of Nativism in California? The Case of Proposition 187 and Illegal Immigration." *Social Science Quarterly* 81, no. 1 (2000) 167–79.

Álvarez, Sonia, Evelina Dagnino, and Arturo Escobar. *Cultures of Politics, Politics of Culture: Re-Visioning Latin American Social Movements*. Boulder, CO: Westview Press, 1998.

Amador, José. *Medicine and Nation-Building in the Americas, 1870–1940*. Nashville, TN: Vanderbilt University Press, 2014.

Amaya, Hector. *Citizenship Excess: Latino/as, Media, and the Nation*. New York: New York University Press, 2013.

American Association of University Women. *The Simple Truth about the Gender Pay Gap*. Washington, DC: American Association of University Women, Breaking through Barriers for Women and Girls, 2017.

American Immigration Council. "Extremists Hijack Immigration Debate: Increased Reports of Hate Crimes and Discrimination Aimed at U.S.- and Foreign-Born Latinos." Washington, DC: Immigration Policy Center, 2008. www.americanimmigrationcouncil.org.

——. "An Immigration Stimulus: The Economic Benefits of a Legalization Program." Washington, DC: Immigration Policy Center, 2013. www.americanimmigrationcouncil.org.

American Psychiatric Association. *Diagnostic and Statistical Manual of Mental Disorders: DSM-5*. Arlington, VA: American Psychiatric Publishing, 2013.

Anaya, Rudolfo A., and Francisco A. Lomelí, eds. *Aztlán: Essays on the Chicano Homeland*. Albuquerque, NM: University of New Mexico Press, 1991.

Anderson, Benedict. *Imagined Communities: Reflections on the Origin and Spread of Nationalism*. London: Verso, 1983.

Anner, Mark S. *Solidarity Transformed: Labor Responses to Globalization and Crisis in Latin America*. Ithaca, NY: Cornell University Press, 2011.

Annino, Antonio, and François-Xavier Guerra. *Inventando la nación: Iberoamérica, Siglo XIX*. Mexico City: Fondo de Cultura Económica, 2003.

Anzaldúa, Gloria E. *Borderlands / La Frontera: The New Mestiza*. San Francisco: Aunt Lute Books, 1987.

——, ed. *Making Face, Making Soul / Haciendo Caras: Creative and Critical Perspectives by Women of Color*. San Francisco: Aunt Lute Books, 1990.

———. *Borderlands / La Frontera: The New Mestiza*, 3rd ed. San Francisco: Aunt Lute Books, 2007.

Anzaldúa, Gloria E., and AnaLouise Keating, ed. *This Bridge We Call Home: Radical Visions for Transformation*. New York: Routledge, 2002.

Aparicio, Frances R. "La vida es un Spanglish disparatero: Bilingualism in Nuyorican Poetry." In *European Perspectives on Hispanic Literature of the United States*, edited by Genevieve Fabre, 147–60. Houston: Arte Público Press, 1988.

———. *Listening to Salsa: Gender, Latin Popular Music, and Puerto Rican Cultures*. Middletown, CT: Wesleyan University Press, 1998.

———. "The Blackness of Sugar: Celia Cruz and the Performance of (Trans)Nationalism." *Cultural Studies* 13, no. 2 (1999a): 223–36.

———. "Reading the 'Latino' in Latino Studies: Toward Re-Imagining Our Academic Location." *Discourse* 21, no. 3 (1999b): 3–18.

———. "La Lupe, La India, and Celia: Toward a Feminist Genealogy of Salsa Music." In *Situating Salsa: Global Markets and Local Meaning in Latin Popular Music*, edited by Lise Waxer, 135–160. New York: Routledge, 2002.

———. "Jennifer as Selena: Rethinking Latinidad in Media and Popular Culture." *Latino Studies* 1, no. 1 (2003a): 90–105.

———. "Latino Cultural Studies." Interview with Juan Zevallos Aguilar. Translated by Dascha Inciarte and Carolyn Sedway. In *Critical Latin American and Latino Studies*, edited by Juan Poblete, 3–31. Minneapolis: University of Minnesota Press, 2003b.

———. "(Re)constructing Latinidad: The Challenge of Latina/o Studies." In *A Companion to Latina/o Studies*, edited by Juan Flores and Renato Rosaldo, 39–48. Malden: Blackwell, 2007.

———. "Embodied Latinidad: Narrating Intralatino/a Lives in Chicago." Unpublished manuscript, 2014.

Aparicio, Frances R., and Susana Chávez-Silverman, eds. *Tropicalizations: Transcultural Representations of Latinidad*. Hanover, NH: Dartmouth College, University Press of New England, 1997.

Aparicio, Frances R., and Cándida Jáquez, eds., with María Elena Cepeda. *Musical Migrations: Transnationalism and Cultural Hybridity in Latin/o America*. New York: St. Martin's Press, 2003.

Aponte, Edwin David. *¡Santo! Varieties of Latino/a Spirituality*. Maryknoll, NY: Orbis Books, 2012.

Appadurai, Arjun. *Modernity at Large: Cultural Dimensions of Globalization*. Minneapolis: University of Minnesota Press, 1996.

Apuzzo, Matt. "Dylann Roof, Charleston Shooting Suspect, Is Indicted on Federal Hate Crime Charges." *New York Times*, July 22, 2015. www.nytimes.com.

Aquino, María Pilar. "Latina Feminist Theology: Central Features." In *A Reader in Latina Feminist Theology: Religion and Justice*, edited by María Pilar Aquino, Daisy L. Machado, and Jeanette Rodríguez, 133–60. Austin: University of Texas Press, 2002.

Aragón, Francisco, ed. *The Wind Shifts: New Latino Poetry*. Tucson: University of Arizona Press, 2007.

Arana, Marie. *American Chica: Two Worlds, One Childhood*. New York: Delta Trade, 2001.

Arciniegas, Germán. *La biografía del Caribe*. 1945. 9th ed. Buenos Aires: Editorial Sudamericana, 1966.

———. *Caribbean, Sea of the New World*. Translated by Harriet de Onís. New York: Alfred A. Knopf, 1946.

———. *Why America? 500 Years of a Name: The Life and Times of Amerigo Vespucci*. Translated by Harriet de Onís. Bogotá: Villegas Editores, 2002.

Arellano, Gustavo. *Taco USA: How Mexican Food Conquered America*. New York: Scribner, 2013.

Arias, Arturo. "Central American-Americans: Invisibility, Power and Representation in the US Latino World." *Latino Studies* 1, no.1 (2003): 168–87.

Arias, Arturo, and Claudia Milian. "U.S. Central Americans: Representations, Agency and Communities." *Latino Studies* 11, no. 2 (2013): 131–49.

Arizona v. United States. U.S. Supreme Court. 567 U.S. (2012). https://supreme.justia.com.

Armas, José. *La Familia de La Raza*. Self-published, 1972.

Armbruster, Ralph, Kim Geron, and Edna Bonacich. "The Assault on California Immigrants: The Politics of Proposition 187." *International Journal of Urban and Regional Research* 19, no. 4 (1995): 655–64.

Arredondo, Gabriela. *Mexican Chicago: Race, Identity and Nation, 1916–1939*. Urbana: University of Illinois Press, 2008.

Arrizón, Alicia. *Latina Performance: Traversing the Stage*. Bloomington: Indiana University Press, 1999.

———. *Queering Mestizaje: Transculturation and Performance*. Ann Arbor: University of Michigan Press, 2006.

Arrizón, Alicia, and Lillian Manzor, eds. *Latinas on Stage: Practice and Theory*. Berkeley, CA: Third Woman Press, 2000.

Artenstein, Isaac, dir. *Ballad of an Unsung Hero*. 1984. Produced and written by Paul Espinosa. New York: Cinema Guild, 2006.

———, dir. *Break of Dawn*. 1988. Los Angeles, CA: Vanguard Cinema, 2002.

Artistic Research. *Texte Zur Kunst* 82 (June 2011). www.textezurkunst.de.

Asencio, Marysol, ed. *Latina/o Sexualities: Probing Powers, Passions, Practices, and Policies*. New Brunswick, NJ: Rutgers University Press, 2009a.

——. "Migrant Puerto Rican Lesbians Negotiating Gender, Sexuality, and Ethnonationality." *National Women's Studies Association Journal* 21, no. 3 (2009b): 1–23.

Avilés-Santiago, Manuel. *Puerto Rican Soldiers and Second-Class Citizenship: Representations in Media*. New York: Palgrave Macmillan, 2014.

Babín, María Teresa, and Stan Steiner, eds. *Borinquen: An Anthology of Puerto Rican Literature*. New York: Knopf, 1974.

Baca Zinn, Maxine. "Political Familism: Toward Sex Role Equality in Chicano Families." *Aztlán* 6, no. 1 (1975): 13–26.

Bada, Xóchitl, Jonathan Fox, and Andrew Selee, eds. *Invisible No More: Mexican Migrant Civic Participation in the United States*. Washington, DC: Woodrow Wilson Center Mexico Institute, 2006.

Bada, Xóchitl, and Shannon Gleeson. "A New Approach to Migrant Labor Rights Enforcement: The Crisis of Undocumented Worker Abuse and Mexican Consular Advocacy in the United States." *Labor Studies Journal* 40, no. 1 (2015): 32–53.

"Background: Development of Directive 15, Appendix." June 9, 1994. www.whitehouse.gov/omb/fedreg_notice_15 (site discontinued).

Báez, Jillian M. "Mexican (American) Women Talk Back: Audience Responses to Latinidad in US Advertising." In *Latina/o Communication Studies Today*, edited by Angharad N. Valdivia, 257–81. New York: Peter Lang, 2008.

Bailey, Benjamin. "Dominican-American Ethnic/Racial Identities and United States Social Categories." *International Migration Review* 35, no. 3 (2001): 677–708.

Baker-Cristales, Beth. "Mediated Resistance: The Construction of Neoliberal Citizenship in the Immigrant Rights Movement." *Latino Studies* 7, no. 1 (2009): 60–82.

Balibar, Étienne. "What We Owe to the Sans-Papiers." In *Social Insecurity*, edited by Len Guenther and Cornelius Heesters, 42–44. Toronto: Anansi, 2000.

Barker, Joanne. *Sovereignty Matters: Locations of Contestations and Possibility in Indigenous Struggles for Self-Determination*. Lincoln: University of Nebraska Press, 2005.

——. "Gender, Sovereignty, and the Discourse of Rights in Native Women's Activism." *Meridians* 7, no. 1 (2006): 127–61.

Barnet, Miguel. *Biografía de un cimarrón*. Havana: Instituto de Etnología y Folklore, Academia de Ciencias de Cuba, 1966.

——. *Biography of a Runaway Slave*. Willimantic, CT: Curbstone Press, 1994.

Barreiro, José. "A Bridge for the Journey: Chronicle of the Indigenous Legacies of the Caribbean Encounters, 1997–2003." In *Indigenous Resurgence in the Contemporary Caribbean: Amerindian Survival and Revival*, edited by Maximilian C. Forte, 235–52. New York: Peter Lang, 2006.

Barrera, Aída. *Looking for Carrascolendas: From a Child's World to Award-Winning Television*. Austin: University of Texas Press, 2001.

Barrera, Mario. *Race and Class in the Southwest: A Theory of Racial Inequality*. South Bend, IN: University of Notre Dame Press, 1989.

Barreto, Matt A., Sylvia Manzano, Ricardo Ramírez, and Kathy Rim. "Mobilization, Participation, and Solidaridad: Latino Participation in the 2006 Immigration Protest Rallies." *Urban Affairs Review* 44, no. 5 (2009): 736–64.

Barreto, Matt A., Stephen A. Nuno, and Gabriel R. Sanchez. "Voter ID Requirements and the Disenfranchisements of Latino, Black, and Asian Voters." Paper presented at the American Political Science Association Annual Conference, Chicago, 2007.

Barreto, Matt, and Gary M. Segura. *Latino America: How America's Most Dynamic Population Is Poised to Transform the Politics of the Nation*. New York: Public Affairs, 2014.

Barreto, Matt A., Gary M. Segura, and Nathan D. Woods. "The Mobilizing Effect of Majority Minority Districts on Latino Turnout." *American Political Science Review* 98, no. 1 (2004): 65–75.

Barrueto, Jorge J. *The Hispanic Image in Hollywood: A Postcolonial Approach*. New York: Peter Lang, 2014.

Bartlett, Lesley, and Ofelia García. *Additive Schooling in Subtractive Times: Bilingual Education and Dominican Immigrant Youth in the Heights*. Nashville, TN: Vanderbilt University Press, 2011.

Bartolomé, Lilia I., and María V. Balderrama. "The Need for Educators with Political and Ideological Clarity: Providing Our Children with 'The Best.'" In *The Best for Our Children: Critical Perspectives on Literacy for Latino Students*, edited by María de la Luz Reyes and John J. Halcón, 48–64. New York: Teachers College Press, 2001.

Basch, Linda, Nina Glick Schiller, and Cristina Szanton Blanc. *Nations Unbound: Transnational Projects, Postcolonial Predicaments, and Deterriotorialized Nation-States*. New York: Routledge, 1994.

Baugh, Scott L. *Latino American Cinema: An Encyclopedia of Movies, Stars, Concepts, and Trends*. Santa Barbara, CA: Greenwood, 2012.

Behar, Ruth. *Translated Woman: Crossing the Border with Esperanza's Story*. Boston: Beacon Press, 1993.

———. *An Island Called Home: Returning to Jewish Cuba*. New Brunswick, NJ: Rutgers University Press, 2007.

Belsey, Catherine. *Critical Practice*. London: Routledge, 1990.

Beltrán, Cristina. *The Trouble with Unity: Latino Politics and the Creation of Identity*. New York: Oxford University Press, 2010.

Beltrán, Mary. *Latina/o Stars in U.S. Eyes: The Making and Meanings of Film and TV Stardom*. Urbana: University of Illinois Press, 2009.

Benitez, Cristina. *Latinization: How Latino Culture Is Transforming the United States*. Ithaca, NY: Paramount Market Publishing, 2007.

Benítez Rojo, Antonio. *La isla que se repite: El Caribe y la perspectiva posmoderna*. Hanover, NH: Ediciones del Norte, 1989.

———. *The Repeating Island: The Caribbean and the Postmodern Perspective*. Translated by James Maraniss. Durham, NC: Duke University Press, 1996.

Benmayor, Rina, Rosa M. Torruellas, and Ana L. Juarbe. "Claiming Cultural Citizenship in East Harlem: 'Si Esto Puede Ayudar a la Comunidad Mía . . .'" In *Latino Cultural Citizenship: Claiming Identity, Space, and Rights*, edited by Wiliam V. Flores and Rina Benmayor, 152–209. Boston: Beacon Press, 1997.

Bennett, Louise. "Colonisation in Reverse." *Caribbean Quarterly* 54, no. 1–2 (2008): 52–53.

Berg, Charles Ramírez. *Latino Images in Film: Stereotypes, Subversion, Resistance*. Austin: University of Texas Press, 2002.

Bergad, Laird W. "Have Dominicans Surpassed Puerto Ricans to Become New York City's Largest Latino Nationality?: An Analysis of Latino Population Data from the 2013 American Community Survey for New York City and the Metropolitan Area." *Latino Data Project, Report 61*. New York: Center for Latin American, Caribbean and Latino Studies, Graduate Center, City University of New York, November 2014.

Bergad, Laird W., and Herbert S. Klein. *Hispanics in the United States: A Demographic, Social, and Economic History, 1880–2005*. New York: Cambridge University Press, 2010.

Bernhardt, Annette, Ruth Milkman, Nik Theodore, Douglas Hekathorn, Mirabai Auer, James DeFilippis, Ana Luz González, Victor Narro, Jason Perelshteyn, Diana Polson, and Michael Spiller. *Broken Laws, Unprotected Workers: Violations of Employment and Labor Laws in America's Cities*. Chicago: Center for Urban Economic Development, National Employment Law Project, and the University of California, Los Angeles, Institute for Research on Labor and Employment, 2009. http://nelp.3cdn.net.

Bernstein, Charles. "Provisional Institutions: Alternative Presses and Poetic Innovation." *My Way: Speeches and Poems*, 145–54. Chicago: University of Chicago Press, 1999.

Betancur, John. "The Settlement Experience of Latinos in Chicago: Segregation, Speculation and the Ecology Model." *Social Forces* 74 (1996): 1299–1324.

Beveridge, Andrew A. "A Century of Harlem in New York City: Some Notes on Migration, Consolidation, Segregation, and Recent Developments." *City and Community* 7, no. 4 (2008): 358–65.

Beverley, John. *Testimonio: On the Politics of Truth*. Minneapolis: University of Minnesota Press, 2004.

Bhabha, Homi K., ed. *Nation and Narration*. New York: Routledge, 1990.

———. *The Location of Culture*. New York: Routledge, 1994.

Bird, Brad, and Jan Pinkava, dirs. *Ratatouille*. Burbank, CA: Disney Pixar, 2007.

Bishop, Claire. "The Social Turn: Collaboration and Its Discontents." *Artforum* 44, no. 6 (2006): 179–85.

Blackwell, Maylei. *¡Chicana Power!: Contested Histories of Feminism in the Chicano Movement*. Austin: University of Texas Press, 2011.

Blauner, Robert. *Racial Oppression in America*. New York: HarperCollins, 1972.

Bloemraad, Irene. *Becoming a Citizen: Incorporating Immigrants and Refugees in the United States and Canada*. Berkeley: University of California Press, 2006.

Bloemraad, Irene, Anna Korteweg, and Gokce Yurdakul. "Citizenship and Immigration: Multiculturalism, Assimilation, and Challenges to the Nation-State." *Annual Review of Sociology* 34 (2008): 153–79.

Bloemraad, Irene, and Christine Trost. "It's a Family Affair: Intergenerational Mobilization in the Spring 2006 Protests." *American Behavioral Scientist* 52, no. 4 (2008): 507–32.

Blumer, Herbert. "Social Movements." In *New Outline of the Principles of Sociology*, edited by Alfred McClung Lee, 199–220. New York: Barnes and Noble, 1949.

Boj Lopez, Floridalma. "Weavings that Rupture: The Possibility of Contesting Settler Colonialism through Cultural Retention among the Maya Diaspora." In *U.S. Central Americans: Reconstructing Memories, Struggles, and Communities of Resistance*, edited by Karina O. Alvarado, Alicia Ivonne Estrada, and Ester E. Hernández, 188–203. Tucson: University of Arizona Press, 2017.

Bolton, Herbert E. "The Epic of Greater America." *American Historical Review* 38, no. 3 (1933): 448–74.

Bonilla, Frank, and Emilio González. "New Knowing, New Practice: Puerto Rican Studies." In *Structures of Dependency*, edited by Frank Bonilla and Robert Girling, 224–34. Stanford, CA: Stanford Institute of Politics, 1973.

Bonilla-Silva, Eduardo. "Reflections about Race by a Negrito Acomplejao." In *The Afro-Latin@ Reader: History and Culture in the United States*, edited by Miriam Jiménez Román and Juan Flores, 445–52. Durham, NC: Duke University Press, 2010.

Borrero, Sonya, Nikki Zite, and Mitchell D. Creinin. "Federally Funded Sterilization: Time to Rethink Policy?" *American Journal of Public Health* 102, no. 10 (2012): 1822–25.

Bosch, Juan. *De Cristobal Colón a Fidel Castro*, 3rd ed. Santo Domingo: Alfa y Omega, 1981.

———. *Social Composition of the Dominican Republic*. New York: Routledge, 2016.

Bosniak, Linda. "Citizenship and Work." *North Carolina Journal of International Law and Commercial Regulations* 27 (2002): 497–521.

Bost, Suzanne and Frances R. Aparicio, eds. *The Routledge Companion to Latino/a Literature*. New York: Routledge, 2013.

Bourdieu, Pierre, and Jean-Claude Passeron. *Reproduction in Education, Society and Culture*. Beverly Hills, CA: Sage, 1977.

Bourne, Randolph S. "Trans-National America." *Atlantic Monthly* (July 1916): 86–97.

Boyarin, Daniel, and Jonathan Boyarin. "Diaspora: Generation and Ground of Jewish Identity." *Critical Inquiry* 19, no. 4 (1993): 693–725.

Brading, David A. *The Origins of Mexican Nationalism*. Cambridge: Centre of Latin American Studies, University of Cambridge, 1985.

Brady, Mary Pat. *Extinct Lands, Temporal Geographies: Chicana Literature and the Urgency of Space*. Durham, NC: Duke University Press, 2002.

Brier, Jennifer. *Infectious Ideas: U.S. Political Responses to the AIDS Crisis*. Chapel Hill: University of North Carolina Press, 2009.

Briggs, Laura. "La Vida, Moynihan, and Other Libels: Migration, Social Science, and the Making of the Puerto Rican Welfare Queen." *CENTRO Journal* 14, no. 1 (2002a): 75-101.

———. *Reproducing Empire: Race, Sex, Science, and U.S. Imperialism in Puerto Rico*. Berkeley: University of California Press, 2002b.

Brimelow, Peter. *Alien Nation: Common Sense about America's Immigration Disaster*. New York: Random House, 1995.

Brown v. Board of Education of Topeka. U.S. Supreme Court. 347 U.S. 483 (1954). https://supreme.justia.com.

Broyles-González, Yolanda. *El Teatro Campesino: Theater in the Chicano Movement*. Austin: University of Texas Press, 1994.

———. *Lydia Mendoza's Life in Music / La Historia de Lydia Mendoza: Norteño Tejano Legacies*. London: Oxford University Press, 2003.

Bruce-Novoa, Juan. *Chicano Poetry: A Response to Chaos*. Austin: University of Texas Press, 1982.

———. *RetroSpace: Collected Essays on Chicano Literature, Theory, and History*. Houston: Arte Público Press, 1990.

Buck-Morss, Susan. *Hegel, Haiti, and Universal History*. Pittsburgh, PA: University of Pittsburgh Press, 2009.

Bureau of Labor Statistics. "National Hispanic Heritage Month: Spotlight on Statistics: U.S. Bureau of Labor Statistics." 2012. www.bls.gov.

———. "BLS Glossary." 2014. www.bls.gov.

Burgett, Bruce, and Glenn Hendler, eds. *Keywords for American Cultural Studies*. New York: New York University Press, 2007.

———. *Keywords for American Cultural Studies*, 2nd ed. New York: New York University Press, 2014.

Burgos, Adrian. *Playing America's Game: Baseball, Latinos, and the Color Line*. Berkeley: University of California Press, 2007.

Burgos, Elizabeth. *Me llamo Rigoberta Menchú y así me nació la conciencia*. 1985. México: Siglo Veintiuno Editores, 2003.

Burnett, Christina Duffy, and Burke Marshall, eds. *Foreign in a Domestic Sense: Puerto Rico, American Expansion, and the Constitution*. Durham, NC: Duke University Press, 2001.

Burnham, Linda, and Nik Theodore. *Home Economics: The Invisible and Unregulated World of Domestic Work*. New York: National Domestic Workers Alliance, Center for Urban Economic Development, University of Illinois at Chicago DataCenter, 2012. www.domesticworkers.org.

Buscaglia-Salgado, José F. *Undoing Empire: Race and Nation in the Mulatto Caribbean*. Minneapolis: University of Minnesota Press, 2003.

Buss, Fran Leeper, ed. *Forged under the Sun / Forjada bajo el sol: The Life of María Elena Lucas*. Ann Arbor: University of Michigan Press, 1993.

Butler, Judith. Preface (1999). In *Gender Trouble: Feminism and the Subversion of Identity*, 2nd ed., vii–xxvi. New York: Routledge, 1999.

Byrd, Jodi. *The Transit of Empire: Indigenous Critiques of Colonialism*. Minneapolis: University of Minnesota, 2011.

Cabán, Pedro A. *Constructing a Colonial People: Puerto Rico and the United States, 1898-1932*. New York: Westview, 1999.

———. "From Challenge to Absorption: The Changing Face of Latina and Latino Studies." *CENTRO Journal* 15, no. 2 (2003a): 127–45.

———. "Moving from the Margins to Where?: Three Decades of Latino/a Studies." *Latino Studies* 1, no. 1 (2003b): 5–35.

Cabranes, José A. *Citizenship and the American Empire*. New Haven, CT: Yale University Press, 1979.

Cadena, Gilbert, and Lara Medina. "Liberation Theology and Social Change: Chicanas and Chicanos in the Catholic Church." In *Chicanas and Chicanos in Contemporary Society*, edited by Roberto M. De Anda, 155–70. Lanham, MD: Rowman and Littlefield, 2004.

Calavita, Kitty. *Inside the State: The Bracero Program, Immigration, and the I.N.S.* New York: Routledge, 1992.

Calvo, Luz. "'Lemme Stay, I Want to Watch': Ambivalence in Borderlands Cinema." In *Latina/o Popular Culture*, edited by Michelle Habell-Pallán and Mary Romero, 73–84. New York: New York University Press, 2002.

Calvo, Luz, and Catriona Rueda Esquibel. *Decolonize Your Diet: Plant-Based Mexican-American Recipes for Health and Healing.* Vancouver: Arsenal Pulp Press, 2015.

Calvo-Quirós, William A. "Driving the Streets of Aztlán: Low 'n Slow." In *One Hundred Years of Loyalty: In Honor of Luis Leal / Cien Años de Lealtad: en Honor a Luis Leal*, vol. 2, edited by Sara Poot Herrera, Francisco A. Lomelí, and María Herrera-Sobek, 1115–34. Santa Barbara: University of California, Santa Barbara, 2007.

Camarillo, Albert M. "Looking Back on Chicano History: A Generational Perspective." *Pacific Historical Review* 82, no. 4 (2013): 496–504.

Caminero-Santangelo, Marta. *On Latinidad: U.S. Latino Literature and the Construction of Ethnicity.* Gainesville: University Press of Florida, 2007.

———. "Latinidad." In *The Routledge Companion to Latino/a Literature*, edited by Suzanne Bost and Frances R. Aparicio, 13–24. New York: Routledge, 2013.

Cammarota, Julio, and Michelle Fine, eds. *Revolutionizing Education: Youth Participatory Action Research in Motion.* New York: Routledge, 2008.

Candelario, Ginetta E. B. *Black behind the Ears: Dominican Racial Identity from Museum to Beauty Shops.* Durham, NC: Duke University Press, 2007.

Cañizares-Esguerra, Jorge. *Puritan Conquistadors: Iberianizing the Atlantic, 1550–1700.* Stanford, CA: Stanford University Press, 2006.

———. Review of *Territories of Empire: US Writing from the Louisiana Purchase to Mexican Independence. Hispanic American Historical Review* 96, no. 1 (2016): 199–200.

Cantú, Lionel, Jr. *The Sexuality of Migration: Border Crossings and Mexican Immigrant Men.* Edited by Nancy A. Naples and Salvador Vidal-Ortiz. New York: New York University Press, 2009.

Cantú, Norma E. *Canícula: Snapshots of a Girlhood in La Frontera.* Albuquerque: University of New Mexico Press, 1995.

Carbado, Devon W. "Racial Naturalization." *American Quarterly* 57, no. 3 (2005): 633–58.

Carr, Raymond. *Puerto Rico: A Colonial Experiment.* New York: Vintage/Random House, 1984.

Carrasco, David. "A Perspective for the Study of Religious Dimensions in Chicano Experience: *Bless Me, Última* as a Religious Text." *Aztlán* 13 (1982): 195–222.

———. *Religions of Mesoamerica: Cosmovision and Ceremonial Centers.* Prospect Heights, IL: Waveland Press, 1990.

Carrillo, Jorge, and Alberto Hernández. *Mujeres fronterizas en la industria maquiladora.* Mexico City: Secretaría de Educación Pública and Centro de Estudios Fronterizos, 1985.

Carrillo, Jorge, and Alfredo Hualde. "Maquiladoras de tercera generación. El caso de Delphi-General Motors." *Espacios: Revista Venezolana de Gestión Tecnológica* 17 (1996): 111–34.

Carrillo, Jorge, and Redi Gomis. "El empleo femenino en multinacionales maquiladoras y no maquiladoras de México." In *Género y trabajo en las maquiladoras de Mexico: Nuevos actores en nuevos contextos*, edited by María Eugenia de la O, 31–54. Mexico: CIESAS, 2013.

Carrillo, Jorge, and Jorge Santibañez Romellón. *Rotación de personal en las maquiladoras*, 2nd ed. Tijuana: Plaza y Valdez Editores, Secretaría del Trabajo y Previsión Social and El Colegio de la Frontera Norte, Tijuana, 2001.

Carter, Thomas P. *Mexican Americans in School: A History of Educational Neglect.* New York: College Entrance Examination Board, 1970.

Casillas, Dolores Inés. *Sounds of Belonging: U.S. Spanish-Language Radio and Public Advocacy.* New York: New York University Press, 2014.

Castañeda, Mari. "The Importance of Spanish Language and Latino Media." In *Latina/o Communication Studies Today*, edited by Angharad N. Valdivia, 51–67. New York: Peter Lang, 2008.

———. "The Role of Media Policy in Shaping the US Latino Radio Industry." In *Contemporary Latina/o Media: Production, Circulation, Politics*, edited by Yeidy M. Rivero and Arlene Dávila, 186–205. New York: New York University Press, 2014.

Castañeda, Xóchitl, and Patricia Zavella. "Changing Constructions of Sexuality and Risk: Migrant Mexican Women Farmworkers in California." *Journal of Latin American Anthropology* 8, no. 2 (2003): 126–51.

Castanha, Tony. *The Myth of Indigenous Caribbean Extinction: Continuity and Reclamation in Borikén (Puerto Rico).* New York: Palgrave Macmillan, 2011.

Castellanos, M. Bianet, Lourdes Gutiérrez Nájera, and Arturo J. Aldama, eds. *Comparative Indigeneities: Towards a Hemispheric Approach.* Tucson: University of Arizona Press, 2012.

Castillo, Ana. *Massacre of the Dreamers: Essays on Xicanisma.* New York: Plume/Penguin, 1995.

Castro, Tony. "Delegate Slaying Mars Convention of La Raza Unida." *Washington Post*, September 1, 1972.

Castro-Klarén, Sara, and John Charles Chasteen, eds. *Beyond Imagined Communities: Reading and Writing the Nation in Nineteenth-Century Latin America*. Washington, DC: Woodrow Wilson Center Press, 2003.

Cavalli-Sforza, Luigi. *Genes, Peoples, and Languages*. Translated by Mark Seielstad. New York: North Point Press, 2000.

CBP Border Security Report Fiscal Year 2014. Washington, DC: U.S. Customs and Border Protection, U.S. Department of Homeland Security, 2014. www.cbp.gov.

Cepeda, María Elena. *Musical ImagiNation: US-Colombian Identity and the Latin Music Boom*. New York: New York University Press, 2010.

Cervantes, Joseph M., and Brians W. McNeill, eds. *Latina/o Healing Practices: Mestizo and Indigenous Perspectives*. New York: Routledge, 2008.

Cervantes, Lorna Dee. "Para un Revolucionario." In *Infinite Divisions: An Anthology of Chicana Literature*, edited by Tey Diana Rebolledo and Eliana S. Rivero, 150–51. Tucson: University of Arizona Press, 1993.

Chabram, Angie, and Rosa-Linda Fregoso, eds. *Chicana/o Cultural Representations: Reframing Alternative Critical Discourses*. Special Issue. *Cultural Studies* 4, no. 3 (1990).

Chabram-Dernersesian, Angie. "I Throw Punches for My Race, but I Don't Want to Be a Man: Writing Us—Chica-nos (Girl, Us) / Chicanas—into the Movement Script." In *Cultural Studies*, edited by Lawrence Grossberg, Cary Nelson, and Paula A. Treichler, 81–111. New York: Routledge, 1992.

———, ed. *Chicana/o Latina/o Cultural Studies: Transnational and Transdisciplinary Movements*. Special issue. *Cultural Studies* 13, no. 2 (1999).

———. "Latina/o: Another Site of Struggle, Another Site of Accountability." In *Critical Latin American and Latino Studies*, edited by Juan Poblete, 105–20. Minneapolis: University of Minnesota Press. 2003.

———. "And, Yes . . . The Earth Did Part: On the Splitting of Chican/o Subjectivity." In *Building with Our Hands: New Directions in Chicana Studies*, edited by Adela de la Torre and Beatríz M. Pesquera, 34–56. Berkeley: University of California Press, 2013.

Chanady, Amaryll. "Identity, Politics and *Mestizaje*." In *Contemporary Latin American Studies*, edited by Stephen Hart and Richard Young, 192–202. London: Arnold, 2003.

Chatterjee, Partha. *The Nation and Its Fragments: Colonial and Postcolonial Histories*. Princeton, NJ: Princeton University Press, 1993.

Chávez, Christopher. *Reinventing the Latino Viewer: Language,* *Ideology, and Practice*. Lanham, MD: Rowman and Littlefield, 2015.

Chávez, Ernesto. *"Mi Raza Primero!" (My People First!): Nationalism, Identity, and Insurgency in the Chicano Movement in Los Angeles, 1966–1978*. Berkeley: University of California Press, 2002.

Chavez, Leo R. *Shadowed Lives: Undocumented Immigrants in American Society*. New York: Cengage, 1997.

———. "A Glass Half Empty: Latina Reproduction and Public Discourse." *Human Organization* 63, no. 2 (2004): 173–88.

———. *The Latino Threat: Constructing Immigrants, Citizens, and the Nation*. Stanford, CA: Stanford University Press, 2008.

———. *The Latino Threat: Constructing Immigrants, Citizens, and the Nation*, 2nd ed. Stanford: Stanford University Press, 2013.

Chávez-García, Miroslava. *States of Delinquency: Race and Science in the Making of California's Juvenile Justice System*. Berkeley: University of California Press, 2012.

Chávez-Silverman, Susana, and Librada Hernández, eds. *Reading and Writing the Ambiente: Queer Sexualities in Latino, Latin American, and Spanish Culture*. Madison: University of Wisconsin Press, 2000.

Chavoya, C. Ondine, and Rita Gonzalez, eds. *Asco: Elite of the Obscure, a Retrospective, 1972–1987*. Williamstown, MA: Williams College Museum of Art, 2011.

Cherokee Nation v. Georgia. Supreme Court of the United States, 30 U.S. 1; 8 L. Ed. 25; 1831 U.S. LEXIS 337.

Chiaramonte, José Carlos. *Nación y estado en Iberoamérica: El lenguaje político en tiempos de las independencias*. Buenos Aires: Editorial Sudamericana, 2004.

Chiaramonte, José Carlos, Carlos Marichal, and Aimer Granados García, eds. *Crear la nación: Los nombres de los países de América Latina*. Buenos Aires: Editorial Sudamericana, 2008.

Chicano Coordinating Council of Higher Education. *El Plan de Santa Barbara: A Chicano Plan for Higher Education*. Oakland / Alta California de Aztlán: La Causa Publications, 1969. www.nationalmecha.org.

Chicano Youth Liberation Conference. "El Plan Espiritual de Aztlán." *In Aztlán: An Anthology of Mexican American Literature*, edited by Luis Valdez and Stan Steiner, 402–6. New York: Vintage, 1972.

Child, Desmond, and Draco Rosa. "Livin' La Vida Loca." *Ricky Martin*. New York: Columbia Records, 1999.

Christman, John H. "Perspectivas para la Industria Maquiladora 2003–2007. Un camino lento hacia el crecimiento." Paper presented at CIV Junta Cuatrimestral Macroeconómica for Global Insight, Mexico City, March 13–14, 2003.

———. "Mexico's Maquiladora Industry Outlook; 2005–2010." Paper presented at LII Maquiladora Industry Outlook Meeting for Global Insight, Mexicali, Baja California, January 28, 2005.

Churchill, Ward, ed. *Marxism and Native Americans*. Boston: South End Press, 1999.

CIEMEX-WEFA. *Maquiladora Industry Outlook* 4, no. 3 (1991).

———. *Maquiladora Industry Outlook* 13, no. 3 (2000).

Cisneros, Sandra. *The House on Mango Street*. Houston: Arte Público Press, 1984.

Clifford, James. "Diasporas." *Cultural Anthropology* 9, no. 3 (1994): 302–38.

Cobas, José, Jorge Duany, and Joe Feagin, eds. *How the United States Racializes Latinos: White Hegemony and Its Consequences*. Boulder, CO: Paradigm Press, 2009.

Cockcroft, Eva Sperling, and Holly Barnet-Sánchez, eds. *Signs from the Heart: California Chicano Murals*. Venice, CA: Social and Public Art Resource Center, 1993.

Cofer, Judith Ortiz. *Silent Dancing: A Partial Remembrance of a Puerto Rican Childhood*. Houston: Arte Público Press, 1980.

———. *The Latin Deli: Telling the Lives of Barrio Women*. New York: W.W. Norton, 1995.

COHA. "The 2014 Presidential Elections in El Salvador and the Transnational Electorate." *Council on Hemispheric Affairs*, 2014. www.coha.org.

Cohen, Cathy. *The Boundaries of Blackness: AIDS and the Breakdown of Black Politics*. Chicago: University of Chicago Press, 1999.

Cohn, D'Vera, Ana Gonzalez-Barrera, and Danielle Cuddington. *Remittances to Latin America Recover—But Not to Mexico*. Washington, DC: Pew Research Center Hispanic Trends Project, 2013. www.pewhispanic.org.

Cohn, Nate. "More Hispanics Declaring Themselves White." *New York Times*, May 21, 2014.

Coleman-Jensen, Alisha, Christian Gregory, and Anita Singh. "Household Food Security in the United States in 2013." *Economic Research Report*, no.173. Washington, DC: Economic Research Service, United States Department of Agriculture, 2014.

Colford, Paul. "'Illegal Immigrant' No More." *AP Blog*, April 2, 2013. https://blog.ap.org.

Coll, Kathleen M. *Remaking Citizenship: Latina Immigrants and New American Politics*. Stanford, CA: Stanford University Press, 2010.

Collins, Jane L. "The Specter of Slavery: Workfare and the Economic Citizenship of Poor Women." In *New Landscapes of Inequality: Neoliberalism and the Erosion of Democracy in America*, edited by Jane L. Collins, Micaela di Leonardo, and Brett Williams, 131–51. Santa Fe, NM: School for Advanced Research Press, 2008.

Collins, Jane L., Micaela di Leonardo, and Brett Williams, eds. *New Landscapes of Inequality: Neoliberalism and the Erosion of Democracy in America*. Santa Fe, NM: School for Advanced Research Press, 2008.

Collister, Brian, and Joe Ellis. "Texas Troopers Ticketing Hispanic Drivers as White." *KXAN News*, Austin, November 6, 2015.

Comas-Díaz, Lillian. "LatiNegra: Mental Health Issues of African Latinas." In *The Multiracial Racial Borders as New Frontier*, edited by Maria P. P. Root, 167–90. New York: Sage Publishers, 1996.

Compton, Elizabeth, Michael Bentley, Sharon Ennis, and Sonya Rastogi. *2010 Census Race and Hispanic Origin Alternative Questionnaire Experiment: Final Report*. Washington, DC: U.S. Census Bureau, 2012.

Conquergood, Dwight. "Performance Studies: Interventions and Radical Research." *TDR* 46, no. 2 (2002): 145–56.

Contreras, Sheila. *Blood Lines: Myth, Indigenism, and Chicana/o Literature*. Austin: University of Texas Press, 2008.

Coontz, Stephanie. *The Way We Never Were: American Families and the Nostalgia Trap*. New York: Basic, 1993.

Cordova, Carrie. "The Mission in Nicaragua: San Francisco Poets Go to War." In *Beyond El Barrio: Everyday Life in Latina/o America*, edited by Gina M. Pérez, Frank A. Guridy, and Adrian Burgos Jr., 211–31. New York: New York University Press, 2011.

Coronado, Raúl. *A World Not to Come: A History of Latino Writing and Print Culture*. Cambridge, MA: Harvard University Press, 2013.

Corral, Eduardo C. *Slow Lightning*. New Haven, CT: Yale University Press, 2012.

Corrin, Lisa G. "Self-Questioning Monuments." In *Felix Gonzalez-Torres: Serpentine Gallery, 1 June–16 July 2000*, 7–15. New York: Serpentine Gallery, 2000.

Cortez, Jaime. *Sexile/Sexilio*. Los Angeles: Institute for Gay Men's Health, 2004.

Cotera, María Eugenia, and María Josefina Saldaña-Portillo. "Indigenous but Not Indian? Chicana/os and the Politics of Indigeneity." In *The World of Indigenous North America*, edited by Robert Warrior, 549–68. New York: Routledge, 2015.

Cotera, Martha P. *Diosa y Hembra: The History and Heritage of Chicanas in the U.S.* Austin: Information Systems Development, 1976.

Crawford, James. *At War with Diversity: U.S. Language Policy in an Age of Anxiety*. Buffalo, NY: Multilingual Matters, 2000.

Crook, Jamie L. "From *Hernandez v. Texas* to the Present:

Doctrinal Shifts in the Supreme Court's Latina/o Jurisprudence." *Harvard Latino Law Review* 11 (2008): 19–83.

Crossley, Nick. *Making Sense of Social Movements*. Buckingham: Open University Press, 2002.

Cruz-Malavé, Arnaldo. *Queer Latino Testimonio, Keith Haring, and Juanito Xtravaganza: Hard Tails*. New York: Palgrave Macmillan, 2007.

Cullen, Deborah, Miki Garcia, and Marysol Nieves, curators. *The S Files (The Selected Files) 05*. Exhibition catalog. New York: El Museo del Barrio, 2005–2006.

Curtin, Deane W., and Lisa M. Heldke, eds. *Cooking, Eating, Thinking: Transformative Philosophies of Food*. Bloomington: Indiana University Press, 1992.

Cutler, John Alba. *Ends of Assimilation: The Formation of Chicano Literature*. Oxford: Oxford University Press, 2015.

Dalleo, Raphael, and Elena Machado Sáez. *The Latino/a Canon and the Emergence of Post-Sixties Literature*. New York: Palgrave Macmillan, 2007.

Darder, Antonia. *Culture and Power in the Classroom: A Critical Foundation for Bicultural Education*. New York: Bergin and Garvey, 1991.

Darity Jr., William, Darrick Hamilton, and Jason Dietrich. "Passing on Blackness: Latinos, Race and Earnings in the USA." *Applied Economics Letters* 9, no. 13 (2010): 847–53.

Davalos, Karen Mary. "'The Real Way of Praying': The Via Crucis, Mexicano Sacred Space, and the Architecture of Domination." In *Horizons of the Sacred: Mexican Traditions in U.S. Catholicism*, edited by Timothy Matovina and Gary Riebe-Estrella, 41–68. Ithaca, NY: Cornell University Press, 2002.

Davies, James C. "Toward a Theory of Revolution." *American Sociological Review* 27, no. 1 (1962): 5–19.

Dávila, Arlene. *Sponsored Identities: Cultural Politics in Puerto Rico*. Philadelphia: Temple University Press, 1997.

———. *Latinos, Inc.: Marketing and the Making of a People*. Berkeley: University of California Press, 2001.

———. *Barrio Dreams: Puerto Ricans, Latinos and the Neoliberal City*. Berkeley: University of California Press, 2004.

———. *Latino Spin: Public Image and the Whitewashing of Race*. New York: New York University Press, 2008.

———. *Culture Works: Space, Value and Mobility across the Neoliberal Americas*. New York: New York University Press, 2012.

Dávila, Arlene, and Yeidy M. Rivero, eds. *Contemporary Latina/o Media: Production, Circulation, Politics*. New York: New York University Press, 2014.

Davis, Angela Y. *Are Prisons Obsolete?* New York: Seven Stories Press, 2003.

De Genova, Nicholas. "The Legal Production of Mexican/Migrant 'Illegality.'" *Latino Studies* 2, no. 2 (2004): 160–85.

———. *Working the Boundaries: Race, Space, and "Illegality" in Mexican Chicago*. Durham, NC: Duke University Press, 2005.

———. "The Queer Politics of Migration: Reflections on 'Illegality' and Incorrigibility." *Studies in Social Justice* 4, no. 2 (2010): 101–26.

De Genova, Nicholas, Sandro Mezzadra, and John Pickles, eds. "New Keywords: Migration and Borders." *Cultural Studies* 29, no. 1 (2015): 55–87.

De Genova, Nicholas, and Ana Y. Ramos-Zayas. *Latino Crossings: Mexicans, Puerto Ricans, and the Politics of Race and Citizenship*. New York: Routledge, 2003.

de la Portilla, Elizabeth. *They All Want Magic: Curanderas and Folk Healing*. College Station: Texas A&M University Press, 2009.

de la Selva, Salomón. *Tropical Town and Other Poems*, 2nd ed. Houston: Arte Público Press, 1999.

de la tierra, tatiana. "Activist Latina Lesbian Publishing: *Esto No Tiene Nombre* and *Conmoción*." *Aztlán* 27, no. 1 (2002): 139–78.

De la Torre, Marisa, and Julia Gwynne. *When Schools Close: Effects on Displaced Students in Chicago Public Schools*. Chicago: Consortium on Chicago School Research, 2009.

De La Torre, Miguel A. *La Lucha for Cuba: Religion and Politics on the Streets of Miami*. Berkeley: University of California Press, 2003.

———, ed. *Hispanic American Religious Cultures*. Santa Barbara, CA: ABC-CLIO, 2009.

de las Casas, Bartolomé. *Brevísima relación de la destrucción de las Indias*. 1552. Barcelona: Planeta, 1994.

———. "Las Casas on the Alleged First Voyage of Amerigo Vespucci." In *The Letters of Amerigo Vespucci*, edited by Clements R. Markham, 68–108. Farnham, UK: Ashgate, 2010.

De León, Arnoldo. *In re Ricardo Rodríguez: An Attempt at Chicano Disenfranchisement in San Antonio, 1896–1897*. San Antonio, TX: Caravel Press, 1979.

———. *They Called Them Greasers: Anglo Attitudes toward Mexicans in Texas, 1821–1900*. Austin: University of Texas Press, 1983.

De León, Jason. *The Land of Open Graves: Living and Dying on the Migrant Trail*. Berkeley: University of California Press, 2015.

de Luna, Anita. *Faith Formation and Popular Religion: Lessons from the Tejano Experience*. Lanham, MD: Rowman and Littlefield, 2002.

de Onís, Catalina (Kathleen) M. "What's in an 'x'?: An Exchange about the Politics of 'Latinx.'" *Chiricú Journal: Latina/o Literatures, Arts, and Cultures* 1, no. 2 (2017): 78–91.

Decena, Carlos Ulises. *Tacit Subjects: Belonging and Same-Sex Desire among Dominican Immigrant Men.* Durham, NC: Duke University Press, 2011.

DeGuzmán, María. *Spain's Long Shadow: The Black Legend, Off-Whiteness, and Anglo-American Empire.* Minneapolis: University of Minnesota Press, 2005.

del Castillo, Adelaida. "Malintzin Tenépal: A Preliminary Look into a New Perspective." In *Essays on La Mujer,* edited by Rosaura Sánchez and Rosa Martinez Cruz, 124–49. Los Angeles: Chicano Studies Center Publications, University of California, Los Angeles, 1977.

del Rio, Vanessa. *Vanessa Del Rio: Fifty Years of Slightly Slutty Behavior.* Edited by Dian Hanson. Köln: Taschen, 2010.

del Valle, José. *A Political History of Spanish: The Making of a Language.* Cambridge: Cambridge University Press, 2013.

del Valle, José, and Ana Celia Zentella. "Lengua, política y la RAE." *Revista Cronopio* 55 (October 2014). www.revistacronopio.com.

Délano, Alexandra. *Mexico and Its Diaspora: Policies of Emigration since 1848.* Cambridge: Cambridge University Press, 2011.

Delgadillo, Theresa. "Forms of Chicana Feminist Resistance: Hybrid Spirituality in Ana Castillo's *So Far from God.*" *Modern Fiction Studies* 44, no. 4 (1998): 888–916.

———. "Hybrid Spiritualities: Resistance and Religious Faith in Contemporary Chicano/a Fiction, Drama, and Film." PhD diss., University of California, Los Angeles, 2000. Ann Arbor, MI: UMI, 2000.

———. *Spiritual Mestizaje: Religion, Gender, Race and Nation in Contemporary Chicana Narrative.* Durham, NC: Duke University Press, 2011.

Delpar, Helen. *Looking South: The Evolution of Latin Americanist Scholarship in the United States, 1850–1975.* Tuscaloosa: University of Alabama Press, 2008.

Demby, Gene. "On the Census, Who Checks 'Hispanic,' Who Checks 'White,' and Why." *Code Switch,* NPR, June 16, 2014.

Denis, Nelson A. *War against All Puerto Ricans: Revolution and Terror in America's Colony.* New York: Nation Books, 2015.

Denton, Nancy A., and Douglas S. Massey. "Racial Identity among Caribbean Hispanics: The Effect of Double Minority Status on Residential Segregation." *American Sociological Review* 54 (1989): 790–808.

Derby, Lauren. *The Dictator's Seduction: Politics and the Popular Imagination in the Era of Trujillo.* Durham, NC: Duke University Press, 2009.

Derrida, Jacques. *Of Grammatology.* Translated by Gayatri Chakravorty Spivak. Baltimore, MD: Johns Hopkins University Press, 1997.

Diaz, David R. *Barrio Urbanism: Chicanos, Planning, and American Cities.* New York: Routledge, 2005.

Diaz, David R., and Rodolfo D. Torres, eds. *Latino Urbanism: The Politics of Planning, Policy and Redevelopment.* New York: New York University Press, 2012.

Díaz, Junot. *Drown.* New York: Riverhead, 1996.

———. *The Brief Wondrous Life of Oscar Wao.* New York: Riverhead, 2007.

Díaz-Cotto, Juanita. *Gender, Ethnicity, and the State: Latina and Latino Prison Politics.* Albany: State University of New York Press, 1996.

———. *Chicana Lives and Criminal Justice: Voices from El Barrio.* Austin: University of Texas Press, 2006.

Díaz-Stevens, Ana María. *Oxcart Catholicism on Fifth Avenue: The Impact of the Puerto Rican Migration upon the Archdiocese of New York.* Notre Dame, IN: University of Notre Dame Press, 1993.

Díaz-Stevens, Ana María, and Anthony M. Stevens-Arroyo. *Recognizing the Latino Resurgence in U.S. Religion: The Emmaus Paradigm.* Boulder, CO: Westview, 1998.

Dinnerstein, Leonard, and David Reimers. *Ethnic Americans: A History of Immigration and Assimilation.* New York: Dodd, Mead, 1975.

Dinzey-Flores, Zaire Z. "Temporary Housing, Permanent Communities Public Housing Policy and Design in Puerto Rico." *Journal of Urban History* 33, no. 3 (2007): 467–92.

Dohan, Daniel. *The Price of Poverty: Money, Work, and Culture in the Mexican-American Barrio.* Berkeley: University of California Press, 2003.

Domínguez, Alberto, Nancy de los Santos, and Susan Racho, dirs. *The Bronze Screen: 100 Years of the Latino Image in Film.* Chicago: Questar, 2002.

Dominguez, Ricardo. "Electronic Civil Disobedience: Inventing the Future of Online Agitprop Theater." *PMLA* 124, no. 5 (2009): 1806–12.

Douglas, Susan J. *Listening In: Radio and the American Imagination.* New York: Times Books, 1999.

Dowdy, Michael. *Broken Souths: Latina/o Poetic Responses to Neoliberalism and Globalization.* Tucson: University of Arizona Press, 2013.

Dowling, Julie A. *Mexican Americans and the Question of Race.* Austin: University of Texas Press, 2014.

Downes v. Bidwell. U.S. Supreme Court. 182 U.S. 244 (1901). https://supreme.justia.com.

Dred Scott v. Sandford. U.S. Supreme Court. 60 U.S. 393 (1856). https://supreme.justia.com.

Duany, Jorge. *The Puerto Rican Nation on the Move: Identities on the Island and in the United States.* Chapel Hill: University of North Carolina Press, 2002.

———. "Nation, Migration, Identity: The Case of Puerto Ricans." *Latino Studies* 1 (2003): 424–44.

Dubatti, Jorge. *Filosofía del teatro III*. Buenos Aires: Atuel, 2014.

Dubos, Jean. *The Mirage of Health: Utopia, Progress, and Biological Change*. Piscataway, NJ: Rutgers University Press, 1987.

Duncan, Brian, V. Joseph Hotz, and Stephen Trejo. "Hispanics in the U.S. Labor Market." In *Hispanics and the Future of America*, edited by Marta Tienda and Faith Mitchell, 228–90. Washington, DC: National Academies Press, 2006. www.nap.edu.

Dussel, Enrique. *Philosophy of Liberation*. Translated by Aquilina Martinez and Christine Morkovsky. Maryknoll, NY: Orbis Books, 1985.

———. *The Invention of the Americas: Eclipse of "the Other" and the Myth of Modernity*. Translated by Michael D. Barber. New York: Continuum, 1995.

———. "Historia del fenómeno religioso en América Latina." In *Religiosidad e historiografía: La irrupción del pluralismo religioso en América Latina y su elaboración metódica en la historiografía*, edited by Hans-Jürgen Prien, 71–82. Frankfurt: Vervuert, 1998.

———. "Europe, Modernity, and Eurocentrism." *Nepantla* 1, no. 3 (2000): 465–78.

Dussel, Enrique, Eduardo Mendieta, and Carmen Bohórquez, eds. *El pensamiento filosófico latinoamericano, del Caribe y "latino" (1300–2000)*. Mexico City: Siglo XXI Editores, 2011.

Dzidzienyo, Anani, and Suzanne Oboler, eds. *Neither Enemies nor Friends: Latinos, Blacks, Afro-Latinos*. New York: Palgrave Macmillan, 2005.

Edin, Kathryn, and Laura Lein. *Making Ends Meet: How Single Mothers Survive Welfare and Low-Wage Work*. New York: Russell Sage Foundation, 1997.

Edin, Kathryn, and Maria Kefalas. *Promises I Can Keep: Why Poor People Put Motherhood before Marriage*. Berkeley: University of California Press, 2005.

Edwards, Brent Hayes. "The Uses of Diaspora." *Social Text* 19, no. 1 (2001): 45–73.

Ekirch, Arthur A. *The Civilian and the Military*. New York: Oxford University Press, 1956.

"El Corrido de Gregorio Cortez." In *"With His Pistol in His Hand": A Border Ballad and Its Hero* by Américo Paredes, 3. Austin: University of Texas Press, 1958.

Elizondo, Virgilio. *Galilean Journey: The Mexican-American Promise*. Maryknoll, NY: Orbis Books, 1983.

Elliott, J. H. *Imperial Spain, 1469–1770*. London: Penguin UK, 2002.

Enck-Wanzer, Darrel, ed. *The Young Lords: A Reader*. New York: New York University Press, 2010.

Ennis, Sharon R., Merarys Ríos-Vargas, and Nora G. Albert. *The Hispanic Population: 2010*. Washington, DC: United States Census Bureau, 2011. www.census.gov.

Erman, Sam. "Meanings of Citizenship in the U.S. Empire: Puerto Rico, Isabel Gonzalez, and the Supreme Court." *Journal of American Ethnic History* 27, no. 4 (2008): 5–33.

Espada, Martín. "Searching for La Revolución in the Streets of Tijuana." In *Alabanza: New and Selected Poems 1982–2002*, 214. New York: W.W. Norton, 2004.

Espenshade, Thomas, and S. Karthick Ramakrishnan. "Immigrant Incorporation and Political Participation." *International Migration Review* 35, no. 3 (2001): 870–909.

Espinosa, Gastón. "'Your Daughers Shall Prophesy': A History of Women in Ministry in the Latino Pentecostal Movement in the United States." In *Women and Twentieth-Century Protestantism*, edited by Margaret Lambers Bendroth and Virginia Lieson Brereton, 25–48. Urbana: University of Illinois Press, 2002.

———. "Mexican-American and Latino Religions." *Oxford Bibliographies Online: Latino Studies*, edited by Ilan Stavans. March 19, 2013. www.oxfordbibliographies.com.

Espinosa, Gastón, Virgilio Elizondo, and Jesse Miranda, eds. *Latino Religions and Civic Activism in the United States*. New York: Oxford University Press, 2005.

Espinosa, Gastón, and Mario T. García, eds. *Mexican American Religions: Spirituality, Activism, and Culture*. Durham, NC: Duke University Press, 2008.

Espinosa, Mariola. *Epidemic Invasions: Yellow Fever and the Limits of Cuban Independence, 1870–1930*. Chicago: University of Chicago Press, 2009.

Espinoza, Dionne. "Revolutionary Sisters." *Aztlán* 26, no. 1 (2001): 17–58.

Esquibel, Catriona Rueda. *With Her Machete in Her Hand: Reading Chicana Lesbians*. Austin: University of Texas Press, 2006.

Estrada, Alicia Ivonne. "(Re)Claiming Public Space and Place: Maya Community Formation in Westlake/MacArthur Park." In *U.S. Central Americans: Reconstructing Memories, Struggles, and Communities of Resistance*, edited by Karina O. Alvarado, Alicia Ivonne Estrada, and Ester E. Hernández, 166–87. Tucson: University of Arizona Press, 2017.

Eustachewich, Lia. "U.S. Court Rules 'Hispanic' Is a Race in Discrimination Suit." *New York Post*, February 16, 2016.

Facio, Elisa, and Irene Lara, eds. *Fleshing the Spirit: Spirituality and Activism in Chicana, Latina, and Indigenous Women's Lives*. Tucson: University of Arizona Press, 2014.

Falcón, Angelo. "Brown, Ramos, Liu, and Garner: Finding the Right Words." *NiLP Newsletter*, December 22, 2014. my-email.constantcontact.com.

BIBLIOGRAPHY

Falcón, Priscilla. *Interview with Freedom Archives*. January 25, 2011. https://vimeo.com.

Falconer, Blas, and Lorraine López, eds. *The Other Latin@: Writing against a Singular Identity*. Tucson: University of Arizona Press, 2011.

Fanon, Frantz. *The Wretched of the Earth*. Translated by Richard Philcox. New York: Grove Press, 2004.

Farmer, Paul. *AIDS and Accusation: Haiti and the Geography of Blame*. Berkeley: University of California Press, 2006.

Fausto-Sterling, Anne. "Is Gender Essential?" In *Sissies and Tomboys: Gender Nonconformity and Homosexual Childhood*, edited by Matthew Rottnek, 52–57. New York: New York University Press, 1999.

Feliciano-Santos, Sherina. "An Inconceivable Indigeneity: The Historical, Cultural, and Interactional Dimensions of Puerto Rican Taino Activism." PhD diss., University of Michigan, Ann Arbor, 2011.

Félix, Adrián. "New Americans or Diasporic Nationalists? Mexican Migrant Responses to Naturalization and Implications for Political Participation." *American Quarterly* 60, no. 3 (2008): 601–24.

Fellner, Astrid M. "The Flavors of Multi-Ethnic North American Literatures: Language, Ethnicity and Culinary Nostalgia." In *Culinary Linguistics: The Chef's Special*, edited by Cornelia Gerhardt, Maximiliane Frobenius, and Susanne Hucklenbroich-Ley, 241–60. Amsterdam: John Benjamins, 2013.

Fernández, Lilia. "From the Near West Side to 18th Street: Un/Making Latina/o Barrios in Postwar Chicago." In *Beyond el Barrio: Everyday Life in Latina/o America*, edited by Gina M. Pérez, Frank A. Guridy, and Adrian Burgos Jr., 233–51. New York: New York University Press, 2011.

Fernández L'Hoeste, Héctor D., and Pablo Vila, eds. *Cumbia!: Scenes of a Migrant Latin American Music*. Durham, NC: Duke University Press, 2013.

Fernández Retamar, Roberto. "Caliban, Notes towards a Discussion of Culture in Our America." 1971. In *Calibán and Other Essays*, translated by Edward Parker, 3–45. Minneapolis: University of Minnesota Press, 1989.

Fields, Virgina M., and Victor Zamudio-Taylor. *The Road to Aztlán: Art from a Mythic Homeland*. Los Angeles: LACMA, 2001.

Figueroa, Luis A. *Sugar, Slavery, and Freedom in Nineteenth-Century Puerto Rico*. Chapel Hill: University of North Carolina Press, 2005.

Findlay, Eileen J. Suarez. *Imposing Decency: The Politics of Sexuality and Race in Puerto Rico, 1870–1920*. Durham, NC: Duke University Press, 1999.

Fine, Janice. *Worker Centers: Organizing Communities at the Edge of the Dream*. Ithaca, NY: ILR Press, 2006.

Fiol-Matta, Licia. *A Queer Mother for the Nation: Gabriela Mistral and the State*. Minneapolis: University of Minnesota Press, 2002.

———. *The Great Woman Singer: Gender and Voice in Puerto Rican Music*. Durham, NC: Duke University Press, 2017.

Fischer, Sibylle. *Modernity Disavowed: Haiti and the Cultures of Slavery in the Age of Revolution*. Durham, NC: Duke University Press, 2004.

Flores, Juan. *Divided Borders: Essays on Puerto Rican Identity*. Houston: Arte Público Press, 1993.

———. "'Salvación Casita': Puerto Rican Performance and Vernacular Architecture in the South Bronx." In *Negotiating Performance: Gender, Sexuality and Theatricality in Latin/o America*, edited by Diana Taylor and Juan Villegas, 121–36. Durham, NC: Duke University Press, 1995.

———. "Pan-Latino/Trans-Latino: Puerto Ricans in the 'New Nueva York.'" *CENTRO Journal* 8, no. 1–2 (1996): 171–86.

———. *From Bomba to Hip-Hop: Puerto Rican Culture and Latino Identity*. New York: Columbia University Press, 2000.

———. *The Diaspora Strikes Back: Caribeño Tales of Learning and Turning*. New York: Routledge, 2009.

Flores, Juan, and George Yúdice. "Living Borders / Buscando America: Languages of Latino Self-Formation." *Social Text* 24 (1990): 57–84.

Flores, Richard. *Los Pastores: History and Performance in the Mexican Shepherd's Play of South Texas*. Washington, DC: Smithsonian Institution Press, 1995.

Flores, William, and Rina Benmayor. *Latino Cultural Citizenship: Claiming Identity, Space and Rights*. Boston: Beacon Press, 1998.

Flores-González, Nilda. *School Kids, Street Kids: Identity and High School Completion among Latinos*. New York: Teachers College Press, 2002.

Flores-Peña, Ysamur. "'Candles, Flowers, and Perfume': Puerto Rican Spiritism on the Move." In *Botánica Los Angeles: Latino Popular Religious Art in the City of Angels*, edited by Patrick Arthur Polk and Donald Cosentino, 88–97. Los Angeles: UCLA Fowler Museum of Cultural History, 2004.

Foley, Neil. *The White Scourge: Mexicans, Blacks, and Poor Whites in Texas Cotton Culture*. Berkeley: University of California Press, 1997.

———. "Becoming Hispanic: Mexican Americans and the Faustian Pact with Whiteness." In *Reflexiones 1997: New Directions in Mexican American Studies*, edited by Neil Foley, 53–70. Austin, TX: Center for Mexican American Studies (CMAS), 1998.

Foucault, Michel. *Archeology of Knowledge*. New York: Pantheon Books, 1972.

———. *Society Must Be Defended*. Translated by David Macey. New York: Picador, 2003.

Foudree, Paja. *Singing for the Dead: The Politics of Indigenous Revival in Mexico*. Durham, NC: Duke University Press, 2013.

Fox, Cybelle. *Three Worlds of Relief: Race, Immigration, and the American Welfare State from the Progressive Era to the New Deal*. Princeton, NJ: Princeton University Press, 2012.

Fox, Jonathan, and Gaspar Rivera-Salgado. *Indigenous Mexican Migrants in the United States*. La Jolla: Center for U.S.-Mexican Studies, University of California, San Diego, 2004.

Fraga, Luis, John A. Garcia, Rodney Hero, Michael Jones-Correa, Valerie Martinez-Ebers, and Gary M. Segura. *Latino Lives in America: Making It Home*. Philadelphia: Temple University Press, 2010.

———. *Latinos in the New Millennium: An Almanac of Opinion, Behavior, and Policy Preferences*. New York: Cambridge University Press, 2012.

Franco, Jean. "Si me permiten hablar: la lucha por el poder interpretativo." *Casa de las Américas* 29, no. 171 (1988): 88–94.

———. "Waiting for a Bourgeoisie: The Formation of the Mexican Intelligentsia in the Age of Independence." In *Critical Passions: Selected Essays*, edited by Mary Louise Pratt and Kathleen Newman, 476–92. Durham, NC: Duke University Press, 1999.

Franqui, Harry. "Fighting for the Nation: Military Service, Popular Political Mobilization and the Creation of Modern Puerto Rican National Identities: 1868–1952." PhD diss., University of Massachusetts, Amherst, 2010.

Freedman, Estelle B. *Their Sisters' Keepers: Women's Prison Reform in America, 1830–1930*. Ann Arbor: University of Michigan Press, 1981.

Fregoso, Rosa-Linda. *The Bronze Screen: Chicana and Chicano Film Culture*. Minneapolis: University of Minnesota Press, 1993.

———, ed. *The Devil Never Sleeps and Other Films by Lourdes Portillo*. Austin: University of Texas Press, 2001.

———. *meXicana Encounters: The Making of Social Identities on the Borderlands*. Berkeley: University of California Press, 2003.

Fregoso, Rosa-Linda, and Cynthia Bejarano. *Terrorizing Women: Feminicide in the Americas*. Durham, NC: Duke University Press, 2009.

Freire, Paulo. *Pedagogy of the Oppressed*. New York: Herder and Herder, 1970.

———. *Pedagogy of Freedom: Ethics, Democracy, and Civic Courage*. New York: Rowman and Littlefield, 1998.

Fritz, Sonia, dir. *The American Dream: Puerto Ricans and Mexicans in New York*. New York: Cinema Guild, 2003.

Fröbel, Folker, Jürgen Heinrichs, and Otto Kreye. *La nueva división internacional del trabajo: Paro estructural en los países industrializados e industrialización de los países en desarrollo*. Mexico City: Siglo XXI, 1981.

Fusco, Coco. *English Is Broken Here: Notes on Cultural Fusion in the Americas*. New York: New Press, 1995.

———. "Observations of Predation in Humans: A Lecture by Dr. Zira, Animal Psychologist." New York: Studio Museum of Harlem, 2013. www.youtube.com.

Fusté, José I. "Unsettling Citizenship/Circumventing Sovereignty: Reexamining the Quandaries of Contemporary Anticolonialism in the United States through Black Puerto Rican Antiracist Thought." *American Quarterly* 66, no. 1 (2014): 161–69.

Galarza, Ernesto. *Merchants of Labor: The Mexican Bracero Story*. Santa Barbara, CA: McNally and Loftin, 1964.

———. *Barrio Boy*. Notre Dame, IN: University of Notre Dame Press, 1971.

Gálvez, Alyshia. *Patient Citizens, Immigrant Mothers: Mexican Women, Public Prenatal Care, and the Birth-Weight Paradox*. Piscataway, NJ: Rutgers University Press, 2011.

Gamboa, Suzanne. "How Can 2020 Census Measure Latino Race-Ethnicity?" *NBC News*, December 2, 2014. www.nbcnews.com.

Gándara, Patricia, and Frances Contreras. *The Latino Education Crisis: The Consequences of Failed Social Policies*. Cambridge, MA: Harvard University Press, 2009.

Gans, Herbert J. "Symbolic Ethnicity: The Future of Ethnic Groups and Cultures in America." *Ethnic and Racial Studies* 2, no. 1 (1979): 1–20.

———. "Ethnic Invention and Acculturation: A Bumpy Line Approach." *Journal of American Ethnic History* 12, no. 1 (1992): 42–52.

García, Alma M. "The Development of Chicana Feminist Discourse, 1970–1980." *Gender and Society* 3, no. 2 (1989): 217–38.

———, ed. *Chicana Feminist Thought: The Basic Historical Writings*. New York: Routledge, 1997.

Garcia, Charles. "Why 'Illegal Immigrant' Is a Slur." CNN, July 6, 2012. www.cnn.com.

García, Cindy. *Salsa Crossings: Dancing Latinidad in Los Angeles*. Durham, NC: Duke University Press, 2013.

Garcia, F. Chris, and Gabriel Sanchez. *Hispanics and the U.S. Political System: Moving into the Mainstream*. New York: Pearson, 2007.

García, Ignacio M. "Juncture in the Road: Chicano Studies

since 'El Plan de Santa Bárbara.'" In *Chicanas/Chicanos at the Crossroads: Social, Economic, and Political Change*, edited by David R. Maciel and Isidro D. Ortiz, 181–203. Tucson: University of Arizona Press, 1996.

———. *Chicanismo: The Forging of a Militant Ethos among Mexican Americans*. Tucson: University of Arizona Press, 1997.

———. *Hector P. García: In Relentless Pursuit of Justice*. Houston: Arte Público Press, 2003.

García, John A. *Latino Politics in America: Community, Culture and Interests*, 3rd ed. Lanham, MD: Rowman and Littlefield, 2016.

García, John A., and Gabriel Sanchez. "Electoral Politics." In *Latino Americans and Participation of Latinos: A Reference Handbook*, edited by Sharon A. Navarro and Armando Mejia, 121–72. Santa Barbara: ABC-CLIO, 2004.

Garcia, Laura, Sandra M. Gutiérrez, and Felicitas Núñez. *Teatro Chicana: A Collective Memoir and Selected Plays*. Austin: University of Texas Press, 2008

García, María Cristina. *Havana, USA: Cuban Exiles and Cuban Americans in South Florida, 1959–1994*. Berkeley: University of California Press, 1996.

García, Ofelia. "Education, Multilingualism and Translanguaging in the 21st Century." In *Multilingual Education for Social Justice: Globalising the Local*, edited by Ajit K. Mohanty, Minati Panda, Robert Phillipson, and Tove Skutnabb-Kangas, 128–45. New Delhi: Orient Blackswan, 2009.

García Bedolla, Lisa. *Latino Politics*, 2nd ed. Cambridge, UK: Polity, 2014.

García Canclini, Néstor. *Hybrid Cultures: Strategies for Entering and Leaving Modernity*. Translated by Christopher L. Chiappari and Silvia L. López. Minneapolis: University of Minnesota Press, 1995.

García Espinosa, Julio. "For an Imperfect Cinema." In *New Latin American Cinema, Volume 1: Theories, Practices, and Transcontinental Articulations*, edited by Michael T. Martin, 71–82. Detroit, MI: Wayne State University Press, 1997.

García-Peña, Lorgia. *The Borders of Dominicanidad: Race, Nation, and Archives of Contradiction*. Durham, NC: Duke University, Press, 2016.

Garza, Roberto J. *Contemporary Chicano Theatre*. Notre Dame, IN: University of Notre Dame Press, 1976.

Gaspar de Alba, Alicia. *Chicano Art Inside/Outside the Master's House: Cultural Politics and the CARA Exhibition*. Austin: University of Texas Press, 1998.

———, ed. *Velvet Barrios: Popular Culture and Chicana/o Sexualities*. New York: Palgrave Macmillan, 2003.

Gaspar de Alba, Alicia, and Alma López, eds. *Our Lady of Controversy: Alma López's "Irreverent Apparition."* Austin: University of Texas Press, 2011.

Gelt, Jessica. "Kogi Korean BBQ, a Taco Truck Brought to You by Twitter." *Los Angeles Times*, February 11, 2009. www.latimes.com.

Georges, Eugenia. *The Making of a Transnational Community: Migration, Development, and Cultural Change in the Dominican Republic*. New York: Columbia University Press, 1990.

Gilb, Dagoberto. *Gritos!* New York: Grove Press, 2003.

Giménez-Smith, Carmen, and John Chávez, eds. *Angels of the Americlypse: An Anthology of New Latin@ Writing*. Denver, CO: Counterpath, 2014.

Girmay, Aracelis. *Kingdom Animalia*. Rochester, NY: BOA, 2011.

Gittell, Noah. "On the Need for a 'Harlem Renaissance' for Latino Cinema." RogerEbert.com, March 21, 2014.

Glasser, Ruth. *My Music Is My Flag: Puerto Rican Musicians and Their New York Communities, 1917–1940*. Berkeley: University of California Press, 1995.

Glazer, Nathan. "Is Assimilation Dead?" *Annals of the American Academy of Political and Social Science* 530, no. 1 (1993): 122–36.

Gleeson, Shannon. "Legal Status as Precarity Multiplier: Social and Economic Consequences of At-Will Employment and Unjust Termination for Unauthorized Workers." Paper presented at the Labor Employment Relations Association Annual Meeting, Portland, OR, 2014.

———. "'They Come Here to Work': An Evaluation of the Economic Argument in Favor of Immigrant Rights." *Citizenship Studies* 19, no. 3–4 (2015): 400–20.

Glenn, Evelyn Nakano. "From Servitude to Service Work: Historical Continuities in the Racial Division of Paid Reproductive Labor." *Signs* 18, no. 1 (1992): 1–43.

———. "Constructing Citizenship: Exclusion, Subordination, and Resistance." *American Sociological Review* 76, no. 1 (2011): 1–24.

Goffman, Erving. *Frame Analysis: An Essay on the Organization of Experience*. New York: Harper and Row, 1974.

Goizueta, Roberto S., ed. *We Are a People! Initiatives in Hispanic American Theology*. Minneapolis, MN: Fortress Press, 1992.

Golash-Boza, Tanya. "Dropping the Hyphen? Becoming Latino(a)-American through Racialized Assimilation." *Social Forces* 85, no. 1 (2006): 27–55.

Golash-Boza, Tanya, and William Darity Jr. "Latino Racial Choices: The Effects of Skin Colour and Discrimination on Latinos' and Latinas' Racial Self-Identifications." *Ethnic and Racial Studies* 31, no. 5 (2008): 899–934.

Golash-Boza, Tanya, and Pierrette Hondagneu-Sotelo. "Latino

Migrant Men and the Deportation Crisis: A Gendered Racial Removal Program." *Latino Studies* 11, no. 3 (2013): 271–92.

Gomberg-Muñoz, Ruth. "Willing to Work: Agency and Vulnerability in an Undocumented Immigrant Network." *American Anthropologist* 112, no. 2 (2010): 295–307.

Gomberg-Muñoz, Ruth, and Laura Nussbaum-Barberena. "Is Immigration Policy Labor Policy?: Immigration Enforcement, Undocumented Workers, and the State." *Human Organization* 70, no. 4 (2011): 366–75.

Gómez, Laura E. *Manifest Destinies: The Making of the Mexican American Race.* New York: New York University Press, 2007.

Gómez-Peña, Guillermo. "A New Artistic Continent." In *Made in Aztlán,* edited by Philip Brookman and Guillermo Gómez-Peña, 88–96. San Diego, CA: Centro Cultural de la Raza, 1986.

Gómez-Quiñones, Juan. *Mexican Students por la Raza: The Chicano Student Movement in Southern California 1967–1977.* Santa Barbara, CA: Editorial La Causa, 1978.

Gómez-Quiñones, Juan, and Irene Velásquez. *Making Aztlán: Ideology and Culture of the Chicana and Chicano Movement, 1966–1977.* Albuquerque: University of New Mexico Press, 2014.

Gonzales, Alfonso. *Reform without Justice: Latino Migrant Politics and the Homeland Security State.* Oxford: Oxford University Press, 2013.

Gonzales, Patrisia. *Red Medicine: Traditional Indigenous Rites of Birthing and Healing.* Tucson: University of Arizona Press, 2012.

Gonzales, Roberto G., and Angie M. Bautista-Chavez. *Two Years and Counting: Assessing the Growing Power of DACA.* Washington, DC: American Immigration Council, 2014.

Gonzales, Rodolfo [Corky]. *I Am Joaquín / Yo soy Joaquín: An Epic Poem.* New York: Bantam, 1972.

Gonzales, Rodolfo, and Alberto Urista. "El Plan Espiritual de Aztlán." *El grito del norte* 2, no. 9 (1969): 5.

González, Jennifer A. *Subject to Display: Reframing Race in Contemporary Installation Art.* Cambridge, MA: MIT Press, 2008.

González, José Luis. *El país de cuatro pisos y otros ensayos.* Río Piedras, PR: Ediciones Huracán, 1980.

———. *Puerto Rico: The Four-Storeyed Country and Other Essays.* Translated by Gerald Guinness. Maplewood, NJ: Waterfront Press, 1990.

González, Jovita. *Dew on the Thorn.* Houston: Arte Público Press, 1997.

———. *Life along the Border: A Landmark Tejana Thesis.* College Station: Texas A&M University Press, 2006.

González, Juan. *Harvest of Empire: A History of Latinos in America.* New York: Penguin, 2001.

———. *Harvest of Empire: A History of Latinos in America,* rev. ed. New York: Penguin, 2011.

González, Juan, and Joseph Torres. *News for All the People: The Epic Story of Race and the American Media.* London: Verso, 2011.

Gonzalez, Michelle A. *Afro-Cuban Theology: Religion, Race, Culture and Identity.* Gainesville: University Press of Florida, 2006.

González, Norma, Luis C. Moll, and Cathy Amanti. *Funds of Knowledge: Theorizing Practices in Households, Communities and Classrooms.* Mahwah, NJ: Lawrence Erlbaum Associates, 2005.

Gonzalez, Rita, Howard N. Fox, and Chon A. Noriega. *Phantom Sightings: Art after the Chicano Movement.* Berkeley: University of California Press, 2008.

González Echevarría, Roberto. "Is 'Spanglish' a Language?" *New York Times,* March 28, 1997.

González-López, Gloria. *Family Secrets: Stories of Incest and Sexual Violence in Mexico.* New York: New York University Press, 2015.

Goode, Judith, and Jeff Maskovsky, eds. *New Poverty Studies: The Ethnography of Power, Politics and Impoverished People in the United States.* New York: New York University Press, 2001.

Gopinath, Gayatri. *Impossible Desires: Queer Diasporas and South Asian Public Cultures.* Durham, NC: Duke University Press, 2005.

Gordillo, Luz. "The Bracero, the Wetback, and the Terrorist: Mexican Immigration, Legislation, and National Security." In *A New Kind of Containment: "The War on Terror," Race, and Sexuality,* edited by Carmen Lugo-Lugo and Mary Bloodsworth-Lugo, 149–66. Amsterdam: Rodopi, 2009.

Gordon, Jennifer. "Holding the Line on Workplace Standards: What Works for Immigrant Workers (and What Doesn't)?" In *What Works for Workers?: Public Policies and Innovative Strategies for Low-Wage Workers,* edited by Stephanie Luce, Jennifer Luff, Joseph A. McCartin, and Ruth Milkman, 134–64. New York: Russell Sage Foundation, 2014.

Gordon, Milton M. *Assimilation in American Life: The Role of Race, Religion and National Origins.* New York: Oxford University Press, 1964.

Gotanda, Neil. "Multiculturalism and Racial Stratification." In *Mapping Multiculturalism,* edited by Avery F. Gordon and Christopher Newfield, 239–50. Minneapolis: University of Minnesota Press, 1996.

Gracia, Jorge J. E. *Hispanic/Latino Identity: A Philosophical Perspective.* Malden, MA: Blackwell, 2000.

Gracia, Jorge J. E., and Elizabeth Millán-Zaibert, eds. *Latin*

American Philosophy for the 21st Century: The Human Condition, Values, and the Search for Identity. Amherst, NY: Prometheus Books, 2004.

Grillo, Evelio. *Black Cuban, Black American: A Memoir*. Houston: Arte Público Press, 2000.

Griswold del Castillo, Richard. *The Los Angeles Barrio, 1850–1890: A Social History*. Berkeley: University of California Press, 1979.

———. *The Treaty of Guadalupe Hidalgo: A Legacy of Conflict*. Norman: University of Oklahoma Press, 1990.

Grob, Gerald. *The Deadly Truth: A History of Disease in America*. Cambridge, MA: Harvard University Press, 2002.

Grobsmith, Elizabeth S. *Indians in Prison: Incarcerated Native Americans in Nebraska*. Lincoln: University of Nebraska Press, 1994.

Groody, Daniel G. *Border of Death, Valley of Life: An Immigrant Journey of Heart and Spirit*. Lanham, MD: Rowman and Littlefield, 2002.

Grosfoguel, Ramón. *Colonial Subjects: Puerto Ricans in a Global Perspective*. Berkeley: University of California Press, 2003.

Gross, Ariela. "Texas Mexicans and the Politics of Whiteness" *Law and History Review* 21, no. 1 (2003): 195–205.

———. "'The Caucasian Cloak': Mexican Americans and the Politics of Whiteness in the Twentieth-Century Southwest." *Georgetown Law Journal* 95 (2007): 337–92.

Gruesz, Kirsten Silva. *Ambassadors of Culture: The Transamerican Origins of Latino Writing*. Princeton, NJ: Princeton University Press, 2002.

———. "Utopia Latina: The Ordinary Seaman in Extraordinary Times." *Modern Fiction Studies* 49, no. 1 (Spring 2003): 54–83.

———. "Cartographies of a Centrocéntrico World." Paper presented at the Central Americans and the Latino/a Landscape: New Configurations of Latina/o America Conference, University of Texas, Austin, February 24, 2012.

Gruzinski, Serge. *The Mestizo Mind: The Intellectual Dynamics of Colonization and Globalization*. Translated by Deke Dusinberre. New York: Routledge, 2002.

Guerra, François-Xavier. *Modernidad e independencias: Ensayos sobre las revoluciones hispánicas*. Mexico City: Fondo de Cultura Económica and Editorial MAPFRE, 1992.

Guerra, François-Xavier, and Annick Lempérière, eds. *Los espacios públicos en Iberoamérica: Ambigüedades y problemas, siglos XVIII–XIX*. Mexico City: Centro Francés de Estudios Mexicanos y Centroamericanos and Fondo de Cultura Económica, 1998.

Guerra, Gilbert, and Gilbert Orbea. "The Argument against the Use of the Term 'Latinx.'" *Swarthmore Phoenix*, November 19, 2015. http://swarthmorephoenix.com.

Guevara, Gema. "La Cuba de ayer / La Cuba de hoy: The Politics of Music and Diaspora." In *Musical Migrations: Transnationalism and Cultural Hybridity in Latin/o America*, edited by Frances R. Aparicio and Cándida Jáquez with María Elena Cepeda, 33–46. New York: St. Martin's, 2003.

Guglielmo, Thomas A. "Fighting for Caucasian Rights: Mexicans, Mexican Americans, and the Transnational Struggle for Civil Rights in World War II Texas." *Journal of American History* 92, no. 4 (2006): 1212–37.

Guidotti-Hernández, Nicole M. *Unspeakable Violence: Remapping U.S. and Mexican National Imaginaries*. Durham, NC: Duke University Press, 2011.

Gunckel, Colin. *Mexico on Main Street: Transnational Film Culture in Los Angeles before World War II*. New Brunswick, NJ: Rutgers University Press, 2015.

Gupta, Akhil, and James Ferguson. *Culture, Power, Place: Explorations in Critical Anthropology*. Durham, NC: Duke University Press, 1997.

Guridy, Frank Andre. *Forging Diaspora: Afro-Cubans and African Americans in a World of Empire and Jim Crow*. Chapel Hill: University of North Carolina Press, 2010.

Guskin, Emily. *"Illegal," "Undocumented," "Unauthorized": News Media Shift Language on Immigration*. Washington, DC: Pew Research Center, June 17, 2013. www.pewresearch.org.

Gutiérrez, David G. *Walls and Mirrors: Mexican Americans, Mexican Immigrants and the Politics of Ethnicity*. Berkeley: University of California Press, 1995.

Gutiérrez, Elena R. *Fertile Matters: The Politics of Mexican-Origin Women's Reproduction*. Austin: University of Texas Press, 2008.

Gutiérrez, Félix, and Jorge Reina Schement. "Chicanos and the Media: A Bibliography of Selected Materials." *Journalism History* 4, no. 2 (1977): 53–55.

———. "Problems of Ownership and Control of Spanish-Language Media in the United States: National and International Policy Concerns." In *Communication and Social Structure: Critical Studies in Mass Media Research*, edited by Emile G. McAnany, Jorge Schnitman, and Noreene Janus, 181–203. New York: Praeger, 1981.

Gutiérrez, Laura G. *Performing Mexicanidad: Vendidas y Cabareteras on the Transnational Stage*. Austin: University of Texas, 2010.

Gutiérrez, Luis. *Still Dreaming: My Journey from the Barrio to Capitol Hill*. New York: W.W. Norton, 2013.

Gutiérrez, Sandra M., and Felicitas Núñez. *Teatro Chicana: A Collective Memoir and Selected Plays*. Austin: University of Texas Press, 2008.

Habell-Pallán, Michelle. *Loca Motion: The Travels of Chicana and Latina Popular Culture*. New York: New York University Press, 2005.

Habell-Pallán, Michelle, and Mary Romero, eds. *Latina/o Popular Culture*. New York: New York University Press, 2002.

Hagan, Jacqueline, Karl Eschbach, and Nestor Rodriguez. "U.S. Deportation Policy, Family Separation, and Circular Migration." *International Migration Review* 42, no. 1 (2008): 64–88.

Hagan, Jacqueline, Nestor Rodriguez, and Brianna Castro. "Social Effects of Mass Deportations by the United States Government, 2000–2010." *Ethnic and Racial Studies* 34, no. 8 (2011): 1374–91.

Hall, Matthew, and Emily Greenman. "The Occupational Cost of Being Illegal in the United States: Legal Status, Job Hazards, and Compensating Differentials." *International Migration Review* 49, no. 2 (2014): 1–37.

Hall, Stuart. "Cultural Identity and Diaspora." In *Identity: Community, Culture, Difference*, edited by Jonathan Rutherford, 222–37. London: Lawrence and Wishart, 1990.

———. "What Is This 'Black' in Black Popular Culture?" In *Black Popular Culture*, edited by Gina Dent, 21–33. New York: New Press, 1998.

Halpern-Meekin, Sarah, Kathryn Edin, Laura Tach, and Jennifer Sykes. *It's Not Like I'm Poor: How Working Families Make Ends Meet in a Post-Welfare World*. Berkeley: University of California Press, 2014.

Hames-García, Michael. "Dr. Gonzo's Carnival: The Testimonial Satires of Oscar Z. Acosta." *American Literature* 72, no. 3 (2000): 463–93.

———. *Fugitive Thought: Prison Movements, Race, and the Meaning of Justice*. Minneapolis: University of Minnesota Press, 2004.

———. *Identity Complex: Making the Case for Multiplicity*. Minneapolis: University of Minnesota Press, 2011a.

———. "Queer Theory Revisited." In *Gay Latino Studies: A Critical Reader*, edited by Michael Hames-García and Ernesto Javier Martínez, 19–44. Durham, NC: Duke University Press, 2011b.

Hames-García, Michael, and Ernesto Javier Martínez, eds. *Gay Latino Studies: A Critical Reader*. Durham, NC: Duke University Press, 2011.

Hamlin, Rebecca. "Immigrants at Work: Labor Unions and Non-Citizen Members." In *Civic Hopes and Political Realities: Immigrants, Community Organizations, and Political Engagement*, edited by S. Karthick Ramakrishnan and Irene Bloemraad, 300–22. New York: Russell Sage Foundation, 2008.

Haney López, Ian. *White by Law: The Legal Construction of Race*. New York: New York University Press, 1996.

———. "White Latinos." *Harvard Latino Law Review* 6 (2003): 1–6.

———. *White by Law: The Legal Construction of Race*, rev.10th anniversay ed. New York: New York University Press, 2006.

Hannaford, Ivan. *Race: The History of an Idea in the West*. Washington, DC: Woodrow Wilson Center Press, 1996.

Hanson, Victor Davis. *Mexifornia: A State of Becoming*. San Francisco: Encounter Books, 2003.

Hardt, Michael, and Antonio Negri. *Empire*. Cambridge, MA: Harvard University Press, 2000.

Harris, Martin, Roberto J. Velásquez, Jerre White, and Teresa Renteria. "Folk Healing and Curanderismo within the Contemporary Chicana/o Community: Current Status." In *The Handbook of Chicana/o Psychology and Mental Health*, edited by Roberto J. Velásquez, Leticia M. Arellano, and Brian W. McNeill, 111–26. Mahwah, NJ: Lawrence Erlbaum, 2004.

Hartney, Christopher. *U.S. Rates of Incarceration: A Global Perspective*. Madison, WI: National Council on Crime and Delinquency, 2006.

Harvey, David. *The New Imperialism*. New York: Oxford University Press, 2003.

———. *A Brief History of Neoliberalism*. New York: Oxford University Press, 2005.

Haughney, Christine. "The Times Shifts on 'Illegal Immigrant,' but Doesn't Ban the Use." *New York Times*, April 23, 2013. www.nytimes.com.

Hayden, Dolores. *Redesigning the American Dream: The Future of Housing, Work, and Family Life*. New York: W. W. Norton, 2002.

Hayes-Bautista, David E. *La Nueva California: Latinos in the Golden State*. Berkeley: University of California Press, 2004.

Hébert, John R. "The Map that Named America." *Library of Congress Information Bulletin* 62, no. 9 (2003). www.loc.gov.

Herchenroeder, Karl. "Michael Bloomberg Blocks Footage of Aspen Institute Appearance." *Aspen Times*, February 13, 2015. www.aspentimes.com.

Hernández, David Manuel. "Pursuant to Deportation: Latinos and Immigrant Detention." *Latino Studies* 6 (2008): 35–63.

Hernández, Ellie. *Postnationalism in Chicana/o Literature and Culture*. Austin: University of Texas Press, 2009.

Hernandez, Jillian. "'Miss, You Look like a Bratz Doll': On Chonga Girls and Sexual-Aesthetic Excess." *NWSA Journal* 21, no. 3 (2009): 63–90.

Hernández, Ramona. *The Mobility of Workers under Advanced Capitalism: Dominican Migration to the United States*. New York: Columbia University Press, 2002.

Hernández, Tanya Katerí. "'Too Black to Be Latino/a': Blackness and Blacks as Foreigners in Latino Studies." *Latino Studies* 1, no. 1 (2003): 152–59.

Hernández-Ávila, Inés. "Tierra Tremenda: The Earth's Agony and Ecstasy in the Work of Gloria Anzaldúa." In *Entre Mundos / Among Worlds: New Perspectives on Gloria Anzaldúa*, edited by AnaLouise Keating, 233–40. New York: Palgrave Macmillan, 2005.

Hernández Castillo, R. Aída. "Indigeneity as a Field Power: Multiculturalism and Indigenous Identities in Political Struggles." In *The Sage Handbook of Identities*, edited by Margaret Wetherell and Chandra Tapalde Mohanty, 379–402. Thousand Oaks, CA: Sage, 2010.

Hernandez v. Texas. U.S. Supreme Court. 347 U.S. 475 (1954). https://supreme.justia.com.

Herr, Richard. *The Eighteenth-Century Revolution in Spain*. Princeton, NJ: Princeton University Press, 1958.

Herrera, Brian Eugenio. *The Latina/o Theatre Commons 2013 National Convening: A Narrative Report*. Boston: HowlRound.com, 2015.

Herrera, Olga. *Towards the Preservation of a Heritage: Latin American and Latino Art in the Midwestern United States*. Notre Dame, IN: Institute for Latino Studies, University of Notre Dame, 2008. http://latinostudies.nd.edu.

Herrera-Sobek, María. *The Mexican Corrido: A Feminist Analysis*. Bloomington: Indiana University Press, 1990.

Hill, Sarah. "Metaphoric Enrichment and Material Poverty: The Making of 'Colonias.'" In *Ethnography at the Border*, edited by Pablo Vila, 141–65. Minneapolis: University of Minnesota Press, 2003.

Hilmes, Michele, and Jason Loviglio, eds. *Radio Reader: Essays in the Cultural History of Radio*. New York: Routledge, 2003.

Hinojosa, Felipe. *Latino Mennonites: Civil Rights, Faith, and Evangelical Culture*. Baltimore: Johns Hopkins University Press, 2014.

Hinojosa, Raul, and Maksim Wynn. "From the Shadows to the Mainstream: Estimating the Economic Impact of Presidential Administrative Action and Comprehensive Immigration Reform." Los Angeles: North American Integration and Development Center, University of California, Los Angeles, 2014.

Hochschild, Jennifer L. *Facing Up to the American Dream: Race, Class, and the Soul of the Nation*. Princeton, NJ: Princeton University Press, 1995.

Hoffman, Abraham. *Unwanted Mexican Americans in the Great Depression: Repatriation Pressures, 1929–1939*. Tucson: University of Arizona Press, 1974.

Hollibaugh, Amber, and Cherríe Moraga. "What We're Rollin Around in Bed With: Sexual Silences in Feminism." In *Powers of Desire: The Politics of Sexuality*, edited by Ann Snitow, Christine Stansell, and Sharon Thompson, 394–405. New York: Monthly Review Press, 1983.

Holmes, Seth. *Fresh Fruit, Broken Bodies: Migrant Farmworkers in the United States*. Berkeley: University of California Press, 2013.

hooks, bell. "Subversive Beauty: New Modes of Contestation." In *Felix Gonzalez-Torres*, edited by Amanda Cruz, 45–49. Washington, DC: Hirshhorn Museum, 1994.

Hopkins, Daniel J. "Translating into Votes: The Electoral Impacts of Spanish-Language Ballots." *American Journal of Political Science* 55, no. 4 (2011): 813–29.

Huerta, Jorge. *Chicano Theater: Themes and Forms*. Tempe, AZ: Bilingual Press, 1982.

———. *Necessary Theater: Six Plays about the Chicano Experience*. Houston: Arte Público Press, 1989.

———. *Chicano Drama: Performance, Society, and Myth*. Cambridge: Cambridge University Press, 2000.

Humphrey, John, and Hubert Schmitz. *Governance and Upgrading: Linking Industrial Clusters and Global Value Chain*. IDS Working Paper 120. Brighton, UK: Institute for Development Studies, 2000.

Huntington, Samuel P. "The Hispanic Challenge." *Foreign Policy* 141 (March–April 2004a): 30–45.

———. *Who Are We? The Challenges to America's National Identity*. New York: Simon and Schuster, 2004b.

Ibarra, María. "Mexican Immigrant Women and the New Domestic Labor." *Human Organization* 59, no. 4 (2000): 452–64.

———. "Emotional Proletarians in a Global Economy: Mexican Immigrant Women and Elder Care Work." *Urban Anthropology* 31, nos. 3–4 (2002): 317–51.

———. "The Tender Trap: Mexican Immigrant Women and the Ethics of Elder Care Work." *Aztlán* 28, no. 2 (2003): 87–113.

Iber, Jorge, and Samuel Octavio Regalado, eds. *Mexican Americans and Sports: A Reader on Athletics and Barrio Life*. College Station: Texas A&M University Press, 2007.

Iceland, John. "Beyond Black and White: Metropolitan Residential Segregation in Multi-Ethnic America." *Social Science Research* 33, no. 2 (2004): 248–71.

Iglesias-Prieto, Norma. *La flor más bella de la maquiladora*. Mexico City: Secretaría de Educación Pública and Centro de Estudios Fronterizos, 1985.

———. *Beautiful Flowers of the Maquiladora: Life Histories of Women Workers in Tijuana*. Austin: University of Texas Press, Institute of Latin American Studies, 1997.

Ignatiev, Noel. *How the Irish Became White*. New York: Routledge, 1995.

Inda, Jonathan Xavier. *Targeting Immigrants: Government, Technology, and Ethics*. New York: Wiley-Blackwell, 2005.

Indych, Anna. "Nuyorican Baroque: Pepon Osorio's Chucherias." *Art Journal* 60, no. 1 (2001): 72–83.

Ingalls, Robert P. *Urban Vigilantes in the New South, 1882–1936*. Knoxville: University of Tennessee Press, 1988.

Ingle, Zachary, ed. *Robert Rodriguez: Interviews*. Jackson: University Press of Mississippi, 2012.

Instituto Nacional de Estadística, Geografía e Informática (INEGI). *Estadísticas Económicas. Industria Maquiladora de Exportación 2006*. www.inegi.org.mx.

———. *Estadística del Programa de la Manufactura, Maquiladora y de Servicios de Exportación (IMMEX) 2010*. www.inegi.org.mx.

———. *Notas informativas: Estadística Integral del Programa de la Industria Manufacturera, Maquiladora y de Servicios de Exportación (IMMEX), 2014*. www.inegi.org.mx.

Isasi-Díaz, Ada María. *Mujerista Theology*. Maryknoll, NY: Orbis Books, 1996.

Jackson, John L., Jr. *Harlemworld: Doing Race and Class in Contemporary Black America*. Chicago: University of Chicago Press, 2001.

Jackson, Robert. *Sovereignty: Evolution of an Idea*. Cambridge, UK: Polity, 2007.

Jacobson, Matthew Frye. *Whiteness of a Different Color: European Immigrants and the Alchemy of Race*. Cambridge, MA: Harvard University Press, 1998.

———. *Roots, Too: White Ethnic Revival in Post-Civil Rights America*. Cambridge, MA: Harvard University Press, 2008.

Jameson, Fredric. *The Political Unconscious: Narrative as a Socially Symbolic Act*. Ithaca, NY: Cornell University Press, 1981.

Janer, Zilkia. "(In)edible Nature: New World Food and Coloniality." *Cultural Studies* 21, no. 2 (2007): 385–405.

———. *Latino Food Culture*. Westport, CT: Greenwood Press, 2008.

Jay, Martin. *Downcast Eyes: The Denigration of Vision in Twentieth-Century French Thought*. Berkeley: University of California Press, 1993.

Jiménez, Lillian. "Moving from the Margin to the Center: Puerto Rican Cinema in New York." In *The Ethnic Eye: Latino Media Arts*, edited by Chon A. Noriega and Ana M. López, 22–37. Minneapolis: University of Minnesota Press, 1996.

Jiménez, Tomás. R. *Replenished Ethnicity: Mexican Americans, Immigration, and Identity*. Berkeley: University of California Press, 2010.

Jiménez Román, Miriam, and Juan Flores, eds. *The Afro-Latin@ Reader: History and Culture in the United States*. Durham, NC: Duke University Press, 2010.

Johansen, Jason C. "Notes on Chicano Cinema." In *Chicanos and Film: Representation and Resistance*, edited by Chon A. Noriega, 303–08. Minneapolis: University of Minnesota Press, 1992.

Johnson, Corey R. "Female Inmates Sterilized in California Prisons without Approval." *Center for Investigative Reporting*, July 7, 2013. http://cironline.org.

Johnson, E. Patrick, and and Ramón H. Rivera-Servera, eds. *Blacktino Queer Performance*. Durham, NC: Duke University Press, 2016.

Johnson, Kevin R. "Fear of an 'Alien Nation': Race, Immigration and Immigrants." *Stanford Law and Policy Review* 7 (1996): 111–18.

———. "The Intersection of Race and Class in U.S. Immigration Law and Enforcement." *Law and Contemporary Problems* 72 (2009): 1–35.

———. "Derrick Bell and the Emergence of LatCrit Theory." *Seattle University Law Review* 36, no. 3 (2013): xxix–xxxi.

Jonas, Suzanne, and Nestor Rodríguez. *Guatemala-U.S. Migration: Transforming Regions*. Austin: University of Texas Press, 2015.

Jones, Oakah L., Jr. *Los Paisanos: Spanish Settlers on the Northern Frontier of New Spain*. Norman: University of Oklahoma Press, 1979.

Jorge, Angela. "The Black Puerto Rican Woman in Contemporary American Society." In *The Puerto Rican Woman*, edited by Edna Acosta-Belén, 134–41. New York: Praeger Publishers, 1979.

Juncker, Kristine. *Afro-Cuban Religious Arts: Popular Expressions of Cultural Inheritance in Espiritismo and Santería*. Gainesville: University Press of Florida, 2014.

Kagan, Richard L. "Prescott's Paradigm: American Historical Scholarship and the Decline of Spain." *American Historical Review* 101, no. 2 (1996): 423–46.

Kalb, Laurie Beth. *Crafting Devotions: Tradition in Contemporary New Mexico Santos*. Albuquerque: University of New Mexico Press, 1994.

Kanellos, Nicolás. "Canto y declamación en la poesía nuyoriqueña." *Confluencia* 1, no. 1 (1985): 102–06.

———. *Mexican American Theatre: Then and Now*. Houston: Arte Público Press, 1989.

———. *A History of Hispanic Theater in the United States: Origins to 1940*. Austin: University of Texas Press, 1990.

———. *Hispanic Immigrant Literature: El Sueño del Retorno*. Austin: University of Texas Press, 2011.

Kanellos, Nicolás, and Jorge A. Huerta, eds. *Nuevos Pasos: Chi-*

cano and Puerto Rican Drama. Houston: Arte Público Press, 1989.

Kaplan, Amy, and Donald E. Pease. *Cultures of United States Imperialism*. Durham, NC: Duke University Press, 1993.

Kasinitz, Philip, Juan Battle, and Inés Miyares. "Fade to Black? The Children of West Indian Immigrants in Southern Florida." In *Ethnicities: Children of Immigrants in America*, edited by Rubén G. Rumbaut and Alejandro Portes, 267–300. Berkeley: University of California Press, 2001.

Kastanis, Angeliki, and Gary J. Gates. "LGBT Latino/a Individuals and Latino/a Same-Sex Couples." Los Angeles: Williams Institute / University of California, Los Angeles School of Law, 2013.

Katz, Michael B. *In the Shadow of the Poorhouse: A Social History of Welfare in America*. New York: Basic Books, 1986.

Kauanui, J. Kehaulani. *Hawaiian Blood: Colonialism and the Politics of Sovereignty and Indigeneity*. Durham, NC: Duke University Press, 2008.

Keefe, Susan E., and Amado M. Padilla. *Chicano Ethnicity*. Albuquerque: University of New Mexico Press, 1989.

Keller, Gary D., ed. *Chicano Cinema: Research, Reviews, and Resources*. Binghamton, NY: Bilingual Review/Press, 1985.

———. *Hispanics and United States Film: An Overview and Handbook*. Tempe, AZ: Bilingual Review/Press, 1994.

Kellner, Douglas M., and Meenakshi Gigi Durham. "Adventures in Media and Cultural Studies: Introducing the KeyWorks." In *Media and Cultural Studies: Keyworks*, edited by Meenakshi Gigi Durham and Douglas M. Kellner, 1–26. New York: John Wiley, 2009.

Kivisto, Peter. "Theorizing Transnational Immigration: A Critical Review of Current Efforts." *Ethnic and Racial Studies* 24, no. 4 (2001): 549–77.

Klor de Alva, J. Jorge. "Aztlán, Borinquen and Hispanic Nationalism in the United States." In *Aztlán: Essays on the Chicano Homeland*, edited by Rudolfo A. Anaya and Francisco A. Lomelí, 135–71. Albuquerque, NM: Academia/El Norte Publications, 1989.

Knauer, Lisa Maya. "Eating in Cuban." In *Mambo Montage: The Latinization of New York*, edited by Agustín Laó-Montes and Arlene Dávila, 425–48. New York: Columbia University Press, 2001.

Kohler-Hausmann, Julilly. "'The Crime of Survival': Fraud Prosecutions, Community Surveillance, and the Original 'Welfare Queen.'" *Journal of Social History* 41, no. 2 (2007): 329-54.

Kraut, Alan. *Silent Travelers: Germs, Genes, and the Immigrant Menace*. Baltimore, MD: Johns Hopkins University Press, 1995.

Krogstad, Jens Manuel, and Mark Hugo Lopez. *Hispanic Nativity Shift: U.S. Births Drive Population Growth as Immigration Stalls*. Washington, DC: Pew Research Center, April 29, 2014. www.pewhispanic.org.

Kroskrity, Paul V. "Identity." In *Key Terms in Language and Culture*, edited by Alessandro Duranti, 106–9. Malden, MA: Blackwell, 2001.

Kunitz, Stephen. *Regional Cultures and Mortality in America*. New York: Cambridge University Press, 2015.

Kwak, Nancy H. *A World of Homeowners: American Power and the Politics of Housing Aid*. Chicago: University of Chicago Press, 2015.

Kynard, Carmen. *Vernacular Insurrections: Race, Black Protest, and the New Century in Composition-Literacing Studies*. Albany: State University of New York Press, 2014.

La Fountain-Stokes, Lawrence. *Queer Ricans: Cultures and Sexualities in the Diaspora*. Minneapolis: University of Minnesota Press, 2009.

———. "Translocas: Migration, Homosexuality, and Transvestism in Recent Puerto Rican Performance." *e-misférica* 8, no. 1 (2011). https://hemi.press.

Lacayo, A. Elena. "The Impact of Section 287(g) of the Immigration and Nationality Act on the Latino Community." *National Council of La Raza* 21 (2010). www.nclr.org.

Lakhani, Sarah Morando. "Producing Immigrant Victims' 'Right' to Legal Status and the Management of Legal Uncertainty." *Law and Social Inquiry* 38, no. 2 (2013): 442–73. doi:10.1111/lsi.12022.

Lanning, John Tate. *Academic Culture in the Spanish Colonies*. New York: Oxford University Press, 1940.

Lara, Ana M. "Uncovering Mirrors: Afro-Latina Lesbian Subjects." In *The Afro-Latin@ Reader: History and Culture in the United States*, edited by Miriam Jiménez Román and Juan Flores, 298–313. Durham, NC: Duke University Press, 2010.

Lasswell, Harold Dwight. *Politics: Who Gets What, When and How?* Whitefish, MT: Literary Licensing LLC, 2011.

Latina Feminist Group. *Telling to Live: Latina Feminist Testimonios*. Durham, NC: Duke University Press, 2001.

Latino Americans. Produced by Adriana Bosch. PBS, 2013. San Francisco: Kanopy Streaming, 2014. www.pbs.org.

Latorre, Guisela. *Walls of Empowerment: Chicana/o Indigenist Murals of California*. Austin: University of Texas Press, 2008.

Laviera, Tato. *Mixturao and Other Poems*. Houston: Arte Público Press, 2008.

Lavrin, Asunción. "Viceregal Culture." In *The Cambridge History of Latin American Literature: Discovery to Modernism*, vol. 1, edited by Roberto González Echevarría and Enrique Pupo-Walker, 286–335. New York: Cambridge University Press, 1996.

Lazarus, Emma. "The New Colossus." In *Emma Lazarus: Selected Poems and Other Writings*. New York: Broadview, 2002.

Lazo, Rodrigo J. "'La Famosa Filadelfia': The Hemispheric American City and Constitutional Debates." In *Hemispheric American Studies*, edited by Caroline F. Levander and Robert S. Levine, 57–74. New Brunswick, NJ: Rutgers University Press, 2008.

Leacock, Eleanor, ed. *The Culture of Poverty: A Critique*. New York: Simon and Schuster, 1971.

Leal, David L., and Ken Meier. *The Politics of Latino Education*. New York: Teachers College Press, 2010.

Lee, Michele Ye Hee. "Donald Trump's False Comments Connecting Mexican Immigrants and Crime." *Washington Post*, July 8, 2015. www.washingtonpost.com.

Lee, Sonia Song-Ha. *Building a Latino Civil Rights Movement: Puerto Ricans, African Americans, and the Pursuit of Racial Justice in New York City*. Chapel Hill: University of North Carolina Press, 2014.

Lee-Pérez, Ramona, and Babette Audant. "Livin' *la Vida Sabrosa*: Savoring Latino New York." In *Gastropolis: Food and New York City*, edited by Annie Hauck-Lawson and Jonathan Deutsch, 209–29. New York: Columbia University Press, 2009.

Leiberson, Stanley. *A Piece of the Pie: Blacks and White Immigrants since 1880*. Berkeley: University of California Press, 1980.

León, Luis D. "Latina/Latino Religious Communities." In *Religion and American Cultures: An Encyclopedia of Traditions, Diversity, and Popular Expressions*, edited by Gary Laderman and Luis León, 177–84. Santa Barbara, CA: ABC-CLIO, 2003.

———. *La Llorona's Children: Religion, Life, and Death in the U.S.-Mexican Borderlands*. Berkeley: University of California Press, 2004.

———. *The Political Spirituality of Cesar Chavez: Crossing Religious Borders*. Berkeley: University of California Press, 2014.

León-Portilla, Miguel. *Time and Reality in the Thought of the Maya*. Translated by Charles L. Boilès, Fernando Horcasitas, and Miguel León-Portilla. Norman: University of Oklahoma Press, 1988.

———. *Aztec Thought and Culture: A Study of the Ancient Nahuatl Mind*. Translated by Jack Emory Davis. Norman: University of Oklahoma Press, 1990.

Leonard, Karen. *Making Ethnic Choices: California's Punjabi Mexican Americans*. Philadelphia: Temple University Press, 1994.

Levine, Elana. "Constructing a Market, Constructing an Ethnicity: U.S. Spanish-Language Media and the Formation of a Syncretic Latino/a Identity." *Studies in Latin American Popular Culture* 20 (2001): 33–50.

Levins Morales, Aurora. *Remedios: Stories of Earth and Iron from the Histories of Puertorriqueñas*. Boston: South End Press, 2001.

Levins Morales, Aurora, and Rosario Morales. *Getting Home Alive*. Ann Arbor, MI: Firebrand Books, 1986.

Levitt, Peggy, and Sanjeev Khagram. "Constructing Transnational Studies." In *The Transnational Studies Reader*, edited by Sanjeev Khagram and Peggy Levitt, 1–22. New York: Routledge, 2008.

Lewis, Oscar. *Five Families: Mexican Case Studies in the Culture of Poverty*. New York: Basic Books, 1959.

———. *The Children of Sanchez: Autobiography of a Mexican Family*. New York: Random House, 1961.

———. "The Culture of Poverty." *Scientific American* 215 (1966a): 19–25.

———. *La Vida: A Puerto Rican Family in the Culture of Poverty—San Juan and New York*. New York, Random House: 1966b.

Light, Michael T., Mark Hugo Lopez, and Ana Gonzalez-Barrera. *The Rise of Federal Immigration Crimes: Unlawful Reentry Drives Growth*. Washington, DC: Pew Research Center, 2014. www.pewhispanic.org.

Lima, Lázaro. *The Latino Body: Crisis Identities in American Literary and Cultural Memory*. New York: New York University Press, 2007.

Limón, José E. "The Folk Performance of Chicano and the Cultural Limits of Political Ideology." *Southwest Educational Development Laboratory* 62 (1979): 1–28.

———. *Mexican Ballads, Chicano Poems: History and Influence in Mexican-American Social Poetry*. Berkeley: University of California Press, 1992.

———. *Dancing with the Devil: Society and Cultural Poetics in Mexican-American South Texas*. Madison: University of Wisconsin Press, 1994.

Lindsay, Arturo. *Santeria Aesthetics in Contemporary Latin American Art*. Washington, DC: Smithsonian Institution Press, 1996.

Lipski, John. *Linguistic Aspects of Spanish-English Language Switching*. Tempe: Arizona State University, Center for Latin American Studies, 1985.

Lira, Natalie, and Alexandra Minna Stern. "Mexican Americans and Eugenic Sterilization: Resisting Reproductive Injustice in California, 1920–1950." *Aztlán* 39, no. 2 (2014): 9–34.

List, Christine. *Chicano Images: Refiguring Ethnicity in Mainstream Film*. New York: Garland, 1996.

Livingstone, Frank B. "On the Non-Existence of Human Races." *Current Anthropology* 3, no. 3 (1962): 279–81.

Lodares, Juan R. "Languages, Catholicism, and Power in the Hispanic Empire (1500-1770)." In *Spanish and Empire*, edited by Nelsy Echávez-Solano and Kenya C. Dworkin y Méndez, 3-31. Nashville, TN: Vanderbilt University Press, 2007.

Logan, John R. *How Race Counts for Hispanic Americans*. Albany, NY: Lewis Mumford Center, Albany University, State University of New York, 2003. http://mumford.albany.edu/.

Logan, John R., and Harvey Luskin Moloch. *Urban Fortunes: The Political Economy of Place*. Berkeley: University of California Press, 1987.

Loh, Katherine, and Scott Richardson. "Foreign-Born Workers: Trends in Fatal Occupational Injuries, 1996-2001." *Monthly Labor Review* (2004): 42-53.

Lomas, Laura. *Translating Empire: Jose Marti, Migrant Latino Subjects, and American Modernities*. Durham, NC: Duke University Press, 2008.

Lomnitz-Adler, Claudio. *Deep Mexico, Silent Mexico: An Anthropology of Nationalism*. Minneapolis: University of Minnesota Press, 2001.

Londoño, Johana. "Aesthetic Belonging: The Latinization and Renewal of Union City, New Jersey." In *Latino Urbanism: The Politics of Planning, Policy and Redevelopment*, edited by David Díaz and Rodolfo D. Torres, 21-46. New York: New York University Press, 2012.

Longeaux y Vásquez, Enriqueta. "The Woman of La Raza." In *Chicana Feminist Thought: The Basic Historical Writings*, edited by Alma M. García, 29-31. New York: Routledge, 1997.

López, Ana M. "Greater Cuba." In *The Ethnic Eye: Latino Media Arts*, edited by Chon A. Noriega and Ana M. López, 38-58. Minneapolis: University of Minnesota Press, 1996.

López, Ann Aurelia. *The Farmworkers' Journey*. Berkeley: University of California, 2007.

López, Antonio. *Unbecoming Blackness: The Diaspora Cultures of Afro-Cuban America*. New York: New York University Press, 2012.

López, David, and Yen Le Espiritu. "Panethnicity in the United States: A Theoretical Framework." *Ethnic and Racial Studies* 13, no. 32 (1990): 198-223.

Lopez, Erika. *Lap Dancing for Mommy: Tender Stories of Disgust, Blame and Inspiration*. Seattle: Seal Press, 1997.

López, Gustavo. *Hispanics of Dominican Origin in the United States, 2013*. Washington, DC: Pew Research Center, 2015. www.pewhispanic.org.

López, Gustavo, and Ana González-Barrera. *Afro-Latino: A Deeply Rooted Identity among U.S. Hispanics*. Washington, DC: Pew Research Center, 2016. www.pewresearch.org.

Lopez, Iris. *Matters of Choice: Puerto Rican Women's Struggle for Reproductive Freedom*. New Brunswick, NJ: Rutgers University Press, 2008.

Lopez, Mark Hugo. *Latinos and Education: Explaining the Attainment Gap*. Washington, DC: Pew Hispanic Center, 2009. www.pewhispanic.org.

Lopez, Mark Hugo, and D'Vera Cohn. *Hispanic Poverty Rate Highest in New Supplemental Census Measure*. Washington, DC: Pew Research Center, 2011. www.pewhispanic.org.

Lopez, Mark Hugo, Rich Morin, and Paul Taylor. *Illegal Immigration Backlash Worries, Divides Latinos*. Washington, DC: Pew Research Center, October 28, 2010. www.pewhispanic.org.

Lorde, Audre. "Learning from the Sixties." In *Sister Outsider: Essays and Speeches by Audre Lorde*, 134-44. Berkeley, CA: Crossing Press, 2007.

Lovelace, Earl. *The Devil Can't Dance*. New York: Persea Books, 1998.

Lovell Banks, Taunya. "Mestizaje and the Mexican Self: No Hay Sangre Negra, So There Is No Blackness." *Southern California Interdisciplinary Law Journal* 15 (2006): 199-233.

Loza, Mireya. "Braceros on the Boundaries: Activism, Race, Masculinity, and the Legacies of the Bracero Program." PhD diss., Brown University, 2011.

Lozano, Rosina A. "Managing a Priceless Gift: Debating Spanish Language Instruction in New Mexico and Puerto Rico, 1930-1950." *Western Historical Quarterly* 44, no. 3 (2013): 271-93.

Lugo, Alejandro. *Fragmented Lives, Assembled Parts: Culture, Capitalism, and Conquest at the U.S.-Mexico Border*. Austin: University of Texas Press, 2008.

Lugones, María. *Pilgrimages/Peregrinajes: Theorizing Coalition against Multiple Oppressions*. Lanham, MD: Rowman and Littlefield, 2003.

———. "Heterosexualism and the Colonial/Modern Gender System." *Hypatia* 22, no. 1 (2007): 186-209.

———. "The Coloniality of Gender." In *Globalization and the Decolonial Option*, edited by Walter D. Mignolo and Arturo Escobar, 369-90. New York: Routledge, 2010.

———. "Methodological Notes towards a Decolonial Feminism." In *Decolonizing Epistemologies: Latina/o Theology and Philosophy*, edited by Ada María Isasi-Díaz and Eduardo Mendieta, 68-86. New York: Fordham University Press, 2012.

Lush, Rebecca. "Introduction: Amerigo Vespucci." *The Early Americas Digital Archive*. College Park: Maryland Institute of Technology in the Humanities at the University of Maryland, n.d. http://eada.lib.umd.edu.

Lyotard, Jean-François. *The Differend: Phrases in Dispute*. Minneapolis: University of Minnesota Press, 1988.

MacDonald, Mary D. "Spirituality." In *Encyclopedia of Religion*, edited by Lindsay Jones, 8718–21. Detroit, MI: Thomson Gale, 2005.

Machado Sáez, Elena. *Market Aesthetics: The Purchase of the Past in Caribbean Diasporic Fiction*. Charlottesville: University of Virginia Press, 2015.

Macías, Anthony. *Mexican American Mojo: Popular Music, Dance, and Urban Culture in Los Angeles, 1935–1968*. Durham, NC: Duke University Press, 2008.

Madrid, E. Michael. "The Latino Achievement Gap." *Multicultural Education* 19, no. 3 (2011): 7–12.

Maffie, James. *Aztec Philosophy*. Boulder: University Press of Colorado Press, 2014.

Magaña, Lisa, and Erik Lee. *Latino Politics and Arizona's Immigration Law SB 1070*. New York: Springer, 2013.

Mahmud, Tayyab, Athena Mutua, and Francisco Valdes. "LatCrit Praxis @XX: Toward Equal Justice in Law, Education and Society." *Chicago-Kent Law Review* 90 (2015): 361–427.

Maira, Sunaina. *Missing: Youth, Citizenship, and Empire after 9/11*. Durham, NC: Duke University Press, 2009.

Maldonado-Torres, Nelson. "The Topology of Being and the Geopolitics of Knowledge: Modernity, Empire, Coloniality." *City* 8, no. 1 (2004): 29–56.

———. "On the Coloniality of Being: Contributions to the Development of a Concept." *Cultural Studies* 21, nos. 2–3 (2007): 240–70.

———. "Religion, Conquest, and Race in the Foundations of the Modern/Colonial World." *Journal of the American Academy of Religion* 82, no. 3 (2014): 636–65.

Manalansan, Martin F. "Queer Intersections: Sexuality and Gender in Migration Studies." *International Migration Review* 40, no. 1 (2006): 224–49. doi:10.1111/j.1747-7379.2006.00009.x.

Manzor, Lillian. *Sites that Speak: Miami through Its Performing Arts Spaces in Spanish*. Los Angeles: Scalar, 2013. http://scalar.usc.edu/hc/sites-that-speak/index.

Manzor, Lillian, and Beatriz Rizk. *Cuban Theater in Miami: 1960–1980*. Miami: Cuban Heritage Collection, University of Miami Libraries, 2012. http://scholar.library.miami.edu.

Marchevsky, Alejandra, and Jeanne Theoharis. *Not Working: Latina Immigrants, Low-Wage Jobs, and the Failure of Welfare Reform*. New York: New York University Press, 2006.

Mares, Teresa M. "Tracing Immigrant Identity through the Plate and the Palate." *Latino Studies* 10, no. 3 (2012): 334–54.

———. "Engaging Latino Immigrants in Food Activism through Urban Agriculture." In *Food Activism: Agency, Democracy and Economy*, edited by Carole Counihan and Valeria Siniscalchi, 31–46. London: Bloomsbury, 2014.

Marez, Curtis. "Signifying Spain, Becoming Comanche, Making Mexicans: Indian Captivity and the History of Chicana/o Popular Performance." *American Quarterly* 53, no. 2 (2001): 267–307.

———. "Cesar Chavez's Video Collection." *American Literature* 85, no. 4 (2013). http://americanliterature.dukejournals.org.

Mariátegui, José Carlos. *Seven Interpretive Essays on Peruvian Reality*. Translated by Marjory Urquidi. Austin: University of Texas Press, 1971.

Mariscal, Jorge. "They Died Trying to Become." *Counterpunch*, April 18, 2003. www.counterpunch.org.

Márquez, Benjamin. *Constructing Identities in Mexican-American Political Organizations: Choosing Issues, Taking Sides*. Austin: University of Texas Press, 2003.

Marshall, Joanna Barszewska. "'Boast Now, Chicken, Tomorrow You'll Be Stew': Pride, Shame, Food, and Hunger in the Memoirs of Esmeralda Santiago." *MELUS* 32, no. 4 (2007): 47–68.

Marston, Sallie A., John Paul Jones III, and Keith Woodward. "Human Geography without Scale." *Transactions of the Institute of British Geographers* 30, no. 4 (2005): 416–32.

Martí, José. *Selected Writings*. Translated by Esther Allen. New York: Penguin, 2002.

Martín, Manuel, Jr. "*Francesco: The Life and Times of the Cencis* (A Play in Two Acts)." *Cuban Theater Digital Archive*. Miami: University of Miami Library, 1973. http://ctda.library.miami.edu.

———. "*Rasputin*." *Cuban Theater Digital Archive*. Miami: University of Miami Library, 1975. http://ctda.library.miami.edu.

Martín, Mario. "*Luna de miel ¡25 años después!*," program. *Cuban Theater Digital Archive*. Miami: University of Miami Library, 1979. http://ctda.library.miami.edu.

Martínez, Anne M. *Catholic Borderlands: Mapping Catholicism onto American Empire, 1905–1935*. Lincoln: University of Nebraska Press, 2014.

Martínez, Elizabeth. "Chingón Politics Die Hard." In *De Colores Means All of Us: Latina Views for a Multi-Colored Century*, 174–181. Cambridge, MA: South End Press, 1998.

Martinez, George A. "The Legal Construction of Race: Mexican Americans and Whiteness." *Harvard Latino Law Review* 2 (1997a): 321–47.

———. "Mexican-Americans and Whiteness." In *Critical White Studies: Looking behind the Mirror*, edited by Richard Delgado and Jean Stefancic, 210–13. Philadelphia: Temple University Press, 1997b.

Martinez, J. Michael. *Heredities*. Baton Rouge: Louisiana State University Press, 2010.

Martínez, Rubén O. "The Impact of Neoliberalism on Latinos." *Latino Studies* 14 (2016): 11-32.

Martínez, Rubén O., and Raymond Rocco. "Neoliberalism and Latinos." *Latino Studies* 14 (2016): 2-10.

Martínez-San Miguel, Yolanda, Ben. Sifuentes-Jáuregui, and Marisa Belausteguigoitia, eds. *Critical Terms in Caribbean and Latin American Thought: Historical and Institutional Trajectories.* New York: Palgrave Macmillan, 2016.

Marx, Karl. *Capital: A Critical Analysis of Capitalist Production* (Volume I). Edited by Frederick Engels. New York: International Publishers, 1984.

Massey, Douglas S., and Brooks Bitterman. "Explaining the Paradox of Puerto Rican Segregation." *Social Forces* 64, no. 2 (1985): 306-31.

Massey, Douglas S., Jorge Durand, and Nolan J. Malone. *Beyond Smoke and Mirrors: Mexican Immigration in an Era of Economic Integration.* New York: Russell Sage Foundation, 2002.

Massey, Douglas S., and Magaly Sánchez R. *Brokered Boundaries: Creating Immigrant Identity in Anti-Immigrant Times.* New York: Russell Sage Foundation, 2010.

Matambanadzo, Sarudzayi M., Francisco Valdes, and Sheila I. Vélez Martínez. "LatCrit Theory @ XX: Kindling the Programmatic Production of Critical and Outsider Legal Scholarship, 1996–2016." *Charleston Law Review* 10 (2016): 297-365.

Matovina, Timothy. *Latino Catholicism: Transformation in America's Largest Church.* Princeton, NJ: Princeton University Press, 2012.

Matovina, Timothy, and Gerald E. Poyo, eds. *Presente! U.S. Latino Catholics from Colonial Origins to the Present.* Maryknoll, NY: Orbis Press, 2000.

Matovina, Timothy, and Gary Riebe-Estrella, eds. *Horizons of the Sacred: Mexican Traditions in U.S. Catholicism.* Ithaca, NY: Cornell University Press, 2002.

Mauer, Marc. *Race to Incarcerate*, rev. ed. New York: New Press, 2006.

Mayer, Vicki. *Producing Dreams, Consuming Youth: Mexican Americans and Mass Media.* New Brunswick, NJ: Rutgers University Press, 2003.

Mayer-García, Eric. "Teatro de la Esperanza." *Cuban Theater Digital Archive.* Miami: University of Miami Library, 2015. http://ctda.library.miami.edu.

Mazón, Mauricio. *The Zoot Suit Riots: The Psychology of Symbolic Annihilation.* Austin: University of Texas Press, 1988.

McCracken, Ellen. *New Latina Narrative: The Feminine Space of Postmodern Ethnicity.* Tucson: University of Arizona Press, 1999.

McKanders, Karla Mari. "Black and Brown Coalition Building during the 'Post-Racial' Obama Era." *Saint Louis University Public Law Review* 29 (2010): 473-99.

Mckiernan-Gonzáles, John. *Fevered Measures: Public Health and Race at the Texas-Mexico Border, 1848–1942.* Durham, NC: Duke University Press, 2012.

———. "American Science, American Medicine, American Latinos." In *American Latinos and the Making of the United States,* 231-48. Washington, DC: National Park Service and Organization of American Historians, 2013.

McNamara, Andrew. *An Apprehensive Aesthetic: The Legacy of Modernist Culture.* Bern, Germany: Peter Lang, 2009.

McNeil, Linda, and Angela Valenzuela. "The Harmful Impact of the TAAS System of Testing in Texas: Beneath the Accountability Rhetoric." In *Raising Standards or Raising Barriers? Inequality and High Stakes Testing in Public Education,* edited by Mindy Kornhaber and Gary Orfield, 127-50. New York: Century Foundation, 2001.

McPherson, Alan L., ed. *Encyclopedia of U.S. Military Interventions in Latin America.* Santa Barbara, CA: ABC-CLIO, 2013.

Mcquade-Salzfass, Lena. "'An Indispensable Service': Midwives and Medical Officials after New Mexico Statehood." In *Precarious Prescriptions: Contested Histories of Race and Health in North America,* edited by Laurie B. Green, John Mckiernan-González, and Martin Summers, 115-41. Minneapolis: University of Minnesota Press, 2014.

Medina, Alberto, José del Valle, and Henrique Monteagudo. "Introduction to the Making of Spanish: Iberian Perspectives." In *A Political History of Spanish: The Making of a Language,* edited by José del Valle, 23-30. Cambridge: Cambridge University Press, 2013.

Medina, Lara. "Los Espíritus Siguen Hablando: Chicana Spiritualities." In *Living Chicana Theory,* edited by Carla Trujillo, 189-213. Berkeley, CA: Third Woman Press, 1998.

———. *Las Hermanas: Chicana/Latina Religious-Political Activism in the U.S. Catholic Church.* Philadelphia: Temple University Press, 2005.

Meléndez, María. *How Long She'll Last in This World.* Tucson: University of Arizona Press, 2006.

Menchaca, Martha. *Recovering History, Constructing Race: The Indian, Black, and White Roots of Mexican Americans.* Austin: University of Texas Press, 2001.

Menchú, Rigoberta. *Me llamo Rigoberta Menchú, y así me nació la conciencia.* Edited by Elizabeth Burgos-Debray. Mexico: Siglo XXI, 1985.

Méndez, Danny. *Narratives of Migration and Displacement in Dominican Literature.* New York: Routledge, 2012.

Mendez v. Westminister School Dist. U.S. District Court for the

Southern District of California. 64 F. Supp. 544 (S.D. Cal. 1946), *aff'd*, 161 F.2d 774 (9th Cir. 1947) (en banc). http://law.justia.com.

Mendieta, Eduardo. *Global Fragments: Globalizations, Latinamericanisms, and Critical Theory*. Albany: State University of New York Press, 2007.

Menjívar, Cecilia. "Liminal Legality: Salvadoran and Guatemalan Immigrants' Lives in the United States." *American Journal of Sociology* 111, no. 4 (2006): 999–1037.

Menjívar, Cecilia, and Leisy J. Abrego. "Legal Violence: Immigration Law and the Lives of Central American Immigrants." *American Journal of Sociology* 117, no. 5 (2012): 1380–1421.

Menjívar, Cecilia, Leisy J. Abrego, and Leah C. Schmalzbauer. *Immigrant Families*. Cambridge, UK: Polity, 2016.

Menjívar, Cecilia, and Daniel Kanstroom, eds. *Constructing Immigrant "Illegality": Critiques, Experiences, and Responses*. New York: Cambridge University Press, 2014.

Mercier, Delphine. "Globalización del trabajo y fábricas mundiales." Paper presented at the IV Congreso Latinoamericano de Sociología del Trabajo (ALAST), Havana, Cuba, September 9–12, 2003.

Mesa-Bains, Amalia. "Contemporary Chicano and Latino Art: Experiences, Sensibilities, and Intentions." *Visions: Los Angeles* 3, no. 4 (1989): 14–19.

———. "'Domesticana': The Sensibility of Chicana Rasquache." *Aztlán* 24, no. 2 (1999): 157–67.

———. "Spiritual Geographies." In *The Road to Aztlán: Art from a Mythic Homeland*, 332–41. Los Angeles: LACMA, 2001.

Messick, Madeline, and Claire Bergeron. "Temporary Protected Status in the United States: A Grant of Humanitarian Relief That Is Less than Permanent." Washington, DC: Migration Policy Institute, 2014. www.migrationpolicy.org.

Mignolo, Walter D. *Local Histories / Global Designs: Coloniality, Subaltern Knowledges and Border Thinking*. Princeton, NJ: Princeton University Press, 2000.

———. *The Idea of Latin America*. Malden, MA: Blackwell, 2005.

———. "Delinking: The Rhetoric of Modernity, the Logic of Coloniality and the Grammar of De-Coloniality." *Cultural Studies* 21, nos. 2–3 (2007): 449–514.

———. *The Darker Side of Western Modernity: Global Futures, Decolonial Options*. Durham, NC: Duke University Press, 2011.

Migration Policy Institute. "Global Remittances Guide." Washington, DC: Migration Policy Institute, 2014. www.migrationpolicy.org.

Milian, Claudia. *Latining America: Black-Brown Passages and the Coloring of Latino/a Studies*. Athens: University of Georgia Press, 2013.

Milkman, Ruth. *L.A. Story: Immigrant Workers and the Future of the U.S. Labor Movement*. New York: Russell Sage Foundation, 2006.

Miner, Dylan A. T. *Creating Aztlán: Chicano Art, Indigenous Sovereignty, and Lowriding across Turtle Island*. Tucson: University of Arizona Press, 2014.

Mines, Richard, Sandra Nichols, and David Runsten. "Final Report of the Indigenous Farmworker Studies (IFS) to the California Endowment." Oakland, CA: California Rural Legal Assistance, 2010. www.crla.org.

Minian, Ana Raquel. "Indiscriminate and Shameless Sex: The Strategic Use of Sexuality by the United Farm Workers." *American Quarterly* 65, no. 1 (2013): 63–90.

Mirabal, Nancy Raquel. *Suspect Freedoms: The Racial and Sexual Politics of Cubanidad in New York, 1823–1957*. New York: New York University Press, 2017.

Mirandé, Alfredo. *Gringo Justice*. Notre Dame, IN: University of Notre Dame Press, 1987.

Mock, Brentlin. "Hate Crimes against Latinos Rising Nationwide." *Southern Poverty Law Center*, November 28, 2007. www.splcenter.org.

Mogul, Joey L., Andrea J. Ritchie, and Kay Whitlock. *Queer (In)Justice: The Criminalization of LGBT People in the United States*. Boston: Beacon Press, 2011.

Mohamed, Heather Silber. "Can Protests Make Latinos 'American'? Identity, Immigration Politics, and the 2006 Marches." *American Politics Research* 20, no. 10 (2012): 1–30.

Molina, Emily T. "Foreclosures, Investors, and Uneven Development during the Great Recession in the Los Angeles Metropolitan Area." *Journal of Urban Affairs* (2015): 1–17.

Molina, Natalia. *Fit to Be Citizens? Public Health and Race in Los Angeles, 1879–1939*. Berkeley: University of California Press, 2006.

———. "'In a Race All Their Own': The Quest to Make Mexicans Ineligible for U.S. Citizenship." *Pacific Historical Review* 79, no. 2 (2010): 167–201.

———. *How Race Is Made in America: Immigration, Citizenship, and the Historical Power of Racial Scripts*. Berkeley: University of California Press, 2014.

Molina-Guzmán, Isabel. *Dangerous Curves: Latina Bodies in the Media*. New York: New York University Press, 2010.

Moloney, Deirdre. *National Insecurities: Immigrants and U.S. Deportation Policy since 1882*. Chapel Hill: University of North Carolina Press, 2012.

Molotch, Harvey. "The City as a Growth Machine: Toward a Political Economy of Place." *American Journal of Sociology* 82, no. 2 (1976): 309–32.

Monsiváis, Carlos. "El hastío es pavo real que se aburre de la luz en la tarde." In *Días de guardar*, 171-192. Mexico City: Ediciones Era, 1970.

Montejano, David. *Anglos and Mexicans in the Making of Texas, 1836-1986.* Austin: University of Texas Press, 1987.

Montero, Oscar. *José Martí: An Introduction.* New York: Palgrave Macmillan, 2004.

Montes, Brian. "No Longer Silent: A Historical Moment of Latino Student Activism." *Latino Studies* 3, no. 2 (2005): 280-87.

Moore, Joan, and Raquel Pinderhughes, eds. *In the Barrios: Latinos and the Underclass Debate.* New York: Russell Sage Foundation, 1993.

Mora, G. Cristina. *Making Hispanics: How Activists, Bureaucrats, and Media Constructed a New American.* Chicago: University of Chicago Press, 2014.

Moraga, Cherríe. "La Güera." In *This Bridge Called My Back: Writings by Radical Women of Color*, edited by Cherríe Moraga and Gloria E. Anzaldúa, 2nd ed., 27-34. New York: Kitchen Table, Women of Color Press, 1983a.

———. *Loving in the War Years: Lo que nunca pasó por sus labios.* Boston: South End Press, 1983b.

———. *The Last Generation: Prose and Poetry.* Boston: South End Press, 1993a.

———. "Queer Aztlán: The Re-Formation of Chicano Tribe." In *The Last Generation*, 145-73. Boston: South End Press, 1993b.

———. *A Xicana Codex of Changing Consciousness: Writings, 2000-2010.* Durham, NC: Duke University Press, 2011.

Moraga, Cherríe, and Gloria E. Anzaldúa, eds. *This Bridge Called My Back: Writings by Radical Women of Color.* Watertown, MA: Persephone Press, 1981.

———, eds. *This Bridge Called My Back: Writings by Radical Women of Color*, 2nd ed. New York: Kitchen Table, Women of Color Press, 1983.

———, eds. *This Bridge Called My Back: Writings by Radical Women of Color*, 4th ed. Albany: State University of New York Press, 2015.

Morawska, Ewa. "In Defense of the Assimilation Model." *Journal of American Ethnic History* 13, no. 2 (1994): 76-87.

Moreiras, Alberto. "The Aura of Testimonio." In *The Real Thing: Testimonial Discourse and Latin America*, edited by Georg M. Gugelberger, 192-224. Durham, NC: Duke University Press, 1996.

Morley, David, and Kuan-Hsing Chen, eds. *Stuart Hall: Critical Dialogues in Cultural Studies.* London: Routledge, 1996.

Mormino, Gary, and George Pozzetta. *The Immigrant World of Ybor City: Italians and Their Latin Neighbors in Tampa, 1885-1985.* Urbana: University of Illinois Press, 1987.

Morris, Norval, and David J. Rothman, eds. *The Oxford History of the Prison: The Practice of Punishment in Western Society.* New York: Oxford University Press, 1998.

Moya, Paula. "Postmodernism, 'Realism,' and the Politics of Identity: Cherríe Moraga and Chicana Feminism." In *Feminist Genealogies, Colonial Legacies, Democratic Futures*, edited by M. Jacqui Alexander and Chandra Talpade Mohanty, 125-50. New York: Routledge, 1997.

Moya Pons, Frank. *Manual de historia dominicana.* 15th ed. Santo Domingo: Ediciones Librería La Trinitaria, 2013.

Mukhija, Vinit, and Anastasia Loukaitou-Sideris. *The Informal American City: From Taco Trucks to Day Labor.* Cambridge, MA: MIT Press, 2014.

Mulvey, Laura. "Visual Pleasure and Narrative Cinema." *Screen* 16, no. 3 (1975): 6-18.

Mundey, Lisa M. *American Militarism and Anti-Militarism in Popular Media, 1945-1970.* Jefferson, NC: McFarland, 2012.

Muñiz, Vicky. *Resisting Gentrification and Displacement: Voices of Puerto Rican Women of the Barrio.* New York: Routledge, 1998.

Muñoz, Carlos. *Youth, Identity, and Power: The Chicano Movement.* London: Verso, 1999.

———. *Youth, Identity, and Power: The Chicano Movement*, rev. ed. London: Verso, 2007.

Muñoz, José Esteban. "Flaming Latinas: Ela Troyano's *Carmelita Tropicana: Your Kunst Is Your Waffen.*" In *The Ethnic Eye: Latino Media Arts*, edited by Chon A. Noriega and Ana M. López, 129-42. Minneapolis: University of Minnesota Press, 1996.

———. *Disidentifications: Queers of Color and the Performance of Politics.* Minneapolis: University of Minnesota Press, 1999.

———. "Feeling Brown: Ethnicity and Affect in Ricardo Bracho's 'The Sweetest Hangover (and Other STDs).'" *Theatre Journal* 52, no. 1 (2000): 67-79.

———. "Feeling Brown, Feeling Down: Latina Affect, the Performativity of Race, and the Depressive Position." *Signs: Journal of Women in Culture and Society* 31, no. 3 (2006): 675-88.

———. "'Chico, What Does It Feel like to Be a Problem?' The Transmission of Brownness." In *A Companion to Latina/o Studies*, edited by Juan Flores and Renato Rosaldo, 441-51. Malden, MA: Blackwell, 2007.

———. *Cruising Utopia: The Then and There of Queer Futurity.* New York: New York University Press, 2009.

———. "Vitalisms After-Burn: The Sense of Ana Mendieta." *Women and Performance* 21, no. 2 (2011): 191-98.

———. "Wise Latinas." *Criticism: A Quarterly for Literature and the Arts* 56, no. 2 (2014): 249-65.

———. "Theorizing Queer Inhumanisms: The Sense of Brown-ness." *GLQ* 21, nos. 2–3 (2015): 209–10.

———. *The Sense of Brown.* Durham, NC: Duke University Press, forthcoming.

Nabhan-Warren, Kristy. *The Virgin of El Barrio: Marian Apparitions, Catholic Evangelizing, and Mexican American Activism.* New York: New York University Press, 2005.

———. *The Cursillo Movement in America: Catholics, Protestants, and Fourth-Day Spirituality.* Chapel Hill: University of North Carolina Press, 2013.

Nadeau, Jean-Benoît, and Julie Barlow. *The Story of Spanish.* New York: St. Martin's Griffin, 2013.

Nance, Kimberly A. *Can Literature Promote Justice? Trauma Narrative and Social Action in Latin American Testimonio.* Nashville, TN: Vanderbilt University Press, 2006.

Nakamura, Lisa. *Digitizing Race: Visual Cultures on the Internet.* Minneapolis: University of Minnesota Press, 2008.

———. "Media." In *Keywords for American Cultural Studies,* edited by Bruce Burgett and Glenn Hendler, 165–68. New York: New York University Press, 2014.

Narro, Victor. "Immigration Reform Alone Will Not End Workplace Violations." *Huffington Post,* April 8, 2013. www.huffingtonpost.com.

Nascimento, Amos. *Building Cosmopolitan Communities: A Critical and Multidimensional Approach.* New York: Palgrave Macmillan, 2013.

National Agricultural Statistics Service. "2012 Census of Agriculture Highlights: Hispanic Farmers." ACH12-11. Washington, DC: United States Department of Agriculture, 2014.

National Immigration Law Center. The Economic Benefits of Legalizing Immigrants' Presence. Los Angeles: National Immigration Law Center, 2014. www.nilc.org

Navarro, Armando. *The Immigration Crisis: Nativism, Armed Vigilantism, and the Rise of a Countervailing Movement.* New York: AltaMira Press, 2009.

Neckerman, Kathryn M. "The Emergence of 'Underclass' Family Patterns, 1900–1940." In *The "Underclass" Debate: Views from History,* edited by Michael B. Katz, 194–219. Princeton, NJ: Princeton University Press, 1993.

Negrón-Muntaner, Frances, dir. *Brincando el Charco: Portrait of a Puerto Rican.* New York: Women Make Movies, 1994.

———. *Boricua Pop: Puerto Ricans and the Latinization of American Culture.* New York: New York University Press, 2004.

———, ed. *None of the Above: Puerto Ricans in the Global Era.* New York: Palgrave Macmillan, 2007.

Negrón-Muntaner, Frances, and Ramón Grosfoguel, eds. *Puerto Rican Jam: Rethinking Colonialism and Nationalism.* Minneapolis: University of Minnesota Press, 1997.

Negrón-Muntaner, Frances, with Chelsea Abbas, Luis Figueroa, and Samuel Robson. *The Latino Media Gap: A Report on the State of Latinos in U.S. Media.* New York: Center for the Study of Ethnicity and Race at Columbia University, the National Association of Latino Independent Producers (NALIP), and the National Hispanic Foundation for the Arts (NHFA), 2014.

NELP, National Employment Law Project. "Independent Contractor Misclassification and Subcontracting." 2009. www.nelp.org.

Nelson, Jennifer. *Women of Color and the Reproductive Rights Movement.* New York: New York University Press, 2003.

Ngai, Mae. *Impossible Subjects: Illegal Aliens and the Making of Modern America.* Princeton, NJ: Princeton University Press, 2004.

Nguyen, Mimi Thi. *The Gift of Freedom: War, Debt and Other Refugee Passages.* Durham, NC: Duke University Press, 2012.

Nicholls, Walter. *The DREAMers: How the Undocumented Youth Movement Transformed the Immigrant Rights Debate.* Stanford, CA: Stanford University Press, 2013.

Nieto, Sonia, Melissa Rivera, Sandra Quiñones, and Jason Irizarry. "Charting a New Course: Understanding the Sociocultural, Political, Economic, and Historical Context of Latino/a Education in the United States." Special issue of *Association of Mexican-American Educators (AMAE) Journal* 6, no. 1 (2012): 1–50.

Nieto-Phillips, John. "Citizenship and Empire: Race, Language, and Self-Government in New Mexico and Puerto Rico, 1898–1917." *CENTRO Journal* 11, no. 1 (1999): 51–74.

Noddings, Nel. *The Challenge to Care in Schools: An Alternative Approach to Education.* New York: Teachers College Press, 1992.

Noel, Urayoán. "For a Caribbean American Graininess: William Carlos Williams, Translator." *Small Axe: A Caribbean Journal of Criticism* 17, no. 3 (2013): 138–50.

———. *In Visible Movement: Nuyorican Poetry from the Sixties to Slam.* Iowa City: University of Iowa Press, 2014.

Noriega, Chon A., ed. *Chicanos and Film: Representation and Resistance.* Minneapolis: University of Minnesota Press, 1992.

———. "'Barricades of Ideas:' Latino Culture, Site-Specific Installation, and the U.S. Art Museum." In *Performing Hybridity,* edited by May Joseph and Jennifer Natalya Fink, 182–95. Minneapolis: University of Minnesota Press, 1999.

———. *Shot in America: Television, the State, and the Rise of Chicano Cinema.* Minneapolis: University of Minnesota Press, 2000.

Noriega, Chon A., and Ana M. López, eds. *The Ethnic Eye: Latino Media Arts.* Minneapolis: University of Minnesota Press, 1996.

Novak, Nicole, Kate O'Connor, Natalie Lira, and Alexandra Minna Stern. *Ethnic Bias in California's Eugenic Sterilization Program, 1920–1945*. Ann Arbor: Population Studies Center, University of Michigan, Research Report 16–866, June 2016.

Nuccetelli, Susana, Ofelia Schutte, and Otávio Bueno, eds. *A Companion to Latin American Philosophy*. Malden, MA: Wiley-Blackwell, 2010.

Núñez Cabeza de Vaca, Álvar. *The Account: Álvar Núñez Cabeza de Vaca's Relación*. 1542. Edited and translated by José Fernández and Martin Favata. Houston: Arte Público Press, 1993.

Nye, Joseph. *Bound to Lead: The Changing Nature of American Power*. New York: Basic Books, 1990.

Nyers, Peter. "No One Is Illegal between City and Nation." *Studies in Social Justice* 4, no. 2 (2010): 127–43.

Oakford, Patrick. *Administrative Action on Immigration Reform: The Fiscal Benefits of Temporary Work Permits*. Washington, DC: Center for American Progress, 2014. www.americanprogress.org.

Obejas, Achy. *Memory Mambo: A Novel*. Pittsburgh, MA: Cleis Press, 1996.

Oboler, Suzanne. *Ethnic Labels, Latino Lives: Identity and the Politics of (Re)Presentation in the United States*. Minneapolis: University of Minnesota Press, 1995.

Ochoa, Gilda L. *Learning from Latino Teachers*. San Francisco: Jossey-Bass, 2007.

Office of the Attorney General. "Attorney General Lynch Delivers Remarks on the Shooting Incident in Charleston, South Carolina." Washington, DC: U.S. Department of Justice, June 18, 2015. www.justice.gov.

Ogbu, John U. *Minority Education and Caste: The American System in Cross-Cultural Perspective*. New York: Academic Press, 1978.

Olalquiaga, Celeste. *Megalopolis: Contemporary Cultural Sensibilities*. Minneapolis: University of Minnesota Press, 1992.

Olea, Héctor, Mari Carmen Ramírez, and Tomás Ybarra-Frausto. *Resisting Categories: Latin American and/or Latino?* Houston: Museum of Fine Arts, 2012.

Olguín, B. V. *La Pinta: Chicana/o Prisoner Literature, Culture, and Politics*. Austin: University of Texas Press, 2010.

Olivas, Alex. *East Metropolis*. Washington, DC: IndyPlanet, 2014.

Olivos, Edward M., Oscar Jiménez-Castellanos, and Alberto M. Ochoa, eds. *Critical Voices in Bicultural Parent Engagement: Advocacy and Empowerment*. New York: Teachers College Press, 2011.

Omi, Michael, and Howard Winant. *Racial Formation in the United States: From the 1960s to the 1990s*. New York: Routledge, 1994.

Ontiveros, Randy. *In the Spirit of a New People: The Cultural Politics of the Chicano Movement*. New York: New York University Press, 2013.

Oquendo, Angel R. "Re-Imagining the Latino/a Race." *Harvard BlackLetter Law Journal* 12 (1995): 110–29.

Orner, Peter. *Underground America: Narratives of Undocumented Lives*. San Francisco: McSweeney's Books, 2008.

Oropeza, Lorena. *¡Raza Si! ¡Guerra No!: Chicano Protest and Patriotism in the Viet Nam Era*. Berkeley: University of California Press, 2005.

Orrenius, Pia M., and Madeline Zavodny. "Do Immigrants Work in Riskier Jobs?" *Demography* 46, no. 3 (2009): 535–51.

Ortiz, Fernando. *Contrapunteo cubano del tabaco y el azúcar*. Havana: Editorial de Ciencias Sociales, 1940.

———. *Cuban Counterpoint: Tobacco and Sugar*. Translated by Harriet De Onis. Durham, NC: Duke University Press, 1995.

Ortíz, Ricardo L. *Cultural Erotics in Cuban America*. Minneapolis: University of Minnesota Press, 2007.

———. "Edwidge Danticat's Latinidad: *The Farming of Bones* and the Cultivation of (Fields of) Knowledge." In *Aftermaths: Exile, Migration, and Diaspora Reconsidered*, edited by Marcus Bullock and Peter Paik, 150–74. New Brunswick, NJ: Rutgers University Press, 2009a.

———. "Writing the Haitian Diaspora: the Trans-National Contexts of Edwidge Danticat's *The Dew Breaker*." In *Imagined Transnationalism: US Latino/a Literature, Culture and Identity*, edited by Kevin Concannon, Francisco A. Lomelí, and Marc Priewe, 237–56. New York: Palgrave, 2009b.

Otheguy, Ricardo. "El llamado espanglish." In *Enciclopedia del español en los Estados Unidos*, edited by Humberto López Morales, 222–46. Madrid: Instituto Cervantes, Santillana, 2009.

Otheguy, Ricardo, and Nancy Stern. "On So-Called Spanglish." *International Journal of Bilingualism* 15, no. 1 (2010): 85–100.

Ouellette, Laurie. *A Companion to Reality Television*. New York: John Wiley, 2013.

Ovalle, Priscilla Peña. *Dance and the Hollywood Latina: Race, Sex, and Stardom*. New Brunswick, NJ: Rutgers University Press, 2010.

Overmyer-Velázquez, Mark. "Good Neighbors and White Mexicans: Constructing Race and Nation on the Mexico-U.S. Border." *Journal of American Ethnic History* 33, no. 1 (2013): 5–34.

Pacini Hernandez, Deborah. *Oye Como Va!: Hybridity and Identity in Latino Popular Music*. Philadelphia: Temple University Press, 2010.

Pacini Hernandez, Deborah, Héctor Fernández L'Hoeste, and Eric Zolov, eds. *Rockin' Las Americas: The Global Politics of Rock in Latin/o America*. Pittsburgh, PA: University of Pittsburgh Press, 2004.

Pacleb, Jocelyn. "Soldiering 'Green Card' Immigrants: Containing the United States Citizenship." In *A New Kind of Containment: "The War on Terror," Race, and Sexuality*, edited by Carmen Lugo-Lugo and Mary Bloodsworth-Lugo, 135–48. Amsterdam: Rodopi, 2009.

Padilla, Felix M. *Latino Ethnic Consciousness: The Case of Mexican Americans and Puerto Ricans in Chicago*. Notre Dame, IN: Notre Dame University Press, 1985.

Padilla, Genaro M. *My History, Not Yours: The Formation of Mexican American Autobiography*. Madison: University of Wisconsin Press, 1994.

Padilla, Raymond V. "High-Stakes Testing and Educational Accountability as Social Constructions across Cultures." In *Leaving Children Behind: How "Texas-Style" Accountability Fails Latino Youth*, edited by Angela Valenzuela, 249–62. Albany: State University of New York Press, 2005.

Padilla, Yesenia. "What Does 'Latinx' Mean?: A Look at the Term that's Challenging Gender Norms." *Complex*, April 18, 2016. www.complex.com.

Pallares, Amalia. *Family Activism: Immigrant Struggles and the Politics of Noncitizenship*. New Brunswick, NJ: Rutgers University Press, 2015.

Pallares, Amalia, and Nilda Flores-González, eds. *¡Marcha! Latino Chicago and the Immigrant Rights Movement*. Champaign: University of Illinois Press, 2010.

Palmer, Deborah K. "Building and Destroying Students' 'Academic Identities': The Power of Discourse in a Two-Way Immersion Classroom." *International Journal of Qualitative Studies in Education* 21, no. 6 (2008): 647–67.

Pantoja, Adrian D., and Gary M. Segura. "Fear and Loathing in California: Contextual Threat and Political Sophistication among Latino Voters." *Political Behavior* 25, no. 3 (2003): 265–86.

Paredes, Américo. *"With His Pistol in His Hand": A Border Ballad and Its Hero*. Austin: University of Texas Press, 1958.

———. *Folklore and Culture on the Texas-Mexican Border*. Austin: University of Texas Press, 1995a.

———. *Texas-Mexican Cancionero: Folksongs of the Lower Border*. Austin: University of Texas Press, 1995b.

Paredez, Deborah. *Selenidad: Selena, Latinos, and the Performance of Memory*. Durham, NC: Duke University Press, 2009.

Parenti, Christian. *Lockdown America: Police and Prisons in the Age of Crisis*, 3rd ed. London: Verso, 2008.

Park, Lisa Sun-Hee. "Assimilation." In *Keywords for Asian American Studies*, edited by Cathy J. Schlund-Vials, Linda Trinh Vo, and Kevin Scott Wong, 14–17. New York: New York University Press, 2015.

Pascual Soler, Nieves, and Meredith E. Abarca, eds. *Rethinking Chicana/o Literature through Food: Postnational Appetites*. New York: Palgrave Macmillan, 2013.

Passel, Jeffrey, and D'Vera Cohn. *A Portrait of the Unauthorized Migrants in the United States*. Washington, DC: Pew Research Center, 2009. www.pewhispanic.org.

Passel, Jeffrey, D'Vera Cohn, and Ana Gonzalez-Barrera. *Population Decline of Unauthorized Immigrants Stalls, May Have Reversed*. Washington, DC: Pew Research Center, 2013. www.pewhispanic.org.

Pastor, Manuel, Jr., and Enrico A. Marcelli. "Men N the Hood: Skill, Spatial, and Social Mismatch among Male Workers in Los Angeles County." *Urban Geography* 21, no. 6 (2000): 474–96.

Pastor, Manuel Jr., and Justin Scoggins. "Working Poor in the Golden State: A Multi-Measure Comparison Using the 2000 and 1990 Public Use Microdata Samples." Santa Cruz: Center for Justice, Tolerance and Community, University of California, 2007.

Paz, Octavio. *El laberinto de la soledad*. Mexico City: Cuadernos Americanos, 1950.

———. *The Labyrinth of Solitude, the Other Mexico, and Other Essays*. Translated by Lysander Kemp. New York: Grove Press, 1985.

Pedraza-Bailey, Silvia. *Political and Economic Migrants in America: Cubans and Mexicans*. Austin: University of Texas Press, 1985.

Pedreira, Antonio S. *Insularismo: ensayos de interpretación puertorriqueña*. 1934. Guaynabo, PR: Editorial Plaza Mayor, 2002.

Peña, Elaine. *Performing Piety: Making Space Sacred with the Virgin of Guadalupe*. Berkeley: University of California Press, 2011.

Peña, Manuel. *The Texas-Mexican Conjunto: History of a Working-Class Music*. Austin: University of Texas Press, 1985.

Peña, Susana. *Oye Loca: From the Mariel Boatlift to Gay Cuban Miami*. Minneapolis: University of Minnesota Press, 2013.

Perdomo, Willie. *Where a Nickel Costs a Dime*. New York: W.W. Norton, 1996.

Perea, Juan F. "Fulfilling Manifest Destiny: Conquest, Race, and the Insular Cases." In *Foreign in a Domestic Sense: Puerto Rico, American Expansion, and the Constitution*, edited by Christina Duffy Burnett and Burke Marshall, 140–66. Durham, NC: Duke University Press, 2001.

———. "The Echoes of Slavery: Recognizing the Racist Origins

of the Agricultural and Domestic Worker Exclusion from the National Labor Relations Act." *Ohio State Law Journal* 72, no. 1 (2011): 95–138.

Pérez, Daniel Enrique. *Rethinking Chicana/o and Latina/o Popular Culture.* New York: Palgrave Macmillan, 2009.

Pérez, Efrén O. "Xenophobic Rhetoric and Its Political Effects on Immigrants and Their Co-Ethnics." *American Journal of Political Science* 59, no. 3 (2015): 549–64.

Pérez, Emma. "Sitios y Lenguas: Chicanas Theorize Feminisms." *Hypatia* 13, no. 2 (1998): 134–61.

———. *The Decolonial Imaginary: Writing Chicanas into History.* Bloomington: Indiana University Press, 1999.

Pérez, Gina. *The Near Northwest Side Story: Migration, Displacement, and Puerto Rican Families.* Berkeley: University of California Press, 2004.

———. *Citizen, Student, Soldier: Latina/o Youth, JROTC, and the American Dream.* New York: New York University Press, 2015.

Pérez, Gina, Frank A. Guridy, and Adrian Burgos Jr., eds. *Beyond el Barrio: Everyday Life in Latina/o America.* New York: New York University Press, 2011.

Pérez, Laura E. *Chicana Art: The Politics of Spiritual and Aesthetic Altarities.* Durham, NC: Duke University Press Books, 2007.

Pérez, Loida Maritza. *Geographies of Home.* New York: Penguin, 1999.

Pérez de Guillén Mariné, Eulalia. "An Old Woman Remembers." Translated by Vivian C. Fisher. *Three Memoirs of Mexican California.* Berkeley, CA: Friends of the Bancroft Library, 1988.

Pérez Firmat, Gustavo. *Life on the Hyphen: The Cuban-American Way.* Austin: University of Texas Press, 1994.

Pew Research Center. *Pew Hispanic Center/Kaiser Family Foundation 2002 National Survey of Latinos.* Washington, DC: Pew Research Center Hispanic Trends Project, 2002. www.pewhispanic.org.

———. *Daily Number Discrimination against Hispanics.* Washington, DC: Pew Research Center, January 19, 2010. www.pewresearch.org.

———. *2010 National Survey of Latinos.* Washington, DC: Pew Research Center Hispanic Trends Project, 2013. www.pewhispanic.org.

———. *The Shifting Religious Identity of Latinos in the United States.* Washington, DC: Pew Research Center, May 7, 2014. www.pewforum.org.

———. *The American Middle Class Is Losing Ground.* Washington, DC: Pew Research Center, 2015a. www.pewsocialtrends.org.

———. *Multiracial in America: Proud, Diverse and Growing in Numbers.* Washington, DC: Pew Research Center, June 11, 2015b. www.pewsocialtrends.org.

———. *Poverty Rate among Hispanic Origin Groups, 2013.* Washington, DC: Pew Research Center, Hispanic Trends, 2015c. www.pewsocialtrends.org.

Philpott, Daniel. *Revolutions in Sovereignty: How Ideas Shaped International Relations.* Princeton, NJ: Princeton University Press, 2001.

Pietri, Pedro. *Puerto Rican Obituary.* New York: Monthly Review, 1973.

Pietrobelli, Carlo, and Roberta Rabellotti, eds. *Upgrading to Compete: Global Value Chains, Clusters, and SMEs in Latin America.* Washington, DC: Inter-American Development Bank and David Rockefeller Center for Latin American Studies, Harvard University, 2006.

Pilcher, Jeffrey M. *Planet Taco: A Global History of Mexican Food.* Oxford: Oxford University Press, 2012.

Pitt, Leonard. *The Decline of the Californios: A Social History of the Spanish-Speaking Californians, 1846–1890.* Berkeley: University of California Press, 1966.

Polikoff, Alexander. *Waiting for Gautreaux: A Story of Segregation, Housing, and the Black Ghetto.* Evanston, IL: Northwestern University Press, 2007.

Poniatowska, Elena. *Hasta no verte Jesús mío.* Mexico City: Ediciones Era, 1969.

Poplack, Shana. "Sometimes I'll Start a Sentence in Spanish Y TERMINO EN ESPAÑOL: Toward a Typology of Code-Switching." *Linguistics* 18 (1980): 581–616.

Portes, Alejandro, Luis E. Guarnizo, and Patricia Landolt. "The Study of Transnationalism: Pitfall and Promise of an Emergent Research Field." *Ethnic and Racial Studies* 22, no. 2 (1999): 217–37.

Portes, Alejandro, and Rubén Rumbaut. *Legacies: The Story of the Second Immigrant Generation.* Berkeley: University of California Press, 2001.

Portes, Alejandro, and Alex Stepick. *City on the Edge: The Transformation of Miami.* Berkeley: University of California Press, 1993.

Portes, Alejandro, and Min Zhou. "The New Second Generation: Segmented Assimilation and Its Variants." *Annals of the American Academy of Political and Social Science* 530, no. 1 (1993): 74–96.

Portillo, Lourdes, dir. *The Devil Never Sleeps / El diablo nunca duerme.* San Francisco: Xochitl Productions, 1994.

———, dir. *After the Earthquake / Despues del Terremoto.* 1979. New York: Women Make Movies, 2010.

Potowski, Kim. *Conversaciones escritas: Lectura y redacción en contexto.* Hoboken, NJ: Wiley, 2011.

Potter, Joseph E., Kari White, Kristine Hopkins, Sarah McKinnon, Michele G. Shedin, Jon Amastae, and Daniel Grossman. "Frustrated Demand for Sterilization among Low-Income Latinas in El Paso, Texas." *Perspectives on Sexual and Reproductive Health* 44, no. 4 (2012): 228–35.

Powell, Philip Wayne. *Tree of Hate: Propaganda and Prejudices Affecting United States Relations with the Hispanic World*. New York: Basic Books, 1971.

Poyo, Gerald Eugene. *"With All, and for the Good of All": The Emergence of Popular Nationalism in the Cuban Communities of the United States, 1848–1898*. Durham, NC: Duke University Press, 1989.

Prashad, Vijay. *The Karma of Brown Folk*. Minneapolis: University of Minnesota Press, 2000.

———. *The Poorer Nations: A Possible History of the Global South*. New York: Verso, 2013.

Pratt, Mary Louise. *"I, Rigoberta Menchú and the Culture Wars."* In *The Rigoberta Menchú Controversy*, edited by Arturo Arias, 29–48. Minneapolis: University of Minnesota Press, 2001.

———. *Imperial Eyes: Travel Writing and Transculturation*, 2nd ed. London: Routledge, 2007.

Prescott, William Hickling. *History of the Reign of Ferdinand and Isabella*. New York: A. L. Burt, 1837.

———. *History of the Conquest of Mexico: With a Preliminary View of the Ancient Mexican Civilization and the Life of the Conqueror, Hernando Cortés*. New York: Harper and Brothers, 1853.

Prewitt, Kenneth. "Fix the Census' Archaic Racial Categories." *New York Times*, August 9, 2013. www.nytimes.com.

Prieto, Jorge. *Harvest of Hope: The Journeys of a Mexican American Physician*. South Bend, IN: University of Notre Dame Press, 1989.

Public Safety Performance Project. *One in 100: Behind Bars in America, 2008*. Washington, DC: Pew Center on the States, 2008. www.pewtrusts.org.

Puente, Henry. *The Promotion and Distribution of U.S. Latino Films*. New York: Peter Lang, 2011.

Pulido, Laura. *Black, Brown, Yellow and Left: Radical Activism in Los Angeles*. Berkeley: University of California Press, 2006.

Quesada, James. "No Soy Welferero: Undocumented Latino Laborers in the Crosshairs of Legitimation Maneuvers." *Medical Anthropology: Cross-Cultural Studies in Health and Illness* 30, no. 4 (2011): 368–408.

Quijano, Aníbal. "Colonialidad de poder y clasificación social." *Journal of World-System Research* 6, no. 2 (2000a): 342–86.

———. "Coloniality of Power, Eurocentrism, and Latin America." *Nepantla: Views from the South* 1, no. 3 (2000b): 533–80.

———. "Coloniality and Modernity/Rationality." *Cultural Studies* 21, nos. 2–3 (March/May 2007): 168–78.

Quijano, Aníbal, and Immanuel Wallerstein. "Americanity as a Concept, or the Americas in the Modern World-System." *International Journal of Social Sciences* 134 (1992): 549–57.

Quiroga, José. *Tropics of Desire: Interventions from Queer Latino America*. New York: New York University Press, 2000.

Rafael, Vicente L. "Welcoming What Comes: Sovereignty and Revolution in the Colonial Philippines." *Comparative Studies in Society and History* 52, no. 1 (2010): 157–79.

Rama, Angel. *The Lettered City*. Edited and translated by John Charles Chasteen. Durham, NC: Duke University Press, 1996.

Ramírez, Catherine S. "Deus ex Machina: Tradition, Technology, and the Chicanafuturist Art of Marion C. Martínez." *Aztlán* 29, no. 2 (2004): 55–92.

———. *The Woman in the Zoot Suit: Gender, Nationalism, and the Cultural Politics of Memory*. Durham, NC: Duke University Press, 2009.

Ramírez, Elizabeth C. *Chicanas/Latinas in American Theatre: A History of Performance*. Bloomington: Indiana University Press, 2000.

Ramirez, Reyna K. *Native Hubs: Culture, Community and Belonging in Silicon Valley and Beyond*. Durham, NC: Duke University Press, 2007.

Ramírez, Susana. "Recovering Gloria Anzaldúa's Sci Fi Roots: Nepantler@ Visions in the Unpublished and Published Speculative Precursors to Borderlands." *Aztlán* 40, no. 2 (2015): 203–20.

Ramirez, Tanisha Love, and Zeba Blay. "Why People Are Using the Term 'Latinx.'" *Huffington Post Latino Voices*, July 5, 2016. www.huffingtonpost.com.

Ramírez, Yasmín. "Nuyorican Visionary: Jorge Soto and the Evolution of an Afro-Taíno Aesthetic at Taller Boricua." *CENTRO Journal* 17 (2005): 22–41.

Ramírez de Arellano, Annette B. *Colonialism, Catholicism, and Contraception: A History of Birth Control in Puerto Rico*. Chapel Hill: University of North Carolina Press, 1983.

Ramirez-Valles, Jesus. *Compañeros: Latino Activists in the Face of AIDS*. Urbana-Champaign: University of Illinois Press, 2011.

Ramos, E. Carmen. *Our America: The Latino Presence in American Art*. Washington, DC: Smithsonian American Art Museum, 2014.

Ramos, Iván. "Spic(y) Appropriations: The Gustatory Aesthetics of Xandra Ibarra (aka La Chica Boom)." *ARARA: Art and Architecture of the Americas* 12 (2015): 1–18.

Ramos, Juanita, ed. *Compañeras: Latina Lesbians: An Anthology*. New York: Latina Lesbian History Project, 1987.

Ramos, Julio. *Divergent Modernities: Culture and Politics in Nineteenth-Century Latin America*. Translated by John D. Blanco. Durham, NC: Duke University Press, 2001.

Ramos-García, Luis. *The State of Latino Theater in the United States*. New York: Routledge, 2002.

Ramos Otero, Manuel. "Vivir del cuento." In *Página en blanco y staccato*, 49–68. Madrid: Editorial Playor, 1987.

Rana, Swati. "Reading Brownness: Richard Rodriguez, Race and Form." *American Literary History* 27, no. 2 (2015): 285–304.

Real Academia Española. "Espanglish." *Diccionario de la lengua española*. Madrid: Real Academia Española, n.d. http://dle.rae.es.

Rechy, John. *City of Night*. New York: Grove Press, 1963.

Reed, Adolph. "The Underclass as Myth and Symbol: The Poverty of Discourse about Poverty." *Radical America* (1992): 21–40.

Reid, Deborah. "Reproductive Justice Advocates: Don't Roll Back Sterilization Consent Rules." *Rewire*, April 2, 2014. https://rewire.news.

Reimers, David M. *Still the Golden Door: The Third World Comes to America*, 2nd ed. New York: Columbia University Press, 1992.

Rentería, Robert. *From the Barrio to the Boardroom*. Mundelein, IL: Writers of the Roundtable Press, 2011.

Reyes, Luis, and Peter Rubie. *Hispanics in Hollywood: An Encyclopedia of Film and Television*. New York: Garland, 1994.

Reyes, Raul A. "Afro-Latinos Seek Recognition and Accurate Census Count." *NBC News*, September 21, 2014. www.nbcnews.com.

Rich, Motoko. "For Young Latino Readers, an Image Is Missing." *New York Times*, December 4, 2012. www.nytimes.com.

Rim, Kathy H. "Latino and Asian American Mobilization in the 2006 Immigration Protests." *Social Science Quarterly* 90, no. 3 (2009): 703–21.

Rincón, Belinda L., and Suzanne Oboler. "Citizenship." In *The Routledge Companion to Latino/a Literature*, edited by Suzanne Bost and Frances R. Aparicio, 133–42. New York: Routledge, 2012.

Rincón, Lina. "Cosmopolitans or New Americans? The Adaptation and Citizenship Meanings of Colombian and Puerto Rican Computer Engineers in the Boston Metropolitan Area after the 'Dot Com.'" In *Migrant Professionals in the City: Local Encounters, Identities and Inequalities*, edited by Lars Meier, 212–31. New York: Routledge, 2015.

Rios, Diana I., and Mari Castañeda, eds. *Soap Operas and Telenovelas in the Digital Age: Global Industries and New Audiences*. New York: Peter Lang, 2011.

Rios, Victor. *Street Life: Poverty, Gangs, and a Ph.D.* North Charleston, SC: CreateSpace Independent Publishing Platform, 2011.

Ríos-Bustamante, Antonio, and Marco Bravo, dirs. *Latino Hollywood: A History of Latino Participation in the Film Industry, 1911–1940*. New York: Cinema Guild, 2005.

Rivas-Rodriguez, Maggie. *Mexican Americans and World War II*. Austin: University of Texas Press, 2005.

Rivera, Raquel Z. *New York Ricans from the Hip Hop Zone*. New York: Palgrave Macmillan, 2003.

Rivera, Raquel Z., Wayne Marshall, and Deborah Pacini Hernandez, eds. *Reggaetón*. Durham, NC: Duke University Press, 2009.

Rivera, Tomás. *. . . Y no se lo tragó la tierra / And the Earth Did Not Devour Him*. 1971. Translated by Evangelina Vigil-Piñón, 3rd ed. Houston: Arte Público Press, 1995.

Rivera Ramos, Efrén. *The Legal Construction of Identity: The Judicial and Social Legacy of American Colonialism in Puerto Rico*. Washington, DC: American Psychological Association, 2001.

Rivera-Servera, Ramón H. *Performing Queer Latinidad: Dance, Sexuality, Politics*. Ann Arbor: University of Michigan Press, 2012.

———. "The Many Legs of Latina/o Theater." In *The Goodman Theatre's Festival Latino*, edited by Henry D. Godinez and Ramón H. Rivera-Servera, xi–xx. Evanston, IL: Northwestern University Press, 2013.

Rivero, Yeidy M. "Interpreting Cubanness, Americanness, and the Sitcom: WPBT-PBS's *¿Qué Pasa, U.S.A.?* (1975–1980)." In *Global Television Formats: Understanding Television across Borders*, edited by Tasha Oren and Sharon Shahaf, 90–107. New York: Routledge, 2012.

Rivero, Yeidy M., and Arlene Dávila, eds. *Contemporary Latina/o Media: Production, Circulation, Politics*. New York: New York University Press, 2014.

Rizk, Beatriz. "Una crónica no anunciada: El 'otro' latino en el ámbito teatral de Estados Unidos." *Aisthesis* 45 (2009): 39–55.

Roberts, Dorothy. *Fatal Invention: How Science, Politics, and Big Business Recreate Race in the 21st Century*. New York: New Press, 2011.

Rocco, Raymond. "Transforming Citizenship: Membership, Strategies of Containment, and the Public Sphere in Latino Communities." *Latino Studies* 2, no. 1 (2004): 4–25.

———. *Transforming Citizenship: Democracy, Membership, and Belonging in Latino Communities*. East Lansing: Michigan State University Press, 2014.

Rodó, José Enrique. *Ariel*. 1900. Madrid: Espasa-Calpe, 1971.

Rodriguez, América. *Making Latino News: Race, Language, Class*. Thousand Oaks, CA: Sage, 1999.

Rodríguez, Ana Patricia. *Dividing the Isthmus: Central American*

Transnational Histories, Literatures, and Cultures. Austin: University of Texas Press, 2009.

Rodríguez, Chantal. *The Latino Theatre Initiative / Center Theatre Group Papers, 1980–2005*. Los Angeles: University of California, Los Angeles, Chicano Studies Research Center Press, 2010.

Rodriguez, Chris. "Another Way of Doing Health: Lessons from the Zapatista Autonomous Communities in Chiapas, Mexico." In *Doing Nutrition Differently: Critical Approaches to Diet and Dietary Intervention*, edited by Jessica Hayes-Conroy, 199–217. Burlington, VT: Ashgate, 2013.

Rodriguez, Clara E., ed. *Latin Looks: Images of Latinas and Latinos in the U.S. Media*. Boulder, CO: Westview Press, 1997.

———. *Changing Race: Latinos, the Census, and the History of Ethnicity in the United States*. New York: New York University Press, 2000.

———. *Heroes, Lovers, and Others: The Story of Latinos in Hollywood*. Washington, DC: Smithsonian Institution, 2004.

———. *Heroes, Lovers, and Others: The Story of Latinos in Hollywood*. New York: Oxford University Press, 2008.

Rodriguez, Clara E., Virginia Sánchez Korrol, and José Oscar Alers, eds. *The Puerto Rican Struggle: Essays on Survival in the U.S.* Maplewood, NJ: Waterfront Press, 1984.

Rodriguez, Jeanette. *Our Lady of Guadalupe: Faith and Empowerment among Mexican-American Women*. Austin: University of Texas Press, 1994.

Rodríguez, Juana María. *Queer Latinidad: Identity Practices, Discursive Spaces*. New York: New York University Press, 2003.

———. "Latino, Latina, Latin@." In *Keywords for American Cultural Studies*, 2nd ed., edited by Bruce Burget and Glenn Hendler, 146–49. New York: New York University Press, 2014a.

———. *Sexual Futures, Queer Gestures, and Other Latina Longings*. New York: New York University Press, 2014b.

Rodriguez, Louie F. "'Everybody Grieves, but Still Nobody Sees': Toward a Praxis of Recognition for Latina/o Students in US Schools." *Teachers College Record* 114, no. 1 (2012): 1–31.

Rodriguez, Luis J. *Always Running: La Vida Loca, Gang Days in L.A.* New York: Touchstone, 1993.

Rodríguez, Malena. "De memorias y manuscritos: César Andreu Iglesias y Bernardo Vega." *Op. Cit.: Revista del Centro de Investigaciones Históricas* 21 (2012–13): 99–151.

Rodríguez, Nestor, and Jacqueline Maria Hagan. "Fractured Families and Communities: Effects of Immigration Reform in Texas, Mexico, and El Salvador." *Latino Studies* 2, no. 3 (2004): 328–51.

Rodriguez, Richard. *Hunger of Memory: The Education of Richard Rodriguez, an Autobiography*. New York: Dial Press, 1982.

———. *Brown: The Last Discovery of America*. New York: Viking, 2002.

Rodríguez, Richard T. *Next of Kin: The Family in Chicano/a Cultural Politics*. Durham, NC: Duke University Press, 2009.

———. "Carnal Knowledge: Chicano Gay Men and the Dialectics of Being." In *Gay Latino Studies: A Critical Reader*, edited by Michael Hames-García and Ernesto Javier Martínez, 113–40. Durham, NC: Duke University Press, 2011.

Rodríguez, Vittoria, and Mary Beltrán. "From the Bronze Screen to the Computer Screen: Latina/o Web Series and Independent Production." In *The Routledge Companion to Latina/o Media*, edited by María Elena Cepeda and Dolores Inés Casillas, 156–70. New York: Routledge, 2017.

Rodríguez Muñiz, Michael. "Grappling with Latinidad: Puerto Rican Activism in Chicago's Pro-Immigrant Rights Movement." In *Marcha!: Latino Chicago and the Immigrant Rights Movement*, edited by Amalia Pallares and Nilda Flores-González, 237–58. Urbana: University of Illinois Press, 2010.

Rodríguez O., Jaime E. *The Independence of Spanish America*. New York: Cambridge University Press, 1998.

———, ed. *Las nuevas naciones: España y México, 1800–1850*. Madrid: Fundación MAPFRE, 2008.

Roediger, David. *The Wages of Whiteness: Race and the Making of the American Working Class*. London: Verso, 1999.

———. *Working toward Whiteness: How America's Immigrants Became White*. New York: Basic Books, 2005.

Rogin, Michael Paul. *Subversive Genealogy: The Politics and Art of Herman Melville*. New York: Knopf, 1983.

Rojas, James. "The Enacted Environment—The Creation of 'Place' by Mexicans and Mexican Americans in East Los Angeles." PhD. diss., Massachusetts Institute of Technology, 1991.

———. "Latino Urbanism in Los Angeles: A Model for Urban Improvisation and Reinvention." In *Insurgent Public Space: Guerrilla Urbanism and the Remaking of Contemporary Cities*, edited by Jeffrey Hou, 36–44. New York: Routledge, 2010.

Román, David. "Latino Performance and Identity." *Aztlán* 22, no. 2 (1997): 151–167.

———. *Performance in America: Contemporary U.S. Culture and the Performing Arts*. Durham, NC: Duke University Press, 2005.

Romano-V., Octavio Ignacio. "The Anthropology and Sociology of the Mexican Americans: The Distortion of Mexican-American History, a Review Essay." *El Grito: A Journal of Contemporary Mexican-American Thought* 2, no. 1 (1968): 13–26.

Romero, Mary, Pierrette Hondagneu-Sotelo, and Vilma Ortiz,

eds. *Challenging Fronteras: Structuring Latina and Latino Lives in the U.S.* New York: Routledge, 1997.

Romo, David Dorado. *Ringside Seat to a Revolution: An Underground Cultural History of El Paso and Juárez, 1883-1932.* El Paso, TX: Cinco Puntos Press, 2005.

Romo, Tere. "Conceptually Divine: Patssi Valdez's Virgen de Guadalupe: Walking the Mural." In *ASCO: Elite of the Obscure, A Retrospective, 1972-1987*, edited by C. Ondine Chavoya and Rita Gonzalez, 276-82. Williamstown, MA: Williams College Museum of Art and Hatje Cantz, 2011.

Rondón, César Miguel. *El libro de la salsa: crónica de la música del Caribe urbano.* Caracas: Editorial Arte, 1980.

Roque Ramírez, Horacio N. "'That's My Place!': Negotiating Racial, Sexual, and Gender Politics in San Francisco's Gay Latino Alliance, 1975-1983." *Journal of the History of Sexuality* 12 (2003): 224-58.

———. "'Mira, yo soy boricua y estoy aquí': Rafa Negrón's Pan Dulce and the Queer Sonic Latinaje of San Francisco." *CENTRO Journal* 19, no. 1 (2007): 274-313.

———. "Gay Latino Histories / Dying to Be Remembered: AIDS Obituaries, Public Memory, and the Queer Latino Archive." In *Beyond El Barrio: Everyday Life in Latina/o América*, edited by Gina M. Pérez, Frank A. Guridy, and Adrian Burgos Jr., 103-28. New York: New York University Press, 2010.

———. "Gay Latino Cultural Citizenship: Predicaments of Identity and Visibility in San Francisco in the 1990s." In *Gay Latino Studies: A Critical Reader*, edited by Michael Hames-García and Ernesto Javier Martínez, 175-97. Durham, NC: Duke University Press, 2011.

Rosaldo, Renato. *Culture and Truth: The Remaking of Social Analysis.* Boston: Beacon Press, 1993.

———. "Cultural Citizenship in San Jose, California." *PoLAR: Political and Legal Anthropology Review* 17, no. 2 (1994): 57-64.

———. "Cultural Citizenship, Inequality, and Multiculturalism." In *Latino Cultural Citizenship: Claiming Identity, Space, and Rights*, edited by William V. Flores and Rina Benmayor, 27-38. Boston: Beacon Press, 1997.

Rosas, Lilia Raquel Dueñas. "(De)sexing Prostitution: Sex Work, Reform, and Womanhood in Progressive Era Texas." PhD diss., University of Texas, Austin, 2012.

Rosenberg, Charles E. "Framing Disease: Illness, Society, and History." In *Framing Disease: Studies in Cultural History*, edited by Charles E. Rosenberg and Janet Golden, i-xxvi. New Brunswick, NJ: Rutgers University Press, 1992.

Rossini, Jon D. *Contemporary Latina/o Theatre: Wrighting Ethnicity.* Carbondale: Southern Illinois University Press, 2008.

Rossini, Jon D., and Patricia Ybarra. "Neoliberalism, Historiography, Identity Politics: Toward a New Historiography of Latino Theater." *Radical History Review* 2012, no. 112 (2012): 162-172.

Roszak, Theodore. *The Making of a Counter Culture: Reflections on the Technocratic Society and Its Youthful Opposition.* Garden City, NY: Doubleday, 1969.

Roth, Wendy. "Racial Mismatch: The Divergence between Form and Function in Data for Monitoring Racial Discrimination of Hispanics." *Social Science Quarterly* 91, no. 5 (2010): 1288-311.

Rúa, Mérida M. *A Grounded Identity: Making New Lives in Chicago's Puerto Rican Neighborhoods.* New York: Oxford University Press, 2012.

Rúa, Mérida M., and Lorena García. "Processing Latinidad: Mapping Latino Urban Landscapes through Chicago Ethnic Festivals." *Latino Studies* 5, no. 3 (2007): 317-39.

Rubin, Gayle. "The Traffic in Women: Notes on the 'Political Economy' of Sex." In *Toward an Anthropology of Women*, edited by Rayna R. Reiter, 157-210. New York: Monthly Review Press, 1975.

Rudolph, Jennifer Domino. *Embodying Latino Masculinities: Producing Masculatinidad.* New York: Palgrave Macmillan, 2012.

Ruiz, Vicki L. *From Out of the Shadows: Mexican Women in Twentieth-Century America.* New York: Oxford University Press, 1998.

———. "El Congreso de Pueblos de Habla Española." In *Latinas in the United States: A Historical Encyclopedia*, vol. 1, edited by Vicki L. Ruiz and Virginia Sánchez Korrol, 226. Bloomington: Indiana University Press, 2006a.

———. "Nuestra América: Latino History as United States History." *Journal of American History* 93, no. 3 (2006b): 655-72.

Ruiz, Vicki L., and Virginia Sánchez Korrol, eds. *Latina Legacies: Identity, Biography, and Community.* New York: Oxford University Press, 2005.

———, eds. *Latinas in the United States: A Historical Encyclopedia*, vols. 1-2. Bloomington: Indiana University Press, 2006.

Rumbaut, Rubén G. "Paradoxes (and Orthodoxies) of Assimilation." *Sociological Perspectives* 40, no. 3 (1997): 483-511.

Rumbaut, Rubén G., Roberto G. Gonzales, Golnaz Komaie, and Charlie V. Morgan. *Debunking the Myth of Immigrant Criminality: Imprisonment among First- and Second-Generation Young Men.* Washington, DC: Migration Policy Institute, 2006.

Rumbaut, Rubén G., and Alejandro Portes, eds. *Ethnicities: Children of Immigrants in America.* Berkeley: University of California Press, 2001.

Russo, Alex. *Points on the Dial: Golden Age Radio beyond the Networks.* Durham, NC: Duke University Press, 2010.

Ryn, Claes G. *A Common Human Ground: Universality and Particularity in a Multicultural World.* Columbia: University of Missouri Press, 2003.

Ryo, Emily. "On Normative Effects of Immigration Law." *Center for Law and Social Science Research Papers Series,* no. CLASS16-11. Los Angeles: USC Gould School of Law, 2016.

Safran, William. "Diasporas in Modern Societies: Myths of Homeland and Return." *Diaspora: A Journal of Transnational Studies* 1, no. 1 (1991): 83–99.

Salazar, Rubén. "Who Is a Chicano? And What Is It the Chicanos Want?" *Los Angeles Times,* February 6, 1970.

Saldaña-Portillo, María Josefina. "Who's the Indian in Aztlán? Re-Writing Mestizaje, Indianism, and Chicanismo from the Lacandon." In *The Latin American Subaltern Studies Reader,* edited by Ileana Rodríguez, 402–23. Durham, NC: Duke University Press, 2001.

———. *The Revolutionary Imagination in the Americas and the Age of Development.* Durham, NC: Duke University Press, 2003.

Saldívar, José David. *The Dialectics of Our America: Genealogy, Cultural Critique, and Literary History.* Durham, NC: Duke University Press, 1991.

———. *Border Matters: Remapping American Cultural Studies.* Berkeley: University of California Press, 1997.

Saldívar, Ramón. *The Borderlands of Culture: Américo Paredes and the Transnational Imaginary.* Durham, NC: Duke University Press, 2006.

Saldívar-Hull, Sonia. "Feminism on the Border: From Gender Politics to Geopolitics." In *Criticism in the Borderlands: Studies in Chicano Literature, Culture, and Ideology,* edited by Héctor Calderón and José D. Saldívar, 203–20. Durham, NC: Duke University Press, 1991.

Salvatore, Ricardo D., and Carlos Aguirre, eds. *The Birth of the Penitentiary in Latin America: Essays on Criminology, Prison Reform, and Social Control, 1830–1940.* Austin: University of Texas Press, 1996.

Sánchez, Franklyn D. "Puerto Rican Spiritualism: Survival of the Spirit." In *Historical Perspective on Puerto Rican Survival in the United States,* edited by Clara E. Rodríguez and Virginia Sánchez Korrol, 167–80. Princeton, NJ: Markus Wiener, 1996.

Sanchez, Gabriel R., Edward D. Vargas, Hannah L. Walker, and Vickie D. Ybarra. "Stuck between a Rock and a Hard Place: The Relationship between Latino/a's Personal Connections to Immigrants and Issue Salience and Presidential Approval." *Politics, Groups, and Identities* 3, no. 3 (2015): 454–68.

Sánchez, George J. *Becoming Mexican American: Ethnicity, Culture, and Identity in Chicano Los Angeles, 1900–1945.* New York: Oxford University Press, 1993.

Sánchez Korrol, Virginia E. *From Colonia to Community: The History of Puerto Ricans in New York City.* Berkeley: University of California Press, 1994.

Sánchez Walsh, Arlene. *Latino Pentecostal Identity: Evangelical Faith, Self, and Society.* New York: Columbia University Press, 2003.

Sanders, Jimy M., and Victor Nee. "Limits of Ethnic Solidarity in the Enclave Economy." *American Sociological Review* 52, no. 6 (1987): 745–73.

Sandoval, Chela. "U.S. Third World Feminism: The Theory and Method of Oppositional Consciousness in the Postmodern World." *Genders* 10 (1991): 1–24.

———. "Mestizaje as Method: Feminists-of-Color Challenge the Canon." In *Living Chicana Theory,* edited by Carla Trujillo, 352–70. Berkeley, CA: Third Woman Press, 1998.

———. *Methodology of the Oppressed.* Minneapolis: University of Minnesota Press, 2000.

Sandoval, Moises. *On the Move: A History of the Hispanic Church in the United States.* Maryknoll, NY: Orbis, 1990.

Sandoval-Sánchez, Alberto. *José, Can You See?: Latinos On and Off Broadway.* Madison: University of Wisconsin Press, 1999.

———. "An AIDS Testimonial: It's a Broken Record / Ese Disco Se Rayó." In *Technofuturos: Critical Interventions in Latino/a Studies,* edited by Nancy Raquel Mirabal and Agustín Laó-Montes, 297–310. Lanham, MD: Lexington Books, 2007.

Sandoval-Sánchez, Alberto, and Nancy Saporta Sternbach, eds. *Puro Teatro: A Latina Anthology.* Tucson: University of Arizona Press, 2000.

———. *Stages of Life: Transcultural Performance and Identity in U.S. Latina Theater.* Tucson: University of Arizona Press, 2001.

Santa Ana, Otto. *Brown Tide Rising: Metaphors of Latinos in Contemporary American Public Discourse.* Austin: University of Texas Press, 2002.

Santiago, Roberto. *Boricuas: Influential Puerto Rican Writings.* New York: Ballantine, 1995.

Sarmiento, Domingo Faustino. *Conflicto y armonía de las razas en América.* Buenos Aires: La Cultura Argentina, 1915.

Sassen, Saskia. *The Mobility of Labor and Capital.* Cambridge: Cambridge University Press, 1988.

Scharrón-del Río, María, and Alan A. Aja. "The Case FOR 'Latinx': Why Intersectionality Is Not a Choice." *Latino Rebels,* December 5, 2015. www.latinorebels.com.

Schechner, Richard. "Restoration of Behavior." In *Between Theatre and Anthropology,* 35–116. Philadelphia: University of Pennsylvania Press, 1985.

Schement, Jorge Reina, and Ricardo Flores. "The Origins of Spanish Language Radio: The Case of San Antonio, Texas." *Journalism History* 4, no. 2 (1977): 56-59.

Schiller, Nina Glick, Linda Basch, and Cristina Blanc-Szanton. *Towards a Transnational Perspective on Migration: Race, Class, Ethnicity, and Nationalism Reconsidered.* New York: Academy of Sciences, 1992.

Schmidt Camacho, Alicia. *Migrant Imaginaries: Latino Cultural Politics in the U.S.-Mexico Borderlands.* New York: New York University Press, 2008.

Schmidt-Nowara, Christopher. *Empire and Antislavery: Spain, Cuba and Puerto Rico 1833-1874.* Pittsburgh, PA: University of Pittsburgh Press, 1999.

Sciorra, Joseph, and Martha Cooper. "'We're Not Here Just to Plant. We Have Culture': An Ethnography of the South Bronx Casita Rincón Criollo." *New York Folklore* 20, no. 3-4 (1994): 19-41.

Scott, David. *Conscripts of Modernity: The Tragedy of Colonial Enlightenment.* Durham, NC: Duke University Press, 2004.

Scott, Joan. "Gender: A Useful Category of Analysis." *American Historical Review* 91, no. 5 (1986): 1053-75.

Secretaría de Economía. "IMMEX Manufacturing, Maquila and Export Service Industry, 2013." www.economia.gob.mx.

Seelke, Clare Ribando. *Afro-Latinos in Latin America and Considerations for U.S. Policy.* Washington, DC: Congressional Research Service, 2008. http://digitalcommons.ilr.cornell.edu.

Seguín, Juan. "A Foreigner in My Native Land." 1858. In *Distant Horizon: Documents from the Nineteenth-Century American West,* edited by Gary Noy, 357-60. Lincoln: University of Nebraska Press, 1999.

Segura, Gary M. *Latino Lives in America: Making It Home.* Philadelphia: Temple University Press, 2010.

———. *Latinos in the New Millennium: An Almanac of Opinion, Behavior, and Policy Preferences.* New York; Cambridge University Press, 2012.

Sendejo, Brenda. "Methodologies of the Spirit: Reclaiming Our Lady of Guadalupe and Discovering Tonantzin within and beyond the Nepantla of Academia." In *Fleshing the Spirit: Spirituality and Activism in Chicana, Latina, and Indigenous Women's Lives,* edited by Elisa Facio and Irene Lara, 81-101. Tucson: University of Arizona Press, 2014.

Sentencing Project. "Incarceration." 2014. www.sentencing-project.org.

Sepúlveda Carmona, Magdalena. "Extreme Poverty and Human Rights, Report of the Special Rapporteur on Extreme Poverty and Human Rights." New York: United Nations, 2011.

Shah, Nayan. *Contagious Divides: Epidemics and Race in San Francisco's Chinatown.* Berkeley: University of California Press, 2001.

Shakespeare, William. *The Tempest.* 1623. Oxford: Oxford University Press, 1998.

Sheridan, Claire. "'Another White Race': Mexican Americans and the Paradox of Whiteness in Jury Selection." *Law and Historical Review* 21 (2003): 109-44.

Sherry, Michael S. *In the Shadow of War: The United States since the 1930s.* New Haven, CT: Yale University Press, 1995.

Shreffler, Karina M., Julia McQuillan, Arthur L. Greil, and David R. Johnson. "Surgical Sterilization, Regret, and Race: Contemporary Patterns." *Social Science Research* 50 (2015): 31-45.

Silva-Corvalán, Carmen, and Kim Potowski. "La alternancia de códigos." In *Enciclopedia del español en los Estados Unidos,* edited by Humberto López Morales, 272-76. Madrid: Instituto Cervantes, Santillana, 2009.

Sinnette, Elinor Des Verney. *Arthur Alfonso Schomburg, Black Bibliophile and Collector.* Detroit, MI: New York Public Library and Wayne State University Press, 1989.

Skinazi, Karen E.H. "Eating the Nations: A Culinary Exploration of Cristina García's *Dreaming in Cuban.*" *Midwestern Folklore* 29, no. 2 (2003): 37-47.

Sklodowska, Elzbieta. "Spanish American Testimonial Novel: Some Afterthoughts." In *The Real Thing: Testimonial Discourse and Latin America,* edited by Georg M. Gugelberger, 84-100. Durham, NC: Duke University Press, 1996.

Small, Mario Luis. *Villa Victoria: The Transformation of Social Capital in a Boston Barrio.* Chicago: University of Chicago Press, 2004.

Small, Mario Luis, David J. Harding, and Michele Lamont. "Reconsidering Culture and Poverty." *Annals of the American Academy of Political and Social Science* 629 (May 2010): 6-27.

Smith, Adam. *An Inquiry into the Nature and Causes of the Wealth of Nations.* New York: Modern Library, 1937.

Smith, Candace. "The White Nationalists Who Support Donald Trump." *ABC News,* March 10, 2016. www.abcnews.go.com.

Smith, Rogers M. *Civic Ideals: Conflicting Visions of Citizenship in U.S. History.* New Haven, CT: Yale University Press, 1997.

———. "The Bitter Roots of Puerto Rican Citizenship." In *Foreign in a Domestic Sense: Puerto Rico, American Expansion, and the Constitution,* edited by Christina Duffy Burnett and Burke Marshall, 373-88. Durham, NC: Duke University Press, 2001.

Smith, Vicki, ed. *Sociology of Work: An Encyclopedia.* Thousand Oaks, CA: SAGE Reference, 2013.

Solórzano, Daniel, and Dolores Delgado Bernal. "Examining Transformational Resistance through a Critical Race and Latcrit Theory Framework: Chicana and Chicano Students in an Urban Context." *Urban Education* 36, no. 3 (2001): 308–42.

Sommer, Doris. *Proceed with Caution, When Engaged by Minority Writing in the Americas*. Cambridge, MA: Harvard University Press, 1999.

Sontag, Susan. "Notes on Camp." In *A Susan Sontag Reader*, 104–119. New York: Vintage, 1983.

Soto, Sandra K. *Reading Chican@ Like a Queer: The De-Mastery of Desire*. Austin: University of Texas Press, 2010.

Sotomayor, Sonia. *My Beloved World*. New York: Knopf, 2013.

Southern Poverty Law Center. *Latina Women Endure Sexual Violence, Discrimination*. 2009. www.splcenter.org.

Spector, Nancy, Amada Cruz, Susanne Ghez, and Ann Goldstein. *Felix Gonzalez-Torres: America*. Exhibition Catalog for the United States Pavillion, 52nd Venice Biennale. New York: Solomon Guggenheim Foundation, 2007.

Spring, Joel. *Deculturalization and the Struggle for Equality: A Brief History of the Education of Dominated Cultures in the United States*, 2nd ed. New York: McGraw-Hill, 1997.

Standing, Guy. *The Precariat: The New Dangerous Class*. New York: Bloomsbury Academic, 2011.

Stanton-Salazar, Ricardo D. "A Social Capital Framework for Understanding the Socialization of Racial Minority Children and Youth." *Harvard Educational Review* 67, no. 1 (1997): 1–40.

Stavans, Ilan. *Spanglish: The Making of a New American Language*. New York: Rayo, 2003.

———, general ed. *The Norton Anthology of Latino Literature*. Edited by Edna Acosta-Belén, Harold Augenbraum, María Herrera-Sobek, Rolando Hinojosa, and Gustavo Pérez Firmat. New York: W.W. Norton, 2011.

Steinberg, Stephen. *Turning Back: A Retreat from Justice in American Race and Policy*. Boston: Beacon Press, 1996.

———. *The Ethnic Myth: Race, Ethnicity, and Class in America*, 3rd ed. Boston: Beacon, 2001.

Stephen, Lynn. *Transborder Lives: Indigenous Oaxacans in Mexico, California, and Oregon*. Durham, NC: Duke University Press, 2007.

Stepler, Renee, and Anna Brown. *Statistical Portrait of Hispanics in the United States*. Washington, DC: Pew Research Center Hispanic Trends, April 19, 2016. www.pewhispanic.org.

Stern, Alexandra Minna. "Buildings, Boundaries, and Blood: Medicalization and Nation-Building on the U.S.-Mexico Border, 1910-1930." *Hispanic American Historical Review*, 79, no. 1 (1999): 41–81.

———. *Eugenic Nation: Faults and Frontiers of Better Breeding in America*. Berkeley: University of California Press, 2005a.

———. "Sterilized in the Name of Public Health: Race, Immigration, and Reproductive Control in Modern California." *American Journal of Public Health* 95, no. 7 (2005b): 1128–38.

Stoll, David. *Rigoberta Menchú and the Story of All Poor Guatemalans*. Boulder, CO: Westview Press, 1999.

Stoltz Chinchilla, Norma, and Nora Hamilton. *Identity Formation among Central American Americans*. Los Angeles: USC Dornsife Center for the Study of Immigrant Integration, 2013.

Stumpf, Juliet. "The Crimmigration Crisis: Immigrants, Crime, and Sovereign Power." *American University Law Review* 56 (2006): 367–419.

Suárez-Orozco, Marcelo, and Mariela Páez, eds. *Latinos: Remaking America*. Berkeley: University of California Press, 2009.

Subervi-Vélez, Federico A. "Mass Media Exposure and Perceived Discrimination among Latinos in Chicago." Paper presented at the 62nd Annual Meeting of the Association for Education in Journalism, Houston, Texas, August 5-8, 1979.

Sundstrom, Ronald. *The Browning of America and the Evasion of Social Justice*. Albany: State University of New York Press, 2008.

Suro, Roberto, and Gabriel Escobar. *2006 National Survey of Latinos: The Immigration Debate*. Washington, DC: Pew Research Center, Hispanic Trends, 2006. www.pewhispanic.org.

Svich, Caridad, and María Teresa Marrero. *Out of the Fringe: Contemporary Latina/Latino Theatre and Performance*. New York: Theatre Communications Group, 2000.

Tafolla, Carmen. "La Malinche." In *Infinite Divisions: An Anthology of Chicana Literature*, edited by Tey Diana Rebolledo and Eliana S. Rivero, 150–51. Tucson: University of Arizona Press, 1993.

Tajima-Peña, Renee, dir. *No Más Bebés*. Produced by Virginia Espino. Los Angeles: Moon Canyon Films, 2015.

Talavera, Victor, Guillermina Gina Núñez-Mchiri, and Josiah Heyman. "Deportation in the U.S.-Mexico Borderlands: Anticipation, Experience, and Memory." In *The Deportation Regime: Sovereignty, Space, and the Freedom of Movement*, edited by Nicholas De Genova and Nathalie Peutz, 166–95. Durham, NC: Duke University Press, 2010.

Tamayo, Jennifer. *You Da One*. Atlanta, GA: Coconut Books, 2014.

Tamez, Margo. "Place and Perspective in the Shadow of the Wall: Recovering Ndé Knowledge and Self-Determination in Texas." *Aztlán* 38, no. 1 (2013): 163–86.

Taussig, Michael. *Mimesis and Alterity: A Particular History of the Senses*. New York: Routledge, 1993.

Taylor, Charles. *A Secular Age*. Cambridge, MA: Harvard University Press, 2007.

Taylor, Diana. *The Archive and the Repertoire: Performing Cultural Memory in the Americas*. Durham, NC: Duke University Press, 2003.

Taylor, Paul, Rakesh Kochhar, Richard Fry, Gabriel Velasco, and Seth Motel. *Twenty-to-One: Wealth Gaps Rise to Record Highs between Whites, Blacks, and Hispanics*. Washington, DC: Pew Research Center, 2011. www.pewsocialtrends.org.

Taylor, Paul, Mark Hugo Lopez, Jessica Martínez, and Gabriel Velasco. *When Labels Don't Fit: Hispanics and Their Views of Identity*. Washington, DC: Pew Research Center, 2012. www.pewhispanic.org.

Telles, Edward E., and Vilma Ortiz. *Generations of Exclusion: Mexican Americans, Assimilation, and Race*. New York: Russell Sage Foundation, 2008.

Tenayuca, Emma, and Homer Brooks. "The Mexican Question in the Southwest." *Communist* (1939): 257–68.

Thackeray, William Makepeace. *The Newcomes*. 1855. New York: Penguin, 1996.

Thomas, Piri. *Down These Mean Streets*. New York: Knopf, 1967.

Thornburgh, Richard. "Puerto Rican Separatism and United States Federalism." In *Foreign in a Domestic Sense: Puerto Rico, American Expansion, and the Constitution*, edited by Christina Duffy Burnett and Burke Marshall, 349–72. Durham, NC: Duke University Press, 2001.

Tilly, Charles. *Regimes and Repertoires*. Chicago: University of Chicago Press, 2006.

Tilly, Charles, and Lesley J. Wood. *Social Movements, 1768–2008*, 2nd ed. Boulder, CO: Paradigm Publishers, 2009.

Tió, Salvador. "Teoría del Espanglish." *Diario de Puerto Rico*, October 28, 1948. https://issuu.com.

Tirres, Christopher D. *The Aesthetics and Ethics of Faith: A Dialogue between Liberationist and Pragmatic Thought*. New York: Oxford University Press, 2014.

Tobar, Héctor. *Translation Nation: Defining a New American Identity in the Spanish-Speaking United States*. New York: Riverhead Books, 2005.

Tonry, Michael. *Punishing Race: A Continuing American Dilemma*. New York: Oxford University Press, 2011.

Toribio, Almeida Jacqueline. "Accessing Bilingual Code-Switching Competence." *International Journal of Bilingualism* 5, no. 4 (2001): 403–36.

Torres, Arlene. "La Gran Familia Puertorriqueña 'Ej prieta de beldá' (The Great Puerto Rican Family Is Really Really Black)." In *Blackness in Latin America and the Caribbean: Social Dynamics and Cultural Transformations*, vol. 2, edited by Arlene Torres and Norman E. Whitten Jr., 285–306. Bloomington: Indiana University Press, 1998.

Torres, Edén E. *Chicana without Apology: The New Chicana Cultural Studies*. New York: Routledge, 2003.

Torres, María de los Angeles. *In the Land of Mirrors: Cuban Exile Politics in the United States*. Ann Arbor: University of Michigan Press, 2001.

Torres-Padilla, José, and Carmen Haydee Rivera, eds. *Writing Off the Hyphen: New Perspectives on the Literature of the Puerto Rican Diaspora*. Seattle: University of Washington Press, 2008.

Torres-Saillant, Silvio. *Caribbean Poetics: Toward an Aesthetic of West Indian Literature*. Cambridge: Cambridge University Press, 1997.

———. "Inventing the Race: Latinos and the Ethnoracial Pentagon." *Latino Studies* 1, no. 1 (2003): 123–51.

———. "Racism in the Americas and the Latino Scholar." In *Neither Enemies nor Friends: Latinos, Blacks, Afro-Latinos*, edited by Anani Dzizienyo and Suzanne Oboler, 281–304. New York: Palgrave Macmillan, 2005.

Torres-Saillant, Silvio, and Ramona Hernández. *The Dominican Americans*. Westport, CT: Greenwood Press, 1998.

TRAC Immigration. *ICE Deportations: Gender, Age, and Country of Citizenship*. Syracuse University, April 9, 2014. http://trac.syr.edu.

Treviño, Roberto R. *The Church in the Barrio: Mexican American Ethno-Catholicism in Houston*. Chapel Hill: University of North Carolina Press, 2006.

Trotter II, Robert T., and Juan Antonio Chavira. *Curanderismo: Mexican American Folk Healing*. Athens: University of Georgia Press, 1997.

Trucios-Haynes, Enid. "Latino/as in the Mix: Applying Gotanda's Models of Racial Classification and Racial Stratification." *Asian Law Journal* 4 (1997): 39–62.

———. "Why 'Race Matters': LatCrit Theory and Latina/o Racial Identity." *Berkeley La Raza Law Journal* 12, no. 1 (2001): 1–42.

Trujillo, Carla. *Chicana Lesbians: The Girls Our Mothers Warned Us About*. Berkeley, CA: Third Woman Press, 1991.

———. "La Virgen de Guadalupe and Her Reconstruction in Chicana Lesbian Desire." In *Living Chicana Theory*, edited by Carla Trujillo, 214–31. Berkeley, MA: Third Woman Press, 1998.

Tuck, Eve, and K. Wayne Yang. "Decolonization Is Not a Metaphor." *Decolonization: Indigeneity, Education and Society* 1, no. 1 (2012): 1–40.

Turner, Kay. *Beautiful Necessity: The Art and Meaning of Women's Altars*. New York: Thames and Hudson, 1999.

Turner, Ralph H. "Sponsored and Contest Mobility and the School System." *American Sociological Review* 25, no. 6 (1960): 855–62.

Tywoniak, Frances Esquibel, and Mario T. García. *Migrant Daughter: Coming of Age as a Mexican American Woman.* Berkeley: University of California Press, 2000.

Urciuoli, Bonnie. "Semiotic Properties of Racializing Discourse." *Journal of Linguistic Anthropology* 21, no. S1 (2011): E113–E122.

Urquijo-Ruiz, Rita E. *Wild Tongues: Transnational Mexican Popular Culture.* Austin: University of Texas Press, 2013.

U.S. Census Bureau. *Hispanic Origin.* July 25, 2013. www.census.gov.

———. *Hispanic Heritage Month 2015.* Profile America Facts for Features CB15-.FF18. September 14, 2015. www.census.gov.

U.S. Department of Labor. *The Latino Labor Force at a Glance.* 2012. www.dol.gov.

Valadez, Jorge. *Deliberative Democracy, Political Legitimacy, and Self-Determination in Multicultural Societies.* Boulder, CO: Westview Press, 2000.

Valdes, Alisa. *The Dirty Girls Social Club.* New York: St. Martin's, 2003.

Valdés, Vanessa K. *Diasporic Blackness: The Life and Times of Arturo Alfonso Schomburg.* Albany: State University of New York Press, 2017.

Valdez, Luis. *Luis Valdez—Early Works: Actos, Bernabé and Pensamiento Serpentino.* Houston: Arte Público, 1990.

Valdez, Luis, and El Teatro Campesino. *La Carpa de los Rasquachi.* New York: New York University Hemispheric Institute Digital Video Library, 2001. http://hidvl.nyu.edu.

Valdez, Luis, and Stan Steiner, eds. *Aztlán: An Anthology of Mexican American Literature.* New York: Vintage, 1972.

Valdivia, Angharad N. *A Latina in the Land of Hollywood and Other Essays on Media Culture.* Tucson: University of Arizona Press, 2000.

———. *Latina/os and the Media.* Cambridge, UK: Polity, 2010.

Valencia, Richard R. *Dismantling Contemporary Deficit Thinking: Educational Thought and Practice.* New York: Routledge, 2010.

Valencia, Richard R., and Bruno Villarreal. "Texas' Second Wave of High-Stakes Testing: Anti-Social Promotion Legislation, Grade Retention, and Adverse Impact on Minorities." In *Leaving Children Behind: How "Texas-Style" Accountability Fails Latino Youth*, edited by Angela Valenzuela, 113–51. Albany: State University of New York Press, 2005.

Valencia, Sonia. "Post-Cyborg Embodiment, Memoir, and Trans-Species Ontologies: Chican@/Latin@ Decolonial, Indigenous, and Eco-Feminist Interventions into Hegemonic Posthuman Discourses." PhD diss. in progress, University of Texas, San Antonio, 2016.

Valentín-Escobar, Wilson. *Bodega Surrealism: Latino Artivists in New York City.* New York: New York University Press, forthcoming.

Valenzuela, Abel, Jr. "Day Labor Work." *Annual Review of Sociology* 29 (2003): 307–32.

———. "Working Day Labor: Informal and Contingent Employment." In *Mexicans in California: Transformations and Challenges*, edited by Ramón A. Gutiérrez and Patricia Zavella, 36–58. Urbana: University of Illinois Press, 2009.

Valenzuela, Abel, Jr., Janette A. Kawachi, and Matthew D. Marr. "Seeking Work Daily: Supply, Demand, and Spatial Dimensions of Day Labor in Two Global Cities." *International Journal of Comparative Sociology* 43, no. 2 (2002): 192–219.

Valenzuela, Abel, Jr., Nik Theodore, Edwin Melendez, and Ana Luz Gonzalez. *On the Corner: Day Labor in the United States.* Los Angeles: University of California, Los Angeles, Center for the Study of Urban Poverty, 2006.

Valenzuela, Angela. *Subtractive Schooling: U.S.-Mexican Youth and the Politics of Caring.* Albany: State University of New York Press, 1999.

———, ed. *Leaving Children Behind: How Texas-Style Accountability Fails Latino Youth.* Albany: State University of New York Press, 2005.

Valenzuela, Angela, and Patricia D. López. "Cultivating a Cadre of Critically Conscious Teachers and 'Taking This Country to a Totally New Place.'" In *U.S. Latinos and Education Policy: Research-Based Directions for Change*, edited by Pedro R. Portes, Spencer Salas, Patricia Baquedano-López, and Paula J. Mellom, 35–44. New York: Routledge, 2014.

Valis, Noël. *The Culture of Cursilería: Bad Taste, Kitsch, and Class in Modern Spain.* Durham, NC: Duke University Press, 2002.

Valle, Victor M., and Rodolfo D. Torres. "The Idea of *Mestizaje* and the 'Race' Problematic: Racialized Media Discourse in a Post-Fordist Landscape." In *Culture and Difference: Critical Perspectives on the Bicultural Experience in the United States*, edited by Antonia Darder, 139–54. Westport, CT: Bergin and Garvey 1995.

———. *Latino Metropolis.* Minneapolis: University of Minnesota Press, 2000.

Vargas, Deborah R. "Representations of Latina/o Sexuality in Popular Culture." In *Latina/o Sexualities: Probing Powers, Passions, Practices, and Policies*, edited by Marysol Asencio, 117–36. New Brunswick, NJ: Rutgers University Press, 2009.

———. *Dissonant Divas in Chicana Music: The Limits of La Onda.* Minneapolis: University of Minnesota Press, 2012.

———. "Ruminations on *Lo Sucio* as a Latino Queer Analytic." *American Quarterly* 66, no. 3 (2014): 715–26. doi:10.1353/aq.2014.0046.

Vargas, José Antonio, dir. *Documented: A Film by an Undocumented American*. United States: Apo Anak Productions, 2013.

Vargas, Lucila. *Latina Teens, Migration, and Popular Culture*. New York: Peter Lang, 2009.

Vargas, Zaragoza. *Crucible of Struggle: A History of Mexican Americans from the Colonial Period to the Present Era*. New York: Oxford University Press, 2010.

Vasconcelos, José. *The Cosmic Race / La Raza Cósmica*. 1925. Translated by Didier T. Jaén. Baltimore, MD: Johns Hopkins University Press, 1997.

Vasquez, Tina. "I've Experienced a New Level of Racism since Donald Trump Went After Latinos." *Guardian*, September 9, 2015. www.theguardian.com

Vazquez, Alexandra T. *Listening in Detail: Performances of Cuban Music*. Durham, NC: Duke University Press, 2013.

Vega, Bernardo. *Memoirs of Bernardo Vega: A Contribution to the History of the Puerto Rican Community in New York*. Edited by César Andreu Iglesias. Translated by Juan Flores. New York: Monthly Review Press, 1984.

Vega, Garcilaso de la, El Inca. *The Royal Commentaries of the Incas and General History of Peru*. 1609, 1617. Translated by Harold V. Livermore. Austin: University of Texas Press, 2014.

Vega, Marta Moreno. *The Altar of My Soul: The Living Traditions of Santería*. New York: One World/Ballantine 2000.

———. *When the Spirits Dance Mambo: Growing Up Nuyorican in El Barrio*. New York: Three Rivers Press, 2004.

Vega, Marta Moreno, Marinieves Alba, and Yvette Modestin, eds. *Women Warriors of the Afro-Latina Diaspora*. Houston: Arte Público Press, 2012.

Velazquez, Loreta Janeta. *The Woman in Battle: The Civil War Narrative of Loreta Janeta Velazquez, Cuban Woman and Confederate Soldier*. Madison: University of Wisconsin Press, 2003.

Vélez-Ibáñez, Carlos G. *Border Visions: Mexican Cultures of the Southwest United States*. Tucson: University of Arizona Press, 1996.

———. *An Impossible Living in a Transborder World: Culture, Confianza, and Economy of Mexican-Origin Populations*. Tucson: University of Arizona Press, 2010.

Veracini, Lorenzo. *Settler Colonialism: A Theoretical Overview*. London: Palgrave Macmillan, 2010.

Vidal, Mirta. "Women, New Voice of La Raza." *Chicanas Speak Out*. New York: Pathfinder Press, 1971.

Viego, Antonio. *Dead Subjects: Toward a Politics of Loss in Latino Studies*. Durham, NC: Duke University Press, 2007.

Vigil, Ernesto B. *The Crusade for Justice: Chicano Militancy and the Government's War on Dissent*. Madison: University of Wisconsin Press, 1999.

Vigil, James Diego. *The Projects: Gang and Non-Gang Families in East Los Angeles*. Austin: University of Texas Press, 2007.

———. "Barrio Genealogy." *City and Community* 7, no. 4 (2008): 366–71.

Vigil, Maurilio E. *Chicano Politics*. Washington, DC: University Press of America, 1977.

Vila, Pablo, ed. *Ethnography at the Border*. Minneapolis: University of Minnesota Press, 2003.

Villa, Raúl Homero. *Barrio-Logos: Space and Place in Urban Chicano Literature and Culture*. Austin: University of Texas Press, 2000.

Villegas, Ana Maria. "Profile of New Hispanic Teachers in U.S. Public Schools: Looking at Issues of Quantity and Quality." Paper presented at the Annual Meeting of the American Education Research Association, Chicago, 2007.

Villegas, Ana Maria, and Jacqueline Jordan Irvine. "Diversifying the Teaching Force: An Examination of Major Arguments." *Urban Review* 42, no. 3 (2010): 175–92.

Vinson, Ben, III, and Matthew Restall, eds. *Black Mexico: Race and Society from Colonial to Modern Times*. Albuquerque: University of New Mexico Press, 2009.

Viramontes, Helena María. *Their Dogs Came with Them: A Novel*. New York: Atria, 2007.

Viruell-Fuentes, Edna. "Beyond Acculturation: Immigration, Discrimination, and Health Research among Mexican Americans." *Social Science and Medicine* 65, no. 7 (2007): 1524–35.

Viruell-Fuentes, Edna, Patricia Y. Miranda, and Sawsan Abdulrahim. "More than Culture: Structural Racism, Intersectionality Theory and Immigrant Health." *Social Science and Medicine* 75, no. 12 (2012): 2099–106.

Vizenor, Gerald. *Manifest Manners: Narratives on Postindian Survivance*. Hanover, NH: University Press of New England, 1994.

Vogeley, Nancy. *The Bookrunner: A History of Early Inter-American Relations—Print, Politics, and Commerce in the United States and Mexico, 1800–1830*. Philadelphia: American Philosophical Society, 2011.

Volpp, Leti. "Civility and the Undocumented Alien." In *Civility, Legality, and Justice in America*, edited by Austin Sarat, 69–106. New York: Cambridge University Press, 2014.

von Hoffman, Alexander. "High Ambitions: The Past and Future of American Low-Income Housing Policy." *Housing Policy Debate* 7, no. 3 (1996): 423–46.

Voss, Kim, and Irene Bloemraad, eds. *Civility, Legality, and Justice in America*. Berkeley: University of California Press, 2011.

Wacquant, Loïc. *Prisons of Poverty*, expanded ed. Minneapolis: University of Minnesota Press, 2009.

Wade, Peter. "Repensando el mestizaje." *Revista colombiana de antropología* 39 (2003): 273–96.

Wanzer-Serrano, Darrell. *The New York Young Lords and the Struggle for Liberation*. Philadelphia: Temple University Press, 2015.

Ward, Peter M. *Colonias and Public Policy in Texas and Mexico: Urbanization by Stealth*. Austin: University of Texas Press, 2010.

Weaver, Vesla M. "Frontlash: Race and the Development of Punitive Crime Policy." *Studies in American Political Development* 21 (Fall 2007): 230–65.

Weber, David J. *The Mexican Frontier, 1821–1846: The American Southwest under Mexico*. Albuquerque: University of New Mexico Press, 1982.

——. *The Spanish Frontier of North America*. New Haven, CT: Yale University Press, 1992.

Weinreich, Uriel. *Languages in Contact*. 1953. The Hague: Mouton, 1968.

Westerman, William. "Central American Refugee Testimonies and Performed Life Histories in the Sanctuary Movement." In *The Oral History Reader*, 2nd ed., edited by Robert Perks and Alistair Thomson, 493–505. New York: Routledge, 1998.

Western, Bruce, and Becky Pettit. "Black-White Wage Inequality, Employment Rates, and Incarceration." *American Journal of Sociology* 111, no. 2 (2005): 553–78.

Whalen, Carmen Teresa. "Bridging Homeland and Barrio Politics: The Young Lords in Philadelphia." In *The Puerto Rican Movement: Voices from the Diaspora*, edited by Andrés Torres and José Velázquez, 107–23. Philadelphia: Temple University Press, 1998.

White, Karl, Kristine Hopkins, Joseph E. Potter, and Daniel Grossman. "Knowledge and Attitudes about Long-Acting Reversible Contraception among Latina Women Who Desire Sterilization." *Women's Health Issues* 23, no. 4 (2014): 257–63.

White, Karletta M. "The Salience of Skin Tone: Effects on the Exercise of Police Enforcement Authority." *Ethnic and Racial Studies* 38, no. 6 (2014): 993–1010.

Whitten, Jr., Norman E., and Arlene Torres, eds. *Blackness in Latin America and the Caribbean: Social Dynamics and Cultural Transformations*, 2 vols. Bloomington: Indiana University Press, 1998.

Wiegman, Robyn. *Object Lessons*. Durham, NC: Duke University Press, 2012.

Williams, Brackette. "A Class Act: Anthropology and the Race to Nation across Ethnic Terrain." *Annual Review of Anthropology* 18 (1989): 401–44.

Williams, Brett. "What's Debt Got to Do with It?" In *The New Poverty Studies: The Ethnography of Power, Politics, and Impoverished People in the United States*, edited by Judith Goode and Jeff Maskovsky, 79–102. New York: New York University Press, 2001.

—— "The Precipice of Debt." In *New Landscapes of Inequality: Neoliberalism and the Erosion of Democracy in America*, edited by Jane L. Collins, Micaela di Leonardo, and Brett Williams, 65–89. Santa Fe, NM: School for Advanced Research, 2008.

Williams, Norma. *The Mexican American Family: Tradition and Change*. Dix Hills, NY: General Hall, 1990.

Williams, Raymond. *Marxism and Literature*. Oxford: Oxford University Press, 1977.

——. *Culture and Society, 1780–1950*. 1958. New York: Columbia University Press, 1983.

Williams, William Carlos. *Al que quiere!* Boston: Four Seas, 1917.

——. *The Embodiment of Knowledge*. New York: New Directions, 1974.

——. "The Defective Record." In *The Collected Poems of William Carlos Williams, Volume 1: 1909–1939*, edited by Christopher MacGowan, 455. New York: New Directions, 1991.

——. "The Defective Record." *PennSound*, 2006. http://writing.upenn.edu.

Wilmoth, Janet M. *Life Course Perspectives on Military Service*. New York: Routledge, 2013.

Wilson, William Julius. *The Truly Disadvantaged: The Inner City, the Underclass and Public Policy*. Chicago: University of Chicago, 1987.

——, ed. *The Ghetto Underclass: Social Science Perspectives*. Newbury Park, CA: Sage, 1993.

Wolfe, Patrick. "Settler Colonialism and the Elimination of the Native." *Journal of Genocide and Research* 8, no. 4 (2006): 387–409.

Woll, Allen. *Latin Image in American Film*. Los Angeles: University of California, Los Angeles, Latin American Center Publications, 1977.

Wynter, Sylvia. "Beyond Miranda's Meanings: Un/Silencing the 'Demonic Ground' of Caliban's Women." In *Out of the Kumbla: Caribbean Women and Literature*, edited by Carole Boyce Davies and Elaine Savory Fido, 355–72. Trenton, NJ: Africa World Press, 1990.

——. "1492: A New World View." In *Race, Discourse, and the*

Origin of the Americas: A New World View, edited by Vera Lawrence Hyatt and Rex Nettleford, 5–57. Washington, DC: Smithsonian Institution Press, 1995.

Yancey, George. *Who Is White? Latinos, Asians, and the New Black/Nonblack Divide*. Boulder, CO: Lynne Rienner, 2003.

Ybarra-Frausto, Tomás. "Rasquachismo: A Chicano Sensibility." In *Chicano Aesthetics: Rasquachismo*, exhibition catalog, 5–8. Phoenix, AZ: MARS Movimiento Artístico del Río Salado, 1989.

———. "Rasquachismo: A Chicano Sensibility." In *Chicano Art: Resistance and Affirmation, 1965–1985*, edited by Richard Griswold del Castillo, Teresa Mckenna, and Yvonne Yarbro-Bejarano, 155–79. Los Angeles: Wright Art Gallery, UCLA, 1991.

———. "The Chicano Movement / The Movement of Chicano Art." In *Exhibiting Culture: The Poetics and Politics of Museum Display*, edited by Ivan Karp and Steven D. Lavine, 128–50. Washington, DC: Smithsonian Institution Press, 1991.

———. "A Panorama of Latino Arts." *American Latinos and the Making of the United States: A Theme Study*. Washington, DC: National Parks Service, 2013. www.nps.gov.

Yarbro-Bejarano, Yvonne. *The Wounded Heart: Writing on Cherríe Moraga*. Austin: University of Texas Press, 2001.

Yosso, Tara J. "Critical Race Media Literacy: Challenging Deficit Discourse about Chicanas/os." *Journal of Popular Film and Television* 30, no. 1 (2002): 52–62.

———. "Whose Culture Has Capital? A Critical Race Theory Discussion of Community Cultural Wealth." *Race Ethnicity and Education* 8, no. 1 (2005): 69–91.

Young Lords Party. *¡Palante! Young Lords Party*. Chicago: Haymarket Books, 2011.

Zambrana, Ruth Enid, and Sylvia Hurtado, eds. *The Magic Key: The Educational Journey of Mexican Americans from K-12 to College and Beyond*. Austin: University of Texas Press, 2015.

Zamora, Emilio. *The World of the Mexican Worker in Texas*. College Station: Texas A&M University Press, 2000.

Zangwill, Israel. *The Melting-Pot*. 1908. Comedy Theatre, New York, September 6, 1909–January 1910. Performance. New York: Macmillan, 1909.

Zavala, Adriana. "Latin@ Art at the Intersection." *Aztlán* 40, no. 1 (Spring 2015): 125–40.

Zavella, Patricia. *Women's Work and Chicano Families: Cannery Workers of the Santa Clara Valley*. Ithaca, NY: Cornell University Press, 1987.

———. *I'm Neither Here nor There: Mexicans' Quotidian Struggles with Migration and Poverty*. Durham, NC: Duke University Press, 2011.

Zeff, Jacqueline. "'What Doesn't Kill You Makes You Fat': The Language of Food in Latina Literature." In *Latina Writers*, edited by Ilan Stavans, 38–47. Westport, CT: Greenwood Press, 2008.

Zentella, Ana Celia. "The 'Chiquita-fication' of U.S. Latinos and Their Languages, or Why We Need an Anthro-Political Linguistics." In *SALSA III: Proceedings of the Symposium about Language and Society at Austin*, 1–18. Austin: Department of Linguistics, University of Texas, 1995.

———. *Growing Up Bilingual: Puerto Rican Children in New York*. Malden, MA: Blackwell, 1997.

———. "TWB (Talking while Bilingual): Linguistic Profiling of Latin@s, and Other Linguistic Torquemadas." *Latino Studies* 12, no. 4 (2014): 620–35.

———. "Spanglish: Language Politics vs *el habla del pueblo*." In *Code-Switching in the Spanish-Speaking Caribbean and Its Diaspora*, edited by Rosa E. Guzzardo Tamargo, Catherine M. Mazak, and M. Carmen Parafita Couto, 11–35. Amsterdam: John Benjamins, 2016.

———. "Bilinguals and Borders: California's Transfronteriz@s and Competing Constructions of Bilingualism." *International Journal of the Linguistic Association of the Southwest* 32, no. 2 (2013) (forthcoming 2017).

Zepeda-Millán, Chris, and Sophia J. Wallace. "Racialization in Times of Contention: How Social Movements Influence Latino Racial Identity." *Politics, Groups, and Identities* 1, no. 4 (2013): 510–27.

Zlolniski, Christian. "Political Mobilization and Activism among Latinos/as in the United States." In *Latinas/os in the United States: Changing the Face of América*, edited by Havidán Rodríguez, Rogelio Sáenz, and Cecilia Menjívar, 352–68. New York: Springer, 2008.

Zolberg, Aristide, and Long Litt Woon. "Why Islam Is Like Spanish: Cultural Incorporation in Europe and the United States." *Politics and Society* 27, no. 5 (1999): 5–38.

Zolov, Eric. *Refried Elvis: The Rise of the Mexican Counterculture*. Berkeley: University of California Press, 1999.

About the Contributors

Linda Martín Alcoff is Professor of Philosophy at the City University of New York. Her most recent book is *The Future of Whiteness*.

Frederick Luis Aldama is University Distinguished Scholar and Arts and Humanities Distinguished Professor at The Ohio State University. His most recent book is *The Routledge Companion to Latina/o Popular Culture*.

Frances R. Aparicio is Professor in the Department of Spanish and Portuguese and Director of the Latina and Latino Studies Program at Northwestern University. She is completing a manuscript entitled "Relational Latinidades: Unearthing Intralatino/a Lives in Chicago."

José F. Aranda Jr. is Associate Professor in the Departments of English and Spanish and Portuguese at Rice University. He has completed a manuscript entitled "The Places of Modernity in Early Mexican American Literature."

Alicia Arrizón is Professor in the Department of Gender and Sexuality Studies at the University of California, Riverside. Her most recent book is *Queering Mestizaje: Transculturation and Performance*.

Manuel G. Avilés-Santiago is Assistant Professor of Communication and Culture at Arizona State University. He is the author of *Puerto Rican Soldiers and Second-Class Citizenship: Representations in Media*.

Mary Beltrán is Associate Professor of Radio-Television-Film at the University of Texas at Austin. She is the author of *Latina/o Stars in U.S. Eyes: The Making and Meanings of Film and TV Stardom*.

Maylei Blackwell is Associate Professor of Chicana/o Studies and Women's Studies at the University of California, Los Angeles. She is the author of *¡Chicana Power!: Contested Histories of Feminism in the Chicano Movement*.

Mary Pat Brady is Associate Professor in the Department of English and Director of the Latino Studies Program at Cornell University. She is the author of *Extinct Lands, Temporal Geographies: Chicana Literature and the Urgency of Space*.

Ginetta E. B. Candelario is Professor of Sociology and Latin American and Latina/o Studies at Smith College. She is the author of *Black behind the Ears: Dominican Racial Identity from Beauty Shops to Museums*.

Dolores Inés Casillas is Associate Professor of Chicana/o Studies at the University of California, Santa Barbara. She is the author of *Sounds of Belonging: U.S. Spanish-Language Radio and Public Advocacy*.

Mari Castañeda is Professor and Department Chair of Communication at the University of Massachusetts, Amherst. She is co-editor of *Soap Operas and Telenovelas in the Digital Age: Global Industries and New Audiences*.

María Elena Cepeda is Professor of Latina/o Studies at Williams College. Her most recent book is *The Routledge Companion to Latina/o Media*.

Sheila Marie Contreras is Associate Professor of English and Associate Dean for Diversity, Inclusion, and Community Engagement at Michigan State University. She is the author of *Blood Lines: Myth, Indigenism and Chicana/o Literature*.

Raúl Coronado is Associate Professor of Ethnic Studies at the University of California, Berkeley. He is the author of *A World Not to Come: A History of Latino Writing and Print Culture*.

María Eugenia Cotera is Associate Professor of American Culture, Latina/o Studies, and Women's Studies at the University of Michigan, Ann Arbor. She is the author of *Native Speakers: Ella Deloria, Zora Neale Hurston, Jovita González, and the Poetics of Culture*.

Arnaldo Cruz-Malavé is Professor of Spanish and Comparative Literature at Fordham University. His most recent book is *Queer Latino Testimonio, Keith Haring, and Juanito Xtravaganza: Hard Tails*.

Arlene Dávila is Professor of Anthropology and Media Studies at New York University. Her most recent book is *El Mall: The Spatial and Class Politics of Shopping Malls in Latin America*.

Nicholas De Genova is Reader in Urban Geography at King's College, London. He is the author of *Working the Boundaries: Race, Space, and "Illegality" in Mexican Chicago*.

Theresa Delgadillo is Professor in the Department of Comparative Studies at The Ohio State University. She is the author of *Spiritual Mestizaje: Religion, Gender, Race, and Nation in Contemporary Chicana Narrative*.

Zaire Z. Dinzey-Flores is Associate Professor of Sociology and Latino and Caribbean Studies at Rutgers University. She is the author of *Locked In, Locked Out: Gated Communities in a Puerto Rican City*.

Julie A. Dowling is Associate Professor of Latina/Latino Studies at the University of Illinois, Urbana-Champaign. She is the author of *Mexican Americans and the Question of Race*.

John A. García is Research Professor Emeritus at the Institute for Social Research at the University of Michigan, Ann Arbor. The third edition of his *Latino Politics in America: Community, Culture, and Interests* appeared in 2016.

Shannon Gleeson is Associate Professor of Labor Relations, Law, and History at the Cornell University School of Industrial and Labor Relations. Her most recent book is *Precarious Claims: The Promise and Failure of Workplace Protections in the United States*.

Rita Gonzalez is Curator and Acting Department Head of Contemporary Art at the Los Angeles County Museum of Art. She has curated numerous exhibitions including *ASCO: Elite of the Obscure, A Retrospective*.

Nicole M. Guidotti-Hernández is Associate Professor of American Studies and Chair of the Department of Mexican American and Latina/o Studies at the University of Texas at Austin. She is the author of *Unspeakable Violence: Remapping U.S. and Mexican National Imaginaries*.

Laura G. Gutiérrez is Associate Professor of Latin American and Latina/o Performance Studies at the University of Texas at Austin. She is the author of *Performing Mexicanidad: Vendidas y Cabareteras on the Transnational Stage*.

Joshua Javier Guzmán is Assistant Professor of English at the University of Colorado, Boulder. He is completing a manuscript tentatively titled "Suspending Satisfaction: Queer Latino Performance and the Politics of Style."

Michael Hames-García is Professor of Ethnic Studies at the University of Oregon. His most recent book is *Identity Complex: Making the Case for Multiplicity*.

Ramona Hernández is Professor of Sociology and Director of the Dominican Studies Institute at the City College of New York. Her book on *Ellis Island Dominicans: Money, Power, and Color* is forthcoming.

Tanya Katerí Hernández is Professor of Law at the Fordham University School of Law. She is the author of *Racial Subordination in Latin America: The Role of the State, Customary Law, and the New Civil Rights Response*.

Norma Iglesias-Prieto is Professor in the Department of Chicana and Chicano Studies at San Diego State University. She is the author of *Beautiful Flowers of the Maquiladoras: Life Histories of Women Workers in Tijuana*.

Zilkia Janer is Professor of Global Studies and Geography at Hofstra University. Her most recent book is *Latino Food Culture*.

Nancy Kang is Assistant Professor of Multicultural and Diaspora Literatures at the University of Baltimore. She is co-author with Silvio Torres-Saillant of *The Once and Future Muse: The Poetry and Poetics of Rhina P. Espaillat*.

Lawrence La Fountain-Stokes is Associate Professor of American Culture, Latina/o Studies, Romance Languages and Literatures, and Women's Studies at the University of Michigan, Ann Arbor. He is the author of *Queer Ricans: Cultures and Sexualities in the Diaspora*.

Lázaro Lima is the E. Claiborne Robins Distinguished Chair in the Liberal Arts at the University of Richmond. His books include *The Latino Body: Crisis Identities in American Literary and Cultural Memory*.

María Lugones is a philosopher and popular educator. She is the author of *Pilgrimages-Peregrinajes: Theorizing Coalition against Multiple Oppressions*.

Nelson Maldonado-Torres is Associate Professor of Latino and Caribbean Studies and Comparative Literature at Rutgers University. He is the author of *Against War: Views from the Underside of Modernity*.

Lillian Manzor is Associate Professor in Modern Languages and Literatures and Director of the Cuban Theater Digital Archive at the University of Miami. She is completing a manuscript entitled "Marginality beyond Return: U.S. Cuban Performances and Politics."

Curtis Marez is Professor of Ethnic Studies at the University of California, San Diego. His most recent book is *Farm Worker Futurism: Speculative Technologies of Resistance*.

Anne M. Martínez is Assistant Professor of American Culture and Cultural Theory at the University of Groningen. She is the author of *Catholic Borderlands: Mapping Catholicism onto American Empire, 1905–1935*.

John Mckiernan-Gonzalez is Associate Professor of History at Texas State University. He is the author of *Fevered Measures: Public Health and Race at the Texas-Mexico Border, 1848–1942*.

Cecilia Menjívar is Foundation Distinguished Professor of Sociology at the University of Kansas. Her most recent publications include the co-authored book *Immigrant Families*.

Nancy Raquel Mirabal is Associate Professor of American Studies and Director of the U.S. Latina/o Studies Program at the University of Maryland, College Park. She is the author of *Suspect Freedoms: The Racial and Sexual Politics of Cubanidad in New York, 1823–1957*.

Sergio de la Mora is Associate Professor of Chicana and Chicano Studies at the University of California, Davis. He is the author of *Cinemachismo: Masculinities and Sexuality in Mexican Film*.

John Nieto-Phillips is Associate Professor of History and Latino Studies at Indiana University. His current book project examines how Latinas/os figured into global Hispanist networks and U.S. language rights struggles.

Urayoán Noel is Associate Professor of English and Spanish and Portuguese at New York University. He is the author of *In Visible Movement: Nuyorican Poetry from the Sixties to Slam*.

B. V. Olguín is Professor in the English Department and Honors College at the University of Texas, San Antonio. His latest book, *Violentologies: Violence and Ontology in Latina/o Literature, Film, and Popular Culture*, is under review.

Randy J. Ontiveros is Associate Professor of English at the University of Maryland. He is the author of *In the Spirit of a New People: The Cultural Politics of the Chicano Movement*.

Ricardo L. Ortíz is Associate Professor of U.S. Latin-x Literature and Culture and Chair of the English Department at Georgetown University. He is currently working on "Testimonial Fictions: Cold War Geopolitics and U.S. Latin-x Literature."

Gina M. Pérez is Professor of Comparative American Studies at Oberlin College. Her most recent book is *Citizen, Student, Soldier: Latina/o Youth, JROTC, and the American Dream*.

Rolando Pérez is Professor in the Romance Languages Department at Hunter College. His most recent book is *Severo Sarduy and the Neo-Baroque Image of Thought in the Visual Arts*.

Gerald E. Poyo is Professor of Latin American and U.S. Latino History at St. Mary's University in San Antonio. His most recent book is *Exile and Revolution: Jose D. Poyo, Key West, and Cuban Independence*.

José Quiroga is Professor of Spanish and Comparative Literature at Emory University. His most recent book is *Mapa callejero: Crónicas sobre lo gay desde América Latina*.

Catherine S. Ramírez is Associate Professor of Latin American and Latino Studies and Director of the Chicano Latino Research Center at the University of California, Santa Cruz. Her current book project is entitled "Assimilation: An Alternative History."

Ramón H. Rivera-Servera is Associate Professor and Chair in the Department of Performance Studies at Northwestern University. He is the author of *Performing Queer Latinidad: Dance, Sexuality, Politics.*

Ana Patricia Rodríguez is Associate Professor in the Department of Spanish and Portuguese and U.S. Latina/o Studies at the University of Maryland, College Park. She is the author of *Dividing the Isthmus: Central American Transnational Histories, Literatures, and Cultures.*

Juana María Rodríguez is Professor of Gender and Women's Studies and Performance Studies at the University of California, Berkeley. Her most recent book is *Sexual Futures, Queer Gestures, and Other Latina Longings.*

Richard T. Rodríguez is Associate Professor of Media and Cultural Studies and English at the University of California, Riverside. He is the author of *Next of Kin: The Family in Chicano/a Cultural Politics.*

Sandra K. Soto is Associate Professor of Gender and Women's Studies at the University of Arizona. She is the author of *Reading Chican@ Like a Queer: The De-Mastery of Desire.*

Alexandra Minna Stern is Professor of American Culture, Obstetrics and Gynecology, History, and Women's Studies at the University of Michigan. Her most recent book is *Telling Genes: The Story of Genetic Counseling in America.*

Silvio Torres-Saillant is Dean's Professor of Humanities at Syracuse University. He is the author of *An Intellectual History of the Caribbean.*

Enid Trucios-Haynes is a Professor of Law at the Louis D. Brandeis School of Law, Interim Director of the Muhammad Ali Institute for Peace and Justice at the University of Louisville, and Co-Director of the Brandeis Human Rights Advocacy Program.

Angela Valenzuela is a Professor of Educational Administration at the University of Texas at Austin. Her most recent book is an edited collection entitled *Growing Critically Conscious Teachers: A Social Justice Curriculum for Educators of Latino/a Youth.*

Deborah R. Vargas is Henry Rutgers Term Chair in Comparative Sexuality, Gender, and Race at Rutgers, the State University of New Jersey, New Brunswick. She is the author of *Dissonant Divas in Chicana Music: The Limits of La Onda.*

Alexandra T. Vazquez is Associate Professor of Performance Studies at New York University. She is the author of *Listening in Detail: Performances of Cuban Music.*

Patricia Zavella is Professor Emerita in the Department of Latin American and Latino Studies at the University of California, Santa Cruz. Her most recent book is *I'm Neither Here Nor There: Mexicans' Quotidian Struggles with Migration and Poverty.*

Ana Celia Zentella is Professor Emerita of the City University of New York and of the University of California, San Diego. She is the author of *Growing Up Bilingual: Puerto Rican Children in New York.*